Violence

Violence

An Interdisciplinary Approach to Causes, Consequences, and Cures

Bandy X. Lee

WILEY Blackwell

This edition first published 2019
© 2019 John Wiley & Sons, Inc.

The right of Bandy X. Lee to be identified as the author of this work has been asserted in accordance with law.

Registered Office
John Wiley & Sons, Inc., 111 River Street, Hoboken, NJ 07030, USA

Editorial Office
9600 Garsington Road, Oxford, OX4 2DQ, UK

For details of our global editorial offices, customer services, and more information about Wiley products visit us at www.wiley.com.

Wiley also publishes its books in a variety of electronic formats and by print-on-demand. Some content that appears in standard print versions of this book may not be available in other formats.

Library of Congress Cataloging-in-Publication Data

Names: Lee, Bandy X., 1970– author.
Title: Violence : an interdisciplinary approach to causes, consequences, and cures / Bandy X. Lee.
Description: First Edition. | Hoboken : Wiley-Blackwell, 2019. | Includes bibliographical
  references and index. |
Identifiers: LCCN 2018051423 (print) | LCCN 2018061188 (ebook) | ISBN 9781119240693
  (Adobe PDF) | ISBN 9781119240709 (ePub) | ISBN 9781119240679 (hardback) |
  ISBN 9781119240686 (paperback)
Subjects: LCSH: Violence. | Violence–Prevention. | Criminology. | BISAC: SOCIAL SCIENCE / Criminology.
Classification: LCC HM1116 (ebook) | LCC HM1116 .L434 2019 (print) | DDC 303.6–dc23
LC record available at https://lccn.loc.gov/2018051423

Cover Design: Wiley
Cover Image: © Museum of Fine Arts, Budapest/Wikimedia Commons

Set in 10/12pt Warnock by SPi Global, Pondicherry, India

Printed in United States of America

10 9 8 7 6 5 4 3 2 1

To my mother, the healer whose work I continue
To Dr. Howard Zonana, in gratitude

Contents

Preface

This volume aims to be an introductory textbook on a single topic that is an offspring of many fields—a topic of rapid growth in information and research but lacking in overall guidance. It may surprise some that a single author should undertake a text of such wide-ranging disciplines. However, as even a thousand-page thesis should be summarizable in a sentence, so should this project be possible. It seems indispensable for coherence and consolidation in this day of disparate scholarship. No doubt there will be compromises, since it will not be possible to do justice to every topic, but my hope is that the benefits are many: what we greatly need in our day is a unified framework capable of bringing our knowledge to completion and not just ever more pockets of complete knowledge.

Such a framework, I believe, is akin to teaching students to fish and feeding them for a lifetime. Students will learn to build a perspective for placing existing knowledge and advancing information in context, and this will prepare them for new developments, which are swiftly to come. It is natural for specialists of every area to believe that theirs is of central importance, but with the burgeoning of fields and subfields, an ability to integrate knowledge and to converse with other fields, more so than knowing more and more about less and less, has become an essential skill. Eventually, students will develop better ways to fish.

Human violence is a phenomenon that disciplines us in this way, due to its complexity and urgency—which require all our capacity for sufficient understanding and efficient application. We now know more than ever about the genetic, interpersonal, cultural, and structural causes of violence. Yet, seldom are the advances of multiple disciplines brought together under a single rubric. The purpose of this text is to present an integrative and interactionist, rather than a reductionist, approach to the study of violence, so as to prepare the student for such integration.

Aristotle observed that the whole is greater than the sum of its parts, to which I would add that synergy works better than fragmentation. While there will always be a need for new and better data, it is equally important to take an occasional pause to appraise the data we already have. A coherent body of knowledge—insofar as is possible—can give the student bearing with respect to what is important, which questions to ask, and how everything fits together. Persistent practice that builds on such groundwork may even go beyond knowledge to achieve wisdom.

This text assumes no previous exposure to the study of violence. It might serve as a comprehensive overview before delving into whatever field students choose: criminal violence reduction, conflict resolution, legal interventions, global health ethics, or human rights advocacy. It can also be a guideline for bringing together the disparate information one ordinarily has to study piecemeal. In order to make the material accessible, as well as to encourage an interdisciplinary conversation, this book has a unique structure: it starts not with a list of topics but domains of research, starting with the most basic but not implying a hierarchy in either direction. Each chapter attempts to explain how its topic relates to the others.

This volume contains enough material for a one-year course. It could also be taught as a semester course, with an emphasis on broad concepts. Each chapter constitutes a unit of understanding with an overview, summary, and discussion questions. The progression of the chapters goes from a general introduction (Part I) to the intra- and interpersonal framework (Part II) to the social and societal framework (Part III) to consequences (Part IV), interventions (Part V) and prevention (Part VI), and then back to a general synthesis and integration (Part VII). Thematically, it covers biological, psychological and symbolic, sociocultural and political, and structural and environmental perspectives on violence; consequences of violence; and legal, medical, and nonviolent approaches to preventing violence, before putting it all together.

The purpose of a textbook is to compile existing information and to present it in the most reasonable way based on current knowledge. I expect that this will entail a letting go of many doctrines inherent in the particular fields and a deeper look at human nature than may be initially comfortable. It will challenge our ordinary notions of responsibility and require us to expand our notion of boundaries to include wider segments of scholarship as well as of society. However, the point is to equip the aspiring student with a broad range of material and an analytical armamentarium that will bolster efforts to arrive at one's own conclusions—and to cultivate that ability.

I believe in my institution's motto: *Lux et Veritas*, or light and truth. The purpose of education is not to inculcate a certain "truth" but to provide the learner with the "light" that is required to see one's own truth. If this text fulfills its purpose, it will not only teach content but the tools for learning, which the student can apply to other areas of life. A body of knowledge can change entirely over the course of a career, but this aptitude remains. True knowledge transcends mere accumulation of facts to become understanding, and inner sight. Therefore, while this is perhaps the first text of its scope for an emerging field, my hope is that it will not be the last—for each new generation has the task of restructuring and redefining knowledge for itself.

No ideas are freshly one's own. This applies especially here, for I am fortunate to stand on the shoulders of many giants: first and foremost, my long-term teacher, mentor, colleague, and friend, Dr James Gilligan, who taught me everything I know, and whose many thoughts I echo, however imperfectly; Dr Robert Jay Lifton, who gave me light in times of darkness; Dr Leon Eisenberg, who was my first inspiration and terrific mentor; Dr Arthur Kleinman, who encouraged me to do my own scholarship; Dr Kathy Sanders, who saw me through that transition; Dr Judith Herman, who accompanied me through another transition; Drs Howard Zonana and Madelon Baranoski, who gave me a home and nurtured my growth; Dr John Young, who came to all my lectures and supported me; and Dr Bruce Wexler, who guided and believed in me from my very beginnings as a medical student. I appreciate Drs Sylvia Kaaya, Jessie Mbwambo, Gad Kilonzo, and the villagers of Chamazi who gave me glimpses of the level of humanity that is possible, in peaceful Tanzania. I am also grateful to Drs Kaveh Khoshnood, James Leckman, and Catherine Panter-Brick for being my chief partners on this topic, as well as Drs Alexander Butchart, Etienne Krug, Christopher Mikton, and Berit Kieselbach at the World Health Organization Violence and Injury Prevention Department. I owe a great debt to the guest lecturers of my course who gave me feedback and offered essential guidance in their disciplines: Drs John Strauss, James Leckman (biology), Elijah Anderson (sociology), Francesca Grandi, David Simon (political science), Thomas Pogge, Atty James Silk (human rights), Dr Amity Doolittle (environmental studies), Prof Jonathan Schell (nuclear violence and nonviolence), Dr Michael Reed-Hurtado, Attys Fiona Doherty (criminal justice), Noah Zatz (public interest law), Drs Maya Prabhu (international law), Kathryn Falb, Kaveh Khoshnood, and Unni

Karunakara (public health). In terms of editorial and research help, I am greatly indebted to Dr Grace Lee, Morkeh Blay-Tofey, James Tierney, Nick Oliver, and Liz Seif. I would also like to acknowledge the student deciding to embark upon this text to get to the heart of a problem that is the source of much of humanity's suffering.

All that I do has one consistent guide: my mother, Dr Inmyung Lee, who taught me half of all the medicine I know, even before I entered medical school; she also showed me that the impulse to serve humanity offers a compass for all knowledge. Because of her, I could model my life after my grandfather, Dr Geun-Young Lee, whom I never met but who came to stir my vision of healing, including of society. My mother came to play a crucial role in the work that culminated in this book. When I was originally aiming for publication in 2015 while teaching and attending a busy clinic, she offered to spend an exceptional few months with me in the spring of 2014 and helped with literature searches, brought me books, collated thousands of pages of notes, and created indices for navigation. Like the parent who helps one to give birth of one's own, she was critical in my giving birth to this book. Most influential was her wellspring of ideas and lifetime of insights, which became the rock and the foundation of this volume. Although I put my name to it, she is more the book's author than I. She would not come to see its publication, but I trust that the student will benefit from her spirit as much as I. Here is one lesson from her: "Play, play with your subject of study—by the time you learn it, this will have been the shortcut!"

To close, I wish to thank all the students, patients, and prisoners who have taught me about human potential, who have shown me reasons for hope and convinced me of possibilities. They, above all, have demonstrated to me how we are all interconnected and could learn from one another. Finally, I also thank all my other colleagues at the Harvard Department of Social Medicine and the Yale Law and Psychiatry Division, my grandmother Eun-Suk Jang, my uncles Drs Soon-Hyung Lee and Sun-Hyung Lee, and my father Dr Yoo Sung Lee, as well as my sister and family: Patricia, Alan, Mirabelle, and Blake. I also cannot leave out my spiritual family: Frank O'Cain, Rebekah Samkuel, Anne Davenport, Leon Golub, Regis DeSilva, Luc Mahieu, Franck Rolin, Sophie Dupey, Hacène-Thierry Larbi, and my beloved J.

Overview

Part I   General Framework

1

Introduction

A Brief Introduction

> Both were remembering. Thinking of Hector, killer of men,
> Priam wept, abased at the feet of Achilles.
> But Achilles wept, now for this father.
> Now for Patroclus. And their sobs resounded through the house.
>
> —*Homer,* Iliad *(Eighth century BCE)*

Human history is mired in violence. Tracing its origins would mean going back to the beginnings of humanity. Being one of the most familiar phenomena around us, hardly any society, community, or individual is immune to its influence. Yet it is also one of the most unfathomable. Even a single instance can be overwhelming—be it homicide, suicide, legal violence in the name of "justice," warfare that devastates a society, terrorism that turns our worldview upside down, or systematic injustices that become a silent killer we call "structural violence." Yet we do not experience one episode at a time but over 3,800 violent deaths per day—1.4 million a year—worldwide. Of these, more than half (56%) are the result of suicide, one-third (33%) are from injuries caused by another person, and slightly more than one-tenth (11%) are due to war or some other form of collective violence (World Health Organization [WHO], 2017). Many millions more suffer from nonfatal injuries, non-injury health consequences, and less visible forms of psychological and social trauma. For every death, there are dozens of hospitalizations, hundreds of emergency room visits, and thousands of clinic appointments (WHO, 2008). Medical technology buffers us from bigger numbers, as a large proportion of wounds that would have been fatal in the past no longer are (MacKenzie et al., 2006; Monkkonen, 2001). The true tragedy is therefore greater than what our imagination can grasp.

For the most vulnerable populations—women, children, and the elderly—nonfatal forms of violence are more frequent and consequential, and its devastating effects reverberate through generations as a major health, human rights, and human development problem. Not yet calculated, furthermore, are the diverted energies for human creativity and civilization. Ninety percent of violent deaths occur in low- and middle-income countries, which draw our attention to the extreme deprivation of certain regions, while alerting us also to the dangers of high economic disparities. More subtle are the effects of concentrated poverty, low education, harsh and inconsistent parenting, and violence-promoting social norms that impede thriving in general.

We need not, however, be fatalistic about violence: as much as it is human-generated, it has human solutions. It is understandable and preventable. To this end, this text is intended to be as comprehensive as possible, bringing together the scholarship on violence that has largely been confined in academic silos until now. We live in an era when violence has reached, perhaps for the first time in history, a level of magnitude and sophistication that is astonishingly close to being incompatible with humanity's ability to continue surviving on earth. Yet, our awareness of the gravity of violence has also grown. If we combine the knowledge we have gained about it in many fields of study, we may attain a level of understanding that equips us with the ability to deal with the problem in new and creative ways. There may be no more urgent task for humankind than to figure out, above all, *how to think about violence* (Gilligan, 1996), which in turn will direct us in *how to understand violence*. Understanding brings clarity, and clarity is power—capable of bringing solutions to problems the way light illumines darkness.

This introductory chapter lays the groundwork, first by developing a broader definition for violence and then by proposing a model that can anchor all the multiple, disparate perspectives that arise from an interdisciplinary study. Along the way, it will delineate how different forms of violence are closely interrelated; help us to recognize that our violent potential changes according to the consciousness we bring to it; and outline a comprehensive course for integrating all research. Our goal is to learn how to think about violence in a ways that suit the complex, *human* nature of human beings. The comprehensive understanding we aim for will require theory, evidence, and storytelling, the last of which the student can expect to encounter in the form of case scenarios and vignettes.

Defining Violence

Violence is vast and varied, and before studying its parts, it is important to have a clear perspective of the whole. The study of violence suffered from a lack of uniform definition for a long time, which hampered measurement, characterization, and even identification. Having no agreed-upon definition can make a field fragmented and chaotic. In pursuing clarity, however, a definition can become too narrow or fixed. An ideal definition would therefore be clear but also be flexible and hold up over time as well as across different domains.

Much confusion ended when the WHO published its landmark *World Report on Violence and Health* (Krug et al., 2002). Assembling all available evidence up to that point, it defined violence as:

> the intentional use of physical force or power, threatened or actual, that either results in or has a high likelihood of resulting in injury, death, psychological harm, maldevelopment or deprivation *(Krug et al., 2002, p. 5).*

This new concept of violence has revolutionized our thinking about violence and has shaped approaches to the topic ever since. This sequence is worth mentioning for understanding the history and trajectory of the field and therefore how best to formulate a future course.

Some of the innovations are as follows. First, the definition emphasizes intentionality, thereby emphasizing process over outcome. Second, it includes not only physical force but also power, widening its scope to include important types of violence that may be hidden but are far more destructive, such as the violence of deprivation or unequal sharing of resources. Third, it states that the intentional act may be threatened or actual, clarifying that the focus should be less on the overt act, which may be incidental, than on the psychological state.

The inclusion of psychological harm, maldevelopment, and deprivation allows for consideration of some of the worst forms of abuse: psychological abuse, rejection, and neglect, which are less visible but may be more enduring than physical abuse (Hildyard & Wolfe, 2002). It has also made clear that sexual violence is not merely violent sexual behavior but primarily a manifestation of violence and domination (Bastick, Grimm, & Kunz, 2007). Whether violence is direct or indirect came to matter less, although intentionality matters: human-generated events are clearly more traumatic than natural calamities (Galea, Nandi, & Vlahov, 2005; Norris et al., 2002). Sociocultural influences play a large role in human behavior and are capable of creating epidemics of individual violence (Lee, Wexler, & Gilligan, 2014).

A broad definition of violence has many advantages. It allows for recognition of the full scope of the phenomenon, which can help prevent neglect of the topic when, for example, a familiar form recedes from view. A common danger of a narrow definition is mistaking the "decline" in one form for an overall decline, when expression may have merely shifted from one type of violence to another (e.g., from interstate wars to low-intensity civil conflict, or from murder epidemics to widespread suicides). Another danger is assuming that different types of violence are unrelated or neglecting to consider large areas because of different labels, when different types can also clearly rise and fall together (e.g., suicides and homicides, or homicides and collective violence) or combine in ways that elucidate larger patterns (Lee et al., 2014). Whether a general tendency for violence directs against the self, another, or a group depends on complex factors, and hence considering all forms together would be the first step to a clearer understanding.

A comprehensive definition helps with this. A consensus needs to develop on how properly to measure and compare concepts across fields of study while such scholarship should adapt to growing bodies of research and shape future inquiry. Where violence begins and where it ends—whether it includes psychological injury, verbal abuse, rape, property damage, or accidents—are questions we have answered through careful examination of research evidence. We now know, for example, that verbal aggression can be just as traumatizing as physical violence; that sexual assault is about dominating and overpowering, not about sexuality; and that harming a person has distinct motivations exceeding those of property damage, unless the latter is to threaten or to intimidate. We also know that accidents due to general recklessness or neglect share risk factors and similar characteristics as violence, even if we do not yet categorize them as violence.

Redefining Violence

We propose a slightly expanded definition, not because of any defect in the WHO definition but because of its strength: it has allowed research to advance widely and rapidly, and therefore may require updating. For example, we know far more about *structural violence*, so called because it refers to the avoidable limitations society places on groups of people through structures that prevent them from meeting their basic needs (Gilligan, 1999). It is the most lethal form of violence and calls for foremost consideration in any definition. Structural violence may at first seem a misnomer, for it concerns structures that are relatively stable and contrasts sharply with the dramatic manifestations of behavioral violence; however, it is a product of human decisions and ultimately has effects similar to those of individual violence (Morgan et al., 2014). Market globalization, furthermore, has given rise to a more rapid flux in existing structures as well as to new ones, creating opportunities for a redistribution of rights and goods.

A second major aspect to consider is our mounting capacity for catastrophic violence, through the proliferation of thermonuclear weapons and the desecration of our natural environment.

These have reached the point of qualifying as *collective suicidal behavior*. It means little to note that we engage in fewer high-intensity battles or deadly warfare when what we now face, more than ever, is the possibility that all of humankind could be wiped out instantaneously (Drell & Goodby, 2008). The extinction of our species—as well as most other life on Earth—will now more likely result from our own actions than from forces over which we have no control. This must be part of our consideration. Human violence, therefore, is not only a serious problem but may be the *most urgent problem* that humanity now confronts, as it places our entire species at greater immediate risk than any other single phenomenon (Rosenbaum, 2011).

An updated definition should reflect this urgency so that it can capture conceptually significant dimensions of violence to guide our thinking, research, and action. The literal definition is not as important as its theoretical ability to stimulate thought and increase awareness, as we will show later in this chapter is of central importance in preventing violence. To suit the complexity of violence, a definition should be broad enough to include the most important types but still specific enough to allow for concrete application. We propose the following new working definition:

> intentional or threatened human action, either direct or through structural neglect and diminution of others, that results in or has a high likelihood of resulting in human deprivation, injury, or death, or contributes to the extinction of the human species *(Lee, personal notes, 2014)*.

This modifies the WHO definition by avoiding use of the word "power," despite the concept being helpful in ways that we noted earlier. Ultimately, violence is *the guise* of power rather than true power, which is its opposite (Arendt, 1970). We will cover in Chapter 3, "The Psychology of Violence," and again in later chapters how violence is a guise to ward off feelings of powerlessness.

Examples of Violence

The Iliad

The Ancient Greek tale of Homer's *Iliad* places humankind in a violent world and depicts one of its recurrent themes: war. War is taken for granted and heroism in war is hailed as the greatest of honorable acts. However, the *Iliad*'s status as a classic perhaps depends on the fact that it does not shy away from ambivalence. In doing so, it illustrates well a central characteristic of violence: *complexity*. Force is as pitiless to its possessor as its victim, and conquerors are inseparable from conquered persons. They have in common only the refusal to believe that they both belong to the same species.

The grand battles of the Trojan War echo through smaller conflicts between characters, while the smaller battles between individuals add up to the larger one. There is disruption of society and everyday life due to war, but the soldiers still carry their skills and their humanity into it. There is brutal chaos of the spirit in the classical hero just as there is in a present-day murderer. At times, warfare is portrayed as murder due to crises of the human condition, such as in the cycle of revenge.

Hector, not expecting Achilles to rejoin the battle, has ordered his men to camp outside the walls of the city of Troy, but when the Trojan army glimpses Achilles, it flees in terror behind the city walls. Achilles kills every Trojan he sees. Finally, Achilles confronts Hector outside the walls, chasing him around the city's periphery three times until Hector finally turns to fight. Achilles kills Hector, attaches the body to the back of his chariot, and drags it across the battlefield to the Achaean camp. Upon his arrival, the triumphant citizens honor Patroclus, whom Hector had slain, with a long series of athletic games. Each of the next nine days, Achilles drags Hector's body in circles around Patroclus' funeral bier. Priam, Hector's father, then tearfully pleads with Achilles to return Hector's body (Homer, 1990).

The Khmer Rouge

The cycle of violence is confined neither to antiquity nor to the Global North. Many societies have endured autocratic and repressive governments in their transition to modern nation-states; among the most notorious is the Khmer Rouge. From 1975 until 1979, they ruled the Democratic Republic of Kampuchea, now Cambodia. Pol Pot and Ieng Sary were prime minister and deputy prime minister under their Communist-based regime. Supporters of the former regime, including soldiers, officials, and civil servants, as well as students, professors, scientists, and members of opposition organizations, were brutally exterminated on a massive scale. Approximately four million people were herded into "communes"—disguised concentration camps where men, women, and children above the age of 10 were put to hard labor.

Mass killings happened alongside the abolition of religion, destruction of economic and cultural structures, and devastation of family and social relations. Tens of thousands were viciously tortured, their bodies cut open and subject to electroshock and live surgery. Forced marriages and rape were commonplace. Children were put to death, eaten, or recruited into armed units to fight. Vietnam launched an attack to overthrow the Khmer Rouge in January 1979, and in August 1979, the Revolutionary People's Tribunal of Cambodia found Pol Pot and Sary guilty of genocide. Executions and the combined effects of strenuous working conditions, malnutrition, and poor medical care had caused the deaths of approximately a quarter of the Cambodian population, or an estimated one to three million people (Boulet, 2009).

A Case of Child Neglect

Some of the most tragic cases of abuse occur within private homes, to those who are the most vulnerable. Allan (the name has been changed for confidentiality purposes) was 4 months old when he was removed from his home by a child service agency following a report of life-threatening neglect. He was placed in foster care, as no relatives were available to take him. Soon thereafter, upon referral to a home-based program by the agency, the court authorized periodic returns home. Despite the services provided to his mother, Allan returned to the foster home after supervised visits with very dirty diapers and the appearance of being underfed, according to the foster parent. Shortly before a court hearing when the mother was expecting Allan to be returned to her custody, the case manager together with an agency worker informed her that they would recommend continued foster home placement with extended visits home. The mother became upset, threatening to kill the case manager. The agency worker called 911, and the police arrived, removing Allan from the mother.

The agency worker reported the conditions of the home: the house was unkempt, and two other children were largely unsupervised and dressed in dirty clothing. There were concerning signs of the mother's unsatisfactory relationship with Allan, whose needs for food and diaper-changing often went unmet. When she interacted with him, she showed little response to his cooing or crying. At the court hearing, the judge ordered that Allan continue in foster care and that visits home be scheduled twice weekly with an evaluation in 1 month to consider overnight visits. At the next court hearing 1 month later, the mother promised that she would be more responsible in caring for Allan. The judge ordered that the child be returned home immediately. Because of budget cuts, the social service agency determined the case closed without follow-up. Five months later, a news report announced that his home had burnt down while he and all family members were in it. Allan and his mother died of smoke inhalation, and the two other children sustained severe burn injuries. It was suspected that the older children, ages five and four, were playing with the stove while the mother was intoxicated with alcohol.

Suicide by Gun

Human violence takes many forms. In 2010 in the US, 19,392 people committed suicide with guns, more than the 11,078 who were killed by others with guns. Though gunshots are not the most common suicide method, they are the most lethal. About 85% of suicide attempts with a firearm end in death (Drexler, 2013).

Emily's 21-year-old husband, Ryan, shot himself with a semiautomatic in November 2008, soon after bringing a lawsuit against a priest who had molested him during his teenage years; the priest had been convicted in 2007 and sentenced to 30 days in jail. Ryan was one of the top five salespeople for a major national company but had struggled with nightmares since the molestation. He had never used a gun before. Pregnant at the time with their second child, Emily walked into the gas station where her husband had bought the gun and asked the owner about the process for selling a gun and whether they screened people for mental illness. The owner showed little emotion, and did not say he was sorry.

Kristyn is a detective. Her father, Bruce, a dentist, shot himself in August 2003, at the age of 63. Bruce had a great sense of humor and a thriving dental practice, but he had suffered for years from undiagnosed depression. After several rounds of drinks late one evening, he took cartridges from an open box of ammunition on a neighbor's refrigerator. He inserted them into an antique hunting rifle that had long been in the family and triggered the deadly blow.

Janyce is a school lunch worker. Her 23-year-old son, Zachary, killed himself with a firearm in 2008—hours after his first drunken driving arrest. He may have been afraid of losing his commercial driver's license, of which he was very proud. He was happy-go-lucky; loved his family, his sisters, and his nephews and nieces; and still lived at home. There were guns in their home because Janyce's husband owned hunting rifles. She was not a gun lover, but several family members owned guns, and she believed there were people who can be trusted with guns for the right purposes. Zachary was impulsive but not particularly more so than others his age. In this instance, an impulsive act cost him his life.

Connecting the Dots

Violence, as a whole, seems a phenomenon of such irrationality and perplexity as to be indecipherable, but putting together the different forms can help. What commonality does suicide have with homicide, and individual violence with warfare? What do the events of global violence as reported in the media have to do with what occurs in the privacy of the home? Much of the study of violence has taken the approach of creating smaller and smaller "niches" in the belief that the narrow scope will circumvent the complexity of the problem. However, with human violence, the exact opposite is true: attempts to divide the field into discreet units of observation have only made the topic more wieldy. The more we accept this complexity and consider the wider context, on the other hand, the more coherent and logical the patterns become. When a student says, "It works in theory but not in practice," one is really saying, "The theory does not work." In the case of violence, a workable theory requires that we relinquish artificial subdivisions in order to confront the complex reality.

For the past couple decades, there has been a growing interest in the study of violence, with an accompanying explosion of information. One of the reasons we have not made more progress in understanding violence so as to prevent it more effectively is that we have fragmented the subject among disciplines that often do not speak with one another. An Indian parable about blind men describing an elephant—the man who feels a leg says it is like a tree trunk; the man who feels the tail says it is like a rope; the man who feels the trunk says it is like a hose; and so forth—implies that a single viewpoint is inherently limited if it fails to account for the totality. This illustrates what has happened in the study of violence: like six blind men (or 60 blind men if we count all the subfields), we have tried to understand the elephant of violence that has been affecting all of humankind throughout history, each according to our own limited point of view. Until very recently, homicide has been studied almost exclusively by criminologists; suicide just as exclusively by psychiatrists; warfare by political scientists and historians; capital punishment by criminal law specialists; and culturally specific forms of violence, such as genital mutilation, by anthropologists, all without much interdisciplinary dialog.

The WHO's *World Report*, by contrast, has placed the different types of violence under the same rubric, welcoming efforts to understand the different types of violence—that is, self-directed, interpersonal, and collective violence—not just separately but in totality, with an ecological perspective (Bronfenbrenner, 1979). Consequently, we have dramatically expanded our understanding of the causes, manifestations, and prevention of violence. This simple concept has generated great progress for the field.

Yet, at a time when we need a global perspective to deal with the problem on a global scale, our information is coming from more and more sharply delineated sources. This obscures the magnitude of the problem. How we bring together the knowledge we now have, and how we think about violence and respond to it, will determine humanity's future—and possibly whether or not we will have one. Returning to the scenarios of the previous section, what do ancient warfare, state oppression, child abuse, and suicides have in common? They may not seem like events that naturally go together, but in the *Iliad*, we see how the Trojan War leads to individual campaigns and vendettas. Observing Cambodia under the Khmer Rouge, we see how entire populations can vanish under dictatorship. In the case of Allan, we see how injury from child maltreatment is tied to the availability of social services. The suicides by firearm show us that what seem largely personal struggles are connected to gun policy. In order to understand fully how violence occurs and how to prevent it effectively, it is necessary to move away from assigning simple causes and solutions to considering multiple risk factors and layers of interventions. Throughout this text, we will explore how to connect seemingly unrelated events and to find commonalities among them.

In order to organize our thinking to this end, we will first propose the *bio-psycho-socio-environmental* model. An extension of the bio-psycho-social model of illness and health (Engel, 1977), this perspective means that human conditions require a broad view involving all of these different levels. The *biological* denotes processes that happen at the level of the physical brain or the body. The *psychological* encompasses the mind's function and human behavior. The *social* involves relationships, social interactions, and society. Finally, the *environmental* implies the surroundings in which all the other processes occur, be they natural or human-produced. This complex model serves as a tentative reminder that many factors contribute to violence and that we can draw from different disciplines to find solutions at multiple levels. No one field of study has all the answers. The study of violence, furthermore, is an art that involves the integration of knowledge and scientific research.

The model is tentative: a complex whole with components in constant interaction is still difficult to conceive. Concerted influences of simultaneous action are characteristic of the environments human beings live in but are not what research designs study the most. Still, the complex nature of violence makes this conceptualization primary in importance. Consistency through simple reductionism, or compilation of data that do not illuminate the whole, does not advance our understanding of violence. Violence studies make clear that knowledge is abundant but wisdom is lacking—but the most critical problem confronting humankind, its own violence, requires no less than the greatest insight of which we are capable. It is best, therefore, to let the nature of violence guide our efforts.

The addition here of the environmental level to the customary schema helps account for effects that are not from direct social interactions, although they may derive from them. There is the natural physical environment, for example. Then there are institutions and "spiritual" traditions we may inherit. Meanwhile, we will prepare to apply the bio-psycho-socio-environmental model to a more systemic representation in the ecological model in Chapter 12's "Public Health Approaches." We conclude that, while there will always be a need for more and better data on the multiple causes and cures for human violence, an even greater need exists for theories capable of integrating the considerable body of information that already exists. The purpose of this book, therefore, is to take an unprecedented but necessary look at violence from an interdisciplinary, global perspective, in order to bring the scholarship of violence to a new stage.

A New Field

While we have made enormous advances in identifying the causes of and cures for most life-threatening processes, from infectious diseases to cancer to heart disease, we are only beginning to make similar progress in understanding causes and cures as they relate to violence. Why is this? Success in other areas of health and medicine have raised the average life expectancy to a level dramatically higher than a century ago, not just in high-income but also in most middle- and low-income countries (Centers for Disease Control and Prevention, 2003). Now, we are in the process of wiping out those gains in some regions of the world because of violence. Why have we failed to prevent violence with anything close to the success we have achieved in preventing or curing other causes of death and disability? The twentieth century was "the most violent century in human history" as measured by the rates of deaths and injuries resulting from violence (Hobsbawm, 1994), and the potential for future violence dwarfs the scale of violence that has already occurred.

Our failure to prevent violence has already resulted in its rise in rankings of worldwide causes of death (Vos et al., 2016). The contrast is even starker if we take into account potential years of life lost (YLL) (Kassebaum et al., 2016), since violence truncates the lives of the young more frequently than degenerative diseases, which primarily kill people nearing the end of their life cycle.

The reasons for our failure to make a more significant dent in our own violence are varied and mutually reinforcing. First, there is the matter of political and economic will. In the United States, for example, despite the fact that violence causes more years of life lost than cancer and heart disease combined, funding for violence research is miniscule compared to other leading causes of death, while funding for gun violence research has been virtually eliminated (Ladapo et al., 2013). Second, violent cultures do not deal with violence seriously. US culture, for instance, treats violence largely as a source of entertainment, pride, or even solution to threats (murder mysteries, violent video games, war heroes, and preemptive defense). Third, powerful economic interests benefit from a continuation of violence. The gun lobby in the US is one of the more explicit examples: no quantity of mass shootings, massacres, innocent deaths, and grieving parents has been able to force passage of substantial gun control laws that would limit commercial profitability (Goss, 2010). The military industry is similarly lucrative, with arms sales of the top one hundred largest arms-producing companies estimating at 395 billion US dollars per year (Stockholm International Peace Research Institute, 2012).

Finally, violence brings political advantage. Certain political groups have risen to power as a result of high levels of violence; in the US, they support racism (against non-whites), sexism (against women), classism (against the poor), ageism (against younger people), and militarism (against the public). Creating divisions in the population also allows for easier control, and given this advantage, there is little real motivation to reduce violence. All of these forces fuel a continued neglect of violence as a valid subject for research and study, perpetuating the problem.

The more we learn about violence and its variations, the more it becomes clear that its study calls for an examination of complex connections within a coherent theory. We go so far as to propose here that *we cannot fully understand even one form of violence without understanding all the others.* This is because these different phenomena are directly related to one another. In order to understand an individual fully, the entire ecological system of the person's development needs to be taken into account; in order to understand individual violence fully, social, structural, and environmental violence must enter the equation.

Another problem with a fragmented approach is that the temptation to abandon the study will be great once the urgency of the topic has passed. Like the individuals who become involved, violence has long been an orphan subject, relegated to the margins of every field. Psychiatry may seem a logical discipline within which to study violence, but it has long considered violent individuals as intractable and outside the domain of healing. Anthropology would appear appropriate, but its researchers have avoided addressing violence with the populations they are trying to befriend. Political science seems natural, but it has not been at ease with violence outside the sanitized structure of war. Law seems practical, but advocates often wish to divert attention from the flaws of those they are representing. While public health has been prominent in some respects, violence is still a marginal topic for the field, and many public health schools do not even teach a course on it. In this manner, everybody's business becomes nobody's business.

Shall we, then, risk being caught off guard if and when another massive world war breaks out, with greater-than-ever lethal potential? Just before the bloodiest battles of the twentieth century, it was believed that humankind had "civilized" itself beyond such violence (Elias, 1939). Following the end of the Cold War, we believed that we had eliminated the major social, historical, political, cultural, and economic risks for worldwide violence (Fukuyama, 1992)—only to be met with a newly fractious and turbulent world. If we have anything to learn from history, it is that violence seldom remains constant—in degree or in form—and each catastrophic eruption has followed a period of complacency. Therefore, it seems that the problem of violence is closely related to our own level of awareness. In recent years, the study of violence has enjoyed a level of popularity as never before (Kurtz, 2008; Wilkinson & Pickett, 2009). Harnessing this opportunity would entail finding a way to establish steady, persistent study so as not only to continue our relatively peaceful interim but to enhance it.

We thus propose here that *violence studies* become a discipline in its own right. With a potential for extreme violence that sets us apart from every other species and from humans at any other point in history, we must take every opportunity for preventing violence seriously. That seriousness could help avert instantaneous annihilation of human civilization, as in the case of thermonuclear war. Or it could help avoid a more gradual but pervasive and permanent destruction of our habitat, as through human-generated climate change. Violence may be the most important subject matter we could study—to prepare during any lull, if we can call it this—to form structured and enduring ways of strengthening the conditions for peace. It is clear that any change to this perennial human problem must happen consciously.

As long as we engage in it, human violence remains a mystery that gives rise to a battery of questions. What makes people violent? What does it take to become nonviolent? What induces humanity's tendency to engage continually in irrational, self-destructive behavior? In spite of mounting research, we do not have the answers to the most basic questions. Therefore, this book is about violence but also, more than that, it is about the fundamental puzzle of human existence: why human beings engage in violence against others and against themselves. What an in-depth study of violence can achieve is the understanding of violence not as an event but as the final outcome of a long developmental process that takes place over the course of an affected individual's lifetime or a community's entire history. We can learn to recognize the many underlying causes that can culminate in a variety of behaviors. Thinking more clearly and consistently about the nature of the multiple causes and manifestations of violence will reduce much of the confusion as well as make prevention more possible.

The field of violence studies should include aspects of criminology but not be confined to that discipline, since most violence is not criminal and most crimes are not violent. It should also include the study of practices causing injuries and deaths that are permitted or even required by the law, as some laws can be violent. It would benefit from the knowledge of human behavior and disease that medicine can provide, since it is the field chiefly concerned with enhancing wellbeing and preventing deaths. It also needs to extend to institutional and structural forms of violence that are far more lethal than any direct violence.

Violence studies ought to complement *peace studies*, which have historically aimed to generate reconciliation and conflict resolution, while violence studies have striven to understand phenomenology and therefore prevention of violence before it happens. Violence studies deal with biological, psychological, sociological, and ecological causes and cures, whereas peace studies have traditionally dealt more with international relations, diplomacy, political science, and economics. That said, the two approaches have been converging as they share a common goal and as the different levels of violence prevention merge. They differ from but are closely related to the study of human rights, which primarily concerns itself with moral principles and may offer a useful perspective on systematic injustice.

All that having been said, the emphasis must lie with the conceptualization of humans as consisting of body, mind, and social-symbolic being, such that fulfilling human needs addresses all these levels as complementary and interacting counterparts. If we are truly to lift ourselves out of violence, we must learn to traverse the full extent of the human experience. By meeting the challenge in its depth and complexity, violence studies can be a foundation for deep-rooted peacebuilding efforts, as it excavates the human capacity not only for curbing violence but for accessing resilience and regenerative creativity.

A New Awareness

We have seen how a change in awareness has been able to produce the kind of scholarship that has drastically curtailed violence around the globe over the past couple decades. We have learned that we have the intelligence and the ability to deal with our own violence, but as is often the case with all-pervasive conditions, our awareness of violence as a problem needing attention has lagged. Indeed, for much of human history, individuals and societies have accepted it as an inevitable part of life, something we needed to tolerate, if not actively engage in. Naturally, the degree to which people participate in it and bystanders condone it (Latane &

Darley, 1970) corresponds to the extent to which it is accepted. Technology has produced the capacity for widespread violence, but our psychology controls the weapons, or fails to control them, and determines what we will do with that physical power. Therefore, a lack of awareness of violence as a problem has contributed to the problem—to the point where it is the most significant source of the problem.

This means that recognizing violence as a problem, not a solution, allows for the beginnings of a solution. As with any change of behavior, acquiring awareness of the behavior affects the behavior itself (Bergin & Garfield, 1994; Grant, Franklin, & Langford, 2002; Prochaska & DiClemente, 1986). As we have noted, we are arriving at a critical time when our level of conscious awareness of violence could determine future human survival. We will term different potential degrees of awareness as alarm consciousness, lack of consciousness, and studied consciousness.

Alarm consciousness is a response to major escalations of violence. Complacency during a period of relative peace gives way to alarm and a sudden awakening to the danger after extreme violence, as with the Napoleonic Wars, whose impact rose to the level of roughly five to seven million deaths (Esdaile, 2014). The most significant escalations in recent history, without doubt, are the two World Wars, the invention of the atom bomb, and the hundreds of regional conflicts that have characterized the hitherto most violent century. The two World Wars claimed over 100 million lives, and many smaller battles additional hundreds of thousands, while governments murdered an estimated 170 million of their own people (Fink, 2010). Toward the end of the century, the US saw an increase in violent crime of more than 560%; around the world, homicide increased by 15% in Organisation for Economic Co-operation and Development (OECD) countries, by 80% in Latin America, and by 100% in the Arab world (WHO, 2015).

Widespread peace movements accompanied the emergence of great thinkers such as Emma Goldman, Simone Weil, Hannah Arendt, Bertrand Russell, Dorothy Day, Martin Luther King Jr., Nelson Mandela, Václav Havel, Eqbal Ahmad, and Rigoberta Menchú, to name just a few. From the shock of the worst wars known to history, this era established a new norm of peace and an awareness that helped to propagate it for decades. Yet it came to a close. Without incorporating the awareness of violence into our institutions, such as adopting it as a field of regular education and study, this consciousness depended on alarm to fight an uphill battle against the structures of war, such as the military-industrial complex. Also, the more that 3000 who perish every day through suicide and homicide, in far greater number than in any war, year after year, do not raise alarms but are tolerated in our homes, our neighborhoods, and our society. Meanwhile, as the memory of the alarm faded, so did the awareness—and a wave of wars (with a US-led "war on terror" in Afghanistan and Iraq ushering in a new era of violent conflict and further need for war) began anew.

In contrast, *lack of consciousness* is due to a psychic numbing (Lifton, 1979), often commensurate with the scale of the problem, when the difficulty, tragedy, and often intimacy of the violence are too much for the mind and lead to denial. It could also manifest as complacency, or, in its latest form, investment in the belief that violence is less and less of a problem because it is declining (Eisner, 2003). Popular "scholars of violence" have seized the opportunity to pander to a public desire for reassurance in ways that contribute to the problem (Pinker, 2011). This response is particularly prevalent in the UK and the US, which are among the regions of the world recently experiencing dramatic relief from epidemics of violence. It is easy to think that violence levels are going down—war deaths, homicides, and the most overt forms of brutality have indeed diminished. However, what sense does it make to quantify violence in this way, when a single nuclear weapon contains the explosive force to wipe out the entire human species, and we continue to amass and to develop these weapons?

Rigorous science requires more than simplistic enumeration of numbers, and where violence is concerned, it may require taking into account our own role in its generation. Counting only a narrow form of violence, such as overt warfare or murder, and extrapolating the trends within Europe and North America to all the world for all time, promotes a Global North-centric view that can become an ingredient for violence. Also, while comforting in thought, the decline does not include suicide, which dwarfs all other types of violence and has reached historic highs, or the far more consequential structural violence present at an unprecedented scale of escalation. Only with undue simplification can we come to the premature and dangerous conclusion that violence is no longer a problem.

Such a claim is also inaccurate. Historians agree that the exact number of even the most objectively measureable violence—deaths—cannot be known with any precision (Gohdes & Price, 2013; Lacina & Gleditsch, 2005): even in the last 150 years, when measurements started to improve, estimates in the most developed parts of the world vary by millions. Thus, drawing conclusions about deaths thousands of years into the past based on current measurements is speculative at best, and to pretend otherwise is irresponsible. Even if the numbers could be known, the changing forms of combat alone make clear the fallacy of such comparisons, since most deaths no longer occur on the battlefield but rather through the famine, disease, dislocation, and insurgencies that accompany war. The toll of war also manifests in upsurges in one-sided violence (e.g., genocidal campaigns such as the Holocaust or the Armenian Genocide), in criminal violence (e.g., increases in crime following the collapse of local policing in post-Baathist Iraq); and in hidden violence (e.g. domestic violence against women and children). As noted, lack of consciousness makes us veer away from serious examination at the present that could help us understand and alleviate the problem where violence rates are rising, such as in Central America (WHO, United Nations Office on Drugs and Crime, & United Nations Development Programme, 2014). Through the omission of important areas, it not only fails to allow for a global assessment (United Nations Office on Drugs and Crime, 2013; Violence Prevention Alliance, 2012) but also misrepresents science (Ferguson, 2013; Mitzen, 2013; Rose, 2013; Stone, 2014) and translates directly into a barrier to moving beyond the problem (Lifton, 1987).

This brings us to the third type of consciousness, which we will call *studied consciousness*: being fully cognizant of the ongoing threat of violence while investigating it thoroughly so as to prevent it effectively. The common approach throughout the world is to wait for spikes of violence to happen, and then to respond retroactively; this approach deals with it proactively. This level of consciousness is especially necessary with the nature of the violence that we face today. We confront perhaps the greatest perils humankind has ever known in the history of human existence in that we have the capacity for instantaneous and complete, or more prolonged but more certain, self-annihilation. However, the sheer magnitude of this unprecedented risk makes it difficult to grasp and tempting to deny and ignore, especially when it is far from everyday experience. A studied consciousness, therefore, also requires steadiness and calm. It is a well-informed awareness of the risks, taking on the vigilance of alarm consciousness and the placidity of lack of consciousness, to approach the topic with composure, even in times of peace. Establishing an independent field devoted to its study can help form a framework for regular practice.

Studied consciousness, through steady research, is likely to reveal processes underlying violence that allow us to focus less on whether overt events of violence are occurring and more on whether the conditions for peace are present, so that we can prevent violence from happening in the first place. Foremost, it accepts that violence is a problem and that existing levels are already unacceptably high—whether or not they are plaguing us in our geographic or chronological moment, since the presence of causal elements means eruptions can occur at any time.

Consistent study detects patterns that are not immediate, such as interrelationships between different types of violence. Suicide and homicide can be the same destructive tendency manifesting differently according to culture or circumstance, for instance, and sometimes the two combine. We all read news stories about somebody who kills a partner or parent and then kills oneself, too. Massacres often conclude with suicide, and suicide bombers combine the two. If we wish to understand these events, we need to understand not only what causes homicide but also what causes suicide. Studied consciousness prepares us for changes in how violence manifests according to situation and time—with change as a constant in all human behavior—so that a change from interstate wars to guerilla warfare and terrorism, or combat warfare to home-grown massacres, does not surprise us.

It takes care not to exclude relevant types of violence that are not obvious on the surface: for instance, the last few decades saw an alarming rise in structural violence between high-income and low- or middle-income countries, as well as within most countries (Ortiz & Cummins, 2011). Structural violence needs consideration not only for causing the greatest rate of excess, premature deaths and damage (Köhler & Alcock, 1976), but because under its conditions, the rise of other forms of violence is only a matter of time (Butchart & Engström, 2002). Educating oneself, therefore, is the preventive against counterproductive actions. Ignorance does not just lead to misdirected action but actively contributes to the problem. A conscious decision to pursue nonviolence allows for preparation, prevents overwhelm, and activates the most effective form of violence reduction, even if the results are not immediately available. Studied consciousness thus ultimately builds on the optimism that violence is not insurmountable, underscoring the extraordinary opportunity to build on our growing understanding and capacity to make a difference.

Further examination will quickly reveal that our era is not placid by any measure. Many countries are struggling with rising food costs, and growing income inequality is affecting high-, medium-, and low-income societies alike. The global financial crisis and recession have generated widespread unemployment and impoverishment. The spread of democracy has had an enormous effect in generating peace (Doyle, 1983), but growing research suggests that this is not a result of the political system *per se* but because of the reduction of structural violence that accompanies it. Caution is therefore necessary when global capitalism shortly follows with a system of privileges capable of offsetting the gains of democracy (Hertz, 2002). The rapid rise in inequality between individuals and between nations not only becomes one of the most important causes of premature deaths and disability, it threatens to be a potent cause of other forms of violence. As the exploitation, intimidation, and greed inherent in structural violence corrode the general health of society, the capacity for a society to examine itself also diminishes. A correction of course then becomes increasingly difficult. Studying and nurturing awareness while we still have the capacity is therefore critical if we are not to be caught off guard in a spiral of violence.

Structure of the Text

With the aim of integrating and synthesizing existing scholarship on violence in an orderly way, this text will progress largely from causes to consequences to cures. We will roughly follow the sequence of studying the major bio-psycho-socio-environmental perspectives on violence. After this current Chapter 1, "Introduction," we present the following chapters:

2) The Biology of Violence
3) The Psychology of Violence

4) The Symbolism (or Spiritual Causes) of Violence
5) The Sociology and Anthropology of Violence
6) The Political Science and Economics of Violence
7) Structural Violence
8) Environmental (and Nuclear) Violence
9) Consequences of Violence
10) Criminal Justice Approaches
11) International Law Approaches
12) Public Health Approaches
13) Global Medicine Approaches
14) Nonviolence Approaches
15) Synthesis and Integration

We can group the progression from an intra- and interpersonal framework (Chapters 2 through 4) to a social and societal one (Chapters 5 through 8), before going into the life cycle (Chapter 9) and the various mechanisms we have at our disposal for preventing violence (Chapters 10 through 14). Our goals are twofold: First, we aim to summarize information that sheds light on a human propensity that takes many forms depending on the context. Doing so also helps to distinguish the diverse etiologies of even a single form of violence. Understanding these requires a multidisciplinary methodology. Second, we aim to change the way we think about violence. This applies both in the way we approach it as a research subject and in what we recognize as violence.

To do so, we give special attention to the most lethal form of violence, structural violence—a term that the Norwegian sociologist Johan Galtung (1969) coined. The inequalities that divide populations into rich and poor, or weak and powerful, determine access to social goods, criminal justice, basic safety, healthcare, and other material and symbolic needs that mitigate if not prevent violence. Relative poverty causes far more deaths than any other form of violence. Studies have shown that the rate of deaths from relative poverty was already in the range of 14–18 million per year 40 years ago (Høivik, 1977), overwhelming the 1.4 million per year from all behavioral violence—such as suicide, homicide, and collective violence—combined (Fitzmaurice et al., 2017). More importantly, as we will demonstrate, structural violence is not only the deadliest form of violence, it is also the most powerful cause of other forms of violence, such as behavioral violence. We call it violence because it is something we as a society choose when we decide on how to distribute or not to distribute, or how to share or not to share, the collective wealth and income that each society produces.

We give urgent attention to the greatest threat of our time, *nuclear* and *environmental violence*, and relate it to the *human* characteristics of violence. First, distinguishing us from other animals, and our time from other periods in history, is the fact that human violence has the potential to bring about the extinction of our species. That is to say, because of the destructive power of the weapons that we have developed, and the extent to which we can alter our environment so as to throw our entire ecosystem off balance, our decisions can have enormous—terminal—consequences. We will address the ramifications of our failure both to learn to curb our own violence and to implement what we have learned so far. We will face squarely our standing as the first species in evolutionary history to risk bringing about its own extinction through its own behavior. Previous extinctions have been due to changes in the natural environment or other uncontrollable forces. Secondly, human violence is complex because of *human* complexity. This lies not just in our ability to attain the technical capacity for violence on a scale that can threaten our collective survival, but also in our capacity to hinder the awareness that is necessary to prevent our own annihilation.

Finally, we will put together information that has its own complex scholarly background. Available violence research comes to us disproportionately from high-income countries, especially the US, for example, such that the priorities of low- and middle-income countries, where the vast majority of violence occurs, are given secondary and tertiary consideration. We call this the 90/10 gap, whereby 90% of published research comes from regions of the world where only 10% of global violence is occurring (Mikton & Butchart, 2009) and resource-poor regions cope with a high burden as well as low attention. With the leadership of the WHO, this gap has begun to close, but the problem remains serious (Lee, Leckman, & Mbwambo, 2014).

What to Expect

Much of this volume will be a basic presentation of established information based on sound research, critical reviews of prevailing theories within each field, and demonstrations through narrative vignettes. However, merging knowledge from different disciplines will allow us to go beyond simply what each field has to offer. Here are some things to expect:

1) *You will challenge assumptions.* The first lesson in violence is that things are not always what they seem. We will be looking at common myths about the nature and definition of violence. Since it is a topic of everyday discourse we may feel we have a certain level of familiarity with it, but this feeling can easily mislead. If your assumptions have not been challenged already, you will soon learn that the deeper your knowledge about violence, the more you will discover that the phenomenon of violence is very different from initial impressions, and in many ways will even seem paradoxical.

2) *You will break down barriers.* In this text, barriers between different forms of violence, different disciplines, and different approaches to prevention will begin to dissolve. Since we will be approaching violence as a human problem that brings with it all the layers of human complexity, this multilayered and complex nature will be the focus and not an annoyance we should explain away or unduly simplify. Recognizing that the various types of human violence relate to one another and that new understanding arises from this synchronous consideration will be a central theme. Because of the interdisciplinary nature of this text, it is inevitable that students will be more comfortable with some subjects than others. Additionally, each field has its own culture and methodology that determine what areas are emphasized and what questions asked—having a conversation that traverses multiple fields of knowledge will require patience and understanding. The student is commended for embarking on this journey that will be, we hope, as rewarding as it is challenging.

3) *You will learn to synthesize.* Violence may ultimately be the most critical quandary of our day. Perpetuating many of our current social, political, and military policies assures that our course of unremitting violence will continue in untenable ways. In order to decipher how to use our energy, creativity, and action in a way that is constructive and not self-destructive, we need to view the issues on a much larger scale than the usual. This entails putting together all the information we have available so as to understand the totality of the problems confronting us, and to taking an integrative and interactionist approach that allows for concerted efforts rather than fragmented, reductionistic ones that can work against one another.

4) *You will learn to criticize.* No matter what we have told ourselves for millennia, we do not have to accept violence as a part of life, any more than we have to accept disease as a part of health. Violence and disease give rise to destruction and premature death,

while health brings life-affirming generativity. Violence is learned, and it can be unlearned—and rechanneled. That a condition has existed for a long time does not make it inevitable, nor does it make it acceptable. That society has followed a violent course till now, to the point where we have come close to, if not arrived at, the brink of calamity, does not mean things should be this way. However, change will require a shift in thinking and a critical assessment of current approaches. You will therefore learn to criticize not only overt acts of violence and injury, but subtler, more enduring ones that emanate from institutional structures. We will also learn to discern which types of violence to prioritize: addressing structural issues, for example, would prevent far more deaths and disability than would tracking every individual and sanctioning every intention, although for now we need to do both.

5) *You will construct better means of prevention.* As we come to a more comprehensive understanding of the nature of violence and its root causes, we will also be able to formulate more effective ways to implement preventive measures. The more we study the topic with care, the more likely we are to develop deeper and more enduring interventions than superficial "Band-Aid" solutions or so-called "solutions" that actually worsen the problem, as we have done throughout history because of a dearth of understanding. The student will have chosen this subject with both concern and hope. The concern is that violence is a serious problem that requires intervention, and the hope is that, as your knowledge, understanding, and wisdom expand, creative and truly productive prevention strategies will become more possible.

As you learn more about the subject, you can expect to be able to answer difficult questions such as these:

1) What explains the unique human tendency toward violence where there is no perceivable instrumental gain?
2) How did Europe, once one of the most violent regions of the world, become one of the most peaceful?
3) How do measures intended to curb violence, such as incarceration or capital punishment, become stimulants of individual violence?
4) How might we explain the observation that, as a general rule, the more violent the act, the less the perpetrator's remorse?
5) What explains the greatest conundrum of all: human actions against the self or one's own species?

Conclusion

The greater the quandary of violence, the more pressing is the need for carefully organized, rigorous inquiry. An urgent imperative of the contemporary study of violence is to describe, analyze, and understand better the phenomenon based on accumulating evidence, so that we might intervene intelligently and constructively. Different forms of violence are closely interlinked, making it essential that we conceptualize violence in an integrated way. It makes no sense to study only one form of violence without the context of the whole, which has given rise to misinterpretations that violence rates are decreasing, when they may have merely morphed from one form to another. A broad definition that is able to connect the multiple, disparate perspectives arising from an interdisciplinary study is necessary. Only then can we solve the problem of violence without substituting one form for another. By no means a straightforward subject, with its emotionally charged nature, human violence elicits reactions to the topic in a way that ignores or underplays its importance—until we are forced to face it.

For this reason, awareness of the problem is an enormous and important step that we cannot overlook but must build into the topic. The study of violence is in essence a study of human beings: through violence, we confront human urgencies and exigencies; encounter the stretches of our nature; and discover our infinite potential for transforming our own behavior. The more knowledge we have, the more tools we can put to use, and the more control we can assert over our destiny. Justice, civil society, human thriving, our collective coexistence, and ultimately our very survival on this planet depend on our ability to understand and to confront violence.

Practically, our response to destruction, oppression, alienation, and other ways in which human beings inflict suffering on one another should not be apathy or further harm. Theoretically, we cannot abstract away the human element or fit the complexity of violence into preconceptions and still be accurate, appropriate, and effective. Just as the causes of violence are simultaneously multifactorial, so are the effective cures necessarily multidimensional, and thus multidisciplinary work is necessary. The topic warrants systematic, serious study, taking into account the full complexity and urgency of the subject and drawing together all that we already know and ought to know. It is the purpose of this wide-ranging text on violence—a human phenomenon so extreme, so bizarre, and so outside the realm of reason, that it brings about the death of oneself and others of one's kind, is not a topic for which we can satisfy ourselves with superficial explanations. It is not only an important subject of study that may determine our survival as a species, but one that warrants serious scholarship as one of the greatest intellectual quandaries of our time.

Questions

Each chapter will end with questions, and students are encouraged to bring their own, for knowing how to ask the right questions will be central to learning how to think about violence.

1 What are some questions we can ask to aid our future survival on the planet?

2 How can we make violence studies a critical area of discourse between public and academic arenas?

3 What are the primary dangers of a limiting definition? Of a definition that is too broad?

4 How does awareness of violence as a problem contribute to solving the problem?

5 How might we organize knowledge across disciplines?

What questions do *you* have?

References

Arendt, H. (1970). *On violence.* New York, NY: Harcourt, Brace, Jovanovich.

Bastick, M., Grimm, K., & Kunz, R. (2007). *Sexual violence in armed conflict: Global overview and implications for the security sector.* Geneva, Switzerland: Geneva Centre for the Democratic Control of Armed Forces.

Bergin, A. E., & Garfield, S. L. E. (1994). *Handbook of psychotherapy and behavior change.* New York, NY: Wiley and Sons.

Boulet, R. C. (2009, August 19). The world's first genocide trial, 30 years on. *Phnom Penh Post.* Retrieved from http://www.phnompenhpost.com/national/worlds-first-genocide-trial-30-years

Bronfenbrenner, U. (1979). *The ecology of human development.* Cambridge, MA: Harvard University Press.

Butchart, A., & Engström, K. (2002). Sex- and age-specific relations between economic development, economic inequality and homicide rates in people aged 0–24 years: A cross-sectional analysis. *Bulletin of the World Health Organization, 80,* 797–805.

Centers for Disease Control and Prevention (2003). Trends in aging—United States and worldwide. *Morbidity and Mortality Weekly Report, 52*(6), 101–104.

Doyle, M. W. (1983). Kant, liberal legacies, and foreign affairs. *Philosophy and Public Affairs, 12*(3), 205–235.

Drell, S., & Goodby, J. (2008). The reality: A goal of a world without nuclear weapons is essential. *Washington Quarterly, 31*(3), 23–32.

Drexler, M. (2013). Guns and suicide: The hidden toll. *Harvard School of Public Health Magazine, 1,* 24–35.

Eisner, M. (2003). Long-term historical trends in violent crime. In M. Tonry (Ed.), *Crime and justice: A review of research* (Vol. *30*) (pp. 83–142). Chicago, IL: University of Chicago Press.

Elias, N. (1939). *Über den Prozeß der Zivilisation. Soziogenetische und psychogenetische Untersuchungen.* Basel, Switzerland: Verlag Haus zum Falken.

Engel, G. L. (1977). The need for a new medical model: A challenge for biomedicine. *Science, 196*(4286), 129–136.

Esdaile, C. J. (2014). *Wars of Napoleon.* New York, NY: Routledge.

Ferguson, R. B. (2013). Pinker's list: Exaggerating prehistoric war mortality. In D. P. Fry (Ed.), *War, peace, and human nature: The convergence of evolutionary and cultural views* (pp. 112–131). Oxford, UK: Oxford University Press.

Fink, G. (Ed.) (2010). *Stress of war, conflict and disaster.* San Diego, CA: Academic Press.

Fitzmaurice, C., Allen, C., Barber, R. M., Barregard, L., Bhutta, Z. A., Brenner, H., … Fleming, T. (2017). Global, regional, and national cancer incidence, mortality, years of life lost, years lived with disability, and disability-adjusted life-years for 32 cancer groups, 1990 to 2015: A systematic analysis for the global burden of disease study. *JAMA Oncology, 3*(4), 524–548.

Fukuyama, F. (1992). *The end of history and the last man.* New York, NY: Free Press.

Galea, S., Nandi, A., & Vlahov, D. (2005). The epidemiology of post-traumatic stress disorder after disasters. *Epidemiologic Reviews, 27*(1), 78–91.

Galtung, J. (1969). Violence, peace, and peace research. *Journal of Peace Research, 6*(3), 167–191.

Gilligan, J. (1996). *Violence: Our deadly epidemic and its causes.* New York, NY: Putnam.

Gilligan, J. (1999). Structural violence. In R. Gottesman (Ed.), *Violence in the United States: An encyclopedia* (pp. 229–233). New York, NY: Scribners and Sons.

Gohdes, A., & Price, M. (2013). First things first: Assessing data quality before model quality. *Journal of Conflict Resolution, 57*(6), 1090–1108.

Goss, K. A. (2010). *Disarmed: The missing movement for gun control in America.* Princeton, NJ: Princeton University Press.

Grant, A. M., Franklin, J., & Langford, P. (2002). The self-reflection and insight scale: A new measure of private self-consciousness. *Social Behavior and Personality: An International Journal, 30*(8), 821–835.

Hertz, N. (2002). *The silent takeover: Global capitalism and the death of democracy.* New York, NY: Simon and Schuster.

Hildyard, K. L., & Wolfe, D. A. (2002). Child neglect: Developmental issues and outcomes. *Child Abuse and Neglect, 26*(6–7), 679–695.

Hobsbawm, E. (1994). *The age of extremes: The short twentieth century, 1914–1991*. London, UK: Abacus.

Høivik, T. (1977). The demography of structural violence. *Journal of Peace Research, 14*(1), 59–73.

Homer (1990). The Iliad. In R. Lattimore, & M. J. Adler (Eds.), *Great books of the Western World* (Vol. 3). Chicago, IL: Encyclopædia Britannica.

Kassebaum, N. J., Arora, M., Barber, R. M., Bhutta, Z. A., & Brown, J. C. A. (2016). Global, regional, and national disability-adjusted life-years (DALYs) for 315 diseases and injuries and healthy life expectancy (HALE), 1990–2015: A systematic analysis for the global burden of disease study 2015. *Lancet, 388*(10053), 1603–1658.

Köhler, G., & Alcock, N. (1976). An empirical table of structural violence. *Journal of Peace Research, 13*, 343–356.

Krug, E. G., Dahlberg, L. L., Mercy, J. A., Zwi, A. B., & Lozano, R. (2002). *World report on violence and health*. Geneva, Switzerland: World Health Organization. Retrieved from http://apps.who.int/iris/bitstream/10665/42495/1/9241545615_eng.pdf

Kurtz, L. R. (2008). *Encyclopedia of violence, peace and conflict*. Amsterdam, The Netherlands: Elsevier.

Lacina, B., & Gleditsch, N. P. (2005). Monitoring trends in global combat: A new dataset of battle deaths. *European Journal of Population, 21*(2–3), 145–166.

Ladapo, J. A., Rodwin, B. A., Ryan, A. M., Trasande, L., & Blustein, J. (2013). Scientific publications on firearms in youth before and after congressional action prohibiting federal research funding. *JAMA, 310*(5), 532–534.

Latane, B., & Darley, J. M. (1970). *The unresponsive bystander: Why doesn't he help*. New York, NY: Appleton.

Lee, B. X., Leckman, J. F., & Mbwambo, J. K. K. (2014). Violence and health: Current perspectives from the WHO violence prevention alliance. *Aggression and Violent Behavior, 19*(6), 609–615.

Lee, B. X., Marotta, P. L., Blay-Tofey, M., Wang, W., & de Bourmont, S. (2014). Economic correlates of violent death rates in forty countries, 1962–2008: A cross-typological analysis. *Aggression and Violent Behavior, 19*(6), 729–737.

Lee, B. X., Wexler, B. E., & Gilligan, J. (2014). Political correlates of violent death rates in the U.S., 1900–2010: Longitudinal and cross-sectional analyses. *Aggression and Violent Behavior, 19*(6), 721–728.

Lifton, R. J. (1979). *The broken connection: On death and the continuity of life*. New York, NY: Touchstone.

Lifton, R. J. (1987). *The future of immortality and other essays for a nuclear age*. New York, NY: Basic Books.

MacKenzie, E. J., Rivara, F. P., Jurkovich, G. J., Nathens, A. B., Frey, K. P., Egleston, B. L., ... Scharfstein, D. O. (2006). A national evaluation of the effect of trauma-center care on mortality. *New England Journal of Medicine, 354*(4), 366–378.

Mikton, C., & Butchart, A. (2009). Child maltreatment prevention: A systematic review of reviews. *Bulletin of the World Health Organization, 87*(5), 353–361.

Mitzen, J. (2013). The irony of Pinkerism. *Perspectives on Politics, 11*(2), 525–528.

Monkkonen, E. (2001). *Murder in New York City*. Berkeley, CA: University of California Press.

Morgan, B., Sunar, D., Carter, C. S., Leckman, J. F., Fry, D. P., Keverne, E. B., ... Olds, D. (2014). Human biological development and peace: Genes, brains, safety, and justice. In J. F. Leckman, C. Panter-Brick, & R. R. Salah (Eds.), *Pathways to peace: The transformative power of children and families* (pp. 95–128). Cambridge, MA: MIT Press.

Norris, F. H., Friedman, M. J., Watson, P. J., Byrne, C. M., Diaz, E., & Kaniasty, K. (2002). 60,000 disaster victims speak: Part I. An empirical review of the empirical literature, 1981–2001. *Psychiatry, 65*(3), 207–239.

Ortiz, I., & Cummins, M. (2011). *Global inequality: Beyond the bottom billion—a rapid review of income.* New York, NY: United Nations Children's Fund.

Pinker, S. (2011). *The better angels of our nature: Why violence has declined.* New York, NY: Viking.

Prochaska, J. O., & DiClemente, C. C. (1986). Toward a comprehensive model of change. In W. R. Miller, & N. Heather (Eds.), *Treating addictive behaviors: Processes of change* (pp. 3–27). New York, NY: Plenum Press.

Rose, H. (2013). Book review symposium: Steven Pinker, the better angels of our nature: A history of violence and humanity. *Sociology, 47*(6), 1227–1229.

Rosenbaum, R. (2011). *How the end begins: The road to a nuclear world war III.* New York, NY: Simon and Schuster.

Stockholm International Peace Research Institute. (2012). *SIPRI Yearbook 2012: Armaments, disarmament, and international security.* Oxford, U.K.: Oxford University Press.

Stone, A. A. (2014). The better angels of our nature: Why violence has declined. *Psychiatric Services, 65*(5), e07–e08.

United Nations Office on Drugs and Crime. (2014). *Global Study on Homicide 2013: Trends, contexts, data.* Vienna, Austria: United Nations. Retrieved from https://www.unodc.org/documents/data-and-analysis/statistics/GSH2013/2014_GLOBAL_HOMICIDE_BOOK_web.pdf

Violence Prevention Alliance. (2012). *Global campaign for violence prevention: Plan of action for 2012–2020.* Geneva, Switzerland: Author. Retrieved from http://www.who.int/violence_injury_prevention/violence/global_campaign/gcvp_plan_of_action.pdf

Vos, T., Allen, C., Arora, M., Barber, R. M., Bhutta, Z. A., Brown, A., … Coggeshall, M. (2016). Global, regional, and national incidence, prevalence, and years lived with disability for 310 diseases and injuries, 1990–2015: A systematic analysis for the global burden of disease study 2015. *Lancet, 388*(10053), 1545–1602.

Wilkinson, R. G., & Pickett, K. (2009). *The spirit level: Why more equal societies almost always do better.* London, UK: Allen Lane.

World Health Organization. (2008). *Global burden of disease 2004 update.* Geneva, Switzerland: Author. Retrieved from http://www.who.int/healthinfo/global_burden_disease/GBD_report_2004update_full.pdf

World Health Organization. (2015). *WHO mortality database.* Geneva, Switzerland. Author. Retrieved from http://www.who.int/healthinfo/mortality_data/en

World Health Organization. (2017). *10 facts about violence prevention.* Geneva, Switzerland. Author. Retrieved from http://www.who.int/features/factfiles/violence/en

World Health Organization, United Nations Office on Drugs and Crime, and United Nations Development Programme. (2014). *Global status report on violence prevention 2014.* Geneva, Switzerland: World Health Organization. Retrieved from http://www.who.int/violence_injury_prevention/violence/status_report/2014/en

Causes

Part II   Intra-/Interpersonal Framework

2

The Biology of Violence

Introduction

> Every living organism is essentially an open system.
> —*Ludwig von Bertalanffy,* General System Theory *(1968)*

Understanding the nature of human beings helps the flourishing of human potential (Eisenberg, 1972). To do this properly, it is important that we broaden and integrate our concepts of violence, which we will attempt to do over the next several chapters as we review the contribution of different disciplines. *Biology* is a basic and sound place to start, for all human behavior entails a physical component, and a bio-psycho-socio-environmental study of violence must examine its biological contributors. Additionally, no other field demonstrates better the diversity and complexity of living beings. Living things reproduce, grow, and respond to changes in the environment, making them impossible to confine to closed systems.

Most students picking up this text will not be biologists or may not even be familiar with biological concepts, but novices need not be worried. As we emphasize throughout this text, there are multiple ways of looking at violence, and their turn will come. Each chapter looks at violence differently and will pose more or less difficulty depending on the experiences the student brings. For example, those with a biology background will feel comfortable with this chapter but not necessarily with political science, and vice versa. By the end of the book, however, all will have been challenged, and that in itself will be a learning experience. Readers are encouraged to immerse themselves in each chapter by using a great human gift—the imagination—and to experience being a biologist, a psychologist, an anthropologist, and so on, as we travel through the text, and sometimes an outsider's view will bring fresh ideas or valuable insights. Far from being external to our purposes, that very act will allow the student not only to accumulate knowledge but to develop a sense of *how to think about violence.*

Returning to biology, it needs to be said that the concept of applying this perspective to violence has a rocky and checkered history. Indeed, the introduction of biology into the discussion has often been a source of violence—think of the justifications for colonial expansion, the extermination of races, discrimination against the morphological "other," and, more recently, the relocation of social problems to the individual (thereby "blaming the victim"). At the same time, the idea of one or another ungovernable biological drive—be it evolutionary, genetic, or biochemical—as absolving humans from responsibility can be appealing to certain people. In this chapter, we will argue that these perspectives arise from a flawed conception of biology and that an updated scientific understanding is necessary. Comprehending biological contributors to violence necessitates a unified bio-psycho-socio-environmental approach to the study of violence to start. This requires us to develop a new concept of biology itself.

Biology has often been assumed to be the definitive answer, but a careful review of human development and human biology argues *against* reducing behavior to biology and against explaining human behavior in terms of animal behavior. More accurately, we see biology as one among many factors that help explain complex behavior. We will review how the principles of biology can be helpful to our overall understanding of violence, in light of other approaches. Biology helps to unify our understanding of the bio-psycho-socio-environmental paradigm by showing how "nature" ties in with "nurture." We will distinguish between aggression and violence, as well as examine the association between mental illness and violence. We will show how recent advances in the neurosciences, such as neuroplasticity and epigenetics, show that the biological cannot be separated from psychology, society, and the environment. Still today many people would like to be *reductionists* with respect to violence and say that, ultimately, the cause of violence is biological, because biology is the most basic of the life sciences that can be used for explanation. This is a mistaken notion of biology that simplifies the field in ways that even biologists would find objectionable.

The Tempting Idea

Historically, the simplification that biology seems to afford has been very tempting. By reducing behavior to biology, biology to physics, and physics to the movement of elementary particles, scientists and pseudo-scientists have tried to reduce the complexity of violent behavior and to explain it in terms of some evolutionary, genetic, neurobiological, neuroendocrine, or morphological process. Nineteenth-century phrenologists sought answers in the shape of the skull, convinced that its outward shape described a person's character, personality, and even the presence of disease—considering the bump behind the ear to be the seat of violence at one stage. Similarly, modern neuroscientists explored localized lesions in the brain, examining in turn the parietal, temporal, and prefrontal lobes in their quest to find the locus for violence. The concept of an ungovernable biological drive—an inevitable consequence of evolutionary, genetic, or biochemical forces—in our nature seemed exonerating and reassuring. We now know that the basic premise of this approach is flawed: the elementary particles that earlier researchers tried to discover have proved elusive, and even if rendered objects of study, they appear to increase rather than decrease in complexity.

Nevertheless, this approach has captured our imagination to such an extent that it continues to dominate discourse on how the brain apparently determines moral, ethical, and even political decisions. Proof of this tendency can be found in courtrooms around the world, where neuroimaging is increasingly being used to "explain" aberrant behavior, determine criminal responsibility, and even decide sentencing policy (Legrenzi & Umilta, 2009). Despite the fact that technological advances have led to impressive methods of viewing neurological contributions to cognition and behavior, the fallacy of the simplistic biology-as-destiny approach is nowhere more obvious than in the study of violence, where every attempt to use a biological approach to provide a single explanation has faltered. By working to create a new biology of violence, we can move away from compartmentalization and reductionism toward integration and synchronization, placing biology within an updated interdisciplinary perspective involving *interaction* of biology with environmental, social, and psychological features.

To review a little history, excitement about correlations between biology and violence reached new levels in the nineteenth century, when Italian criminologist Cesare Lombroso authored *Criminal Man* (1876). He asserted that criminality was a genetic throwback to primitive states and that a "criminal type" of person was recognizable through physical features such as a large jaw or cheekbones, a sloping forehead, long arms, and flat feet. At that time, "physiognomy" was in fashion—it was believed that one could determine a person's character and personality and even whether he or she had a disease from outer appearances, especially from the shape of the skull. Lombroso's work was strongly and justifiably criticized (Wolfgang, 1955), but the idea of violence and criminal leanings being rooted in biology was so compelling that his criminological theory influences investigations of crime to this day.

In the US, sociologist Richard Dugdale's (1877) genealogical study of families with histories of criminal involvement, mental health problems, and poverty, and then eugenicist Henry Goddard's (1912) investigation of genealogical "feeblemindedness" seemed to support a hereditary component to crime. In England, physician Charles Goring (1913) compared convicts to noncriminal citizens and found that criminals were shorter and weighed less; however, Goring had not taken into account environmental differences, which invalidated his conclusions. Then in the 1930s, American physical anthropologist Ernest Hooten (1939) stated that biological inferiority was the cause of crime: you could see this from criminal individuals' physical characteristics, such as low foreheads, long necks, and crooked jaws. That was also the time when Nazi ideology claiming the superiority of the Aryan race based on appearances was gaining ground.

In the 1940s and 1950s, American criminologists Glueck and Glueck (1950) were the first to perform studies of chronic juvenile offenders; they claimed that potential deviants could be identified as young as 6 years old—but the approach was fraught with subjective and thus unreliable assessments. The methodological flaws of this lopsided reliance on biology are apparent to us today. In order to argue for biological determinism, one would have to push dangerously toward pseudoscience and ideology and away from scientific consensus. The failure of strictly biological theories led to the popularity of social theories in the 1960s, which then swung the pendulum to the other extreme. While an improvement in instruments and technology has renewed hopes once again for biological explanations, an enlightened approach cannot ignore the context of psychological, social, and environmental interactions, as we have mentioned.

Other popular theories that should be mentioned include the idea that those who resort to criminal behavior are less intelligent than other people (Hirschi & Hindelang, 1977), but since intelligence quotient (IQ) tests are not valid across racial and class lines, their results were unreliable. Studies of chromosome abnormalities looked at the "XYY" syndrome's relationship to violent crime, postulating that the Y, or the designated "male" chromosome, must be responsible for violent behavior, given the higher prevalence of violence in males as opposed to females across cultures and time (and therefore two Y chromosomes should yield more "Y characteristics"). The results, however, were inconclusive: no difference in levels of violence emerged between XY and XYY chromosome bearers (Schiavi et al., 1984). While the relationship between hormones and aggression in nonhumans is well established, the putative effect in humans is more complex, and the direction of the effect is usually unclear (Kingston et al., 2012). Meanwhile, substantial evidence indicated that biological development is strongly associated with socioeconomic, environmental, and racial factors; for example, black and lower socioeconomic status mothers had a higher incidence of pregnancy and delivery complications, premature births, and infants with low birth weights relative to mothers in other race and socioeconomic groups (National Center for Health Statistics, 1980).

Despite the absence of any genetic confirmation, evolutionary theories for violent behavior continued to develop: American ethologist Konrad Lorenz's *On Aggression* (1966) and biologist E. O. Wilson's *Sociobiology: The New Synthesis* (1975) still powerfully grip the imagination. Based on his observation of animals, Lorenz argued that aggression, having evolutionary advantages, is biologically programmed into human beings and is responsible for the propensity to kill and to torture. Wilson claimed that since social behavior results from evolution—the success of an organism seen in the extent to which its genes are represented in the next generation—aggression must have some adaptive function. Sociobiologists after Wilson have tried to explain aggressive behavior as individual efforts in devotion to a "selfish gene" (Dawkins, 1976; de Waal, 1996).

The appeal of evolutionary theory is that it simplifies, but there is the danger of oversimplification to the point of caricature. Even the most impressive indicator of heredity (the high-monoamine-oxidase-A-activity genotype) cannot be more than one of many risk factors (Deater-Deckard, Ivy, & Smith, 2005), and not even a universal one. The plethora of available neuroscientific evidence encounters a lack of in-depth biographical studies, creating a deficit in research regarding the relationship between trauma, environment, and brain functioning. Evolutionary theory has the effect of replacing the individual past with the human past as an alternative to biographical research, or replacing human research with animal research, unduly generalizing without evidence (Niehoff, 1999). Yet only human beings uniquely kill members of their own species with such regularity. Theory requires consideration of complexity (Bowles, 2009), and premature efforts to simplify beyond the evidence paradoxically lead to a need for contorted explanations to justify. In this manner, while the structural elegance of an explanation based on pure biology is tempting, we must recognize when it does not hold up to evidence, especially when it comes to human violence.

Reductionism as an ideology has emerged mostly from a narrow interpretation of the scientific method. It is the practice of describing and analyzing a complex phenomenon in terms of another set of phenomena that are held to represent a simpler or more fundamental level, with the assumption that the latter would provide an adequate and better explanation. Biologists themselves have advocated thinking of living organisms as systems that we should observe in their entirety in order to understand properly (Bertalanffy, 1934). The past 30 years, in particular, have seen remarkable progress in understanding the effects of environment on gene expression, social influences on the brain, and the malleability of nerve matter itself, such that it is no longer possible to conceive of a biology apart from "soft" influences. This holds particularly true for human beings, who have overdeveloped forebrains that are highly susceptible to these factors. Our brains not only develop well into adulthood but continually change over our full lifespan. We can no longer hope that the biological sciences will yield a "marker" or an underlying substrate responsible for human violence, but we can be certain that biology will play a role.

Case Vignettes

The Case of Phineas Gage

The prefrontal brain region is thought to play a large role in "executive function," or planning, decision-making, goal-setting, and moderating social behavior, all of which appear to be involved in inhibiting disruptive behavior (Yang & Raine, 2009). A famous case that led to this postulation is that of Phineas Gage. We review the case here while keeping in mind that, while this may be one of the most graphic examples of what damage to an area of the brain can do, it does not negate the fallacies of reductionism, which would try to claim that this explains the mechanisms of violence in all cases for all time. Gage was a railroad worker who lived in the middle of the nineteenth century. According to the town physician, he was "a perfectly healthy, strong and active young man, 25 years of age … possessing an iron will as well as an iron frame"

(Harlow, 1868). During a rock-blasting accident, a premature explosion sent a large iron rod into the left side of Gage's face through his jaw, passing behind the left eye and exiting the left frontal side of the brain. He was thrown onto his back and briefly convulsed but spoke within minutes, walked with little assistance, and rode in a carriage to the clinic. "Doctor, here is business enough for you," he said, and expressed hope that he would return to work in a few days.

Recovery was long and uneven, however, and there were changes in his personality: others described him at times as "uncontrollable" and at others as "weak and childish." A professor of surgery at Harvard Medical School invited Gage to Boston for several weeks in what may have been one of the earliest instances of a patient entering a hospital for medical education rather than for treatment. Although unable to reclaim his post with the railroad, he continued to work in several jobs for 12 years, until epileptic seizures impaired him from doing very much. One day, the convulsions repeated frequently until he died in *status epilepticus*, or a continual seizure. While records are scarce, before the injury he was considered hard-working, responsible, and a "great favorite" among the men in his charge, and his employers regarded him as "the most efficient and capable foreman in their employ." Afterward, while his memory and general intelligence were intact, he became "fitful, irreverent, indulging at times in the grossest profanity (which was not previously his custom), manifesting but little deference for his fellows, impatient of restraint or advice when it conflicts with his desires, at times pertinaciously obstinate, yet capricious and vacillating, devising many plans of future operations, which are no sooner arranged than they are abandoned in turn for others appearing more feasible.... In this regard his mind was radically changed, so decidedly that his friends and acquaintances said he was 'no longer Gage'" (Harlow, 1868). While the precise facts remain unclear, Gage became a hypothetical case for changes in "higher mental functions" such as moral judgment being due to brain injury, or localized brain function, whereby the prefrontal cortex and the amygdala are implicated in increased aggression, although the risk of violence seems less than is widely presumed (Brower & Price, 2001). Again, while interesting as a case, multiple factors should always enter into consideration, as not all persons with a localized brain injury will turn violent, and not all violent persons will have suffered a brain injury.

Familial Depression

Parental depression is a risk factor for depression and drug disorders in children of both genders, making it another possible area where biology may have a role in the transmission of conditions. Mary's father died by swallowing poison when she was a preteen. He was away from home for long periods of time when Mary and her brothers were young. Mary believed her mother had an affair while her father was away. Before his death, her father was unemployed, alcoholic, and ill; he was also an illegal bookmaker. Mary grew up in a strict Catholic family and strongly held to the church's ethics and teaching. She attended a Catholic college and felt shamed because of her family's poverty, the necessity of accepting financial aid, and her deceased father's illegal activities, which had the potential to become known to the police or the public. She became very anxious and was torn between her feelings of love and support for her father and her fear that his wrongdoing might bring shame and punishment upon the family. Mary believed she was the only one in her family who loved her father. As a child she watched helplessly as he sickened before his suicide.

An autopsy revealed his spinal fluid to be low in serotonin, a nerve chemical that acts to calm brain activity. When serotonin levels are low, individuals are less able to stop their violent impulses, including suicide. A well-functioning frontal lobe is also required, as it is the behavioral control center in the brain. It allows a person to feel guilt or remorse, to develop empathy, and to have a "conscience" (Anderson et al., 1999). This area is damaged when a person is subject to repeated stressors (Liston et al., 2006) and can have reduced volume in cases of major mental disorders requiring antipsychotics, suicide (Rajkowska, 1997), imprisonment, sociopathic behavior, and lead poisoning (Cecil et al., 2008). Alcohol is the substance that most increases the risk of violence by disabling the frontal behavioral control center. The multiple biological aspects of clinical depression, alcohol use disorder, and suicidality are interesting to note, although none of them should be considered apart from environmental, social, and psychological factors. As an adult, Mary married two men she knew were alcoholics, feeling it was her responsibility to rescue them from their addiction. Both marriages ended badly, however, with Mary becoming a victim of domestic violence and an alcohol abuser herself. After years of attempting to achieve sobriety, she, too, perished through an overdose of pain medication.

Traumatic Brain Injury and Posttraumatic Stress

Paul was a model teenager and captain of his high school football team who aspired to be a police officer like his father. Soon after he started college, however, the Iraq War broke out, and he decided to "serve in [his] country's military police." He successfully completed training, but his experience in Iraq was stressful from the start. Upon arrival, he soon came under mortar attack without adequate shelter or equipment. He witnessed violence and death all around him. On one occasion, momentarily unconscious, he fell out of a Humvee, landing on his forehead. When his companion shook him back to consciousness, Paul said he was "okay" and did not seek immediate medical attention. When his companion forced him to see a medical officer, he received stitches but underwent no other examination. The rest of Paul's deployment was a blur, even though he was minimally able to carry out his duties. When he returned home several months later, however, his family noticed he was no longer the same person: he was easily distracted and irritable, had memory problems, and isolated himself. He frequently woke up in the middle of night, believing he was back in Iraq, and experienced intense distress, sweating, a pounding heart, and shortness of breath. In the daytime, he had frequent headaches and ringing in his ears. Once, while his father was urging him to go to the hospital, Paul tackled his father to the ground and beat him up badly enough that the father needed to receive treatment.

Aggression is a common, fluctuating, and long-term problem following traumatic brain injuries (TBI's) (Baguley, Cooper, & Felmingham, 2006), and combined with posttraumatic stress disorder (PTSD) in veterans can worsen the propensity for violent behavior (Fontana & Rosenheck, 2008). The symptoms of TBI and PTSD can be difficult to differentiate and seem to compound each other. Both can cause psychological and physiologic symptoms. Both cause memory problems, difficulty concentrating, disordered sleep, anxiety, depression, personality changes, and irritability or aggression. Thorough evaluation of the head trauma as well as the psychological symptoms is warranted, in addition to learning strategies for coping with stress or conflict (Raine, 2014).

Paul refused any treatment, and as his symptoms seemed to improve over the next year, he wished to put the past behind him. When the time came for his next deployment, he embarked with great resolution, but before he could reach the army base, he had a panic attack, feeling like he was "going to die" if he returned to Iraq. He went "absent without leave" and drove around for several days before returning home, after which he shut himself in his room, refusing to face his family or to answer any calls from the army. He eventually agreed to evaluation and treatment, which revealed severe posttraumatic stress disorder and continued severe headaches and ringing in his ears as a result of his head injury. He had to fight for his disability benefits because of a history of being "absent without leave," which added years of suffering. He eventualy received the therapy he needed and was able to hold minimally stressful jobs and to live with some independence, although he continued to avoid reminders of his deployment.

Postpartum Depression and Psychosis

At one time Jenny was a high school valedictorian, champion swimmer, and college-educated registered nurse. Then she murdered three of her five children by systematically drowning them in the bathtub after her husband left for work. She had a long history of severe postpartum depression and postpartum psychosis. Postpartum depression is a mood disorder that typically begins 1 week to 1 month after childbirth and leads to symptoms such as extreme sadness, low energy, anxiety, changes in sleeping or eating patterns, crying episodes, and irritability. Postpartum psychosis is a psychiatric emergency in which symptoms of high mood and racing thoughts, depression, severe confusion, loss of inhibition, paranoia, hallucinations, and delusions set in, beginning suddenly in the first 2 weeks after delivery; it often requires hospitalization.

Jenny, after giving birth to each of her children, displayed extreme psychotic behavior that included hallucinations, suicide attempts, self-mutilation, and an irresistible impulse to hurt her children. Both pregnancy and the postpartum period involve multiple hormonal changes. The sex hormones estrogen and progesterone circulate at very high levels during pregnancy and precipitously drop in the postpartum period, and therefore are candidates for explaining the biology of postpartum depression and postpartum psychosis (Bloch, Daly, & Rubinow, 2003). Management should include intensive monitoring of psychological and social factors, as well as strict control of the environment as necessary. Jenny had been in and out of psychiatric institutions over the years. Just weeks before the murders, she was released from a psychiatric hospital because her insurance had run out. After two trials, she was found not guilty by reason of insanity.

Aggression versus Violence

The first important distinction in the biology of violence might be between aggression and violence. While these terms have been used interchangeably in much scholarly and ordinary discourse, emerging evidence has called for a clearer distinction between them. *Aggression* as defined here is a neutral energy that can help humans (or animals) to fight or flee when vital interests are threatened; the word derives from the Latin root *aggredi* ("to approach"), which stems from *gradi* ("to step"), without implying a value judgment on its own. Assertive behavior to defend oneself or one's offspring, energy or zeal for the achievement of goals, or the determination to confront and overcome challenges—without necessarily resulting in an injury to self or others—are all considered adaptive and count in this definition. For example, surgery and dental procedures are often "aggressive" but not violent, as the actor intends benefit rather than harm. The hormone that produces such states of arousal is *cortisol*.

In contrast, *oxytocin* is a chemical that nurtures and promotes attachment, suppresses anxiety and stress and generally reduces violence (Tops et al., 2007). But in the case of defensive aggression reverses its effect: when protecting offspring from intruders, for example, higher oxytocin levels can lead to greater "violence" (DeWall et al., 2014). In this manner, aggression can be biologically and socially adaptive, serve the survival of the individual and the species, and cease when threat disappears. When a society makes available nonviolent means of aggressive expression (such as opportunities to exert and to attain success through education, training, and employment), aggression can be placed in the service of prosocial, productive, and creative aspirations and may even result in a net decrease in the amount of violence in a society.

When nonviolent means of achieving goals are not perceived to be available, then an aggressive drive for these things can deteriorate into becoming maladaptive and pathogenic. Behavior then degenerates into *violence*. *Violentia* in Latin denotes "vehemence" and relates to the verb *violare*, "to violate." Violence does not serve an adaptive purpose, is cruel and destructive, is specific to the human species, and is not biologically adaptive. Mammals, especially primates, possess a good deal of defensive aggression but are not killers and torturers like humans. Although similar to aggression on the surface, violence has a different motivation and quality.

Violence can sometimes appear when more adaptive, productive energies are absent. As one gene–environment interaction study revealed, children with a certain gene predisposing them to violence became violent only when the triggering environment was present; absent the environment, the child was actually *less* active than the norm (Jaffee et al., 2002). In other words, a child with potentially violent tendencies is more passive or *lacks aggressive energy* without the triggering environment. We will see how this is important in Chapter 3 on the psychology of violence. Aggression is plentiful in other primates, but violence is almost uniquely human.

Like any disorder, violence can be acute or chronic, a single episode or repetitive. It has been divided into two other contrasting syndromes: a high-arousal and impulsive, affective type and a low-arousal, premeditated predatory type. Although the biological basis of these two types remains poorly understood, the former pattern appears more physiologically driven, associated with low serotonin levels, for example (Virkkunen et al., 1995), whereas the latter seems more cognitively driven (Anderson et al., 2002). Impulsive violence is thought to be based on anger and is sometimes labeled hostile or reactive, while premeditated violence is more instrumental and can be difficult to detect. Different forms of neurocognitive models may eventually be necessary to explain these different forms (Blair, 2001). Distinguishing among different types of violence can be difficult, as they often appear together or have multiple motives (Bushman & Anderson, 2001). Nevertheless, developing awareness about the existence and perniciousness of the premeditated type is important, for it can infiltrate far-reaching systems and schemes, even policies, without much dramatic behavioral display but do greater harm. "Smart," usually "white collar," criminals, for example, perpetrate structural violence more often than direct violence, as they are more likely to infiltrate leadership positions with more discreet but devastating intentions.

Mental Illness and Violence

Is there a relationship between mental illness and violence? Media and public perception often overplays the link, but a large-scale violence risk assessment study in the US. that followed more than 1,000 people for a year after they left psychiatric hospitals compared them with the general population and found no difference in levels of violence—unless drugs or alcohol were used (Steadman et al., 1998). Mental illness by itself is not necessarily a cause for violence (Fazel et al., 2009): most mentally ill persons never commit a serious act of violence, and almost all those who commit violent crimes do so because of factors other than mental illness (Angermeyer, 2000). Rather, "deinstitutionalized" mentally ill persons, many of whom become homeless after release from hospitals, are more often victims of violent crimes than perpetrators (Hiroeh et al., 2001). Furthermore, if one counts the treatment society has available and yet does not offer to them, they are already victims of structural violence (Kohn et al., 2004).

As with any other group, social stress and environmental pressures can sometimes provoke violence in mentally ill individuals. In mental illness, most of the excess risk appears with simultaneous substance abuse, which more than doubles the risk of violence among those who are mentally ill (Swartz et al., 1998). Insufficient access to medication and other forms of psychiatric therapies, together with a lack of community supports, contributes to symptom exacerbation, which can increase the probability of "self-medication" through substance abuse (Arboleda-Florez, Holley, & Crisanti, 1998). Still, the one form of violence that is most common among those with mental illness, especially those meeting the criteria for schizophrenia or a major mood disorder, is suicide. In addition, the people who commit collective or political violence (warfare, genocide, and terrorism) are not, for the most part, mentally ill by any standard definition.

A social phenomenon of note is the disastrously mismanaged deinstitutionalization of mentally ill persons in the US, which has shunted them into jails and prisons, a phenomenon more accurately described as "trans-institutionalization" (Munetz, Grande, & Chambers, 2001). Since mental illness does not have much to do with increased violence, simply locking away those who are mentally ill produces little result. Rather, it will do harm and potentially cause increases in violence. Just like their non-mentally-ill peers, those with mental illness acculturate into violent mores in the criminal justice system. Furthermore, they are disproportionately incarcerated for longer, receiving greater penalties for their debility and becoming vulnerable targets of other inmates and guards (Fellner, 2006). If we do not adequately reduce symptoms that cause suffering and instead constantly expose people to settings that cause stress and worsen mental health, violence will increase in those people whether they were mentally ill to begin with or not.

Those with mental illness are more likely to be victims of violence also by their own hand. Worldwide, the burden of disease attributable to mental illness is rising rapidly, especially in low- and middle-income countries: the global burden of disease attributable to depression rose 37%. In terms of *disability-adjusted life years* (DALYs)—a measure of overall disease burden that takes into account the number of years lost due to ill health, disability, or early death— depression moved up from being the 15th leading cause to the 11th over the span of 20 years (Murray et al., 2012). At over 800,000 every year, suicide is also the leading cause of violent deaths, far greater in number than murders and wars combined (400,000 and 50,000 per year, respectively) (Haagsma et al., 2016). It is also the second-leading cause of death among 15- to 29-year-olds globally (World Health Organization, 2014). All persons with mental disorder, therefore, require urgent treatment if they are at risk of self-directed violence.

Mental disorders not only carry independent mortality risk, but they also increase mortality and morbidity by contributing to other diseases: substance misuse, maternal and reproductive problems, developmental problems, cardiovascular disease, cancer, and adverse effects on immune function (Prince et al., 2007). Mental illness, especially during childhood and adolescence, predicts poorer educational and economic outcomes as well as increased legal and criminal justice involvement in adulthood (Murray et al., 2013). The more we know of the biology of violence, the more it will point to the importance of proper treatment of illness, general healthcare, and prevention through improvement of social conditions over investment in criminal justice.

It is important to note how violence contributes to mental illness. Child maltreatment, for example, can lead to an inability to regulate emotion, difficulty forming attachment, memory disorder, and other mental health problems. Emotionally, a history of abuse predicts unstable and negative emotional states and socially inappropriate expressions of emotion (Shields & Cicchetti, 1998). Abuse or neglect disrupts child–parent attachment and subsequent "coherence of mind" (Grossmann, Grossmann, & Waters, 2006), which are necessary for memory, cognition, and identity formation. Physical abuse and neglect cause greater levels of several major psychiatric illnesses, including posttraumatic stress disorder, major depression, anxiety disorders, and sleep disorders (Wolfe, 1999), as well as attention deficit hyperactivity disorder, oppositional disorder, and conduct disorder (Famularo, Kinscherff, & Fenton, 1992). Maltreatment in childhood not only affects an individual emotionally but also cognitively, impairing memory and information processing (Alexander, Quas, & Goodman, 2002). The exact consequences will depend on familial and social context, as well as on the timing, severity, and chronicity of the abuse.

The Neuroplastic Brain

While an ever-expanding pool of knowledge in recent decades seemed to promise simplification around the biological basis for human behavior the opposite has been true: the brain itself turns out to be a highly complex, flexible, and changeable organ. *Neuroplasticity* (*neuro-* is Greek for "nerve," and *plastikos* the Greek word meaning "able to be molded" or "fit for molding") describes these observations. Studies of brain development have dramatically increased our understanding of how the environment shapes the brain even before birth, setting the stage for the child's presentation later in life, including propensity for violence (Dong & Krohn, 2015). Early experiences thus become exponential in their expression over time. Recent discoveries that the brain is plastic well into adulthood make social shaping all the more important to the brain's biology (Rakic, 2002). Brain anatomy undergoes modification every day, with pathways and connections shifting with new experiences in a process called *neurogenesis*. Changes in behavior and in neural input from the environment, as well as a remapping of the brain after injury, all contribute to fashioning brain pathways and signal transmission throughout life (Pascual-Leone et al., 2011).

In addition, what is most significant about the brain's evolution is that the proportion devoted to the cerebral cortex is vastly more prominent in primate species, so much so that it has to fold in on itself to stay within the skull—and this is exponentially more true in human beings. Most pronounced in the human brain is the frontal part of this cortex, which is responsible for social attaching and bonding, regulating emotion and planning, advanced cognition, and a self-aware identity (Sowell et al., 2003). All these aspects are important for controlling impulses for violence and for making prosocial choices.

Early patterns of attachment to a caregiver—or their absence—shape an individual's expectations in later relationships (Bowlby, 1969). These have direct interactions with the anatomy, physiology, and genetics of the developing brain (Filley et al., 2001). Exposure to bad experiences, or worse, a lack of key input, causes not only the person but the brain to suffer (Nelson et al., 2011). Damage to the frontal lobe can lead to a lack of restraint, or behavioral *disinhibition*, and impulsivity. Other anatomic insults to the central nervous system, especially including prenatal and perinatal trauma, are also associated with increased violence (Raine et al., 2000). Still, actual manifestations of violence usually require the presence of an environmental trigger or adverse social circumstances, in addition to brain damage. For example, one study showed that the presence of violent behaviors was associated not with the total size of the lesion or whether the patient had seizures, but rather with a disruption of family activities (Grafman et al., 1996).

Furthermore, while violent prison inmates have been reported to show elevated rates of traumatic brain injury or seizure disorders compared with nonviolent prisoners and the general public, many of these head injuries appear to be the result of violent lifestyles that produces higher rates of head injuries and brain lesions than in the general population (Mirsky & Siegel, 1994). Neuroimaging literature is converging on a set of brain regions and circuits that are consistently implicated in violence (Anderson & Kiehl, 2012), but correlation does not imply causation: brain plasticity further complicates the relationship between differences in brain imagery and differences in behavior, nor can one rule out a third factor that may be influencing differences in both brain and behavior.

Physiologic factors most associated with violence include the stress hormonal and nerve signaling systems. The *hypothalamic–pituitary–adrenal* (HPA) system, responsible for producing cortisol at times of stress (Shonkoff et al. 2012) goes through major developmental changes throughout childhood (Gunnar & Donzella, 2002). If chronically exposed to stress, such as in settings of family abuse or in war zones where the "fight or flight" response is constantly activated, it can alter how the brain responds in future contexts (Gunnar & Vazquez, 2006). The response is typically exaggeration or suppression: some individuals become hyperstressed, which can lead to overreaction to the smallest provocation, while others turn numb toward stress or require a lot of stimulation (Lupien, McEwen, Gunnar, & Heim, 2009). This dysregulation contributes to violent behaviors as well as other damaging effects on health (Sapolsky, Romero, & Munck, 2000).

The hormonal end products of the HPA system, cortisol and testosterone, are highly interactive with each other as well as with the social environment in the production of violent behavior (Montoya et al., 2012). Serotonin, on the other hand, is responsible for social regulation and helps decrease impulsive violence (Nelson & Chiavegatto, 2001). An absence of attachment with a parent or caregiver may decrease the serotonin channels that allow the flow of social information and experience later in life. But biological systems are rarely dependent on one biological factor. Usually, there are inhibitory and excitatory influences that interact among themselves and other hormones, whose combination then interacts with the environment before there is any observable behavior.

Environment and Epigenetics

How can a single genetic code, which the entire human race shares, give rise to the immense variation among individuals? How do human beings have such multiple ways of adapting to surroundings, of solving problems, and of imagining and creating? For a single individual, how does the fertilized egg cell divide and differentiate into all the different cell types of an organism, including nerve cells, muscle cells, and immune cells—not to mention all the different body parts, such as eyes, brain, and limbs? The answer, in part, lies in *epigenetics*. Epigenetic (*epi-* is from the Greek prefix that means "over," "outside of," or "around") mechanisms refer to heritable and other long-term changes in gene activity that are not part of the deoxyribonucleic acid (DNA) or ribonucleic acid (RNA) codes. These have the effect of turning genes "on" or "off"; in other words, genes do not decide outcome, but may or may not depending on the environment. This variation happens through DNA "tagging" (methylation), "wrapping" (histone modification), inhibition (repressor proteins), or environmental signaling (chemicals, drugs, or diet).

All cells in the body contain the same genetic material, but something in the environment signals (turns "on" or "off") what the genes must do, when, and how much. The environment intervenes in an organism's development, persisting through divisions of a single cell or an organism's lifetime and beyond, without altering the underlying DNA (Bird, 2007). The modifications, by activating some genes and inhibiting others, are all based on signals coming from the surrounding cells and the environment (Reik, 2007). The number of possibilities are so large that, with every step, the expressive variability of a given organism's entire hereditary information (genome) is seen as potentially infinite. Epigenetic events interconnect molecules and cells so that they function together as a whole, which can in turn influence the parts. As we mentioned, the organism may also play a role through its own actions and choices, as has been observed in maize (McClintock, 1950).

These epigenetic changes vary across brain regions and over the course of neural development (Provençal et al., 2013). They may last through the duration of a cell's life, or for the life cycle of the organism, or even exert influence across generations (Petronis, 2010). This complexity means that the majority who have a "high-risk combination" of genes for violence will never become violent (Tiihonen et al., 2015). Adoption studies show that the interaction between a family history of personality disorders and an adverse home environment is a better predictor of violence than either unfavorable biology or an adverse environment alone (Cadoret et al., 1995). In other words, genetic disposition needs to be in interaction with environmental events, such as child abuse, for there to be outward expression of violence; in the absence of child abuse, the genetic disposition did not significantly affect violence (Caspi et al., 2002). Since the environment shapes nature at every step, those who become violent can alter gene expression across generations or through the sharing of an environment. As such, genes are not reliable for predicting dangerousness or as markers for therapeutic intervention (Vassos, Collier, & Fazel, 2014).

An implication of this characteristic is that human beings are capable of shaping the very environment that molds their brains and gene expression to a degree that is without parallel among other animals, through physical structures, laws, and other codes of behavior, as well as language and the arts (Wexler, 2006). This ability and malleability has allowed human life to evolve in extraordinarily versatile ways in environments that are vastly different from the origins that shaped us. Culture, therefore, rather than being added onto a finished animal, is a central ingredient in the production of the human animal (Geertz, 1973).

This level of malleability means that adverse experiences can leave behind highly consequential changes in the anatomy and physiology—and even affect future generations (Felitti et al., 1998). Childhood experiences determine the organization and function of the adult brain in many ways (Perry et al., 1995), and for some symptoms, there can be a lag of many years, even decades, before early adverse experiences are expressed in the form of disease (Shonkoff, Boyce, & McEwen, 2009). This also means that organisms—especially highly complex ones such as human beings—can be very resilient in bouncing back from adversity, given the right conditions. They can also adjust to disruptive environmental changes and play a modifying role (West-Eberhard, 2003). Shifts in the environment or changes in approach can modify connections between existing brain cells or generate new ones, altering the way these cells fire (Ponti et al., 2008).

The Interconnected Whole

In gene translation, it was once assumed that a person born with a certain pattern of methylation, for example, would die with that pattern. This meant that, if one had a given gene, one would exhibit behavior corresponding to that gene. It also meant that those who are violent likely had their behavioral pattern fixed very early in life. However, as we develop more sophisticated ways of examining the genes that generate violent tendencies in early childhood (DiLalla, 2002) that continue into adulthood (Hofstra, van der Ende, & Verhulst, 2000; Moffitt et al., 2002), we find that the quest for the one, linear, gene-to-phenotype transcription for violence eludes us (Miczek et al., 2001). The formula, rather, has continually grown more complex. It is no longer:

gene– > phenotype (such as violence)

But:

genes and epigenetics (environment) + organizing (open) characteristics of living organisms, emergent properties, and ecosystems + neuroplastic (environment-responsive) pathways of the human brain + higher-level (subjective, intentional) organizing principles + nearly infinite, complex ramifying effects = violent behavior

Under these circumstances, a formula is virtually meaningless, and trying to create a linear model a fool's errand. Rigorous science will have to require that all of nature build nurture into its model and all of nurture build in nature, for they shape each other in tandem and as a unit. In other words, genetic manifestations may be both a cause and an effect of behaviors and experiences, and nowhere is this more apparent than in violence.

Studying the biology of violence thus has the paradoxical effect of revealing how social human beings are. We are only beginning to come to terms with the enduring ways in which the social environment during early childhood has consequences throughout the lifespan even for such characteristics as intelligence, emotions, behavior, and health (Black et al., 2017). Violence stems from such a tightknit weave of both biological and environmental influences on behavior that the dominance of any single discipline in explaining it cannot be justified (Denno, 1990).

The caregivers' ability to protect, nurture, and stimulate the child can lead to physically, psychologically, and socially healthy developmental trajectories. Social and societal support structures that allow for safe, stable, and stress-free environments for families and communities can in turn improve caregivers' ability to protect, nurture, and stimulate the child. Thus, the nurturance children receive through their immediate surroundings, as well as the society in which they grow up, well into adulthood, matter in regard to whether or not they become violent. As genes and environment are an inseparable whole, and a generation's experience is heritable through epigenetic means, improvements in environmental conditions can also multiply over time to contribute to long-lasting peace (Leckman, Panter-Brick, & Salah, 2014). These are the emerging conclusions from the new, interdisciplinary collaboration between the fields of violence studies and early childhood development (Lannen & Ziswiler, 2014).

What does all this mean with respect to agency and free will (a legal question that often arises in relation to assigning responsibility)? Lest one mistake locating violent behavior in the brain rather than the soul to mean undermining autonomy of the will, British molecular biologist Francis Crick (1994) has suggested that free will is possible because of the enormously large number of neural connections in the brain. If what we describe as "the soul" were entirely detached from biological substrates and psychological and social influences, "free will" would be an aimless, random act. On the other hand, if it were sufficiently grounded in the biology of current observation, which is in every moment generative of a near-infinite number of new combinations, then it would be more reflective of the free will that we experience at the human level: grounded in experience and connected to the past but capable of conceiving an infinite number of combinations for the future. The openness and complexity of biology allows for a foundation that is far from rigid, deterministic, simplistic, and separate from all other experience. Interdisciplinary conversations, in this manner, can help "connect the dots" and guide our understanding of how violence arises but also how to think about violence.

Conclusion

Any serious student of the biology of violence would have to conclude that biology is not destiny. Reductionism is an ideology, not science, and unhelpful as a method for conceiving the complexity of violence, or the complexity of human beings or any other living organisms. Biologists were hence the first to recognize the need for whole-system thinking and open models for living organisms, and increasing evidence has supported them. In this chapter, we showed how biology helps to unify our understanding of the bio-psycho-socio-environmental paradigm by resisting reductionism. We distinguished between aggression and violence, as well as clarified the misimpression of mental illness as a cause of violence, when it is more often the other way around. We showed how neuroscience, especially in the past 30 years, has seen remarkable progress in understanding the effects of the environment on gene expression, subsequent social influences on the brain, and the malleability of human nature itself. This characteristic is particularly pronounced for human beings, who have overdeveloped forebrains that develop well into adulthood and over the full lifespan in response to social, psychological, and environmental experiences.

We can no longer hope that the biological sciences will yield a "marker" or an underlying substrate responsible for human violence, but we can be certain that biology plays an essential role among the bio-psycho-socio-environmental determinants and intervention methods. This means that the lawyer in the courtroom will not be able to see radiographic images as the definitive source of evidence to determine responsibility for a violent crime, but rather will have to place them in context. The political scientist will not have to be concerned that conflict is inevitable because of our evolutionary predisposition but will consider a range of possibilities. However, as to whether there should be a biology of violence, the recommendation in this text is an unequivocal *yes*—and for all students of violence. Just as reductionism to biology can mislead, so will "reductionism" to any other field. For example, reducing violence to psychological or social causes alone can bring misconceptions of another kind, given human complexity. We will therefore consider scholarship from any field not in isolation but in interaction with other areas of knowledge, just as we have seen in this chapter how biology interacts with other levels of the human experience.

Great advances in the field of biology have occurred, and perhaps one of the greatest has been a change in paradigm. The entire foundation for understanding the basics of biology—anatomy, physiology, genetics, and behavioral determinants—has changed. It can no longer be assumed that biology unidirectionally determines behavior, and physics and chemistry determine biology; behavior not only also shapes biology but is inseparable from it. There is no "bottom" of all knowledge from which we can begin, for all knowledge begins with premises that are, essentially, assumptions. What the field of biology demonstrates is that, while we need to start somewhere, a constant interchange of confirmation and testing between data and theory, and comparing and contrasting different approaches and methods, must continue to bring us closer to the actual picture.

Biology, through close observations of living organisms, has highlighted the importance of shifting from linear causations to multifaceted predispositions. No particular field has primacy over others, but a practice of interchange and exchange can develop out of communication between the disciplines. This helps guard against devolving into ideology-driven pseudoscience while finding solutions that are evidence-based and principle-defining for the future. This is the reason why a comprehensive study of violence must include all the relevant fields, as this text tries to do, from biology, psychology, sociology, anthropology, political science, economics, and environmental studies to criminal justice, law, public health, medicine, philosophy, religion, and the arts. Integration of human inquiry is seldom attempted in any field, and yet the time is ripe for more substantive progress in our understanding of the human condition and its problems. Where violence is concerned, this level of understanding, far from being a fanciful pastime, may be a matter of life or death, or biological survival of our species.

In sum, attempting to tease out biology from other influences in the human sphere is no longer practically or theoretically tenable; thus, even for the non-biologist it has become impossible to ignore biological aspects in all areas of human engagement. Nowhere is this more apparent than in the study of violence. We are only beginning to come to grips with the enduring ways in which poor attachment, toxic stress, and other adverse conditions during early childhood have consequences throughout the lifespan, with ramifications throughout society. Biology, once the field many turned to for reductionism, is now demonstrating that genes and environment are intertwined in ways that have long-lasting and wide-ranging effects. Already with a long history of providing an open systems model through the observation of living organisms, it is now among the fields leading the way in a paradigm shift. Adverse environments, such as those that structural violence can cause, affect parents' ability to rear their children and have negative consequences for social harmony and health. Biological correlates for behavior are thus predisposing but insufficient conditions for shaping the bio-psycho-socio-environmental sphere we inhabit, and a more flexible but also more consequential concept of a biology of violence is necessary.

Questions

1 Why is understanding biology important to the understanding of human violence?

2 What role do biological "markers" or substrates have in predicting violence?

3 What do we mean when we say that brain–environment interactionism supersedes the "nature versus nurture" controversy?

4 What do brain plasticity, epigenetics, and hormonal–behavioral interactions say about the biology of violence?

5 What place do psychological, social, and environmental factors have in the biology of violence?

References

Alexander, K. W., Quas, J. A., & Goodman, G. S. (2002). Theoretical advances in understanding children's memory for distressing events: The role of attachment. *Developmental Review*, *22*(3), 490–519.

Anderson, N. E., & Kiehl, K. A. (2012). The psychopath magnetized: Insights from brain imaging. *Trends in Cognitive Sciences*, *16*(1), 52–60.

Anderson, S. W., Bechara, A., Damasio, H., Tranel, D., & Damasio, A. R. (1999). Impairment of social and moral behavior related to early damage in human prefrontal cortex. *Nature Neuroscience*, *2*(11), 1032–1037.

Anderson, S. W., Bechara, A., Damasio, H., Tranel, D., & Damasio, A. R. (2002). *Impairment of social and moral behavior related to early damage in human prefrontal cortex. Foundations of social neuroscience.* (pp. 333–343). Cambridge, MA: MIT Press.

Angermeyer, C. (2000). Schizophrenia and violence. *Acta Psychiatrica Scandinavica*, *102*(s407), 63–67.

Arboleda-Florez, J., Holley, H., & Crisanti, A. (1998). Understanding causal paths between mental illness and violence. *Social Psychiatry and Psychiatric Epidemiology*, *33*(1), S38–S46.

Baguley, I. J., Cooper, J., & Felmingham, K. (2006). Aggressive behavior following traumatic brain injury: How common is common. *Journal of Head Trauma Rehabilitation*, *21*(1), 45–56.

Bertalanffy, L. v. (1934). Untersuchungen über die Gesetzlichkeit des Wachstums. I. Allgemeine Grundlagen der Theorie; mathematische und physiologische Gesetzlichkeiten des Wachstums bei Wassertieren. *Arch. Entwicklungsmech.*, *131*, 613–652.

Bertalanffy, L. v. (1968). *General system theory: Foundations, development, applications*. New York, NY: Braziller.

Bird, A. (2007). Perceptions of epigenetics. *Nature*, *447*(7143), 396.

Black, M. M., Walker, S. P., Fernald, L. C., Andersen, C. T., DiGirolamo, A. M., Lu, C., ... Devercelli, A. E. (2017). Early childhood development coming of age: Science through the life course. *Lancet*, *389*(10064), 77–90.

Blair, R. J. R. (2001). Neurocognitivemodels of aggression, the antisocial personality disorders, and psychopathy. *Journal of Neurology, Neurosurgery and Psychiatry*, *71*(6), 727–731.

Bloch, M., Daly, R. C., & Rubinow, D. R. (2003). Endocrine factors in the etiology of postpartum depression. *Comprehensive Psychiatry*, *44*(3), 234–246.

Bowlby, J. (1969). *Attachment and loss: Vol. I Attachment*. London, UK: Hogarth.

Bowles, S. (2009). Did warfare among ancestral hunter-gatherers affect the evolution of human social behaviors? *Science*, *324*(5932), 1293–1298.

Brower, M. C., & Price, B. H. (2001). Neuropsychiatry of frontal lobe dysfunction in violent and criminal behaviour: A critical review. *Journal of Neurology, Neurosurgery and Psychiatry*, *71*(6), 720–726.

Bushman, B. J., & Anderson, C. A. (2001). Media violence and the American public: Scientific facts versus media misinformation. *American Psychologist*, *56*(6–7), 477.

Cadoret, R. J., Yates, W. R., Troughton, E., Woodworth, G., & Stewart, M. A. (1995). Gene-environmental interaction in the genesis of aggressivity and conduct disorders. *Archives of General Psychiatry*, *52*(11), 916–924.

Caspi, A., McClay, J., Moffitt, T. E., Mill, J., Martin, J., Craig, I. W., ... Poulton, R. (2002). Role of genotype in the cycle of violence in maltreated children. *Science*, *297*, 851–854.

Cecil, K. M., Brubaker, C. J., Adler, C. M., Dietrich, K. N., Altaye, M., Egelhoff, J. C., ... Lanphear, B. P. (2008). Decreased brain volume in adults with childhood lead exposure. *PLoS Medicine*, *5*(5), e112.

Crick, F. (1994). *The astonishing hypothesis: The scientific search for the soul*. New York, NY: Scribner.

Dawkins, R. (1976). *The selfish gene*. New York, NY: Oxford University Press.

De Waal, F. (1996). *Good natured: Origins of right and wrong in humans and other animals*. Cambridge, MA: Harvard University Press.

Deater-Deckard, K., Ivy, L., & Smith, J. (2005). Resilience in gene-environment transactions. In S. Goldstein, & R. B. Brooks (Eds.), *Handbook of resilience in children* (pp. 49–63). New York, NY: Springer.

Denno, D. W. (1990). *Biology and violence: From birth to adulthood*. New York, NY: Cambridge University Press.

DeWall, C. N., Gillath, O., Pressman, S. D., Black, L. L., Bartz, J. A., Moskovitz, J., & Stetler, D. A. (2014). When the love hormone leads to violence: Oxytocin increases intimate partner violence inclinations among high trait aggressive people. *Social Psychological and Personality Science*, *5*(6), 691–697.

DiLalla, L. F. (2002). Behavior genetics of aggression in children: Review and future directions. *Developmental Review, 22*(4), 593–622.

Dong, B., & Krohn, M. D. (2015). Exploring intergenerational discontinuity in problem behavior: Bad parents with good children. *Youth Violence and Juvenile Justice, 13*(2), 99–122.

Dugdale, R. (1877). *"The jukes": A study in crime, pauperism, disease and heredity.* New York, NY: Putnam's Sons.

Eisenberg, L. (1972). The *human* nature of human nature. *Science, 176*(4031), 123–128.

Famularo, R., Kinscherff, R., & Fenton, T. (1992). Psychiatric diagnoses of maltreated children: Preliminary findings. *Journal of the American Academy of Child and Adolescent Psychiatry, 31*(5), 863–867.

Fazel, S., Gulati, G., Linsell, L., Geddes, J. R., & Grann, M. (2009). Schizophrenia and violence: Systematic review and meta-analysis. *PLoS Medicine, 6*(8), e1000120.

Felitti, V. J., Anda, R. F., Nordenberg, D., Williamson, D. F., Spitz, A. M., Edwards, V., ... Marks, J. S. (1998). Relationship of childhood abuse and household dysfunction to many of the leading causes of death in adults: The Adverse Childhood Experiences (ACE) study. *American Journal of Preventive Medicine, 14*(4), 245–258.

Fellner, J. (2006). Corrections quandary: Mental illness and prison rules. *Harvard Civil Rights-Civil Liberties Law Review, 41*, 391–412.

Filley, C. M., Price, B. H., Nell, V., Antoinette, T., Morgan, A. S., Bresnahan, J. F., ... Kelly, J. P. (2001). Toward an understanding of violence: Neurobehavioral aspects of unwarranted physical aggression: Aspen neurobehavioral conference consensus statement. *Cognitive and Behavioral Neurology, 14*(1), 1–14.

Fontana, A., & Rosenheck, R. (2008). Treatment-seeking veterans of Iraq and Afghanistan: Comparison with veterans of previous wars. *Journal of Nervous and Mental Disease, 196*(7), 513–521.

Geertz, C. (1973). *The interpretation of cultures.* New York, NY: Basic Books.

Glueck, S., & Glueck, E. (1950). *Unraveling juvenile delinquency.* New York, NY: Commonwealth Fund.

Goddard, H. (1912). *The Kallikak family: A study in the heredity of feeble-mindedness.* New York, NY: Macmillan.

Goring, C. (1913). *The English convict: A statistical study.* London, UK: HMSO.

Grafman, J., Schwab, K., Warden, D., Pridgen, A., Brown, H. R., & Salazar, A. M. (1996). Frontal lobe injuries, violence, and aggression: A report of the Vietnam head injury study. *Neurology, 46*(5), 1231.

Grossmann, K. E., Grossmann, K., & Waters, E. (Eds.) (2006). *Attachment from infancy to adulthood: The major longitudinal studies.* New York, NY: Guilford Press.

Gunnar, M. R., & Donzella, B. (2002). Social regulation of the cortisol levels in early human development. *Psychoneuroendocrinology, 27*(1), 199–220.

Gunnar, M. R., & Vazquez, D. (2006). Stress neurobiology and developmental psychopathology. In D. Cicchetti, & D. J. Cohen (Eds.), *Developmental psychopathology: Developmental neuroscience* (Vol. 2) (pp. 533–577). Hoboken, NJ: Wiley and Sons.

Haagsma, J. A., Graetz, N., Bolliger, I., Naghavi, M., Higashi, H., ... Ameh, E. A. (2016). The global burden of injury: Incidence, mortality, disability-adjusted life years and time trends from the global burden of disease study 2013. *Injury Prevention, 22*(1), 3–18.

Harlow, J. M. (1868). Recovery from the passage of an iron bar through the head. *Publications of the Massachusetts Medical Society, 2*(3), 327–347.

Hiroeh, U., Appleby, L., Mortensen, P. B., & Dunn, G. (2001). Death by homicide, suicide, and other unnatural causes in people with mental illness: A population-based study. *Lancet, 358*(9299), 2110–2112.

Hirschi, T., & Hindelang, M. J. (1977). Intelligence and delinquency: A revisionist review. *American Sociological Review, 42*, 571–587.

Hofstra, M. B., van der Ende, J., & Verhulst, F. C. (2000). Continuity and change of psychopathology from childhood into adulthood: A 14-year follow-up study. *Journal of the American Academy of Child and Adolescent Psychiatry, 39*(7), 850–858.

Hooten, E. A. (1939). *Crime and the man.* Cambridge, MA: Harvard University Press.

Jaffee, S. R., Moffitt, T. E., Caspi, A., Taylor, A., & Arseneault, L. (2002). Influence of adult domestic violence on children's internalizing and externalizing problems: An environmentally informative twin study. *Journal of the American Academy of Child and Adolescent Psychiatry, 41*(9), 1095–1103.

Kingston, D. A., Seto, M. C., Ahmed, A. G., Fedoroff, P., Firestone, P., & Bradford, J. M. (2012). The role of central and peripheral hormones in sexual and violent recidivism in sex offenders. *Journal of the American Academy of Psychiatry and the Law Online, 40*(4), 476–485.

Kohn, R., Saxena, S., Levav, I., & Saraceno, B. (2004). The treatment gap in mental health care. *Bulletin of the World Health Organization, 82*(11), 858–866.

Lannen, P., & Ziswiler, M. (2014). Potential and perils of the early years: The need to integrate violence prevention and early child development (ECD+). *Aggression and Violent Behavior, 19*(6), 625–628.

Leckman, J. F., Panter-Brick, C., & Salah, R. (Eds.) (2014). *Pathways to peace: The transformative power of children and families* (Vol. *15*, J. Lupp, Series Ed.) Strüngmann Forum Reports. Cambridge, MA: MIT Press.

Legrenzi, P., & Umilta, C. (2009). *Neuro-mania: Il cervello non spiega chi siamo.* Bologna, Italy: Il Mulino.

Liston, C., Miller, M. M., Goldwater, D. S., Radley, J. J., Rocher, A. B., Hof, P. R., ... McEwen, B. S. (2006). Stress-induced alterations in prefrontal cortical dendritic morphology predict selective impairments in perceptual attentional set-shifting. *Journal of Neuroscience, 26*(30), 7870–7874.

Lombroso, C. (1876). *L'Uomo delinquente: Studiato in rapporto alla antropologia alla medicina legale ed alle discipline carceriae.* Milano, Italy: Hoepli.

Lorenz, K. (1966). *On aggression.* New York, NY: Harcourt, Brace and World.

Lupien, S. J., McEwen, B. S., Gunnar, M. R., & Heim, C. (2009). Effects of stress throughout the lifespan on the brain, behaviour and cognition. *Nature Reviews Neuroscience, 10*(6), 434–445.

McClintock, B. (1950). The origin and behavior of mutable loci in maize. *Proceedings of the National Academy of Sciences, 36*(6), 344–355.

Miczek, K. A., Maxson, S. C., Fish, E. W., & Faccidomo, S. (2001). Aggressive behavioral phenotypes in mice. *Behavioural Brain Research, 125*(1), 167–181.

Mirsky, A. F., & Siegel, A. (1994). The neurobiology of violence and aggression. In A. J. Reiss, Jr., & J. A. Roth (Eds.), *Understanding and preventing violence* (Vol. *III*) (pp. 59–172). Washington, DC: National Academy Press.

Moffitt, T. E., Caspi, A., Harrington, H., & Milne, B. J. (2002). Males on the life-course-persistent and adolescence-limited antisocial pathways: Follow-up at age 26 years. *Development and Psychopathology, 14*(1), 179–207.

Montoya, E. R., Terburg, D., Bos, P. A., & van Honk, J. (2012). Testosterone, cortisol, and serotonin as key regulators of social aggression: A review and theoretical perspective. *Motivation and Emotion, 36*(1), 65–73.

Munetz, M. R., Grande, T. P., & Chambers, M. R. (2001). The incarceration of individuals with severe mental disorders. *Community Mental Health Journal, 37*, 361–372.

Murray, C. J., Vos, T., Lozano, R., Naghavi, M., Flaxman, A. D., ... Aboyans, V. (2012). Disability-adjusted life years (DALYs) for 291 diseases and injuries in 21 regions, 1990–2010: A systematic analysis for the Global Burden of Disease Study 2010. *Lancet, 380*(9859), 2197–2223.

National Center for Health Statistics (1980). *The international classification of diseases, 9th revision, clinical modification.* Washington, DC: U.S. Department of Health and Human Services.

Nelson, C. A., Bos, K., Gunnar, M. R., & Sonuga-Barke, E. J. (2011). The neurobiological toll of early human deprivation. *Monographs of the Society for Research in Child Development, 76*(4), 127–146.

Nelson, R. J., & Chiavegatto, S. (2001). Molecular basis of aggression. *Trends in Neurosciences, 24*(12), 713–719.

Niehoff, N. (1999). *Biology of violence: How understanding the brain, behavior, and environment can break the vicious circle of aggression.* New York, NY: Free Press.

Pascual-Leone, A., Freitas, C., Oberman, L., Horvath, J. C., Halko, M., Eldaief, M., & Vahabzadeh-Hagh, A. M. (2011). Characterizing brain cortical plasticity and network dynamics across the age-span in health and disease with TMS-EEG and TMS-fMRI. *Brain Topography, 24,* 302–315.

Perry, B. D., Pollard, R. A., Blakley, T. L., Baker, W. L., & Vigilante, D. (1995). Childhood trauma, the neurobiology of adaptation, and use dependent development of the brain: How states become traits. *Infant Mental Health Journal, 16*(4), 271–291.

Petronis, A. (2010). Epigenetics as a unifying principle in the aetiology of complex traits and diseases. *Nature, 465*(7299), 721–727.

Ponti, G., Peretto, P., Bonfanti, L., & Reh, T. A. (2008). Genesis of neuronal and glial progenitors in the cerebellar cortex of peripuberal and adult rabbits. *PLoS One, 3*(6), e2366.

Prince, M., Patel, V., Saxena, S., Maj, M., Maselko, J., Phillips, M. R., & Rahman, A. (2007). No health without mental health. *Lancet, 370*(9590), 859–877.

Provençal, N., Suderman, M. J., Caramaschi, D., Wang, D., Hallett, M., Vitaro, F., … Szyf, M. (2013). Differential DNA methylation regions in cytokine and transcription factor genomic loci associate with childhood physical aggression. *PLoS One, 8*(8), e71691.

Raine, A. (2014). *Anatomy of violence: The biological roots of crime.* London, UK: Penguin Books.

Raine, A., Lencz, T., Bihrle, S., LaCasse, L., & Colletti, P. (2000). Reduced prefrontal gray matter volume and reduced autonomic activity in antisocial personality disorder. *Archives of General Psychiatry, 57*(2), 119–127.

Rajkowska, G. (1997). Morphometric methods for studying the prefrontal cortex in suicide victims and psychiatric patients. *Annals of the New York Academy of Sciences, 836*(1), 253–268.

Rakic, P. (2002). Neurogenesis in adult primate neocortex: An evaluation of the evidence. *Nature Reviews Neuroscience, 3*(1), 65–71.

Reik, W. (2007). Stability and flexibility of epigenetic gene regulation in mammalian development. *Nature, 447*(7143), 425–432.

Sapolsky, R. M., Romero, L. M., & Munck, A. U. (2000). How do glucocorticoids influence stress responses? Integrating permissive, suppressive, stimulatory, and preparative actions. *Endocrine Reviews, 21*(1), 55–89.

Schiavi, R. C., Theilgaard, A., Owen, D. R., & White, D. (1984). Sex chromosome anomalies, hormones, and aggressivity. *Archives of General Psychiatry, 41*(1), 93–99.

Shields, A., & Cicchetti, D. (1998). Reactive aggression among maltreated children: The contributions of attention and emotion dysregulation. *Journal of Clinical Child Psychology, 27*(4), 381–395.

Shonkoff, J. P., Boyce, W. T., & McEwen, B. S. (2009). Neuroscience, molecular biology, and the childhood roots of health disparities. *JAMA, 301*(21), 2252–2259.

Shonkoff, J. P., Garner, A. S., Siegel, B. S., Dobbins, M. I., Earls, M. F., McGuinn, L., … Committee on Early Childhood, Adoption, and Dependent Care (2012). The lifelong effects of early childhood adversity and toxic stress. *Pediatrics, 129*(1), e232–e246.

Sowell, E. R., Peterson, B. S., Thompson, P. M., Welcome, S. E., Henkenius, A. L., & Toga, A. W. (2003). Mapping cortical change across the human life span. *Nature Neuroscience, 6*(3), 309–315.

Steadman, H. J., Mulvey, E. P., Monahan, J., Robbins, P. C., Appelbaum, P. S., Grisso, T., ... Silver, E. (1998). Violence by people discharged from acute psychiatric inpatient facilities and by others in the same neighborhoods. *Archives of General Psychiatry, 55*, 393–401.

Swartz, M. S., Swanson, J. W., Hiday, V. A., Borum, R., Wagner, R., & Burns, B. J. (1998). Taking the wrong drugs: The role of substance abuse and medication noncompliance in violence among severely mentally ill individuals. *Social Psychiatry and Psychiatric Epidemiology, 33*(1), S75–S80.

Tiihonen, J., Rautiainen, M. R., Ollila, H. M., Repo-Tiihonen, E., Virkkunen, M., Palotie, A., ... Saarela, J. (2015). Genetic background of extreme violent behavior. *Molecular Psychiatry, 20*, 786–792.

Tops, M., van Peer, J. M., Korf, J., Wijers, A. A., & Tucker, D. M. (2007). Anxiety, cortisol, and attachment predict plasma oxytocin. *Psychophysiology, 44*(3), 444–449.

Vassos, E., Collier, D. A., & Fazel, S. (2014). Systematic meta-analyses and field synopsis of genetic association studies of violence and aggression. *Molecular Psychiatry, 19*(4), 471–477.

Virkkunen, M., Goldman, D., Nielsen, D. A., & Linnoila, M. (1995). Low brain serotonin turnover rate (low CSF 5-HIAA) and impulsive violence. *Journal of Psychiatry and Neuroscience, 20*(4), 271–275.

West-Eberhard, M. J. (2003). *Developmental plasticity and evolution.* New York, NY: Oxford University Press.

Wexler, B. E. (2006). *Brain and culture: Neurobiology, ideology, and social change.* Cambridge, MA: MIT Press.

Wilson, E. O. (1975). *Sociobiology: The new synthesis.* Cambridge, MA: Belknap Press.

Wolfe, D. A. (1999). *Child abuse: Implications for child development and psychopathology.* Thousand Oaks, CA: Sage.

Wolfgang, M. E. (1955). Cesare Lombroso: 1835–1909. In H. Mannheim (Ed.), *Pioneers in criminology.* Montclair, NJ: Patterson Smith.

World Health Organization. (2014). *Preventing suicide: A global imperative.* Geneva, Switzerland: Author. Retrieved from http://apps.who.int/iris/bitstream/10665/131056/1/9789241564779_eng.pdf

Yang, Y., & Raine, A. (2009). Prefrontal structural and functional brain imaging findings in antisocial, violent, and psychopathic individuals: A meta-analysis. *Psychiatry Research: Neuroimaging, 174*(2), 81–88.

3

The Psychology of Violence

Introduction

> The ego is not master in its own house.
> —*Sigmund Freud,* A Difficulty in the Path of Psycho-Analysis *(1953)*

In Chapter 2, we saw how giving a biological dimension to human behavior enriches our understanding of violence, not by reducing social or moral aspects to their "building blocks" but through understanding how it interacts and integrates other fields of knowledge. This, in turn, implies that we can have some control over biology and the physical world that was in the past assumed to be fixed: even our biology does not make human violence inevitable. Conversely, the same principle in *psychology* entails some humility, as understanding our psychology in depth means that we give up notions that we are fully the cause of our own thoughts and behavior. Thus, the notion of an open system in interaction with the environment applies just as much to psychology, with sociocultural, politicoeconomic, and environmental factors at play, whether we perceive them or not. While leaving open what emerges from the whole of these processes (which we leave for the next chapter), we will study human psychology as another facet of the bio-psycho-socio-environmental formulation of the causes and cures of violence.

Psychology allows for intimate encounters, as in clinical situations, and external observations, as in a laboratory. It is the most systematic study of human beings and the things they do, including how we react and think. It can help us to understand the minds of violent individuals, those who have experienced trauma, and how both sometimes combine in the same individual. At the same time, few fields have embraced reductionism as eagerly, veering far from its original subject of study (*psyche* is the Greek word for "breath," "spirit," or "soul"). This is to be cautioned against. If biology has historically tried to reduce behavior to genetics, physiology, and anatomy, psychology has tried to reduce it to stimulus–response units, or the mind when it is disordered (when faculties deteriorate or simplify).

The reason for this approach is that, for more than a hundred years, classical physics served as "the gold standard" for all scientific fields, including psychology (Andersson, 1994). In the same way that biology has tried to reduce life processes to physiology, chemistry, and ultimately physics, the discipline of psychology has felt that, in order to be considered properly scientific, it would need to reduce it to behavior and then to brain science. We now know that this reductionism by favoring lower levels no longer holds for physics, much less for the study of human beings: reductionistic biology fails to explain life, as reductionistic psychology fails to

Violence: An Interdisciplinary Approach to Causes, Consequences, and Cures, First Edition. Bandy X. Lee.
© 2019 John Wiley & Sons, Inc. Published 2019 by John Wiley & Sons, Inc.

explain the human mind. Human beings are far more complex than this approach will allow, and a proper understanding lies in *embracing complexity* rather than in finding a way to explain it away. This becomes especially true in the study of human violence. An evolution in methodology reflects this progression: moving away from exclusive reliance on randomized controlled trials that can yield answers from large amounts of quantitative data, intimate human contact as a source of knowledge and qualitative data, to guide which questions to ask in the first place, have also come to be valued. Psychotherapy or psychodynamic studies is the observation is one-on-one contact with an individual, where is ethnography is intimate contact with a culture.

Therefore, while much of contemporary psychology concentrates on behavior and biology, this chapter will return to a level of understanding once again considered radical: *psychodynamics*, or the systematic study of inner forces that drive human behavior, feelings, and emotions. *Psychodynamic theory* has helped to identify various defense mechanisms, paradoxical aspects of the mind, and the importance of early experiences. How these forces play out in psychodynamics, especially in conscious and unconscious motivation, is relevant to the study of violence—even if it requires the resurrection of some "outdated" notions (Mitchell, 1988).

Psychodynamic theory, once central in the effort to understand and to intervene in human psychological affairs, has largely been relegated to the sidelines in a renewed drive for the field to become more "scientific." Unfortunately, for the last few decades, this has meant becoming more "biological" and adopting a more closed-system approach (Molenaar, 2004). Topics within psychology have consequently become indistinguishable from those in biology and neuroscience, with inferences from animal studies, treatments that reduce symptoms through chemicals, and computational models based on machines (O'Reilly, 2006). Given what we know about psychosocial influences on biology, we propose that psychodynamics needs an update that reflects brain processes just as studies of the nervous system now reflect mental processes (Shepherd, 1991). There should also be a much wider application of psychodynamics to society at large. We will conceptualize this in the context of *how to think about violence* across the bio-psycho-socio-environmental spectrum.

An emphasis on psychodynamics should not repeat what has happened in their heyday: the reduction of biology to interpersonal relations. At the time, theorists attributed highly biological illnesses such as schizophrenia to early parent-child dynamics alone, which created concepts such as a "schizophrenogenic" parent and tragic blaming when support was in order for a complex, largely uncontrollable situation (Neill, 1990). If we do not discard the essence with the mistakes that have been made, but rather revisit the core of these principles in revised form in the context of many other processes, then we may benefit from the knowledge.

A systematic study of the psychological forces that shape human emotion, thought, and behavior can shed light on violence. Knowledge of two characteristics of the human mind is especially helpful: (a) the presence of the unconscious and the paradoxes that it engenders; and (b) the access to enormous inner resources when self-defeating mechanisms are understood and overcome. Thinking more deeply allows us to get past the notion that violent individuals are simply bizarre and doing inexplicably aberrant things to the knowledge that people who are prone to violence share our psychology and can help us grasp how our own minds work. Since violence often occurs outside the realm of conscious or long-term thought (Toch, 1969) and is ultimately self-defeating and paradoxical, explanations that account for this complexity are necessary. Particularly relevant to perplexing behavior is the psychodynamic principle that the capacity to observe ourselves and to have self-knowledge (Markus, 1983) helps us to observe others. Making human beings the object of study is no different than the rest of science, which tests hypotheses against external observations, taking into account potential internal biases (Cooke, 1991). Subjecting the human mind to this method has allowed for great advances in understanding and, as a result, the person is more able to be master of one's own mind, precisely through the concession that there are other forces at play.

One Among Many

Violence is always a tragedy, but explanations can vary according to perspective. There are many models in psychology, of which psychodynamic theory is only one. The question is, why are there so many? What makes psychology so complex? While philosophical interest in mind and behavior dates back to the great ancient civilizations of Egypt, China, India, and Greece, psychology as a major scientific discipline is relatively young, and theories about the mind have changed many times (Goodwin, 2008). The mind as a subject of study is vastly complex, and it is clear that our knowledge about it is still miniscule. Furthermore, there is the difficulty of the mind trying to observe itself, whereby what is hidden from the mind will also likely be hidden from observation. Nevertheless, ways to tackle these challenges have slowly developed.

Psychology first became an experimental science through German physician Wilhelm Wundt's (1911) breakdown of mental processes into basic components. American psychologist William James (1918) then responded by theorizing how the mind went beyond its components to function as one, a question we explore to this day. Psychodynamic approaches began in the 1890s, and Austrian physician Sigmund Freud (1910) developed the field of psychoanalysis—a way of using theories about how the mind works and psychotherapy to treat issues that stem from inner conflict.

Freud's approach was largely based on observations, introspection, and interpretations. While this sounds subjective, it was an experimental approach in the sense that an external observer collected "objective" data on a person, rather than taking for granted the person's report (Freud, Bonaparte, Freud, and Kris, 1954). This approach yielded valuable information on the human mind, especially in its ability to explain inexplicable behavior. However, because these observations are not fully amenable to *quantitative* study—objective measurements that can be analyzed numerically—it led to a decline in the field (Kernberg, 2006). Nevertheless, psychoanalysis is now seeing a mild resurgence due to the development of *qualitative* methods, which explore the appropriate questions to ask (regardless of measurability) and observe changes in quality. In this text, we emphasize the application of methods *appropriate to the phenomenon* and warn of potentially misleading results when applying simplistic, quantitative methods to human complexity.

Psychodynamic approaches were developed and refined over many decades: while Freud broke down mental functions to make them experimental, Swiss psychiatrist Carl Jung (1913) developed a more integrative approach. Erik Erikson (1950) added theories of development, Melanie Klein (1950) and Donald Winnicott (1964) relational theories, and John Bowlby (1988) attachment theory in early life—all of which add to our understanding of violence. In the United States, *behaviorism*, headed by John Watson (1930) and later by B. F. Skinner (1976), became the dominant school of thought by the mid-twentieth century; it focused on conditioned responses and rejected any notion of "mind."

The currently popular paradigm is *cognitivism*, which derives from a renewed interest in mental states and information processing due to advances in computer technology. *Cognitive science* is the study of thought, learning, and mental organization and shares its subject matter not only with psychology but with other disciplines such as computer science, neuroscience, linguistics, and philosophy of mind. A counterpart of psychodynamics, cognitivism helps to circumvent delving into the unconscious or a traumatic past, and in cases of extreme trauma, can avoid some of the risks of emotional overwhelm. Coupled with behavioral modification, *cognitive-behavioral therapy* (CBT) helps to regulate emotions for coping (Beck, 1993). While this can be a practical tool for finding relief in the absence of an ability or adequate support to get to "the source" of the problem, it does not deal with the deeper layers that play an important role in violence.

As mentioned, psychodynamic approaches, once the center of all psychological and psychiatric practice and now in their outskirts, are now experiencing a modest resurgence as research methods to show validity and efficacy have improved (Leichsenring et al., 2013; de Maat et al., 2013). Furthermore, neuroscientific evidence has been able to give anatomical confirmation of psychodynamics' theoretical grounds (Damasio, Everitt, & Bishop, 1996; Sacks, 1984; Solms & Turnbull, 2002). Biologists have observed that the unconscious part of the mind is "a million times more powerful" than the conscious mind, and that we operate 95 to 99 percent of our lives from subconscious programming (Lipton, 2005). Rather than debating whether psychodynamics should again take a leading role in psychology, we will note simply that emotional logic warrants its own study, and the complexity of the human makeup makes it possible to conceive of biological and psychological events as concurrences in a multi-faceted system rather than a linear causality from one domain to another.

Given the central role of emotional life in development, attachment formation, meaning making, and identity, we will review its principles here for their sheer explanatory power with respect to human violence. We deem studies of both cognition and emotion to be useful as long as we do not assume that validity of one explanation overturns the other: we can avoid perpetual pendulum swings by taking a broader, more integrated approach. Rigor lies not in reducing phenomena into a singular mechanism but in acknowledging that different levels will interweave in a manner appropriate to the complexity we observe.

A linear approach, for example, would not be able to detect the fragmentation that occurs as a sign of poor mental health (the Old English word for health, *hælp*, denotes "wholeness" or "being whole"). In other words, health and illness might be seen in a spectrum of wholeness to fragmentation. While schism and a loss of unity are most pronounced in serious mental illness (e.g., schizophrenia denotes a split between reason and emotion), human beings with reasonable health also experience varying levels of fragmentation within the self that give rise to inner *conflict*. Therefore, psychodynamic theory is not just a study of fragments but of how the mind as a whole functions less effectively when it is in conflict with itself, such as happens between *conscious* and *unconscious* processes. Reducing this conflict by bringing in as much of the unconscious mechanisms into consciousness is a principal goal of psychodynamics and how it heals.

Wholeness heals in other ways: an awareness of psychodynamic principles in the general culture throughout North America and Western Europe has arguably reduced to the point of disappearance many afflictions related to emotional repression, whereas they are still highly prevalent in some other regions of the world. On the other hand, the Global North has traditionally suffered more from the problems of atomization and the disintegration of communities. Diverse approaches to psychological treatment, furthermore, seem preferable to a singular theory; called an *eclectic* approach, employing multiple methods simultaneously is more effective in restoring wholeness.

Case Vignettes

Clinical Depression

Ryan is an extremely high achiever. Academically, he has done well in all of his activities, but he suffers from acute anxiety about his academic performance, personal achievement, and appearance. The onset of his symptoms began when he started studying hard for examinations around the age of 16. There are occasions when he becomes emotional and breaks down under the strain. Once, when Ryan received his examination results, he broke down in tears in the back of the car. When his parents see the results, they are puzzled: he did very well and is at the top of his class. Not only that, he writes for the school newspaper, and some of his articles on current affairs seem almost professional level. His parents are very attentive to him and seem to be doing everything to provide the best for their son, and this makes Ryan feel worse about himself. Despite achieving excellent results, Ryan is unable to enjoy his success and finds the whole experience exhausting rather than gratifying.

Ryan's self-doubt initially seemed normal for a teenager, but it begins to dominate other aspects of his life. His parents worry that his perfectionistic tendencies are a problem and seek professional help. Ryan's doctor diagnoses him with clinical depression and prescribes antidepressant medication. He starts the medication but feels no better. During exam periods, he repeats the same pattern of getting his results and bursting into tears, unable to derive a sense of satisfaction from his successful performance. Two weeks after seeing the doctor, he is still feeling empty and depressed, and his next appointment is another week away. Feeling guilty about not feeling better despite getting treatment, he sees no point in living. Anxious, depressed, and feeling doomed to a life of unhappiness, he swallows all his pills to take his own life. Waking up in a hospital with his parents by his side, he decides to take a semester off to relieve some of the stress and focus on his recovery. Along the way, he is told that depression can happen in the context of stress but also without any reason. Medications take time to start working, but with the help of a counselor, he stays with his treatment plan and experiences a full recovery. Clinical depression is often difficult for the afflicted person or those in the surrounding environment to understand, for it exceeds any "normal" sadness; one can experience intense, intolerable suffering in the absence of any objective problems or abnormal appearances (Sadock et al., 2017).

Antisocial Personality

Vincent is a white man who at the age of 30 begins to kill female prostitutes, most of them white. He was adopted as a child and grew up in a large urban area. He has a limited history of dating women his age and has had no lasting romantic relationships, though he has a few social friends of both sexes. He has no record of treatment for psychological disorders. As an adult, he has taken some college courses but drops out and later resumes living in his family home. He has had a few sporadic low-paying jobs and fails in several business ventures. He has grown accustomed to using prostitutes to satisfy his sexual urges, having done so routinely for several years. He meets them on inner-city streets, pays for their services, and carries out his sexual interactions with them inside his car. Occasionally, he brings a prostitute home for a longer stay when his mother is away. During these years of frequenting prostitutes, he has been arrested once for solicitation but has never been charged with any violent crimes.

The 17 women he kills range in age from 21 to 41. He strangles all of them. He varies his method of disposing of the victims' bodies: he buries some, places some under discarded items such as mattresses, dumps some in bodies of water, and hides some in wooded areas. He dismembers three, scattering their remains in and around the metropolitan area where he lives. No patterns or discernable changes over time are noted in these disposals. He later states he simply took advantage of opportunities that arose that allowed him to avoid detection. He sometimes keeps the personal belongings of his victims, including jewelry and photo identification. His murders span a period of a little over 4 years. The time between murders varies from one to 18 months. He does not know why he chooses certain victims over other potential ones. He sometimes leaves home knowing that he will kill later that day, whereas at other times, he does not know until just before the opportunity presents itself. His relative degree of stealth, his selection of vulnerable victims with a transient lifestyle, and the variations in his methods of body disposal allow him to remain undetected for many months.

When arrested, he confesses to the murders, expressing little feeling. In his interview, he displays all the symptoms of antisocial personality disorder: failure to conform to social norms by repeatedly performing acts that are grounds for arrest; deceitfulness, lying, and conning others for profit or pleasure; impulsive behavior; irritability and aggressiveness leading to assaults; blatant disregard for the safety of self and others; a pattern of irresponsibility; and a lack of remorse (American Psychiatric Association, 2013). Antisocial individuals are difficult to identify for untrained persons, since they are often charming and may even come across as empathic, for they are highly attuned to others' feelings and needs—not to help, but to prey upon and to exploit. They often have backgrounds of trauma, although the specific trauma can be hard to identify. Vincent's history is remarkable for family instability, the death of his father 2 years before the first murder, social isolation, and a deep resentment of young women. He claims his sexual intercourse with the victims was consensual, and although he cannot articulate any specific reasons for the murders, he professes an intense interest in watching them die. He admits that his killings have become a "problematic hobby" for him. He describes having a high degree of mobility, from which the interviewers infer that driving around to evaluate and map each area gives him the thrill of strategizing about how he will obtain and dispose of future victims.

Extreme Narcissism

On December 6, 1989, at just a little after four in the afternoon, 25-year-old Marc Lépine arrives at the École Polytechnique, an engineering school affiliated with the Université de Montréal. He is armed with a Mini-14 rifle and a hunting knife. Lépine is familiar with the layout of the building since he has visited the École Polytechnique many times before. Lépine sits for a time in the office of the registrar on the second floor. He does not speak to anyone, even when a staff member asks if she can help him. He leaves the office and goes around the building before entering a second-floor mechanical engineering class of about 60 students in the middle of a presentation. After approaching the student giving the presentation, he asks everyone to stop everything and orders the women and men to opposite sides of the classroom. No one moves at first, believing it to be a joke until he fires a shot into the ceiling.

Lépine separates the nine women from the approximately 50 men and tells the men to leave the classroom. He asks the women whether they knew why they are here. When one student replies that she doesn't know, Lépine answers: "I am fighting feminism." One of the students says: "Look, we are just women studying engineering, not necessarily feminists ready to march on the streets to shout we are against men, just students intent on leading a normal life." Lépine responds: "You're women; you're going to be engineers. You're all a bunch of feminists. I hate feminists." He then opens fire on the students from left to right, killing six and wounding three. Lépine moves toward the financial services office, where he shoots and kills a woman through the window of the door she just locked. Next, he goes down to the first-floor cafeteria, in which about a hundred people are gathered. The crowd scatters after he shoots a woman standing near the kitchens and wounds another student. Entering an unlocked storage area at the end of the cafeteria, Lépine shoots and kills two more women hiding there.

Lépine walks up to the third floor where he shoots and wounds one female and two male students in the hall. He enters another classroom, fires on students in the front row, and then kills two women who are trying to escape the room. He moves toward some of the female students, wounding three of them and killing another. He changes the magazine in his weapon and moves to the front of the class, spraying the classroom. At this point, one of the wounded women asks for help and, after unsheathing his hunting knife, Lépine stabs her three times, killing her. He takes off his cap, wraps his coat around his rifle, and fatally shoots himself in the head. His jacket pocket contains a suicide letter, in which he has written that he blames feminists for ruining his life, for they seek social changes that "retain the advantages of being women ... while trying to grab those of the men." He has shot 28 people, killing 14 women, including 12 engineering students, one nursing student, and a school employee. A police psychiatrist who interviewed Lépine's family and entourage suggests that he may have had "extreme narcissistic vulnerability," as shown by his methods of killing, fantasies of power and success, and feelings of incompetence that he would compensate for through violent and grandiose imaginations (Sourour, 1991). In this manner, extreme narcissism can lead to violence. When a person has an exaggerated need for admiration and affirmation, as well as a grandiose image of self-importance to counteract intolerable feelings of incompetence and worthlessness, then violent rage can result when reality fails to fulfill one's fantasies.

Heat of Passion

Othello woos his wife Desdemona with stories of his adventures in travel and war. The Duke of Venice tells Othello that he must go to Cyprus to aid in the defense against the Turks, who are heading for the island. Desdemona insists that she accompany Othello on his trip, and they make preparations to depart that night. Upon landing in Cyprus, Iago, a man who hates Othello and his standing in the army, plans to destroy him and puts a plan into play to convince Othello that Desdemonda is having an affair. Iago suggests that Cassio, a recently disgraced soldier, is her lover. After a meeting with Cassio, Desdemona pleads with Othello to reinstate Cassio as lieutenant. This impassioned defense adds to Othello's growing suspicion. Othello speaks with Iago, after which Desdemona comes to call Othello to supper and finds him feeling unwell. She offers him her handkerchief to wrap around his head, but he finds it to be too small and lets it drop to the floor. Iago retrieves the handkerchief and plants it in Cassio's room. When Othello demands visual proof that his wife is unfaithful, Iago says that he saw Cassio wipe his beard with Desdemona's handkerchief—the first gift Othello ever gave her. Othello vows to take vengeance on his wife and on Cassio. When Othello sees Desdemona later that evening, he demands that she give him the handkerchief, but she tells him that she does not have it with her and attempts to change the subject by continuing her plea on Cassio's behalf. This drives Othello into a further rage, and he storms out.

Jealousy so consumes Othello, he falls into a trance and has a seizure. Cassio comes by, and Iago tells him to come back in a few minutes to talk. Once Othello recovers, Iago tells him of the meeting he has planned with Cassio. He instructs Othello to hide nearby and watch as Iago extracts the story of his affair with Desdemona from Cassio. While Othello stands in hiding, Iago fishes information from Cassio about a prostitute, Bianca, causing Cassio to laugh and confirm Othello's suspicions. Bianca herself then enters with Desdemona's handkerchief, reprimanding Cassio for making her copy out the embroidery of a love token given to him by another woman. Later, when Desdemona and Othello are together, Othello is given a letter from Venice calling him home and instating Cassio as his replacement. Othello strikes Desdemona and accuses Desdemona of being a whore. He ignores her protestations. Meanwhile, Iago instructs a conspirator, Roderigo, to ambush Cassio, but Roderigo misses his mark. Iago wounds Cassio and runs away. Meanwhile, Othello stands over his sleeping wife in their bedchamber, preparing to kill her. Desdemona wakes and attempts to plead with Othello, asserting her innocence. Othello smothers her. Afterward, Othello learns that Cassio is alive and is mortified. Emilia, Iago's wife, asks Othello what happened, and Othello tells her that he has killed Desdemona for her infidelity, which Iago brought to his attention (Shakespeare, 1990). Othello is a Moor, or a black man in Venice, and therefore many contributors to his violent response can be hypothesized, including culturally induced insecurity and doubt, discrimination and trauma, and intense love that can turn into hate for the belief that one does not deserve what one desires.

The Mind as Iceberg

The first principle of psychodynamics is that only a very small portion of the mind consists of conscious activity. In other words, what we are conscious of is not all there is. Freud used the analogy of an iceberg to explain how little of the mind is actually within our awareness, with only one-seventh of its bulk above water. The implication is that there is great depth to the human psyche, far more than is immediately apparent. The "discovery" of the unconscious was significant enough for American historiographer Henri Ellenberger (1970) to write an epic tome chronicling the culmination of a collective psychological evolution that even predated psychoanalysis. The conscious part of our minds, or the tip of this enormous iceberg, is the straightforward part: this is where we decide to do something and then do it. In plenty of situations, however, we observe that we may decide to do something but do not follow through, or we act in ways that contradict what we say we intend or sometimes even sabotage our goals. We know of the existence of the unconscious only by this gap, for by definition, the unconscious does not easily let itself be known.

The *ego* is like the head of a large household, or the captain of an enormous ship whose crew have taken over the steering but, rather than letting the captain know this, will do whatever they can to make the captain believe oneself in charge. The crew may believe that they are doing what is best for the welfare of the whole ship, but none of them have the vista of the captain so they scramble in scattered directions and often steer in the direction exactly opposite to the intended destination. The moment the ego becomes aware of this dynamic, the divide will dissolve and operations will unite toward a more integrated goal. On rare occasions, individuals may be able to recognize the discrepancy in their thoughts or actions on their own. However, it often takes an outside observer to accomplish this, since the unconscious is by definition not consciously accessible. Greater integration at the conscious level and less "takeover" by unconscious processes is a sign of health.

Fragmentation occurs because, underneath our conscious existence, there are regulatory mechanisms in place just as in the body: mechanisms that protect us and help keep us alive. The body keeps itself alive through automatic regulatory mechanisms, so we do not constantly have to remember to breathe in order to survive—or to keep the heart beating, or to respond to danger when there is no time for reflection. Similarly, unconscious mechanisms try to aid the survival of the psyche by avoiding mental pain or by controlling unacceptable impulses—which, all at once, can become overwhelming. The problem arises when it tries to do so to the exclusion of an effective resolution, for unconscious drives are necessarily more primitive than conscious, considered ones. Therefore, while their purpose is to protect and to promote survival, to leave important decisions to these lower mechanisms can result in rigid, self-defeating, and maladaptive choices. However, if the conscious mind is capable of integrating the unconscious to become more whole, the alignment allows one to grasp "higher" goals that are more productive and adaptive. The presence of these layers means that problems such as violent behavior and violent psychology will require more than superficial solutions.

Mental functions are often divided between the cognitive (information processing) and the psychodynamic (emotional processes), sometimes called the cool "know" system and the hot "go" system (Metcalfe & Mischel, 1999). These are akin to the two types of violence we discussed in Chapter 2, "The Biology of Violence": the low-arousal and premeditated, predatory type versus the high-arousal and impulsive, affective type. Generally, we like to believe that we are rational beings, but this view takes into account only the surface. Psychoanalysis, through a focus on actions we cannot explain through rational means becomes one of the chief methods by which we delineate emotional logic and the "irrational" mind's use of defense mechanisms to hide motives from the "rational" mind.

Some Defense Mechanisms

One way in which the unconscious manifests itself is in the strategies it employs "to defend" one's view of oneself against painful feelings, conflicting impulses, or outside criticisms. Sometimes this is deliberate, but most times, and more likely, it is unconscious and outside one's control. The unconscious might manipulate or distort reality, repress and bury emotions that later erupt, and choose courses that are not very socially acceptable or adaptive. We see this often in violent individuals: some of the specific examples of defenses we will talk about here include acting out, projection, reaction formation, and return of the repressed.

Acting out is a direct expression of an unconscious wish or impulse in action, occurring without conscious awareness of the emotion that is driving the behavior. People who become violent are often acting out extreme experiences, memories, or emotions that they feel otherwise incapable of expressing. Putting actions before words in the form of language, violent persons are often said to "talk with their fists." One may pick fights with random people or punch holes in walls as a way of saying: "I am angry about my situation" (Walker, 1995). When thinking about one's feelings is especially painful, acting out short-circuits the thought by moving directly into action. By learning to put these feelings into words, one can reduce this urge. In fact, a central aim of psychotherapy in the *Global North*—although by no means the only one—is to convert feelings and actions into words. This way, one can be more aware of them, manage them, and begin to resolve them by developing more constructive responses (Streeck, 1999).

Projection is taking intolerable feelings or thoughts about oneself and putting them onto others. It enables one to disown unacceptable thoughts, feelings, and impulses such that another person is perceived as possessing those qualities, and one can lay blame on another instead. This can include projecting feelings of self-hatred onto others, thereby perceiving others as faulting, ridiculing, or otherwise judging the person. One can also reverse severe self-rebuke into false accusations or intolerance toward others (Casement, 1990). Bullies are almost always masking their own sense of personal insecurity and vulnerability by projecting these feelings onto the victim so that they can ridicule "the other" (Gilbert, 1999). Studies of bullies in Finland, for example, revealed them frequently to have more handicaps and to be unpopular among their peers (Lagerspetz et al., 2008), if not at risk for various mental disorders in adolescence (Kaltiala-Heino et al., 2000). Bullies are notable for their dislikability, isolation, and poor academic performance (Veenstra et al., 2005). Other aggressive projections can take the form of hypervigilance against some external danger, or paranoia, as well as severe jealousy and prejudice. These can occur anywhere from the micro-level of interpersonal relationships all the way up to the macro-level of international politics or even international armed conflict (Jung, 1978). These dynamics are powerful, especially as they are unconscious even as their effects are unfolding.

Reaction formation is a defense that consists of converting unconscious feelings that one perceives to be unacceptable into the opposite belief or behavior. For example, someone who is attracted to people of the same sex may choose to become a "neo-Nazi" who openly persecutes homosexual persons in order to suppress those feelings in oneself. Or, a person with a history of murder may harshly criticize another who has committed pedophilia in a display of moral indignation that convinces onself (and others) of his or her uprightness. Similarly, narcissism is a reaction against feelings of low self-love that involves forming exaggerated, grandiose notions of the self (Baumeister, Smart, & Boden, 1996). Sociopathy, or antisocial behavior, can be an attempt to eliminate feelings of lifelessness or of a void inside by dramatically assaulting signs of life outside, and is sometimes seen as an extreme end of the narcissistic scale (Kernberg, 1995). We may consider violence itself a reaction formation against catastrophic feelings of powerlessness: many are violent not because they feel strength, but rather because they experience a desperate lack of it. Destructive rage occurs when their grandiose or inflated self-image, put in place as a compensation, is threatened (Kohut, 1972). American political theorist Hannah Arendt (1970) correctly perceived that power and violence are opposites: the extremity of violence, employed to mask subjective feelings of powerlessness, often mirrors the intensity of those feelings. In other words, the greater the experience of feeling inferior, the more violent the emotional agitation and urge to conquest (Adler, 1924). This sense of weakness or vulnerability come with a vigilance or fear that one's inadequacy will be exposed, and since the greatest shame is to be feeling such shame, shame and humiliation are potent sources of violence (Gilligan, 1996). When feelings reach such catastrophic levels as to cause violence, then we know what is critical to human existence: the antidote to shame is self-love, which turns out to be essential to the survival of the soul. While the extreme lack of regard or empathy for others make sociopathy seem outside the realm of ordinary human psychology, the underlying extreme lack of self-regard makes it comprehensible through psychodynamics.

Return of the repressed refers to the fact that unacceptable feelings, be they anger, sadness, or shame, do not disappear when we push them far into the unconscious. They build up, somewhat like a pressure cooker, so that eventually they push forth with greater strength, overcoming the energy it took to repress them. These feelings then return with a vengeance (Aronson, 1992). They may emerge as outbursts or as explosions of unexpected form, but they inevitably appear. This is different from emotional *suppression*, which is conscious and more adaptive; for example, one may temporarily choose to suppress feelings of grief after losing a parent in order to be able to carry out responsibilities toward one's children. Because this is done with conscious awareness, feelings will not "catch one by surprise." Such are the dynamics of mind, with complexities that defy understanding unless conceived of in terms of layers, levels, and dimensions—which may need to be deciphered singly but are still occurring in the context of whole individuals, families, communities, and society. Of these dynamics each has its function with a logic of its own level. In an unintegrated human being, fragmentation can lead to the dominance of one level over others, sometimes defying general wellbeing—and this is how human behavior becomes paradoxical.

The Mind as Paradox

The word *paradox* originates from the Greek, where *para-* (παρα-) means contrary and *doxa* (δόξα) means opinion or expectation. The *Oxford English Dictionary* (Stevenson, 2010) defines it as a "statement or tenet contrary to received opinion or belief" or an "apparently absurd or self-contradictory statement or proposition, or a strongly counterintuitive one, which investigation, analysis, or explanation may nevertheless prove to be well-founded or true." The mind is not just complex but paradoxical. As we have seen in the Section "Some Defense Mechanisms," the paradoxes are difficult to explain without taking into account unconscious processes—and nowhere do they become more pronounced than in violence. Underneath the guise of smug self-assurance may lie chronic self-destructiveness and attraction to "bad" behavior that as a whole lead to disaster for the individual; violent persons are, so to speak, successful in failing (Meninger, 1938).

Even where the violent actions are not impulsive but premeditated, the results are often self-defeating: one may believe that one is getting ahead at the moment, but violence seldom ends well for anyone involved. One may be blind to the imminent consequences that will befall one personally or damage the very ecology of which one is part, leading to consequences for children and community, if not for oneself. Some of this tendency can be observed even in "nonviolent" situations: physicians discover routinely, for example, that some patients do not behave as if they wish to get better, no matter what they say or believe; a portion of doctors' work therefore involves keeping patients from doing things that favor disease over recovery. It is not surprising, then, if outwardly destructive individuals do everything possible to obstruct family and friends who are trying to help them or their attorney who is attempting to defend them, or refrain from acting in ways that would help them avoid punishment. They will skillfully sabotage any efforts to give them opportunities for improvement or rehabilitation.

Observation of these tendencies led Freud to formulate the theory of a "death drive" as an innate impulse in human beings (Freud, 1923), later termed *thanatos* after the Greek word for death. He contrasted this to his theory of *eros*, the Greek word for love, indicating the source of *libido*, or life force that favors vitality, creativity, and procreation (Freud, 1922). This force has several layers: at the lowest, libido or the drive for pleasure; intermediately, a drive for the preservation of self, of kin, and of society; and at the highest, concern for all of humankind and the universe. Jung (1916) endowed libido with psychic energy and a spiritual force, moving it closer to the more universal drive. This vital force has also appeared in various philosophical phrases: the *élan vital* of French philosopher Henri Bergson (1907), the *Wille zum Leben*, or will to live, of German philosopher Arthur Schopenhauer, or the *will to meaning* of Austrian psychiatrist Victor Frankl (1963). There seems almost no limit to what the mind can overcome when there is sufficient "life impulse," but absent it, the capacity for destruction also seems limitless. The death drive, therefore, is directed against life. It came to represent the human tendency to engage in self-destructive behaviors that could lead to self-damage and death (Roazen, 1975). Hence, the field of psychodynamics establishes a spectrum of human propensities, from the life-enhancing to the death-inducing, in contrast to the more popular but simplistic notion that all human beings would always favor self-interest under the *rational choice theory*. The human mind is more complex than this, capable of driving itself to destruction just as much as to procreation and generativity.

However, Freud conceived the death drive to be as innate as the drive for life, and did not go further. Mirroring the sociobiological theory of "instincts" as inborn drives that are inherited through evolutionary advantage, he saw them as drives simply searching for opportunities for release. However, this theory does not hold up to what we know about biology and psychology; healthy drives are different than pathological ones, and only the latter are destructive. Furthermore, past translations into English as life and death "instincts" have removed their meaning further from the original German word *Trieb*, which is "drive" or "impulse" (Fenichel, 1946). Drives for human behavior are not inborn but rather are borne from a complex interplay of biological, psychological, social, and environmental factors, including symbolic and cultural. Examining more closely, the death drive appears more as a life drive gone awry: violence, no matter how self-defeating, will have come from some propensity for life that has been misdirected as a result of harmful environments or misplaced meanings.

To be more precise, just as we can speak about health versus disease, in mental health, we can talk about urges that affirm life versus those that draw toward death. Human beings choose the former when they are healthy, resourceful, and capable of making choices, whereas they gravitate toward the latter when they are ill or under stress and perceive few options. In mental illness, a person with symptoms beyond a certain level of severity will also lose the ability to restore health, actively fighting against getting better and avoiding at all cost doctors, medications, and hospitals. Many countries that emphasize civil liberties still permit forced treatment of such persons—until they regain their agency and choice, at which time they often begin accepting their own therapy again. Involuntary hospitalization, restraint, and medication are allowed because, once they feel better, the patients are able to articulate that, had they been in their right state of mind—their "own" mind—they would have accepted it, and society protects this as a *right to treatment* (Rachlin, Pam, & Milton, 1975).

Suicide is forcibly prevented for the same reasons; in the course of healing, the individual who feels better frequently reverses the decision. Getting better, or the transition from self-destruction to life promotion, can be a scary prospect, evoking *regression* or pulling back. Violent or hostile individuals are even harder to engage, for the destructive impulse is directed outward, which can alienate, if not hurt, the caregiver or treater. This dynamic is amplified multifold in the criminal justice system, where guards are not adequately trained in de-escalation methods and are not there to engage in positive, prosocial interactions.

The paradox of self-destructiveness speaks to the complexity and the power of the mind. The mind's multidimensional layers allow for dissonance and contradictions but also make possible the logic of greater order. Disorder in the mind can, without awareness, turn death into life, dark into light, destruction into construction, and harm into help in agile feats to meet emotional needs. The mind has the power, for example, to detach from plain reality, to cling to false beliefs, and to hear and see things that are not there, or even to paralyze the entire body. In other words, "madness" has methods that can be maddening for rational goals, devolving easily into violence against oneself or others.

Once we understand and align this powerful but unconscious force with our powerful intellect, we can tap into greater potential, and the possibilities there are equally enormous. "Life drive" can be a source of passion that fuels a person's pursuits, facilitates love for others, and motivates personal growth. It is, therefore, more useful to build an awareness of these dynamics than to pretend that they do not exist, since they play a hidden role in all human affairs. A healthy psyche brings cognition and emotion into harmony in ways that promote functioning as a whole rather than in opposition. Preventing human violence follows the same principle, resulting not only in the absence of violence but in the release of generativity, creativity, and abundance of emotional resource.

A Developmental Matter

Psychodynamics first brought attention to the influence of early childhood experience on later adult life—an important concept in violence prevention. A vast amount of literature has appeared about the consequences of poor attachment in early childhood (Butchart, Mikton, & Krug, 2014; Lannen & Ziswiler, 2014). Since Bowlby's (1944) seminal study on a group of young boys without parents who engaged in delinquent behavior, a wealth of research has shown that the absence of strong attachment is associated with poor interpersonal relationships, antisocial behavior, use of hard drugs, and youth violence (Kobak et al., 2001). More significant than verbal and physical abuse against the child is neglect, or the absence of love, which later manifests in the paradox of rejecting through violence the very thing one needs: intimacy and care.

Neglect in childhood is thus linked with antisocial personality disorders in later life (Hildyard & Wolfe, 2002), which are associated with increased violence (Granic & Patterson, 2006). While constitutional, psychological, and social resilience factors may overcome many consequences of trauma, severe trauma can become highly consequential (de Bellis, 2001). The trauma is greater when the perpetrator of abuse or neglect is the primary caregiver, which is most often the case (Graham et al., 1999). Developmental trauma can be "cumulative" in an ongoing impairment of the attachment relationship (Schore, 2001). We can predict violence as an adult most commonly by there having been behavioral problems in childhood and youth, and secondly through violence between parents in the home (Ehrensaft et al., 2003). Children who experience rejection by their parents are more likely to be bullies or victims than others (Boulton & Smith, 1994). Males, ethnic minorities, and urban residents who are more likely to witness violence have higher rates of disorders from stress, depression, and violence.

There is a strong link between early trauma and adult violence (Mersky & Reynolds, 2007; Smith, Timothy, & Thornberry, 2005; Widom, 1989). In other words, we can safely assume that most perpetrators are victims, even if they try to push the experience out of consciousness by denying it and adopting a tough and careless exterior. Family support can thus modify the impact of neglect and exposure to violence (Buka et al., 2001; van der Kolk et al., 2005). The availability of positive, stable supports is one of the most important determinants for increasing resilience in traumatized individuals across the life cycle (DuMont, Widom, & Czaja, 2007; Kaufman, 2007). *Resilience* means that if one has experienced a certain level of trauma, the degree of pathology is not commensurate with the level of trauma; it is the ability to bounce back after misfortune happens. The lack of positive, stable supports substantially diminishes resilience and contributes to violent behavior among traumatized youth. Social cohesion among neighbors, combined with their willingness to intervene on behalf of the common good, is also linked to reduced violence, and can mediate the effects of concentrated disadvantage and residential instability (Sampson, Raudenbush, & Earls, 1997).

Positive Psychology

The counterpart to psychodynamics, as mentioned in the Section "One Among Many," is cognitive science, but there is another dichotomy between traditional and positive psychology that needs mending. With respect to cognitive science, just as we cannot begin to know the whole human being without considering both body and mind, we must conceive of the whole human mind as both emotion and cognition in order to understand it properly. Emotion regulation, for example, has cognitive consequences (Richards & Gross, 2000), and an enduring personality arises from a set of stable knowledge structures for interpreting the world and guiding behavior (Anderson & Bushman, 2002). Cognitive processes are an important management tool for behavior and emotions, as we see in *dialectical behavior therapy* (DBT), which helps to reduce suicide attempts and self-harm (Sherman & Cohen, 2006). In turn, dealing with emotions such as through *insight-oriented therapy* (a form of modified psychoanalysis) can free up the mind to make rational, conscious choices. This close relationship does not mean that one area is reducible to another. We can, again, prevent wide pendulum swings by taking a broader, integrated approach. Rigor lies not in the ability to diminish phenomena into a singular mechanism, but in knowing that, in human affairs, different levels will interact with great complexity and interweaving.

Additionally, another integration that has been happening in the psychological fields is between a disease-oriented approach, which focuses on relieving misery, and *positive psychology*, which emphasizes building wellbeing (Sheldon & King, 2001). The way biology is not destiny, psychological principles are also not rules, and the human psyche has great potential for resilience, flexibility, and creativity (Panter-Brick & Eggerman, 2012). Positive psychology has its earliest origins in *humanistic psychology*, which critiqued traditional psychology for breaking things down rather than taking a more holistic approach to human existence (Horney, 1937; May, 1940). It advocated for a more person-centered approach that emphasized that all organisms, including humans, have an underlying flow of movement toward constructive fulfillment of their inherent possibilities (Rogers, 1951). American psychologist Abraham Maslow (1954) originated the concept of a positive psychology, noting that the science of psychology had revealed much about our shortcomings, our illness, and our sins, but little about our potentialities, our virtues, our achievable aspirations, or our full psychological height.

Intervening were calls to look for not just the origins of disease but the origins of health (Antonovsky, 1979); to focus on the human capacity to be open to new mindsets (Langer, 1989); and to find the strengths of people (Cannon & Stone, 1997). While a necessary concept, positive psychology still requires more development and a rigorous research program with methods of measurement before it can form a scientific foundation in its own right. Concepts such as *resilience*, or the ability to "bounce back" after adversity, trauma, or stress (Luthar, Cicchetti, & Becker, 2000), and *posttraumatic growth*, or positive transformation following trauma (Tedeschi & Calhoun, 1996), have helped to add different dimensions. The reason this development is important for us is not only that it supports our tenet that a broader perspective is helpful, but also in violence prevention, learning how to start being constructive is integral to learning how to stop being destructive. Indeed, the best antidote to a negative behavior is to foster positive, prosocial, and self-affirming behavior that better aligns and rechannels the inner drive that led to the destructive behavior in the first place. Instead of just looking to repair damage, a positive outlook begins to discover what allows a person or a community to improve, to build strength, and to thrive.

Addressing and relieving pathology is important, but so is understanding human strength and self-regenerative power. These build on wellbeing and satisfaction in the past; flow, joy, and pleasure in the present; and faith, hope, and optimism in the future. Developing a capacity for love, vocation, and creativity at the individual level can lead to altruism, civility, and cooperation at the community level (Gillham & Seligman, 1999). In other words, positive psychology emphasizes *positive prevention* and *positive therapy* through systematically building competency and strength, not just combating weakness (Masten et al., 2002). In sum, there is much to gain in understanding the psychology of violence through how different elements *interact* and *integrate* into a whole. This allows for an *irreducible complexity* that takes into account multiple layers of the mind, emotive and cognitive mechanisms, and an understanding of pathology as well as positive health.

Conclusion

Psychology has a lot to offer in our quest of how to think about violence beyond the usual determination of harm and simple criminal intent (Hart, 2011). Psychology delves into psychodynamic and cognitive processes that can vastly expand our understanding of violence and our ability to prevent it. Rather than engage in the struggle to become more "scientific" through reductionistic approaches—be they biomedical, neuroscientific, information-processing, or disease-oriented models—psychology can tell us a lot about the complexity of the human mind through the dynamics of its layers and how the mind works. Psychodynamic theory is but one among many but is particularly helpful in illuminating violence. We might therefore consider adding onto insightful approaches of the past rather than replacing them with newer approaches:

currently, information processing and neuroscience. In other words, psychodynamic theory itself needs updating and development. At the same time, incorporating the brain and its mechanisms should help us to understand the mind, in the same way that psychological and social processes have informed biology. While all the different "schools" of psychology are informative and helpful in some way, without integration of the field and interchange with other fields, psychology will continue its pendulum swings, of going from the mind to the brain, and psychiatry will similarly swing, from psychoanalysis to pharmacotherapy, only to swing back again. This deprives patients of the best care, which involves the treatment of both the mind and the brain, while what also suffers is the prevention of violence, which includes larger-scale, social policy interventions and not just individual physical restraint.

We emphasize psychodynamic theory as a unique contribution of psychology toward studying human beings and why they do the things they do, especially when it does not make obvious sense. This is particularly useful for the understanding of human violence. We advocate abandoning an approach that looks for an explanation of psychological phenomena through reducing psychology to behavior and then to brain science in order to meet an ideological concept of what science is supposed to be. A proper appreciation of the human mind lies in acknowledging its full complexity. The study of violence shows that if we entered the brain looking for "the biological origins" of violence, we would find them, and likewise for "the psychological origins" or "the social origins"—we would be able to explain the rest away like a hammer that sees what it discovers only as a nail. Not only that, if we sought only to uncover "disease-producing elements," we would find only disease. It is therefore important to ensure that we bring all perspectives to a problem, including a search for "health-generating elements," with the intent to identify and enhance ways of thriving. Psychodynamic theory requires further development—and a merging with the biological and the social sciences—but for now it sheds useful light on violence. It provides a systematic study of the psychological forces that shape human emotion, thought, and behavior that is essential to deciphering the conundrum of violence. Acknowledging the presence of the unconscious, and not just the conscious, allows for an understanding of the mind's paradoxes and possibilities. Psychological principles, like all others, are not ultimate explanations but aspects of a complex whole that includes the biological, the social, and the environmental. Each is important, but the perspective that holds together the whole is even more so. The overall perspective is what allows for a true understanding of human destructiveness, where all factors are co-occurring, by necessity in synchronicity, to produce or to prevent the outcome of violence.

Questions

1   Why is understanding psychology important to the understanding of human violence?

2   What does psychodynamic theory offer that cognitive science or information processing do not?

3   What are the many layers of the mind, and what does it mean when we say the mind is like an iceberg?

4   How do defense mechanisms and paradoxes of the mind help explain violence?

5   What is the difference between traditional and positive psychology, and what are some of the ways they can inform each other?

References

Adler, A. (1924). Progress in individual psychology. *British Journal of Medical Psychology*, *4*(1), 22–31.

American Psychiatric Association. (2013). *Diagnostic and statistical manual of mental disorders* ((5th ed.). ed.). Washington, DC: Author.

Anderson, C. A., & Bushman, B. J. (2002). Human aggression. *Annual Review of Psychology*, *53*(1), 27–51.

Andersson, G. (1994). *Criticism and the history of science: Kuhn's, Lakatos's and Feyerabend's criticisms of critical rationalism*. Leiden, Netherlands: Brill.

Antonovsky, A. (1979). *Health, stress, and coping: New perspectives on mental and physical well-being*. San Francisco, CA: Jossey-Bass.

Arendt, H. (1970). *On violence*. New York, NY: Harcourt, Brace, Jovanovich.

Aronson, E. (1992). The return of the repressed: Dissonance theory makes a comeback. *Psychological Inquiry*, *3*(4), 303–311.

Baumeister, R. F., Smart, L., & Boden, J. M. (1996). Relation of threatened egotism to violence and aggression: The dark side of high self-esteem. *Psychological Review*, *103*(1), 5–33.

Beck, A. T. (1993). Cognitive therapy: Past, present, and future. *Journal of Consulting and Clinical Psychology*, *61*(2), 194–198.

Bergson, H. (1907). *L'Évolution créatrice*. Paris, France: Alcan.

Boulton, M. J., & Smith, P. K. (1994). Bully/victim problems in middle-school children: Stability, self-perceived competence, peer perceptions and peer acceptance. *British Journal of Developmental Psychology*, *12*(3), 315–329.

Bowlby, J. (1944). Forty-four juvenile thieves: Their characters and home life. *International Journal of Psychoanalysis*, *25*(19–52), 107–127.

Bowlby, J. (1988). *A secure base: Clinical applications of attachment theory*. London, UK: Routledge.

Buka, S. L., Stichick, T. L., Birdthistle, I., & Earls, F. J. (2001). Youth exposure to violence: Prevalence, risks, and consequences. *American Journal of Orthopsychiatry*, *71*(3), 298–310.

Butchart, A., Mikton, C., & Krug, E. (2014). Governments must do more to address interpersonal violence. *Lancet*, *384*(9961), 2183–2185.

Cannon, M., & Stone, P. J. (1997). *Organizational psychology*. Aldershot, UK: Ashgate.

Casement, P. (1990). *Further learning from the patient: The analytic space and process*. London, UK: Tavistock/Routledge.

Cooke, R. M. (1991). *Experts in uncertainty: Opinion and subjective probability in science*. New York, NY: Oxford University Press.

Damasio, A. R., Everitt, B. J., & Bishop, D. (1996). The somatic marker hypothesis and the possible functions of the prefrontal cortex. *Philosophical Transactions of the Royal Society, B: Biological Sciences*, *351*(1346), 1413–1420.

De Bellis, M. D. (2001). Developmental traumatology: The psychobiological development of maltreated children and its implications for research, treatment, and policy. *Development and Psychopathology*, *13*(3), 537–561.

de Maat, S., de Jonghe, F., de Kraker, R., Leichsenring, F., Abbass, A., Luyten, P., … Dekker, J. (2013). The current state of the empirical evidence for psychoanalysis: A meta-analytic approach. *Harvard Review of Psychiatry*, *21*(3), 107–137.

DuMont, K. A., Widom, C. S., & Czaja, S. J. (2007). Predictors of resilience in abused and neglected children grown-up: The role of individual and neighborhood characteristics. *Child Abuse and Neglect*, *31*(3), 255–274.

Ehrensaft, M. K., Cohen, P., Smailes, E., Chen, H., & Johnson, J. G. (2003). Intergenerational transmission of partner violence: A 20-year prospective study. *Journal of Consulting and Clinical Psychology*, *7*(4), 741–753.

Ellenberger, H. (1970). *The discovery of the unconscious: The history and evolution of dynamic psychiatry*. New York, NY: Basic Books.

Erikson, E. (1950). *Childhood and society*. New York, NY: Norton.

Fenichel, O. (1946). *Psychoanalytic theory of neurosis*. London, UK: Routledge and Kegan Paul.

Frankl, V. E. (1963). *Man's search for meaning*. Boston, MA: Beacon Press.

Freud, S. (1910). *Five lectures on psycho-analysis*. London, UK: Hogarth Press.

Freud, S. (1922). *Beyond the pleasure principle*. London, UK: Vienna International Psycho-Analytical Press.

Freud, S. (1923–1925). *The standard edition of the complete psychological works of Sigmund Freud*. London, UK: Hogarth Press.

Freud, S. (1953). A difficulty in the path of psycho-analysis [Eine Schwierigkeit der Psychoanalyse]. In S. Freud, & A. Freud (Eds.), *The standard edition of the complete psychological works of Sigmund Freud: Jensen's Gradiva and other works* (Vol. *17*) (pp. 135–145). London, UK: Hogarth Press.

Freud, S., Bonaparte, M., Freud, A., & Kris, E. (1954). Project for a scientific psychology. In Freud, S., Bonaparte, M., Freud, A., and Kris, E. (Eds.) *The origins of psycho-analysis: Letters to Wilhelm Fliess, drafts and notes: 1887–1902* (pp. 347–445). New York, NY: Basic Books.

Gilbert, P. (1999). *Overcoming depression: A step-by-step approach to gaining control over depression*. New York, NY: Oxford University Press.

Gillham, J. E., & Seligman, M. E. (1999). Footsteps on the road to a positive psychology. *Behaviour Research and Therapy, 37*, S163–S173.

Goodwin, C. J. (2008). *A history of modern psychology*. Hoboken, NJ: Wiley.

Graham, Y. P., Heim, C., Goodman, S. H., Miller, A. H., & Nemeroff, C. B. (1999). The effects of neonatal stress on brain development: Implications for psychopathology. *Development and Psychopathology, 11*, 545–565.

Granic, I., & Patterson, G. (2006). Toward a comprehensive model of antisocial development: A dynamic systems approach. *Psychological Review, 13*(1), 101–131.

Hart, S. D. (2011). The role of psychopathy in assessing risk for violence: Conceptual and methodological issues. *Legal and Criminological Psychology, 3*(1), 121–137.

Hildyard, K. L., & Wolfe, D. A. (2002). Child neglect: Developmental issues and outcomes. *Child Abuse and Neglect, 26*(6–7), 679–695.

Horney, K. (1937). *Collected works of Karen Horney*. New York, NY: Norton.

James, W. (1918). *The principles of psychology*. New York, NY: Dover Publications.

Jung, C. G. (1913). Psycho-analysis. In *Transactions of the psycho-medical society* (Vol. *4*, Part 2). Cockermouth, UK: Brash Bros.

Jung, C. G. (1916). *Psychology of the unconscious: A study of the transformations and symbolisms of the libido—A contribution to the history of the evolution of thought*. New York, NY: Moffat, Yard, and Company.

Jung, C. G. (Ed.) (1978). *Man and his symbols*. London, UK: Picador.

Kaltiala-Heino, R., Rimpelä, M., Rantanen, P., & Rimpelä, A. (2000). Bullying at school—An indicator of adolescents at risk formental disorders. *Journal of Adolescence, 23*(6), 661–674.

Kaufman, J., Yang, B. Z., Douglas-Palumberi, H., Houshyar, S., Lipschitz, D., Krystal, J. H., & Gelernter, J. (2004). Social supports and serotonin transporter gene moderate depression in maltreated children. *Proceedings of the National Academy of Sciences of the United States of America, 101*(49), 17316–17321.

Kernberg, O. F. (1995). *Aggression in personality disorders and perversions*. New Haven, CT: Yale University Press.

Kernberg, O. F. (2006). Psychoanalytic controversies: The pressing need to increase research in and on psychoanalysis. *International Journal of Psychoanalysis, 87*(4), 919–936.

Klein, M. (1950). *The psycho-analysis of children*. London, UK: Hogarth Press.

Kobak, R., Little, M., Race, E., & Acosta, M. C. (2001). Attachment disruptions in seriously emotionally disturbed children: Implications for treatment. *Attachment and Human Development, 3*(3), 243–258.

Kohut, H. (1972). Thoughts on narcissism and narcissistic rage. *Psychoanalytic Study of the Child, 27*(1), 360–400.

Lagerspetz, K. M., Björkqvist, K., Berts, M., & King, E. (2008). Group aggression among school children in three schools. *Scandinavian Journal of Psychology, 23*(1), 45–52.

Langer, E. J. (1989). *Mindfulness*. Reading, MA: Addison-Wesley.

Lannen, P., & Ziswiler, M. (2014). Potential and perils of the early years: The need to integrate violence prevention and early child development. *Aggression and Violent Behavior, 19*(6), 625–628.

Leichsenring, F., Abbass, A., Luyten, P., Hilsenroth, M., & Rabung, S. (2013). The emerging evidence for long-term psychodynamic therapy. *Psychodynamic Psychiatry, 41*(3), 361–384.

Lipton, B. (2005). *The biology of belief: Unleashing the power of consciousness, matter and miracles*. Carlsbad, CA: Hay House.

Luthar, S. S., Cicchetti, D., & Becker, B. (2000). The construct of resilience: A critical evaluation and guidelines for future work. *Child Development, 71*(3), 543–562.

Markus, H. (1983). Self-knowledge: An expanded view. *Journal of Personality, 51*(3), 543–565.

Maslow, A. H. (1954). *Motivation and personality*. New York, NY: Harper.

Masten, A. S., Reed, M. G. J., Snyder, C. R., & Lopez, S. J. (2002). *Handbook of positive psychology*. Oxford, UK: Oxford University Press.

May, R. (1940). *The springs of creative living: A study of human nature and god*. New York, NY: Abingdon-Cokesbury.

Meninger, K. (1938). *Man against himself*. New York, NY: Harcourt, Brace.

Mersky, J. P., & Reynolds, A. J. (2007). Child maltreatment and violent delinquency: Disentangling main effects and subgroup effects. *Child Maltreatment, 12*, 246–258.

Metcalfe, J., & Mischel, W. (1999). A hot/cool-system analysis of delay of gratification: Dynamics of willpower. *Psychological Review, 106*(1), 3–19.

Mitchell, S. A. (1988). *Relational concepts in psychoanalysis*. Cambridge, MA: Harvard University Press.

Molenaar, P. C. (2004). A manifesto on psychology as idiographic science: Bringing the person back into scientific psychology, this time forever. *Measurement, 2*(4), 201–218.

Neill, J. (1990). Whatever became of the schizophrenogenic mother? *American Journal of Psychotherapy, 44*(4), 499–505.

O'Reilly, R. C. (2006). Biologically-based computational models of high-level cognition. *Science, 314*(5796), 91–94.

Panter-Brick, C., & Eggerman, M. (2012). Understanding culture, resilience, and mental health: The production of hope. In M. Ungar (Ed.), *The social ecology of resilience* (pp. 369–386). New York, NY: Springer.

Rachlin, S., Pam, A., & Milton, J. (1975). Civil liberties versus involuntary hospitalization. *American Journal of Psychiatry, 132*(2), 189–192.

Richards, J. M., & Gross, J. J. (2000). Emotion regulation and memory: The cognitive costs of keeping one's cool. *Journal of Personality and Social Psychology, 79*(3), 410–424.

Roazen, P. (1975). *Freud and his followers*. New York, NY: Alfred A. Knopf.

Rogers, C. (1951). *Client-centered therapy: Its current practice, implications and theory*. London, UK: Constable.

Sacks, O. (1984). *A leg to stand on*. New York, NY: Simon and Schuster.

Sadock, B. J., Sadock, V. A., Ruiz, P., & Kaplan, H. I. (2017). *Kaplan and Sadock's comprehensive textbook of psychiatry*. Philadelphia, PA: Wolters Kluwer.

Sampson, R. J., Raudenbush, S. W., & Earls, F. (1997). Neighborhoods and violent crime: A multilevel study of collective efficacy. *Science, 277*, 918–924.

Schore, A. N. (2001). The effects of early relational trauma on right brain development, affect regulation, and infant mental health. *Infant Journal of Mental Health, 22*, 201–269.

Shakespeare, W. (1990). Othello, the Moore of Venice. In R. Lattimore, & M. J. Adler (Eds.), *Great books of the Western world* (Vol. *27*). Chicago, IL: Encyclopædia Britannica.

Sheldon, K. M., & King, L. (2001). Why positive psychology is necessary. *American Psychologist, 56*(3), 216–217.

Shepherd, G. M. (1991). *Foundations of the neuron doctrine*. New York, NY: Oxford University Press.

Sherman, D. K., & Cohen, G. L. (2006). The psychology of self-defense: Self-affirmation theory. *Advances in Experimental Social Psychology, 38*, 183–242.

Skinner, B. F. (1976). *About behaviorism*. New York, NY: Random House.

Smith, C. A., Timothy, O. I., & Thornberry, T. P. (2005). Adolescent maltreatment and its impact on young adult antisocial behavior. *Child Abuse and Neglect, 29*, 1099–1119.

Solms, M., & Turnbull, O. (2002). *The brain and the inner world: An introduction to the neuroscience of subjective experience*. New York, NY: Other Press.

Sourour, T. K. (1991). Report of Coroner's Investigation. Retrieved from http://www.diarmani.com/Montreal_Coroners_Report.pdf

Stevenson, A. (2010). *Oxford dictionary of English*. New York, NY: Oxford University Press.

Streeck, U. (1999). Acting out, interpretation and unconscious communication. *International Forum of Psychoanalysis, 8*(2), 135–143.

Tedeschi, R. G., & Calhoun, L. G. (1996). The posttraumatic growth inventory: Measuring the positive legacy of trauma. *Journal of Traumatic Stress, 9*(3), 455–471.

Toch, H. (1969). *Violent men: An inquiry into the psychology of violence*. Chicago, IL: Aldine Publishing.

Van der Kolk, B. A., Roth, S., Pelcovitz, D., Sunday, S., & Spinazzola, J. (2005). Disorders of extreme stress: The empirical foundation of a complex adaptation to trauma. *Journal of Traumatic Stress, 18*(5), 389–399.

Veenstra, R., Lindenberg, S., Oldehinkel, A. J., De Winter, A. F., Verhulst, F. C., & Ormel, J. (2005). Bullying and victimization in elementary schools: A comparison of bullies, victims, bully/victims, and uninvolved preadolescents. *Developmental Psychology, 41*(4), 672–682.

Walker, H. M. (1995). *Antisocial behavior in school: Strategies and best practices*. Pacific Grove, CA: Brooks/Cole Publishing.

Watson, J. B. (1930). *Behaviorism*. New York, NY: Norton.

Widom, C. S. (1989). The cycle of violence. *Science, 244*, 160–166.

Winnicott, D. W. (1964). *The child, the family, and the outside world*. Harmondsworth, UK: Penguin Books.

Wundt, W. (1911). *Einleitung in die psychologie*. Leipzig, Germany: Engelmann.

4

The Symbolism (or Spiritual Causes) of Violence

Introduction

> No longer in a merely physical universe, man lives in a symbolic universe.
> —*Ernst Cassirer,* An Essay on Man *(1944)*

In Chapter 3, we discussed the vast depth and complexity of the mind, and yet it does not end there. Studying the symbolism of violence and, further, addressing its spiritual aspects will initially seem to lie outside the domain of a scientific study of violence. Nevertheless, it will increasingly become clear that it is difficult, if not impossible, to address the problem without this consideration. Again, violence heightens our understanding of what is important in being human.

First, the biology of our overdeveloped frontal brains makes us highly social; that overly social nature makes us highly communicative; and that overly communicative nature propels us to create symbolic universes far beyond our biological origins. Asking the most basic questions about violence, therefore, will lead us to discover that symbolism lies at its heart (Schwartz & Friedrichs, 1994). For instance: Why do humans commit violence? Given that it does not serve a practical purpose much of the time—indeed, most of the time—what is its function? Why do human beings go to war to their mutual destruction or, as is mostly the case, for what is at best a pyrrhic victory? Why the drive toward nuclear warfare, at the risk of the species' extinction? What enables human beings to become suicide bombers? Why is the killing of another person sometimes not enough, such that one must torment and mutilate? What about self-injury, or suicide?

Many quandaries are difficult to answer with ordinary logic. If someone takes a gun to the head or walks in front of a tank in protest, at the risk of dying, we wonder why. Even when an action serves a "predatory" purpose, what are the reasons underlying the purpose, which is often self-defeating or, indeed, defeating of the whole system of which the actor is a part? Why do massacres hold such poignancy? Why are human beings far more likely to take their own lives than they are to take the lives of others? Answers to these questions will ever be elusive without considering what violence symbolizes. Far from being random, violence organizes around a principle that makes humans unique as well as the most violent of beings: hence German philosopher Ernst Cassirer's (1944) description of human beings as *homo symbolicum,* or "representational animals."

While we have believed since Aristotle's time that human beings are "rational animals," an alternative logic is necessary when that characterization fails. We may need to interpret human actions as *symbolic language*—that is, events that are explainable only by "symbolic logic." Emanating from highly symbolic beings, the seemingly irrational act may find its method in making meaning (Frankl, 1962), even if creating that meaning requires one's own sacrifice. In other words, actions are symbolic representations of thoughts, whereby violent acts are a signaling of desperate need. Much of violence does not result in tangible gains but is motivated by symbolic meanings more important than survival itself. This chapter, an extension of the last, "The Psychology of Violence," attempts to complete conventional psychology by giving a brief overview of what might arguably be the most relevant question concerning how to think about violence. If there are remaining mysteries about violence from psychology, we can look for answers in symbolism or spirituality.

We will discuss how violence points to the most poignant aspects of human existence, which center around the need for love, or the source of spirit and meaning. Indicating the fundamental areas of healthy development, violence results when the longing for life goes awry. We will show how religion and art become potent arenas for violent expression. Channeled correctly, they are also the vehicles for developing compassion and creativity. Few actions point to what is of central importance to human beings as violence does, since it occurs in a heightened state of exigency. This forces us to accept the reality of higher human needs, such as the impulse to actualize, not just to sustain, the self and a love for the highest values (Maslow, 1962).

The willingness to destroy oneself and as many other people as possible, in a desperate attempt to fulfill those needs, reveals the urgency of the needs. Individuals or groups engaging in violent behavior may not always be aware of or be able to articulate these reasons. Actions, however, are very telling. Even if the individual is unable to "translate" symbolic action into words, the underlying symbolism is detectable in the act, for human beings use symbolism to explain and to enact what is important to them.

Violence and Meaning

What is symbolism? The *Oxford English Dictionary* (Swartz, 2013) defines symbolism as "the practice of representing things by symbols, or of giving a symbolic character to objects or acts." The *Merriam-Webster Dictionary* (Merriam-Webster, 2011) says that it is "the art or practice of using symbols especially by investing things with a symbolic meaning or by expressing the invisible or intangible by means of visible or sensuous representations, as: (a) artistic imitation or invention that is a method of revealing or suggesting immaterial, ideal, or otherwise intangible truth or states; or (b) the use of conventional or traditional signs in the representation of divine beings and spirits." The field of study that concerns itself with symbols and signs is *semiotics*, the plural of *semiotic*; in the original Greek, *semeiotikos* means "significant" or "observant of signs," from *semeion* "a sign, a mark" (Liddell et al., 2011).

The use of the term semiotics in English began in the seventeenth century to denote the medical practice of interpreting symptoms or signs of diseases (Stubbe, 1670), and more recently, legal theorists have described law as a system of combative signs and language (Boshoff, 2013). In the nineteenth century, the importance of signs as a part of social life led American philosopher Charles Sanders Peirce and Swiss linguist Ferdinand de Saussure to designate semiotics as a science in its own right (Nöth, 1990). With increasing recognition of the importance of symbols in human life, American philosopher Susanne Langer (1942) put forth ideas that are now commonly accepted: human beings have a basic and pervasive need to symbolize, to invent meanings, and to imbue their world with meaning.

Throughout the twentieth century, the field of semiotics became very influential (Eco, 1976). A great deal revolves around symbols and the symbolic meaning that we communicate, pointing to how crucial meaning is in human life. French thinkers Roland Barthes (1957), Jacques Lacan (1966), and Claude Lévi-Strauss (1958) applied these ideas in literary studies, psychoanalysis, and anthropology respectively. The concept of a language as a system of signs has expanded into and influenced virtually every field. The study of *linguistics* became prominent (Vendler, 1979), as has the study of ritual and of art (Babcock, 1978). As in everyday human language, signs signal something other than what they are; there is no intrinsic meaning in the sounds or syllables we create to communicate a deeper meaning, or to make a "mark" (Chandler, 2007).

In human violence, a meaning deeper than the overt words or actions is present in its expression of heightened urgency. Whatever is the most meaningful will engrave itself in the mark of an extreme act in which a person is willing to give up their own life and the lives of others (Achebe, 1958). Also implicit will likely be a person's or a group's worldview, or attitude of mind. Some may wish to believe that what they cannot explain does not exist, but actions are a form of communication (Dickens, 1859), and it is human nature to convey a shared significance (García Márquez, 1966). Just as the everyday language we use to communicate to others draws from a system of signs that we inherit, violent acts draw from their sociocultural contexts when they terrorize (Retsikas, 2006). They use words and myths that intensify the act (Ritscher, 2005) and even make use of visual iconography (Ushie, 2012). Thus, art and religion become frequent vehicles for violence (Ellens, 2007; Fraser, 1974), either in depiction or in enactment, even though–or precisely because—both these fields embody some of the highest human attainments that are the farthest removed from violence.

Case Vignettes

Mythological Violence

Uranus, the sky, despises many of the children his wife Gaia, the earth, bore. On her own, Gaia gave birth to Uranus along with the mountains and the sterile sea, Pontus. Soon, Uranus covers Gaia on all sides and becomes her mate and equal. Unlike the beautiful Titans whom Uranus adores, the one-eyed Cyclops and many-armed Hekatonkheires are monstrous in form and in nature. Uranus puts these unfavored children into the prison of Tartarus, enraging Gaia. She colludes with her son, Cronus, who is a Titan, to depose Uranus. She fashions a serrated sickle from a mythic metal called adamant. Cronus uses adamant to sever the genitals of his father.

As Uranus's blood falls to the earth, the Furies, who punish crimes, the Ash-Tree Nymphs, and the race of Giants arise. Cronus heaves Uranus's genitals into the sea, and from the foam rises Aphrodite, the beautiful goddess of love, who floats along and steps ashore at Cyprus. The mutilated Uranus has to withdraw forever from the earth, or perish. Uranus promises revenge for his son's unforgivable act. Cronus grows paranoid that he will be supplanted by his own child in the future. His wife Rhea gives birth to many children, but Cronus refuses to allow them to grow large enough to defeat him in combat. He devours his children as soon as they are born, imprisoning them in his stomach, just as Uranus had imprisoned his and Gaia's children. Cronus also fails to release his siblings from their prison, which gives both Gaia and Uranus reason to seek revenge against him. The two of them help Rhea to save her next child, Zeus, raising the child in secret until he's strong enough to defeat his father.

When Zeus grows up, he conspires with Metis, daughter of the ocean, to free his siblings. Metis slips Cronus a powerful emetic, and Cronus throws up the future Olympic gods, who join Zeus in a great war against the Titans. The war goes on for 10 years, until Zeus frees the children of Gaia from Tartarus, which tips the odds in favor of the Olympians. Armed with lightning and superior weaponry, the Olympic gods defeat the Titans and imprison them in Tartarus. When Zeus romantically pursues Metis, she morphs her appearance in an attempt to escape from him; he eventually overpowers and impregnates her. Gaia and Uranus predict that, after giving birth to Zeus's daughter, Metis will bear a son who will supplant Zeus. The forces in power generate their opposites and the generational fear of the young overtaking the old is illustrated in the violence of those in power against their future counterparts. The relationship between the sexes is inherently troubled, and the decisive factor in losing control of the world is mistreating one's children in the hope of not to have to fight them when they are older and strong. The wives play a major role. In their anger, they help their sons dethrone their husbands. The forces of nature are rendered in terms of struggle within the family. Zeus prevents Metis from conceiving again. Later, Zeus suffers from a powerful headache and his son Hephaestus cleaves his skull open, allowing Zeus's daughter Athena, fully grown and armed, to escape. However, Metis remains trapped, and Zeus maintains his leadership, leaving the prophecy unfulfilled (Hesiod, 1966). This tale illustrates the use of violence in ancient times on a mythological level. Full of symbolism, it accounts for and gives order to basic aspects of existence, including the perpetration of violence.

Cycle of Revenge

In Queen Gertrude's room, Polonius hides behind a tapestry. When Prince Hamlet arrives, he verbally and physically confronts his mother, shouting at her to sit down and not move. The queen is alarmed by Hamlet's hostility and, fearing for her life, she cries out, "Thou wilt not murder me? Help ho!" Hamlet holds a fervent obsession and resentment toward his mother for betraying him and his dead father through her convenient marriage to Claudius, Hamlet's uncle. Previously, Hamlet was hesitant to act. He was unsure whether to believe the ghost of his father, who told him that he was murdered by Claudius and needs revenge in order to be released from purgatory. Hamlet's initial fear of what dreams may come after death prevents him from killing himself. Hamlet had the chance to kill King Claudius, but backed down when he saw that the King was praying with the excuse that killing Claudius at that moment would send him to heaven. Upon hearing the queen's wails, Polonius confusedly yells back. Hamlet thinks that the unseen spy is his father, the King. Hamlet blindly strikes out at the tapestry, killing Polonius. Hamlet does not even stop to ponder who the person behind the tapestry might be, or why he might be there. Although he may think that it is Claudius, it is clear that Hamlet is more interested in lashing out at someone, anyone, than in killing Claudius.

What are appearances and what is reality is questioned by casting doubt about whether Hamlet is "mad in craft" or whether he has indeed lost his mind. It can be said that the price of being the "wretched, rash, intruding fool" is Polonius's own life. Hamlet expresses no guilt for the death. Appearances and reality are brought together again as his mother cries out, "What rash and bloody deed is this!" Hamlet fires back without remorse: "A bloody deed— almost as bad, good mother, as to kill a king and marry his brother," redirecting guilt away from himself, at fault in Polonius's death, to the older crime of the queen in agreeing to marry Hamlet's uncle, Claudius. This lashing out is the pivot point for Hamlet. Until then, he has only brooded and pondered, taking almost no action despite many opportunities to act. Killing Polonius is his first critical act; it disturbs the system and starts events along their ultimate irrevocable course. After Hamlet kills Polonius, an important member of the court, he cannot afford to stop and analyze everything any longer. If he broods over what he has done, then he will be destroyed—if not by Claudius then by his own guilt. Polonius's death also has great consequences for others. Ophelia, Polonius's daughter, goes mad and commits suicide after hearing of her father's death.

After this event, Claudius begins to fear his nephew Hamlet and starts to plot against him. The deaths of both his father Polonius and his sister Ophelia move Laertes to hate Hamlet, formerly his friend, and he thus becomes an instrument of Claudius's schemes to kill Hamlet. As a result of Hamlet's rash action and Claudius's schemes, Hamlet and Laertes are poisoned in their swordfight, the queen drinks herself to death, and Hamlet kills Claudius with the very poison that Claudius intended for Hamlet. Hamlet's "rash and bloody deed" of killing Polonius when his pent-up emotions "snap" propel the story toward its bloody all-consuming finale (Shakespeare, 1990).

The first lines of this tragedy forebode the application of violence. Hamlet's words: "To be or not to be, that is the question," in themselves suggest a "living or dying," a "giving life or taking life." As it becomes obvious, the plot requires action from Hamlet, upon which he chooses inaction. Violence ensues, not from overt action but the passivity of not choosing life.

Cult Violence

The Waco siege was at a compound belonging to a religious group that David Koresh led, the Branch Davidians, at Mount Carmel Center Ranch northeast of Waco, Texas. The Branch Davidians is a religious group that originated in 1955 from a schism in the Seventh-day Adventist Church of the Shepherd's Rod (Davidians) following the death of Shepherd's Rod founder Victor Houteff. Houteff founded the Davidians based on his prophecy of an imminent apocalypse involving the Second Coming of Jesus Christ and the defeat of the evil armies of Babylon. As the Davidian group gained members, its leadership moved the church to a hilltop northeast of Waco, Texas, which they named Mount Carmel. In 1959, the widow of Victor Houteff, Florence Houteff, announced that the expected Armageddon was about to take place, and members were told to gather at the center to await this event. Many built houses, while others stayed in tents, trucks, or busses. Most sold their possessions. Following the failure of the prophecy, which many attributed to Mrs. Houteff setting her own private date for its fulfillment, control of the site fell to Benjamin Roden. He promoted different doctrinal beliefs than Mr. Houteff's original Davidian Seventh-day Adventist organization. On Roden's death, control fell to his wife, Lois Roden, who groomed a young man named Vernon Howell as her chosen successor. In 1984, a meeting divided the group, with Howell leading one faction (calling themselves the Davidian Branch Davidians) and George Roden, Mrs. Roden's son, leading the competing faction. After this split, George Roden ran Howell and his followers off Mount Carmel. Howell and his group relocated to Palestine, Texas, but Howell was able to return and regain control of the group.

On August 5, 1989, Howell released the "New Light" audio tape, in which he stated that he had been told by God to procreate with the women in his group to establish a "House of David" of his "special people." This involved separating married couples in the group and agreeing that only he could have sexual relations with the wives, while the men observed celibacy. He also claimed that God had told him to start building an "army for God" to prepare for the end of days. Howell filed a petition in the Supreme Court of California on May 15, 1990, to legally change his name to David Koresh. By 1992, most of the land belonging to the Branch Davidians had been sold, leaving a core of 77 acres. Koresh took several "wives" at Mount Carmel and fathered at least 12 children with them; several of the "wives" were as young as 12 or 13 when they become pregnant. A central aspect of Koresh's religious teachings was his claim that the apocalyptic events predicted in the Bible's Book of Revelation are imminent so the Davidians must stockpile weapons and explosives in preparation.

On February 28 1993, at Mount Carmel, agents of the US Bureau of Alcohol, Tobacco, Firearms and Explosives (ATF) launch a raid against the Branch Davidian compound as part of an investigation into illegal possession of firearms and explosives. As the agents attempt to penetrate the complex, gunfire erupts, beginning an extended gun battle that leaves four ATF agents dead and 15 wounded. Six Branch Davidians are killed, and several more injured, including Koresh. After 55 min of shooting, the ATF agents withdraw, and a cease-fire is negotiated over the telephone. Following the unsuccessful ATF raid, the US Federal Bureau of Investigation (FBI) takes over. A standoff with the Branch Davidians stretches into 51 days as little progress is made in the telephone negotiations. On April 18, 1993, US Attorney General Janet Reno approves a tear-gas assault on the compound, and at six in the morning on April 19, the Branch Davidians are informed of the imminent attack and told to surrender. They do not. Then, two FBI combat vehicles begin inserting gas into the building. The Branch Davidians, many with gas masks on, refuse to evacuate. Just after noon, a fire erupts in the compound. The compound is completely ablaze. Koresh and at least 80 of his followers, including 22 children, die. The FBI and the U.S. Department of Justice maintain that there is conclusive evidence that the Branch Davidian members ignited the fire themselves. Regarding gunfire reported during the fire, the government argues that the Davidians killed one another as part of a suicide pact or killed dissenters attempting to escape (Department of the Treasury, 1993).

The violent tendencies of dangerous cults can be classified into two general categories: offensive violence and defensive violence; the latter is used to defend a compound or enclave that was created to eliminate contact with the dominant culture (FBI, 2000). This example shows a manifestation of defensive violence, following the well-known crucifixion of Jesus Christ. The counterpart of this is offensive violence, such as mob violence. Both examples can manifest in cults.

Mob Violence

A man of the church in Nigeria comes to Lagos to visit some rich parishes and beg for aid for the Niger Delta mass burials after an oil fire has killed hundreds of people. He negotiates with the leaders of the scores of tribes that make up his church to ensure that everybody's burial ritual is represented during their week of mourning. He is staying with his brother in Ikotun, a neighborhood of Lagos, and is using his brother's car to drive into town in the middle of morning traffic. Nigeria is undergoing a fuel scarcity, but he not going to let that stop him, as he knows where black market dealers are selling fuel. This is how it is for Lagos and Lagosians, and as his grampa used to say: "If you know the people, you know the place." He sees a woman being accosted in a nearby bus on the road and the woman fighting back. She jumps out of the bus and squats to drain blood from her ear, making sure that none of it spills on her dress. The man has heard of an earring thief around town. A group of children whose schools are on strike gather around her, consoling the woman. Part of the traffic is a group of people dancing among the cars. They carry amulets, clubs, and locally made hunting rifles. They are members of the Oodua People's Congress (OPC). They chant that Lagos belongs to the Yorubas, so that the other ethnic groups in Nigeria understand that they are just guests in the city and act accordingly. The group says they will not tolerate armed robbers or corrupt police anymore in the city, and as it is the year of 1999, it is their turn to rule Nigeria.

During this time in Nigeria, the country has recently transitioned to democratic rule with the election of Obasanjo, and competition for oil—wealth—fueled violence between ethnic groups. This causes the militarization of nearly the entire region by ethnic militia groups as well as the Nigerian military and police forces. Suddenly, people are converging upon the scene, with drivers and passengers alike exiting busses to watch a boy struggling in a fire. The boy is known as the earring thief and he has been caught. He is surrounded by tires, doused in gas, and set ablaze. The crowd around the boy aflame is celebrating like a goal has been scored in a soccer match. The man of the church notes from his car: "No matter how scarce fuel is, there's always enough for the thief." There can be two interpretations of this: from one point of view, it means that the thief will find oil no matter what the situation is, as with the black market; from the other, it means that oil is not being wasted when used on a thief. The event of the burning of the boy near traffic is an example of collective violence being propagated as vigilante justice against a potential thief, one who is most likely not Yoruba, given the symbolism of the violence in the open and the use of a scarce resource to punish the boy for his crime (Akpan, 2010).

A Longing for Life

Violence, ironically, reveals the importance of life. If creative, procreative, and life-generating energy are on one side of the spectrum of possibilities, then the impulse for destruction, desecration, and death-generation are on the other. Why and how, then, does violence happen? We may find clues in the cultural history of words: the etymology of "violence" and "creation" reveal the forces at work within the human being. *Violence* comes from a thirteenth-century French word deriving from *vis*, or "strength, force, power, energy," with the same Latin root behind the expression "vim and vigor." The word "vitality" also expresses the same impetus for life. From the Proto-Indo-European root, it means "to go after, strive after, pursue vigorously, desire" (Watkins, 2011).

The same root in Greek goes further to transforms into *bióō* ("to live") or *bíos* ("life") itself (Rendich & Davis, 2016). The term "vi-olence," therefore, bears within it a quest and a force that may offer a way of understanding the shared core that is harbored within such opposing acts as violence and creation. In a positive sense, *vi*-olence testifies to a force that seeks to permeate something alive and new; however, it does so through destruction rather than through creation. Responding to the intensity of the creative urge, innovative individuals are described as "violent" to the extent that they exercise their power to impose their thoughts or visions on others (McDougall, 1999). However, this "violence" is of a different nature than the kind that destroys, on the battlefield or in the inner city—which does not generate something new but is injurious and traumatic. It is the kind of violence that crept into *vir* ("man") as in "virile," a particular kind of force that can easily turn into a vehicle for validating one's existence (Freud, 1920) with even the aid of ethics and esthetics (Apollon, 2002).

Why this similarity? We learned in "The Psychology of Violence" of the paradoxical mind. Critically in need of life force and not finding it, or not believing that it is available, a person may turn to symbolism instead. Scorning or destroying the very thing one needs is a symbolic gesture that one performs to impress upon oneself and others that one does not need it. Or one may exaggerate that which it is too painful to admit that one lacks. This can lead to the kind of exaggeration of force that is violence. In extreme violence, we sometimes see ritualistic symbolic aspects, such as carving out the eyes or cutting the tongue, for killing a person is not enough to get rid of the feeling of shame, or to eliminate the feeling of weakness or lack of worth as a human being that the person has revealed. Even after one goes through acts of mutilation, the feeling remains, for the feeling is not possible to eradicate this way. Serial acts of murder may follow, including serial rituals, and becomes repetitive and self-destructive, not to mention highly destructive of others.

Understanding the underlying drive toward life and how a lack of life force manifests can allow for interventions that address the core problem. More so than teaching "social skills," which are strategies for managing behavior, recognizing the deeper, unconscious, and symbolic communications behind behavior is becoming important (O'Loughlin & Johnson, 2010; Rogers, 2006). Approaches that acknowledge and engage, often in the face of participants' resistance or acting out, get to the core of the need: affirmation and demonstration of meaning for the individual (Gilligan & Lee, 2004).

A Forbidden Concept

It is tempting to believe that violent acts are random, or a pure discharge of energies (Berkowitz, 1962). From a practical perspective, violence is often excessive, superfluous, and self-destructive. However, people who act in extreme ways, taking drastic measures that put themselves at risk, are trying to tell us something. They are stating what is important to them. They indicate to us to what length human beings will go in their search—and this search is for meaning. Violence is an area where the centrality of meaning in human life becomes manifest. Where, then, does this sought-for meaning come from? Meaning is often placed in the self, in one's identity, or the internalized sense of one's place in the world. Every cognitive concept has an emotional counterpart (Ellis, 1991), and this manifests in the craving to be loved.

A German author expresses this very succinctly:

> *Eine Blume kann nicht blühen ohne Sonnenschein, und ein Mensch kann nicht leben ohne Liebe* [A flower cannot bloom without sunshine, and a human cannot live without love]. *(Müller, 1871, p. 15)*

American psychiatrist and violence scholar James Gilligan (1996) has articulated that love is as essential to the soul as oxygen is to the body, noting the centrality of love. In acts of desperation, what is most essential to human life comes to light. We learn from violence the central requirement for healthy emotional development and the survival of the soul: love. Where love is lacking, violence dominates (Jung, 1916). American psychologist Harry Harlow (1959) showed through an experiment with rhesus monkeys that, when given the choice, infant macaques overwhelmingly gravitated toward terrycloth-covered mother surrogates without food than bare-wire mother surrogates with food. If caregiver contact and warmth are more important to primates than even food, then how much more is this true for human beings, whose social brains are vastly more developed? Indeed, we see that well-fed human infants can experience *failure to thrive* when there is a lack of touch or signs of love (Scholler & Nittur, 2012), as adults may sacrifice all manner of material comfort for meaning (Glucklich, 2001).

Love gives rise to life and all that is good in the world; if one cannot have that, then the next best way to gain power over life is to kill it. Violence contains fantasies of absolute power, of infinite destruction and omnipotence capable of countering the actual, unbearable feelings of impotence. Deadly action-power negates the need for dependence by elevating the killer to a god-like superiority. We choose the plebeian term *love* here because it is all-encompassing and general (it comes from the Old English word *lufu*, meaning "affection" as well as "friendliness," a product of the Proto-Germanic *lubo*, which is related to joy and praise), encompasses the different Greek distinctions of love (e.g., *agape, eros, philia,* and *storge*), and has a longer tradition in literary sources than in the scientific literature. Scholarly sources more commonly use technical terms such as "attachment," "bonding," "sexual desire," or "cathexis," which serve to fragment and underplay its centrality. After all, love is the language of poetry, and scholars often find that, after a lot of wandering, they return to where poets have been. What scholars add is scientific confirmation.

When love is absent at the societal, communal, familial, or personal level, or in any combination thereof, this humanity may not have a chance to grow. The psyche is at risk, may die in a way that becomes difficult to revive, or revolt violently against this "death" in ways that can cause literal death. Individuals who commit heinous crimes often report that they feel "dead" inside (Toch, 1969), and we know that this is more than metaphorical. Those capable of harming others are also prone to harming themselves, sometimes through self-mutilation. A common explanation one hears is that injury to the self confirms that they are alive—for example, the sight of blood convinces them that there is life in them, even though they feel so dead and numb that they do not even feel the pain of cutting (Bohus et al., 2000). We thus have evidence of human existence that is experienced as worse than physical or even psychic pain: nonexistence.

Contrasting with this is a feeling of fullness in "spirit," of being "spirited" or even "spiritual"— an inner experience of heightened life that comes from having meaning. The *Oxford English Dictionary* (Swartz, 2013) defines the "spirit" as: "the animating or vital principle in man (and animals); that which gives life to the physical organism, in contrast to its purely material elements; the breath of life." Deriving from the Old French *espirit*, it has its roots in the Latin word *spiritus*, or "a breathing (respiration, and of the wind), breath; breath of a god," hence "inspiration; breath of life." This vital breath is what gives vibrancy and distinguishes the living from the dead and the animate from the inanimate. Vitality and health yield energy for positive action: for fighting against injustice or other forms of violence, and for activities that build and generate conditions for peace. It differentiates the dynamic state of health that arises from proper physical and psychological development from an absence of it. The Old English word for health, *hælþ*, is similarly related to *halig*, which means "holy".

We noted in the chapter "The Psychology of Violence" that violent persons are rather lacking in general activity and energy, whereas a state of health allows one to feel spirited, sacred, creative, and alive, and ultimately at peace. Lacking this state, violence becomes a proxy for fulfillment of existential needs. Hence, violence will try to mimic generativity, exerting exaggerated energy where genuine life force is lacking. Even though the life-enhancing vitality, integration, and joy are diametrical opposites of destructiveness and cruelty, the latter are as much a solution to the problem of human existence as the former, responding to essential human needs. True strength does not require extravagant displays; it manifests quietly in the actual works of creativity, productivity, and other qualities that inspire societal respect. In other words, if one does not have legitimate and socially acceptable means of achieving self-worth, then one resorts to illegitimate means, such as violence. Through displays of force, one can at least inspire fear if not respect to fend off the feeling of dearth temporarily, even at one's later peril. For example, if the world valued productive and beneficial members of society, but did not make available avenues for attaining this, then one might still obtain meaning by inverting the notions of what is good and what is bad, what is truly productive and what is powerless (Anderson, 1999).

If violence is mimicry of a spiritual, or an animated, state, negative symbols are guises of meaning. Making violence brave, powerful, and active makes up for the intolerable feelings of despair, inadequacy, and poor productivity that often plague individuals who become violent. Changing these notions helps to fulfill the need for meaning. Furthermore, perpetrators of violence will try to convince themselves and others that they are opting for violence out of choice—rather than out of a feeling of desperation upon seeing few choices. They often target signs of life (Felthous & Kellert, 1986), sometimes with a desire to decipher what they do not have, in the process of destruction, although sometimes in an attempt to wipe out reminders of their lack. This is sometimes interpreted as a wish to destroy goodness (Meloy, 1988), resulting from an overwhelming envy of those who live in love and are full of life.

Love, on the other hand, animates the spiritual tendency to desire a larger life, to want to care for more than just oneself and to belong to something greater. The presence of love fills emptiness and nurtures growth in ways that violence never can. Meanwhile, an absence of love results in a contraction and a groping toward death, sometimes literally of the self or of others, and thus readily leads to violence. To know where the absence of love has been, one needs only to follow the damage (Meloy & Meloy, 2002). Love from the family can mitigate some lack of love from society or community, but it cannot replace it, and vice versa; nurturance and acceptance are critical at all levels (Gorman-Smith, Henry, & Tolan, 2004).

When one is deprived of love, one does not become neutral to it. A psychological defense system develops in a way that makes the dearth more endurable, but then this psychology rejects love in other settings. As American psychologist, Abraham Maslow, noted that human beings become "perpetually wanting animals" by thwarting actual or imminent basic needs, which leads to psychopathy (Maslow, 1943). Human dependency on love is a fact of life, and yet those who are violent, who most need it, will be the first to sneer at the idea of it (they may consider care and affection to be for "sissies" and "wusses"—weaklings with whom one is too strong to share rank). The academic world itself is not immune to this, for in the desire to appear serious and rigorous, as mentioned above, it fails to include in its inquiry the most central aspect of human existence. Finally, we know the existence of what cultures commonly call "evil", which may be seen as envy and ultimately rejection of the good, from which we can deduce our core human yearning.

Violence in Religion and Art

When one feels loved, it translates into having personal meaning and a place in the world. We see that the centrality of meaning becomes clear in *posttraumatic stress disorder* (PTSD), which is a trauma-induced syndrome that manifests in physiologic symptoms of anxiety, hypervigilance, and loss of sleep. These symptoms are notoriously resistant to medications or any other treatment. But if one is able to establish new meaning in one's life that incorporates the trauma, for example, by seeking to learn from the experience or by adopting a new purpose in the world or a mission based on the experience, the symptoms diminish. PTSD results from a "ruptured worldview," or the view of life as safe and meaningful. As with many other illnesses, the capacity for recovery begins with questioning: *What is the meaning of what has happened? What is my purpose in this context?* Many other conditions, even physical ones, respond variably to meaning and purpose, and a will to live (Rosenkranz et al., 2003).

In the more individual-oriented modern societies, one often derives meaning from self-identity; in the more communal regions, one might attain it from diminution of the self in favor of the community, but the importance of meaning remains the same. Religion provides meaning through a shared cosmology, while art does it through the elevation of individual expression. At the heart of religion are compassion, ethical deeds, peace, harmony, and love, which also articulate the human qualities associated with heightened emotional health. At the center of art are creativity, generativity, inventiveness, and celebration of civilization's highest accomplishments as exemplified in the human spirit. These domains represent expressions of love and life-giving energy as well as avenues for cultivating their development.

What, then, accounts for the violence that has often appeared in these domains since their very beginnings (Girard, 1977; Harding, 2000)? The Crusades, the Jihads, the Inquisition, the Thuggee murders of India, the Buddhist mass burials in Burma, Aztec and Incan sacrifices, the Islamic State of Iraq and Syria (ISIS), the conflict between Israel and Palestine, and the legitimization of preemptive war by means of Christian-fundamentalist eschatologies make it obvious that violent practice in the name of religion is common (Juergensmeyer, 2001; Richardson, 2001). Similarly, in the arts, one need only look at depictions of horror in the portrayals of self-mutilation, carnage, genocide, and—worse—surrealistic denial of life or dehumanization through scale or the negation of a personal touch. Media and the internet have been criticized and widely investigated for similarly displaying violence (Coyne, 2007; Tahir & Chaudhary, 2011). But do these expressions in the context of religion or art negate their original purpose? These illustrate not so much the character of religion or of art but rather their meaning for the highly symbolically driven human mind: where the human soul places the greatest significance and source of meaning, we will find the most extreme reactions when there is a lack.

We have discussed concepts such as reaction formation in Chapter 3, "The Psychology of Violence": the mind will produce *hyperreligiosity* where deeper religious feeling is lacking, *fundamentalism* where uncertainty abounds, and *veneration of destructivity* where one cannot build in genuinely constructive ways. Religion is seen as a way to give morality to violent acts, thus legitimizing violence (Weisbrod, 2002); thus, using religion to judge and condemn others constitutes symbolic violence (Swartz, 1996). There is an enlarging body of literature that deals with religion and terrorism (Al-Khattar, 2003; Jones & Smith, 2014). Similarly, art can be used to legitimize oppression through social class distinctions (Bourdieu, 1979), or alternatively as a way to "aestheticize" violence, instilling violence-promoting values (Nelson, 2011). This does not mean that displays of courage and depictions of human suffering always oppose the advancement of life; art as a means of catharsis or of mobilizing social action has also been amply described (Perlmutter & Koppman, 1999), although recognizing the difference requires subtlety.

Meaning and Moral Development

Violence, being replete with symbols, has an intimate connection with emotional and cognitive development (Yakeley & Meloy, 2012). When the need for love is fulfilled, the symbolic nature of human beings imbues the tangible world with cognitive meaning (Jung, 1964). The need of truth, then, becomes more central than any other need, though it is seldom mentioned (Bousquet & Weil, 1950). When one is not able to find meaning, what happens? One sees violence. This is the deeper dynamic that underlies the quest to avoid shame and to find self-love. If one cannot find meaning, a sense of self-worth, then the desperation drives a person to do anything to obtain it, including give up one's life. We see this in suicide bombers, prisoners who go on hunger strikes, or violent offenders who feel the need to do what they do even if it means they will pay for it the rest of their lives.

In normal development, the striving for meaning gives rise to a moral compass of right or wrong, good or bad, and, implicitly, enhancement of health or induction of illness. Human morality is an issue of considerable import both individually and collectively; internalization of a set of standards is integral to a sense of purpose in everyday life (Bandura, 1991). Swiss developmental psychologist Jean Piaget (1924) first articulated, and American psychologist Lawrence Kohlberg (1971) elaborated, on how moral stages progress over a lifespan. They showed that psychological health and maturity find expression in the emergence, evolution, and culmination of moral sensibilities across the human lifespan. Attitudes and understandings that arise from this development help to instill a sense of justice, respect for others' rights, and finally an ability to care for others.

Piaget divided the stages of moral development into *premoral* (0–5 years), *moral realism* (5–9 years), and *moral relativity* (9+ years)—that is, before morality; absolute morality (authority figures such as parents, teachers, and God determine the rules); and morality whose rules can change according to circumstance (people make the rules and therefore can break them). Kohlberg referred to these stages as *preconventional* (childhood), *conventional* (adolescence and adulthood), and *postconventional* (advanced adulthood), which he further distinguished into:

1a) Obedience and punishment (*how can I avoid punishment?*).
1b) Self-interest (*what's in it for me? – you scratch my back, and I'll scratch yours*).
2a) Interpersonal accord and conformity (*keeping the rules allows me to be liked and thought well of*).

2b) Authority and social order (*obeying laws and conventions keeps society from falling apart*).

3a) Social contract (*agreement among people increases the welfare of all*).

3b) Universal ethical principles (*the fallibility of humans demands mutual respect and understanding*).

Kohlberg also speculated about a more advanced stage, "transcendental morality," which has a cosmic orientation and is linked with religion (Kohlberg & Power, 1981). It is important to note that this progression does not depend solely on the individual but also on socialization, such as gender differences in upbringing (Gilligan, 1982).

Each of these stages, when communally shared, forms a culture that reflects a moral paradigm as well as an implicit world view. Russian novelist Leo Tolstoy (2004) effectively described this phenomenon in a narrative:

> It is usually imagined that a thief, a murderer, a spy, a prostitute, acknowledging his or her profession to be evil, is ashamed of it. But the contrary is true. People whom fate and their sin-mistakes have placed in a certain position, however false that position may be, form a view of life in general which makes their position seem good and admissible. In order to keep up their view of life, these people instinctively keep to the circle of those who share their views of life and of their own place in it. This surprises us where the persons concerned are thieves bragging about their dexterity, prostitutes vaunting their depravity, or murderers boasting of their cruelty. But it surprises us only because the circle, the atmosphere, in which these people live, is limited, and chiefly because we are outside of it. Can we not observe the same phenomenon when the rich boast of their wealth—robbery; when commanders of armies pride themselves of their victories—murder; and when those in high places vaunt their power—violence? That we do not see the perversion in the views of life held by these people, is only because the circle formed by them is larger and we ourselves belong to it (pp. 131–132).

We see similar dynamics playing out today: while there may be no greater violence than limiting the opportunity for human beings to realize their full, symbolic potential, such as a full identity and self-meaning, society condones—if not rewards—such violence at increasingly systemic scales (Fanon, 1963). And if we justify war, it is because peoples justify the traits of which they find themselves possessed, not because war will endure an objective examination of merit. At the same time, they will condemn individuals who commit a single murder. In the face of this discrepancy, it is of little wonder that the average offender of criminal violence considers oneself a victim who is further victimized when the criminal justice system penalizes (Stevenson, 2014). This failure of symbolic function on the part of the justice system, rather than deterring offenses, has the unintended effect of reverting the offender to preconventional morality ("might makes right") through its own example (Andrews & Bonta, 2010).

The converse of this is that, as Scottish philosopher David Hume (1764) noted, the boundaries of justice grow larger, in proportion to the largeness of human views and the force of our mutual connection. This larger sense of justice might include not just conventional ("law and consent") but also postconventional ("fairness and compassion") morality, thus not just prohibiting wrongdoing but also encouraging proactive right-doing. The postconventional stage is about moving toward principles from rules, thereby increasing in flexibility and humility in the face of human fallibility and incomplete knowledge. Russian novelist Fyodor Dostoyevsky (1912) noted that it is unjust for any human being to claim complete judgment on another, for none is perfect but, rather, all are responsible for all.

The moral code of most religions, regardless of interpretation, does not stop at the level of rules but aspires to principles: the Hebrew word for "justice" (*Tzedek*), for example, is also the root of "charity" (*Tzedakah*) (Donin, 1991); Buddhist teachings say, "Hatred does not cease by hatred, but only by love" (Cleary, 1994); Christianity interprets the spirit of the written law as "Love your neighbor as you love yourself" (Mark 12:31, New International Version Bible); Islam urges one to "Spend of the good things that you have earned [in alms]" (al-Baquarah 2:267, the *Holy Qur'ān*, translated by M. Sher 'Alī); and Hinduism teaches that loving all leads to perceiving all living beings as a part of oneself (Madhavananda, 1935). Finally, laws are only necessary where love is lacking (Richards, 2016).

Compassion and Creativity

In Kohlberg's stages of moral development, we see a pattern: the principle of order based on force (obedience and punishment) gradually gives way to organization based on empathy, compassion, and love (universal ethical principles). The accompanying emotional, psychosocial development, as American developmental psychologist Erik Erikson (1980) articulated, follows a similar sequence:

1a) Trust vs. mistrust (*can I trust this person to take care of me?*).
1b) Autonomy vs. shame (*am I capable of doing things myself?*).
2a) Initiative vs. guilt (*can I make choices on my own?*).
2b) Industry vs. inferiority (*am I as competent as others?*).
2c) Identity vs. role confusion (*what is my purpose, and how do I fit in?*).
3a) Intimacy vs. isolation (*how can I experience love and intimacy?*).
3b) Generativity vs. stagnation (*how might I better care for others, and contribute in my career?*).
3c) Ego integrity vs. despair (*now that my own life does not matter as much, what does?*).

Although Erikson's eight stages denote much (and the above groupings are for our own illustration), emotional development, in broad strokes, can be characterized as an expansion of "ego boundaries," or what one counts as oneself or one's own (Bronfenbrenner, 1977). This is the highest state of emotional development and maturation whereby the unit of identity for the individual may expand into the whole of society. We move from the self to the self in relation to society and others beyond the self. Ultimately, as a Persian poet (Jalāl al-Dīn Rūmi, 1994) put it: "When your chest is free of your limiting ego, /Then you will see the ageless Beloved." At this stage of development is a sense of oneness with the world and with all of humanity, and these individuals have an expanding ability to give love in the form of: (a) compassion (charity, service to relieve suffering, and spiritual support); or (b) creation (children, work for the world's betterment, and art). In their ideal, healthy manifestations, therefore, religion and art can be great avenues for cultivating and expressing empathy, compassion, love, generativity, and creativity—and for gaining a sense of oneness with others and the world, and of peace, benevolence, and abundance.

The principles or "spirit" of compassion and creativity, of course, go beyond the domains of religion and art; secular ethics and charity have sometimes shown greater generosity of spirit, while science and technology have been incubating grounds for creativity. Almost any domain can be an outlet for the expression of heightened emotional health, or states of health that are higher than a mere absence of disease (World Health Organization, 1946). In other words, any domain can build health, even if not every domain can eliminate disease. Health, whether individual or societal, often comes from resilience, or the ability to overcome hardship or trauma, which is a process rather than a trait (Masten, 2001). Resilient individuals are capable of coping with negative thoughts or emotions, without denying them, and working through difficult experiences to develop flexibility and coping strategies (Werner & Smith, 1992). This ability comes from perceiving oneself as having choices and exercising them creatively to take part in shaping one's reality.

An individual can develop this process throughout one's life span (Rutter, 2008) to fulfill an important human potential. While this capacity is dormant in everyone, and perhaps the most unique characteristic of human beings (described as "free will" in religion and law, or as "leaps of imagination" in art and science), the degree to which it can be accessed may depend on the environment. The bio-psycho-socio-environmental model incorporates the "environmental," obviously including the natural environment, but also including the larger human-made physical and symbolic worlds. An environment of symbols may initially derive from social interactions, but as symbols can exist among us and beyond us, they go on to establish a wealth of codes that have a life of their own (Freyenhagen, 2013). Semiotics completes individual psychology by representing influences that can promote advanced human capabilities as well as limit individual identity, and may alternatively comprise a *bio-psycho-socio-spiritual* model. It illustrates the source and the capacity for self-love; a feeling of interconnectedness with the world; a reference for feeling empathy for others; and a faculty for finding meaning in life, the origin or life, and the universe—all of which mitigate the propensity for violence.

Conclusion

The emotional centrality of love has a cognitive counterpart, which is meaning. These terms can carry semiotic or linguistic significance, but here we reviewed their deeper roots in human development. We showed how violence points to the most poignant aspects of being human, which center around these concepts. Love, which connotes meaning, worth, and personal value, gives rise to emotional vitality and a cognitive sense of importance. As symbolic animals, humans are not limited by that of which they are capable but that of which they conceive is possible—and this potential can go in either direction. In the absence of love, a longing for life is thwarted in ways that can give rise to extremities such as violence. We showed how religion and art, as embodiments of these essential human longings, can become potent vehicles for violent expression. However, they also allow for the cultivation of compassion and creativity, which powerfully prevent and mitigate violence. Adequate coverage of this topic would require a whole book, but we introduce it briefly here rather than omitting it, for the central importance it has in how we should think about violence. To summarize simply, in human development, the experience of love in the home, in the community, and as a valued member of society gives rise to a system of thoughts, beliefs, and expectations about the self and others. The heightened vitality that results from proper emotional and cognitive development is therefore important to channeling human impulse away from violence and toward life.

In the presence of sufficient love, one sees meaning in oneself and one's relation to others, and this becomes an important cognitive counterpart to the emotional experience of love. While meaning is highly personal and can take almost any form, heightened psychological health is experienced cognitively as meaning, self-worth, and social legitimacy. Meaning is therefore a social construction of self: there are societies that construct its identities at a level far beyond the individual, while others construct identities at levels below the individual person, such that they facilitate the appearance of many identities within a single person. This important cognitive need is something for which one will fight to one's death. This is the reason why, the more deprived the individual, the community, or nation, the more it is preoccupied with principles, identity, or international recognition: it is the struggle for survival of the symbolic self (Burris & Rempel, 2004). In this context, violence can be (mis)used to convey quick meaning, through action or depiction, as a proxy for fulfilling this need.

Violence is the endpoint of a long process, an almost accidental event that aggregates the more enduring attitudes, predispositions, and tendencies of an individual, while the individual is a repository of much wider societal symbolism and proclivity. Because of the symbolic nature of human violence, it can change in form and manifestation depending on the environment around the event itself, the originator, the audience, and the cultural context. Different symbols can promote or discourage violence. Therefore, no particular iconography, style of art, religion, or ideology is immune from the capacity for violence, harm, subjugation, and oppression. Nevertheless, religious groups that employ violence are relatively rare (Sprinzak, 1993), and art and iconography used for violent political aims (Cavanaugh, 2004) are misguided examples rather than the essence of these fields. Art and religion, as any domain of intense human aspiration, can be a means of developing and channeling compassion and creativity through powerful symbolism.

Questions

1 How does symbolism contribute to the understanding of human violence?

2 What is the relationship between meaning and moral development?

3 What place does love hold in human development?

4 What is a death drive, and how is it different from an impulse for life?

5 What are the mechanisms by which religion and art become vehicles for violence?

References

Achebe, A. (1958). *Things fall apart*. London, UK: Heinemann.
Akpan, U. (2010, January 4). Baptizing the gun. *New Yorker*. Retrieved from https://www.newyorker.com/magazine/2010/01/04/baptizing-the-gun
Al-Khattar, A. M. (2003). *Religion and terrorism: An interfaith perspective*. Westport, CT: Praeger.
Anderson, E. (1999). *Code of the street: Decency, violence, and the moral life of the inner city*. New York, NY: Norton and Company.
Andrews, D. A., & Bonta, J. (2010). Rehabilitating criminal justice policy and practice. *Psychology, Public Policy, and Law, 16*(1), 39–55.
Apollon, W. (2002). The jouissance of the other and the sexual division in psychoanalysis. In W. Apollon, D. Bergeron, & L. Cantin (Eds.), *After Lacan: Clinical practice and the subject of the unconscious*. Albany, NY: State University of New York.
Babcock, B. A. (1978). *The reversible world: Symbolic inversion in art*. Ithaca, NY: Cornell University Press.
Bandura, A. (1991). Social cognitive theory of self-regulation. *Organizational Behavior and Human Decision Processes, 50*(2), 248–287.
Barthes, R. G. (1957). *Mythologies*. Paris, France: Seuil.
Berkowitz, L. (1962). *Aggression: A social-psychological analysis*. New York, NY: McGraw-Hill.

Bohus, M., Limberger, M., Ebner, U., Glocker, F. X., Schwarz, B., Wernz, M., & Lieb, K. (2000). Pain perception during self-reported distress and calmness in patients with borderline personality disorder and self-mutilating behavior. *Psychiatry Research, 95*(3), 251–260.

Boshoff, A. (2013). Law and its rhetoric of violence. *International Journal for the Semiotics of Law, 26*(2), 425–437.

Bourdieu, P. (1979). *La distinction: Critique sociale du jugement.* Paris, France: Éditions de minuit.

Bousquet, J., & Weil, S. (1950). *Correspondance entre Simone Weil et Joë Bousquet (avril-mai 1942).* Marseille, France: Cahiers du Sud.

Bronfenbrenner, U. (1977). Toward an experimental ecology of human development. *American Psychologist, 32*(7), 513–531.

Burris, C. T., & Rempel, J. K. (2004). "It's the end of the world as we know it": Threat and the spatial-symbolic self. *Journal of Personality and Social Psychology, 86*(1), 19–42.

Cassirer, E. (1944). *An essay on man: An introduction to a philosophy of human culture.* New Haven: Yale University Press.

Cavanaugh, W. T. (2004). Sins of omission: What "religion and violence" arguments ignore. *Hedgehog Review, 6*(1), 34–50.

Chandler, D. (2007). *Semiotics: The basics.* New York, NY: Routledge.

Cleary, T. (1994). *Dhammapada: The sayings of the Buddha.* New York: Bantam Books.

Coyne, S. M. (2007). Does media violence cause violent crime? *European Journal on Criminal Policy and Research, 13*(3–4), 205–211.

Department of the Treasury. (1993). *Report of the Department of the Treasury on the Bureau of Alcohol, Tobacco, and Firearms investigation of Vernon Wayne Howell, also known as David Koresh.* Washington, DC: Author.

Dickens, C. (1859). *A tale of two cities.* London, UK: Chapman and Hall.

Donin, H. (1991). *To be a Jew: A guide to Jewish observance in contemporary life.* New York, NY: Basic Books.

Dostoyevsky, F. (1912). *The brothers Karamazov* (C. Garnett, Trans.). London, UK: Heinemann.

Eco, U. (1976). *A theory of semiotics.* Bloomington, IN: Indiana University Press.

Ellens, J. H. (2007). *The destructive power of religion: Violence in Judaism, Christianity, and Islam.* Westport, CT: Greenwood.

Ellis, A. (1991). The revised ABC's of rational-emotive therapy (RET). *Journal of Rational-Emotive and Cognitive-Behavior Therapy, 9*(3), 139–172. doi:10.1007/BF01061227

Erikson, E. H. (1980). *Identity and the life cycle.* New York, NY: Norton.

Fanon, F. (1963). *The wretched of the earth.* New York, NY: Grove Press.

Federal Bureau of Investigation. (2000). *Project Megiddo.* Washington, DC: U.S. Department of Justice.

Felthous, A. R., & Kellert, S. R. (1986). Violence against animals and people: Is aggression against living creatures generalized? *Bulletin of the American Academy of Psychiatry and the Law, 14*(1), 55–69.

Frankl, V. E. (1962). *Man's search for meaning: An introduction to logotherapy.* New York, NY: Simon and Schuster.

Fraser, J. (1974). *Violence in the arts.* New York, NY: Cambridge University Press.

Freud, S. (1920). *Beyond the pleasure principle.* London, UK: International Psycho-Analytical Press.

Freyenhagen, F. (2013). *Adorno's practical philosophy: Living less wrongly.* Cambridge, UK: Cambridge University Press.

García Márquez, G. (1966). *One hundred years of solitude* (G. Rabassa, Trans.). New York, NY: Harper and Row.

Gilligan, C. (1982). *In a different voice: Psychological theory and women's development.* Cambridge, MA: Harvard University Press.

Gilligan, J. (1996). *Violence: Our deadly epidemic and its causes.* New York, NY: Putnam.

Gilligan, J., & Lee, B. (2004). Beyond the prison paradigm: From provoking violence to preventing it by creating "anti-prisons" (residential colleges and therapeutic communities). *Annals of the New York Academy of Sciences, 1036*(1), 300–324.

Girard, R. (1977). *Violence and the sacred.* Baltimore, MD: Johns Hopkins University Press.

Glucklich, A. (2001). *Sacred pain: Hurting the body for the sake of the soul.* New York, NY: Oxford University Press.

Gorman-Smith, D., Henry, D. B., & Tolan, P. H. (2004). Exposure to community violence and violence perpetration: The protective effects of family functioning. *Journal of Clinical Child and Adolescent Psychology, 33*(3), 439–449.

Harding, A. (2000). *European societies in the Bronze Age.* Cambridge, UK: Cambridge University Press.

Harlow, H. F. (1959). Love in infant monkeys. *Scientific American, 200*(6), 68–75.

Hesiod (1966). *Theogony* (M. L. West, Trans.). New York, NY: Clarendon Press.

Hume, D. (1764). *Essays and treatises on several subjects.* London, U.K.: Millar.

Jalāl al-Dīn Rūmi, M. (1994). *Masnavi I Ma'Navi: Teachings of Rumi: The spiritual couplets of Maulańa Jalálu-'D-Dín Muhammad I Rúmí.* (E. H. Whinfield, Trans.). London, UK: Octagon.

Jones, D. M., & Smith, M. L. R. (2014). *Sacred violence: Political religion in a secular age.* Basingstoke, UK: Palgrave Macmillan.

Juergensmeyer, M. (2001). The logic of religious violence. In D. C. Rapoport (Ed.), *Inside terrorist organizations* (pp. 172–193). Portland, OR: Frank Cass.

Jung, C. G. (1964). *Man and his symbols.* New York, NY: Doubleday.

Kohlberg, L. (1971). *From is to ought: How to commit the naturalistic fallacy and get away with it in the study of moral development.* New York, NY: Academic Press.

Kohlberg, L., & Power, C. (1981). Moral development, religious thinking, and the question of a seventh stage. *Zygon, 16*(3), 203–259.

Krug, E. G., Dahlberg, L. L., Mercy, J. A., Zwi, A. B., & Lozano, R. (2002). *World report on violence and health.* Geneva, Switzerland: World Health Organization. Retrieved from http://apps.who. int/iris/bitstream/10665/42495/1/9241545615_eng.pdf

Lacan, J. M. E. (1966). *Ecrits.* Paris, France: Seuil.

Langer, S. K. (1942). *Philosophy in a new key: A study in the symbolism of reason, rite, and art.* Cambridge, MA: Harvard University Press.

Lévi-Strauss, C. (1958). *Anthropologie structurale.* Paris, France: Plon.

Liddell, H. G., Scott, R., Jones, H. S., & MacKenzie, R. (2011). *Online Liddell-Scott-Jones Greek-English lexicon.* Irvine, CA: University of California.

Madhavananda, S. (1935). *Brihadaranyaka Upanishad.* (S. Madhavananda, Trans.). Belur Math, India: Advaita Ashrama.

Maslow, A. H. (1943). A theory of human motivation. *Psychological Review, 50*(4), 370–396.

Maslow, A. H. (1962). *Toward a psychology of being.* Princeton, NJ: Van Nostrand.

Masten, A. S. (2001). Ordinary magic: Resilience processes in development. *American Psychologist, 56*(3), 227–238.

McDougall, J. (1999). Violence and creativity. *Scandinavian Psychoanalytic Review, 22,* 207–217.

Meloy, J. R. (1988). *The Psychopathic Mind: Origins, Dynamics, and Treatment.* Northvale, NJ: Aronson.

Meloy, J. R., & Meloy, M. J. (2002). Autonomic arousal in the presence of psychopathy: A survey of mental health and criminal justice professionals. *Journal of Threat Assessment, 2*(2), 21–33.

Merriam-Webster (2011). *Merriam-Webster's collegiate dictionary* (11th ed.). Springfield, MA: Author.

Müller, M. (1871). *Deutsche Liebe: Aus den Papieren eines Fremdlings.* Leipzig, Germany: Brockhaus.

Nelson, M. (2011). *The art of cruelty.* New York, NY: Norton and Company.

Nöth, W. (1990). *Handbook of semiotics*. Bloomington, IN: Indiana University Press.

O'Loughlin, M., & Johnson, R. (2010). *Imagining children otherwise: Theoretical and critical perspectives on childhood subjectivity*. New York, NY: Peter Lang.

Perlmutter, D., & Koppman, D. (1999). *Reclaiming the spiritual in art: Contemporary cross-cultural perspectives*. Albany, NY: State University of New York Press.

Piaget, J. (1924). *Le Jugement moral chez l'enfant*. Paris, France: Delachaux et Niestlé.

Rendich, F., & Davis, G. (2016). *Comparative etymological dictionary of classical Indo-European languages: Indo-European-Sanskrit-Greek-Latin*. Charleston, SC: CreateSpace.

Retsikas, K. (2006). The semiotics of violence: Ninja, sorcerers, and state terror in post-Soeharto Indonesia. *Bijdragen tot de Taal-, Landen Volkenkunde, 162*(1), 56–94.

Richards, D. A. J. (2016). *Why love leads to justice: Love across the boundaries*. New York, NY: Cambridge University Press.

Richardson, J. T. (2001). Minority religions and the context of violence: A conflict/interactionist perspective. *Terrorism and Political Violence, 13*(1), 103–133.

Ritscher, L. A. (2005). *The semiotics of rape in renaissance English literature*. Santa Cruz, CA: University of California.

Rogers, A. G. (2006). *The unsayable: The hidden language of trauma*. New York, NY: Random House.

Rosenkranz, M. A., Jackson, D. C., Dalton, K. M., Dolski, I., Ryff, C. D., Singer, B. H., ... Davidson, R. J. (2003). Affective style and in vivo immune response: Neurobehavioral mechanisms. *Proceedings of the National Academy of Sciences, 100*(19), 11148–11152.

Rutter, M. (2008). Developing concepts in developmental psychopathology. In J. J. Hudziak (Ed.), *Developmental psychopathology and wellness: Genetic and environmental influences* (pp. 3–22). Washington, DC: American Psychiatric Publishing.

Scholler, I., & Nittur, S. (2012). Understanding failure to thrive. *Paediatrics and Child Health, 22*(10), 438–442.

Schwartz, M. D., & Friedrichs, D. O. (1994). Postmodern thought and criminological discontent: New metaphors for understanding violence. *Criminology, 32*(2), 221–246.

Shakespeare, W. (1990). Tragedy of Hamlet, Prince of Denmark. In R. Lattimore, & M. J. Adler (Eds.), *Great books of the Western world* (Vol. 27). Chicago, IL: Encyclopædia Britannica.

Sprinzak, E. (1993). *Three models of religious violence: The case of Jewish fundamentalism in Israel. Fundamentalisms and the state*. (pp. 462–490). Chicago, IL: University of Chicago Press.

Stevenson, B. (2014). *Just mercy: A story of justice and redemption*. New York, NY: Spiegel and Grau.

Stubbe, H. (1670). *The plus ultra reduced to a non plus, or, a specimen of some animadversions upon the plus ultra of Mr Glanville*. London, UK.

Swartz, D. (1996). Bridging the study of culture and religion: Pierre Bourdieu's political economy of symbolic power. *Sociology of Religion, 57*(1), 71–85.

Swartz, J. J. (2013). *Oxford English dictionary* (2nd ed.). Oxford, UK: Per Linguam.

Tahir, M. A., & Chaudhary, M. A. (2011). The prevalence of violent and aggressive behavior in students with computer and internet use at Balochistan University of IT, Engineering, and Management Sciences, Quetta, Pakistan. *Pakistan Journal of Clinical Psychology, 10*(2), 3–15.

Toch, H. (1969). *Violent men: An inquiry into the psychology of violence*. Chicago, IL: Aldine Publishing.

Tolstoy, L. (2004). *Resurrection* (L. Maude, Trans.). New York, NY: Dover Publications.

Ushie, G. O., & Nta, E. G. (2012). Descriptive focus as a semiotic marker in Festus Iyayi's violence. *Studies in Literature and Language, 5*(3), 45–48.

Vendler, Z. (1979). *Linguistics in philosophy*. Ithaca, NY: Cornell University Press.

Watkins, C. (2011). *The American dictionary of indo-European roots*. Boston, MA: Houghton Mifflin Harcourt.

Weisbrod, B. (2002). Fundamentalist violence: Political violence and political religion in modern conflict. *International Social Science Journal, 54*(4), 499–508.

Werner, E., & Smith, R. S. (1992). *Overcoming the odds: High risk children from birth to adulthood.* Ithaca, NY: Cornell University Press.

World Health Organization (1946). Preamble to the Constitution of the World Health Organization as adopted by the International Health Conference, New York, 19–22 June. Geneva, Switzerland: Author.

Yakeley, J., & Meloy, J. R. (2012). Understanding violence: Does psychoanalytic thinking matter? *Aggression and Violent Behavior, 17*(3), 229–239.

Causes (Continued)

Part III   Social and Societal Framework

5

The Sociology and Anthropology of Violence

Introduction

> Man is by nature a social animal.
>
> —*Aristotle,* Politics *(Trans. 1568)*

Until now, we have discussed violence within an *intra- and interpersonal framework*, interpreting violence from the viewpoint of what happens within and between individuals. The next several chapters discuss the broader *social and societal framework* for thinking about violence. Obviously, an intra- or interpersonal framework is limiting when it comes to collective violence; we do not expect to and cannot decipher all the dynamics of individual violence so as to add them up to equal the whole of collective violence. Certainly, individuals affect the whole, but we learn from the social sciences that the opposite is also true: personal decisions—including the most private and personal ones—have a social and cultural component to them. In other words, individual decisions that we consider to be "free" and "independent" are inevitably linked not only to unconscious elements within ourselves but also to invisible forces outside of ourselves. The bio-psycho-socio-environmental paradigm tells us that every individual decision has not only biological and psychological contributors, but also social and environmental ones. We are highly interconnected, to the extent that collective problems become personal problems—and for this reason, no study of violence is complete without the study of society and societal dynamics.

Awareness of the forces at communal, societal, and even global levels that affect our decisions gives us the possibility of greater agency and empowerment, not only through knowing what forces have influence but also through the awareness that an individual's influence can reverberate through society. *Sociological imagination* refers to the ability of the researcher to look at a personal problem and conceive of it as a public issue. In seeking behavioral change, it is useful to recognize that solving a personal problem may involve not just changing personal circumstances but also making larger changes—and to recognize that those larger changes can lead to a web of changes. To elucidate how this works, it is useful to study the related but separate disciplines of sociology and anthropology. To help us consider how to think about violence, this chapter will present some examples, the histories of the two fields, some major sociological theories, and some perspectives of anthropology before finally bringing them altogether.

Sociology concerns the scientific study of human society and social behavior, including the origins and development of societies and interactions within societies. The importance of sociology in the study of violence is that it demonstrates, through the study of relationship,

Violence: An Interdisciplinary Approach to Causes, Consequences, and Cures, First Edition. Bandy X. Lee.
© 2019 John Wiley & Sons, Inc. Published 2019 by John Wiley & Sons, Inc.

community, and society, that the actions of individuals do not take place in isolation but rather are extensions and manifestations of the cultural forces and pressures acting on humans as part of a social structure. In other words, sociology can be a useful tool to explain why actions that seem random or inexplicable when we only look at the individual can be more understandable when we consider them in relation to society as a whole. We know this from the fact that violent death rates vary according to social group, and even in the same society there are epidemics of homicide and suicide (Lee, Wexler, & Gilligan, 2014). Many have considered sociology to be "psychology writ large," in the same manner that Ruth Benedict (1934) described anthropology as "personality writ large."

Anthropology, conversely, is the scientific study of humans, humanity, and culture. Generally speaking, anthropology concerns the study of cultures outside one's own, either geographically or historically, and the comparison of cultural differences. Anthropology encompasses a variety of fields, including social and cultural anthropology (the study of cultural variation among humans), linguistic anthropology (the study of how language can influence culture, communication, and thought), biological anthropology (the study of the physical and aspects of humanity and primate behavior), and archeology (Scupin & DeCorse, 2016).

Although sociology and anthropology have developed independently of each other and function as individual disciplines, their methods of gathering information and the populations they study have converged over time. For this reason, we consider them together here even though the large body of violence research from each field would each merit more than a chapter; in fact, each would probably require an entire book to do justice to its importance in the study of violence. The two areas bring great potential as our understanding of the complexity of violence grows; we will show how ecological conditions and the need for social belonging can give rise to individual violence, while culture helps to explain the symbolic and subjective nature of even collective violence. We hope that the student will draw inspiration from this chapter and go on to study these fields beyond the brief survey this chapter can offer.

Evolution of Sociology

Social analysis of cultures and societies began far before the existence of any discipline. In Western tradition, it was the Ancient Greek philosopher Plato (1763) who first recorded any form of social analysis as part of his study of proper government and the correct application of laws. In East Asia, the Ancient Chinese philosopher Confucius (1861) examined culture and society with the intention of avoiding chaos and violence through an emphasis on social roles. In medieval Islam, the North African scholar Ibn Khaidun investigated social cohesion and conflict (Enan, 2007), and is now considered to be the father of sociology. It is interesting to note that these three great scholars had similar approaches to the study of their own societies— as separated as they were by time and distance—and laid down principles that we draw upon to this day.

However, it was not until 1848 that French philosopher Auguste Comte coined the term sociology. By emphasizing what he called social positivism, Comte postulated a philosophical framework for the alleviation of the specific social ills arising from the French Revolution. Considered by many to be the first philosopher of science, Comte's utopianism found an echo in the works of Émile Durkheim (1897), who is best remembered for his study of suicide rates among Catholic and Protestant populations. His painstaking collection and analysis of the data established sociology as a science in its own right, separate from both psychology and philosophy. His studies showed that the frequency of suicides was statistically lower in Catholic communities than in neighboring Protestant communities, from which he inferred that the forces at work were neither personal nor psychological, but social (Wacquant, 1993). According to Durkheim, his studies could show if a society was healthy or potentially self-destructive, and could propose solutions to social breakdowns. Durkheim was concerned with the effects of modernization and industrialization on society and its members.

Durkheim (1894) rejected Comte's (1848) logic that sociological positivism is a remedy for social ills, but along with Karl Marx and Max Weber from Germany formally established the field as a science of social institutions. Durkheim posited that through studies like his on suicide rates, sociology would be able to determine whether any given society is "healthy" or "pathological" and seek social reform to counter organic breakdown or social *anomie* (a lack of moral standards in an individual or a group as a result of the loss of social bonds). After Durkheim, sociology swiftly attained the status of a legitimate science and became increasingly popular as the nineteenth century drew to a close. It developed quickly as an academic response to the social challenges of modernity, such as industrialization, urbanization, secularization, and the process of "rationalization" (Habermas, 1987). The fields of psychology, economics, jurisprudence, and philosophy drew to an increasingly greater extent from the growing body of sociological research (Giddens, Duneier, & Applebaum, 2007). More recently, American sociologists George Herbert Mead (1934) and Charles Cooley (Cooley & Angell, 1930) influenced the rise of social psychology and the symbolic interactionism of the influential Chicago School.

The Chicago School is sometimes called the ecological school, as it was the first major body of work that researched the urban environment. *Symbolic interactionism* was an important breakthrough, as it emphasizes the meanings that people create in their lives and in society through their interactions (Dennis & Martin, 2005). American anthropologist Clifford Geertz (1983) called it "local knowledge," and in W. I. Thomas's words: "If men define situations as real, they are real in their consequences" (Thomas & Thomas, 1928). These radical ideas elevated members of society from being merely passive entities conforming to social pressures to active participants in their own understanding of their communities.

Broadly speaking, the study of modern sociology is divided into two competing theoretical frameworks (Abend, 2008). *Functionalists* writing after Durkheim believe that society functions together as an organized whole (one frequent analogy is of society as a biological organism, with separate parts of the body working together) to ensure the continuation and stability of the society (Jones, 2007). Contrasting with this is *conflict theory*, which emphasizes differences—be they social, political, or material—as the defining force of a social structure, and change through competition for power (Dahrendorf, 1958). Marx's theory of class struggle is a classic example of the latter perspective, although the field has fragmented in recent years and now influences feminist theory, postmodern theory, postcolonial theory, and many others.

Evolution of Anthropology

The field of anthropology also began from more or less humble beginnings. As far back as 440 BCE, father of history Herodotus wrote his *Histories*. Not merely a collection of stories about the Persian Wars, *Histories* is the first documented instance of cross-cultural comparisons and the forerunner of modern anthropology. Herodotus's facts are often incorrect and contradictory, but his methods of information gathering and his aims in compiling his data are clear precursors of a science that would flourish some two thousand years later.

Other cross-cultural records exist from around the world, in literature ranging from that of Mesopotamia (Third Dynasty of Ur) to the Sanskrit texts of Hindu cosmology (the Purāṇas), to the annals of China (Qin Dynasty), but it was not until 1647 that Caspar and Thomas Bartholins, co-founders of the University of Copenhagen, coined the term anthropology as "the science that treats of man." Writing more than a century later, French philosopher Jean-Jacques Rousseau (1755) formulated ideas about the natural human free from the oppressive effects of civilization that had profound effects on the field. While the institution of slavery was fast falling out of favor in Europe and America, his work informed a new generation of anti-slavery, pro-human rights philosophers.

The way Durkheim has shown through sociology that even the most private act of violence, suicide, has more to do with societal than individual characteristics, anthropology has revealed through its study of the ethnicity-, gender-, and class-based dimensions and cultural contributions to violence (Rylko-Bauer, Whiteford, & Farmer, 2009). We will later see how violent deaths, or suicide and homicide together, can also serve as barometers of the socioeconomic health of a society. Anthropology has also allowed for a break in a near-exclusive focus on the Global North, both geographically and in its point of view. American anthropologist Franz Boas (1938), for example, by withholding theory because of the complexity of cultures, encouraged detailed, objective recording and study of ethnographic findings; this led to the pioneering approach of studying cultures from their own historical background and perspective (Moore, 2008).

Ethnological Societies of Paris, London, and New York maintained international connections and published their own journals until the twentieth century, when many thousands of higher educational institutions established anthropology departments (Eriksen & Nielsen, 2001). The work of Boas and Polish anthropologist Bronisław Malinowski (1944) established the discipline's framework of long-term, in-depth examination of societies, with emphasis on immersion by the researcher. Drawing inspiration from these early works, anthropologists have used these findings and more modern methodologies to frame cultural critiques of racial ideologies, gender inequality, and, more recently, postcolonial oppression in favor of multiculturalism (Eriksen, 2004).

The cultural anthropological tradition is said to have originated in North America, while the social anthropological tradition has its roots in Europe (Rapport, 2014). *Cultural anthropology* emphasizes culturally patterned thought and behavior, placing great emphasis on the meanings that people make from, and the way they express themselves in, symbolic expressions such as art and myth (Winthrop, 1991). *Social anthropology*, on the other hand, is dedicated to the study of distant civilizations in their traditional as well as contemporary forms (Lewis, 2009).

As we begin our examination of these two disciplines, it is important to keep in mind that both have limitations when it comes to the study of violence. Sociology to date has largely avoided investigations of violence, leaving it out of its examination of social dynamics (Walby, 2012). It covers violence more consistently in the subfield of criminology, which does not deal with all of violence, since most crimes are not violent, and not all violence is criminal. Anthropology, on the other hand, is limited because of its intimate and field research methods. Because anthropologists often gather information while living within the culture they are studying or exploring formerly inhabited sites, the context of violent conflicts is difficult to research. Anthropology's purview being largely anti-theoretical and relativistic has made it blind to genocides about to happen (Scheper-Hughes, 2004). Despite some drawbacks, these two disciplines are indispensable to a broader understanding of violence.

Case Vignettes

A Cult of End Times

Aum Shinrikyo began as a 15-person meditation group in 1984 in Japan and grew into a movement with almost 50,000 members. Its financial assets amount to hundreds of millions of dollars, and it has facilities in several different countries, including the US,

Germany, Russia, Taiwan, and Sri Lanka. It also engages in assassinations, assembles unconventional weapons programs, and plots to overthrow the Japanese government. The scale and scope of the threat the group poses are not realized until the Tokyo subway sarin attack in 1995.

Shoko Asahara, Aum's self-proclaimed guru, leads the group according to a philosophy that combines elements of Buddhism, Hinduism, certain scientific matters, Nostradamus, and millennialism. Over the course of 8 years, Aum Shinrikyo evolves from a small organization offering yoga and meditation classes to a rich and destructive multinational entity. In the initial stage, Aum is an embryonic religious group that attracts Japanese adherents, mostly young people seeking spiritual and personal fulfillment. When asked about the initial appeal of Aum, followers recall that everyone in Aum was aiming for the same thing—raising their spiritual level. Aum members are seeking a more peaceful state of being and freedom from earthly troubles. Members attain a heightened level of spirituality through an ascetic lifestyle and meditation. This formative period lasts until the group's first known killing.

In October 1988, a young group member dies during a harsh initiation ceremony in front of Asahara and several other group members. This death calls into question the legitimacy and safety of the organization's practices. Additionally, Aum leaders fear that the death might adversely influence government authorities who are considering an appeal of their decision to delay granting the group certification as a religious organization. The leaders secretly dispose of the deceased member's body, which only adds to the discomfort of the members who witness the death. In April 1989, Asahara's most devoted followers kill a group member who witnessed the earlier fatal incident and wanted to leave the organization. Asahara justifies this killing as necessary to allow Aum to flourish and fulfill its mission of salvation. Asahara and his closest followers harbor an intense sense of grandiosity and mission. His righteousness and the divine destiny that he prophesizes enable them to justify violence and pave the way for more murders.

The time period following the group's defeat in the 1990 elections is marked by an increasing sense of paranoia in Aum and the development of an even more delusional worldview. Sometime after the elections, in 1992–1993, the group embarks on an ambitious weapons development and procurement program, using its offices abroad to amass weapons capabilities. Also during this period, Aum's violence extends beyond attacks on its own members and discrete assassinations, and includes indiscriminate attacks in the locales of its opponents. The group progresses from the killing of members for a higher purpose to assassinations of outside critics and, eventually, to larger and less-focused attacks. In July 1994, Aum members release a poisonous chemical agent, sarin, near a dormitory that houses three judges who are to rule on a land dispute between Aum and local citizens in Matsumoto who seek to prevent the group from entering their community. The attack kills seven people and injures several hundred, including the judges. The case is postponed. In 1995, the group uses liquid sarin in an attack on the Tokyo subway during morning rush hour. This attack marks a fundamental shift in the threat posed by terrorist groups: before it, terrorists rarely used chemical agents as weapons to inflict indiscriminate mass casualties. The attack is also unexpected, as the group is still not a recognized terrorist organization, but rather a religious group that many view as a cult. Japanese authorities are surprised by the scale of the killing, which claims 12 lives and injures a thousand more (Kaplan & Marshall, 1996).

Cults are groups with socially deviant or novel beliefs and practices that form around religious, spiritual, or philosophical themes or around a personality, object, or goal. They have been the object of sociological study in the context of the study of religious behavior since the 1930s. Examples may include political cults, doomsday cults, destructive cults, racist cults, polygamist cults, and terrorist cults.

Social Exclusion

John Durbeyfield, a poor peddler, is shocked to learn that he is the descendent of an ancient noble family, the d'Urbervilles, while Tess, his eldest daughter, joins the other village girls in the May Day dance, where Tess briefly exchanges glances with a young man named Angel Clare. Mr. Durbeyfield and his wife decide to send Tess to the d'Urberville mansion, where they hope Mrs. d'Urberville will make Tess's fortune and help the family. In reality, Mrs. d'Urberville is no relation to Tess: her husband, the merchant Simon Stokes, simply changed his name to d'Urberville after he retired. But Tess does not know this. The coquettish and forceful Alec d'Urberville, Mrs. d'Urberville's son, gets Tess a job tending fowl on the d'Urberville estate, and Tess has no choice but to accept because of an earlier accident involving her family's horse, her family's only means of income, for which she blames herself.

Tess spends several months at this job, all the while resisting Alec's attempts to seduce her. On the way to the d'Urberville estate one day, Alec drives his horse recklessly, and Tess pleads with him to stop. He continues at a fast pace and tells her to hold on to his waist. She complies only out of fear for her safety. Traveling down the next steep hill, he urges her to hold onto him again, but she refuses and pleads with him to slow down. He agrees to drive more slowly, but only if she will let him kiss her. Tess allows him to kiss her on the cheek. She wipes the kiss off with her handkerchief, and he becomes angry at her unwillingness to submit to his advances. They argue, and Tess finishes the journey on foot. Though she is dependent economically on Alec and is socially inferior to him, Tess tells him that his kissing her angers her, that she does not love him, and that his intercourse with other women offends her.

After several weeks at the d'Urbervilles, Tess goes to the market. Tess has not frequented this market very often but realizes that she likes it and plans to return to it. Several months later, she goes to the market and discovers that her visit coincides with a local fair. That evening, she waits for some friends to walk her home and declines Alec's offer to take her himself. When her friends are ready to leave, Tess finds that some of them are drunk, and they express their irritation that she has Alec's attention all to herself, growing increasingly coarse. Alec arrives on his horse, and Tess agrees to ride with him back to the d'Urbervilles estate. Alec lets the horse wander off the path deep into the woods, where he tries to convince Tess to take him as a lover. Tess continues to be reticent, and Alec realizes that they have become lost in the emerging fog. He gives Tess his coat and goes to look for a landmark. Still trying to win her favor as a lover, he tells Tess that he has bought her father a new horse. When he returns, Tess is asleep, and Alec uses the opportunity to take advantage of her in the forest. In Victorian England, any kind of premature sexual encounter would earn a young woman moral rebuke and social condemnation, regardless of how the man involved conducted himself. Soon, Tess returns home to her family to give birth to Alec's child, whom she names Sorrow, and a life of torment begins (Hardy, 1891).

Tess falls victim to the sexual double standard of society despite being a good woman, and suffers through no fault of her own. In this manner, societal conditions and standards, which generations have developed and applied throughout society, can override and determine the fate of an individual. Other interpretations highlight the tension between industrialization and peasantry, whereby Tess is an educated member of the rural working class, whom landed bourgeoisie, liberal idealism, and Christian moralism of a village thwart.

Social Negation

Deon is a man in his early thirties living with his mother. While he likes to tell everyone that he is taking care of her, the truth is, like many others in the inner-city ghetto, he has few prospects for supporting himself. Still, he will not tolerate anyone "dissing" (disrespecting) him by not treating him right or not granting him his "props" (proper deference). He has few friends but keeps a band of "homies" (those who would watch his back in a "jam"). In order to maintain their respect, he must be appropriately violent and manifest "nerve"; hence he would periodically take another person's possessions, mess with someone's woman, throw the first punch, or "get in someone's face." He is well aware that these displays can provoke a life-threatening response—many in his neighborhood have guns—but more important to him is to show that he lacks fear of death. Ten years ago, another man simply looked at him the wrong way, and he gratuitously beat the man with a metal pipe until he was bloody and unconscious. He served 18 months in jail, but this incident has earned him respect like never before. It also gave him a "ticket" to proving his manhood at the same time as having his basic needs met, such as food, clothing, and shelter, whenever the thought of depending on his mother or not counting in the eyes of society became too shameful (at least in jail he was "counted").

While growing up, he was said to be a "bright kid," but he could never focus well enough to get a decent education. His father was hardly around but according to rumors had set up two other families elsewhere; when he did appear, he beat him and his mother, who then had to take time off from her three jobs while everyone went hungry. The neighborhood offered little hope for a future, and now, one of his younger brothers is serving 40 years for killing two people, and the other is in jail more often than not for using and selling drugs. Deon, too, is familiar with the correctional system, having already served time for robbery, extortion, and aggravated assault.

The prison subculture hardened Deon's predisposition to violence further. He has learned to give unmistakable messages that he is capable of violence, even mayhem, whenever the situation calls for it. His facial expressions, his gait, and his aggressive talk, as well as his tattoos and clothing, are meant to ward off any attempts to challenge him. Even so, there are no guarantees, since people are always looking for a fight in order to increase their share of "juice," or the respect that is so hard to come by. If he is assaulted, he must show he is capable of avenging himself, or he risks being "tried" (challenged) or "rolled on" (physically assaulted)—even by his homies if he lost their respect. Deon would not give up on his honor, which depended entirely on his status on the street, and, like many others, would more than willingly risk dying than be dissed (Anderson, 1999).

Deon is a casualty of social forces beyond his control. "The code of the street" is as old as the world, where the law of the jungle reigns when dignity and identity are urgently at stake. Similar attitudes are increasingly seen at global scale, as entire countries and regions experience marginalization and negation in the new world order.

Warring Peoples

The Vikings were seafarers whose raids are recorded from the late eighth to the late eleventh centuries, and covered all the Atlantic shore down to the Portuguese coast. They were a beguiling combination of weapons, warrior ethos, and strategy, who mobilized on swift deployment. According to custom, all free Norse men were required to own and permitted to carry weapons at all times, which usually consisted of an iron helmet, a wooden round shield, an iron-chain mail shirt, and a sword (Fedrigo et al., 2017). Other offensive weapons were the wooden long bow, the spear, the dagger, and the battle-axe. However, probably the most important item in Viking raids was their ship, commonly known as the *drakkar*. It allowed sailing along the coast, and the Viking warfare strategy was land and take by surprise cities and monasteries that they would then pillage. During the Viking era, the Atlantic coast of Europe was almost permanently under siege (Barnard & Spencer, 2009). In combat, Vikings are thought to have engaged in a frenetic, furious style of fighting known as *berserkergang*, for which they have been termed *berserkers* (Wernick, 1979).

Another example of extremely effective use of swift and nimble light infantry is the Zulu army in the early nineteenth century. The Zulus are a Bantu ethnic group of Southern Africa who, toward the end of the eighteenth century, started a deep transformation that changed them from peaceful shepherds into one of the most formidable armies of the time. This occurred under the command of Shaka, who united what was once a confederation of tribes into an imposing empire. All young men were engaged in the army from youth until the age of 40, thus becoming particularly well-trained in fighting and enduring barefoot running over long distances. Their only weapon was a newly designed *assegai*, or a large blade halfway between a short spear and a long-handled dagger, which they handled like a sword. Specializing in lightning-fast approach and charge, their battle strategy was simple: the Zulu army presented a strong center to hold the enemy's attention, and then two wings to encircle the flanks, in addition to a reserve holding the army's rear (Barnard & Spencer, 2009). They faced and even defeated the British army with far superior firearms (David, 2005).

A people known for high levels of violence are the Yanomamö of South America, who have been described as being in a state of "chronic warfare." This culture values men who are strong, belligerent, and fierce. Yanomami warfare consists of ambushes and raiding of enemy villages. Disputes between men are resolved through club fights, where opponents alternately wallop each other on the head, usually until one man collapses. The scars on the head resulting from such exchanges are displayed with pride as signs of their aggressiveness (Chagnon, 1968). Interest in them has sparked a debate around whether violence and warfare are an inherent part of the culture, or a response to specific historical situations. Yanomami males are in constant conflict with neighboring tribes over local resources, and violence remains one of the leading causes of death. When Yanomami tribes fight and raid nearby tribes, they sometimes kill the children and rape and abduct the women (Ferguson, 1995). Wives are beaten with clubs, sticks, and machetes, and burning with a branding stick occurs often, symbolizing a man's dominance over his wife (Good & Chanoff, 1991).

Warriors from simple societies in the past and the present, as a whole, seemed more engaged in the performance than the killing aspect of warfare. They were experts with their choice weapons and with decorating their bodies. Armies faced each other for hours at a safe distance in a choreographic display of their fierce body-paintings and gear, hurling and shouting abuse, but hostilities tended to cease once someone was injured (Barnard & Spencer, 2009).

Domestic Terrorism

On April 15, 2013, two bomb blasts, 12 seconds apart, rock the finish line of the Boston Marathon, killing at least three people instantly and wounding more than 260, and leaving the street covered in blood. Medical professionals on hand to care for blisters and sore knees suddenly find themselves treating life-threatening lacerations and lost limbs. Emergency workers rush to the scene, despite the possibility of more blasts. The explosions blow out windows, send smoke into the sky, and leave victims piled on each other. About 30 people are transferred to hospitals under a Code Red for life-threatening injuries. The White House deems the bombing an act of terror. The attack truncates the world's most prestigious road race, which draws runners from across the globe. Three days later, the US Federal Bureau of Investigation releases photographs and surveillance videos showing two suspects walking near each other, each carrying a backpack. The suspects are identified as brothers whose family had emigrated to the US from Chechnya as asylum-seekers around 2002: 26-year-old Tamerlan Tsarnaev and 19-year-old Dzhokhar Tsarnaev. After a carjacking and a shootout with police, Tamerlan is shot by the police and run over by Dzhokhar as he attempts to escape in a car. Dzhokhar is found the next day, April 19, in a boat in a suburban backyard and taken into custody.

The investigators piece together a portrait of two brothers who were motivated by extremist Islamic beliefs but not acting with known terrorist groups—and who may have learned to build bombs from information on the internet. The two brothers represent a kind of emerging threat that federal authorities have long feared: angry and alienated young men who train themselves, unaffiliated with any particular terrorist group, but are able to use the internet to learn a lethal craft. The older brother, in particular, had been using internet sources to learn not only the philosophical beliefs of radical Islamist fundamentalist terrorists, but also components of how to build explosive devices from the online English magazine of the Qaeda affiliate in Yemen. The magazine's first issue came out in mid-2010 and contained bomb-making instructions in articles with titles such as: "Make a Bomb in the Kitchen of Your Mom." In February 2013, Tamerlan bought fireworks at a store about an hour's drive north of Boston. After looking for the most powerful kind, he settled on a reloadable mortar kit called a Lock and Load, which comes with a launch tube and shells. Tamerlan's ex-brother-in-law says Tamerlan had been enamored of conspiracy theories, and the wars in the Middle East also concerned him, as he looked for their connection to the oppression of Muslim populations around the globe (Cooper, Schmidt, & Schmitt, 2013).

Contrary to popular perception, radicalization into terrorism is not always the product of poverty, youth, ignorance, lack of education, lack of employment, criminality, or mental illness (Sageman, 2008). The internet, rather, can be a radicalizing forum, providing an anonymous way for like-minded, conflicted individuals to build on extremist ideologies they encounter. Other social networks that support radical beliefs can have similar effects. Prison systems can be such a place, as a study of ex-convicts who attended training camps in Yemen has shown (Johnson, 2011).

Sociological Theories

While human society is highly complex, it is possible to formulate theories about it and test them against empirical data. This is what makes sociology a science, one that is very valuable to the study of violence. Many of the topics sociologists have studied are closely related to the study of violence, including the root causes of poverty and crime and the problems associated with them. Sociology examines violence in the context of society: violence arises not from the individual but from the pressures and forces acting on the individual as a result of environment, institutions, and relationships. It is, in fact, impossible to study violence without taking the sociological viewpoint into consideration, for without the wider context even individual violence remains inexplicable and unpredictable. Central to the study of violence from a sociological point of view are the contending principles of functionalism and conflict theory. Let us examine each of these in turn.

The first approach we will study is functionalism. As far back as 1876, British philosopher Herbert Spencer suggested that the norms and institutions of any society function in much the same way as the organs of a body perform their separate functions to the benefit of the whole. In fact, *systems theory* in biology is still widely accepted as a working model for sociological research; it emphasizes drawing comparisons that allow researchers to visualize structures that are greater than their parts, but still part of a complete system (Giddens, 1984). Specifically human faculties, such as the power of speech, cultural traditions, and norms of morality evolve in the context of well-organized communities. Under this theory, societies and cultures can possess collective agency and work as a single, indivisible unit. Sociology can thus be a systematic study of social life that is important to the study of violence.

Unlike functionalist theories that emphasize the cohesiveness of systems, conflict theory critiques the inequality between particular groups, as in the fragmented states of pathology. Dissatisfied with the then-prevailing explanations of social problems in terms of the shortcomings of individuals, Marx and his collaborator Friedrich Engels defined *class consciousness*. As workers' awareness of themselves as a unified class in opposition to a capitalist system that oppresses them, it is the driving force behind social reform as the conflict between workers and oppressors finds expression in social conflict and change. History is a natural course of evolution that succeeds or fails in correcting these ills (Marx & Engels, 1848). Within this larger scope, *interactionism* has developed and become one of the dominant sociological perspectives of the modern age. It explores how humans interact in any given society and how social processes such as conflict, cooperation, and identity-formation arise from these interactions.

An important extension of this theory has been *symbolic interaction*, which focuses on the meaning that individuals make from their surroundings, and which reached its full bloom in the Chicago School before and after World War II (Fine, 1995). Instead of giving greater weight to the broader macro-level of society, symbolic interaction studies instead the more intimate micro-level, analyzing society in terms of the shared meanings and reality that people construct through their interactions. According to this particular school of thought, people use symbolic communication to navigate their surroundings, creating a complex, ever-changing web of collective meaning-construction (Macionis & Gerber, 2010). Shaped by Weber (1922), Mead (1964), and Erving Goffman (1959), among others, this perspective best bridges the symbolic character of human beings as discussed in Chapter 4 "The Symbolism (or Spiritual Causes) of Violence" and the social reality we construct through meaningful symbols.

Relevant to the theory of symbolism is the concept of *social belonging*, which Weber articulated as a fundamental human need that is essential for optimal functioning (Easterbrook & Vignoles, 2013). Factors within society that create a strong sense of belonging include relationships that have the characteristics of interdependence, frequent interactions, and intimacy (Baumeister & Leary, 1995). A lack of belonging has been connected to an increased risk of self-harm and suicide (Timmons et al., 2011). Closely related to a sense of belonging are the concepts of *social inclusion and exclusion*, which have strong links to beliefs in equality and inequality (Richmond & Saloojee, 2006). Movement toward political inclusion, for example, is a way to reduce political violence and violent protests (Osakwe, 2012). Similarly, reducing inequalities in gender norms can help reduce violence against women (Hilbert & Krishnan, 2000), and having strong cross-ethnic friendships is correlated with positive attitudes toward other racial groups (Tropp & Prenovost, 2008).

The next major sociological theory that is useful in the understanding of violence is *utilitarianism*, also known as *exchange theory*. It relies on two major assumptions: (a) viewing social interactions as an ongoing process of negotiations and exchange between parties, cost–benefit analyses and comparisons of alternatives are their constant basis; and (b) individuals, in interacting with others, will always seek to maximize their wins. Similar to rational choice theory in economics, people are assumed to be rational actors who have knowledge of the alternatives; knowledge of the possible consequences of each alternative; an ordering by preference of outcomes; and the ability to select among these alternatives (Whitford, 2002). However, unlike the standard economic model, the factors that affect social exchanges vary both over time and between individuals, and are therefore not reducible to a single quantitative exchange rate (West & Turner, 2007). Proponents of this theory include George C. Homans (1961), Peter Blau (1964), and Richard Emerson (1976). March and Simon (1958) brought nuances to the theory by noting that an individual's rationality is bounded by the context or organizational setting.

Various syntheses have emerged from these approaches, and sociology is helpful in its contribution of the *ecological framework* of violence, wherein levels of the individual, relationships, community, and society are in dynamic interrelation. By helping to navigate the difficult-to-resolve dichotomies of structure and agency, subjectivity and objectivity, and statistics and dynamics, sociology can raise questions concerning the ability of individuals to make free choices as well as the nature of observation, topics that have important implications to our understanding of violence. In other words, do individuals make free choices, or are there factors that limit these choices? Is observation primarily based in individual perception, or are there external, shared realities? Lastly, is it more useful to employ methods of historical evolution, or snapshots of social life? The ecological framework of sociology shows us that answers are neither simple nor mutually exclusive, but rather require careful consideration in matters such as our attempt to understand violence.

Anthropological Perspectives

While sociology has originated from attempts to describe the workings of society through the use of grand theories, anthropology is more concerned with demonstrating the variety of human societies, having cataloged and respected the ways in which these societies choose to characterize themselves. Broadly speaking, in our progression along the bio-psycho-socio-environmental paradigm of human affairs, we are moving from the intrapersonal to the interpersonal, and then from within society to the between-society comparisons of anthropology. Anthropology has been more concerned with showing than telling, although what it tells has grown more complex with time, allowing local stories to emerge on their own terms and interweaving them with local history and circumstances as they relate to global structures. A large body of research from biological anthropology demonstrates, for example, that violence results from competition neither automatically nor inevitably; rather, conflicts are settled by preventive or compensatory strategies far more often than by violent confrontation (Albers, 1993). Even the objective of war is not violence but the related profits.

While traditional anthropology has dealt with distant cultures, looking "across the tracks," such as in urban anthropology in the US, is becoming more popular (Hannerz, 1980). Whether studying local or distant cultures, certain principles and methodologies remain important. One of them is the use of both *emic* (insider) and *etic* (outsider) observations while studying a culture. These derive from the linguistic terms *phonemic* and *phonetic*: the former relates to language-specific sound units that a native speaker recognizes (but a foreigner does not), while the latter refers to objective, universal sounds that are common across languages. Phonemes solidify in the brain after a certain age range, and therefore when one tries to learn a foreign language, one carries the phonemes of one's own language to the new language, resulting in an "accent." Widening this distinction to cultures, insiders can reveal meanings and nuances of particular cultural features, while outsiders can identify the uniqueness and commonality of those features.

Cultural context needs to be examined both sensitively and critically, since traditions are sometimes used to justify practices that perpetrate violence, such as violence against women, female genital mutilation, or the use of severe corporal punishment at school. The pervasive nature of culture makes it difficult to describe when one is too close, while understanding its intricate meanings is difficult from the outside. These concepts then lead to universalist versus relativist notions. *Universalists* would argue that violence, like any illness, is innate (e.g., a biological "instinct") and ubiquitous, and differences are superficial because culture is "added onto" the universal core. Psychiatric disorders, for example, were once considered universal at the core with different expressions only because of different cultural conventions. However, even schizophrenia, which has an almost uniform prevalence of 1% throughout the world, is found to look vastly different with a far better prognosis in less economically developed countries

(Jablensky et al., 1994). *Relativists* emphasize the studies that increasingly underscore how culture not only shapes individual meaning and significance but also determines the causes, manifestations, and final course of many major psychiatric illnesses. Similarly, anthropology provides insights into violence that pertain to conceptual issues, cross-cultural variation, the relative influence of biology and culture, gender differences, and transmission of conflict.

Human cultures exhibit marked variations in violence, and there are many peaceful ones: the Anabaptists of North America, the Buid of the Philippines, the Chewong of Malaysia, the Piaroa of Amazonia, the Semai of Malaysia, the Toraja of Indonesia, and some Zapotec communities of Mexico are examples. Even the most violent societies are not violent all the time, and even societies at war have more areas at peace than at war, and it seems productive to consider the cultural characteristics of peaceful societies to help inform possible means of prevention. A review of 24 peaceful societies (Bonta, 1996) has shown, for example, that their methods of resolving conflict differ greatly from those of other, more violent societies, while their worldviews of peacefulness create structures that reinforce those views. The review reveals that over half of peaceful societies have no recorded violence; they rarely punish other adults (apart from the threat of ostracism); they handle conflicts with outside societies in the same peaceful ways that they approach internal conflicts; they do not look to governments to handle internal disputes; and they have a highly negative view of conflict. Peaceful societies are also more likely to solve conflicts through diplomacy and dialogue, while prolonged periods of peace enable them to achieve new levels of development (Fleishman, Gerard, & O'Leary, 2008).

The existence of peaceful societies supports the highly *symbolic* and *subjective*, rather than practical and objective, nature of violence. Human nature is both potentially aggressive and destructive and potentially orderly and constructive (Mead, 1942). The notion of *violent imaginaries* arises from the view that violence needs to be imagined before it is carried out (Schmidt & Schröder, 2001). As we saw with the symbolic nature of human beings in Chapter 4, cultures, like individuals, do not strike out at random but follow cultural norms of appropriate action, shared moral imperatives, rites, rituals, and meaning. One feature of violence we might highlight is its *performative* quality. Violent acts are meaningful because they stage power and legitimacy, which is socially more important than the actual physical results. American anthropologist Veena Das (2000) notes that a new form of violence has emerged in the last few decades, going beyond contractual violence to involve global flows of images, capital, and people within the same local world. That is to say, wars are no longer fought *over* resources, but are rather *themselves* resources for making and remaking worldviews. A good example of this is the violence in Northern Ireland, which has had the effect of sharply dividing Protestants and Catholics, rather than being merely a symptom of existing differences (Feldman, 1991). The Israeli-Palestinian conflict is another, where victims and perpetrators frame the experience of violence quite differently in order to reclaim agency and political identity (Peteet, 1994).

Stories can keep alive the memory of past glories (Meeker, 1979; Rosaldo, 1980) or perceived injustices (Malkki, 1995; Swedenburg, 1995), which states can capitalize on to promote violence to their own ends (Čolović, 1995). In real terms, this means that all forms of mass media as well as public rituals can dramatize and intensify antagonism (Jarman, 1997); examples are the arousal of war frenzy in fascist Germany and Italy and in post-September 11 United States (Kellner, 2010). These forms of mass appeal do not only occur in the context of war, however; they can apply wherever symbolic representations are perceived to be under threat. Because globalization has made it more difficult for individuals to retain an identity based on place and history, nationalism, ethnicity, and religion have become high currencies in conflict (Appadurai, 1998; Kapferer, 1988). To study contemporary ethnic and religious conflict outside of these symbolic interpretations is to ignore their meaning, as *violent imaginaries* only become violent actions as a result of their cultural and social importance and interpretation. While these are seldom entirely new inventions or discontinuous from realities, a reframing for current application instigates action. State failure can sometimes facilitate subsequent political violence by making these representations more prominent (Kosmatopoulos, 2011).

Need for Belonging

One of the central themes of sociology is the relationship between self and society. We are far more connected than apparent, and the basic human need, the need for love, is relevant not only at the interpersonal but also at the societal level. It manifests in the form and experience of a need for social belonging. We exist in an ecology, with individual, relationship, community, and societal levels, and love at all those levels is necessary for healthy growth. Just as the Greeks identified different kinds of love (e.g., *storge, philia, eros,* and *agape*), there are different kinds of needs (e.g., self-directed, relationship, community, and societal). A sense of belonging in society fulfills the need for love and fuels a capacity to love others. A culture of exploitation, deprivation, and defense, on the other hand, acts much like the dynamic of shame at the individual level. Whereas the most vulnerable portions of the population fall victim to violence first, the entire structure of society has a role, and a society that is divided against itself is no less self-destructive than an individual who is less than "whole" (we have spoken of the characteristic of wholeness in health in "The Psychology of Violence"). Anomie, poverty, social segregation, and marginalization are the conditions that make the struggle for identity, belonging, power, and recognition predominate in the pursuit of meaning. Violence rates, therefore, serve as a barometer for the overall health of a society, and we know well from the high water marks of civilization that peace usually accompanies creativity and productivity in the arts and compassion and sharing in social policies.

Violent societies vary greatly, but a common characteristic is inequality. Strict hierarchies such as Japan before World War I, the Kwakiutl Native American society, the Yanomami people of South America, and the American South, particularly in the nineteenth century, were all highly stratified societies, with privileged classes. This means there were always groups that belonged less and shared less in the resources and the prestige. In these societies, violence became a great source of honor and pride, while cowardice was a source of shame. Social codes that often emphasized honor to the death led to high rates of war and violence.

The same dynamic occurs in male violence: in patriarchies, strict gender roles and cultural norms cause men to establish masculinity and especially violent masculinity to set themselves apart from women as well as from other men (Meuser, 2002). This occurs also with age: where age groups are segregated, violent behavior peaks in individuals in their late teens and early twenties, and then quickly tapers off. We see it in ethnic variations: communities with substantial minority populations have higher rates of violence, even when accounting for other influences (Hipp, 2010). Finally, we see it in relative poverty (Merton, 1938). Violence is thus more about identity and recognition, not survival—about attention and approval, not gratification. Consequently, the claims of belonging and exclusion are used as a strategy for escalation in these social pursuits. Violence is thus a barometer for social and economic inequalities and is "individualized" insofar as it exposes the loss of social bonding forces on the one hand, and on the other, the variation in extent of individual ways of coping with social problems (Heitmeyer & Hagan, 2003). This is the *social truth* we live in, according to Durkheim (1893).

Social solidarity, on the other hand, is a feeling of participation in and connection to a group that provides cohesion and meaning. It transcends individual relationships, even though it in large part derives from them. Peaceful societies are also diverse but have in common characteristics of equality and community togetherness. Examples include the Inuits of Greenland, the Ladakhi of India, the Nubians of Egypt, and the Kibbutzim societies in Israel. A lack of social hierarchy and rivalry marks them, as well as community-centeredness and equal sharing. "Primitive" societies provided a sense of belonging automatically based on likeness and similarity of situation. Modern societies give value to one another more out of recognition of need: interdependence can create social solidarity. In modern times, this may happen through a shared belief in individual dignity, in human rights—which are powerful concepts for the United Nations, international law, and other universal norms and customs (Steiner & Alston, 2000). As American Reformed theologian Reinhold Niebuhr noted, and as American philosopher Cornell West echoed, love takes the form of justice in public (Sharlet, 2009). Personal relationships cannot entirely supplant love at the societal level, and the shame experience we observe in individuals who become violent (Gilligan, 1996) has its origins in the discrimination, marginalization, and humiliation of entire groups.

Anthropological research has contributed, at a global level, to a sense of belonging for all cultures. As a field, it has a pronounced tradition of advocacy and activism, going back at least to the days when Boas challenged "scientific" racism to insist on racial equality and advocated that cultures be understood in their own terms. Through showing that marginalized or repressed cultures matter, and the encouragement of multicultural and value-free thinking, the discipline has been at the forefront of promoting *cultural justice.* American anthropologist Margaret Mead, who also believed that anthropology had a role in social activism, is famous for saying: "Never doubt that a small group of thoughtful, committed citizens can change the world. Indeed, it is the only thing that ever has" (Sommers & Dineen, 1984).

Conclusion

It is interesting to note how sociology and anthropology have converged over time, and how they now share many of the same methodologies and areas of study. Despite this, neither has yet produced groundbreaking theories or explanations of violence and the role that violence plays in society or for the individual (Accomazzo, 2012; Malesevic, 2010). Violence therefore remains an area of great potential exploration for these critical fields. In this chapter, we showed how sociology and anthropology are important in illuminating the vast social and cultural influences on the individual. We explored how, bringing complexity to our understanding of violence, the two fields can add to the various theories about societal dynamics as well as cultural variety. Above all, a better awareness of these fields can help us to develop a bio-psycho-socio-environmental perspective that is more comprehensive. Indeed, understanding how local, national, and global processes interlink at micro- and macro-levels has become critical for understanding how violence arises at any level.

A better understanding of both sociology and anthropology can reveal a lot about the social and cultural dynamics of violence. Although the study of violence in these disciplines is only beginning to develop, the growing emphasis on the Global South, on minorities and gender-related issues, and on the changes in form and visibility that violence creates make these areas especially valuable. For example, research on violence in relation to inequalities of gender, ethnicity, sexuality, and religion is advancing our understanding of new forms of violence (Ertürk & Purkayastha, 2012; Iganski, 2008). Experiences of postcolonialism, war, and conflict zones are important in these new forms of violence (Caforio & Kümmel, 2005; Fanon, 1990). As this body of knowledge grows, we are becoming more aware of how local, national, international, and global processes are all interconnected, linking macro- and micro-levels in ways that can influence violence rates at all levels.

Sociological and anthropological models are useful in the study of violence, as they high-light the interactions between these different levels (Purkayastha, 2009) and subsequently how different types of violence are interconnected (Lee et al., 2014). Their uniquely inti-mate and detailed ethnographic methods are also revealing (Moore, 2008). Recent attempts to analyze violence from perspectives other than merely the criminal or the political (Malesevic, 2010; Ray, 2011; Scheper-Hughes & Bourgois, 2004; Wieviorka, 2009) offer hope to the possibility that sociology and anthropology will offer ways to elucidate impor-tant dynamic relationships between these different spheres.

Questions

1 What does it mean to say that human violence occurs in a social and cultural context?

2 What are the major ways in which sociology theorizes about human society?

3 What are some of the ways anthropology demonstrates the variety among human societies?

4 How does the need for social belonging help explain individual violence?

5 How do cultural symbols help explain the subjective and "imaginary" nature of violence?

References

Abend, G. (2008). The meaning of "theory". *Sociological Theory, 26*(2), 173–199.

Accomazzo, S. (2012). Anthropology of violence: Historical and current theories, concepts, and debates in physical and socio-cultural anthropology. *Journal of Human Behavior in the Social Environment, 22*(5), 535–552.

Albers, P. (1993). Symbiosis, merger, and war: Contrasting forms of intertribal relationships among historic plains Indians. In J. H. Moore (Ed.), *The political economy of north American Indians*. Norman, OK: University of Oklahoma Press.

Anderson, E. (1999). *Code of the street: Decency, violence, and the moral life of the Inner City*. New York, NY: Norton and Company.

Appadurai, A. (1998). Dead certainty: Ethnic violence in the era of globalization. *Development and Change, 29*(4), 905–925.

Aristotle (1598). *Aristotles politiques, or discourses of gouernment* (A. Islip, Trans.). London, England: Islip.

Barnard, A., & Spencer, J. (2009). *Encyclopedia of social and cultural anthropology*. Florence, KY: Routledge.

Bartholin, C., & Bartholin, T. (1647). *Preface. Institutions anatomiques de Gaspar Bartholin, augmentées et enrichies pour la seconde fois tant des opinions et observations nouvelles des modernes*. Paris, France: Hénault et Hénault.

Baumeister, R. F., & Leary, M. R. (1995). The need to belong: Desire for interpersonal attachments as a fundamental human motivation. *Psychological Bulletin, 117*(3), 497–529.

Benedict, R. (1934). *Patterns of culture*. Boston, MA: Mifflin Company.

Blau, P. M. (1964). *Exchange and power in social life*. New York, NY: Wiley.

Boas, F. (1938). *The mind of primitive man*. New York, NY: Macmillan.

Bonta, B. D. (1996). Conflict resolution among peaceful societies: The culture of peacefulness. *Journal of Peace Research, 33*(4), 403–420.

Caforio, G., & Kümmel, G. (2005). *Military missions and their implications reconsidered: The aftermath of September 11th.* Amsterdam, Netherlands: Elsevier.

Chagnon, N. A. (1968). *Yanomamö: The fierce people.* New York, NY: Holt, Rinehart and Winston.

Čolović, I. (1995). *Bordell der Krieger: Folklore, Politik und Krieg.* Osnabrück, Germany: Fibre.

Comte, A. (1848). *Discours sur l'ensemble du positivisme. Ou, Exposition sommarie de la doctrine philosophique et sociale propre à la grande république occidentale, etc.* Paris, France.

Confucius (1861). *Confucian analects, the great learning, and the doctrine of the mean* (J. Legge, Trans.). London, UK: Trübner.

Cooley, C. H., & Angell, R. C. (1930). *Sociological theory and social research: Selected papers of Charles Horton Cooley.* New York, NY: Holt and Company.

Cooper, M., Schmidt, M. S., & Schmitt, E. (2013, April 23). Boston suspects are seen as self-taught and fueled by Web. *New York Times.* Retrieved from http://www.nytimes.com/2013/04/24/us/boston-marathon-bombing-developments.html?hpandpagewanted=allandmtrref=en

Dahrendorf, R. (1958). Toward a theory of social conflict. *Journal of Conflict Resolution, 2*(2), 170–183.

Das, V. (2000). *Violence and subjectivity.* Berkeley, CA: University of California Press.

David, S. (2005). *Zulu, the heroism and tragedy of the Zulu war of 1879.* London, UK: Penguin Books.

Dennis, A., & Martin, P. J. (2005). Symbolic interactionism and the concept of power. *British Journal of Sociology, 56*(2), 191–213.

Durkheim, E. (1893). *De la Division du travail social: Étude sur l'organisation des sociétés supérieures.* Paris: Presses universitaires de France.

Durkheim, E. (1894). Les règles de la méthode sociologique. *Revue Philosophique de la France et de l'Étranger, 37*, 465–498.

Durkheim, E. (1897). *Le suicide, étude de sociologie.* Paris, France: Alcan.

Easterbrook, M., & Vignoles, V. L. (2013). What does it mean to belong? *European Journal of Social Psychology, 43*(6), 455–462.

Emerson, R. M. (1976). Social exchange theory. *Annual Review of Sociology, 2*, 335–362.

Enan, M. A. (Ed.) (2007). *Ibn Khaldun: His life and works.* Kuala Lumpur, Malaysia: Other Press Sdn Bhd.

Eriksen, T. H. (2004). *What is anthropology?.* London, UK: Pluto.

Eriksen, T. H., & Nielsen, F. S. (2001). *A history of anthropology.* London, UK: Pluto Press.

Ertürk, Y., & Purkayastha, B. (2012). Linking research, policy and action: A look at the work of the special rapporteur on violence against women. *Current Sociology, 60*(1), 142–160.

Fanon, F. (1990). *The wretched of the earth.* London, UK: Penguin.

Fedrigo, A., Grazzi, F., Williams, A. R., Panzner, T., Lefmann, K., Lindelof, P. E., … Strobl, M. (2017). Extraction of archaeological information from metallic artefacts—A neutron diffraction study on Viking swords. *Journal of Archaeological Science: Reports, 12*, 425–436.

Feldman, A. (1991). *Formations of violence: The narrative of the body and political terror in Northern Ireland.* Chicago, IL: University of Chicago Press.

Ferguson, R. B. (1995). *Yanomami warfare: A political history.* Seattle, WA: University of Washington Press.

Fine, G. A. (1995). *A second Chicago school? The development of a postwar American sociology.* Chicago, IL: University of Chicago Press.

Fleishman, R., Gerard, C., & O'Leary, R. (2008). *Pushing the boundaries: New frontiers in conflict resolution and collaboration.* Bingley, U.K.: Emerald Group Publishing.

Geertz, C. (1983). *Local knowledge: Further essays in interpretive anthropology*. New York, NY: Basic Books.

Giddens, A. (1984). *The constitution of society: Outline of the theory of structuration*. Cambridge, UK: Polity Press.

Giddens, A., Duneier, M., & Applebaum, R. (2007). *Introduction to sociology* (6th ed.). New York, NY: Norton and Company.

Gilligan, J. (1996). *Violence: Our deadly epidemic and its causes*. New York, NY: Putnam.

Goffman, E. (1959). *The presentation of self in everyday life*. Garden City, NY: Doubleday.

Good, K., & Chanoff, D. (1991). *Into the heart: One man's pursuit of love and knowledge among the Yanomama*. New York, NY: Simon and Schuster.

Habermas, J. (1987). *The philosophical discourse of modernity: Modernity's consciousness of time*. Cambridge, UK: Polity Press.

Hannerz, U. (1980). *Exploring the City: Inquiries toward an urban anthropology*. New York, NY: Columbia University Press.

Hardy, T. (1891). *Tess of the D'Urbervilles, a pure woman*. London, UK: Collins.

Heitmeyer, W., & Hagan, J. (2003). *International handbook on violence research*. Dordrecht, Netherlands: Kluwer.

Hilbert, J. C., & Krishnan, S. P. (2000). Addressing barriers to community care of battered women in rural environments: Creating a policy of social inclusion. *Journal of Health and Social Policy*, *12*(1), 41–52.

Hipp, J. (2010). A dynamic view of neighborhoods: The reciprocal relationship between crime and neighborhood characteristics. *Social Problems*, *57*(2), 205–230.

Homans, G. C. (1961). *Human behavior: Its elementary forms*. New York, NY: Harcourt.

Iganski, P. (2008). *"Hate crime" and the city*. Bristol, UK: Policy Press.

Jablensky, A., Sartorius, N., Cooper, J. E., Anker, M., Korten, A., & Bertelsen, A. (1994). Culture and schizophrenia. *British Journal of Psychiatry*, *165*, 434–436.

Jarman, N. (1997). *Material conflicts: Parades and visual displays in Northern Ireland*. Oxford, UK: Berg.

Johnson, T. (2011). *Threat of homegrown Islamist terrorism*. New York, NY: Council on Foreign Relations. Retrieved from https://www.cfr.org/backgrounder/threat-homegrown-islamist-terrorism#p4

Jones, S. S. (2007). Functionalism of mind and functionalism of society: The concept of conscience and Durkheim's division of social labour. *Durkheimian Studies*, *13*(1), 85–104.

Kapferer, B. (1988). *Legends of people, myths of state: Violence, intolerance, and political culture in Sri Lanka and Australia*. Washington, DC: Smithsonian Institution Press.

Kaplan, D. E., & Marshall, A. (1996). *The cult at the end of the world: The terrifying story of the Aum doomsday cult, from the subways of Tokyo to the nuclear arsenals of Russia*. New York, NY: Random House.

Kellner, D. (2010). *Cinema wars: Hollywood film and politics in the Bush-Cheney era*. West Sussex, UK: Wiley-Blackwell.

Kosmatopoulos, N. (2011). Toward an anthropology of "state failure": Lebanon's Leviathan and peace expertise. *Social Analysis*, *55*(3), 115–142.

Lee, B. X., Marotta, P. L., Blay-Tofey, M., Wang, W., & de Bourmont, S. (2014). Economic correlates of violent death rates in forty countries, 1962–2008: A cross-typological analysis. *Aggression and Violent Behavior*, *19*(6), 729–737.

Lee, B. X., Wexler, B. E., & Gilligan, J. (2014). Political correlates of violent death rates in the U.S., 1900–2010: Longitudinal and cross-sectional analyses. *Aggression and Violent Behavior*, *19*(6), 721–728.

Lewis, I. M. (2009). *Social and cultural anthropology in perspective: Their relevance in the modern world*. New Brunswick, NJ: Transaction Publishers.

Macionis, J. J., & Gerber, L. M. (2010). *Sociology*. Toronto, ON: Pearson Education Canada.

Malesevic, S. (2010). *The sociology of war and peace*. Cambridge, UK: Cambridge University Press.

Malinowski, B. (1944). *A scientific theory of culture and other essays*. Chapel Hill, NC: University of North Carolina Press.

Malkki, L. H. (1995). *Purity and exile: Violence, memory, and national cosmology among Hutu refugees in Tanzania*. Chicago, IL: University of Chicago Press.

March, J. G., & Simon, H. A. (1958). *Organizations*. New York, NY: Wiley.

Marx, K., & Engels, F. (1848). *The manifesto of the communist party*. London, UK: Workers' Educational Association.

Mead, G. H. (1934). *Mind, self, and society*. Chicago, IL: University of Chicago Press.

Mead, G. H. (1964). *On social psychology: Selected papers*. Chicago, IL: University of Chicago Press.

Mead, M. (1942). *And keep your powder dry: An anthropologist looks at America*. New York, NY: Morrow and Company.

Meeker, M. E. (1979). *Literature and violence in North Arabia*. Cambridge, UK: Cambridge University Press.

Merton, R. (1938). Social structure and anomie. *American Sociological Review, 3*(5), 672–682.

Meuser, M. (2002). Doing masculinity. Zur Geschlechtslogik männlichen Gewalthandelns. In R.-M. Dackweiler, & R. Schäfer (Eds.), *Gewalt-Verhältnisse. Feministische Perspektiven auf Geschlecht und Gewalt* (pp. 53–78). New York, NY: Campus.

Moore, J. (2008). *Visions of culture: An introduction to anthropological theories and theorists*. Lanham, MD: Altamira Press.

Osakwe, E. (2012). The dynamics of citizenship participation and inclusion in Nigeria. *International Journal of Interdisciplinary Social Sciences, 6*(11), 53–61.

Peteet, J. (1994). Male gender and rituals of resistance in the Palestinian intifada: A cultural politics of violence. *American Ethnologist, 21*(1), 31–49.

Plato (1763). *The republic*. (H. Spens, Trans.). Glasgow, UK: R. and A. Foulis.

Purkayastha, B. (2009). Many views on peace. In G. Caforio (Ed.), *Advances in military sociology: Essays in honor of Charles C. Moskos*. Bingley, UK: Emerald.

Rapport, N. (2014). *Social and cultural anthropology: The key concepts*. London, UK: Routledge.

Ray, L. (2011). *Violence and society*. London, UK: Sage.

Richmond, T., & Saloojee, A. (2006). *Social inclusion: Canadian perspectives*. Chicago, IL: Independent Publishers Group.

Rosaldo, R. (1980). *Ilongot headhunting, 1883–1974: A study in society and history*. Stanford, CA: Stanford University Press.

Rousseau, J. J. (1755). *Discours sur l'origine et les fondements de l'inegalité parmi les hommes*. Amsterdam, The Netherlands: Rey.

Rylko-Bauer, B., Whiteford, L. M., & Farmer, P. (2009). *Global health in times of violence*. Santa Fe, NM: School for Advanced Research Press.

Sageman, M. (2008). *Leaderless Jihad: Terror networks in the twenty-first century*. Philadelphia, PA: University of Pennsylvania Press.

Scheper-Hughes, N. (2004). Ishi's brain, Ishi's ashes: Anthropology and genocide. In N. Scheper-Hughes, & P. Bourgois (Eds.), *Violence in war and peace: An anthology* (pp. 61–68). Oxford, UK: Blackwell.

Scheper-Hughes, N., & Bourgois, P. (2004). Introduction: Making sense of violence. In N. Scheper-Hughes, & P. Bourgois (Eds.), *Violence in war and peace: An anthology* (pp. 1–27). Oxford, UK: Blackwell.

Schmidt, B. E., & Schröder, I. (2001). *Anthropology of violence and conflict*. New York, NY: Routledge.

Scupin, R., & DeCorse, C. R. (2016). *Anthropology: A global perspective*. Boston, MA: Pearson.

Sharlet, J. (2009). The supreme love and revolutionary funk of Dr. Cornel West, philosopher of the blues. Rolling Stone, May 28, 54–61.

Sommers, F. G., & Dineen, T. (1984). *Curing nuclear madness: A new-age prescription for personal action*. Toronto, ON: Methuen.

Spencer, H. (1876). *The principles of sociology*. London, UK: Williams and Norgate.

Steiner, H. J., & Alston, P. (2000). *International human rights in context: Law, politics, morals*. Oxford, UK: Oxford University Press.

Swedenburg, T. (1995). *Memories of revolt: The 1936–1939 rebellion and the Palestinian National Past*. Minneapolis, MN: University of Minnesota Press.

Thomas, W. I., & Thomas, D. S. (1928). *The child in America: Behavior problems and programs*. New York, NY: Knopf.

Timmons, K. A., Selby, E. A., Lewinsohn, P. M., & Joiner, T. E. (2011). Parental displacement and adolescent suicidality: Exploring the role of failed belonging. *Journal of Clinical Child and Adolescent Psychology, 40*(6), 807–817.

Tropp, L. R., & Prenovost, M. A. (2008). The role of intergroup contact in predicting children's interethnic attitudes: Evidence from meta-analytic and field studies. In S. R. Levy, & M. Killen (Eds.), *Intergroup attitudes and relations in childhood through adulthood* (pp. 236–248). New York, NY: Oxford University Press.

Wacquant, L. (1993). Positivism. In W. Outhwaite, & T. B. Bottomore (Eds.), *Blackwell dictionary of twentieth-century social thought*. Oxford, UK: Blackwell.

Walby, S. (2012). Violence and society: Introduction to an emerging field of sociology. *Current Sociology, 61*(2), 95–111.

Weber, M. (1922). *Die protestantische Ethik und der Geist des Kapitalismus: Die protestantischen Sekten und der Geist des Kapitalismus; Die Wirtschaftsethik der Weltreligionen*. Tübingen, Germany: J.B.C. Mohr.

Wernick, R. (1979). *Vikings*. Alexandria, VA: Time-Life Books.

West, R., & Turner, L. (2007). *Introducing communication theory: Analysis and application*. Boston, MA: McGraw-Hill.

Whitford, J. (2002). Pragmatism and the untenable dualism of means and ends: Why rational choice theory does not deserve paradigmatic privilege. *Theory and Society, 31*(3), 325–363.

Wieviorka, M. (2009). *Violence: A new approach*. London, UK: Sage.

Winthrop, R. (1991). *Dictionary of concepts in cultural anthropology*. Westport, CT: Greenwood.

6

The Political Science and Economics of Violence

Introduction

> Peace is not an absence of war, it is a virtue, a state of mind, a disposition for benevolence, confidence, justice.
>
> —*Baruch de Spinoza,* A Theologico-Political Treatise *(1670)*

Political and economic forces are such important and ubiquitous factors in the modern world that we can hardly leave them out of any analysis of violence. The disciplines that deal with these forces have made useful contributions to elucidating the relationship between human societal structures and the phenomenon of violence. Political science is the study of systems of government and the analysis of political activity and political behavior. The study of violence in political science has boomed in the past couple of decades, catapulting from being a peripheral topic to one of central concern. Most notably, the field's innovative multidisciplinary perspective has allowed it to accomplish in practice what public health has asserted in theory. It is a useful model for adapting the bio-psycho-socio-environmental perspective of violence. Economics is a social science that studies the various factors that affect the production, distribution, and consumption of goods and services. Because the field has many important implications at all levels of society, its analyses on how economies work and how economic agents behave and interact within economies has become important to the study of human violence. It is interesting and informative to note the overlap that exists between the study of violence in these two fields, as economics drive the dominant political forces in society while those same political forces largely determine the distribution of power and resources.

Political science has been adaptable in the face of the changing forms of human violence. Traditionally, international relations was the first subfield to address the issue of violence systematically, and it focused almost exclusively on the most obvious manifestation of violence: interstate war. Since the middle of the twentieth century, however, incidents of interstate conflict and organized civil war have steadily decreased, and the emphasis of study has gradually changed (Urdal, 2006). While interstate violence has been declining, the threat of violence, the use of violence for political ends, and the unpredictable forms and consequences of violence—such as terrorism—have become perhaps more pervasive throughout the world. Amid this landscape, political science has been one of the first disciplines to understand that the complex, multifaceted nature of violence is impossible to understand in isolation, and it has adapted to these changing realities by drawing from the broader literature on crime, gang wars, riots, rebellions, revolution, state repression, and genocide to help explain violence in the political sphere. As a result, political science has been instrumental in bringing together scholars of international security, area studies, comparative politics, development, ethnography, international law, and military studies.

The field of economics has in recent years also been making similar progress in its attempt to understand violence, but using a very different approach. Accumulating research shows a correspondence between income or growth measures and conflict or behavioral violence. In an effort to explain these links, the field has tried to advance theories along the lines of *behavioral economics*, or a method of economic analysis that applies psychological insights into human behavior to explain economic decision-making. Although the simplicity of singular theories may seem to undermine the complex nature of violence, they are important illustrators of *systemic contributors* to violence: violence is not something that "just happens;" instead, often, economic problems and crises create the grounds for eventual violent expressions. The violence that arises, in turn, can then have a destabilizing effect on society and contribute to economic decline. Viewed in this light, the study of economics can provide useful insight as to how human-created systems and forces can influence violent behavior.

This chapter will therefore show how the disciplines of political science and economics have made useful contributions to understanding the relationship between human societal structures and violence. We will review how political science has brought diverse fields together, while economics has endeavored to develop coherent theories. We will examine the concept of power and how it can turn into domination or build on economic wealth, leading to conflict.

Evolution of the Two Disciplines

Although political science has roots going back more than 2000 years, to the writings of Chanakya, Plato, and Aristotle, a formal approach to the study of political science began with Italian diplomat Niccolò Machiavelli (1469–1527) and became codified during the nineteenth century. Machiavelli, however, formulated his political theory around the notion of a powerful prince or state that would not hesitate to use immoral or even criminal means to gain power and emphasized fear over being loved. He argued for the role of a strong military—concepts that shape political practice and realities to this day. Fascination with the characteristics that determine an ideal state had held sway for as long as societies have existed, and fields such as political and moral philosophy, political theology, history, and political economy arose. It was not until the early twentieth century, however, that American political science broke from the more traditional fields of history and economics through a desire to advance a more scientific study of politics (Gunnell, 2006). Political science is a branch of knowledge that deals with systems of government and analyzes political bodies to identify patterns, draw conclusions, and formulate theories. However, because it is essentially a study of human behavior within the context of real political situations that are difficult to control, it is an observational, as opposed to an experimental, science (Lowell, 1910).

The field gained more popularity and developed its own language after World War I (Blatt, 2009). Political science is more complex than political history. It incorporates the study of political activity and behavior, as well as the distribution of power and resources (Stoner, 2008). The 1950s and 1960s introduced a shift in focus by emphasizing the systematic and scientific study of governance, the dynamics of political activity, and political thought and behavior in place of the conventional focus on institutions and legal texts (Converse, 1970; Dahl, 1961). This resulted in the development of experimental political science (Druckman et al., 2011), which uses experimental methods, statistical analyses, and model building. This progressive thinking continued through the 1960s and 1970s, borrowing heavily from *game theory* of economics as the analytical basis for studying political institutions and behavior (Riker & Ordeshook, 1973). Game theory uses mathematical models of conflict and cooperation between "intelligent and rational" decision-makers. The field has made considerable progress using these approaches, but a unified systematic theory has been slow to develop (Hill, 2012), and more recently, it has had to allow for psychology and "irrational" elements in order to explain events. In view of this, it has adopted *methodological pluralism*—drawing inspiration from a wide variety of methods and theoretical approaches—which has become its defining feature as well as its strength.

Economic writings date back to the earliest civilizations, but the thirteenth-century Italian theologian and jurist Thomas Aquinas founded scientific economics when he used a natural-law perspective to explain monetary, interest, and value theory (Schumpeter, 1954). The disappearance of feudalism and the rise of economic nationalism in Europe set the stage for two contending economic perspectives. *Mercantilists* argued for the use of gold or silver and trade as the basis of wealth accumulation, typically under state regulation to the detriment of rival national powers. In contrast to this, *physiocrats* advocated the importance of land, agriculture, and labor as responsible for wealth creation, and were in favor of a laissez-faire policy of economics with minimal involvement by the government (Blaug, 1997).

In *The wealth of nations*, Scottish moral philosopher Adam Smith (1786) formalized economic thought and laid the foundation of classic free market economic theory, signaling the birth of economics as a discipline (Blaug, 2007). His *resource-allocation theory* states that the interaction of supply, demand, and prices in the market will result in an equal rate of return that eventually achieves a general equilibrium (Stigler, 1976). English cleric and scholar Thomas Malthus (1798), however, argued a theory of diminishing returns, postulating that the geometrically growing population will eventually outstrip food production, which increases arithmetically. In contrast to Smith's emphasis on production, English political economist David Ricardo (1817) focused on distribution and pointed out that the population and capital growth would inevitably press against a fixed supply of land, pushing up rents and holding down wages, while John Stuart Mill (1871) maintained that markets are not as efficient in distributing income as in allocating resources, which makes societal intervention necessary.

Marxian economics follows the reasoning set out in *Das Kapital* (Marx, 1867), which, through the *labor theory* of value (the labor that goes into commodity production determines its value) and *surplus value* (workers only receive a proportion of their work value), explained capital exploitation of labor (Roemer, 1987). The growth of neoclassical economic theory systematized supply and demand as crucial determining factors of price and quantity for markets (Campos, 1987). A fundamental concept in the study of economics is the assumption that economic actors or agents act *rationally*: amid multiple desirable ends and limited resources, they are capable of having a set of preferences and a guiding objective, and of making rational decisions. John Maynard Keynes (1936) ushered in contemporary *macroeconomics*, which was soon adopted by the Chicago School of economics, from Milton Friedman to former chairman of the Federal Reserve Ben Bernanke, who have advocated free market and monetarist ideas in a modern version of Adam Smith's principles.

Case Vignettes

A Separatist Movement

Politics has often played a role in collective violence, including civil conflicts and war. Basque nationalism is a movement that asserts that Basques, an indigenous ethnic group of the western Pyrenees, are a nation and promotes political unity among the Basques. Euskadi Ta Askatasuna (ETA) is an armed Basque nationalist and separatist organization in northern Spain and southwestern France. The group evolved from a group promoting traditional Basque culture into a paramilitary group engaged in a violent campaign of bombing, assassinations, and kidnappings in the Spanish Basque country and throughout Spanish territory.

ETA is born in 1952 because of hostilities directed against the Basque region and people by Francisco Franco both during and after the Spanish Civil War. The Basque people believe Franco is trying to root them out and turn their homeland into an industrial wasteland. After the end of the Spanish Civil War and World War II, anti-Basque measures are not eased but are institutionalized under the Franco regime. Over time, the ETA promotes Basque nationalism. Before Franco's death in 1975, Basque pressure for an independent nation becomes more serious under ETA's influence. In 1968, following recruitment and political radicalization by ETA and repression by Spanish authorities, particularly the Guardia Civil police, the first killings take place. At a roadblock, "Txabi" Etxebarrieta, a member of the three-man ETA executive committee, is stopped by the Spanish Guardia Civil. Etxebarrieta kills the man who stops him and is later himself killed by the authorities.

More ETA killings, and retaliation by the authorities, soon follow. During this period, ETA is careful to target figures who are identified with the Franco regime and the repression of Basques. In the early days, the assassination of such figures gives ETA an image borrowed from the days of heroic Basque resistance to fascism, even to the point of other governments petitioning the Spanish government not to execute convicted ETA murderers. In 1973, ETA targets the prime minister, Admiral Luis Carrero Blanco. It launches Operation Ogre in an attempt to prevent Carrero Blanco from succeeding Franco and ensuring the continuation of his policies. With the help of 165 pounds of dynamite planted in the street under Blanco's car, which is parked outside a church every morning in the same spot while the prime minister attends mass, it explodes on December 20, 1973, killing him. After that, the violence, arrests, and killings in the Basque region multiply, complicating the logic of violence for a singular purpose. ETA has killed more than 800 people since 1968. Over the years, ETA attempts several times to murder King Juan Carlos. The organization's targets go far beyond the unpopular figures from the Franco period who were the early victims of their wrath. More recently, they have targeted politicians, reporters, businessmen who refuse to pay their extortion demands, and, increasingly, the public at large. As with the Blanco assassination, such killings show their determination but narrow their appeal, uniting the Spanish nation and most Basques against them. Recent ETA attempts and bombings have included international airports in Spain that are geographically removed from the Basque region. There are now some five hundred of its members in Spanish prisons. They are scattered for security reasons throughout the nation.

In September 1998, ETA declares a total and indefinite ceasefire. The ceasefire lasts around fourteen months; in November 1999, ETA announces the end of the ceasefire. In the year 2000, the ETA kills 23 people. In order to finance its operations, ETA engages in kidnappings for ransom, extortion, and robberies. The main targets of such money-raising activities are Basque entrepreneurs, who are beginning to abandon the Basque Country in large numbers in order to escape extortion or abduction by the terrorist group. In addition, the terrorist conflict is cited as deterring domestic and foreign direct investment in the Basque Country. In March 2001, ETA issues warnings discouraging tourist travel in the Basque region, and in August 2001, a car bomb explodes in an underground parking lot at Madrid's Barajas airport, continuing the violence. In September 2010, ETA declares a new ceasefire, announcing, in October 2011, a "definitive cessation of its armed activity." Politicians cite the efforts of security and intelligence forces in Spain and France as the primary reasons for the weakening of ETA. In November 2012, the group is ready to negotiate a "definitive end" to its operations and to disband. The group announces on April 7, 2017, that it has given up all its weapons and explosives and will officially be a disarmed organization as of the following day. The French police finds 3.5 tons of weapons on April 8, 2017, at the caches ETA hands over (Shepard, 2002).

Apartheid

Apartheid, which in Afrikaans means "separateness," was an institutionalized racial segregation system in South Africa that existed from 1948 until the early 1990s. It was an authoritarian political culture of white supremacy that encouraged state repression of black, Asian, and other non-white Africans in favor of the nation's minority white population. During the 1970s and 1980s, internal resistance to apartheid became increasingly militant, and brutal crackdowns by the government followed. Protracted sectarian violence left many dead or in detention.

Vlakplaas is a farm west of Pretoria that served as the headquarters of the South African Police counterinsurgency unit working for the apartheid government in South Africa. From the late 1970s, Vlakplaas functioned as a paramilitary hit squad, capturing political opponents of the apartheid government and either turning (so they became *askaris*, or police officers) or executing them. The Vlakplaas farm was the site of multiple executions of political opponents of the apartheid government. Joyce Seipei, the mother of Stompie Seipei, a man killed at Vlakplaas, testifies at the first hearing of the Truth and Reconciliation Commission (TRC) in Durban on May 8, 1996, describing how she identified his body: On the 29th of December in 1988, Stompie was taken from the Methodist Church with his friends. A month later, two ministers from Johannesburg Methodist Church arrived at Joyce's house. The minister took Stompie's mother to Diepkloof Mortuary, where she identified his body, which was decomposed, with no hair at the back and his eyes gouged. After being killed, he was thrown into a river. Joyce knew it was her son. "This is Stompie," she said.

Between 1983 and 1993, Vlakplaas operatives are responsible for undercover operations, which include the infiltration of African National Congress (ANC) organizations and the abduction, torture, and murder of thousands of anti-apartheid activists. The bodies of their victims are buried secretly, burned, or dumped in the nearby Hennops River. Dirk Coetzee is the first commander of the special counter-insurgency unit at Vlakplaas. He orders the deaths of many ANC activists, including Griffiths Mxenge, a human rights lawyer, who is stabbed 40 times at Umlazi Stadium in Durban, and Sizwe Kondile, a young law graduate from the Eastern Cape, who is interrogated, beaten, and then handed over to Coetzee, who has him shot and his body burned. Coetzee's career at Vlakplaas is short-lived. He is demoted first to the narcotics division and then to the flying squad, and in 1986 is discharged from the police force. Colonel Eugene de Kock, the next commander at Vlakplaas between 1985 and 1993, is known among his colleagues as "Prime Evil." He and his group of trained killers are responsible for some of the worst atrocities committed during the apartheid years. For the next 10 years, de Kock is in charge of groups of trained *askaris* and his units carry out numerous killing raids and ambushes of alleged ANC and Pan Africanist Congress guerrillas. Another collaborator, Brigadier Willem Schoon, heads the C Section, the anti-terrorism unit of the South African Police security branch responsible for liaising with the commanders of the undercover unit at Vlakplaas. He is involved in numerous cases of murder and abduction and also implicated in the bombing of the Congress of South African Trade Unions headquarters in Johannesburg in 1987.

One of the immediate results of the TRC hearings is that some of the perpetrators, particularly members of the white security police and specialized forces who confess to the abduction and murder of anti-apartheid activists, disclose where the bodies of their victims are buried. For the victims' families who waited for years without knowing what happened to their spouses, parents, or children, this is the first confirmation that their missing relatives are actually dead. Once the locations are known, exhumations supervised by officials from the TRC take place all over South Africa. One *askari*, Brian Ngqulunga, becomes deeply disturbed by his work for the Vlakplaas commanders. He becomes unhinged by the organized murder he is involved in and goes on a drunken binge. Ngqulunga goes home and shoots his pregnant wife three times.

He is later killed. His wife survives, and after his exhumation, takes her husband's remains back to the family home for a proper funeral (Edelstein, 2002).

Social Engineering

The Great Leap Forward of the People's Republic of China was an economic and social campaign by the Communist Party of China from 1958 to 1961 that ends in catastrophe, resulting in tens of millions of deaths. Mao Zedong leads the campaign, aiming to transform the country from an agrarian economy into a socialist society through rapid industrialization and collectivization so as to rival America by 1988. Mao tours China and concludes that industry can only prosper if the work force is well fed, while agricultural workers need industry to produce the modern tools required for modernization. Mao announces a Five Year Plan, which reforms China into a series of communes. The geographical size of a commune varies but most contain about five thousand families. People in a commune give up their ownership of tools and animals so that everything is owned by the commune, including the life of each resident. The commune provides all that is needed—including schools, nurseries, and entertainment. It provides healthcare, and the elderly are moved into "houses of happiness" so that they can be looked after. Soldiers work alongside civilians. The population in a commune is subdivided into 12 families that form a work team. Twelve work teams form a brigade. Each subdivision is given specific work to do. Party members oversee the work of a commune to ensure that it follows Party decisions.

In 1959, things start to decline. The orders of the Party officials become more and more impossible, and commune leaders, who know what their commune is and is not capable of doing, can be charged with being "reactionary" and imprisoned if they complain. Hastily produced farm machinery falls to pieces during use. Many thousands of workers suffer injuries after long working hours and falling asleep at their jobs. Steel produced in backyard furnaces is frequently too weak to be of any use and cannot be used in construction. Buildings constructed with substandard steel do not last long. Also, the production method takes many workers away from their fields: food is not harvested. The year 1958 has good weather for growing food, but a very poor growing year follows in 1959. The harvest is well below what China needs at the most basic level. In parts of China, starvation occurs. Things are even worse in 1960. Around nine million people starve to death, and many millions more fall ill from a lack of food. The government introduces rationing.

In one story from the central Henan province, one in eight are wiped out by starvation and violence over three short years. In one area, officials attempt to take possession of more grain than farmers have grown, and in nine months, a third of the inhabitants die in a single commune. Thirteen children who beg officials for food are dragged deep into the mountains to die from exposure and starvation. A teenage orphan kills and eats her four-year-old brother. Forty-four of a village's forty-five inhabitants die, and the last remaining resident, a woman in her sixties, goes insane. Others are tortured, beaten, or buried alive for declaring realistic harvests, refusing to hand over what little food they have, stealing scraps, or simply angering officials. By 1959, the Party deems the Great Leap Forward a failure. Some Party members place the blame solely on Mao, who resigns from his position as Head of State. Private ownership of land is reinstated, and communes are cut down to manageable sizes. Peasants are given incentives to produce as much spare food as possible, but damage has already been done: it is estimated that 45 million Chinese have lost their lives between 1959 and 1962 (Dikötter, 2010).

Aspiring to compete with Western industrialized nations, the Great Leap Forward represents a massive economic and social attempt to transform an agrarian economy into a modern society rapidly. Leaping into it unprepared, with poor central planning and little expertise, the experiment has ended in catastrophe.

Rape as a Weapon of War

Rape or other forms of sexual violence during war, armed conflict, or military occupation were often viewed as spoils of war, but now they are increasingly recognized as weapons of war itself. Particularly in ethnic conflict, sexual violence may take the form of gang rape or rape with objects. It includes instances where an occupying power forces girls and women into prostitution or sexual slavery. As a weapon of psychological warfare, its purpose is to humiliate and demoralize the enemy.

During the Bosnian War from 1992 to 1995, the violence includes widespread rape. While men from all ethnic groups engage in rape, the great majority of such crimes are perpetrated by Bosnian Serb forces, who use rape as an instrument of terror in their program of ethnic cleansing, on Bosniaks, or Bosnian Muslims. Before 1980, the lack of ethnic conflict in Yugoslavia was primarily due to Marshal Josef Broz Tito's effective suppression of nationalism. In 1989, Serbian president Slobodan Milošević inflames Serbian nationalist sentiment. He stirs up feelings of victimhood and aggression toward Bosniaks with exaggerated tales about the role a small number of Bosniaks played in the persecution of Serbs during the Ustaše genocide in the 1940s. Bosniaks in Eastern Bosnia begin to be removed from their employment and ostracized, and to have their freedom of movement curtailed. The horrors of the Bosnian war begin in early June and July 1992 when Serbian forces start arresting young men in the area of Gacko. Around 37% of the region's 10,000 population is Muslim, but Muslims form the middle classes and constitute a majority inside the town. One day, 120 young men are arrested and 10 of them have their throats cut in the street. Altogether, 136 people in Gacko are killed, mostly men but some women and children. Bosniak houses and apartments are looted or razed to the ground. The civilian population is rounded up and some people are physically abused or murdered. Men and women are separated and then held in concentration camps.

As a tactic of ethnic cleansing, rape ensures that the targeted population will not return to the area. The assailants tell their victims they will bear a child of the assailant's ethnicity. The Serb forces set up "rape camps," where they subject women to repeated rapes, torture, and humiliation, and only release them when they become pregnant. Even then they detain pregnant women until it is too late to abort the fetus. Victims are told they will be hunted down and killed if they report what has transpired. These women are often raped by their former neighbors. Gang rape and public rapes in front of villagers and neighbors are common. Estimates of the number of women and girls raped range from 12,000 to 50,000; the vast majority are Bosniaks raped by Bosnian Serbs. In Kalinovik camp, where roughly one hundred women are detained, the Serbian soldiers continually tell their victims: "You are going to have our children. You are going to have our little Chetniks," implying that the reason for their being raped is "to plant the seed of Serbs in Bosnia." All sides of the conflict are reported to have committed rape, but the largest number of reported victims are Bosniaks and the largest number of alleged perpetrators are Bosnian Serbs. There are few reports of rape and sexual assault between members of the same ethnic group (*Prosecutor v. Zelenović*, 2007).

Military Dictatorship

Military dictatorship is a form of government in which a military force takes full or substantial control of political authority. It differs from civilian dictatorship in that it organizes its rule around the military and usually forms after a *coup d'état* has overthrown the previous government. Viewing themselves as saving the nation from corrupt or myopic civilian politicians, military dictators often justify their position as "neutral arbiters" outside of the political system.

In addition to holding arms, the cohesion and institutional structure of the military often give it immediate advantage over civilian institutions.

In September 1991, the Haitian Armed Forces overthrow the president, Jean Bertrand Aristide. Between the end of September 1991 and October 1994, Haiti is under a de facto military regime. An estimated number of 4,000 civilians are killed and several hundred thousand tortured, imprisoned, or forced into exile by the Haitian Armed Forces and Revolutionary Front for the Advancement and Progress of Haiti (FRAPH), a paramilitary organization that persecutes supporters of President Aristide. The founder and former leader of FRAPH is Emmanuel Toto Constant. Constant commits torture, crimes against humanity, and the systematic use of violence against women during the FRAPH regime. Members of FRAPH kill, imprison, and abuse supporters of President Aristide, working in concert with the Haitian military to terrorize and repress the civilian population. FRAPH members receive weapons, training, and financial support from the Haitian military troops, while Constant exercises command and control over FRAPH forces. Constant, whose father was an army commander under the former Haitian Dictator François Duvalier, used Duvalier's notorious "Tonton Macoutes" paramilitary units as a model for the formation of FRAPH. Under Duvalier, the Tonton Macoutes were officially labeled National Security Volunteers (VSN). The VSN operated parallel to and in conjunction with the army while reporting directly to Duvalier. Constant recruits many former VSN members into the ranks of FRAPH.

With the financial and logistical support of the Haitian Armed Forces and certain Haitian civilians, FRAPH loots, burns, and destroys homes in an effort to break the resistance of the population to military rule. FRAPH uses rape and sexual assault to punish and intimidate women for their actual or imputed political beliefs, or those of their husbands, or to terrorize them during violent sweeps of pro-Aristide neighborhoods. Constant is also accused of being involved in the Raboteau massacre, which takes place April 18–22, 1994, in Raboteau, Haiti. There is an attack by military and paramilitary units on pro-democracy activists, killing at least six people. In September 1994, the United States military arrives in Haiti to secure the return of the democratically elected government headed by President Aristide. The high command of the military regime flees Haiti, escaping to nearby countries. In December 1994, the Haitian government issues a warrant for Constant's arrest. Constant has fled to the Dominican Republic and then to the United States. A judge orders Constant to be deported to Haiti in September 1995, but that order is never executed. On October 28, 2008, Constant is sentenced to 12–37 years in prison for his role in a criminal mortgage fraud scheme in New York after being found guilty on all six felony counts against him in a July 2008 trial (*Doe v. Constant*, 2009).

Macro-Scale Political Science Theories

Some of the central questions that political science has asked about violence include: How, why, and when do political actors use violence as strategies against one another? And what conditions cause conflict to take the form of violence and not some other means of contest? Political science has addressed many important questions that are central to our examination of violence. The form of violence that has traditionally been the subject of focus is interstate war. Applying the *rationalist argument*—the belief or theory that decisions and actions should be based on reason and knowledge alone (Durlauf & Blume, 2008)—the question is why wars occur at all, given that they are costly and potentially devastating. One proposed explanation is *information failure*, whereby states miscalculate the costs and benefits of waging war versus peaceful settlement. An alternative explanation is the *security dilemma*, which posits that violence results from the fact that leaders are incapable of credibly guaranteeing that they will maintain their commitment not to attack. According to this model, actions designed to safeguard the security of the state result in similar actions by other states and a general increase in tension that eventually creates conflict, even if the nations involved do not particularly desire it. Curiously, there is very little talk of actual violence, either within these states or among their people, in these arguments, as the states are regarded as strategic, rational units operating within an idealized international system. Still others have argued that a "realist" account of motivation—self-preservation or self-aggrandizement—is not as applicable as concerns over accountability and integrity (Welch, 1995).

With the decline of interstate warfare in the last half of the twentieth century, the focus of the study of violence in politics has changed to a more local model. Especially after the end of the Cold War, when civil wars became virtually the only wars where actual fighting occurs, one of the more important questions that has occupied political scientists has been the causes of violence. From the 1960s to the 1980s the *frustration theory* was a popular approach to studying the phenomenon, particularly in relation to rebellions and insurgencies (Weinstein, 2007). This argument states that rising expectations, coupled with relative deprivation, are the root cause of violent contestation of the established political order (Gurr, 1970). This *demand-based* theory postulates that violence occurs because there is a demand for it through group-level grievances. However, the fact exists that civil war remains rare, even though grievances exist everywhere. The 1990s saw the rise of the *supply-based* theory, which draws conclusions from studies by the World Bank. British economist Paul Collier and German social scientist Anke Hoeffler (2004) argued that an abundance of natural resources creates fertile ground for internal discontent by financing rebellion, while poverty lowers the opportunity cost of joining a rebel group (Weinstein, 2007). In sum, the control of resources can turn insurgent groups into criminal organizations, and fighting continues because it is a lucrative activity.

Modern comparative politics has moved beyond a strict *supply-versus-demand* model, otherwise known as the *greed-versus-grievance* model. Now, the field embraces a wide range of variables. One of the many questions we now ask is whether a link exists between *weak states* and intrastate violence (Fearon & Laitin, 2003). Returning to the rationalist explanation that war follows a lack of credible agreements, the question arises: Is the lack of administrative capacity, or the state's inability to arbitrate between groups, responsible? While it may seem self-evident that developing countries experience more violence than wealthier states, no causal link has been proven (Chenoweth & Lawrence, 2010). The state often actively participates in violence (e.g., Central America in the 1980s, Sudan, East Timor, and Sri Lanka). Research shows that there is little correlation between a country's per capita gross domestic product (GDP) and its capacity for violent coercion. North Korea, for example, remains terribly impoverished by contemporary standards but retains a formidable apparatus of oppression, while equally poor countries such as Laos and Botswana have long and relatively stable histories of refraining from violence. Even in countries where intrastate conflict and even civil wars occur, violence does not occur everywhere at all times. While theories that attempt to explain outbreaks of violence include *primordial hatreds* (ancient enmity between groups) or *fixed identities* (identities that are destined or do not change). While these factors can promulgate policies of exclusion within the state, or result in conflict as geographic ethnicities desire their own independence, these differences often arise as a *result* of conflict, not as a cause of it.

Certain theorists assert that elites are frequently the initiators of violence, often playing on concepts of identity and blame to discount their own role in exploitation. In Rwanda, for example, members of the Hutu majority government instigated intrastate conflict out of the political motivation of genocide against the Tutsi. That this tactic has inherent risks that could well be antithetical to their stability does not seem to have deterred them. Others suggest that it is the type of government that determines the probability of violence: *authoritarian* states repress all forms of political or social dissent and demonstrate no blatantly violent characteristics, while mature democracies will find peaceful resolutions to social tensions (Huntington, 2006). Authoritarian or, worse, *totalitarian* governments may reduce visible violence through the control of all aspects of public and private life, but the resulting political repression, regulation of speech, mass surveillance, and widespread use of terror consist of greater violence, as we have defined it in Chapter 1, "Introduction."

Another common explanation is the *youth bulge*, which proposes that an increase in the youth population is a contributing factor to the prevalence of political violence such as terrorism (Urdal, 2006). An ever-increasing pool of youth with little social opportunity makes the cost of recruitment to violence much lower. Another political factor is humiliating foreign interventions, such as the anti-Armenian violence that broke out in Turkey in 1915 when the population believed that the Armenians living there were acting as agents for the Russian invasion (Verdeja, 2012). And political scientists are beginning to recognize income disparity as a significant contributor to both political violence and violence in general (Muller, 1985). Sometimes, economic tensions can merge with a political transition as in the post-Mao movement that gave rise to student-led protests and the Tiananmen Square massacre (Human Rights Watch, 2009).

Micro-Scale Political Science Theories

In general, the study of *macro-indicators*, which draws its conclusions by comparing countries that have experienced civil wars with those that have not, fails to explain how violence emerges. Researchers who prefer to utilize a *micro-level* approach criticize this assumption that violence is either present or absent as crude and unreliable. The *micro-level* approach examines questions such as: Who are the actual actors using violence? What forms does that violence take? And who are the victims? A study of nationalist movements in colonial Morocco demonstrated that violence levels rose even higher after the execution of rebel leaders, as aspiring leaders fought among themselves in the struggle for ascendancy (Lawrence, 2010).

Research in both Colombia and Sri Lanka has shown that some combatant groups use narrow repertoires and targeting (Wood, 2009). In Colombia, paramilitary groups were responsible for a disproportionally higher number of civilian victims than the Revolutionary Armed Forces of Colombia (FARC). In combat zones such as Afghanistan and Iraq, the distinction between combatants and civilians has become exceedingly difficult. The micro-level perspective is thus responsible for bringing about two major theoretical innovations in the study of violence: disaggregation and the recognition that violence is complex and dynamic.

The *micro-dynamic* approach gives particular attention to *civilian behavior* during times of war. Rebels recruit from this population, and any combatant group must at some point rely on the compliance of or collaboration by the people. The most parsimonious model comes from the study of peasants in Vietnam (Popkin, 1979): with the basic premise being that civilians are rational, calculating actors, the peasant will always act to maximize wellbeing, which in war situations consists of survival. This means that in a combat zone the civilian will support whichever armed group can guarantee survival and security, and thus cooperation accrues to the militarily predominant. The great flaws of this approach are that it ignores the sociopolitical importance of attitudes, loyalties, preexisting identities, and civilian decision-making, while being incapable of describing any actions that do not make sense from a strictly rational point of view, such as resistance.

Others have looked at the relationship between civilians and rebels as being a *spectrum* of behavior ranging from collaboration to resistance (Staniland, 2012), taking into account that both civilians and rebels can move from one behavior to another, which makes cooperation a continuous bargaining process. When Al Qaeda established itself in Afghanistan and Mali, it had no indigenous support base and had to rely on local ties for support and recruitment, which in turn gave the civilian authorities a certain amount of bargaining power with the insurgents. Kalyvas and Kocher (2007) assert that nonparticipation with an armed group can be riskier than affiliation, particularly if the nature of the violence includes indiscriminate civilian targeting.

The conflict between Tibet and China is another example of politically driven civilian violence. In 1960, the Tibetan Uprising was an attempt to overthrow the Chinese government. Over the course of 3 years, 94 Tibetans had self-immolated in Tibet and China as an attempt of Tibetan Monks to bring awareness to the international community regarding the human rights violations in Tibet (International Campaign for Tibet, 2012). China's point of view is that it is liberating the Tibetans from their serf and feudal lifestyle by modernizing the infrastructure through urbanization and stimulation of the economy by creating jobs, but Tibetans are facing economic and political oppression by the Chinese government, protesting economic distress, poverty, unemployment, and famine. In this manner, political science now embraces the study of "fine-grain" causal processes; of political radicalization and polarization; of violence and nonviolence as opposite poles of a wide spectrum of options; of violence as a joint outcome; and of the distinction between war and violence (Kalyvas & Balcells, 2010).

Microeconomic Perspectives

Moving away from political science, let us examine the prevailing economically based theories surrounding the manifestation of violence. The economic perspective is important to the study of violence for obvious reasons: the most deprived and vulnerable nations experience the greatest amounts of violence. The *World Development Report* (World Bank, 2011) suggests that violence is not only among the many causes of poverty but is the primary cause. Economists have thus looked at how poverty affects not only the behavior of people living in a society, but also creates a politically unstable nation. They have noted how violence and poverty affect each other at all levels of society: conflicts leading to violence begin as a result of economic hardships on the micro level, but then potentially develop into civil and international clashes on the macro level. These theories derive from both the study of *microeconomics*, which is concerned with the behavior of individuals as they negotiate the difficulties of obtaining resources in the midst of scarcity (Baumol & Blinder, 2011), and *macroeconomics*, which is a more extensive overview of economic activity, including growth, inflation, and economic policies such as taxation and unemployment (Sims, 1980).

In their most basic manifestation, economic theories posit that violent behavior is a result of a cost–benefit analysis leading to the conclusion that violence will be desirable (Rachlin, 2004). Working from this assumption, an economic theory of violence will argue that any changes within groups will affect intergroup conflict: for instance, raising the income levels of low-income groups will reduce the amount of violence associated with that group (Mitra & Ray, 2014). While violence is multifactorial and does not always follow a linear model, some research into domestic violence in India indicates that poor women are more likely to be victims of domestic violence than rich women (Dalal, 2011). Other approaches to viewing the economic causes of violence also exist. Research into violent coups in Latin America used economic theory to compare *coups d'état* to management shakeups within corporations (Chaffee, 1992), because a *coup* is a manifestation of political competition within a state (Stanley, 1998).

However, though a unified economic theory may be attractive, the underlying assumptions about human behavior that inform these dynamics (having choices, accessing those choices, and making the correct cost–benefit analyses to act upon) do not always hold.

One of the more influential microeconomic theories is *consumer demand theory*, the theory that indicates that there exists a relationship between consumer preference and expenditure (Hicks, 1939). If a fall in consumer income influences purchasing patterns, a shift in preferences can happen, and violence can result. Society may dwindle, and market participants may be in trouble, if an equilibrium no longer guards consumer choice (Lancaster, 1966) giving rise to potential violence. *Game theory* is another useful attempt to explain violence through conflict- and cooperation-based decision-making among rational actors within a framework of structured competition. As the players utilize different strategies to maximize returns, suppliers may begin to violate cooperative agreements in order to protect their own interests. They may employ any method, even coercion and violence, to stay ahead of the game (Vagliasindi, 2004). Game theory thus helps explain strategic decision-making to compete in the market, with a basic assumption being that human beings will use all means, even at the expense of fairness, to win the game (Neumann, 1944).

Another microeconomic theory called *rational choice theory* also tries to explain violent behaviors. The theory assumes that humans are rational beings who are capable of understanding their situations, formulating a set of probable outcomes, and applying a cost-to-benefit assessment of alternatives before choosing a course of action. From this perspective, violence and criminality are intentional choices actors engage in to advance their personal goals. Both suppliers and buyers will exhibit a natural tendency to act violently under conditions of scarcity as a result of the available options and the imperative to maximize their own happiness. The English philosopher Henry Sidgwick noted that individuals in pursuit of pure self-interest can create imbalances that lead to economic inefficiency, as humans are not always rational when it comes to making choices (Simon, 1957). Since economic behavior depends on choice (Barros, 2010), violence comes into play when there is irrational pursuit of self-interest. However, violence is precisely where the scheme of rational self-interest does not always hold, and an interdisciplinary perspective could be helpful.

Understanding the economic nature of violence, different organizations have conducted studies on estimating the cost of violence (Day, McKenna, & Bowlus, 2005; Skeperdas et al., 2009). Studies have found that the cost of violence may vary depending on the method used to measure violence. However, these costs are not negligible and may have both direct and indirect effects on the economy.

Macroeconomic Perspectives

From a macroeconomic perspective, the African Development Bank has determined that the risk factors for violence include: the presence of natural resources, low income, low economic growth, competition for scarce resources, and high military spending, among other noneconomic factors (Brauer & Dunne, 2011). We see high levels of violence in countries like South Africa, Zimbabwe, and resource-rich Democratic Republic of Congo. For this reason, a growing number of economic theorists consider the fostering of economic empowerment and financial security to be an important method of reducing violence (Postmus et al., 2013). A *Keynesian approach* indicates that in a consumer society, consumer spending declines along with wages cuts, at the same time as government revenues decrease when elites evade taxes. This burdens the workers, who are the ultimate consumers, at the same time as public services decline (Keynes, 1936). A typical Keynesian solution to this situation is to call for cooperation between the private sector and the government in the implementation of fiscal policy that responds to economic ills such as market unrest (Keynes, 1923). Earlier *classical theories* reject any form of government intervention in the market system (Harris, 1975), but little to no government intervention often leads to capitalist abuses.

Other correlational studies have attributed lack of economic growth and a decline in real GDP, together with a rise in income inequality, to explain outbreaks of humanitarianism emergencies (Auvinen & Nafziger, 1999). Sudan in the 1980s, for example, experienced turmoil because a lack of economic development led to food being withheld from groups that criticized the government, as well as the direct use of force against these groups (Keen, 2000). War and interpersonal violence, although consequences of economic turmoil and uncertainty, can hinder economic development and thus become responsible for a cycle of violence and economic decline (Krug et al., 2002).

In terms of *political economy*, Marx's *theory of revolution* describes the inevitable conflict that arises from capitalism, which divides people into polarized economic classes: the bourgeoisie and the proletariat (Marx, 1864). The different economic circumstances lead to conflict, and when the labor force's insurrection becomes too powerful for bourgeois society to resist, existing oppressive systems are destroyed and new markets are created (Marx & Engels, 1848). *Neoclassical theory* maintains that the improvement of material conditions is the most important priority of human beings and with consumer and producer surpluses should lead to the highest levels of satisfaction (Caldari, 2004). However, with scarcity, forces attempting to right abuses may in turn increase the level of violence in society (Marshall, 1890). The *labor theory of value* demonstrates that differences in labor quality and efficiency can lead to inequality of labor (Ricardo, Sraffa, & Dobb, 1951). When a market participant exploits labor, violence in the market can occur, resulting in poor production and economic unrest (Human Rights Watch, 2006). As the various economic approaches to the causes of violence indicate, the basic issues appear to be inequality and a low standard of living, and addressing these factors could well be the most effective way of raising security and preventing violence (Sraffa, 2004).

Concepts of Power

Power, a central concept in political science, is the capacity to achieve values in collaboration with and in opposition to others. It can be an end in itself, but it is primarily instrumental in attaining other objectives. Within a group or between groups, this capacity often has an uneven distribution, so that more powerful people and groups have more autonomy than others as well as more influence over others. When there is uneven distribution, it becomes *domination*. On the other hand, dominated individuals, groups, and political units may act autonomously to organize a powerful resistance and to seek to increase their capacity. Contention and conflict of this kind consist of politics, while interactions with others make power essentially relational. Power relations shape political activities, but are often embedded perceptibly in institutions or invisibly in structures. We will return to this concept in greater detail in Chapter 7, "Structural Violence".

The classical political theorists concerned themselves primarily with concepts such as justice, virtue, and the good life. At the same time, they also understood that power was instrumental to the achievement of these values. In the fourth century BCE, Aristotle (1598) used the distribution of power as the criterion by which to distinguish governments of the one, the few, and the many. In the fifth century BCE, Thucydides (1550) affirmed that the strong do what they will, and the weak suffer what they must because of the inequality of power and its consequences. Roman writers occupied themselves with gaining control of and regulating power. Power became a concept for analysis with the work of Machiavelli (1532), who elucidated how princes and states could exploit its mechanisms. English political philosopher Thomas Hobbes (1651) held the view that power should be concentrated and institutionalized in a sovereign. Enlightenment philosophers John Locke, Charles-Louis Montesquieu, and the authors of *The Federalist Papers*, Alexander Hamilton, John Jay, and James Madison (1788), devised their institutional arrangements of dividing, sharing, and separating power with the aim of avoiding any concentration of power.

For the most part, monarchies and aristocratic societies provide for inherited offices, titles, privileges, and wealth that confer power on those holding positions. In contrast, democratic electoral systems offer more widespread opportunities to contenders who may seek, win, or lose office. Meanwhile, capitalist economic arrangements are based on competition, with rewards for success and the ever-present risk of failure. Patriarchal social arrangements place men in positions of power over women, whereas egalitarian societies aim for more nearly equal allocation of authority. Slave societies confer on masters nearly complete power over slaves, but as slave revolts and political revolutions attest, those who are dominated sometimes resist and overthrow an unjust social and political order.

There can be antidotes to abuses of power. American political theorist Robert Dahl (1989) has named *democracy*—or a system of government where the whole population shares power— as a central guideline. Political values that human beings seek may include policy objectives but also more enduring principles such as order and justice, equality and freedom, security and stability, and the checks and balances that prevent despotism and arbitrary rule. Certain individual characteristics may breed power. German sociologist Max Weber (1921) analyzed the concept of *charisma*, an attribute of a person that inspires others to defer to him. The individual is able to amass power by commanding respect and deference, by means of intellect and will, through the use of knowledge, through rhetoric, by guile, and by the performance of brave and admirable deeds. Traditional authority of inherited leadership and legitimate authority based in law and orderly procedure, on the other hand, stem from social and political arrangements that are institutionalized.

Power is also built upon material resources, such as economic wealth, production facilities, and military might. Accumulated wealth and income can purchase commodities and services to ensure autonomy, to gain the cooperation of others, and to amass and exercise power over others. Production facilities can similarly be mobilized to extract, grow, and manufacture instruments for achieving political ends. Meanwhile, the last part of the twentieth century and continuing into the twenty-first century, *neoliberal* ideology in favor of privatizing what had previously been public functions has produced a trend toward allocating authority to private groups and firms, thus strengthening the structural power of nongovernmental institutions and weakening public accountability of democratic systems and facilitating the abuse of power.

Military capability also creates an imbalance of power, both domestically and internationally, through threats as well as actual use. American economist Thomas Schelling (1967) has tried to delineate the efficacy and the limitations of using violence to exercise influence, while political thinkers such as Hannah Arendt (1970) have drawn a sharp distinction between power and violence: the latter consists of domination and brute force that signals power in jeopardy. A clearer concept of power may come from the original French *pouvoir*, which means "to be able" denoting a creative, generative, and cohesive force. The word for "power" in Greek, *dunamis*, illustrates this: loosely meaning "strength, power, or ability," it is the root for the English words "dynamite," "dynamo," and "dynamic." Those lacking in true ability may succeed in forcing subjugation through brute force but not in persuasion—which is why states that lack legitimate power or are in a decline are more likely to resort to violence.

Individuals and groups contend to shape the behavior of those in power, and this conflict characterizes political life as one group or political unit strives to achieve goals at the expense of others who may possess the values at stake or who hold incompatible values. Democratic politics create space for conflict to occur through rhetoric, deliberation through constitutional means, resolution by legislative and judicial processes, elections, and internationally through cooperative institutions. On the other hand, armed struggle commonly occurs in situations where there is little provision of such space, or where governance is a more arbitrary exercise by elites, leading to noncompliance, clandestine behavior, and civil war situations if not insurrections. This text aims in part to describe, explain, and analyze how health and the absence of violence, locally and globally, relate to the organization of political and economic activity and the distribution of power and wealth. German anarchist Gustav Landauer argued that government is not an institution that can be destroyed by a revolution but a condition, a certain relationship between human beings, which we destroy by contracting other relationships (Ward, 2004).

Conclusion

This chapter demonstrated that political science and economic theory not only give us useful insights into the causes and consequences of violence, but can also offer viable options for the prevention of violence on many levels. In this chapter, we discussed how these two fields have made useful contributions to our understanding of how major societal structures relate to violence. Political science has been effective in synthesizing the different fields that have studied violence, while economics has tested a number of different theories to try to bring coherence to the topic. Both converge on power or wealth differentials that give rise to conflict or behavioral violence. In these discoveries, we may uncover not only the causes and consequences of violence but also the cures.

Political science, which has adopted an exceptionally flexible approach in light of the changing manifestations of violence, has demonstrated that despite the complexity of the causal connections it postulates, two major factors repeatedly appear to be important to outbreaks of violence. These factors are inequalities in power (such as foreign invasions and the mistreatment of outgroups as with the Armenians in Turkey) and the failure of political institutions to provide opportunities (such as for youth in the Islamic terrorism context). Further exacerbation results from the fact that political decision-makers are often anonymous and have competing interests with respect to the prevention of violence.

Economic theory might recognize that it does not merely explain independently occurring phenomena but determines ways of managing the world economy. At a time when decisions from one part of the world have repercussions everywhere, there is a need to address shared responsibility. In light of this, a growing number of prominent economists argue that we should not just leave economies to "market forces" but rather take the shaping and enforcement of regulations and laws into account (Krugman, 2012; Stiglitz, 2012). Other major intellectuals and writers (Hacker & Pierson, 2010; Lessig, 2011; Noah, 2012) argue that the inequality that the current system engenders not only violates moral values but colludes with a money-driven political system to concentrate undue power among the affluent, who then use that power to insulate themselves from competition and win unwarranted tax favors or government-protected market shares through *rent seeking*, or increasing their share of wealth without creating wealth. These actions damage the apparatus of capitalism and create a volatile environment, stimulating crises, undermining productivity, eroding infrastructure, and retarding growth. While these dynamics may appear to bear no direct relationship to violence, we will see in the following chapters of this book that inequality itself constitutes violence, causes damage to people, and is a potent stimulant to other forms of violence (Gilligan, 1996). Indeed, as local solutions for the enormous global problems that overwhelm local politics become increasingly difficult to find, what we need at this political and economic juncture are more effective ways of interacting that offer political respect and ensure the economic wellbeing of all players, not just a few. Political science and economics can help us to conceive of them.

Questions

1   How do political and economic forces contribute to human violence?

2   What are some of the ways political science helps to synthesize violence studies?

3   What are some of the ways economics has tried to bring about a coherent picture of violence?

4   What is the difference between power and domination?

5   How does political or economic equality mitigate violence?

References

Arendt, H. (1970). *On violence.* New York, NY: Harcourt, Brace and World.

Aristotle (1598). *Aristotles Politiques, or discourses of gouernment.* (A. Islip, Trans.). London, UK: Islip.

Auvinen, J., & Nafziger, E. W. (1999). The sources of humanitarian emergencies. *Journal of Conflict Resolution, 43*(3), 267–290.

Barros, G. (2010). Herbert A. Simon and the concept of rationality: Boundaries and procedures. *Revista de Economia Política, 30*(3), 455–472.

Baumol, W., & Blinder, A. (2011). *Microeconomics: Principles and policy.* Boston, MA: Cengage Learning.

Blatt, J. (2009). *How political science became modern: Racial thought and the transformation of the discipline, 1880–1930.* New York, NY: New School University.

Blaug, M. (2007). The social sciences: Economics. In *Encyclopædia Britannica,* The New Encyclopædia Britannica (Vol. 27) (pp. 343). Edinburgh, UK: Encyclopædia Britannica.

Blaug, M. (Ed.) (1997). *Economic theory in retrospect.* Cambridge, UK: Cambridge University Press.

Brauer, J., & Dunne, J. P. (2011). Macroeconomics and violence. In D. Braddon, & K. Hartley (Eds.), *Handbook on the economics of conflict.* Cheltenham, UK: Elgar.

Caldari, K. (2004). Alfred Marshall's idea of progress and sustainable development. *Journal of the History of Economic Thought, 26*(4), 519–536.

Campos, A. (1987). Marginalist economics. In J. Eatwell, M. Milgate, & P. Newman (Eds.), *The New Palgrave: A dictionary of economics* (Vol. 3) (pp. 320). London, UK: Macmillan Stockton Press Maruzen.

Chaffee, W. A. (1992). *The economics of violence in Latin America: A theory of political competition.* Westport, CT: Praeger.

Chenoweth, E., & Lawrence, A. (2010). *Rethinking violence: States and non-state actors in conflict.* Cambridge, MA: MIT University Press.

Collier, P., & Hoeffler, A. (2004). Greed and grievance in civil war. *Oxford Economic Papers, 56*(4), 563–595.

Converse, P. E. (1970). Attitudes and non-attitudes: Continuation of a dialogue. In E. R. Tulte (Ed.), *The quantitative analysis of social problems* (pp. 168–189). Reading, MA: Addison-Wesley.

Dahl, R. A. (1961). The behavioral approach in political science: Epitaph for a monument to a successful protest. *The American Political Science Review, 55*(04), 763–772.

Dahl, R. A. (1989). *Democracy and its critics.* New Haven, CT: Yale University Press.

Dalal, K. (2011). Does economic empowerment protect women from intimate partner violence. *Journal of Injury and Violence Research, 3*(1), 35–44.

Day, T., McKenna, K., & Bowlus, A. (2005). *The economic costs of violence against women: An evaluation of the literature.* New York, NY: United Nations. Retrieved from http://www.un.org/womenwatch/daw/vaw/expert%20brief%20costs.pdf

Dikötter, F. (2010). *Mao's great famine: The history of China's most devastating catastrophe, 1958–62.* New York, NY: Walker Publishing.

Doe v. Constant, 08–4827-cv (2nd Cir. 2009).

Druckman, J. N., Green, D. P., Kuklinski, J. H., & Lupia, A. (2011). *Cambridge handbook of experimental political science.* Cambridge, UK: Cambridge University Press.

Durlauf, S. N., & Blume, L. (2008). *The New Palgrave dictionary of economics.* Basingstoke, UK: Palgrave Macmillan.

Edelstein, J. (2002). *Truth and lies: Stories from the truth and reconciliation commission in South Africa.* London, UK: Granta Books.

Fearon, J. D., & Laitin, D. (2003). Ethnicity, insurgency, and civil war. *American Political Science Review, 97*(1), 75–90.

Gilligan, J. (1996). *Violence: Our deadly epidemic and its causes.* New York, NY: Putnam.

Gunnell, J. G. (2006). The founding of the American political science association: Discipline, profession, political theory, and politics. *American Political Science Review, 100*(4), 479–486.

Gurr, T. R. (1970). *Why men rebel.* Princeton, NJ: Princeton University Press.

Hacker, J. S., & Pierson, P. (2010). *Winner-take-all politics: How Washington made the rich richer—and turned its back on the middle class.* New York, NY: Simon, and Schuster.

Hamilton, A., Madison, J., & Jay, J. (1788). *The federalist papers.* New York, NY: M'Lean.

Harris, D. J. (1975). The theory of economic growth: A critique and reformulation. *American Economic Review, 65*(2), 329–337.

Hicks, J. R. (1939). *Value and capital.* Oxford, UK: Oxford University Press.

Hill, K. Q. (2012). In search of general theory. *Journal of Politics, 74*(4), 917–931.

Hobbes, T. (1651). *Leviathan.* London, UK: Crooke.

Human Rights Watch. (2006). *Building towers, cheating workers: Exploitation of migrant construction workers in the UAE.* New York, NY: Author. Retrieved from https://www.hrw.org/reports/2008/bhr0208/3d.htm

Human Rights Watch. (2009). *The Tiananmen legacy: Ongoing persecution and censorship.* New York, NY: Author. Retrieved from https://www.hrw.org/sites/default/files/related_material/The%20Tiananmen%20Legacy_3.pdf

Huntington, S. P. (2006). *Political order in changing societies.* New Haven, CT: Yale University Press.

International Campaign for Tibet. (2012). *Storm in the grasslands: Self-immolations in Tibet and Chinese policy.* Washington, DC: International Campaign for Tibet.

Kalyvas, S. N., & Balcells, L. (2010). International system and technologies of rebellion: How the end of the cold war shaped internal conflict. *American Political Science Review, 104*(3), 415–429.

Kalyvas, S. N., & Kocher, M. A. (2007). How "free" is free riding in civil wars? Violence, insurgency, and the collective action problem. *World Politics, 59*(2), 177–216.

Keen, D. (2000). War, crime, and access to resources. In E. W. Nafziger, F. Stewart, & R. Väyrynen (Eds.), *War, hunger, and displacement: The origins of humanitarian emergencies* (pp. 283–304). Oxford, UK: Oxford University Press.

Keynes, J. M. (1923). *A tract on monetary reform*. London, UK: Macmillan and Company.

Keynes, J. M. (1936). *The general theory of employment, interest and money*. London, UK: Macmillan.

Krug, E. G., Mercy, J. A., Dahlberg, L. L., & Zwi, A. B. (2002). The world report on violence and health. *Lancet, 360*(9339), 1083–1088.

Krugman, P. R. (2012). *End this depression now*. New York, NY: W.W. Norton and Company.

Lancaster, K. J. (1966). *A new approach to consumer theory*. Chicago, IL: University of Chicago Press.

Lawrence, A. (2010). Triggering nationalist violence: Competition and conflict in uprisings against colonial rule. *International Security, 35*(2), 88–122.

Lessig, L. (2011). *Republic, lost: How money corrupts Congress—and a plan to stop it*. New York, NY: Twelve.

Lowell, A. L. (1910). The physiology of politics. *American Political Science Review, 4*(1), 1–15.

Machiavelli, N. (1532). *Il Principe*. Rome, Italy: Antonio Blado d'Asola.

Malthus, T. R. (1798). *An essay on the principle of population*. London, UK: J. Johnson.

Marshall, A. (1890). *Principles of economics* (Vol. 5). Leuven, Belgium: Macmillan.

Marx, K. (1864). *Why revolution? The inaugural address of the international workingmen's association*. Glasgow, UK: Socialist Labour Party of Great Britain.

Marx, K. (1867). *Das Kapital: Der Produktionsprocess des Kapitals* (Vol. 1). Hamburg, Germany: Meissner.

Marx, K., & Engels, F. (1848). *Manifest der kommunistischen Partei*. London, UK: Communistischer Arbeiterbildungsverein.

Mill, J. S. (1871). *Principles of political economy*. London, UK: Longmans, Green.

Mitra, A., & Ray, D. (2014). Implications of an economic theory of conflict: Hindu-Muslim violence in India. *Journal of Political Economy, 122*(4), 719–765.

Muller, E. N. (1985). Income inequality, regime repressiveness, and political violence. *American Sociological Review, 50*(1), 47–61.

Neumann, V. (1944). *Theory of games and economic behavior*. Princeton, NJ: Princeton University Press.

Noah, T. (2012). *The great divergence: America's growing inequality crisis and what we can do about it*. New York, NY: Bloomsbury.

Popkin, S. L. (1979). *The rational peasant: The political economy of rural society in Vietnam*. Berkeley, CA: University of California Press.

Postmus, J. L., Plummer, S., Mcmahon, S., & Zurlo, K. A. (2013). Financial literacy: Building economic empowerment with survivors of violence. *Journal of Family and Economic Issues, 34*(3), 275–284.

Prosecutor v. Zelenović, IT-96-23/2-S, International Criminal Tribunal for the Former Yugoslavia (2007).

Rachlin, H. (2004). The behavioral economics of violence. *Annals of the New York Academy of Sciences, 1036*(1), 325–335.

Ricardo, D. (1817). *On the principles of political economy and taxation*. London, UK: J. Murray.

Ricardo, D., Sraffa, P., & Dobb, M. H. (1951). *The works and correspondence of David Ricardo*. Cambridge, UK: Cambridge University Press.

Riker, W. H., & Ordeshook, P. C. (1973). *An introduction to positive political theory*. Englewood Cliffs, NJ: Prentice Hall.

Roemer, J. E. (1987). Marxian value analysis. In J. Eatwell, M. Milgate, & P. Newman (Eds.), *The New Palgrave: A dictionary of economics* (Vol. *3*) (pp. 383). London, UK: Macmillan Stockton Press Maruzen.

Schelling, T. C. (1967). *Arms and influence.* New Haven, CT: Yale University Press.

Schumpeter, J. A. (1954). *History of economic analysis.* Oxford, UK: Psychology Press.

Shepard, W. S. (2002). The ETA: Spain fights Europe's last active terrorist group. *Mediterranean Quarterly, 13*(1), 54–68.

Simon, H. A. (1957). *Models of man.* New York, NY: Wiley and Sons.

Sims, C. A. (1980). Macroeconomics and reality. *Econometrica: Journal of the Econometric Society, 48*(1), 1–48.

Skeperdas, S., Soares, R., Willman, A., & Miller, S. C. (2009). *The costs of violence.* Washington, DC: World Bank. Retrieved from http://siteresources.worldbank.org/ EXTSOCIALDEVELOPMENT/Resources/244362-1239390842422/6012763-1239905793229/ costs_of_violence.pdf

Smith, A. (1786). *An inquiry into the nature and causes of the wealth of nations.* London, UK: Strahan and Cadell.

Spinoza, B. (1670). *A theologico-political treatise.* Amsterdam, Netherlands: Apud Henricum Künraht.

Sraffa, P. (2004). *The works and correspondence of David Ricardo.* Ann Harbor, MI: Edwards Brothers.

Staniland, P. (2012). States, insurgents, and wartime political orders. *Perspectives on Politics, 10*(02), 243–264.

Stanley, W. (1998). The economics of violence in Latin America: A theory of political competition. *Studies in Comparative International Development, 32*(4), 121–122.

Stigler, G. J. (1976). The successes and failures of Professor Smith. *Journal of Political Economy, 84*(6), 1199–1213.

Stiglitz, J. E. (2012). *The price of inequality: How today's divided society endangers our future.* New York, NY: Norton and Company.

Stoner, J. R. (2008). Political science and political education. Paper presented at the annual meeting of the APSA Teaching and Learning Conference. San José, CA: American Political Science Association.

Thucydides (1550). *The hystory writtone by Thucidides.* (T. Nicolls, Trans.). London, UK: Tylle.

United Nations. (2015). *Transforming our world: The 2030 agenda for sustainable development.* New York, NY: United Nations. Retrieved from https://sustainabledevelopment.un.org/content/ documents/21252030%20Agenda%20for%20Sustainable%20Development%20web.pdf

Urdal, H. (2006). A clash of generations? Youth bulges and political violence. *International Studies Quarterly, 50*(3), 607–629.

Vagliasindi, P. A. (2004). *Uncertainty and game theory: Private choices and public choices.* Borgo Lalatta, Italy: Collegio Europo di Parma.

Verdeja, E. (2012). The political science of genocide: Outlines of an emerging research agenda. *Perspectives on Politics, 10*(2), 307–321.

Ward, C. (2004). *Anarchism: A very short introduction.* Oxford, UK: Oxford University Press.

Weber, M. (1921). *Wirtschaft und gesellschaft.* Tübingen, Germany: Mohr.

Weinstein, J. M. (2007). *Inside rebellion: The politics of insurgent violence.* Cambridge, UK: Cambridge University Press.

Welch, D. A. (1995). *Justice and the genesis of war.* Cambridge University Press.

Wood, E. J. (2009). Armed groups and sexual violence: When is wartime rape rare? *Politics and Society, 37*(1), 131–161.

World Bank. (2011). *World development report: Conflict, security, and development.* Washington, DC: Author. Retrieved from http://siteresources.worldbank.org/INTWDRS/Resources/ WDR2011_Full_Text.pdf

7

Structural Violence

Introduction

> Few tragedies can be more extensive than the stunting of life, few injustices deeper than the denial of an opportunity to strive or even to hope, by a limit imposed from without, but falsely identified as lying within.
>
> —*Stephen Jay Gould*, The Mismeasure of Man *(1996)*

Structural violence, though mostly hidden and unrecognized, is a concept important enough in any study of violence to warrant a full chapter in this volume, even though it is not a field of study in its own right. In light of its scope, importance, and implications—in causing other forms of violence, we may even argue that it is a central concept. Structural violence refers to the avoidable limitations that society places on groups of people that constrain them from meeting their basic needs and achieving the quality of life that would otherwise be possible. These limitations, which can be political, economic, religious, cultural, or legal in nature, usually originate in institutions that exercise power over particular subjects. Because these limitations are embedded in social structures that operate normatively, people tend to overlook them as nothing more than ordinary difficulties that they encounter in the course of their daily lives. For example, many people desperately need education, healthcare, political power, or legal assistance but are unable to access them easily due to restrictions in the existing social order.

Unlike more visible and obvious forms of violence, where a person or a group of persons physically harms someone, structural violence occurs through economically, politically, or culturally driven processes that work together in such a way as to limit victims from achieving full quality of life (Gupta, 2012). At first glance, structural violence may seem a misnomer, for inequality and injustice are characteristics within very stable social structures where there is little overt disruption, but persistent and insidious damage results. For example, if someone dies of tuberculosis, autoimmune deficiency syndrome (AIDS), or another curable disease in the modern world, where advanced medications exist but are not accessible to them, then that is a form of structural violence (Ho, 2007). We classify it as a form of violence because these deaths are preventable and only occur because of disparities in distribution of health care among different strata or regions. The harm is structural because it is a product of institutions and other structures; it is violent because it causes injury and death. It is human violence because these are human decisions and not natural occurrences, and because it is correctable and preventable through human agency (Winter and Leighton, 2001).

Violence: An Interdisciplinary Approach to Causes, Consequences, and Cures, First Edition. Bandy X. Lee.
© 2019 John Wiley & Sons, Inc. Published 2019 by John Wiley & Sons, Inc.

A key aspect of structural violence is that it is often subtle, invisible, and accepted as a matter of course; even more difficult than detecting it is assigning culpability for it, since the actors are often impossible to identify, hidden as they are behind anonymous institutions or long disappeared while the violence continues. There are no concrete operators directly attacking others, as when one person kills another. However, if we took into account the victim's and not just the perpetrator's perspective, structural violence has similar effects as behavioral violence, including death (Morgan et al., 2014). Structural violence, in fact, is by far the most lethal form of violence as well as the most potent cause of other forms of violence (Butchart & Engström, 2002). The magnitude of damage warrants calling it violence rather than simply social injustice or oppression. The excess rates of death and disability resulting from the social and economic structures of our society—that is, its division into rich and poor, powerful and weak, and superior and inferior—are measurable using life expectancy data, as we will see later in this chapter. Calculations show that between 10 and 20 million deaths per year can be attributed to structural violence (Høivik, 1977), more than ten times the number due to suicide, homicide, and warfare *combined*. The numbers are even greater now, and the Commission on Social Determinants of Health of the World Health Organization (WHO, 2008) has declared that social injustice is killing people on a grand scale.

A cause of this omission is an incomplete definition: without a clear definition of what constitutes violence, important—even central—occurrences will be missed, and many a fallacious conclusion become possible. This text therefore begins and ends with definitions: from a holistic, ecological perspective, all forms of violence originate from a continuum of bio-psycho-socio-environmental causes. This means that no violence is entirely individual or entirely without agency, making structural violence just as much a collective responsibility as any other type of violence. We choose our societal structures when we decide, as every society does, how to distribute or not to distribute, or how to share or not to share, the collective income and wealth that the society produces—as well as which arrangements we will accept and maintain. Indian economist Amartya Sen (1982) won the Nobel Prize in economics in part for demonstrating that the mass deaths that occur during famines are not the result of food shortage, but rather of the poor's shortage of purchasing power—they cannot afford to buy the food that is already available in their countries.

Similarly, the millions of deaths occurring because of the AIDS epidemic in low-income nations, such as those of sub-Saharan Africa, are not the result of natural causes but of poverty: poor people with AIDS cannot afford to pay for the medicines that save the lives of millions of similar victims in high-income countries. The effects of unequal control over the distribution of resources worsen if those low in income are also low in education, in health, and in power—as is frequently the case, as these dimensions interlink within the societal structure. In order to account for all these areas of harm, we must adopt a larger definition of violence not limited to existing fields of inquiry, one that will adapt inquiry to the need for understanding.

Origins of the Concept

Although an embryonic and incomplete understanding of structural violence may be as old as injustice and conflict themselves, the concept as a topic of scientific study gained salience as the result of a seminal essay by the Norwegian sociologist Johan Galtung (1969). He defined structural violence as a deliberate impairment of fundamental human needs by actors of power. He rejected the narrow definition of violence as somatic incapacitation or deprivation of health alone, with killing as the extreme form, at the hands of an actor who intends the consequence. If this were all violence is about, he argued, highly unacceptable social orders would still be compatible with peace. If people are starving when starvation is objectively avoidable, then violence has occurred, regardless of whether there is a clear subject–action–object relationship, which is becoming less and less relevant to contemporary world economic relations.

In simpler terms, violence is present whenever social, economic, and cultural forces influence human beings in such a way that they are unable to attain their potential, physically or mentally or both. In other words, violence is the cause of the difference between the *potential* and the *actual*, or what could have been and what is, regardless of whether a clearly identifiable actor is present. Galtung (1985) acknowledges his inspiration by the leader of the Indian independence movement, Mohandas Gandhi, who called poverty "the worst form of violence" and commented that by moving away from the actor-oriented perspective of most Western social sciences, he could focus on the situations where individuals can do enormous harm to other human beings without ever intending to, merely by performing their regular duties as defined by the prevailing social, political, and economic structures. Structural violence is a process that works slowly through general misery, diminishing the dignity of human beings and ultimately killing them, sometimes without anyone being aware that it is happening. According to this perspective, people can avoid much structural violence if they become aware of the limitations their social structures impose on them (Beyer, 2008).

The concept also developed in the 1950s and 1960s through liberation theologians in the Catholic Church in Latin America, principally as a moral reaction to the poverty and social injustices in the region (Gutiérrez, 1973). Meanwhile, Canadian peace researchers Gernot Kohler and Norman Alcock (1976) devised ways to quantify social, political, and economic inequalities. In the first of two measures, they used Sweden as a model because it had come closest to eliminating structural violence, with the most equal standards of living and the highest life expectancy of all nations. They asked how many deaths could be avoided if all countries enjoyed the same living conditions as Sweden. The second measure they used was "the egalitarian model," for which they calculated a complete and equal redistribution of the available global wealth. They then asked how many deaths could be avoided if this kind of equitable sharing could ever be achieved. The results were stark. When the authors compared life expectancies elsewhere in the world with those in Sweden, they calculated that some 18 million deaths each year could be attributed to structural violence, or the socioeconomic inequalities that exist globally.

They worked from the assumption that life expectancy is a function of relative socioeconomic position (Galtung & Høivik, 1971). Then, plotting gross national product (GNP) per capita for each nation on earth, they were able to show that life expectancy in nations with a GNP per capita equal to the world average was 68.3 years in the year 1965. A remarkable finding from this model of life expectancy is its magnitude. Spreading wealth and resources equally *raised* the average life expectancy by approximately 40 years for the country with the lowest life expectancy, which in 1965 was 27 years in Guinea. Meanwhile, it *lowered* life expectancy by only 6 years for the country with the highest life expectancy, which was 74.7 years in Sweden. In other words, achieving conditions of complete global equality would produce only a marginal loss in life expectancy in richer countries while creating a tremendous number of extra years of life in poorer nations.

Today, the differences are starker: a child born in a suburb of Glasgow in Scotland can expect a life 28 years shorter than another living only 13 km away. A girl in Lesotho is likely to live 42 years less than another in Japan. In Sweden, the risk of a woman dying during pregnancy and childbirth is 1 in 17,400; in Afghanistan, the odds are one in eight (WHO, 2008). It is a violence that is built into the structure of the society and constitutes differences in life chances while manifesting in infant mortality, slow starvation, disease, despair, and humiliation that destroys almost every aspect of life. In this manner, social and economic policies that create and augment the differences between—and within—countries are crucial factors in whether a child will grow and develop to full potential and live a flourishing life, or whether its life will be blighted. British social epidemiologists Richard Wilkinson and Kate Pickett (2008) similarly conclude that egalitarian societies would do enormously better overall with only minor compromises from the wealthy. The association between income distribution and population health is remarkable, as in the example of the US. Despite being the richest nation on earth, it has wider income disparities than other developed countries and, as expected, a lower average life expectancy than those countries (Kulkarni, Levin-Rector, Ezzati, & Murray, 2011).

One of the greatest problems encountered by any student of structural violence is the fact that this type of violence is barely perceptible when compared with behavioral violence. The tolls of street violence or war seem at first glance much higher, but in reality the "tranquil" waters of structural violence are much more harmful. We might even go as far as to say that the *least* damaging forms of violence are the most overt, while the most destructive forms are hidden. American violence scholar James Gilligan (1999) compared structural violence with the most deadly military conflicts in history. Estimating a total of 49 million military and civilian fatalities from World War II, or about eight million deaths per year from 1939 to 1945, and also considering the death toll from a hypothetical nuclear exchange between the US and the former Soviet Union to be 232 million, Gilligan concluded that these numbers could not even begin to compare with the harm of structural violence. The latter continues year after year, during times of peace as well as of war, and roughly every 15 years, on average, as many people have died because of relative poverty as would die in a nuclear war that caused 232 million deaths. This is, in effect, the equivalent of an ongoing, unending but rather accelerating thermonuclear war or genocide perpetrated on the weak, the poor, and the underprivileged every year of every decade, throughout the world.

Gilligan also described structural violence in terms of increased rates of disabilities and deaths among people who occupy the bottom class; the suffering of people from the lower strata of society is a function of the more privileged classes having collective bargaining power to determine how and where resources will be allocated. Unlike behavioral violence, the lethal effects of structural violence operate continuously rather than sporadically. It can occur independently of any intention to kill anyone; for example, it can be a byproduct of wishing to maximize one's own wealth and power. It is usually invisible, in the sense that deaths from structural violence may appear to have other causes, be they natural or violent. More recent figures bear out these conclusions even more startlingly, as we will see later in this chapter. Gilligan (2001) also maintained that feelings of shame, humiliation, and inferiority, which become pronounced as the disparity between classes increases, are the most potent cause of behavioral violence such as suicide, homicide, warfare, and capital punishment (Bloom, 2001).

More recently, American anthropologist Paul Farmer (2003) developed the concept of structural violence further by first defining structure as a *pattern of collective social actions* that occur within institutional practices, laws, economic policies, and other habitual elements. Not just collective thoughts and beliefs, these structures can materially manifest through facilities such as roads, server systems, hospitals, and schools. From Farmer's perspective, violence is suffering that results from social arrangements that put individuals in harm's way. In this case, given that the exertion of structural violence is systematic—that is to say, *indirectly applied* by all members of a given social order—no particular individual is fully at fault, while at the same time *everyone* in that order is partly at fault. Cumulative historical forces and processes work together to constrain individual agency, if not always neatly, from being able to resist marginalization and oppression, and deny them the benefits of social progress.

Case Vignettes

A Prison Inmate's Predicament

Structural violence can take the form of discrimination against poor, minority, and mentally ill individuals. Those who experience further marginalization through entry into a correctional system are at even greater risk. Correctional inmates are generally treated poorly, even more so if they are a member of a minority group and mentally ill, which can lead to increased incidences of death. Terrill Thomas, a 38-year-old mentally ill black man, is such an example. He dies of dehydration in April 2016 in Milwaukee, Wisconsin, while being held in solitary confinement in part due to his behavior in jail.

According to the *Milwaukee Journal Sentinel*, inmates near Thomas heard him beg for water days before his death. Correction officers are said to have turned off the water supply as punishment for his flooding his previous cell and for his erratic behavior. Thomas had bipolar disorder, for which a psychiatrist was prescribing medication, and he was "not operating in a world of reality" when he entered the institution. Yet, instead of making sure that he received treatment for his very serious mental health condition, the jail responded by punishing him for acting out. Treating his mental illness as a behavioral problem, the jailers disciplined him. He had been arrested on charges of shooting a man and later firing a gun inside a hotel and casino, and had been placed in a cell at the Milwaukee County Jail with no mattress, blanket, or pillow. There was a toilet, but it would not flush after the water was turned off. Thomas was not given drinks with his food, an unsavory, brick-shaped dish called "nutraloaf" that some states have banned. He did not eat and lost at least 30 pounds, according to his lawyer. Other inmates told correction officers that Thomas needed water, but Thomas could not ask for it himself, and 9 days after his arrest, he is found dead on the floor of his cell.

Thomas's case is not unusual for abuse that occurs behind bars. Families who believe their loved ones were abused often have difficulty getting prosecutions. Although public interest in police shootings has grown in the US, abuse in the prison system is more likely to remain hidden, partly because police shootings in public spaces are often captured by videos that go viral and stoke widespread calls for justice. That type of evidence is rare in jail-related deaths: the video footing allegedly showing the guards shutting off the water and not turning it back on in Thomas's case have been recorded over or deleted. Hence, the same level of accountability is difficult to obtain. Poor investigation leads to less awareness of what is happening (Victor, 2017). The sheriff led a "tough on crime" campaign that year, but the jail was found to be dangerous, with four inmate deaths that year.

A Poor Child's Martyrdom

Bonded child labor is the slavery of and structural violence against individuals below the age of majority. Throughout history, many children have been sold into slavery so as to repay family debts or crimes or to earn some money. The enslavement and trafficking of children continues today, especially in low-income countries. Iqbal Masih, a boy from a small, rural village outside of Lahore in Pakistan, suffered such a fate.

Shortly after Iqbal's birth, his father abandoned the family, and his mother found it difficult to make enough money to feed all her children. In 1986, Iqbal's older brother was to be married, and the family needed money to pay for a celebration. For a very poor family in Pakistan, the only way to borrow money was to ask a local employer. Iqbal's family borrowed 600 rupees (about 12 US dollars) from a man who owned a carpet-weaving business. Without asking or consulting Iqbal, who was just 4 years old, his family sold him into bondage through a *peshgi* (loans) system. Iqbal had to work an entire year without wages in order to learn the skills of a carpet weaver. During and after his apprenticeship, his employer added the cost of the food he ate and the tools he used to the original loan. When he made mistakes, he was fined, which also added to the loan. In addition to these costs, the employer added interest. It was not unusual for employers to pad the total, keeping the children in bondage for life. By the time Iqbal was 10 years old, the loan had grown to 13,000 rupees (about 260 US dollars). Iqbal worked 6 days a week, at least 14 hours a day, in terrible conditions and sweltering heat. If he or the other apprentices talked back, ran away, were homesick, or were physically sick, they were severely beaten, chained to their loom, isolated in a dark closet, or hung upside down. After all this, Iqbal was paid 60 rupees (about 20 cents) a day after his apprenticeship ended.

After working 6 years as a carpet weaver, Iqbal heard about a meeting of the Bonded Labor Liberation Front (BLLF), which was working to help children like Iqbal. After work, he snuck away to attend the meeting. There, he learned that the government had outlawed *peshgi* in 1992. Shocked, Iqbal spoke to the president of the BLLF, who helped him get the paperwork he needed to show his employer that he should be free. Not content just to be free himself, he worked also to get his fellow workers free. Iqbal studied very hard, finishing 4 years of schoolwork in two. He eventually helped over 3,000 Pakistani children who were in bonded labor to escape to freedom and made speeches about child labor throughout the world. He expressed a desire to become a lawyer to better equip him to free bonded laborers, and he attended conferences in Sweden and in the US to encourage others to help eradicate child slavery. Iqbal's growing popularity and influence led to him receiving numerous death threats. In April 1995, Iqbal was shot dead while he and some friends were cycling in Muridke. He was 12 years old. The problem of bonded child labor continues today, with millions of children in Pakistan and India working in factories to make carpets, mud bricks, cigarettes, jewelry, and clothing—all in horrific conditions similar to those Iqbal experienced (Rosenberg, 2017).

A Lead Into Collective Violence

Structural violence, or systematic subjugation, can lead to a greater chance of overt violence. A civil rights campaign arose in Northern Ireland, UK, in the mid-1960s with grievances calling for an end to job, housing, and voting discrimination, as well as an end to gerrymandering that reduced voting power, a reduction in police brutality and the allowance for police to search without a warrant, arrest, and imprison people without charge or trial—which favored Loyalists (supporters of continued English involvement) over Republicans (opponents of English involvement who desire unification of Northern Ireland with the Irish Republic). The movement was largely nonviolent at the start, but the emergence of armed paramilitary organizations led to warfare over the next three decades.

The Irish Republican Army (IRA) is any of several armed movements in Ireland dedicated to Irish Republicanism, or the belief that all of Ireland should be an independent republic. It is also characterized by the belief that political violence is necessary to achieve that goal. The conflict in Northern Ireland between Loyalists and Republicans has claimed many lives throughout the years of violence. The conflict in Northern Ireland between Loyalists and Republicans is also a division between Protestants and Catholics, and the violence in many cases is as much about brutal sectarianism as about political goals. The Provisional Irish Republican Army (PIRA) develops in 1969, splitting from the rest of the Republican movement due to differences in political and military strategy.

Violent conflict over British involvement in Ireland has an extensive history even as the political landscape shifts. The British withdrew from the majority of the Irish island in 1921, the part that became the independent Republic of Ireland in 1948, and the island was geographically partitioned to form Northern Ireland, a part of the waning British Empire. The PIRA operates as an insurgent terrorist organization, carrying out operations in Northern Ireland, in the Irish Republic, on the British mainland, and in other areas, including continental Europe and the United States. Their goal is to force a British withdrawal from Ireland and to establish a Democratic Socialist Republic based on the Easter Proclamation of 1916. As it pursues these goals, the group seeks to maintain the allegiance of the Catholic population in Northern Ireland and the Republic, its primary support community. The PIRA also draws on Republican traditions that call for brutal force as the means by which to achieve the goal of Irish unification.

Included in the IRA's violence is directed political assassinations. Lord Mountbatten is a legendary British statesman and a naval officer, as well as an uncle of Prince Philip, Duke of Edinburgh, and cousin to Elizabeth II. Despite security advice and warnings, in August 1979, Mountbatten goes fishing in his wooden boat, which IRA member Thomas McMahon had slipped into the previous night and attached a radio-controlled bomb. When Mountbatten is a few hundred yards from the shore, the bomb detonates. The IRA claims responsibility for the death of Lord Mountbatten. They say that the operation is one of the ways they can bring the continuing occupation of their country to the attention of the English people. The many tributes to Mountbatten, they note, will sharply contrast with the indifference of the British government and the English people to the deaths of Irish men, women, and children, as well as Irish soldiers at the hands of the British forces. Gerry Adams, one of the leaders of the IRA, says that what the IRA did to Lord Mountbatten is what Mountbatten has been doing all his life to other people. With his war record, Adams argues, Lord Mountbatten could not object to dying in what is clearly a war situation (Jackson, Baker, & Cragin, 2005).

A Lead Into Self-Directed Violence

Structural violence can also lead to higher suicides. When the first of three Free Trade Zones (FTZ) in Sri Lanka was established in the town of Katunayake in 1978 under the World Bank/International Monetary Fund (IMF) structural adjustment program, it was expected that rural, unemployed women who have little chance to find wage employment elsewhere would fill the newly created assembly-line jobs. They would work for only a few years before marriage to accumulate money and jewelry for their dowry. The assumption was that the women working in the zones would accept employment under any conditions, leading to rigorous work schedules and minimal wages. By 1995, Sri Lanka records the highest rate of suicide in the world at 48 deaths per 100,000, and the rate is two and a half times greater in rural areas than in metropolitan centers, corresponding to the rural–urban disparity in agricultural development and economic stagnation. More than half of all suicides in Sri Lanka are committed by young people, age 15 to 29, of both sexes.

A wailing woman, Ramya, threatens to kill herself but is restrained and pushed onto a bed. When Ramya's wailing and physical struggles do not stop, another woman pins her to the wall and tells her sternly to stop behaving like an ignorant fool and act like the educated woman she is. Ramya seems to consider this and quiets down for a while. A few hours later, she starts wailing again. Another resident, Malika, talks to her in a soft voice, asking her to "be a good child, and listen to what others say." Ramya again quiets down and falls asleep with her head on a friend's lap. Women casually mention committing suicide at the factories. It is common for them to point to a stressful situation and to say that the only thing left for them to do is to put a rope around their necks and hang themselves or to pour a bottle of poison in their mouths. These suicidal expressions usually come at the end of a long story and appear to provide relief and a symbolic closure to their concerns. Listeners offer comforting words, praising the storyteller for having the courage not to commit suicide despite the problems. Often the story-teller adds a few more sentences about how hard resisting the impulse for self-harm is, and how they are strong women who can negotiate an unfair world with quiet resolve. They overcome their difficulties through a common identity as migrant transnational factory workers and the sisterhood the women develop with their housemates.

In a short story by one of the FTZ workers, a worker who has committed suicide narrates the following story from her coffin, surveying her own funeral: "Both *amma* [mother] and *thatha* [father] are crying now. You would not have to cry so much if you had been more understanding of my problems. Look at the way boarding [house] auntie is grieving. I hope at least now she will be more sympathetic toward girls' problems. Ah, here comes Kumar. He is crying now. He should. He is the reason why I am lying here." In the story, the dead woman takes her revenge by making all those who have wronged her regret their actions. The story grows haunting at the end as she screams in fear, pleading with her relatives and friends not to leave her alone in the cold, dark cemetery (Hewamanne, 2010).

Healthcare, Nutrition, and Liberty Disparities

As we have already stated, structural violence can take many forms and can be so entrenched in the social order that it is difficult to recognize. In this section, we will examine a few of the more widespread and recognizable ways in which structural violence can manifest in society. One of the most pressing ways in which structural violence causes morbidity and mortality in people is through *healthcare disparities*. Preventable diseases such as diarrhea and pneumonia kill approximately two million children worldwide every year, simply because they are too poor to afford the effective treatment that is available (United Nations Children's Fund [UNICEF], 2012). As of 2013, nearly 22 million children under the age of one had not received proper vaccinations against diphtheria, tetanus, and pertussis (UNICEF & WHO, 2014). In 2010, almost 300,000 childbirth-related deaths occurred globally, most of them in low- and middle-income countries, and most of them avoidable (WHO, UNICEF, United Nations Population Fund [UNFPA], & The World Bank, 2012). Over the past 50 years, the maternal mortality rate of black women in the US has been four times as high as that of white women (Tucker, Berg, Callaghan, & Hsia, 2007). In 2007, the infant mortality rate for non-Hispanic black women was 2.4 times that of non-Hispanic white women (Mathews & MacDorman, 2011).

One of the deadlier healthcare disparities pertains to the human immunodeficiency virus (HIV) infection. Studies indicate that 88% of all children and 60% of all women infected with HIV live in sub-Saharan Africa, where nations are typically low-income and underdeveloped. In 2007, an estimated 40 million people were living with HIV, more than 90% of them from low-income countries with limited access to prevention and treatment facilities. Reasons for inadequate resources can be variable: in Northern Uganda, for example, which has been terrorized by the resistance army for over 15 years, an internal displacement of 1.8 million people has led to the virtual collapse of public services in the refugee camps. Consequently, the HIV prevalence in this northern region is twice that of the rest of the country (Mukherjee, 2007). Even in the US, infection rates among women of color are higher than among white women. In the Syracuse area of New York, African-American women have 12.5 times more cases of AIDS than whites (Lane et al., 2004).

Increasing poverty is another symptom and indication of structural violence. The inability to afford basic nutrition for survival is a mark of extreme poverty, but according to the United Nations World Food Programme (UNWFP, 2016), malnutrition is the leading cause of death globally, killing more people each year than HIV/AIDS, malaria, and tuberculosis *combined*. More than three billion people—nearly half of the world's population—live in poverty (on less than 2.5 US dollars per day), while more than 1.3 billion live in extreme poverty (on less than 1.25 US dollars per day) (United Nations Development Programme [UNDP], 2014). Nearly half of all deaths in children under the age of 5 are attributable to undernutrition, amounting to almost three million unnecessary deaths every year (UNICEF, WHO, & World Bank Group, 2015). Approximately 800 million people—almost 11% of the world's population, 98% of whom live in low-income countries—lack adequate food (Food and Agriculture Organization [FAO] of the UN, International Fund for Agricultural Development [IFAD], & UNWFP, 2014).

More than 750 million people lack access to clean, drinkable water, and low sanitation alone kills an estimated 842,000 people every year (WHO & UNICEF, 2014). Haiti, for example, is one of the poorest countries in the Western hemisphere. In that country, more than 54% of the population lives on less than one US dollar per day, and cholera outbreaks are endemic, as only 63% of the citizens have access to safe water sources (Alsan et al., 2011). According to Oxfam International (2013), it would take an estimated 60 billion US dollars annually to eradicate extreme global poverty. This figure seems unattainable and unrealistic until one considers that the world's 10 richest billionaires own some 505 billion US dollars in combined *private* wealth (Peterson-Withorn, 2015) and that the top 1% of earners holds more wealth than the rest of the planet combined (Credit Suisse, 2016) (see Figure 7.1). Charity and aid to the unfortunate, in this context, does little to solve the deformed statecraft that magnifies and accelerates such cruelty.

The related but more extreme form of structural violence is *contemporary slavery*, which exists in the form of underpayment and the withholding of wages and salaries, especially to workers from low-income countries. An estimated 35.8 million people are victims of contemporary slavery (Walk Free Foundation, 2014), and 10 nations account for 76 percent of this number, including India, China, Pakistan, and Nigeria. Although accurate figures are difficult to calculate, this multibillion-dollar industry reaps up to 150 billion US dollars annually in illegal profits (International Labour Organization, 2008). Approximately 70 percent of modern-day slaves are female, and up to 50 percent are minors (United States Department of State,

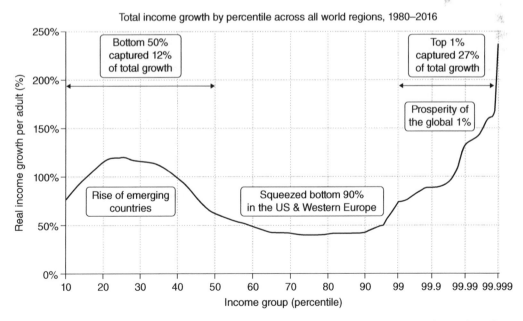

Figure 7.1 Although the poorest half of the global population has seen some income growth, mainly in China and in India, the top 1% richest individuals in the world captured twice as much growth as the bottom 50% individuals since 1980.

2005). Women and girls are forced to work primarily in the domestic sector or as commercial sex workers, while men and boys work primarily in agriculture, construction, and mining. The root causes of contemporary slavery are disparities in economic power that force citizens from low-income economies to submit to forms of slavery and human trafficking in exchange for better standards of living.

The problem is not restricted to underdeveloped countries: there are case reports in the U.S. of illegal Mexican immigrants being lured into the country with promises by wealthy American families who then deny them wages (Barner, Okech, and Camp, 2014). Similarly, many citizens from developing West African nations have become victims of human trafficking in other high-income economies. These unfortunate laborers are typically enticed to foreign destinations with promises of a better income, only to experience exploitation as commercial sex workers or as free laborers. Given the lack of privileges of these victims, they cannot access justice for the damages they have endured. More generally, with global industrialization, the exploitation of child and female labor, urban crowding, slums, poverty, disease, prostitution, and family breakdown have grown. World conflict now occurs largely in the form of differences in interests between elites who run economic and political systems and the majority of people who do not benefit from their policies and actions. Consequently, slavery is in rapid resurgence in the context of extreme inequality.

Gender, Racial, and Voting Rights Disparities

Structural violence is persistent also in the form of *gender disparities*. Although the lives of women around the world have improved noticeably in recent decades, gaps in access to rights, education, health, and jobs still remain. One of the worst disparities is the rate at which girls and women die relative to males in low-income, developing countries, where an estimated 3.9 million excess deaths occur each year, purely as a result of gender inequality. Almost two-fifths of all female fetuses worldwide are never allowed to grow due to a preference for sons, one-sixth of all girls die in childhood, and over one-third of women die in their reproductive years (World Bank, 2012). An important facet of this gender-biased structural violence is the fact that it leads to, and encourages, behavioral violence. Countries in the Middle East, Central and Southern Asia, and North Africa record higher rates of gender-based violence than the rates in Organisation for Economic Co-operation and Development (OECD) countries. The South Asia region, known for its poor economic status, contains 69% of the world's population but suffers 96% of the world's structural violence. In Bangladesh, men propagate violence on women mainly because they have witnessed violence in their families of origin, and because social systems and structures condone such violence (Cross, 2013). Similar studies have shown that women with little education in Egypt are far more likely to tolerate violence from their husbands, especially if they are dependent on them for sustenance.

Not all gender-based structural violence is necessarily behavioral; statistics of income differences in the US show that in 2012 the wage rate for men was 23% higher than that for women, the difference being attributable to cultural biases that deny women the same opportunities as men to explore their potential. Women 1 year out of college and working full time earned on average 35,296 US dollars per year, while their male counterparts earned 42,918 dollars per year (Kesley, 2013). Another aspect of this gender disparity is the statistics on maternal deaths. In the 1980s, half a million maternal deaths occurred annually, of which 99% were in poor countries. Although the number of annual maternal deaths has been declining since then, a 2010 survey report by the UN Population Fund (FPA) showed that pregnancy- and birth-related complications are still the leading causes of death among 15- to 19-year-olds in low-income countries (Mukherjee et al., 2011).

Structural violence can also operate through systematic *racial disparities*. The United States is home to systematic racial discrimination; the US incarcerates 2.4 million people, and although African-Americans make up only 13% of the population, they comprise 41% of the country's prison population. And while drug-use figures are similar for blacks and whites in the US, the former are 2.8 to 5.5 times more likely to be arrested and to receive longer and harsher sentences for this kind of crime than the latter (Human Rights Watch, 2009).

A recent US Department of Justice report (2015) on the police department of Ferguson, Missouri, following an investigation of the 2014 police killing of an unarmed African-American teenager, revealed that the impact on African-Americans is disproportionate at all levels of justice, a trend that is widespread throughout the entire country (Malcolm X Grassroots Movement, 2012). This kind of disparity is directly attributable to structural racism, which facilitates negative stereotypes and legitimizes keeping minority groups from defending themselves. Many of the U.S. practices, particularly in the areas of criminal justice, immigration, and national security, violate international human rights standards in this manner (Human Rights Watch, 2015).

A more hidden but similar trend is apparent in unemployment figures: data from a 2013 Center for Economic and Policy Research survey showed that the overall unemployment rate among 22- to 27-year-old college graduates in the US was 5.6%, while for African-American graduates, it was 12.4% (Jones & Schmitt, 2014). At the same time, African-Americans exhibit elevated rates of mortality for 8 out of the 10 major causes of death, most of which have an association with disparities in healthcare access (Williams & Collins, 2001). In 2008, white Americans with 16 years or more of schooling had life expectancies far greater than African-Americans with fewer than 12 years of education—14.2 years for men and 10.3 years for women (Olshansky et al., 2012). Europe also has a number of disturbing trends in the area of racial disparity, which are now threatening to enter mainstream politics through far-right parties, thereby further entrenching discriminatory structures. Sentiments against immigration are running particularly high, with most Europeans viewing immigrants as an economic burden, as not assimilating, and as perpetrating crimes—these attitudes are a side effect of global structural violence, which divides rich countries and poor countries roughly over racial lines.

Another form of structural violence is the *control of voting rights* and the denial of political power. This can occur either within sovereign states, as in the Apartheid regime of South Africa, or within international bodies like the International Monetary Fund, in which countries such as Japan, Germany, the United Kingdom, and the United States exert excessive influence. For example, the US treasury funds more than half of the World Bank and therefore has numerous fiscal privileges, while low-income countries like those in Africa have little hope of enjoying the same privileges and thus the benefits of trade liberalization (Global Envision, 2007). Global institutions can also facilitate and encourage corruption in national governments and institutions: in the face of extreme inequalities, it is far more lucrative for the latter to cater to the interests of foreign governments and firms than to the interests of their impoverished compatriots (Pogge, 2002). In this manner, the power to choose and to change unjust structures is unavailable to those who do not have the power in the first place.

Expansion of the Concept

Earlier in this book we discussed how the World Report on Violence and Health (Krug et al., 2002) has been instrumental in shaping global discourse on violence, beginning with a standard definition. The definition reflected the progression in violence studies to recognize psychological violence as potentially more damaging than physical violence. It also included neglect because, for human beings, deprivation of care can be more consequential than adverse but still-present human contact. Finally, it opened room for inclusion of structural violence, which causes far greater excess deaths than all the overt killings combined, is the most destructive violence of our era. One of the strengths of the definition in the *World Report* is that it reflects the broader understanding that violence is not just physical force; it includes the critical concept of power. Structural violence is therefore an illustration of a power system wherein social structures or institutions cause harm to people in a way that results in maldevelopment and other deprivations, akin to abuse or neglect at systemic scale.

Galtung distinguishes between structural, direct, and cultural violence. By this definition, *direct violence* occurs through physical and verbal abuse, but it is also in synergy with structural and cultural violence (Galtung Institut, 2016). The concept of *cultural violence* includes the beliefs and attitudes of a group of people that define their heritage; aspects of culture such as religion, art, ideology, language, science, and other communal, symbolic elements that embody these beliefs are used to justify or legitimize either direct or cultural violence. A good example of this kind of violence is a history tale that glorifies war victories and makes people overlook the value of collaboration (Fink, 2010). Bourgois (2001) summarizes research to date and identifies three additional types of violence, namely political, symbolic, and everyday, normalized violence. *Political violence* refers to the direct perpetration of violent acts in the name of a political ideology, movement, or state, or as a part of resistance to the state (Farmer et al., 2006). *Symbolic violence* is a term that applies to power structures that result in the internalization of humiliations and legitimizations of the hierarchy, resulting in self-blame for misfortunes and a naturalization of the status quo.

American anthropologist Nancy Scheper-Hughes (1996) has further developed the concept of *everyday violence* in an effort to draw attention to the process by which out-of-the-ordinary events like death and torture become normal and accepted because of the sheer ubiquity of brutality. By these definitions, careful observation is necessary, as those with the greatest interest in maintaining the status quo do not have to exert themselves much to defend it. They can mobilize the army, the police, mercenaries, and even the behavioral violence of the underclass to strengthen the existing order: in these instances, "security forces" are just doing their jobs when the establishment orders them into action through established structural expectations.

Most groups conceal their naked domination under a veil of ideological or esthetic purity. French philosopher Pierre Bourdieu (1979) has described this vicious competition as a form of symbolic violence in which different groups and individuals use their different positions in society to employ different social strategies. People at the top, for example, may adopt a reserved and understated style to show that they are far above the assertive, attention-seeking strategies that expose the pretensions of the less "refined." People at the bottom, however, do not have a lot of accomplishment to brandish but can use irony and sarcasm to demonstrate their upper hand. The drive to be superior to others under conditions of inequality is an endemic condition that propels its members, consciously or not, to commit violence against others. It manifests in trying to gain status and cultural affirmation in ways that advance oneself at the expense of others, in developing tastes, promoting lifestyles, and advancing "class" in ways that separate one's own group further from those of others.

Although cultural inequality does not create economic inequality as much as it widens and legitimizes it, cultural capital and economic capital have become ever more intertwined with time. Acts of *microaggression* are brief, everyday exchanges that send denigrating messages to certain individuals because of their group membership, be it minority, poor, disabled, or some other marginalized status (Pierce, 1995; Sue, 2010). Because underlying them are far more pervasive structures that denigrate human beings and diminish self-esteem, the effects exceed the specific abuses. Meanwhile, individuals or classes that have mastered the cultural "code" dominate the places where financial opportunities are richest. These add to the widening social distances, which then serve to widen geographic and economic gaps. Therefore, it almost takes a conscious, *countercultural* noncompliance on the part of the individual to reverse some of this relentless trend.

Scheper-Hughes (2006) emphasizes that structural violence refers to the ease with which humans are capable of reducing the socially vulnerable to expendable "non-persons." This implicitly gives them the license—even duty—to kill them. She shows how ubiquitous and normal even the most brutal forms of violence can become—through examples such as the operation of a death squad in Northeast Brazil that mobilized the support of ordinary people in an almost genocidal attack against Afro-Brazilian street "marginals," and the incomplete integration of "dangerous and endangered" youth still living in squatter camps and shack communities of urban South Africa. In this manner, elimination of entire groups of people can become "everyday" as a result of a change in conceptualization (Haslam, 2006).

The Most Potent Stimulant

In addition to being the deadliest form of violence, structural violence is also the most potent stimulant of behavioral violence. American civil rights activist Martin Luther King Jr. (1967) was prescient in calling the "deplorable crimes" of African-Americans to be "derivative crimes"—born of the greater crimes of the white society. Gilligan (1996) has drawn a relationship between structural violence—or divisions into superiority and inferiority, by whatever means—and the shame, stress, discrimination, and denigration that result from a lower status. This underlying psychology in turn stimulates murders, wars, suicides, and deaths from stress-induced illness. Others have framed it in terms of an erosion of social networks and trust (Elgar & Aitken, 2010). The increase in rates of death and disability that arise from structural violence often results from overt violence in the form of family violence, gender violence, racial violence, hate crimes, police violence, state violence, massacres, terrorism, and war. Indeed, a World Bank-sponsored study proved that in 39 nations around the world, homicide rates increased with inequality (Fajnzylber, Lederman, & Loayza, 2002).

By using rates of employment as a measure of inequality (Galbraith, 1998), we discover that unemployment brings greater mortality (Martikainen & Valkonen, 1996). The figures are valid even among the more developed countries. For 26 European nations, from 1970 to 2007, every 1% increase in unemployment indicated a 0.79% rise in suicides and a 0.79% rise in homicides (Stuckler et al., 2009). Globalized corporate management, with a rising percentage of layoffs, downsizing, and impersonal management styles has seen rises in workplace violence, usually ending with the perpetrator's suicide (Noer, 2009).

Another cross-sectional study of 165 countries showed that economic development, inequality, and poverty are significant predictors of homicide, although there are many variations in homicide for lower-income countries (Ouimet, 2012). Some researchers have taken excess deaths and poor health outcomes to be indicators of unequal development (Pickett & Wilkinson, 2015), while others have approached the question from a feminist perspective (Anglin, 1998; Brock-Utne, 1989), or in terms of human rights (Eisler, 1997). Economic decline, income inequality, and pervasive rent seeking by ruling elites can generate a reduced surplus in the larger population that can threaten entire nations. Weakening states, alongside competitions for control of goods, eventually give rise to humanitarian emergencies due to war and state violence (Nafziger & Auvinen, 2002). There is also political decay in relation to relative deprivation or a perception of injustice arising from a growing discrepancy between expectations and economic and social realities. The structural violence of domination, exploitation, and humiliation also needs to draw on physical violence in order to coerce its victims to submit to the more powerful party. Some have shown that well-established democracies do not make war (Rummel, 2003; Weart, 1998), while power and inequality among nations are associated with interstate wars (Hinsley, 1967; van Evera, 2013).

Perhaps in need of special emphasis are the effects of economic inequality on suicide. Unemployment (Voss et al., 2004) and frequency of bankruptcy (Weyerer & Wiedenmann, 1995) are highly associated with increased suicide, with a twofold to threefold increase in relative risk (Blakely, Collings, & Atkinson, 2003). However, what is important is not absolute but relative poverty, pointing to factors other than material deprivation. In settings of high economic inequality, suicide among the poor rises drastically, but so does suicide among the rich, to a lesser degree (Daly, Wilson, & Johnson, 2013). With rising inequalities, a concern for human rights becomes more prominent. *Human rights* are moral principles or norms that outline standards for the treatment of others, in recognition of the inherent dignity and equal and inalienable rights of all members of the human family (United Nations, 1948). The topic has entered into international dialog over the last century in the effort to understand how violence, terrorism, war, poverty, inequality, development, and democracy relate to one another. In the context of rising inequalities (Piketty & Goldhammer, 2014), the drive for a more humane and inclusive kind of globalization and development has led to the 1993 World Conference on Human Rights, which animated the fiftieth anniversary celebrations of the 1948 *Universal Declaration of Human Rights* and ultimately influenced the drafting of the *2030 Agenda for Sustainable Development* (United Nations, 2015).

Conclusion

At a time when areas such as healthcare, education, and communications are advancing rapidly, the majority of humankind is increasingly left behind, with consequences that amount to life and death. In this chapter, we called this condition structural violence and noted how it is by far the most lethal form of violence. We also showed how, because these limitations are embedded within social structures, they may seem as nothing more than the ordinary difficulties of life. We gave examples as health, economic, gender, and racial disparities, and highlighted how structural violence is also the most potent stimulant of behavioral violence. Global and national communities often hold poor countries and the poor responsible for violence, but with unjust socioeconomic structures at its root, sporadic violence will find fertile ground for growth that no surveillance systems or law enforcement forces will be able to quell. Weapons and recourse to military means only exacerbate the problem by creating new and more serious conflicts. As a result, structural violence is one of the most critical areas of violence studies of our time.

An understanding of this form of violence should lead to a reevaluation of social movements and social change, in an effort to reduce or eliminate structural harm. In many cases the agents of structural violence are not detectable, mainly because structures have been set in motion long ago and the players are no longer present—or in the case of corporations, the perpetrators are not visible from the start—but the effects continue through the structures they have set up. Unfortunately, inequality is a self-sustaining form of violence, as marginalized and violent communities have fewer opportunities for growth and improvement. Vulnerable groups are also the first to succumb to behavioral violence, preventing further development at the personal, local, national, and global levels. As a result, the gap separating the minority who grow exponentially through exclusion and inequality, and the majority who must make do with little, grows apace. A similar dynamic occurs at the global level: in a structure where advantage monopolizes on further advantage, more countries are de-developing as a result. Structural violence is therefore more than mere exploitation or oppression: it is a systematic and entrenched way for the powerful to feed upon the powerless.

Capitalism becomes a squandering principle that leaves populations impoverished while paradoxically leading them to believe it will make them richer, when the reverse is true for the vast majority. The twentieth century has observed a significant loss in social connectedness and sense of wellbeing. Residents of countries with higher income inequality have worse health (Beckfield, 2004), not just of the poor (Wilkinson, 1992) but of the rich (Subramanian & Kawachi, 2004). Greater income inequality is also associated with higher levels of mental illness (Burns, Tomita, & Kapadia, 2014); depression (Messias, Eaton, & Grooms, 2011); murder and assault (Hsieh & Pugh, 1993); obesity and obesity-related death (Pickett, 2005); as well as drug abuse, teenage pregnancy, racism, incarceration, and a number of other societal problems (Wilkinson & Pickett, 2009). These countries also have more sociopolitical instability in the form of assassinations, coups, and riots (Alesina & Perotti, 1996); worse institutions in terms of less efficient governments, higher regulatory burdens, and weaker rule of law (Easterly, 2007); and more corruption (Jong-Sung & Khagram, 2005). The wealthy have stronger motivations to keep institutions weak in order to minimize redistribution, while at the same time having more power to influence institutions, given the relatively higher share of their resources (Buttrick & Oishi, 2017).

In the face of this, we cannot justify mere pacification of those who are suffering as meaningful peace. American political scientist Quincy Wright (1942) rejected a simplistic, *negative* definition of peace as the mere absence of war in favor of a more complex, *positive* definition that views peace as international justice and a spirit of cooperation. Galtung expanded this idea of a positive peace to include the integration of human society (Galtung, 1964) and egalitarian distribution of power and resources (Galtung, 1968). These modified definitions of peace should lead us eventually to a parallel distinction between violence and nonviolence, wherein nonviolence indicates a state that is more than just the absence of violence (Gregg, 1936). The goal of peace researchers is to provide a scientific study of structures and institutions in an effort to convert those that are pregnant with violence into peaceful ones, and to transform harmful ones into healthy ones. In light of this, we need to modify our definition of violence as the manifestations of violence change over time, so that we can conceptualize, cope with, and eventually cure it. We are all responsible, for in terms of structural violence, any perpetuation of the status quo becomes a perpetration, but at the same time we are all capable of instituting change for the better, with far greater influence than we may initially realize.

Questions

1 How is structural violence the most lethal form of violence?

2 What are examples of contemporary forms of structural violence?

3 What are the mechanisms of structural violence, and how does it cause its own increase?

4 How does structural violence stimulate behavioral violence, that is, homicides, suicides, mass murders, and war?

5 How does conceptualizing structural violence help us to consider conditions that could add to positive peace?

References

Alesina, A., & Perotti, R. (1996). Income distribution, political instability, and investment. *European Economic Review, 40*(6), 1203–1228.

Alsan, M., Westerhaus, M., Herce, M., Nakashima, K., & Farmer, P. E. (2011). Poverty, global health, and infectious disease: Lessons from Haiti and Rwanda. *Infectious Disease Clinics of North America, 25*(3), 611–622.

Anglin, M. K. (1998). Feminist perspectives on structural violence. *Identities: Global Studies in Culture and Power, 5*(2), 145–151.

Barner, J., Okech, D., & Camp, M. (2014). Socio-economic inequality, human trafficking, and the global slave trade. *Societies, 4*(2), 148–160.

Beckfield, J. (2004). Does income inequality harm health? New cross-national evidence. *Journal of Health and Social Behavior, 45*(3), 231–248.

Beyer, C. (2008). *Violent globalisms: Conflict in response to empire.* Aldershot, UK: Ashgate.

Blakely, T. A., Collings, S. C. D., & Atkinson, J. (2003). Unemployment and suicide: Evidence for a causal association. *Journal of Epidemiology and Community Health, 57*(8), 594–600.

Bloom, S. L. (2001). *Violence: A public health menace and a public health approach.* London, UK: Karnac Books.

Bourdieu, P. (1979). *La Distinction: Critique sociale du jugement.* Paris, France: Éditions de minuit.

Bourgois, P. (2001). The power of violence in war and peace: Post-Cold War lessons from El Salvador. *Ethnography, 2*(1), 5–34.

Brock-Utne, B. (1989). Women and third world countries—What do we have in common? *Women's Studies International Forum, 12*(5), 495–503.

Burns, J. K., Tomita, A., & Kapadia, A. S. (2014). Income inequality and schizophrenia: Increased schizophrenia incidence in countries with high levels of income inequality. *International Journal of Social Psychiatry, 60*(2), 185–196.

Butchart, A., & Engström, K. (2002). Sex- and age-specific relations between economic development, economic inequality, and homicide rates in people aged 0–24 years: A cross-sectional analysis. *Bulletin of the World Health Organization, 80*(10), 797–805.

Buttrick, N. R., & Oishi, S. (2017). The psychological consequences of income inequality. *Social and Personality Psychology Compass, 11*(3), e12304.

Credit Suisse. (2016). *Global wealth databook 2016.* Zurich, Switzerland: Author. Retrieved from http://publications.credit-suisse.com/tasks/render/file/index.cfm?fileid=AD6F2B43-B17B-345E-E20A1A254A3E24A5

Cross, K. (2013). The gendered effects of structural violence, Paper presented at the APSA annual meeting, Chicago, IL. Retrieved from http://papers.ssrn.com/sol3/papers.cfm?abstract_id=2300717##

Daly, M. C., Wilson, D. J., & Johnson, N. J. (2013). Relative status and well-being: Evidence from U.S. suicide deaths. *Review of Economics and Statistics, 95*(5), 1480–1500.

Easterly, W. (2007). Inequality does cause underdevelopment: Insights from a new instrument. *Journal of Development Economics, 84*(2), 755–776.

Eisler, R. (1997). Human rights and violence: Integrating the private and public spheres. In J. E. Turpin, & L. R. Kurtz (Eds.), *The web of violence: From interpersonal to global* (pp. 161–185). Urbana-Champaign, IL: University of Illinois Press.

Elgar, F. J., & Aitken, N. (2010). Income inequality, trust and homicide in 33 countries. *European Journal of Public Health, 21*(2), 241–246.

Fajnzylber, P., Lederman, D., & Loayza, N. (2002). Inequality and violent crime. *Journal of Law and Economics, 45*(1), 1–40.

Farmer, P. (2003). *Pathologies of power: Health, human rights, and the new war on the poor.* Berkeley, CA: University of California Press.

Farmer, P. E., Nizeye, B., Stulac, S., & Keshavjee, S. (2006). Structural violence and clinical medicine. *PLoS Medicine, 3*(10), e449.

Fink, G. (2010). *Stress of war, conflict and disaster*. Amsterdam, Netherlands: Academic Press.

Food and Agriculture Organization of the United Nations, International Fund for Agricultural Development, and United Nations World Food Programme. (2014). *The state of food insecurity in the world 2014: strengthening the enabling environment for food security and nutrition*. Rome, Italy: Food and Agriculture Organization of the United Nations. Retrieved from http://www.fao.org/3/a-i4030e.pdf

Galbraith, J. K. (1998). *Created unequal: The crisis in American pay*. New York, NY: Free Press.

Galtung, J. (1964). A structural theory of aggression. *Journal of Peace Research, 1*(2), 95–119.

Galtung, J. (1968). A structural theory of integration. *Journal of Peace Research, 5*(4), 375–395.

Galtung, J. (1969). Violence, peace, and peace research. *Journal of Peace Research, 6*(3), 167–191.

Galtung, J. (1985). Twenty-five years of peace research: ten challenges and some responses. *Journal of Peace Research, 22*(2), 141–158.

Galtung, J., & Høivik, T. (1971). Structural and direct violence: a note on operationalization. *Journal of Peace Research, 8*(1), 73–76.

Galtung Institut. (2016). *Understanding Galtung's violence triangle and structural violence*. Retrieved from https://www.galtung-institut.de/en/network/groups/anything-galtung/forum/topic/understanding-galtungs-violence-triangle-and-structural-violence

Gilligan, J. (1996). *Violence: Our deadly epidemic and its causes*. New York, NY: Putnam.

Gilligan, J. (1999). Structural violence. In R. Gottesman (Ed.), *Violence in the United States: An encyclopedia* (pp. 229–233). New York, NY: Scribners and Sons.

Gilligan, J. (2001). *Preventing violence*. London, UK: Thames and Hudson.

Global Envision. (2007). The IMF and World Bank are major causes of poverty in Africa. Retrieved from https://www.globalenvision.org/library/23/1524

Gould, S. J. (1996). *The mismeasure of man*. New York, NY: W.W. Norton.

Gregg, R. B. (1936). *The power of non-violence*. London, UK: Routledge.

Gupta, A. (2012). *Red tape: Bureaucracy, structural violence, and poverty in India*. Durham, NC: Duke University Press.

Gutiérrez, G. (1973). *A theology of liberation: history, politics, and salvation*. Maryknoll, NY: Orbis Books.

Haslam, N. (2006). Dehumanization: An integrative review. *Personality and Social Psychology Review, 10*(3), 252–264.

Hewamanne, S. (2010). Suicide narratives and in-between identities among Sri Lanka's global factory workers. *Ethnology, 49*(1), 1–22.

Hinsley, F. H. (1967). *Power and the pursuit of peace: Theory and practice in the history of relations between states*. Cambridge, UK: Cambridge University Press.

Ho, K. (2007). Structural violence as a human rights violation. *Essex Human Rights Review, 4*(2), 1–17.

Høivik, T. (1977). The demography of structural violence. *Journal of Peace Research, 14*(1), 59–73.

Hsieh, C.-C., & Pugh, M. D. (1993). Poverty, income inequality, and violent crime: A meta-analysis of recent aggregate data studies. *Criminal Justice Review, 18*(2), 182–202.

Human Rights Watch. (2009). *Decades of disparity: Drug arrests and race in the United States*. New York, NY: Author.

Human Rights Watch. (2015). *World report 2015: Events of 2014*. New York, NY: Author. Retrieved from https://www.hrw.org/sites/default/files/world_report_download/wr2015_web.pdf

International Labour Organization. (2008). *ILO action against trafficking in human beings 2008*. Geneva, Switzerland: Author. Retrieved from http://www.ilo.org/wcmsp5/groups/public/@ed_norm/@declaration/documents/publication/wcms_090356.pdf

Jackson, B. A., Baker, J. C., & Cragin, K. (2005). *Aptitude for destruction: Case studies of organizational learning in five terrorist groups* (Vol. 2). Santa Monica, CA: Rand Corporation.

Jones, J., & Schmitt, J. (2014). *A college degree is no guarantee* (pp. 1–14). Center for Economic and Policy Research.

Jong-Sung, Y., & Khagram, S. (2005). A comparative study of inequality and corruption. *American Sociological Review, 70*(1), 136–157.

Kesley, C. (2013). Gender inequality: Empowering women. *Journal of Legal Issues and Cases in Business, 3*, 1–7.

Köhler, G., & Alcock, N. (1976). An empirical table of structural violence. *Journal of Peace Research, 13*(4), 343–356.

Krug, E. G., Dahlberg, L. L., Mercy, J. A., Zwi, A. B., & Lozano, R. (2002). *World report on violence and health*. Geneva, Switzerland: World Health Organization. Retrieved from http://apps.who.int/iris/bitstream/10665/42495/1/9241545615_eng.pdf

Kulkarni, S. C., Levin-Rector, A., Ezzati, M., & Murray, C. J. (2011). Falling behind: Life expectancy in U.S. counties from 2000 to 2007 in an international context. *Population Health Metrics, 9*(1), 16.

Lane, S., Rubinstein, R., Keefe, R., Webster, N., Cibula, D., Rosenthal, A., & Dowdell, J. (2004). Structural violence and racial disparity in HIV transmission. *Journal of Health Care for the Poor and Underserved, 15*(3), 319–335.

Malcom, X., & Grassroots Movement. (2012). *Report on the extrajudicial killings of 120 black people: January 1 to June 30, 2012*. Brooklyn, NY: Malcom X Grassroots Movement. Retrieved from https://www.scribd.com/document/100830487/Report-on-the-Extrajudicial-Killing-of-120-Black-People-Fast

Martikainen, P. T., & Valkonen, T. (1996). Excess mortality of unemployed men and women during a period of rapidly increasing unemployment. *Lancet, 348*(9032), 909–912.

Martin, T. C. (1995). Women's education and fertility: Results from 26 demographic and health surveys. *Studies in Family Planning, 26*(4), 187–202.

Mathews, T. J., & MacDorman, M. F. (2011). Infant mortality statistics from the 2007 period linked birth/infant death data set. *National Vital Statistics Reports, 59*(6), 1–30.

Messias, E., Eaton, W. W., & Grooms, A. N. (2011). Income inequality and depression prevalence across the United States: An ecological study. *Psychiatric Services, 62*(7), 710–712.

Morgan, B., Sunar, D., Carter, C. S., Leckman, J. F., Fry, D. P., Keverne, E. B., ... Olds, D. (2014). Genes, brains, safety, and justice. In J. F. Leckman, C. Panter-Brick, & R. Salah (Eds.), *Pathways to peace: The transformative power of children and families* (pp. 95–128). Cambridge, MA: MIT Press.

Mukherjee, J. (2007). Structural violence, poverty and the AIDS pandemic. *Society for International Development, 50*(2), 115–121.

Mukherjee, J., Barry, D., Satti, H., Raymonville, M., Marsh, S., & Smith-Fawzi, M. (2011). Structural violence: A barrier to achieving the millennium development goals for women. *Journal of Women's Health, 20*(4), 593.

Nafziger, E. W., & Auvinen, J. (2002). Economic development, inequality, war, and state violence. *World Development, 30*(2), 153–163.

Noer, D. M. (2009). *Healing the wounds: Overcoming the trauma of layoffs and revitalizing downsized organizations*. New York, NY: Wiley and Sons.

Olshansky, S. J., Antonucci, T., Berkman, L., Binstock, R. H., Boersch-Supan, A., Cacioppo, J. T., ... Jackson, J. (2012). Differences in life expectancy due to race and educational differences are widening, and many may not catch up. *Health Affairs, 31*(8), 1803–1813.

Ouimet, M. (2012). A world of homicides: The effect of economic development, income inequality, and excess infant mortality on the homicide rate for 165 countries in 2010. *Homicide Studies, 16*(3), 238–258.

Oxfam International. (2013). *The cost of inequality: How wealth and income extremes hurt us all*. Oxford, UK: Author. Retrieved from https://www.oxfam.org/sites/www.oxfam.org/files/cost-of-inequality-oxfam-mb180113.pdf

Peterson-Withorn, C. (2015). Forbes billionaires: Full list of the 500 richest people in the world 2015. *Forbes*, March 2. Retrieved from https://www.forbes.com/sites/chasewithorn/2015/03/02/forbes-billionaires-full-list-of-the-500-richest-people-in-the-world-2015/#47e3bc6845b9

Pickett, K. E. (2005). Wider income gaps, wider waistbands? An ecological study of obesity and income inequality. *Journal of Epidemiology and Community Health, 59*(8), 670–674.

Pickett, K. E., & Wilkinson, R. G. (2015). Income inequality and health: A causal review. *Social Science and Medicine, 128*(1), 316–326.

Pierce, C. M. (1995). Stress analogs of racism and sexism: Terrorism, torture, and disaster. In C. V. Willie, P. P. Rieker, B. M. Kramer, & B. S. Brown (Eds.), *Mental health, racism, and sexism* (pp. 277–293). New York, NY: Routledge.

Piketty, T., & Goldhammer, A. (2014). *Capital in the twenty-first century*. Cambridge, MA: Harvard University Press.

Pogge, T. (2002). *World poverty and human rights: Cosmopolitan responsibilities and reforms*. Cambridge, MA: Polity.

Rosenberg, J. (2017). Pakistani martyr Iqbal Masih, biography of a 10-year-old activist. Thought Co., April 14. Retrieved from https://www.thoughtco.com/10-year-old-activist-iqbal-masih-1779425

Rummel, R. J. (2003). *Power kills: Democracy as a method of nonviolence*. Piscataway, NJ: Transaction Books.

Scheper-Hughes, N. (1996). Small wars and invisible genocides. *Social Science and Medicine, 43*(5), 889–900.

Scheper-Hughes, N. (2006). Dangerous and endangered youth: Social structures and determinants of violence. *Annals of the New York Academy of Sciences, 1036*(1), 13–46.

Sen, A. (1982). *Choice, welfare, and measurement*. Cambridge, MA: MIT Press.

Stuckler, D., Basu, S., Suhrcke, M., Coutts, A., & McKee, M. (2009). The public health effect of economic crises and alternative policy responses in Europe: An empirical analysis. *Lancet, 374*(9686), 315–323.

Subramanian, S. V., & Kawachi, I. (2004). Income inequality and health: What have we learned so far? *Epidemiologic Reviews, 26*(1), 78–91.

Sue, D. W. (2010). *Microaggressions in everyday life: Race, gender and sexual orientation*. New York, NY: Wiley.

Tucker, M. J., Berg, C. J., Callaghan, W. M., & Hsia, J. (2007). The Black-White disparity in pregnancy-related mortality from 5 conditions: differences in prevalence and case fatality rates. *American Journal of Public Health, 97*(2), 247–251.

United Nations. (1948). *Universal declaration of human rights*. New York, NY: Author. Retrieved from http://www.ohchr.org/EN/UDHR/Documents/UDHR_Translations/eng.pdf

United Nations. (2015). *Transforming our world: The 2030 agenda for sustainable development*. New York, NY: Author. Retrieved on from https://sustainabledevelopment.un.org/content/documents/21252030%20Agenda%20for%20Sustainable%20Development%20web.pdf

United Nations Children's Fund. (2012). Pneumonia and diarrhoea: Tackling the deadliest diseases for the world's poorest children. Retrieved from http://www.unicef.org/eapro/Pneumonia_and_Diarrhoea_Report_2012.pdf

United Nations Children's Fund & World Health Organization. (2014). *Immunization summary: A statistical reference containing data through 2013*. New York, NY: United Nations Children's Fund. Retrieved from http://www.who.int/immunization/monitoring_surveillance/Immunization_Summary_2013.pdf

United Nations Children's Fund, World Health Organization, & World Bank Group. (2015). *Levels and trends in child malnutrition: UNICEF, WHO, World Bank Group joint child malnutrition estimates. Key findings of the 2015 edition*. New York, NY: United Nations Children's Fund Retrieved from https://data.unicef.org/wp-content/uploads/2015/12/JME-2015-edition-Sept-2015_203.pdf

United Nations Development Programme. (2014). Human development report 2014. *Sustaining human progress: Reducing vulnerabilities and building resilience*. New York, NY: United Nations Development Programme. Retrieved from http://hdr.undp.org/sites/default/files/hdr14-report-en-1.pdf

United Nations World Food Programme. (2016). *Zero hunger*. Rome, Italy: Author. Retrieved from http://www.wfp.org/hunger/causes

United States Department of Justice. (2015). *Investigation of the Ferguson police department*. Washington, DC: Author.

United States Department of State. (2005). *Trafficking in persons report*. Washington, DC: Author.

Van Evera, S. (2013). *Causes of war: Power and the roots of conflict*. Ithaca, NY: Cornell University Press.

Victor, D. (2017, April 25). Milwaukee inmate died after being deprived of water for 7 days. *New York Times*. Retrieved from https://www.nytimes.com/2017/04/25/us/milwaukee-inmate-died-after-being-deprived-of-water-for-7-days.html

Voss, M., Nylén, L., Floderus, B., Diderichsen, F., & Terry, P. D. (2004). Unemployment and early cause-specific mortality: A study based on the Swedish twin registry. *American Journal of Public Health, 94*(12), 2155–2161.

Walk Free Foundation. (2014). *Global Slavery Index 2014*. Broadway Nedlands, Australia: Author. Retrieved from https://cdn.walkfreefoundation.org/content/uploads/2017/05/14093942/2014-Global-Slavery-Index.pdf

Weart, S. R. (1998). *Never at war: Why democracies will not fight one another*. New Haven, CT: Yale University Press.

Weyerer, S., & Wiedenmann, A. (1995). Economic factors and the rates of suicide in Germany between 1881 and 1989. *Psychological Reports, 76*(3S), 1331–1341.

Wilkinson, R. G. (1992). Income distribution and life expectancy. *British Medical Journal, 304*(6820), 165–168.

Wilkinson, R. G., & Pickett, K. E. (2008). Income inequality and socioeconomic gradients in mortality. *American Journal of Public Health, 98*(4), 699–705.

Wilkinson, R. G., & Pickett, K. E. (2009). *The spirit level: Why more equal societies almost always do better*. London, UK: Penguin.

Williams, D., & Collins, C. (2001). Racial residential segregation: A fundamental cause of racial disparities in health. *Association of Schools of Public Health, 116*(5), 404–416.

Winter, D. D. N., & Leighton, D. C. (2001). Structural violence. In D. J. Christie, R. V. Wagner, & D. D. N. Winter (Eds.), *Peace, conflict, and violence* (pp. 585–599). New York, NY: Prentice Hall.

World Bank. (2012). *The world development report 2012: Gender equality and development*. Washington, DC: Author. Retrieved from https://siteresources.worldbank.org/INTWDR2012/Resources/7778105-1299699968583/7786210-1315936222006/Complete-Report.pdf

World Health Organization. (2008). *Health equity through action on the social determinants of health*. Geneva, Switzerland: Author. Retrieved from http://apps.who.int/iris/bitstream/handle/10665/43943/9789241563703_eng.pdf?sequence=1

World Health Organization & United Nations Children's Fund. (2014). *Progress on drinking water and sanitation: 2014 Update*. New York, NY: United Nations Children's Fund. Retrieved from https://www.unicef.org/publications/files/JMP_report_2014_webEng.pdf

World Health Organization, United Nations Children's Fund, United Nations Population Fund, & World Bank. (2012). *Trends in maternal mortality: 1990 to 2010: WHO, UNICEF, UNFPA and The World Bank estimates*. Geneva, Switzerland: World Health Organization Retrieved from http://apps.who.int/iris/bitstream/handle/10665/44874/9789241503631_eng.pdf?sequence=1

Wright, Q. (1942). *A study of war*. Chicago, IL: University of Chicago Press.

8

Environmental (and Nuclear) Violence

Introduction

> To corrupt or destroy the natural environment is an act of violence not only against the earth but also against those who are dependent on it, including ourselves.
> —*Wendell Berry,* The Long-Legged House *(1969)*

Although not yet a full-fledged area of study, environmental violence is another aspect of our study of violence that is important enough to warrant a chapter. Of the topics considered in our bio-psycho-socio-environmental model, the natural environment has the most all-encompassing influence on human beings, making it a crucial place to complete our exploration of how to think about violence. Of all violence studies, it is perhaps the least considered but the most urgent topic. We could even argue that addressing environmental violence is the most urgent task facing humanity today, as it continues to the extinction of our species. Given the critical importance of the environment to human survival, the disproportionate lack of concern regarding scientific warnings of human-driven catastrophic changes, and acting in ways like a species intending not to survive, places it in the category of *collective suicide.*

When we speak of *environmental violence* in this chapter, we are referring to any violence that people(s) do to one another with a cause or effect in the environment. This includes the direct damage to the environment by humans but also the violent response from the natural world as a result of human degradation of the environment and the violence humans do to one another because of their effects on the climate. Damage to the environment is a *human* issue, for our survival is at stake, along with that of other species; the planet itself will continue. Our apparent lack of concern about it, demonstrated by the major pushback we see against changing our behavior to rectify the problem, is an indication that we need—critically—a global psychology or global psychiatry that not only addresses cross-cultural issues and geographic disparities, but also can help with the diagnosis, prognosis, and treatment of the unhealthy tendencies of humankind as a whole. Such a field has yet to exist, despite the fact that we are imperiling our very existence—and perhaps the field of violence studies can be a start (and hence this volume on its pathogenesis, processes, and prevention). This being the case, a proper treatment of environmental violence would be too extensive for the scope of this book, and to the student is encouraged to go beyond the overview of the problem we present here.

Environmental science is a group of sciences that together attempt to explain how life is sustained on earth, examining, among other things, the causes of environmental problems and possible solutions to them. Since the focus of this chapter is to review the rich and varied

Violence: An Interdisciplinary Approach to Causes, Consequences, and Cures, First Edition. Bandy X. Lee.
© 2019 John Wiley & Sons, Inc. Published 2019 by John Wiley & Sons, Inc.

contributions of this field to our understanding of human violence, we will return to global environmental violence only at the end. We will also consider nuclear violence in this context, not only because, together with environmental destruction, it is the most urgent problem confronting humankind, but also because the underlying mindset is connected. Meanwhile, we will interpret environmental violence in many ways; for example, it can include the way urban environments can oppress and can also include the choice to build specific settings such as prisons. Nevertheless, we limit our discussion here to: (a) primary violence or direct damage humans do to the environment that threatens our survival; (b) secondary violence from the natural world (in the form of excess earthquakes, tsunamis, heat waves, and hurricanes) as a result of human degradation of the earth; and (c) tertiary violence between people(s) in conflict over natural resources or through environmental policies that violate people.

Clarifying Misconceptions

With regard to violence relating to the environment, the most obvious and urgent contributing factors would seem to be *overpopulation* and *resource scarcity*. For centuries, people have argued that, if there were enough natural resources and space for everyone, there would be no reason for environmental conflict. One of the first proponents of this idea was English cleric and scholar Thomas Malthus, who wrote about the looming crisis in *An Essay on the Principle of Population* (Malthus, 1798). He correctly showed that population grows exponentially while food production does not—but he used that understanding to advocate that society should not provide for those in poverty but rather should let them die, before disease, famine, and war check growth in a natural form of population control. This logic has been a justification for perpetrating even greater violence.

This classic *Malthusian catastrophe* model led to the development of the *environmental security* thesis, which views environmental scarcity as a future cause of strife. It is an ideology that continues to provide a rationale for violence against groups of people by promoting the view that resources are scarce, that groups will need to struggle for limited resources, and that a security crisis will result. This concept became prominent through *The Population Bomb* (Ehrlich, 1968), which foretells a coming crisis from overpopulation and the resulting struggles. Similarly, *The Coming Anarchy* (Kaplan, 2000) argues that the developing world, especially "the Dark Continent," represents a threat to the developed world as rising populations and undernourishment set the stage for barbaric acts of violence to follow.

These works have brought needed attention to important issues such as a surging population, air pollution, water depletion, spreading disease, deforestation, soil erosion, and mass migrations leading to conflict and violence. However, the problem of this model is that overpopulation and waste of resources always happen with *other* people in *other* places, with implicit contempt for them. More importantly than absolute scarcity, blatantly uneven resource accumulation and consumption require greater focus. Political maneuvering or mismanagement of resources that instigates war also needs to enter into the equation as potent causes of environmental violence (Peluso & Watts, 2001). Furthermore, greater distribution of opportunities and the education of women, in particular, are associated with lower fertility rates (Martin, 1995). Hence, rather than there being a linear cause-and-effect linkage, problems of the environment, populations, and violence revolve around issues of *power*, not around real scarcity (Robbins, 2011).

Political economy concerns production and trade and their relations with law, custom, government, and the people. Resources constitute and depend on the political economy of access and control (de Castro, 1952). Unlike behavioral violence, which is site-specific, environmental violence has both localized and global impacts, such as air and water pollution, which can migrate from one country to the next. Currently, there is enough to feed everyone on the planet (Oniang'o, 2017). Most of the world's starvation and famine are the result of entitlements that individuals, communities, and nations possess and how they choose to use them to reallocate them or to procure more privilege (Hossain, 2017). These entitlements determine how the world distributes, reproduces, transforms, and fights over its resources, as well as who performs the labor and who bears the burden in the process of accumulation. For this reason, power—especially in the form of domination—is the main source of environmental violence, in any of the myriad ways in which it manifests.

Furthering the Concept

Human beings have been degrading the environment and causing *climate change* since the mid-twentieth century through the emission especially of carbon dioxide, (Intergovernmental Panel on Climate Change, 2013). We can conceive of it as in Figure 8.1. Figure 8.2 reveals that the rapid rise in carbon levels are not in the least part of a natural cycle. Figure 8.3 illustrates

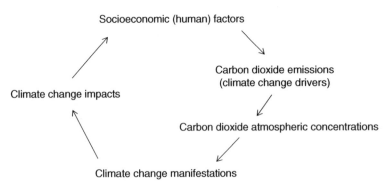

Figure 8.1 Cycle of human causes of climate change.

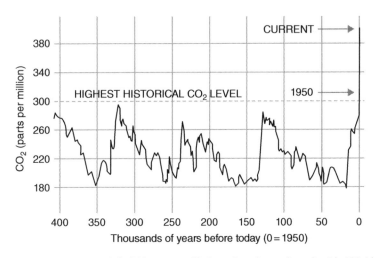

Figure 8.2 Ancient air bubbles trapped in ice tell us that carbon dioxide (CO_2) levels in the atmosphere are higher than they have been at any time in the past 400,000 years.

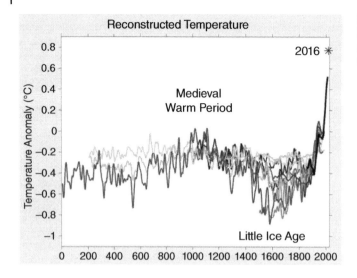

Figure 8.3 For the northern hemisphere, temperatures in recent decades appear to be the warmest since at least about 1000 CE.

how extreme the climate change has been since human intervention. *Global warming* on the part of humans is a major form of environmental violence not only because of scale but also because of the degree to which the sharing of benefits and consequences are unequal: in fact, they have an inverse relationship, which makes it a particularly pernicious form of intergroup violence. Also, it threatens all life on earth and is thus a form of self-directed violence. The failure to change our behavior, not to mention recognize our contribution to climate change, constitutes a part of environmental violence.

One of the major causes of global warming is the accumulation of *greenhouse gasses*, such as carbon dioxide, methane, and nitrous oxide, which prevent the warmth of the sun's rays from leaving the earth's atmosphere (Lashof & Ahuja, 1990). While it is true that there are many other factors, such as volcanic activity, variations in the earth's orbit and axis, and the solar cycle, few respectable scientific bodies and national science academies disagree that most global warming is directly attributable to human activity (Cook et al., 2013). The impacts of these climate changes will occur in the form of changes in mean temperatures over long time periods as well as extreme events becoming more frequent and even more extreme (Rowhani et al., 2011).

Warming of the climate affects the carbon cycle and creates a vicious loop that aggravates the situation even more (United Nations Environment Programme, 2001), leading to both direct and indirect consequences. Some direct consequences are heat waves, droughts and floods, expanding deserts, rising sea levels, the disappearance of plant and animal species, diminished food production, and a generally catastrophic impact on the survival of vast populations around the planet (Union of Concerned Scientists, 2010). Indirect consequences of climate change include mass migrations, wars over depleted resources, and the exacerbation of sectarian tensions (Zhang et al., 2007), together with profound health consequences in the form of infectious diseases, physical harm, psychological trauma, anxiety, and depression (Berry, Bowen, & Kjellstrom, 2010; McMichael, Woodruff, & Hales, 2006).

Major damage and displacement due to climate change disproportionately affect those who live in the Global South—defined as Africa, Latin America, and developing Asia, including the Middle East—because of climatic vulnerability as well as poorer infrastructure and emergency-response readiness. As a consequence, those who have contributed the least to the problem and have the fewest resources to deal with it will suffer more of its negative repercussions (Mohai, Pellow, & Roberts, 2009). At the same time, there is no accountability on the part of the corporations and governments of the Global North—defined as the US, Canada, Western Europe, developed parts of Asia, Australia, and New Zealand—that have benefited most from the system of high consumption, export of toxic waste, and environmental damage while contributing the most to human-generated climate change (Agarwal & Narain, 1991).

Poor, minority, elderly, and homeless people, who have few resources or mobility to allow them to evacuate suffer the most, while government relief measures are slow to assist them (Giroux, 2006). More broadly, climate change is a threat to the human species as a whole, putting our very existence at risk. The current destruction of the natural environment, at rates never before seen on this planet (United Nations Environment Programme, 2001), is a threat to our habitat with its complex systems that provide the necessary conditions for human life. As a tragic consequence of our unchecked exploitation of nature, humans are now at risk of becoming victims of our own devastation.

Case Vignettes

Violence Over Diminishing Resources

Greed and the perception of scarcity create and escalate the experience of scarcity on the ground, and therefore also determine the manifestation of environmental violence in the form of violent conflict. The most vulnerable are often the first to succumb to this form of violence.

The people of Nimbo, Nigeria, knew that an attack was coming. The villagers mobilized young men and hired police to protect their farming community. One of them said nomadic herdsmen had kidnapped him before returning him home with a letter threatening bloodshed. At daybreak, the police left, and the attackers emerged, shooting and hacking 15 people to death. "I never believed they can enter the town," said a man who escaped the attack with machete wounds all over his body. "We were running and running and running." Villagers from Nimbo had been feuding with herdsmen in the area for years. They accuse the nomads of chasing them from their farmland, while ethnic Fulani herdsmen leaders say the villagers harass and attack them.

The raid was part of a series of brutal attacks and kidnappings stretching from Nigeria's southern Niger Delta to its northwest corner that have been blamed on Fulani herdsmen. The president, himself a Fulani who declared cattle as being among his possessions after taking office in the previous year, puts out a statement vowing to deal with "rampaging herdsmen." But experts say there is no common cause of these attacks and that most farmers and herdsmen coexist peacefully. When relations sour and turn violent, it is usually due to local disputes that go unresolved, in combination with competition for increasingly scarce land and resources. Researchers believe that there are growing ecological and demographic pressures in the rural areas of Nigeria, and political authorities are not very effective at managing the resulting conflicts.

Nimbo residents remember a time when herdsmen would sell villagers unhealthy cows for slaughter at a discount, but those days are long gone. Relations are hostile. About 6 years ago, herdsmen shot a well-liked hunter from the village after he caught a cow in one of his traps. Villagers said it was an accident, but the incident set off a cycle of tit-for-tat violence. "Sometimes, our people, they fight together. You understand? They kill our people and our people kill them," said a former government councillor who bore deep gashes on his head and back from machete attacks as he fled Nimbo (Stein, 2016).

Premature Deaths due to Lack of Water

Water is essential to human life. We use it for everything from drinking and bathing to growing crops and livestock to maintaining communities and industries. Global warming is already having measurable impact on the amount, distribution, timing, and quality of water, creating an excess in some areas while depleting sources in others. Because our activities depend so much on water, even slight changes in its availability can result in great hardship and stress, and again the most vulnerable are the most affected.

From the banks of the huge Kollidam River, Selvaraju's farm is barely a mile away. The river is a tributary of the Tamil Nadu's Cauvery delta that drains surplus water into the sea. Water, regardless of how much rain fell, was never a problem next to this river, until it suddenly was. Selvaraju takes his own life, hanging himself from a tree on his farm, after his old borewell ran dry for the first time in two decades. The new one he had commissioned just a month earlier also bore no water. The 65-year-old, who owned a 7-acre farm, left behind unpaid debts and a family—a wife and three sons—with many questions. Could he not have waited for a few more months for the rains? Why did he need to kill himself? Water, his son Karti observes, has suddenly become a luxury in and around the village.

In a neighboring village, a similar story unfolds. Veermani was not the right age to have a heart attack, and yet he did and passed away. "When I rushed to check what the matter was, he was not responding," his widow Kavitha says. She called for help and took him to the nearby cottage hospital in an ambulance. It was, doctors said, a shock death: something she still does not understand. "It did not rain this year. It was our bad luck," she says. "It was the first year we decided to lease land, and it turned out to be the worst year for farming."

In the same village, Arokyamary narrates a similar tale. No one in the family thought that her husband, Azhagesan, would die of a heart attack. He was only 36 years old. He went to his farm in the afternoon and died of sudden shock in the middle of his wilting crops. Azhagesan, a landless farmer, had leased two acres of farmland. His sudden demise threw his family into a financial and emotional quagmire. His elderly mother, Amruthavalli, is now the only working member of the family—she works as a sweeper in a nearby school for about 1.5 US dollars a day. These shock deaths are a consequence of emotional stress and economic troubles, says a practicing cardiologist and social worker in a once-prosperous paddy bowl in the Delta region. When the monsoon failed, farmers in village after village in the region talked about failed crops, mounting debts, and the lack of work (Hardikar, 2017).

Migrations Due to Climate Change

Some areas in the world are becoming less habitable because of changes in extreme climate-related hazards and other environmental conditions. While the link between global warming and migrations may be complex, we can look at overarching patterns to decipher a relationship. *Climate refugees* are people who are forced to leave their home regions in response to a compromise in their wellbeing and livelihood due to sudden or long-term local changes in the environment. They may alternatively be called environmental refugees, ecological refugees, climate change refugees, disaster refugees, eco-refugees, ecologically displaced persons, environmentally displaced persons, and forced environmental migrants, among others.

Parul traveled across Bangladesh to escape the flood waters, but they seem to have followed her. The shack she shares with her husband and four children in Dhaka, the nation's capital, sits on the edge of a sprawling slum next to a lake. When it rains, dank water sloshes into their shelter. Only the bed, raised up on bricks, stays dry. "This room is all we have, so we need to stay here no matter what happens," says Parul. Seven years ago, a monsoon flood left nothing standing in their village, located on the country's southwest coast. "We had no option but to climb up the banks with our belongings immediately," said Parul. "Within a week, we moved to Dhaka to start a new life."

Every day, some 2,000 people settle in the Bangladeshi capital. It is nothing new: for generations the city has been a magnet for men and women escaping rural poverty. But now there is another driver that experts say has accelerated the race to the capital: the earth's changing climate, which has already made life extremely difficult in stretches of this flat country threaded with rivers. In the coming decades, millions more climate refugees around the world are expected to make similar journeys. Bangladesh contributes just 0.4 metric tons per capita to the carbon emissions fueling climate change, while the US produces 17 and the UK 7.1, but will be severely affected by it. Within three decades, the country is expected to be at least two degrees Celsius hotter. By 2080, the seas could be 2 ft higher. The glaciers in the Himalayas will melt faster, sending more floodwaters to batter the Bay of Bengal. Cyclones will wrack the coast more frequently, and with greater intensity. Salty seawater will pollute drinking supplies and destroy fertile land. In a cruel irony, many refugees will wind up in cities even more ill-equipped to withstand the changing climate (McPherson, 2015).

It is difficult to attribute Bangladesh's rural exodus indisputably to climate, but the majority of migrants hail from coastal areas that are already experiencing rising sea levels, increased salinity, destructive floods, and cyclones. At least 400,000 people move to Dhaka every year, according to the World Bank (Kabir & Parolin, 2012). The International Organization for Migration estimates that 70% of Dhaka's slum-dwellers moved there fleeing some sort of environmental shock (Cities Alliance, 2016). In 2012, Moniruzzaman Khan, the director of the Centre for Climate Change and Environmental Research at BRAC University, tracked 1,500 families migrating to cities, mostly Dhaka. They were struggling to find fresh water to drink as rising seas spilled into rivers.

Nuclear Devastation

Hibakusha is the Japanese term for the surviving victims of the 1945 atomic bombings of Hiroshima and Nagasaki. The word literally means "explosion-affected people." The medical injuries can range from thermal and blast effects to deaths within weeks from ionizing radiation to the delayed effects of infertility, blood disorders, and cancers. Yet these are only the surface injuries; the psychological injuries and memories are no doubt among the most damaging that humanity has known.

In rooms throughout his home, 90-year-old Masakazu Saito has dozens of old clocks indicating it is 8:15 a.m.—the time an atomic bomb flattened Hiroshima and nearly killed him seven decades ago. They keep him remembering the event that he believes should never happen again. Although he was stationed in Hiroshima as an army lieutenant at the time and survived injuries from the bombing, he still suffers from the aftereffects. When the atomic bomb was dropped on Hiroshima on the morning of August 6, 1945, Saito, then 21, was in a barracks about 1.8 kilometers from ground zero. About 90% of the 400 soldiers in the camp were killed immediately. Saito suffered severe burns to his back and arms. As he struggled out of the barracks, he was confronted with hellish scenes, such as girls lying on the ground crying for help. He saw some with their eyeballs hanging out of their eye sockets and intestines protruding from their bodies. He tended to victims as best he could but then lost consciousness. When he came to, Saito found that he was lying with corpses in a large hole dug in a schoolyard ahead of a mass incineration. He shouted and was able to escape the hole just in time. After the war, when Saito returned to his hometown, local people discriminated against him because of their fears of radiation. Because of this, despair about his future and suicidal thoughts obsessed him (Shintomi, 2014).

One of the notable aftermaths of the two bombings was an increased occurrence of leukemia among the survivors, especially 5–6 years after the bombing. Years later, the survivors started suffering from breast, lung, thyroid, and other cancers at alarming rates (Sawada, Chaitin, & Bar-On, 2004). Most of the pregnant women who were exposed to the bombings experienced miscarriages and infant deaths. Most of the children born in this period had impaired growth, increased risk of cancer, and intellectual disabilities (Shimizu et al., 2010). In addition to the harm they caused human beings, the two bombings also had dire environmental effects. The immediate effects included extremely high temperatures of about 10 million degrees Celsius, and a crushing wind as a result of the blast. The detonation of the bombs created a radioactive dust that fell from the sky. Water and wind spread the dust more widely, and it contaminated the water supply, food chain, and ground.

Saito only regained a sense of optimism when he started communicating with other atomic bomb survivors. Later, he established a group of survivors in his hometown and organized activities to raise awareness about the horrors of nuclear weapons. Despite no sign that any of the nuclear-armed countries are ready to abandon their arsenals, he continues to wish for the abolition of nuclear weapons. "I'll make my last appeal to the world's leaders," he said before attending the 2015 Review Conference of the Parties to the Treaty on the Non-Proliferation of Nuclear Weapons, held every 5 years since the treaty entered into force in 1970.

Political Economy and Scarcity

The role of the political economy is central in environmental violence. Conflicts over resources have multiple layers of determinants, and the bio-psycho-socio-environmental model is useful here. We stated in Chapter 4 that the "environmental" aspect of this model encompasses the environment of symbols we generate as a consequence of our social interactions. As in the rest of violence, the symbolic domain, or the *perception* of scarcity, is predominant (Behnassi, Draggan, & Yaya, 2011). When different groups lay claim to the same land based on historical rights, for example, they would probably not be very inclined toward war—which generates greater overall depletion—if there were not a perception of scarcity (Southwick, 1996).

While the distinction between scarcity of resources and the perception of scarcity may seem subtle, it can have important consequences. A perceived crisis in the food supply, for example, can lead to scarcity claims that prompt investment schemes, out of greed or fear, rather than planning for equitable food distribution (Timmer, 2015). Vulnerable populations end up receiving even less food, as the perceived shortage fosters hoarding. An obvious example is the long history of European colonialism. Nations looked for food and raw materials beyond the borders of Europe as its population started to grow, and the great empires began—as a result of the fear, not the pain, of scarcity (Ponting, 1991). Colonialism destroyed many indigenous populations and drastically changed the lives of others. Unsettling Latin America, Africa, and Asia, this era essentially created "the Third World" and is responsible for many of the conflicts that still plague us today (Hoogvelt, 2001).

Nations that have suffered violence in this way have other characteristics that further impoverish them and make them vulnerable to outbreaks of violence and conflict: they have less effective management systems and less capacity to meet their population's social demands. Their poor infrastructure can destabilize governmental and economic processes (Esfahani & Ramírez, 2003). This contributes to *relative* scarcity and disparity on a large scale, breeding discontent and diffuse subnational violence (Homer-Dixon & Deligiannis, 2009). Environmental violence, therefore, simultaneously constitutes and results from structural violence (Conca & Dabelko, 2002). International security is at risk when these countries further fragment due to internal conflict that often leads to large-scale emigration and they are unable to negotiate effectively or participate in international agreements (Gordon, 2007). Because all human affairs lie within the natural environment, environmental factors easily tie into justifications for violence or human rights abuses (Homer-Dixon, 2010), but this does not imply a simplistic relationship between scarcity and violence. As we have noted, the origins lie in the political economy.

Resource Curse and Violent Dispossession

The lack of a direct link between scarcity and violence is nowhere more apparent than in situations where the abundance of resources becomes a source of violence. One of the best contemporary examples of conflict over natural resources is the case of "blood diamonds," otherwise known as "conflict diamonds" (Lujala, Gleditsch, & Gilmore, 2005). The relative abundance of these stones has made it possible for military insurgents to fund the proliferation and trafficking of arms, the recruitment of mercenaries, and the continuation and intensification of conflict, resulting ultimately in a massive death toll and an ongoing refugee crisis throughout much of Central and West Africa (Ross, 1999). Similar situations with other resources (e.g., the "conflict minerals" of the Democratic Republic of Congo), as well as the realization that valuable commodities can prolong conflict in war zones, have led to the concept of the *resource curse*, otherwise known as "the paradox of plenty" (Basedau & Lacher, 2006).

Another good example of an abundance of resources fueling conflict is the situation in Colombia, where the local population has engaged in artisanal gold mining for centuries. This relatively stable situation changed with the 2008 global economic crisis and subsequent rise in gold prices. In a very real sense Colombia experienced a modern-day gold rush, with high-stakes conflict developing among migrant workers, leftist guerrillas, paramilitary groups, foreign investors, and the local population. A lack of internal stability in the area made it possible for well-organized criminal cartels to use whatever force they deemed necessary to protect their interests and to deal directly with US and Canadian companies to the sum of over 2 billion dollars a year. Meanwhile, the region's annual homicide rate rose to over 420 homicides per 100,000 residents, while many of the traditional miners disappeared as a result of death or displacement (Idrobo, Mejía, & Tribin, 2014). The national government finally deployed its security forces and regained a measure of control, only to turn over the mining industry to multinational conglomerates, which has further deepened resentment and resistance on the part of the local population.

Illegal logging is another source of environmental violence that not only causes irreparable degradation to forests but endangers various animal species as well as local people. Between 2002 and 2013, more than 900 defenders of the forest—including activists, rangers, and indigenous people—were killed in violence related to illegal logging (Global Witness, 2014). These numbers do not even include the journalists who were killed in the process of investigating the illicit trade. In Thailand, armed groups enter from Cambodia to smuggle out illegally extracted trees to China (Nuwer, 2016). Paramilitary cartels continue to operate with impunity around the globe, and their activities support several ruling regimes across Asia, Latin America, and Eastern Europe (Galeotti, 2014).

An example of environmental policies that are violent against people is *forced evictions* for national parks in the name of conservation. In the United States at the end of the nineteenth century, for instance, the creation of Yosemite National Park in California and Yellowstone National Park in Wyoming for conversation purposes required a series of forced displacements, which were resisted, resulting in the killing of hundreds of Native Americans. Worldwide, the establishment of more than 108,000 officially protected conservation areas, about half with indigenous peoples living in or regularly using them, has led to numerous violent conflicts and environmental refugees (Dowie, 2009). Yet, the global need for conservation arises not from indigenous populations but from the disruption of ecosystems as a result of the stripping of natural forests, the destruction of wetlands, and the contamination of the elements in the pursuit of profit.

Violent dispossession occurs in realms outside of conservation: also turning violent are large-scale acquisitions of land made in the name of industrial food and biofuel production—the rapidly growing phenomenon of *land grabbing*. Once again, indigenous peoples, who lack secure tenure of the land they inhabit, are the victims of domestic and transnational companies, governments, and individuals who benefit at their expense. Water resources are often critical to these acquisitions, and thus they often occur in association with *water grabbing* (Rullia, Savioria, & D'Odorico, 2013). These trends have accelerated in recent years in response to concerns about food security in high-income countries and the promulgation of investment opportunities in the Global South (Borras et al., 2011).

Governments grant large concessions to transnational companies for agricultural development at the expense of peoples who have lived on the land for centuries. Over the course of 1 year in Ethiopia alone, approximately 1.5 million people were displaced in the name of agricultural development, many of them coerced through beatings, torture, and the bulldozing or burning down of their homes (Human Rights Watch, 2012). Another aspect of this is the fact that, in many countries, would-be investors benefit more from learning how to navigate the mostly ad hoc process and paying off corrupt government officials than from developing viable, sustainable business plans (Deininger & Byerlee, 2011). Violent resistance can arise as people recognize these actions as unjust, undemocratic decision making on the part of powerful elites working in their own interest against those who depend on the resources in question for a livelihood.

Secondary Violence from the Environment

To return to our categories of environmental violence, there are: (a) primary violence or direct damage humans do to the environment; (b) secondary violence from the natural world as a result of this degradation; and (c) tertiary violence between people(s) in conflict over natural resources. Our topic here will be natural disasters, which are not "natural" but are largely resulting from human alteration of nature—a hazard we ourselves have created (Carson, 1962). This area is complex, as there is also the intertwining of poor urban planning and engineering, for example, which the impact of an earthquake and tsunami can amplify. Nevertheless, arising out of the natural environment, these disasters can kill, destroy land, cause migrations and wars, and have profound implications for mental and physical health (Klein, 2014). As it is now 95% certain that human beings are the main cause of global warming, ensuing extreme weather conditions, and the destruction of natural ecosystems (Pachauri et al., 2014) (here, we distinguish between human global warming and the resulting effect of climate change), many are now dubbing the phenomenon "human-made disasters" or "the boomerang effect": human actions affect the environment in ways that rebound with unintended negative consequences for humans. Migration due to natural disasters, furthermore, may cause conflict in receiving areas (Reuveny, 2002).

A good illustration of this kind of secondary environmental violence is the effects of deforestation, including *mudslides* and *dust storms*. Loose soil from deforestation can turn into mudslides when it rains, as happened in Venezuela in 1999: the resulting devastation killed tens of thousands of people, destroyed thousands of homes as well as whole towns, and led to the complete collapse of Vargas State's infrastructure (Larsen et al., 2001). Deforestation also causes dust storms that arise because of the removal of windbreaks and the consequent scouring of topsoil from previously arable land. In 1935, a dust storm swept across the Plains States of the US, displacing an estimated 300 million tons of topsoil, forcing hundreds of thousands of people to relocate, killing others, and worsening the effects of the Great Depression (Lockeretz, 1978).

Another example of "the boomerang effect" can be seen in the unintended effects of destructive fishing practices and ocean warming on coral reefs, which lead to a decrease of shoreline protection. The damage caused by the 2004 Indian Ocean earthquake and the resulting *tsunami,* which killed an estimated 228,000 people and had an economic impact of 10 billion dollars (Bernard & Robinson, 2009), is now largely recognized to have resulted from human damage to the region's coral reefs. Computer models have demonstrated that healthy coral reefs can offer a coastline at least twice as much protection as dead reefs in this kind of situation (Kunkel, Hallberg, & Oppenheimer, 2006), meaning that much of the damage could have been avoided with proper environmental management.

Another problem experienced in connection with human-made disasters is *pollution,* which not only directly causes natural disasters but also indirectly worsens their impact. For example, a flood is more damaging if the water is polluted (Messner & Meyer, 2006): it can have negative consequences for the land and people's health for years after the immediate crisis has passed. The yellow sandstorms that travel across China to Korea and Japan are all the more dangerous because of the industrial toxins they carry (Choi, Bone, & Zhang, 2016). Another inescapable observation concerning environmental damage is that rates of certain diseases to which the environment significantly contributes, such as cancer, are rising. Variations of this dreaded disease, almost non-existent 150 years ago, now affect over one in two of those born in the UK after 1960 (Ahmad et al., 2015) and demonstrate an increasingly younger onset (Brinton et al., 2008).

The Perils of Nuclear War

We touch upon nuclear violence here, not only because a nuclear war would cause devastation to the environment—although new evidence on climate disruption renews arguments for a nuclear weapons ban (Helfand, 2017)—but because the two forms of violence are closely connected. In this case, both environmental degradation and nuclear proliferation represent a mounting potential for the greatest, most consequential human violence: total annihilation of the human species. It is also similar in terms of its underlying, circular dynamics: (a) nuclear war would represent primary violence against the environment; (b) much of human loss of life would result from the secondary consequences of nuclear devastation rather than direct targeting; and (c) a kind of tertiary violence is already occurring among nations, be it in the form of a race toward proliferation and accumulation of weapons, or a "climate" of hostility and mistrust.

Therefore, as the final aspect of our examination of environmental violence, we now turn briefly to the possible consequences of interstate war, especially nuclear war, a looming specter that is becoming increasingly possible. Wars have degraded and damaged the environment since the beginning of recorded history, but the dangers of war are much greater now, with the introduction of biological, chemical, and nuclear weapons. We will briefly touch on these before proceeding to nuclear weapons, the apex of the risks we face in our violence against ourselves.

Biological weapons, in relation to conventional, chemical, or even nuclear weapons, are potentially the greatest threat to the environment and humanity relative to mass and costs of development and storage. These weapons, which are capable of altering the very balance of nature itself, are difficult to control effectively, and although outlawed following the *Biological Weapons Convention* (1972) have been used for bioterrorism in both the US and Chile in 2001 (Wheelis, Rózsa, & Dando, 2006). The situation is very similar with chemical weapons, which are extremely volatile and hazardous to both humans and the environment, with the capacity to cause sensory irritation, temporary incapacitation, injury, or death. Despite the *Chemical Weapons Convention* (1993), which forbids the production, storage, or stockpiling of chemical weapons, large arsenals of these weapons continue to exist around the world, constituting an ongoing threat to human life and the environment (Evison, Hinsley, & Rice, 2002).

By far the most menacing of our modern weapons, however, are nuclear arms, which derive tremendous explosive force from very small amounts of matter. These weapons can be of the fission ("atomic") variety, or a combination of fission and fusion (thermonuclear or "hydrogen"). The destructiveness of these weapons is almost inconceivable. The bombings of the Japanese cities of Hiroshima and Nagasaki during World War II resulted in an estimated 200,000 civilian and military deaths from acute injuries alone (Manhattan Engineer District and US Army, 1957). Since that time, over 2,000 nuclear weapon detonations have occurred for testing and demonstration purposes, each having an unspecified but detrimental effect on the environment. Furthermore, despite the end of the Cold War and the *Treaty on the Non-Proliferation of Nuclear Weapons* (1968), countries around the world still continue to develop, expand, and stockpile nuclear arsenals—which prompted the *Treaty on the Prohibition of Nuclear Weapons* (2017), for which the International Campaign to Abolish Nuclear Weapons (ICAN) won the Nobel Peace Prize.

Currently, there are over 15,000 known nuclear weapons in the possession of the US, Russia, the UK, France, China, India, Pakistan, Israel, and North Korea, many of them ready for immediate use (Nuclear Threat Initiative, 2015). After almost 20 years of warnings about the dangers of "accidental nuclear war," nearly 2,000 weapons remain on "launch-on-warning" hair-trigger alert, and nuclear disarmament has stalled (Wright, MacDonald, & Gronlund, 2016). Meanwhile, these weapons systems are increasingly vulnerable to cyberattack (Forrow et al., 1998).

The use of these weapons would be catastrophic on a global scale. A recent study has found that a *regional* nuclear war between developing Third-World nuclear powers, using less than 0.03% of the total explosive yield of the current global nuclear arsenal, would result in tens of millions of deaths, together with global temperature crashes and an inability to grow crops in most of the world for more than 5 years—the dreaded *nuclear winter* (Robock et al., 2007). A slightly larger nuclear war that is more likely based on the capacity of the nine nuclear-armed states would ignite massive firestorms capable of releasing millions of tons of smoke and soot into the atmosphere, which would block the sun's rays and create massive *global cooling*, with drying and darkening for more than a decade (Turco et al., 1983). This would disrupt food production worldwide, creating a *nuclear famine*, which would put more than two billion people at risk of dying from starvation (Helfand et al., 2016).

The US publicly committed in 2009 to the abolition of nuclear weapons, but 8 years later it had a 1.25 trillion-dollar, 30-year budget to modernize its nuclear arsenal. More than anything, this is a problem of human violence at a national if not global scale, with the future of humanity in jeopardy because of a seeming inability to adjust our thoughts and actions to the objective conditions of this age. The source of the problem is psychological as much as it is military or political, and therefore should be considered much like all the other forms of violence we have discussed in this text: as a human problem, with bio-psycho-socio-environmental contributors. For more than a quarter of a century, the two major nuclear powers were extremely careful not to approach the brink of war too closely, finally accepting the self-defeating absurdity of nuclear war (Mehan, Nathanson, & Skelly, 1990). Now, there has been an irrational reversion to brinkmanship, denial, minimization, and misconception about the degree of danger. At the same time, the US withdrew from the 2015 Paris climate accord, which had as its central aim curbing global temperature rises (Tollefson, 2017). From these facts, we can see that the greatest immediate danger to human survival is not natural scarcity or technology but rather, overwhelmingly, the direct effects of human intention.

Conclusion

It is now obvious that, through the influence we have on the environment and the technological capability we have for destruction, human beings have become, for the first time in evolutionary history, a species at risk of making itself extinct as a result of its own actions. As we ourselves are our own greatest threat, it is now human consciousness that will be the main factor that determines whether we continue on this path of violence to our own destruction or become able to change our behavior toward a path of survival. It will determine whether we can stop: (a) plundering the earth's resources with shortsighted approaches to the economy, production, and commerce; (b) reallocating resources away from areas that are vulnerable and in dire need; (c) obstructing access to information about our critical environmental situation, while at the same time promoting a false and superficial ecology that serves to conceal problems and to engender a carefree recklessness; and (d) avoiding the injustice of the highest-income countries causing the majority of climate change while the lowest-income countries suffer the worst consequences and benefit the least (Nanda & Pring, 2013).

To review, we opened this chapter with the argument that the inclusion of environmental violence is necessary for a course on violence to be complete. It is, nevertheless, an uncomfortable topic that requires humanity to face not only a form of violence by one group against another—the Global North against the South—but self-directed violence that threatens the annihilation of the human species. Its problems reflect a deeper dynamic, whereby if we were to gain insight into what we are hiding from ourselves, then we could finally find solutions to our problems: climate change, population explosion, collective violence, and so on, are all within our grasp. We emphasized that environmental violence is a human issue, whereby it is not the planet or "the environment" that need saving, but ourselves. We defined environmental violence as any violence that is associated with the environment and identified primary, secondary, and tertiary forms of environmental violence. We discussed the link between the political economy, the perception of scarcity, access to resources, and ensuing conflicts. We noted how nuclear violence is very similar to environmental violence in terms of the scale of damage they can effectuate on our habitat and threaten our survival as a species. Even though one is instantaneous and the other more gradual, these two forms are capable of a kind of destruction that is total and irreversible and constitute the double, human-caused emergency of our time.

Where do we go from here? While the current prospects are grim, there is great reason for hope and possibility, since the recognition of our tragic role in our violence is the first step to ending that tragedy. Therefore we can ask: Will we break down divisions that we make among ourselves to meet a common threat confronting humankind now that our survival is at stake? Will we consider reparations and rights, knowing that those who are least responsible for climate change suffer its gravest consequences, and that caring for these rights will protect all our security and survival? Will we turn from our current course to take the necessary steps toward disarmament and the dismantling of a culture of violence that gives legitimacy to "rogue states" and terrorists? Our common ecology makes clear that humanity is one, and even where there is mistaken belief that one is thriving at the detriment of others, like cancer cells that flourish without realizing that they are killing their host, and our shortsightedness may make us blind to the fact that we are altering society in a manner that will be destructive to all. Environmental science helps us to recognize that, rather than politics that are subject to financial and special interests, an evidence-based approach to policy will help protect the common good as well as our only habitat.

Climate justice addresses the fact that global warming is not a purely environmental or physical problem but an ethical and political one (Page, 2007). It calls for attention to the issues of social justice, equality, human rights, and the historical responsibilities for climate change that underlie the current climate crisis. Just as structural violence has an intimate link with behavioral violence, a lack of climate justice has a close relationship with all different forms of environmental violence. The fact that those who did not contribute to global warming are the first to suffer from it, and the disinformation campaign by the countries and corporations that do the most polluting, while threatening mass murder of all life on earth, make environmental violence one of the most egregious forms of violence.

The study of environmental violence, like the study of violence in general, brings us face-to-face with the stark reality that preventing violence is no longer a matter of a difference of opinion or priority of interests but a matter of life or death—and whether we all live together or die together. The study of environmental violence gives us a framework for understanding the form of violence that most urgently needs intervention, against powerful interests that will do everything possible to maintain the current global economic and military system, even at the long-term expense of everyone. We have the tools at our disposal; the question now is whether we will allow ourselves to transform our pathological drive toward violence into a healthy one of peace and survival.

Questions

1   Why is environmental violence an important topic in the study of human violence?

2   What influence does the political economy have on violence due to conflict over resources?

3   What are the ways in which damage to the environment can cascade into other forms of violence?

4   What is the double emergency of our time?

5   How can concepts of climate justice and of collective suicide prevention help us deal with environmental violence?

References

Agarwal, A., & Narain, S. (1991). *Global warming in an unequal world: A case of environmental colonialism*. New Delhi, India: Centre for Science and Environment.

Ahmad, A. S., Ormiston-Smith, N., & Sasieni, P. D. (2015). Trends in the lifetime risk of developing cancer in Great Britain: Comparison of risk for those born from 1930 to 1960. *British Journal of Cancer, 112*(5), 943–947.

Basedau, M., & Lacher, W. (2006). *A paradox of plenty? Rent distribution and political stability in oil states*. GIGA Working Paper No 21. doi:10.2139/ssrn.909189

Behnassi, M., Draggan, S., & Yaya, S. (2011). *Global food insecurity: Rethinking agricultural and rural development paradigm and policy*. Berlin, Germany: Springer Science and Business Media.

Bernard, E. N., & Robinson, A. R. (2009). *Tsunamis* (Vol. *15*). Cambridge, MA: Harvard University Press.

Berry, H. L., Bowen, K., & Kjellstrom, T. (2010). Climate change and mental health: A causal pathways framework. *International Journal of Public Health, 55*(2), 123–132.

Berry, W. (1969). *The long-legged house*. New York, NY: Harcourt, Brace and World.

Biological Weapons Convention. (1972). Retrieved from http://disarmament.un.org/treaties/t/bwc/text

Borras, S. M., Hall, R., Scoones, I., White, B., & Wolford, W. (2011). Towards a better understanding of global land grabbing: An editorial introduction. *Journal of Peasant Studies, 38*(2), 209–216.

Brinton, L. A., Sherman, M. E., Carreon, J. D., & Anderson, W. F. (2008). Recent trends in breast cancer among younger women in the United States. *Journal of the National Cancer Institute, 100*(22), 1643–1648.

Carson, R. (1962). *Silent spring*. Boston, MA: Houghton Mifflin.

Chemical Weapons Convention. (1993). Retrieved from https://treaties.un.org/doc/Treaties/1997/04/19970429%2007-52%20PM/CTC-XXVI_03_ocred.pdf

Choi, Y., Bone, C., & Zhang, N. (2016). Sustainable policies and strategies in Asia: Challenges for green growth. *Technological Forecasting and Social Change, 112*(1), 134–137.

Cities Alliance. (2016). *Climate migration drives slum growth in Dhaka*. Brussels, Belgium: Author. Retrieved from http://www.citiesalliance.org/node/420

Conca, K., & Dabelko, G. D. (2002). *Environmental peacemaking*. Washington, DC: Woodrow Wilson Center Press.

Cook, J., Nuccitelli, D., Green, S. A., Richardson, M., Winkler, B., Painting, R., ... Skuce, A. (2013). Quantifying the consensus on anthropogenic global warming in the scientific literature. *Environmental Research Letters, 8*(2), 024024.

De Castro, J. (1952). *Geography of hunger*. Boston, MA: Gollancz.

Deininger, K., & Byerlee, D. (2011). *Rising global interest in farmland: Can it yield sustainable and equitable benefits?*. Washington, DC: The World Bank.

Dowie, M. (2009). *Conservation refugees: The hundred-year conflict between global conservation and native peoples*. Cambridge, MA: MIT Press.

Ehrlich, P. R. (1968). *The population bomb*. New York, NY: Ballantine Books.

Esfahani, H. S., & Ramírez, M. T. (2003). Institutions, infrastructure, and economic growth. *Journal of Development Economics, 70*(2), 443–477.

Evison, D., Hinsley, D., & Rice, P. (2002). Chemical weapons. *British Medical Journal, 324*(7333), 332–335.

Forrow, L., Blair, B. G., Helfand, I., Lewis, G., Postol, T., Sidel, V., ... Cassel, C. (1998). Accidental nuclear war—A post-Cold War assessment. *New England Journal of Medicine, 338*(18), 1326–1332.

Galeotti, M. (2014). *Global crime today: The changing face of organised crime*. New York, NY: Routledge.

Giroux, H. A. (2006). Reading Hurricane Katrina: Race, class, and the biopolitics of disposability. *College Literature, 33*(3), 171–196.

Global Witness (2014). *Deadly environment*. London, UK: Author.

Gordon, R. (2007). Climate change and the poorest nations: Further reflections on global inequality. *University of Colorado Law Review, 78*(4), 1559–1624.

Hardikar, J. (2017, June 21). With no water and many loans, farmers' deaths are rising in Tamil Nadu. *The Wire*. Retrieved from https://thewire.in/agriculture/drought-tamil-nadu-farmers-deaths

Helfand, I., Haines, A., Ruff, T., Kristensen, H., Lewis, P., & Mian, Z. (2016). The growing threat of nuclear war and the role of the health community. *World Medical Journal, 62*(3), 86–94.

Helfand, I. (2017). Climate disruption and global famine: Nuclear weapons impact on the environment. In United Nations, Civil society and disarmament 2016: *Civil society engagement in disarmament processes—The case for a nuclear weapons ban* (pp. 16–25). New York, NY: United Nations.

Homer-Dixon, T., & Deligiannis, T. (2009). Environmental scarcities and civil violence. In H. G. Brauch, N. C. Behera, P. Kameri-Mbote, J. Grin, U. Oswald Spring, B. Chourou, et al. (Eds.), *Facing global environmental change* (Vol. 4)Hexagon Series on Human and Environmental Security and Peace. Berlin, Heidelberg: Springer.

Homer-Dixon, T. F. (2010). *Environment, scarcity, and violence.* Princeton, NJ: Princeton University Press.

Hoogvelt, A. (2001). *Globalization and the postcolonial world: The new political economy of development.* Baltimore, MD: Johns Hopkins University Press.

Hossain, N. (2017). Inequality, hunger, and malnutrition: Power matters. In K. von Grebmer, J. Bernstein, N. Hossain, T. Brown, N. Prasai, Y. Yohannes, et al. (Eds.), *2017 Global Hunger Index* (pp. 24–29). Washington, DC: International Food Policy Research Institute.

Human Rights Watch (2012). *Ethiopia: Army commits torture, rape.* New York, NY: Author. Retrieved from https://www.hrw.org/news/2012/08/28/ethiopia-army-commits-torture-rape

Idrobo, N., Mejía, D., & Tribin, A. M. (2014). Illegal gold mining and violence in Colombia. *Peace Economics, Peace Science and Public Policy, 20*(1), 83–111.

Intergovernmental Panel on Climate Change (2013). Summary for policymakers. In T. F. Stocker, D. Qin, G.-K. Plattner, M. Tignor, S. K. Allen, J. Boschung, et al. (Eds.), *Climate change 2013: The physical science basis. Contribution of working group I to the fifth assessment report of the intergovernmental panel on climate change.* Cambridge, UK: Cambridge University Press.

Kabir, A., & Parolin, B. (2012). Planning and development of Dhaka—A story of 400 years. 15th International Planning History Society Conference. Washington, DC: World Bank. Retrieved from http://www.fau.usp.br/iphs/abstractsandpapersfiles/sessions/09/kabir_parolin.pdf

Kaplan, R. D. (2000). *The coming anarchy: Shattering the dreams of the Post Cold War.* New York, NY: Random House.

Klein, N. (2014). *This changes everything: Capitalism versus the climate.* New York, NY: Simon and Schuster.

Kunkel, C. M., Hallberg, R. W., & Oppenheimer, M. (2006). Coral reefs reduce tsunami impact in model simulations. *Geophysical Research Letters, 33*(23), L2361e2.

Larsen, M. C., Wieczorek, G. F., Eaton, L. S., Morgan, B. A., & Torres-Sierra, H. (2001). Venezuelan debris flow and flash flood disaster of 1999 studied. *Eos, Transactions American Geophysical Union, 82*(47), 572–573.

Lashof, D. A., & Ahuja, D. R. (1990). Relative contributions of greenhouse gas emissions to global warming. *Nature, 344*(6266), 529–531.

Lockeretz, W. (1978). The lessons of the dust bowl: Several decades before the current concern with environmental problems, dust storms ravaged the Great Plains, and the threat of more dust storms still hangs over us. *American Scientist, 66*(5), 560–569.

Lujala, P., Gleditsch, N. P., & Gilmore, E. (2005). A diamond curse? Civil war and a lootable resource. *Journal of Conflict Resolution, 49*(4), 538–562.

Malthus, T. R. (1798). *An essay on the principle of population, as it affects the future improvement of society with remarks on the speculations of Mr. Godwin, M. Condorcet, and other writers.* London, Great Britain: Johnson.

Manhattan Engineer District and U.S. Army. (1957). *The atomic bombings of Hiroshima and Nagasaki.* Report of June 29.

McMichael, A. J., Woodruff, R. E., & Hales, S. (2006). Climate change and human health: Present and future risks. *Lancet, 367*(9513), 859–869.

McPherson, P. (2015, December 1). Dhaka: The city where climate refugees are already a reality. *The Guardian*. https://www.theguardian.com/cities/2015/dec/01/dhaka-city-climate-refugees-reality

Mehan, H., Nathanson, C. E., & Skelly, J. M. (1990). Nuclear discourse in the 1980's: The unravelling conventions of the cold war. *Discourse and Society, 1*(2), 133–165.

Messner, F., & Meyer, V. (2006). Flood damage, vulnerability and risk perception—Challenges for flood damage research. In J. Schanze, E. Zeman, & J. Marsalek (Eds.), *Flood risk management: Hazards, vulnerability and mitigation measures* (pp. 149–167). Dordrecht, Netherlands: Springer.

Mohai, P., Pellow, D., & Roberts, J. T. (2009). Environmental justice. *Annual Review of Environment and Resources, 34*(1), 405–430.

Nanda, V., & Pring, G. R. (2013). *International environmental law and policy for the 21st century*. Leiden, Netherlands: Nijhoff Publishers.

Nuclear Threat Initiative (2015). *The nuclear threat*. Washington, DC: Author Retrieved from http://www.nti.org/learn/nuclear

Nuwer, R. (2016). Illegal logging has become more violent than ever. *National Geographic*. Retrieved from https://news.nationalgeographic.com/2016/02/160202-Illegal-loggers-murders-violence-defending-land

Oniang'o, R. (2017). Will the G7 deliver on their promise to commit resources to end world hunger by 2030? From the first World Food Conference in 1974, no resolutions or pledges have ever been fulfilled. So, what guarantees are there that this one will be? *African Journal of Food Agriculture Nutrition and Development, 17*(1).

Pachauri, R. K., Allen, M. R., Barros, V. R., Broome, J., Cramer, W., Christ, R., … Dubash, N. K. (2014). *Climate change 2014: Synthesis report. contribution of working groups I, II and III to the fifth assessment report of the intergovernmental panel on climate change*. Geneva, Switzerland: Intergovernmental Panel on Climate Change.

Page, E. A. (2007). *Climate change, justice and future generations*. Cheltenham, UK: Edward Elgar Publishing.

Peluso, N. L., & Watts, M. (2001). *Violent environments*. Ithaca, NY: Cornell University Press.

Ponting, C. (1991). *A green history of the world*. London, UK: Sinclair-Stevenson.

Reuveny, R. (2002). Economic growth, environmental scarcity, and conflict. *Global Environmental Politics, 2*(1), 83–110.

Robbins, P. (2011). *Political ecology: A critical introduction*. New York, NY: Wiley.

Robock, A. (2010). Nuclear winter. *Climate Change, 1*(3), 418–427.

Robock, A., Oman, L., Stenchikov, G. L., Toon, O. B., Bardeen, C., & Turco, R. P. (2007). Climatic consequences of regional nuclear conflicts. *Atmospheric Chemistry and Physics, 7*(8), 2003–2012.

Ross, M. L. (1999). The political economy of the resource curse. *World Politics, 51*(2), 297–322.

Rowhani, P., Degomme, O., Guha-Sapir, D., & Lambin, E. F. (2011). Malnutrition and conflict in East Africa: the impacts of resource variability on human security. *Climatic Change, 105*(1–2), 207–222.

Rullia, M. C., Savioria, A., & D'Odorico, P. (2013). Global land and water grabbing. *Proceedings of the National Academy of Sciences, 110*(3), 892–897.

Sawada, A., Chaitin, J., & Bar-On, D. (2004). Surviving Hiroshima and Nagasaki—experiences and psychosocial meanings. *Psychiatry, 67*(1), 43–60.

Shimizu, Y., Kodama, K., Nishi, N., Kasagi, F., Suyama, A., Soda, M., … Hayashi, M. (2010). Radiation exposure and circulatory disease risk: Hiroshima and Nagasaki atomic bomb survivor data, 1950–2003. *British Medical Journal, 340*, b5349.

Shintomi, T. (2014, December 30). A-bomb survivor, 90, intent on attending NPT confab. *Japan Times*. Retrieved from www.japantimes.co.jp/news/2014/12/30/national/bomb-survivor-90-intent-attending-npt-confab/#.WxV162dMfGV

Southwick, C. H. (1996). *Global ecology in human perspective*. New York, NY: Oxford University Press.

Stein, C. (2016, May 11). Farmer-herder conflict rises across Nigeria. *Voa News*. Retrieved from https://www.voanews.com/a/farmer-herder-conflict-rises-across-nigeria/3326151.html

Timmer, C. P. (2015). *Food security and scarcity: Why ending hunger is so hard*. Philadelphia, PA: University of Pennsylvania Press.

Tollefson, J. (2017). Trump pulls United States out of Paris climate agreement. *Nature News, 546*(7657), 198.

Treaty on the Non-Proliferation of Nuclear Weapons. (1968). Retrieved from https://www.un.org/disarmament/wmd/nuclear/npt/text

Treaty on the Prohibition of Nuclear Weapons. (2017). Retrieved from http://undocs.org/A/CONF.229/2017/8

Turco, R. P., Toon, O. B., Ackerman, T. P., Pollack, J. B., & Sagan, C. (1983). Nuclear winter: Global consequences of multiple nuclear explosions. *Science, 222*(4630), 1283–1292.

Union of Concerned Scientists (2010). *Climate change and mental health: Extreme weather takes a toll*. Cambridge, MA: Author.

United Nations Environment Programme. (2001). Vital Climate Graphics. Retrieved from https://www.grida.no/resources/6885

Wheelis, M., Rózsa, L., & Dando, M. (2006). *Deadly cultures: Biological weapons since 1945*. Cambridge, MA: Harvard University Press.

Wright, D., MacDonald, E., & Gronlund, L. (2016). *Reducing the risk of nuclear war taking nuclear weapons off high alert*. Cambridge, MA: Union of Concerned Scientists.

Zhang, D. D., Brecke, P., Lee, H. F., He, Y.-Q., & Zhang, J. (2007). Global climate change, war, and population decline in recent human history. *Proceedings of the National Academy of Sciences of the United States of America, 104*(49), 19214–19219.

Consequences

9

Consequences of Violence

Introduction

> Violence ends by defeating itself. It creates bitterness in the survivors and brutality in the destroyers.
>
> —*Martin Luther King Jr.*, Nobel Peace Prize Lecture *(1964).*

The consequences of violence are vast and varied, far exceeding what we can measure or perceive. They include not only the obvious traumas resulting from being a victim or a witness, but also the less recognizable social, cultural, and economic repercussions that embed deeply in victims' physical and psychological lives. Then there is the unquantifiable human cost of grief and pain. Also, the more common the form of violence, the less it is recognized or seen. In this chapter, we will review the extent of the consequences of violence, and attempt to demonstrate that, while violence is costly, it is also *worth preventing*. We will do so while reviewing the common categories of violence: self-directed violence; youth, intimate partner, and sexual violence; child maltreatment and elder abuse; and collective violence. In the coming chapters, we will evaluate what interventions could alleviate the pain and suffering of those already coping with the consequences of violence. Reducing violence in a given society or around the world does more than curb its direct impact; it allows for human thriving and an upsurge of life that are greater than the mere absence of the problem. On a global scale, we can gauge a population's general state of health, or ability to thrive, by the level of all forms of violence—self-directed, interpersonal, and collective—in totality (Lee et al., 2014).

Because violence affects human health and wellbeing in complex and innumerable ways, the ways in which reducing it allow an individual, a family, or a community to flourish are equally numerous. Knowing all the costs of violence is impossible, but it is necessary to establish some measures that can help identify areas of need and track the progress of our efforts. The most obvious measure, still in need of standardization, is death rates, but we must keep in mind that they are only the tip of the iceberg of true harm and suffering (Mayor, 2002). Tracking consequences can also help contrast the very small costs of prevention with the large costs of response (Sharp et al., 2014). For example, the Institute for Economics and Peace (2014) reported that the responses necessary to remedy past violence and contain further spread amount to some 9.46 trillion dollars, or 11% of Gross World Product. The US Centers for Disease Control and Prevention (CDC, 2010), analyzing medical and work consequences of homicide and suicide, estimated their cost as 70 billion dollars for almost 55,000 deaths in a year.

Violence: An Interdisciplinary Approach to Causes, Consequences, and Cures, First Edition. Bandy X. Lee.
© 2019 John Wiley & Sons, Inc. Published 2019 by John Wiley & Sons, Inc.

The costs in terms of time away from work, medical expenses, legal fees, security budgets for entire nations also translate to losses of developmental opportunities for whole regions. This is all the more pronounced because violence mainly impacts young people at the height of their productivity, especially among men aged 15 to 44 years. The impact of violence is also not limited to physical injury. Causes of early death and lifelong ill health include depression, posttraumatic stress disorder, suicide attempts, chronic pain syndromes, substance misuse, unwanted pregnancies, and sexually transmitted infections. War and civil conflict lead to further wars as well as to interpersonal violence, destroyed infrastructure, forced displacement, and weak states where further wars and exploitation can flourish. The most common forms of violence, however, are hidden from view, and there are also the less quantifiable costs: the loss of sense of safety, curtailed dreams and aspirations, abandoned hopes for humanity. As one puts up guard, defends, and prepares for the next attack, what opportunities is one detracting from, and what potentials are diminishing? The loss may never be calculable. When we put together the human consequences of violence at all levels, we begin to grasp the enormity of the issue. Violence cuts into the very heart of the person, but it also causes entire civilizations to suffer.

Although violence affects every continent and country and virtually every community, its effects are disproportionately felt in low- and middle-income countries, where resources are already scarce and fall further behind as a result. Furthermore, studies of its social and economic impact are lacking (Waters et al., 2005), with most of the available information about the effects of violence comeing from high-income nations, most notably the United States (Wolf, Gray, & Fazel, 2014). This makes international comparisons of economic consequences even further removed, since the calculation of losses involves foregone wages and income. While each life in a high-income country costs more in dollars, each dollar in lower-income countries constitutes a greater economic loss. Since violence never occurs in isolation but reverberates as other types of harm and other forms of violence, we need to consider how the physical, psychological, social, and societal effects of violence will be magnified and exacerbated in resource-poor settings (Haugen & Boutros, 2015). Meanwhile, although an economic analysis of violence is useful, it cannot begin to account for all the ways in which different forms of violence compromise psychological wellbeing, public health, human rights, and sociopolitical development (Taylor et al., 2013).

Case Vignettes

Child Abuse and Neglect

Jacques was born in Port-au-Prince, Haiti, where he lived until age seven with his sister and a woman he believed to be mother, but who he later learned was his maternal grandmother. He was told sometime later that his biological father, a married pharmacist with children, had raped his mother. When he was about a year old, Jacques' mother deserted him and emigrated to Canada. While living with his grandmother, Jacques witnessed violence and murder, and believes he was sexually molested by two neighbors. He witnessed voodoo rituals at home, which included the slaughter of animals, drinking of their blood, and torture of "possessed" people. Children, including him, were offered to be beaten with whips by people in costumes. He lived across the street from a prison, where inmates were regularly brought out into the street for public punishment, and he believes he witnessed amputation and decapitation. At age seven, his stepfather brought him and his sister to New York City, where he was reunited with his mother. Only then did he learn who his biological mother was. While living with his mother and stepfather, Jacques suffered severe physical and emotional abuse, including being beaten with electrical cords and occasionally with boards studded with nails, as well as being burned with scalding water. His mother forced him to kneel on graters for hours at a time and burned his hands on the stove. He was often absent from school because of his injuries. At the age of nine, while he was hospitalized for serious burns from being placed in a bath of boiling water, the New York State Family Court issued an order to have him and his sister removed from his mother's custody.

His years in state institutional care in a series of numerous foster homes and institutions were not much better. At many of these facilities, he again endured physical, sexual, and emotional abuse. In one of his foster homes, when he was about age 10, he was locked in the basement whenever his foster parents left the home, once for 3 days without food. He suffered innumerable beatings in foster and group homes. When he was 9 or 10 years old, he was sexually molested many times by a counselor he had trusted. At age 14, while in a juvenile facility, he was stabbed with a coil bedspring, which resulted in a lengthy hospitalization. As a ward of the state, Jacques lived in a total of 36 homes over an 8-year period, and his behavior has come to reflect his experience of instability and abuse. He became difficult to place in foster homes due to behavioral problems and poor adjustment. Despite multiple failed attempts to reunite him with his biological mother, he constantly ruminated about her and longed to be accepted, and he would sometimes become incapacitated in everyday life because of this. He frequently felt unwanted because families did not wish to take him, while he continued to feel rejected by his mother, who seldom visited him.

Jacques began breaking the law when he found out that he could not get a job because he had no green card or social security number. He went from foster care to state prison as a youth offender and then received a felony drug conviction at age 25 and served state prison time for it. When he was about to be released, the Office of Homeland Security transferred him to a facility in Pennsylvania and initiated proceedings to deport him to Haiti as an illegal alien. Jacques has no personal connections to Haiti and does not speak French or Creole, and his last known relative has left the country. Most significantly, he will likely undergo Haiti's documented practice of indefinitely detaining American deportees from prison.

Jacques has not been able to obtain an identity card despite his 21 years in America. He was eligible for adjustment to legal immigration status under special provisions for children placed in foster care, but his caretakers failed to file for it. Meanwhile, his biological mother became a US citizen, as did his sister who came with him and was also in state custody. Facing deportation, he made numerous suicide attempts, the last time hanging himself while in the custody of the Office of Homeland Security. He continued to have passive suicidal ideations. Once, he admitted to having wanted to kill another inmate, and correctional officers restrained him. He came upon many duels "unexpectedly," especially while incarcerated. He states that he used to "talk with [his] fists" but is now able to suppress his anger, because he does not wish to lose any chance he has. He has nightmares of Haiti, envisioning people rioting and open firing, and he sometimes forgets or delusionally denies the possibility of his being deported.

Child abuse is one of the most terrifying and traumatic experiences one can have. Children who experience maltreatment have ongoing difficulties with emotional security, self-esteem, and ordinary development. Later in life, they continue to have difficulties with trust, social interactions, school performance, and relationships, which can in turn provoke or exacerbate abuse. Victims of child abuse and neglect are more likely to commit crimes as juveniles and as adults and more likely to suffer from depression, anxiety, and irritability. Witnesses of domestic violence are more likely to engage in felony assault.

Veteran Partner Violence

"If you don't hear from me in the next 24 hours, call the police," Wendy whispers to Linda before hanging up. Linda's phone shows it is 2:12 a.m., and it is the third call in as many minutes. Linda tries to call Wendy back, but there is no answer. She goes back to sleep, angry at the phone call in the middle of the night. The next morning, she lets out her anger in an email: "I cannot, for the love of God, imagine what you were thinking when you called last night. Please tell me." Linda and Wendy became "battle buddies" at home while their husbands were serving in Iraq in the mid-2000s. They cried together each time a military family member called with word of a soldier's death or suicide; they grieved at funerals and gravesites; and they wept with each other when they learned that one of their husbands had been mobilized for another deployment. Wendy's husband had served three combat tours since 2002. The last one, the shortest, was 10 months. Wendy wrote in an email that "he actually came back pretty normal this time!" That was nearly 4 months ago.

Earlier in the year, when Linda picked up the phone, Wendy had blurted out: "Tom tried to strangle me last night." She later explained: "I called you from the bathroom. I locked myself in with the pets. I didn't want him to hurt my puppy. I'm sorry I called. I was just so scared, and I didn't have anyone else to call. I couldn't call the cops." Linda had gotten other midnight calls from other military wives, cowering in closets and under dining room tables, dialing for a lifeline to someone outside of their domestic war zone. But Wendy had worked at a women's shelter nearly a decade ago and knew all the warning signs. Tom adored his wife. He had no history of domestic violence and no pattern of abuse; he had not tried to isolate her from friends, family, or finances. His most recent post-deployment mental health assessment had not indicated any issues. There was not a single red flag before he wrapped his hands around Wendy's throat and squeezed—which is what makes veterans' household violence unique.

Abuse by combat veterans often does not follow the recurring power-and-control cycle of abuse that is common in other intimate partner abuse stories. Veteran interpersonal violence often occurs suddenly, with only one or two extremely violent and frightening abusive episodes that trigger them to seek treatment. Studies of treatment-seeking veterans with posttraumatic stress disorder (PTSD) or combat-related mental health issues report that at least half of those veterans commit family violence. Veterans Affairs data show that male veterans with PTSD are two to three times more likely than veterans without PTSD to engage in intimate partner violence, and the majority of veterans with combat stress commit at least one act of spousal abuse in their first year following deployment.

Wendy reached out to another military spouse who lived off post and was married to an Iraq war veteran. She told her what happened, and her friend said that she and her husband had gotten into so many fights, hitting and screaming and throwing things at each other, that she ended up going to the domestic violence shelter. Most family victims of veteran violence do not file reports with the police or their husband's command. The military is stepping up domestic violence programs and education at military installations, but the pressure on spouses within the active duty and retired military culture and much of the civilian population to remain silent is especially intense during a time of war. Speaking out about veteran violence at home seems to be perceived as more of a betrayal than the violence itself. Still, since 2003, there has been a 75% increase in reports of domestic violence in and around Fort Hood, Texas, where the number of soldiers diagnosed with PTSD rose from 310 in 2004 to 2,445 in 2009.

Wendy says to Linda that she has quit praying that she and Tom "would get their old lives back. That's gone." According to military statistics, nearly half of active-duty National Guard members, 38% of Army soldiers, and 31% of Marines report mental health problems upon return from Middle East deployments. The majority of studies of treatment-seeking veterans with PTSD or combat-related mental health issues report that at least 50% of those veterans engage in intimate partner violence and family violence. As combat operations wind down on the war front, they are just beginning for thousands of military family members (Bannerman, 2010).

Financial and Physical Elder Abuse

Sherry was widowed early and has been living alone for many years. Still, she has been very active and is friendly with her neighbors. She does not have children of her own, but has visited with her nieces and nephews frequently until they became occupied with families of their own. She worked hard most of her life and has retired with a large nest egg. While she has been independent most of her life, at the age of 79, she needs help with home repairs and yard work. She hires Stan, a middle-aged man, to give her a hand with jobs that have become difficult to do herself. When she is about 81, Sherry begins exhibiting signs of dementia and needs assistance with more than just odd jobs around the house. She tells Stan that she is planning to hire an aide since she has no family near enough to assist her with her daily needs. Stan tells Sherry that she does not need to spend any money in hiring a caregiver, as he will gladly do it.

Stan seizes the opportunity to move into Sherry's large home. He first convinces Sherry to give him power of attorney for her healthcare under the pretense of providing assistance with her medications and doctor's appointments. He then stops mailing the checks Sherry writes for payment of utility bills and, when past due notices arrive, begins to berate her for being forgetful, insisting that she does not have the capacity to handle her own finances. Sherry resists at first, but eventually he convinces her to make him her agent under a durable power of attorney. He then takes control of her pension checks. He uses some of the money to pay for her food, doctor's bills, and medications but deposits the rest into his own account. He also adds his name as joint owner on all of her bank accounts to gain access to the rest of her funds.

Over the next several months, Stan stops taking care of the yard and making repairs to the home. The neighbors begin to suspect something is amiss. When they stop by the house to check up on Sherry, Stan tells them that she is asleep or does not wish to speak with them. Stan changes the locks on the doors to keep relatives out and makes sure that those who called to ask about Sherry do not speak with her. The only "outside" person Sherry ever talks to is her physician during occasional medical checkups, but Sherry does not complain to her doctor about the abuse because Stan has convinced her that he is the only person willing to care for her. Sherry's mental and physical state begins to deteriorate. Stan finds it difficult to care for her and yells at her whenever she falls or cannot make it to the bathroom. He begins to give Sherry sleeping pills to quiet her when she complains. He eventually confines her to her bedroom and then her bed. Her health declines rapidly, and eventually Stan feels he has no choice but to take her to the hospital. Sherry dies within days of being hospitalized.

Sherry had always told her nieces and nephews that she would leave each of them an equal part of her estate, since she had no children. She had even shown them a copy of her will. However, after she dies, the family discovers that a new will has been executed, which names Stan as the beneficiary of her entire estate. The family files a will contest, and most of Sherry's estate is depleted by the years of litigation between the family and Stan. Many such cases of elder abuse, neglect, and financial exploitation occur but are never reported. Often, elder abusers are not strangers but family members, keeping the issue further hidden from view. With the older adult populations exploding globally, elder abuse is now recognized internationally as a serious problem, urgently requiring the attention of healthcare systems, social welfare agencies, policymakers, and the general public. There has been a lack of reliable data regarding elder abuse as a consequence of low priority given to this group, but this trend has been gradually changing over the last decade (United Nations Office of the High Commissioner for Human Rights, 2010, World Health Organization, United Nations Office on Drugs and Crime [UNODC], & United Nations Development Programme [UNDP], 2014).

Medical Consequences of Rape

The Democratic Republic of the Congo, especially the eastern part of the country, has been described as "the rape capital of the world" in the twenty-first century, because of the prevalence and intensity of all forms of sexual violence. These are stories from women who have required fistula repairs (surgery to repair unnatural openings in internal organs) following brutal rape.

Bupole lives on what she cultivates in the fields in harmony with her parents and her four brothers. None of the children can read or write because the nearest school is more than a 12-hr walk away through dense forest. Because of the war and insecurity, the family members visit their house only during the day, and only for storage of food, never for rest. They spend their nights out in the forest not far from their fields. In the mornings, they gather food. At noon, they return to the village for 2 or 3 hr, just enough time to prepare a meal that they eat quickly for fear of being ambushed and captured by armed militia scavenging for women and food. By four in the afternoon, everyone routinely treks back to the forest to seek refuge for the night. The day they fear comes. The men they dread and against whom they took all their precautions suddenly appear earlier than expected. They surround the entire village and begin firing in every direction, killing anyone who attempts to flee. A bullet hits Bupole's father in the neck and he falls, dying. Another bullet hits her mother in the thigh as they try to escape. Bupole stops. She cannot abandon her. Five men catch up with her as she tries to help her mother. They tie Bupole up and stuff a gag into her mouth. Then they rape her again and again. Bupole remains unconscious for hours. They finally leave. Much later, a different group of armed men comes to the rescue. However, it is too late for Bupole's mother who has slowly bled to death. They bring her mother's body to a neighboring village, along with Bupole and five other women who were also brutalized. On that day, Bupole's village buries 25 of its members. Bupole's mind is in anguish, her entire body is in terrible pain, and she is bleeding from her private parts. Over the next 2 days, she realizes she cannot hold her urine, even though she has no sensation of needing to urinate. Everything flows out of her as soon as she drinks. She is beyond depression. No one can stand to be near her because of the stench. Later, she finds some hope after hearing from two women who have suffered from the same ailment. They were treated for urine leakage and healed after going to a hospital in Goma. Their reassurance helps her to seek care. Bupole survived the gang-rape, but with a complex vesico-vaginal fistula. She has severe adhesions of the vaginal walls, causing almost complete obliteration and absence of the vaginal cavity and requiring difficult surgery.

Byamungu brings palm oil to the market. She walks with her family 4 hr on foot with merchandise on her back. If she has no buyer, she leaves her jerry can there because the distance is so great. But when business is good, she buys soap and brings the remaining money to her parents. One day, Byamungu returns from the market with a group of women and feels the need to relieve her bowels. Since the only place to go is in the forest, she tells the others not to leave her. She finishes her business and quickly returns to the path. Suddenly, a group of men appears behind her. One of them grabs her by the hand. She screams, but her frightened companions are already running away. The more she screams, the faster they run. Abandoned, she faces eight men who first rob her of the money and packets of soap. Then, three of them drag her into the bush, strip her naked and rape her repeatedly. The other five do not approve of their brothers' brutality and try to stop them, but only half-heartedly. When they finish, they leave Byamungu there bleeding, moaning in pain, until a group of women find her slumped on the ground. One of them carries Byamungu on her back until they reach a health center. The lady's entire back is covered in Byamungu's blood. Another woman from Byamungu's village goes to inform her parents. That night, the entire village comes to the health center to see the damage: feces and urine flow out of the same opening in her body. After a week at the health center, Byamungu spends another 3 weeks at home before going to the hospital in Goma for surgery. She can control her bladder, but cannot completely control her bowels (Longombe, Claude, & Ruminjo, 2008).

Rape is a serious public health problem, and it has short- and long-term adverse physical and psychological consequences on an individual. After effects can include gynecological complaints, chronic lower abdominal pain, abnormal vaginal bleeding, infertility, genital sores, and swellings in the abdomen. In extreme cases, as above, a rupture of the walls that separate the vagina and bladder or rectum can heal incorrectly, such that fistulas form, creating connections between the different tracts. Human immunodeficiency virus (HIV) infections and surgical complications can result. Consequences also include severe psychological distress, substance abuse, and attempted suicides.

Wartime Collective Sexual Violence

Collective sexual violence commonly accompanies war. One of the less-known crimes during World War II relates to the Japanese army's "comfort system," a state-sanctioned arrangement of mass sexual slavery and sexual violence against hundreds of thousands of women and girls captured in occupied territories. The Japanese government for a long time refused to acknowledge its responsibility, contending that the "comfort women" were voluntary prostitutes. The number of women forced into sexual service by the Japanese army is estimated to be from 20,000 to 400,000, with a conservative estimate between 50,000 and 100,000. They were predominantly Chinese and Korean, but also Filipinas, Indonesian, Dutch, Taiwanese, and Japanese. Private operators ran many of the comfort stations, although in some areas the Japanese military directly operated them. These accounts are from the 2001 Women's International War Crimes Tribunal against nine high-ranking Japanese military and government officials and Emperor Hirohito.

One of the Chinese witnesses recalls that a local woman deceived her into becoming a comfort woman as a teenager. The woman told her that she was beautiful and offered her a lucrative job. She did not wish to take the job, but the woman warned her that she would be sorry. She was very poor and supported five of her family members, and so she decided to take the job. She was driven to a Japanese army base where soldiers stood holding their guns. She tried to resist getting out of the car and being taken inside, but the soldiers and comfort station managers hit her and abused her. She was sexually abused continuously for 15 months. The system worked in such a way that soldiers would purchase a ticket to get access to her. Most of the soldiers, according to her, were inhumane. They would change condoms up to four times during sexual intercourse, and it hurt so much that she could not sit. She was also forced to have sex with soldiers without condoms because they believed that the women were free of sexual diseases, and often the intercourse came with additional abuse if she did not obey every command.

Another witness from Korea was lured into the comfort facilities when a Japanese police officer visited her at work and told her about a better job in a factory. When she applied and moved for the new job, soldiers from the Japanese military captured her and made her a comfort woman. She serviced 30 men a day. She tells of 1 day when she was in great pain. When she did not respond to the demands of the officer she was servicing, the soldier beat her with his fists, kicked her, and took out a long knife and held it on her throat and cut her. Blood poured out of her, soaking her body, as the soldier satisfied his lust. She witnesses that other women caught diseases, became malnourished, and were carted out or dumped into the river to drown. She saw two Japanese soldiers stab a pregnant woman in the belly, killing her.

A Malaysian witness describes being brought in as a comfort woman at age 13. She would work 10 hr a day and through the night. She faced torture and abuse. When she became pregnant, 5 months into it, a Japanese soldier pushed on her abdomen until the fetus came out. She was told that if she held onto the tickets that the Japanese soldiers provided her for services, she could exchange them for money. She was not able to do so. Escape was punished with torture. One witness testifies that she escaped twice from the cave where soldiers kept her and other women as sex slaves. After the second escape, she was taken out of the cave naked and unconscious, and hung. Then, she was thrown into freezing water. Another person from the cave was tortured with a hot iron rod on her lips, tongue, and breasts after escaping.

Those charged include persons of the highest levels of authority in Japan during the period the crimes had been committed, 1937–1945, including Emperor Hirohito, the official Head of State at the time, and some of the highest ranking military commanders in the Japanese army. The Tribunal finds them all guilty of rape and sexual slavery as crimes against humanity during World War II for the development of the Comfort Women system. The Tribunal's decision has no binding effect on Japan but it makes recommendations, including that the victims be given an apology and reparations (Chinkin, 2001).

Wartime sexual violence happens in the form of rape or other forms of sexual violence, which combatants commit during armed conflict, war, or military occupation. It is often considered as spoils of war, but it can sometimes occur in the form of gang rape, forced prostitution, or sexual slavery by an occupying power. During armed conflict, it can be a means of waging psychological warfare in order to humiliate and demoralize the enemy. Rape is also recognized as a form of genocide or ethnic cleansing when it is performed with the intent to destroy a target group, in whole or in part.

Self-Directed Violence

Self-directed violence includes *suicide* and all other nonfatal intentional acts of self-injury irrespective of the degree of suicidal intent. It has received worldwide attention because of the general upward trend in both suicide rates and absolute numbers of suicidal behavior across the lifespan (World Health Organization [WHO], 2002). The WHO (2006) noted that suicide rates around the world rose by 60% over the last half century. With close to 800,000 suicides every year, as well as many more people attempting suicide or engaging in self-injurious behavior, self-directed violence has become the most prevalent form of behavioral violence worldwide (Borges et al., 2010). In 2012, suicide was the second leading cause of death worldwide among 15- to 29-year-olds, with 75% occurring in low- and middle-income countries (WHO et al., 2014).

The tragedy of suicide affects not only the immediate victim, but also the families, communities, and entire societies it leaves behind, and there are growing concerns about the pain, societal disruption, and economic drain that these deaths create (Hoven, Mandell, & Bertolote, 2010). Suicide rates are likely to be underestimated, because reports of death by suicide often cause stigmatization and other negative consequences for the remaining family and are likely to be unrecognized, misclassified, or deliberately hidden in official records (Bertolote & Fleischmann, 2002). Suicide attempts—although the data are far less reliable and more local—are estimated to be 10–20 times more frequent than completed suicides (DeLeo et al., 2004). In addition to the fact that attempted suicide often causes permanent impairment and disability, there is growing concern about the rising prevalence of mental disorders such as depressive disorders and other risk factors for suicide (Thapar et al., 2012).

While research on the societal and economic burden of suicide is scanty, the estimated average cost of each suicide in the US is over 1.16 million dollars in medical expenses and lost productivity (Centers for Disease Control and Prevention, 2010). This amount includes direct costs, including treatment, hospitalization, funeral costs, and psychological costs, and indirect costs from loss of productivity and work output, the reduction of life expectancy, and other quality-of-life losses (Butchart et al., 2008). The total fiscal loss resulting from suicides was estimated to be 16 billion dollars for 2005, with nonfatal attempts costing another 4.7 billion dollars (Yang & Lester, 2007). A report from New Zealand calculated the total cost of suicide in 2002 at 1.4 billion dollars, an average of 2.5 million dollars per suicide (O'Dea & Tucker, 2005). Data on the costs of nonlethal suicide attempts are relatively lacking, and direct medical costs are only a part of the picture. Each suicide leaves behind between 6 and 32 family members and friends, while surviving the loss of a loved one to suicide is a risk factor for suicide in itself (Ali, Dwyer, & Rizzo, 2011). Surviving family members and close friends suffer a range of complex grief reactions, including guilt, anger, abandonment, denial, helplessness, and shock (Jordan, 2001). Worldwide, the incidences, burdens, and cultural meanings of suicide vary among different countries and among different ethnic groups within countries.

Youth, Intimate Partner, and Sexual Violence

There are many kinds of interpersonal violence, each of which can have profound effects on the victim. The first type of violence we will examine is *youth violence*, which is defined as violence that involves persons between the ages of 10 and 29, either as victims or as perpetrators (Krug et al., 2002). Globally, youth violence is the fourth leading cause of death for people in this age group with an estimate of 200,000 homicides each year, which constitute 41% of the total global homicides (WHO, 2008). Eighty-three percent of youth homicide victims are male, as are the majority of the perpetrators. However, it should be noted that youth homicide rates vary dramatically between countries, as well as within countries by socioeconomic indicators, among other factors. Statistics indicate that youth homicide rates decreased in most countries around the world from 2000 to 2012, although the decrease was greater in high-income countries, where the problem is less serious and where there are more resources to implement prevention programs.

For every young person who dies from violence, 20–40 more sustain injuries that require hospital treatment (Krug et al., 2002). Firearm attacks are more often fatal than assaults involving knives, fists, feet, and blunt objects (Cerda, 2016). Sexual violence affects a significant proportion of youth; in a WHO survey of women, 3–24% reported their first sexual experience as forced (Garcia-Moreno et al., 2005). Physical fighting and bullying are also common in this age group; a study of 40 countries showed an average of 42% of boys and 37% of girls had experienced bullying (Craig et al., 2009). Youth homicide and nonfatal violence contribute greatly to the global burden of premature death, injury, and disability (Granero et al., 2011). It also has a serious, often lifelong, impact on a person's psychological and social functioning (Le & Blum, 2011), which can in turn affect victims' families, friends, communities, and society (Cooley-Strickland et al., 2009).

Youth violence increases healthcare and welfare costs, as well as the need for criminal justice services, while reducing productivity, thus generally undermining the fabric of society

(World Health Organization, 2015). Interventions to prevent high-risk youth from becoming career offenders are therefore likely to be highly cost-effective, and preventive measures to keep youths from becoming high-risk in the first place even more so. One study in the US calculated preventive measures to cost little more than 17 dollars per averted youth violence incident, with the highest estimate being 55 dollars. Compare this to the cost of treating a victim in the emergency room: an average of over 1,300 dollars for general wounds and over 3,600 dollars for gunshot wounds (Sharp et al., 2014).

The second type of violence we review here is *intimate partner violence* (IPV), which is one of the most common forms of violence against women; in sharp contrast, men are far more likely to be the victim of violence by a stranger or an acquaintance than by an intimate partner. Research has shown that 40–70% of female murder victims are killed by their husband or boyfriend, often in the context of an abusive relationship (Krug et al., 2002). IPV is widespread and takes many forms, including physical, sexual, and emotional abuse, as well as controlling behavior. Between 13 and 61% of women admit to having experienced physical violence by a partner; 4–49% reported having experienced severe physical violence by a partner; 6–59% reported sexual violence by a partner at some point in their lives; and 20–75% report experiencing one or more emotionally abusive acts from a partner (Garcia-Moreno et al., 2005). Research also suggests that different types of violence often coexist: physical IPV often predicts accompanying sexual IPV as well as emotional abuse. The consequences of IPV are profound, affecting the health and happiness of the persons immediately involved and encompassing their entire families and the community at large.

Living in a violent relationship affects more than short- and long-term physical and mental health; it also influences a woman's self-esteem, her ability to gain access to information and services, and her ability to participate in private and in public life. Furthermore, being a victim of violence becomes a risk factor for a variety of diseases and medical conditions, as well as risky behaviors such as physical inactivity and substance abuse (Dickinson et al., 1999; Follette, Polusny, Bechtle, & Naugle, 1996). In addition to immediate injuries and trauma, women in these relationships are three to five times more likely to report mental health issues such as suicidality, substance abuse, posttraumatic stress disorder, and depression (Eshelman & Levendosky, 2012). Additionally, the costs and consequences do not remain with the direct victim. Exposure to IPV against the mother is one of the strongest predictors of male perpetration and female experience of IPV later in life (Kishor & Johnson, 2004), while IPV is also strongly predictive of child abuse within the home (Holt, Buckley, & Whelan, 2008).

The third type of violence we study is *sexual violence*, defined as any sexual act or an attempt to obtain a sexual act by violence or coercion. This form of violence disproportionately affects women and girls (International Committee of the Red Cross, 2013), although it can happen to anybody at any age. Rarely a crime of passion, sexual violence is an exertion of power and dominance over the victim (Herman, 1992) and is one of the most traumatic, pervasive, and common forms of violence (Kalra & Bhugra, 2013). Although this is a neglected area of research (Puri, Frost, Tamang, Lamichhane, & Shah, 2012), available data suggest that nearly one in four women experience sexual violence by an intimate partner in some countries (Hakimi et al., 2001), and up to one-third of adolescent girls report their first sexual experience as forced (Jewkes et al., 2001). Other contexts in which sexual violence may occur include sexual trafficking, female genital mutilation, child marriage, and rape as a weapon of war (Swiss et al., 1998). Sexual violence can carry a high level of social stigma for the victim, with profound implications for short- and long-term mental, as well as physical, sexual, and reproductive health, and social well-being (Holmes, Resnick, Kilpatrick, & Best, 1996). Death can also result from sexual violence, through suicide, the transmission of the HIV, or murder—whether during the sexual assault or as an "honor killing" (Sev'er & Yurdakul, 2001). A rape victim may also undergo humiliation, shaming, and abandonment by her family and community with deep socioeconomic consequences (Josse, 2010).

Child Maltreatment and Elder Abuse

A fourth type of interpersonal violence, that we discuss here, is *child maltreatment*, or the abuse and neglect of children under the age of 18. This can take the form of physical and emotional mistreatment, sexual abuse, neglect, and exploitation, and can result in actual or potential harm to the child's health, survival, development, or dignity (Consultation on Child Abuse Prevention, World Health Organization, & Global Forum for Health Research, 1999). Global figures indicate that up to a quarter of adults report having suffered from some form of physical abuse as children, with one in five women and one in 13 men reporting sexual abuse. As these numbers show, girls are particularly vulnerable to sexual violence, especially in conditions of armed conflict or in refugee settings, where exploitation and abuse can come from combatants, community members, aid workers, and others. Child maltreatment can result not only in psychological abuse and neglect, but also in death. Global research indicates that up to 41,000 annual fatalities result from the maltreatment of children under the age of 15, but this number almost certainly underestimates the true extent of the problem, due to the fact that a significant proportion of these deaths are incorrectly attributed to falls, burns, drowning, and other causes (Krug et al., 2002).

It should not be a surprise that violence in childhood has substantial, long-term consequences, including impaired physical and mental health, poor school performance, and job and relationship difficulties. However, emerging research is proving these consequences to be even more pernicious and pervasive than previously believed. For example, we have known about poor psychosocial adjustment, psychiatric problems including antisocial and self-destructive behavior, and emotional difficulties in adulthood (Fergusson, Horwood, & Lynskey, 1996). Now there is evidence of negative influences on cognitive, neural, and immune development, and even genomic repercussions that last beyond a single life cycle to affect future generations (Heim et al., 2002). Furthermore, child abuse increases the risk of major illnesses as an adult, including life-threatening conditions such as heart disease, cancer, sexually transmitted infections, and suicide (Springer et al., 2007). It also increases the chance of chronic illnesses such as irritable bowel syndrome and fibromyalgia, which cause pain and debilitation (Romans, Belaise, Martin, Morris, & Raffi, 2002). These conditions seem to result not only from adopting risky behaviors such as substance abuse, poor diet, and neglect of self-care, but from direct disruptions of early brain development. In this manner, child abuse can have major consequences for the child's physical, emotional, academic, and economic prospects (Twardosz & Lutzker, 2010), and ultimately, the slowing of a country's social and economic development.

The financial aspects are one measure of the consequences. Child abuse and neglect directly necessitate enormous costs for treatment in the form of visits to the hospital and other health services, mental health treatment, child welfare, disability, low productivity, criminal justice, longer-term health costs, and premature death. An extensive analysis in the US showed an estimated average lifetime cost per victim of nonfatal child maltreatment to be over 210,000 dollars, with each fatality costing an estimated 1.27 million dollars. The lifetime economic burden resulting from new cases of fatal and nonfatal child maltreatment is estimated at approximately 124 billion dollars, while sensitivity analyses indicate that the total burden could be as high as 585 billion dollars (Fang et al., 2012).

The final form of interpersonal violence that we examine is *elder abuse*. This manifests as physical acts of violence and as neglect occurring in any relationship where there is an expectation of trust. The age at which elder abuse begins varies by culture but is typically at the retirement age of 60–65 years in high-income countries and at the onset of physical decline in others. Elder abuse can take many forms apart from physical violence, including sexual, psychological, and emotional abuse, as well as financial and material abuse, neglect, abandonment, and the violation of dignity and respect.

Elder abuse occurs in countries of all income levels, and yet there is typically little response to—or even recognition of—the problem. Prevalence rates are available only in select high-income countries, ranging from 1 to 10% (Kleinschmidt, 1997; Switzer & Michienzi, 2012), despite its obvious social and moral significance. This kind of abuse is difficult to research accurately because of a number of factors. There is a widespread reluctance to report on the part of the victims, for fear of retaliation, institutionalization, and loss of social support. This is commonly exacerbated by a difficulty in self-reporting due to cognitive decline and ill health, together with service providers having difficulty recognizing the symptoms due to a lack of awareness and proper training. The implications of elder abuse vary widely according to history, culture, tradition, economic capacity, and the perceptions of older people by the elder's family, community, and society as a whole. Generational shifts in notions of family and the place of older members can also play a role.

The consequences of this kind of violence can be particularly serious because older people are physically weaker and more vulnerable than younger adults, as well as isolated and often dependent on limited incomes. This form of abuse often results not only in physical harm, but in a series of emotional and psychological consequences. A decline in the victim's functional abilities, increased dependency, an increased sense of helplessness and stress, depression, dementia, malnutrition, and premature death may all result from elder abuse (Dong, Simon, Odwazny, & Gorbien, 2008). According to research in New Zealand, Canada, and the UK, approximately 67–70% of victims of elder abuse are women. Domestic violence later in life may be a continuation of long-term IPV, as a higher proportion of spousal homicides reveals, or abuse that begins with retirement or an illness (Hightower, Hightower, & Smith, 2001). And while the risk of homicide for older men is far greater outside the family than within (Health Canada, Statistics Canada, & Canadian Institute for Health Information, 1999), the risk of death for victims of elder abuse is three times higher than for non-victims (Hendee, 1990).

Collective Violence

According to the WHO definition, *collective violence* is the instrumental use of violence by people who identify themselves as members of a group—whether the group is transitory or permanent—against another group or set of individuals, in order to achieve political, economic, or social aims (Krug et al., 2002). Collective violence receives much public attention. It includes violent conflicts between nations and groups, state and group terrorism, torture, genocides, rape as a weapon of war, the movements of large numbers of people displaced from their homes, and gang warfare. The deaths, physical illnesses, disabilities, and mental anguish resulting from each instance are stunning, even if the total number is the smallest among the different types of violence. Approximately 31,000 war-related fatalities are recorded every year, with a vast majority of these deaths taking place in lower-income countries. In 2000, the figures for related deaths varied from less than 1 per 100,000 population in high-income states, to 6.2 per 100,000 in low- and middle-income countries, with the WHO African Region recording the highest numbers: 32 per 100,000.

Besides the many thousands who die in violent conflicts, huge numbers suffer from physical injuries, sometimes in the form of permanent disability or mutilation. Higher mortality rates among civilians during times of violent conflict are usually due to injuries, but may also be due to factors such as poor access to food, increased rates of infectious diseases, diminished access to healthcare, poor environmental conditions, and psychological distress. Under such conditions, infants and refugees are particularly vulnerable to disease and death. Civilians are vulnerable in times of unrest; a study of young women with acquired immunodeficiency syndrome (AIDS) in Haiti, for example, demonstrated that their condition was the result of sexual abuse by military or paramilitary forces (Farmer, 1996).

Others suppress the trauma they have suffered from the cruelty of conflict to avoid recall or stigma, which can easily lead to anxiety, posttraumatic stress disorder, and suffer from depression, suicidal behavior, and substance abuse (Steel et al., 2009). Collective violence also has consequences that extend far beyond the immediate. Conflict often disrupts economic and social development, diverting vital resources to defense. It displaces thousands of people from their homes and disrupts food production. Famine due to war and genocide is estimated to have caused 40 million deaths in the last century (Krug et al., 2002). It is worth keeping in mind, however, that although armed conflict between nations and groups, state and group terrorism, massacres, and gang warfare receive much more public attention, far greater damage and more deaths result from the more habitually accepted conditions of inequality and injustice in everyday violence.

Consequences of Trauma

The concept that violence begets violence has been confirmed with strong empirical evidence linking childhood maltreatment and violent behavior later in life (Widom, 1989). Children whose caregivers are victims of IPV are at increased risk for physical, mental, and behavioral problems (Bensley, Van Eenwyk, & Simmons, 2003). Family violence is one of the most consistent predictors of children becoming victims or perpetrators of violence in their own relationships (Cui, Ueno, Gordon, & Fincham, 2013; Wolfe, Scott, & Crooks, 2005). Violence in relationships begins early (Simon, Miller, Gorman-Smith, Orpinas, & Sullivan, 2010). For children who have been exposed to violence, supportive and responsive parenting is one of the strongest predictors of thriving despite their adverse experiences (Graham-Bermann et al., 2009).

However, the *cycle of violence* hypothesis generally supports the idea that caregivers perpetrate violence against their own children as a result of parental childhood victimization. It provides a model for how violence might transmit across generations as well as across sociological layers, such as from society to family, or family to individual, as well as from individual to society. It is all the more reason to help heal perpetrators as well as victims, for it is the tortured who turn into torturers. In a post-conflict context, one such pathway can be the transmission of violence from society to family, whereby war-related trauma translates to family violence (Catani, 2010). Although traumatized caregivers may be at an increased risk of perpetration, children living in highly adverse environments may also elicit negative responses as they display a variety of behavioral and emotional problems. The family with exposure to higher levels of organized violence, therefore, may as a whole be at increased risk of experiencing maltreatment at home (Haj-Yahia & Abdo-Kaloti, 2003).

Victimization also contributes to adverse health outcomes across domains of self-reported health, morbidity, and utilization of health services. Victimized children, for example, are more likely to engage in health-compromising behaviors, including cigarette smoking, substance use, and high-risk sexual activity (Dube et al., 2002). Persons who have experienced traumatic events have higher rates than the general population of a wide range of serious and life-threatening illnesses. The mechanism might be that traumatic events can cause changes in regulation of the stress-response or immune system, which can affect a variety of diseases such as cardiovascular disease, diabetes, gastrointestinal disorders, and cancer (Kendall-Tackett, 2009).

A large-scale Adverse Childhood Experiences (ACE) study has been done to describe the relationship of exposure to emotional, physical, or sexual abuse and household dysfunction during childhood to health risk behavior and disease in adulthood (Felitti et al., 1998). It revealed that extreme, traumatic, or repetitive childhood stressors such as experiencing abuse, witnessing domestic violence, and serious household dysfunction are common, often kept secret, and largely unrecognized by the outside world. Also, a strong relationship exists between the breadth of exposure to abuse or household dysfunction during childhood and multiple risk factors for several of the leading causes of death in adults. The relationship is dose-dependent: in other words, the more adverse experiences one has had, the worse the health outcomes. Poor physical health is therefore just as important as mental health problems and impaired psychosocial functioning as an outcome of traumatic experience (Schnurr & Green, 2004).

Conclusion

The consequences and costs of violence are startling. The full toll of violence is impossible to decipher, as each form of violence gives rise to other forms, with short-term and long-term consequences that interweave and reproduce. Although the estimate of 10 trillion US dollars annually, of which 51% is for military spending and another 15% the result of homicides (Institute for Economics and Peace, 2014), is a large figure, it likely does not even account for intangible costs of the emotional and psychological results of violence. As studies in structural and sexual violence demonstrate, stigmatization and isolation resulting from violence have an immense effect on the sociopolitical strength and economic capability of victims. In this chapter, we reviewed the common categories of violence: self-directed violence; youth, intimate partner, and sexual violence; child maltreatment and elder abuse; and collective violence. We learned that the effects on the health and wellbeing of the victims, witnesses, and perpetrators can be profound.

The measurable effects hardly touch upon the true extent of the consequences in terms of our common humanity. The rippling effect of each and every act of violence throughout our ecology is almost impossible to assess, as the loss of potentials, the dampening of aspirations, the diversion of resources into defense systems, and the compromises in our collective quality of life result in personal, sociopolitical, and developmental consequences that we are only now beginning to understand. Our growing pool of knowledge suggests that the different types of violence are interrelated and can influence one another, meaning that every act of violence can reinforce and encourage more violence, snowballing in effect until it encounters conditions that mitigate it. It is therefore not an exaggeration to say that we live in a violent world where violence touches virtually everyone, and our choice at each stage is either to perpetuate or to mitigate it.

In view of this, prevention is an important way to reverse the trends. The general tendency to intervene only after highly visible violence occurs, through "immediate," short-term projects that target easily identifiable groups, or worse, police and prison "crackdowns," are extremely expensive and ineffective (Foster & Jones, 2006). Not only that, they add to the collective ecology of violence in ways that could potentially make the problem worse. More effective are *upstream* interventions, which means that we intervene at much earlier stages of prevention, when the problem is small or has not yet occurred, rather than only after highly visible incidents of violence have happened. Not only is this approach highly cost-effective, it also reduces enormous suffering and other human costs.

The benefits of preventing problems before they appear, or preventing the spread of existing problems, require research and education. We need first to recognize violence as a problem.

We need to have proper understanding that can guide research, knowledge application, and action. At the same time, it is important to prevent further damage and distress by strengthening services for victims of violence. Demonstratating the burden of violence can support the need for its reduction through prevention. However, the consequences of violence are a particularly challenging area of study. Because violence disproportionately affects resource-poor settings, where reliable health registration systems are difficult to establish and where violence may disrupt whatever surveillance system exists, it is a responsibility we must all take on and not just the victims. The fact that there are many who suffer in silence because of stigma or isolation makes the study all the more urgent. Only by building accurate data collection and research capacity, so as to reflect the nature and extent of the problem, will we become capable of improving all our safety.

Questions

1   How extensive are the consequences of violence in society?

2   What are the major types of violence that we have discussed?

3   How extensively is violence kept secret, and which types are most hidden?

4   Why are the consequences of violence difficult to perceive or measure?

5   In what way can low levels of violence be a measure of societal health?

References

Ali, M. M., Dwyer, D. S., & Rizzo, J. A. (2011). The social contagion effect of suicidal behavior in adolescents: Does it really exist? *Journal of Mental Health Policy and Economics, 14*(1), 3–12.

Bannerman, S. (2010, September 25). PTSD and domestic abuse: Husbands who bring the war home. *Daily Beast.* Retrieved from https://www.thedailybeast.com/ptsd-and-domestic-abuse-husbands-who-bring-the-war-home

Bensley, L., Van Eenwyk, J., & Simmons, K. W. (2003). Childhood family violence history and women's risk for intimate partner violence and poor health. *American Journal of Preventive Medicine, 25*(1), 38–44.

Bertolote, J. M., & Fleischmann, A. (2002). Suicide and psychiatric diagnosis: A worldwide perspective. *World Psychiatry, 1*(3), 181–185.

Borges, G., Nock, M. K., Abad, J. M. H., Hwang, I., Sampson, N. A., Alonso, J., ... Bruffaerts, R. (2010). Twelve-month prevalence of and risk factors for suicide attempts in the WHO World Mental Health Surveys. *The Journal of Clinical Psychiatry, 71*(12), 1617–1628.

Butchart, A., Brown, D., Khanh-Huynh, A., Corso, P., Florquin, N., & Muggah, R. (2008). *Manual for estimating the economic costs of injuries due to interpersonal and self-directed violence.* Geneva, Switzerland: World Health Organization. Retrieved from http://apps.who.int/iris/bitstream/10665/43837/1/9789241596367_eng.pdf

Catani, C. (2010). War in the home: A review of the relationship between family violence and war trauma. *Verhaltenstherapie, 20*(1), 19–27.

Centers for Disease Control and Prevention. (2010). Data and Statistics (WISQARS): Cost of Injury Reports. Retrieved from https://wisqars.cdc.gov:8443/costT

Cerda, M. (2016). Editorial: Gun violence—Risk, consequences, and prevention. *American Journal of Epidemiology, 183*(6), 516–517.

Chinkin, C. M. (2001). Women's international tribunal on Japanese military sexual slavery. *The American Journal of International Law, 95*(2), 335–341.

Consultation on Child Abuse Prevention, and World Health Organization, and Global Forum for Health Research (1999). *Report of the consultation on child abuse prevention*, 29–31 March 1999, WHO, Geneva. Geneva, Switzerland: World Health Organization. Retrieved from http://apps.who.int/iris/handle/10665/65900

Cooley-Strickland, M., Quille, T. J., Griffin, R. S., Stuart, E. A., Bradshaw, C. P., & Furr-Holden, D. (2009). Community violence and youth: Affect, behavior, substance use, and academics. *Clinical Child and Family Psychology Review, 12*(2), 127–156.

Craig, W., Harel-Fisch, Y., Fogel-Grinvald, H., Dostaler, S., Hetland, J., Simons-Morton, B., ... Pickett, W. (2009). A cross-national profile of bullying and victimization among adolescents in 40 countries. *International Journal of Public Health, 54*(S2), 216–224.

Cui, M., Ueno, K., Gordon, M., & Fincham, F. D. (2013). The continuation of intimate partner violence from adolescence to young adulthood. *Journal of Marriage and the Family, 75*(2), 300–313.

DeLeo, D., Bille-Brahe, U., Kerkhof, A., & Schmidtke, A. (2004). *Suicidal behavior: Theories and research findings*. Göttingen, Germany: WHO Regional Office for Europe.

Dickinson, L. M., de Gruy, F. V., Dickinson, W. P., & Candib, L. M. (1999). Health-related quality of life and symptom profiles of female survivors of sexual abuse. *Archives of Family Medicine, 8*(1), 35–43.

Dong, X. Q., Simon, M., Odwazny, R., & Gorbien, M. (2008). Depression and elder abuse and neglect among a community-dwelling Chinese elderly population. *Journal of Elder Abuse, and Neglect, 20*(1), 25–41.

Dube, S. R., Anda, R. F., Felitti, V. J., Edwards, V. J., & Williamson, D. F. (2002). Exposure to abuse, neglect, and household dysfunction among adults who witnessed intimate partner violence as children: implications for health and social services. *Violence and Victims, 17*(1), 3–18.

Eshelman, L., & Levendosky, A. A. (2012). Dating violence: Mental health consequences based on type of abuse. *Violence and Victims, 27*(2), 215–228.

Fang, X., Brown, D. S., Florence, C. S., & Mercy, J. A. (2012). The economic burden of child maltreatment in the United States and implications for prevention. *Child Abuse and Neglect, 36*(2), 156–165.

Farmer, P. (1996). On suffering and structural violence: A view from below. *Daedalus, 125*(1), 261–283.

Felitti, V. J., Anda, R. F., Nordenberg, D., Williamson, D. F., Spitz, A. M., Edwards, V., ... Marks, J. S. (1998). Relationship of childhood abuse and household dysfunction to many of the leading causes of death in adults: The adverse childhood experiences (ACE) study. *American Journal of Preventive Medicine, 14*(4), 245–258.

Fergusson, D. M., Horwood, M. T., & Lynskey, L. J. (1996). Childhood sexual abuse and psychiatric disorder in young adulthood II: Psychiatric outcomes of childhood sexual abuse. *Journal of the American Academy of Child and Adolescent Psychiatry, 35*(10), 1365–1374.

Follette, V. M., Polusny, M. A., Bechtle, A. E., & Naugle, A. E. (1996). Cumulative trauma: The impact of child sexual abuse, adult sexual assault, and spouse abuse. *Journal of Traumatic Stress, 9*(1), 25–35.

Foster, E. M., & Jones, D. (2006). Can a costly intervention be cost-effective? An analysis of violence prevention. *Archives of General Psychiatry, 63*(11), 1284–1291.

Garcia-Moreno, C., Jansen, H. A. F. M., Watts, C., Ellsberg, M., & Heise, L. (2005). *WHO multi-country study on women's health and domestic violence against women: Initial results on prevalence, health outcomes and women's responses.* Geneva, Switzerland: World Health Organization. Retrieved from http://www.who.int/gender/violence/who_multicountry_study/summary_report/summary_report_English2.pdf

Graham-Bermann, S. A., Gruber, G., Howell, K. H., & Girz, L. (2009). Factors discriminating among profiles of resilience and psychopathology in children exposed to intimate partner violence (IPV). *Child Abuse and Neglect, 33*(9), 648–660.

Granero, R., Poni, E. S., Escobar-Poni, B. C., & Escobar, J. (2011). Trends of violence among 7th, 8th and 9th grade students in the state of Lara, Venezuela: The global school health survey 2004 and 2008. *Archives of Public Health, 69*(1), 7.

Haj-Yahia, M. M., & Abdo-Kaloti, R. (2003). The rates and correlates of the exposure of Palestinian adolescents to family violence: toward an integrative-holistic approach. *Child Abuse and Neglect, 27*(7), 781–806.

Hakimi, M., Hayati, E. N., Marlinawati, V. U., Winkvist, A., & Ellsberg, M. C. (2001). *Silence for the sake of harmony: Domestic violence and women's health in central Java.* Yogyakarta, ID: Gadjah Mada University.

Haugen, G. A., & Boutros, V. (2015). *The locust effect: Why the end of poverty requires the end of violence.* New York, NY: Oxford University Press.

Health Canada, Statistics Canada, and Canadian Institute for Health Information. (1999). *Statistical report on the health of Canadians.* Ottawa, Canada: Health Canada.

Heim, C., Newport, J., Wagner, D., Wilcox, M. M., Miller, A. H., & Nemeroff, C. B. (2002). The role of early adverse experience and adulthood stress in the prediction of neuroendocrine stress reactivity in women: A multiple regression analysis. *Depression and Anxiety, 15*(12), 117–125.

Hendee, W. R. (1990). American Medical Association white paper on elderly health: Report of the council on scientific affairs. *Archives of Internal Medicine, 150*(12), 2459–2472.

Herman, J. L (1992). *Trauma and recovery: The aftermath of violence—from domestic abuse to political terror.* New York, NY: Basic Books.

Hightower, J., Hightower, H. C., & Smith, G. (2001). *Silent and invisible: A report on abuse and violence in the lives of older women in British Columbia and Yukon.* Vancouver, Canada: BC/Yukon Society of Transition Houses.

Holmes, M. M., Resnick, H. S., Kilpatrick, D. G., & Best, C. L. (1996). Rape-related pregnancy: Estimates and descriptive characteristics from a national sample of women. *American Journal of Obstetrics and Gynecology, 175*(2), 320–325.

Holt, S., Buckley, H., & Whelan, S. (2008). The impact of exposure to domestic violence on children and young people: A review of the literature. *Child Abuse and Neglect, 32*(8), 797–810.

Hoven, C. W., Mandell, D. J., & Bertolote, J. M. (2010). Prevention of mental ill-health and suicide: Public health perspectives. *European Psychiatry, 25*(5), 252–256.

Institute for Economics and Peace. (2014). *The economic cost of violence containment.* Sydney, Australia: Author. Retrieved from http://economicsandpeace.org/wp-content/uploads/2015/06/The-Economic-Cost-of-Violence-Containment.pdf

International Committee of the Red Cross. (2013). *Advancement of women: ICRC statement to the United Nations, 2013.* Geneva, Switzerland: Author. Retrieved from https://www.icrc.org/eng/resources/documents/statement/2013/united-nations-women-statement-2013-10-16.htm

Jewkes, R., Vundule, C., Maforah, F., & Jordaan, E. (2001). Relationship dynamics and teenage pregnancy in South Africa. *Social Science and Medicine, 52*(5), 733–744.

Jordan, J. (2001). Is suicide bereavement different? A reassessment of the literature. *Suicide and Life-threatening Behavior, 31*(1), 91–102.

Josse, E. (2010). They came with two guns: The consequences of sexual violence for the mental health of women in armed conflicts. *International Review of the Red Cross, 92*(877), 177–195.

Kalra, G., & Bhugra, D. (2013). Sexual violence against women: Understanding cross-cultural intersections. *Indian Journal of Psychiatry, 55*(3), 244–249.

Kendall-Tackett, K. (2009). Psychological trauma and physical health: A psychoneuroimmunology approach to etiology of negative health effects and possible interventions. *Psychological Trauma: Theory, Research, Practice, and Policy, 1*(1), 35.

King, M. L. Jr. (1964). *Nobel peace prize lecture: The quest for peace and justice.* Stockholm, Sweden: Nobel Foundation. Retrieved from http://www.nobelprize.org/nobel_prizes/peace/laureates/1964/king-lecture.html

Kishor, S., & Johnson, K. (2004). *Profiling domestic violence—A multi-country study.* Calverton, MD: ORC Macro.

Kleinschmidt, K. C. (1997). Elder abuse: A review. *Annals of Emergency Medicine, 30*(4), 463–472.

Krug, E. G., Dahlberg, L. L., Mercy, J. A., Zwi, A. B., & Lozano, R. (2002). *World report on violence and health.* Geneva, Switzerland: World Health Organization. Retrieved from http://apps.who.int/iris/bitstream/10665/42495/1/9241545615_eng.pdf

Le, L. C., & Blum, R. W. (2011). Intentional injury in young people in Vietnam: Prevalence and social correlates. *MEDICC Review, 13*(3), 23–28.

Lee, B. X., Marotta, P. L., Blay-Tofey, M., Wang, W., & de Bourmont, S. (2014). Economic correlates of violent death rates in forty countries, 1962–2008: A cross-typological analysis. *Aggression and Violent Behavior, 19*(6), 729–737.

Longombe, A. O., Claude, K. M., & Ruminjo, J. (2008). Fistula and traumatic genital injury from sexual violence in a conflict setting in Eastern Congo: Case studies. *Reproductive Health Matters, 16*(31), 132–141.

Mayor, S. (2002). WHO report shows public health impact of violence. *British Medical Journal, 325*(7367), 731.

O'Dea, D., & Tucker, S. (2005). *The cost of suicide to society.* Wellington, New Zealand: Ministry of Health. Retrieved from https://www.health.govt.nz/system/files/documents/publications/thecostofsuicidetosociety.pdf

Puri, M., Frost, M., Tamang, J., Lamichhane, P., & Shah, I. (2012). The prevalence and determinants of sexual violence against young married women by husbands in rural Nepal. *BMC Research Notes, 5*(1), 291.

Romans, S., Belaise, C., Martin, J., Morris, E., & Raffi, A. (2002). Childhood abuse and later medical disorders in women. *Psychotherapy and Psychosomatics, 71*(3), 141–150.

Schnurr, P. P., & Green, B. L. (2004). Understanding relationships among trauma, post-tramatic stress disorder, and health outcomes. *Advances in Mind-Body Medicine, 20*(1), 18–29.

Sev'er, A., & Yurdakul, G. (2001). Culture of honor, culture of change: A feminist analysis of honor killings in rural Turkey. *Violence Against Women, 7*(9), 964–998.

Sharp, A. L., Prosser, L. A., Walton, M., Blow, F. C., Chermack, S. T., Zimmerman, M. A., & Cunningham, R. (2014). Cost analysis of youth violence prevention. *Pediatrics, 133*(3), 448–453.

Simon, T. R., Miller, S., Gorman-Smith, D., Orpinas, P., & Sullivan, T. (2010). Physical dating violence norms and behavior among sixth-grade students from four U.S. sites. *Journal of Early Adolescence, 30*(3), 395–409.

Springer, K., Sheridan, J., Kuo, D., & Carnes, M. (2007). Long-term physical and mental health consequences of childhood physical abuse: Results from a large population-based sample of men and women. *Child Abuse and Neglect, 31*(5), 517–530.

Steel, Z., Chey, T., Silove, D., Marnane, C., Bryant, R. A., & Van Ommeren, M. (2009). Association of torture and other potentially traumatic events with mental health outcomes among populations exposed to mass conflict and displacement: A systematic review and meta-analysis. *Journal of the American Medical Association, 302*(5), 537–549.

Swiss, S., Jennings, P. J., Aryee, G. V., Brown, G. H., Jappah-Samukai, R. M., Kamara, M. S., ... Turay-Kanneh, R. S. (1998). Violence against women during the Liberian civil conflict. *JAMA, 279*(8), 625–629.

Switzer, J., & Michienzi, A. (2012). Elder abuse: An update on prevalence, identification, and reporting for the orthopaedic surgeon. *Journal of the American Academy of Orthopaedic Surgeons, 20*(12), 788–794.

Taylor, L. K., Merrilees, C. E., Cairns, E., Shirlow, P., Goeke-Morey, M., & Cummings, E. M. (2013). Risk and resilience: The moderating role of social coping for maternal mental health in a setting of political conflict. *International Journal of Psychology, 48*(4), 591–603.

Thapar, A., Collishaw, S., Pine, D. S., & Thapar, A. K. (2012). Depression in adolescence. *Lancet, 379*(9820), 1056–1067.

Twardosz, S., & Lutzker, J. R. (2010). Child maltreatment and the developing brain: A review of neuroscience perspectives. *Aggression and Violent Behavior, 15*(1), 59–68.

United Nations Office of the High Commissioner for Human Rights. (2010). *Human rights of older persons: Summary of the report of the secretary-general to the general assembly (report a/66/173).* New York, NY: United Nations.

Waters, H. R., Hyder, A. A., Rajkotia, Y., Basu, S., & Butchart, A. (2005). The costs of interpersonal violence—An international review. *Health Policy, 73*(3), 303–315.

Widom, C. S. (1989). The cycle of violence. *Science, 244*(4901), 160–166.

Wolf, A., Gray, R., & Fazel, S. (2014). Violence as a public health problem: An ecological study of 169 countries. *Social Science and Medicine, 104*(100), 220–227.

Wolfe, D. A., Scott, K. L., & Crooks, C. V. (2005). Abuse and violence in adolescent girls' dating relationships. In D. Bell, S. L. Foster, & E. J. Mash (Eds.), *Handbook of behavioral and emotional problems in girls* (pp. 381–414). New York, NY: Plenum Publishers.

World Health Organization. (2002). *Multisite intervention study on suicidal behaviours—SUPRE-MISS.* Geneva, Switzerland: Author.

World Health Organization. (2006). *Preventing suicide: A resource at work.* Geneva, Switzerland: Author. Retrieved from http://whqlibdoc.who.int/publications/2006/9241594381_eng.pdf

World Health Organization. (2008). *The global burden of disease: 2004 update.* Geneva, Switzerland: Author. Retrieved from http://www.who.int/healthinfo/global_burden_disease/GBD_report_2004update_full.pdf

World Health Organization. (2015). *Preventing youth violence: An overview of the evidence.* Geneva, Switzerland: Author. Retrieved from http://apps.who.int/iris/bitstream/10665/181008/1/9789241509251_eng.pdf

World Health Organization, United Nations Office on Drugs and Crime, & United Nations Development Programme (2014). *Global status report on violence prevention 2014.* Geneva, Switzerland: World Health Organization. Retrieved from http://www.who.int/violence_injury_prevention/violence/status_report/2014/en

Yang, B., & Lester, D. (2007). Recalculating the economic cost of suicide. *Death Studies, 31*(4), 351–361.

Cures

Part V   Intervention Framework

10

Criminal Justice Approaches

Introduction

> The degree of civilization in a society can be judged by entering its prisons.
> —*Fyodor Dostoyevsky,* The House of the Dead *(1862)*

Until now, this book has focused on the nature of violence; we now transition from the causes and consequences of violence to interventions. Perhaps one of the most defining characteristics of any human society is what levels of violence it finds acceptable. Beyond that, the apparatus of the state usually intervenes. This has been the way a civilized society tries to protect its own safety. Until very recently, the primary way societies have dealt with problematic violence has been through criminal justice, or the system of practices and institutions that a government employs in order to uphold social order, deter crime, and sanction those who violate laws through the exercise of penalties and rehabilitative efforts. As such, one of the main functions of the criminal justice system is to regulate violence within society. It attempts to do so by employing legal systems that authorize the police and the military to use violence within prescribed parameters while penalizing those who use it in other ways (David, 2006). According to German sociologist Max Weber (1919), the state claims a monopoly on the legitimate use of force within a specific territory in order to control nonmilitary, or criminal, use of violence. Civil society generally grants this authority in order to enforce laws and to maintain order. However, there are dangers inherent in such exercise of power over a population, in that it can be abused. When working well, it is the foundation of civilization, responsible for the general peace and flourishing of the state; at its worst, it is the instrument by which governments can commit democide through police brutality, executions, massacres, slave labor camps, and intentional famine (Rummel, 1994).

Thus far in our study of violence, we have focused on examining and understanding the various types and causes of violence. This chapter will be the first in this volume to offer concrete solutions, and the criminal justice approach is the first among the methods of intervention we will explore. We will address its problems as well as its advantages. Then, we will compare it with the newer, public health approach, which aims to improve population health and to prevent injuries before they begin. The criminal justice approach focuses primarily on interpersonal, or occasionally collective, criminal violence. It is the predominant approach to situations that require a swift response, without having a full understanding of violence as a bio-psycho-socio-environmental event. With the advent of a public health approach to human violence, emphases have begun to shift, but the transition has been neither universal nor complete: thus, there exist two competing and complementary approaches to intervention: the criminal justice (or "law

Violence: An Interdisciplinary Approach to Causes, Consequences, and Cures, First Edition. Bandy X. Lee.
© 2019 John Wiley & Sons, Inc. Published 2019 by John Wiley & Sons, Inc.

and order") approach and the health (or "recovery and restoration") approach. Both approaches are necessary, but it is an unpleasant reality that the former is overblown, while the latter hardly enters discussion, when the balance should perhaps be in reverse. As part of our ongoing exploration of how to think about and deal with violence, a study of the criminal justice approach is essential not only to understand its function, but also to comprehend its shortcomings and the problems that it inadvertently generates.

In this chapter, we will show how, through a system of penalties and rehabilitative efforts, governments have endeavored to uphold social order and reduce crime. We will also show how implementation has been different from theory. In particular, we will review how the US has engaged in a massive experiment of ever-increasing incarceration rates with little effect, while racial disparities and class favoritism undermine legitimacy. While punitive measures such as solitary confinement and the death penalty have proven to be self-defeating, several other nations have done better with community intervention, individual development, and restorative justice.

Consequently, we will discover that it is only by grappling with and understanding the complexities of criminal justice that we can explore possible alternative approaches to preventing violence within societies. By changing the way in which we think about violence, and making ourselves aware of the different ways in which violence manifests, we can begin to formulate more effective solutions to problems. Chapters following this one will cover the ways in which the international law approach can be a tool for preventing or mitigating collective and structural violence. We will then examine the public health approach, which aims to improve population health and to prevent injuries and violence before they begin. Finally, we will review a more intimate medical approach, which instead of treating whole populations considers how to treat each individual with the whole self—taking into account human complexity and cultural sensitivity. As part of our study, we will extrapolate this human-centered principle and expand it to the level of nonviolent social action, in order to review its surprising successes against violence at all levels before integrating our knowledge and concluding. We begin here with criminal justice.

Historical Overview

Laws, police, courts, and correction institutions have evolved gradually with large human settlements and enlarging societies, and continue to change with evolving needs and norms of social customs, political ideals, and economic conditions. With the development of agriculture and the end of a migratory existence for most of humanity, and with growing numbers of people living together in closer quarters, customary laws such as those of Ancient Egypt, originating with the unification of Upper and Lower Egypt in 2925 BCE, gave way to more formal codes. This happened independently in many places around the world, and in others based on prominent codes such as those of Sumerian king Ur-Nammu, established in 2050 BCE, or the Babylonian ruler Hammurabi of 1,700 BCE (VerSteeg, 2002). In Ancient China, local magistrates or "prefects," through appointment by the head of state, enforced Chinese traditional law, operative at least since the eleventh century BCE.

One of the earliest attempts to create an all-encompassing set of guidelines for social behavior came from Athenian statesman Draco in 621 BCE. It did not meet with great success, and left an imprint in the English language through the word "draconian," meaning harsh or severe. Beyond simply creating codes, Roman Emperor Augustus established law enforcement through the creation of wards in the capital and squads of men to protect them (Eck, 2003). The Roman emperor Justinian, understanding the need for a centralized and equally applicable framework, divided the capital into 14 wards, each with squads of armed men responsible for their safety and protection, under the guidelines of the Twelve Tablets of 450 BCE. In 529 CE, the *Justinian Code* became a touchstone of Roman law, thereby giving the world the concept of "justice" after the emperor's name. Similar developments took place throughout the world, with Egypt, Greece, India, China, and other civilizations all adopting legal codes of criminal jurisprudence in order to strengthen the power and legitimacy of kings and aristocrats. The administration of justice solidified with statutes such as the *Lex Calpurnia de Repetundis* of the Roman Empire, which introduced the jury trial in 149 BCE.

The Middle Ages saw a virtual collapse of criminal jurisprudence, with the maintenance of law and order becoming a function of local lords and heads of state. Torture and execution without recourse to trial became the norm and were carried out publicly, without remorse, pity, or centralized code. The rise of absolute monarchs and the Enlightenment saw a return to an adherence to a centralized body of laws and codes relating to crime and punishment, and this slowly led to the forms of criminal law we are familiar with today.

Despite the existence of legal codes, a great deal of the punishment for crime and criminality has, since earliest times, fallen on the lowest ranks of society. The history of criminal jurisprudence is a history of adaptation and compromise, with legislating bodies continually finding it necessary to ensure additional rights and responsibilities for both victims and offenders and to professionalize police forces. Views on punishment have vastly changed over time: although prisons and jails have existed since the rise of civilization, typically for detaining prisoners before trial or for confining people without judicial process, incarceration became widespread only in the nineteenth century. Led by a group of Quakers in Pennsylvania, reform movements advocated for the abolition of cruel corporal punishments in favor of imprisonment in jails and prisons. This led to a marked drop in the state's crime rate (McKelvey, 1977), and a general trend in this direction throughout the world.

The growth of modern nation-states, which the US and France exemplify, led to a proliferation of modern criminal justice systems. In theory, such systems consist of three main parts: (a) law enforcement, or police; (b) government entities for resolving legal disputes, or courts; and (c) a system for implementing the decisions of the courts, or corrections. The police enforce the laws in its state, county, or jurisdiction. Law enforcement officers and agencies are responsible for upholding laws by enforcing them and maintaining public order and public safety. Their work may include the prevention, detection, and investigation of crimes, and apprehending and detaining members of the public whom they suspect of violating the law. The courts are responsible for adjudicating laws in ways that prevent individuals from breaking them in the future. When law enforcement charges individuals with violating laws, the courts then determine if the charges are valid and should proceed to convictions. They also determine the appropriate punishments to accompany the convictions. Correctional systems are responsible for implementing punishments, or in some cases rehabilitation programs. When the courts impose their sentences, correctional branches—typically jails, prisons, probation, and parole—carry them out. In the US, federal and state correctional facilities are referred to as *prisons*, and county or municipal institutions are *jails*, which usually hold offenders for less than a year.

These distinct agencies exist independently of representative politics and function together under the rule of law as the principal means of maintaining civic order. The guiding principles underlying most criminal judicial systems are usually a mixture of incapacitating dangerous offenders, punishing the offense, deterring others who would commit crimes, and rehabilitating offenders. Much research on deterrence has focused on the influence of social controls on criminal behavior. In particular, incarceration and probation are highly controlled environments that intend to provide the control and structure that offenders may not have had before entering the system in an effort to deter violence (Sherman, 1993; Silver & Miller, 2004). However, young offenders in the US become further schooled in antisocial behavior in a setting with few meaningful programs and almost no programs that help them reintegrate into society. Many critics charge that large flaws afflict nearly every part of the system and that the entire system requires an overhaul. In Europe and other regions of the world, radical reforms are already underway.

Restoration versus Retribution

There are two broad philosophies within the approach to the question of crime and punishment. The first can be termed *restorative justice*, and it emphasizes that crime is an act against another person and the community; that crime control should rest in the community; and that accountability should be direct as well as involve reparation. The second is *retributive justice*, and it reflects the view that crime is against the state or a violation of the law; that the criminal justice system should control crime; and that offender accountability lies primarily in taking the punishment. Restorative justice takes into account the needs of the victim, the offender, and society and seeks to repair harms through apologizing, making amends, or doing community service. Retributive justice considers punishment to be morally acceptable if it is proportionate and thus provides gratification to the victim; justice is achieved when the wrongdoer is justly punished. The former is more social, requiring greater involvement of victims and communities, while the latter is more individual with individual responsibility.

Germany and the Netherlands increasingly exemplify the former style of dealing with criminality, while the US, which currently has the highest percentage of people incarcerated in correctional facilities of any nation on earth, remains an example of the latter. Thus, despite the many variations of laws, court systems, and social customs throughout the world, the unique lessons from the successes and errors of the US system are worth mentioning. Foremost among them is its leading role in *mass incarceration*. Beginning around the mid-1970s, the US embarked on an unprecedented experiment for the US or the world, which within 40 years resulted in the highest imprisonment rate of any nation on record, and sevenfold greater than the average in its history up to that point. With up to 756 people per 100,000 population behind bars at its peak, and over two million behind bars or seven million adults under some kind of correctional supervision, the scale has been large enough to influence the nation's culture (Travis, Western, & Redburn, 2014) (see Figure 10.1).

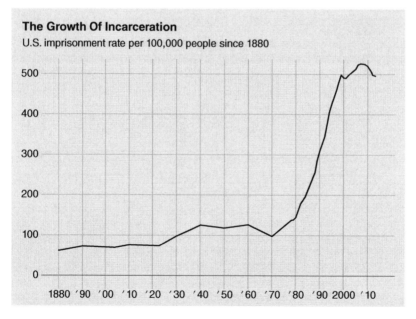

Figure 10.1 For most of US history, incarceration rates remained relatively stable, at more or less 100 per 100,000 population, until the 1970s.

Apart from the sheer magnitude of the figures, the demographics of the situation also point to critical and deep-seated flaws in the approach to justice that the US practices. Members of ethnic minorities are incarcerated at far higher rates than others: African-Americans are incarcerated at nearly seven times the rate of white males (Pettit, Sykes, & Western, 2009), while Hispanic males are incarcerated at nearly three times the rate of white males (Guerino, Harrison, & Sabol, 2012). Just as shocking are the rates of youth incarcerations: peaking at 381 per 100,000, nearly 2.2 million juveniles were arrested in 2007 alone (Puzzanchera, 2009). While comprising a mere 5% of the world's population, the US has supported approximately one quarter of the world's prisoners (Deady, 2014), a statistic that sets it far apart from the rest of the world (Walmsley, 2016).

While purporting to protect the public, even after the national crime rate dropped by more than 40% in the last 25 years, the rise in the incarceration rate since the mid-1970s remained steady. A profound shift in ideology had taken place, leading to the introduction of harsher punishments, sentencing guidelines requiring longer sentences, less discretion for parole authorities, and—perhaps most importantly—the elimination of rehabilitation programs (Taxman, Byrne, & Pattavina, 2005). To give just one example of this trend, the average offender served an 18-month sentence in 1990; a decade later, the same offender could expect to serve 25 months (Bureau of Justice Statistics, 2004). Yet without rehabilitation, sanctions and incarceration alone increases rates of reoffending (Chen & Shapiro, 2007). Of course, such drastic actions are not without profound economic effects: in many states, public investment in prisons outpaces that in higher education, raising questions about priorities and efficacy (Scott-Hayward, 2009). The social experiment of unprecedented scale in both cost and magnitude (Zimring & Hawkins, 1993) notwithstanding, the massive attempt to be "tough on crime" did not seem to make a dent in violence rates (Mendes & McDonald, 2001; Weisberg, 2012). Rather, imprisonment and violence rates rose together through the 1970s, 1980s, and until the mid-1990s, when finally violence rates dropped dramatically—during a period that saw an equally dramatic drop in rates of unemployment (Lee, Wexler, & Gilligan, 2014).

Though not on the scale of the US, many countries around the world variably adopted this race to incarcerate as a solution to social problems. The British Ministry of Justice noted that between 1995 and 2009, the prison population in England and Wales increased by 66% (Fox, Fox, & Marsh, 2013). Canada "hardened" its physical conditions of confinement to make them more punitive and more restrictive; those changes have no relationship to changes in community crime rates (Sapers & Zinger, 2009). A release of figures in Norway showed that a 52% increase in the prison population did nothing to reduce or even stabilize crime rates—in fact, quite the opposite: there had been a 500% increase in overall crime and a 900% increase in violent crime over the same period (Hartvig & Kjelsberg, 2009). It is becoming apparent to all that mass incarcerations and community sanctions, whose ostensible purpose is to deter crime and serve justice, are having the opposite effect. Perhaps most important are the negative social influences that they are having on poor and minority groups, whose disproportionate share of broken families, difficulty in finding post-prison employment, and loss of voting and other political rights of participation are just a few of the more obvious results. Repeat offenders are common, while medical and mental health problems are rising (Wilper et al., 2009). Meanwhile, spending billions on prisons every year diverts funds from alleviating the poverty that fuels criminal activity in the first place (Drucker, 2013).

Certainly, there are nations with far more notorious prison conditions, such as Venezuela, Thailand, Russia, and China. However, the US criminal justice system has some disturbing features in its retributive approach. The first that needs mentioning is double confinement, otherwise known as *solitary confinement*. Throughout the 1990s, the use of segregation, or confinement in single cells, became popular across the US. Whether the reasons were punitive, protective, or for administrative purposes, the incarceration of those inmates the authorities considered to be too dangerous or disruptive to remain in the general prison population were sent to small (often 6 by 8 ft), steel-doored cells for 22–23 hr a day. By 2004, 44 of the nation's states had "supermax" facilities consisting entirely of such cells and collectively housed approximately 25,000 prisoners (Mears, 2005). The truth is that such facilities are more commonly used for reasons of convenient prison management and profit, in the case of private prisons (Herivel & Wright, 2003), than for actual misconduct, and without due process.

The dysfunction of solitary confinement was already evident in the nineteenth century, causing prisons to close down or to change approaches because prisoners only became more unruly and even insane (Friedman, 1994). Knowing what we do now about human neurological and psychological needs, one might say that there is no more cruel punishment. The finding that such social deprivation increases psychotic symptoms (Hafemeister and George, 2012) and induces a "psychiatric syndrome" in previously healthy persons (Grassian, 2006) is unsurprising. Yet, in the U.S., inmates are still subject to the brutality of isolation for months, years, and even decades at a time. One particularly disturbing feature of double incarceration is the high rate at which it leads to self-harm. At Rikers Island of New York City, approximately 7% of inmates were in solitary confinement at some point during their incarcerations, but that small population accounted for more than 53% of over 1,000 acts of self-harm (Kaba et al., 2014). This trend has also been noticed in other countries, such as South Africa (Louw & O'Brien, 2007). The United Nations Committee against Torture has gone as far as declaring that more than 15 days in solitary confinement violates human rights standards (Cloud et al., 2015). We can therefore state that solitary confinement, far from reducing recidivism, causes inmates in many cases to become more dangerous, with greater mental health consequences and increases in violent recidivism (Gordon, 2013). Along similar lines, other harsh and punitive measures, such as boot camps, electronic monitoring, and "scared straight" programs for young offenders, have been a disastrous failure in terms of recidivism (Petrosino et al., 2000).

The ultimate in this approach is *capital punishment*, also known as the death penalty, which is the legally authorized killing of persons as punishment for crime. In the US, there were no implementations of the death penalty between 1967 and 1977, but in time, coinciding with the proliferation of prisons, more and more states instituted new death penalty statutes, and almost 1,440 executions have taken place since then (Death Penalty Information Center, 2016). The US is currently the only country in the Western hemisphere that applies the death penalty, and as of 2015, lags behind only China, Iran, Pakistan, and Saudi Arabia (Death Penalty Worldwide, 2016). In spite of numerous statistical analyses, many flawed, trying to prove the deterrent effects of capital punishment, none have emerged that are convincing (Donohue & Wolfers, 2006; Liu, 2004), while there is evidence that executions actually *increase* murder rates (Cochran, Chamlin, & Seth, 1994).

Capital punishment remains controversial worldwide, leading to a United Nations resolution in 2007 calling for its universal suspension (UN, 2007). Many criticize the death penalty as inhumane and a violation of the United Nations *Convention against Torture* (Swartz, 2012). Additionally, it leads to many wrongful executions of innocent persons (Dieter, 2004). Some claim that as many as 39 executions were performed in the US in the face of compelling evidence of innocence between 1992 and 2004, while newly available deoxyribonucleic acid (DNA) evidence prevented more than 15 executions in the same period; as of 2015, 20 of the 347 people exonerated through DNA served time on death row (Innocence Project, 2016). Also problematic is the more frequent use of this punishment against perpetrators from racial and ethnic minorities or from lower socioeconomic backgrounds, and the influence of the background of the victim on the outcome (Amnesty International, 2003): African-American defendants are more likely to receive a death sentence if the case involves a white victim (Eberhardt et al., 2006). There is also evidence that the death penalty may totally lack any deterrent value and instead encourage a culture of violence: those who commit lethal violence are almost never attuned to distant consequences, but the death penalty legitimizes their "killer" tendencies. According to US Supreme Court justice Louis Brandeis (1928), the government is a potent, omnipresent teacher, and punishment is an implicit condoning of violence; thus, it is not surprising that the states that have instituted capital punishment, or state-sanctioned murder, would have higher rates of street murder. In the face of these problems and astronomical cost—not to mention human cost—capital punishment is growing increasingly unpopular in the US.

Discrimination and Legitimacy

The topic of *legitimacy* is of growing theoretical and practical importance in the criminal justice field. It distinguishes criminal justice from brute, "might makes right" principles and is the hallmark of a civilized society. Public trust in policing, adjudication, and corrections is important because, for justice to be effective, citizens must see it as legitimate and fair. Even when people do not get what they want or feel they deserve, the fairness of procedures is important to them—sometimes five or six times as much as the nature of the outcome (Tyler & Huo, 2002). Institutional legitimacy is the foundation of public compliance with the law and societal commitment to the rule of law. Undermining the legitimacy of the US justice system are racial and economic factors, which we will examine here in detail.

Due to *racial profiling*, which in law enforcement refers to suspecting individuals of wrongdoing based on stereotypes about their race rather than on their behavior, ethnic minorities are far more likely to be arrested than white Americans. Once arrested, they are more likely to be convicted; and once convicted, they are more likely to face stiff sentences for the same crimes. African-American males are six times more likely to receive prison sentences than white males and almost three times more likely to receive them than Hispanic males (United States Bureau of Justice Statistics, 2012). Tougher sentencing laws have also hit African-Americans the hardest: they account for 41% of the prison population while comprising only 13% of the population (West & Sabol, 2008). Nationally, police are three times more likely to search stopped cars of African-American drivers than those of white drivers and about two times more likely to search stopped cars of Hispanic drivers than those of white drivers (Eith & Durose, 2011). African-Americans are arrested for drug use at three times the rate of whites, and for drug sale or manufacture at four times the rate of whites, despite the fact that they use and sell drugs at comparable rates (Snyder, 2011).

Furthermore, African-Americans are twice as likely as whites to be imprisoned for the same robbery charge, and their number on death row has not changed in 20 years even though the homicide rate among African-Americans has decreased (Tonry & Melewski, 2008). Even though African-Americans and whites are homicide victims in nearly equal numbers, four out of five executions since the reinstatement of the death penalty have involved white victims (Baldus, Woodworth, & Pulaski, 1990). Beyond just an issue of legitimacy, this bias has led some scholars to call mass incarceration a system of racialized social control: bringing in entire segments of minority communities and branding them as criminals relegates them to a permanent second-class status upon release, stripping them of the right to vote, to serve on juries, to be free of legal and employment discrimination, and to access education and other public benefits (Alexander, 2010). Furthermore, the practice of leasing out mostly African-American convicts for negligible or no income into abysmal working conditions has been called "slavery by another name" (Blackmon, 2008). In this manner, it becomes a vehicle of violence that systematically injures individuals and tears apart communities, rather than a mode of prevention. Due to these racial disparities in law enforcement, sentencing practices, and imprisonment, the deterrence effect of the criminal system has weakened among affected populations (Taxman et al., 2005).

Another factor that undermines the legitimacy of criminal justice in the US is class: researchers have noted that some of the effects of race and ethnicity may be attributable to class and the crucial importance of considering also the class status of both the offender and the victim (Zatz, 2000). Corporate crime, for example, causes twice as many deaths each year through preventable accidents or illnesses as "violent crime," which includes only direct, behavioral violence. Yet executives who, for profit, make concrete decisions that result in widespread suffering and death rarely receive punishment as criminals. By punishing only individual violent crimes and individual property crimes, the criminal justice system works to make the poor seem scary and violent. This distortion is useful to those in positions of power, because it deflects the discontent and potential hostility of the average citizen away from the classes above them and toward the classes below them (Reiman, 1979). Lacking legitimacy has a profound effect on eroding compliance and cooperation, and the social inequities that contribute to this distortion also contribute to *recidivism*, or the tendency of a convicted criminal to reoffend, which leads to rearrests (Bottoms & Tankebe, 2012). Rather, a state that acts brutally against human beings legitimizes brutality instead. A multistate study in the US has shown that those who experienced more of the criminal justice system were the least likely to be deterred (Bhati & Piquero, 2007).

Furthermore, the acculturation to, and normalization of, criminality for the children of those convicted to jail sentences, through the constant exposure to prison facilities and parole supervisors, is a cause for great concern. When inmates "return to society," those convicted of even nonviolent offenses often have difficulty finding a job, which augments a cycle of social exclusion, criminal behavior, and recidivism (Wright, 2010). The disadvantages generated by the criminal justice system and its distortions heighten racial tensions, resentment directed at immigrants, and a whole host of divisions, amounting to a strategy of "divide and rule": that is, the abetting of animosity between deprived groups so that the ruling party can continue to rule and divert them from recognizing the real source of their deprivation. Distorting the image of what hurts people allows people to keep getting hurt. As the process entrenches itself in structures and institutions, it becomes not only culturally acceptable but reinforced: the media endlessly feeds back images of the poor as criminally violent, and the police continually target the economically disfavored. In this manner, the criminal justice system becomes a perpetuator and aggravator of existing injustices.

Prisoner recidivism rates—a key indicator of a correctional system's performance—have stubbornly remained at 40% despite pouring more money into prisons, and four to six out of 10 adult offenders still return to prison within 3 years of release (Pew Center on the States, 2011). In criminology, this is sometimes called the "Pyrrhic defeat" theory: as opposed to a "Pyrrhic victory," where one ostensibly wins at great cost, a Pyrrhic defeat is where one loses at great cost, but some part of the system benefits enough—for example, private prisons profit (Coyle, 2003)—to keep it going despite the great overall cost. The beginnings of a remedy might include: confronting the underlying sources of crime, such as poverty; making punishments fit crimes (e.g., doing away with class exemptions); treating addiction as a medical problem and legalizing most drugs; implementing correctional programs that promote rather than undermine personal responsibility; and limiting the power while increasing the accountability of the criminal justice system, so that practice can better match purported purpose.

Reform versus Abolition

Prisons have served a purpose in organizing violence for civilization, but in the contemporary era, when the tendency toward prison proliferation and harsher punishment has led to gross violations of human rights, questions arise as to whether they contribute more to disorder and harm than to good. In order to address the problem, several countries are attempting reform. It is now clear from a robust body of evidence that rehabilitative efforts are effective in reducing recidivism (Andrews & Bonta, 2010).The British criminal justice system, while emphasizing deterrence over detention, has had success following the "risk, need, and responsivity" principles, developing standardized programs to address specific aspects of an offender's behavior (Fox et al., 2013). In a similar vein, Supporting Offenders through Restoration Inside (SORI) tries to increase offender empathy for victims to motivate behavioral change and has found that offenders who complete the programs show more concern for their victims and more motivation to change behavior, although not taking more responsibility for their actions (Beech & Chauhan, 2013). According to Germany's Prison Act (1977), the sole aim of incarceration is to enable prisoners to lead a life of social responsibility free of crime upon release, and therefore prison life is organized in·such a way as to facilitate rehabilitation and reintegration into society. Similarly, the aim of the Netherlands' Penitentiary Principles Act (1998) is the resocialization of prisoners, whereby the principle of association (both inside prisons and between prisoners and the community) holds over separation.

A European–American comparison appears to suggest that these principles translate into greater efficiency and reduction of recidivism (Subramanian & Shames, 2013). The prison systems in Norway, Sweden, Finland, and Denmark also appear to be more efficient at reducing recidivism, providing educational services, and rehabilitating prisoners (Ward et al., 2013). While the Chinese criminal justice system has been criticized for valuing substantive outcomes over procedure, as observed in the wave of enforced disappearances during the "Jasmine Revolution" of 2011 (Rosenzweig, 2013), it has been found that juvenile offenders in the Bang-Jioo informal community-based rehabilitation program had few reoffenses (Zhang, 2008). In the US, even jail-based restorative programs such as the Resolve to Stop the Violence Project have shown large reductions in violent recidivism (Gilligan & Lee, 2005). Simply punishing offenders does little for moral development and the motivation not to reoffend, whereas a complex process of transformation and reintegration may help restore whole communities (Braithwaite, 1989; Rossner, 2013). An upsurge of interest in restorative justice has taken into consideration psychological models of early development (Gavrielides, 2015).

Another side effect is that prisons have become a repository for the social ills we do not wish to face. As a result of low societal investment in mental health care, mentally ill individuals make up 64% of US jail inmates; in state and federal prisons that figure is 56% and 45%, respectively (James & Glaze, 2006). Because of the great cost and low efficacy associated with treating mental illness in correctional settings, few jails are equipped to provide services (Lee and Prabhu, 2015); accordingly, illnesses go untreated, leading to more severe symptoms, erratic behavior, recidivism, and suicide (Osher & Steadman, 2007). In one study, there was a positive correlation between arrests and both prior involuntary psychiatric hospitalizations and the absence of outpatient mental health treatment. Those who did not receive outpatient services, especially, were 23% more likely to be arrested for a misdemeanor and 12% more likely to be arrested for a felony (Constantine et al., 2010). Integrated mental health and substance abuse services are important, as such conditions are commonly co-occurring or may mask symptoms of underlying mental illness.

For women in the criminal justice system, 60–80% of whom have children (Pollock, 2002), a recent study has suggested that the often more positive relationship between women and parole and probation officers (as compared to men's relationships with these officials) can offer opportunities for interventions outside of the system (Hall, Golder, Conley, & Sawning, 2013). Thailand has employed restorative justice programs with a "society-centered approach" that serves as an alternative to the modern criminal justice system and attempts to restore the place of the community in crime prevention (Ua-amnoey & Kittayarak, 2004). The Thai pilot project has resulted in 10% of juvenile offenders having their cases referred to restorative justice programs rather than traditional incarceration. Alternative programs have also received support in Indiana, where the "pulling levers" intervention program has used a deterrence-based message to specifically target high-risk offenders and social community groups to engage potential offenders, resulting in significant reductions in homicide rates among 15- to 24-year-old males (the highest-risk population) (Corsaro & McGarrell, 2010). After decades of cripplingly costly investment in incapacitation and retribution, many states are now recognizing that the mass incarceration experiment has failed, and that theoretically sound and carefully implemented community strengthening programs can produce better public safety outcomes than purely punitive measures.

For these and other reasons, the call for abolishing prisons altogether has been growing (McLeod, 2015). Within the US context, it is no longer the conjunction between crime and punishment that is consistent, but that between race, class, and punishment (Pettit & Western, 2004). In 1926, the first year of such a national recording, 21% of prison admissions were black. By 1970, black people constituted 39% of admissions, and in 1992, 54% (Irwin & Austin, 1997). In 1995, almost one-third of young black men were either in prison or directly under the control of a correctional system (Bureau of Justice Statistics, 2003). Given that the criminal justice system touches only a small fraction of criminal activities in society, it ensues that one has a greater likelihood of being incarcerated if one is a young black man than if one has actually broken the law (Rotman, 1990). If this is the case, then it also follows that many who are incarcerated pose no threat of harm to society. If a system does not serve its purported function—to deter crime—but operates a caste-like system that targets minorities and serves as a surrogate ghetto (Wacquant, 2000), then the whole system is inherently destructive and requires reconsideration. A system grounded in racism and classism does not correct itself by changing sentencing laws or training police better; thus, in addition to working to mitigate harm, it is necessary to consider an approach that is different from the foundation.

Case Studies

Scandinavian Prisons

The most interesting fact about Scandinavian prisons is that many are barely prisons at all. Incarceration in Scandinavian countries focuses on restorative justice. Correctional facilities focus on the care of the offender and making sure he or she can become a functioning member of society again, and they have one of the lowest recidivism rates and one of the lowest crime rates in the world. Norway is home to the world's most humane prison: Halden Prison, a 75-acre facility that maintains as much "normalcy" as possible. There are no bars on the windows, kitchens are fully equipped with sharp objects, and friendships occur between guards and inmates. Norway's prison system is designed with three core values in mind: normality, humanity, and rehabilitation. The country does not have the death penalty or a life sentence; the maximum custodial sentence is 21 years. When criminals in Norway leave prison, they usually stay out; the country has one of the lowest recidivism rates in the world at 20% (Kolind et al., 2014).

The Danish island of Falster is now home to the world's most humane maximum security penal institution, Storstrøm Prison, which can hold up to 250 people. It is designed to be a mini-community where inmates can spend their time in an environment that replicates life outside as much as possible. The prison layout spans an area the size of 18 football fields and is centered around social activities. There are options for the inmates to spend their time exercising, studying, creating art, or praying in the onsite church. In addition, they buy their own food at the grocery store. The cells are 13 square meters and come equipped with a refrigerator, closet, and 22-in. television (Reiter, Sexton, & Sumner, 2017).

Sweden's prison system boasts impressive numbers: in the past decade, the number of Swedish prisoners has dropped from 5,722 to 4,500 out of a population of 9.5 million. Sweden has closed a number of prisons, and the recidivism rate is around 29% (Hedstrom, 2018). Most remarkable is the use of "open" prisons. Prisoners stay in housing that often resembles college dormitories and are able to commute to a job and visit families while under electronic monitoring. Prisoners and staff eat together in community spaces throughout the prison. There are many factors that contribute to the effectiveness of their prison systems in comparison to many other countries in the West. The larger context of relatively inclusive societies with widely shared prosperity contributes to their success, but the low rates of recidivism hint at an alternative model for violence prevention: the humane treatment of prisoners.

Prison Meditation

Meditation programs in prison have been the subject of research since the 1970s, and the programs are generally viewed positively by prison administrators seeking to reduce aggressive behavior. Early research focused on transcendental meditation. Unlike mindfulness meditation, whose goal is awareness and acceptance of the whole field of consciousness, transcendental meditation consists of repeating a mantra silently to oneself. A small US study suggests that prisoners who practice transcendental meditation twice a day experience less stress and fewer mental health issues than inmates who do not meditate. Inmates in an Oregon state prison underwent a five-session training program in meditation, which asked that they practice the technique twice a day for 20 min. After 4 months, all the men showed some improvement in symptoms as well as significant reductions in perceived stress, anxiety, depression, dissociation, and sleep disturbances (Nidich et al., 2016).

The prison Stress Management and Rehabilitation Training (SMART) in India teaches prisoners how to manage their stress, aggression, and trauma, building a foundation for a new life. More than 120,000 inmates have undergone the SMART program with spectacular results, and over 100 prisons have implemented the program. Now, this program is active in over 45 countries and continues to grow. The cornerstone of the program is advanced breathing techniques, including Sudarshan Kriya, which removes stress and has been shown to have numerous physical and mental health benefits. It focuses on the individual's responsibility to manage effectively his or her own mind and negative emotions, through breathing techniques, physical stretches, meditations, and cognitive behavioral techniques for maintaining positive behaviors and attitudes. Its techniques have been proven to be an effective treatment for posttraumatic stress disorder, depression, and anxiety. Additionally, it has been shown that practitioners experience a decrease in violent behavior (Brown & Gerberg, 2005).

Prison Animal Therapy

Prison-based animal programs (PAPs) have shown promise when it comes to increased sociability, responsibility, and levels of patience of inmates who participate in them. The majority of programs pair animals, most commonly dogs, with inmates 24 hr a day. Trials of animal-assisted therapy interventions, a form of human–animal interaction therapy most often used with populations affected by depression or anxiety, mental illness, and trauma, may provide models for how PAP research can have widespread implementation in jail and prison settings, whose populations have high rates of mental health problems. There is a correctional facility in Canon

City, Colorado, that mixes dogs on "doggie death row" with inmates as varied as murderers and recluses (Loe, 2015). The dogs have a therapeutic effect, drawing inmates out of their cells to therapy sessions. These dogs give and receive love without fear among some of Colorado's most dangerous inmates. In many cases, the program also helps rehabilitate the animals, or at least train the animals for adoption or more specific training. There is a variety of PAPs that are aimed at helping offenders build personal and emotional skills, the lack of which could lead to violent behavior. Animal-assisted therapy is rooted in the idea that the human–animal bond and interactions are beneficial and therapeutic. The major results of these programs indicate that they benefit not only the inmates but also the institution, the animals, the community, and the people who later receive the animals. PAPs have been around for many years, but rigorous empirical studies are still lacking (Swyers, 2014).

Youth Violence Prevention

In Sweden, there is no concept of punishment for young people who commit crimes. The notion of care and treatment is at the heart of the Swedish approach to working with young offenders and social services are pivotal to any action plan for a young offender. Although the age of criminal responsibility is 15, anybody under the age of 18 is treated as a child in need of guidance and support. Young offenders rarely receive custodial sentences and are usually handled in accordance with the Care of Young Persons Act. Where closed institutional care is mandated by a court, usually following a prosecution for a serious crime under the Secure Youth Care Act, it is for a fixed term and focused on care and treatment.

The approach in the Netherlands is about finding the right balance between punishment and care for each individual young person. Specialist youth prosecutors are responsible for all investigations and for recommending appropriate penalties for less serious offenses. Only a judge can sentence a juvenile to custody. The age of criminal responsibility is 12, but young people aged 16–23 may be tried either as adults or as juveniles depending on their level of maturity. Juveniles currently make up around 1.7% of the prison population and custodial sentences are usually followed by periods of community supervision.

For the vast majority of young people involved in violence, violent behavior will have manifested in adolescence and will be influenced by peer or environmental factors. National policymakers give consideration to the value of restorative justice elements, such as the Halt penalty, which views young people who offend as part of a group. It is important to move toward a more sophisticated understanding of drivers of violence, as not all violent young people are violent for the same reasons, and not all will respond to the same interventions.

The youth system in France is founded on a set of principles set out in legislation enacted in 1945. The most important of these is the principle of education alongside punishment. The legislation also sets out a requirement for specialist child judges and for consideration of the personality and circumstances of any minor before deciding on an appropriate punishment or intervention. There is no age of criminal responsibility as such in French law, but a child under the age of 13 cannot be sentenced to custody. Juveniles currently make up around 1.1% of the prison population. The youth justice system combines criminal and child protection processes, and the youth judge is responsible for decisions about both. As in the Netherlands, the youth prosecutor can make decisions about punishment in minor cases (Waddell, 2013).

Prison Violence Prevention Programming

In the US, a program by the name of Resolve to Stop the Violence Project (RSVP) has been implemented in the San Francisco County Jail since 1997 in an attempt to reduce recidivism by focusing on rehabilitation and restorative justice principles rather than on retribution for the past. The highly interactive and intensive, comprehensive program includes acupuncture for stress, cognitive-behavioral techniques for dismantling a "male role belief system" that predisposes to violence, "victim impact" sessions for building empathy, a drama program for role play, and a mentorship program that allows participants the chance to become facilitators at a later date. Given the concentration of violent offenders in an open dormitory, predictions of riots and mayhem gave way to the opposite: it has become the safest dormitory in the entire county jail system, with violent incidents all but ceasing after the first month (Lee & Gilligan, 2005). Out in the community, inmates who participated in RSVP have had 46% lower rearrest rates for violent crimes and have spent 43% less time in custody. The decline in violent rearrests increased with greater lengths of stay: 53% if the participants stayed for 12 weeks or more, and 83% if they stayed 16 weeks or more (Gilligan & Lee, 2005). The greater the exposure, the better the outcome, in contrast to traditional imprisonment, in which the opposite is true.

When RSVP was first instituted, the US was at a crossroads but chose to increase solitary confinement of violent offenders instead of instituting programs that allow for socialization and interaction. Now, after massive investment without productive result, multiple states have turned to the RSVP model and have replicated it with considerable success. The program has long been replicated around the world in countries such as the United Kingdom, Poland, New Zealand, Singapore, and Mexico. The use of prisons just for punishment and incapacitation is costly, ineffective, and ultimately self-defeating. Violent offenders often engage in destructive behaviors because they never had a chance to socialize in the first place. Restoration of offenders, alongside restorative justice components that hold them accountable with opportunities to mend the harm they have done, is a rapidly growing model in a time when an alternative to traditional incarceration in the US is much needed.

Conclusion

Transitioning from the causes and manifestations of violence to interventions, in this chapter we reviewed the success and failures of the criminal justice system. Criminal justice is, in a sense, a mark of a civilization that seeks to control problematic human behavior in a systematic manner to maintain collective security. We discussed how, through a system of penalties and rehabilitative efforts, a government endeavors to uphold social order and to deter crime. However, when the implementation turns into a means of social control, exacerbating existing injustices and adding more violence to existing violence, then it becomes a source of harm. The US experiment with mass incarceration, solitary confinement, and the death penalty has now been well-studied and has become a lesson in how short-sightedness leads to short-term solutions in the best case scenario, but to counterproductive measures in the worst case scenario. Racial disparities and class favoritism have not only compromised the system but may represent abuses of the very kind that a justice-serving, law-bound system is expected to curb.

Decades of ideology-driven investment have clearly shown what does not work: a steadily increasing prison population at great social and financial cost, fewer alternatives to incarceration for those with mental illness or substance problems, the abolition of parole in 16 states, and expanding uses of solitary confinement or the death penalty, not to mention systemic failures and perceived injustices that lose legitimacy, especially for high-risk populations. Meanwhile, institutional, corporate, and governmental violence are neglected. By adding injustice to injustice, or violence to violence, the system fails in its fundamental purpose: to protect public safety and to reduce violence. This highlights the need to view violence from a proactive, preventive, and health-promoting perspective rather than in a reactive, reactionary, and destruction-propagating way. Crime is a legal concept, in that the law "creates" the crimes it punishes based on social judgment and consensus. This is another area where definition is important: if we defined crimes as conditions in need of rehabilitation and community-based programs, different results might be possible. Indeed, alternative systems used in Great Britain, Thailand, China, and the US that focus on community intervention, individual development, and restorative justice have been shown to reduce recidivism. Furthermore, rehabilitation-focused correctional systems in Northern and Western Europe appear not only to reduce recidivism but to improve socialization and public safety as well.

That said, abolition as an aspirational horizon to which we might commit ourselves may be worth considering for the good it could do to improve criminal justice. It would require us to imagine a constellation of alternative strategies and institutions, with the ultimate aim of preventing all forms of crime, such that correctional institutions will no longer be necessary. Stagnant ideas, mammoth institutions, and profit-driven designs that exploit prisoners have been allowed to persist without transparency or accountability; meanwhile, police and prose-cutorial abuses go unchecked, fueling violence and acting as a form of violence. An abolitionist approach would require that we look far beyond the current prison model to imagine a dif-ferent structuring of society. This might include a change of culture that reduces the informal caste system that limits the opportunities of many according to location and ethnicity; deploy-ing police in a way that does not stoke conflict between the community and the police; focusing more on reducing recidivism, which entails rehabilitation efforts; and finally resorting less to violent means that require maintaining the largest military in the world and waging war in many places. Research tells us that all these forms of violence are interrelated.

Removing prisons from our ideological landscape would not only remove the self-defeating, logical conclusion to which we drive ourselves—more prisons within prisons, more punitive sentencing, more prisons in society, and a society-wide "prison culture"—but force us to con-sider evidence of effectiveness and the society we wish to shape. In other words, we would not be looking for prison-like substitutes but rather decarceration as an overarching strategy, in a multisectoral collaboration that advances our societal structure toward general public security and wellbeing. We would envision a continuum of alternatives to imprisonment: demilitariza-tion of schools, revitalization of education at all levels, a health system that provides free physi-cal and mental care for all, and a justice system based on reparation and reconciliation rather than retribution and vengeance (Davis, 2003). Research shows that, far from being a utopian ideal, this is the more effective and cost-effective approach for whole communities (Nation et al., 2003). Throwing more resources at prisons while providing little to address the sources of crime, such as poverty, lack of educational attainment, hopelessness, and poor health care rather reveals a glaring weakness in public policy. The plan of prison abolition would therefore become part of a plan for societal improvement that, instead of spreading suffering and dam-age, could help reduce the total human toll and change the larger culture in positive ways.

Questions

1   How has criminal justice evolved as a way for society to contain violence?

2   What are its major competing tenets?

3   How does mass incarceration diminish its ability to deter?

4   How are solitary confinement and the death penalty self-defeating?

5   Which approaches in the US and internationally have shown promise?

References

Alexander, M. (2010). *New Jim Crow: Mass incarceration in the age of colorblindness.* New York, NY: New Press.

Amnesty International. (2003). *United States of America: Death by discrimination—The continuing role of race in capital cases.* London, UK: Author. Retrieved from http://www.amnesty.org/en/documents/AMR51/046/2003/en

Andrews, D. A., & Bonta, J. (2010). Rehabilitating criminal justice policy and practice. *Psychology, Public Policy, and Law, 16*(1), 39–55.

Baldus, D. C., Woodworth, G., & Pulaski, C. A. (1990). *Equal justice and the death penalty: A legal and empirical analysis.* Boston, MA: Northeastern University Press.

Beech, A., & Chauhan, J. (2013). Evaluating the effectiveness of the Supporting Offenders through Restoration Inside (SORI) programme delivered in seven prisons in England and Wales. *Legal and Criminological Psychology, 18*(2), 229–239.

Bhati, A., & Piquero, A. (2007). Estimating the impact of incarceration on subsequent offending trajectories: Deterrent, criminogenic, or null effect. *The Journal of Criminal Law and Criminology, 98*(1), 207–253.

Blackmon, D. A. (2008). *Slavery by another name: The re-enslavement of black Americans from the Civil War to World War II.* New York, NY: Anchor Books.

Bottoms, A., & Tankebe, J. (2012). Beyond procedural justice: A dialogic approach to legitimacy in criminal justice. *The Journal of Criminal Law and Criminology, 102*(1), 119–170.

Braithwaite, J. (1989). *Crime, shame and reintegration.* Cambridge, UK: Cambridge University Press.

Brandeis, L. (1928). Dissenting, Olmstead v. United States, 277 U.S. 438.

Brown, R. P., & Gerbarg, P. L. (2005). Sudarshan Kriya Yogic breathing in the treatment of stress, anxiety, and depression: Part II—Clinical applications and guidelines. *Journal of Alternative and Complementary Medicine, 11*(4), 711–717.

Bureau of Justice Statistics. (2003). *Criminal offenders statistics.* Washington, DC: U.S. Department of Justice.

Bureau of Justice Statistics. (2004). *Compendium of federal justice statistics, 2002.* Washington, DC: U.S. Department of Justice.

Chen, M. K., & Shapiro, J. M. (2007). Do harsher prison conditions reduce recidivism? A discontinuity- based approach. *American Law and Economics Review, 9*(1), 1–29.

Cloud, D. H., Drucker, E., Browne, A., & Parsons, J. (2015). Public health and solitary confinement in the United States. *American Journal of Public Health, 105*(1), 18–26.

Cochran, J. K., Chamlin, M. B., & Seth, M. (1994). Deterrence or brutalization? An impact assessment of Oklahoma's return to capital punishment. *Criminology, 32*(1), 107–134.

Constantine, R., Andel, R., Petrila, J., Becker, M., Teague, G., Boaz, T., & Howe, A. (2010). Characteristics and experiences of adults with a serious mental illness who were involved in the criminal justice system. *Psychiatric Services, 61*(5), 451–457.

Corsaro, N., & McGarrell, E. (2010). Reducing homicide risk in Indianapolis between 1997 and 2000. *Journal of Urban Health, 87*(5), 851–864.

Coyle, A. (2003). Editorial: A human rights approach to prison management. *Criminal Behavior and Mental Health, 13*(2), 77–80.

David, J. E. (2006). The one who is more violent prevails—Law and violence from a Talmudic legal perspective. *Canadian Journal of Law and Jurisprudence, 19*(2), 385–406.

Davis, A. Y. (2003). Racialized punishment and prison abolition. In T. L. Lott, & J. P. Pittman (Eds.), *Blackwell Companions to Philosophy: A companion to African-American philosophy* (pp. 360–369). Hoboken, NJ: Blackwell.

Deady, C. W. (2014). *Incarceration and recidivism: Lessons from abroad.* Newport, RI: Pell Center for International Relations and Public Policy. Retrieved from https://salve.edu/sites/default/files/filesfield/documents/Incarceration_and_Recidivism.pdf

Death Penalty Information Center (2016). *Facts about the death penalty.* Washington, DC: Author.

Death Penalty Worldwide (2016). *DPW executions and death sentences monitor.* Ithaca, NY: Cornell Center on the Death Penalty Worldwide.

Dieter, R. C. (2004). *Innocence and the crisis in the American death penalty.* Washington, DC: Death Penalty Information Center.

Donohue, J. J., & Wolfers, J. (2006). *Uses and abuses of empirical evidence in the death penalty debate.* Cambridge, MA: National Bureau of Economic Research.

Dostoyevsky, F. (1862). *The house of the dead.* Saint Petersburg, Russia: Vremya.

Drucker, E. (2013). *A plague of prisons: The epidemiology of mass incarceration in America.* New York, NY: New Press.

Eberhardt, J. L., Davies, P. G., Purdie-Vaughns, V. J., & Johnson, S. L. (2006). Looking deathworthy: Perceived stereotypicality of black defendants predicts capital-sentencing outcomes. *Psychological Science, 17*(5), 383–386.

Eck, W. (2003). *The age of Augustus.* Oxford, UK: Blackwell Publishing.

Eith, C., & Durose, M. R. (2011). *Contacts between police and the public, 2008.* Washington, DC: U.S. Department of Justice.

Fox, A., Fox, C. l., & Marsh, C. (2013). Could personalization reduce re-offending? Reflections on potential lessons from British social care reform for the British criminal justice system. *Journal of Social Policy, 42*(1), 721–741.

Friedman, L. (1994). *Crime and punishment in American history.* New York, NY: Basic Books.

Gavrielides, T. (2015). *The psychology of restorative justice.* Farnham, UK: Ashgate Publishing.

Gilligan, J., & Lee, B. X. (2005). The resolve to stop the violence project: Reducing violence in the community through a jail-based initiative. *Journal of Public Health, 27*(2), 143–148.

Gordon, S. E. (2013). Solitary confinement, public safety, and recidivism. *University of Michigan Journal of Law Reform, 47*(1), 495–528.

Grassian, S. (2006). Psychiatric effects of solitary confinement. *Washington University Journal of Law and Policy, 22*(1), 325–383.

Guerino, P., Harrison, P. M., & Sabol, W. J. (2012). *Bureau of justice statistics bulletin: Prisoners in 2010.* Washington, DC: U.S. Department of Justice.

Hafemeister, T., & George, J. (2012). The ninth circle of hell: An eighth amendment analysis of imposing prolonged supermax solitary confinement on inmates with a mental illness. *Denver University Law Review, 90*(1), 1–54.

Hall, M. T., Golder, S., Conley, C., & Sawning, S. (2013). Designing programming and interventions for women in the criminal justice system. *American Journal of Criminal Justice, 38*(1), 27–50.

Hartvig, P., & Kjelsberg, E. (2009). Penrose's law revisited: The relationship between mental institution beds, prison population, and crime rate. *Nordic Journal of Psychiatry, 63*(1), 51–56.

Hedstrom, J. (2018). *The American and Swedish criminal justice system: A comparative study.* Johnson City, TN: East Tennessee State University.

Innocence Project (2016). *Innocence list.* New York, NY: Author.

Irwin, J., & Austin, J. (1997). *It's about time: America's imprisonment binge.* Belmont, CA: Wadsworth Publishing.

James, D. J., & Glaze, L. E. (2006). *Bureau of justice statistics special report: Mental health problems of prison and jail inmates.* Washington, DC: U.S. Department of Justice.

Kaba, F., Lewis, A., Glowa-Kollisch, S., Hadler, J., Lee, D., Alper, H., ... Venters, H. (2014). Solitary confinement and risk of self-harm among jail inmates. *American Journal of Public Health, 104*(3), 442–447.

Kolind, T., Frank, V. A., Lindberg, O., & Tourunen, J. (2014). Officers and drug counsellors: New occupational identities in Nordic prisons. *British Journal of Criminology, 55*(2), 303–320.

Lee, B. X., & Prabhu, M. (2015). Reflection on the madness in prisons. *Stanford Law and Policy Review, 26*(1), 253–268.

Lee, B. X., & Gilligan, J. (2005). The resolve to stop the violence project: Transforming an in-house culture of violence through a jail-based programme. *Journal of Public Health, 27*(2), 149–155.

Lee, B. X., Wexler, B. E., & Gilligan, J. (2014). Political correlates of violent death rates in the U.S., 1900–2010: Longitudinal and cross-sectional analyses. *Aggression and Violent Behavior, 19*(6), 721–728.

Liu, Z. (2004). Capital punishment and the deterrence hypothesis: Some new insights and empirical evidence. *Eastern Economic Journal, 30*(2), 237–258.

Loe, A. M. (2015). *Prison-based animal programs: A descriptive analysis.* Greeley, CO: University of Northern Colorado.

Louw, J., & O'Brien, C. (2007). The psychological effects of solitary confinement: An instance of psychology in South African courts. *South Africa Journal of Psychology, 37*(1), 96–106.

McKelvey, B. (1977). *American prisons: A history of good intentions.* Montclair, NJ: Patterson Smith.

McLeod, A. M. (2015). Prison abolition and grounded justice. *UCLA Law Review, 62*(1), 1156–1239.

Mears, D. P. (2005). A critical look at supermax prisons. *Corrections Compendium, 30*(5), 6–7.

Mendes, S. M., & McDonald, M. D. (2001). Putting severity of punishment back in the deterrence package. *Policy Studies Journal, 29*(4), 588–610.

Nation, M., Crusto, C., Wandersman, A., Kumpfer, K. L., Seybolt, D., Morrissey-Kane, E., & Davino, K. (2003). What works in prevention: Principles of effective prevention programs. *American Psychologist, 58*(6–7), 449.

Nidich, S., O'Connor, T., Rutledge, T., Duncan, J., Compton, B., Seng, A., & Nidich, R. (2016). Reduced trauma symptoms and perceived stress in male prison inmates through the transcendental meditation program: A randomized controlled trial. *The Permanente Journal, 20*(4), 43–47.

Osher, F., & Steadman, H. (2007). Adapting evidence-based practices for persons with mental illness involved with the criminal justice system. *Psychiatric Services, 58*(11), 1472–1478.

Penitentiary Principles Act of 1998. Article 2 (1998).

Petrosino, A., Turpin-Petrosino, C., & Finckenauer, J. O. (2000). Well-meaning programs have harmful effects! Lessons from experiments of programs such as scared straight. *Crime and Delinquency, 46*(3), 354–379.

Pettit, B., & Western, B. (2004). Mass imprisonment and the life course: Race and class inequality in US incarceration. *American Sociological Review, 69*(2), 151–169.

Pettit, B., Sykes, B., & Western, B. (2009). *Technical report on revised population estimates and NLSY 79 analysis tables for the pew public safety and mobility project.* Cambridge, MA: Harvard University.

Pew Center on the States (2011). *State of recidivism: The revolving door of America's prisons.* Washington, DC: Pew Charitable Trusts.

Pollock, J. M. (2002). Parenting programs in women's prisons. *Women and Criminal Justice, 14*(1), 131–152.

Prison Act (Strafvollzugsgesetz) of 1977 § 2 and 3(1977).

Puzzanchera, C. (2009). *Juvenile justice bulletin: Juvenile arrests 2008.* Washington, DC: U.S. Department of Justice.

Reiman, J. H. (1979). *The rich get richer and the poor get prison: Ideology, class and criminal justice.* New York, NY: Wiley.

Reiter, K., Sexton, L., & Sumner, J. (2017). Negotiating imperfect humanity in the Danish penal system. In P. S. Smith, & T. Ugelvik (Eds.), *Scandinavian penal history, culture and prison practice: Embraced by the welfare state?* (pp. 481–508). Berlin, Germany: Springer.

Rosenzweig, J. (2013). Disappearing justice: Public opinion, secret arrest, and criminal procedure reform in China. *China Journal, 70,* 73–97.

Rossner, M. (2013). *Just emotions: Rituals of restorative justice.* Oxford, UK: Oxford University Press.

Rotman, E. (1990). *Beyond punishment: A new view on the rehabilitation of criminal offenders.* New York, NY: Greenwood Press.

Rummel, R. J. (1994). *Death by government.* New Brunswick, NJ: Transactions Publishers.

Sapers, H., & Zinger, I. (2009). Ombudsman as a monitor of human rights in Canadian federal corrections. *Pace Law Review, 30*(5), 1512–1528.

Scott-Hayward, C. S. (2009). *The fiscal crisis in corrections: Rethinking policies and practices.* New York, NY: Vera Institute of Justice.

Sherman, L. W. (1993). Defiance, deterrence, and irrelevance: A theory of the criminal sanction. *Journal of Research in Crime and Delinquency, 30*(4), 445–473.

Silver, E., & Miller, L. L. (2004). Sources of informal social control in Chicago neighborhoods. *Criminology, 42*(3), 551–583.

Snyder, H. N. (2011). *Arrest in the United States, 1980–2009.* Washington, DC: U.S. Department of Justice.

Subramanian, R., & Shames, A. (2013). *Sentencing and prison practices in Germany and the Netherlands: Implications for the United States.* New York, NY: Vera Institute of Justice.

Swartz, N. (2012). Does capital punishment amount to cruel, inhuman, and degrading punishment: A reflection on Botswana and South Africa. *Journal of Politics and Law, 5*(4), 100–110.

Swyers, K. (2014). *Prison-based animal programs (PAPs) and mental health outcome measures.* Portland, OR: University of Portland.

Taxman, F., Byrne, J. M., & Pattavina, A. (2005). Racial disparity and the legitimacy of the criminal justice system: Exploring consequences for deterrence. *Journal of Health Care for the Poor and Underserved, 16*(4), 57–77.

Tonry, M., & Melewski, M. (2008). The malign effects of drug and crime control policies on black Americans. *Crime and Justice, 37*(1), 1–44.

Travis, J., Western, B., & Redburn, F. S. (2014). *The growth of incarceration in the United States: Exploring causes and consequences.* Washington, DC: The National Academies Press.

Tyler, T. R., & Huo, Y. J. (2002). *Trust in the law: Encouraging public cooperation with the police and courts.* New York, NY: Russell-Sage Foundation.

Ua-amnoey, J., & Kittayarak, K. (2004). Restorative justice: A paradigm shift in the Thai criminal justice system. *Corrections Today, 66*(7), 86–91.

United Nations (2007). *Moratorium on the use of the death penalty.* New York, NY: Author. Retrieved from http://www.un.org/en/ga/search/view_doc.asp?symbol=A/RES/62/149

United States Bureau of Justice Statistics. (2012). *Prisoners in 2011.* Washington, DC: United States Department of Justice.

VerSteeg, R. (2002). *Law in the ancient world.* Durham, NC: Carolina Academic Press.

Wacquant, L. (2000). The new "peculiar institution": On the prison as surrogate ghetto. *Theoretical Criminology, 4*(3), 377–389.

Waddell, S. (2013). *Preventing youth violence: Lessons from three European countries.* London, UK: Winston Churchill Memorial Trust.

Walmsley, R. (2016). *World prison population list.* London, UK: Institute for Criminal Policy Research.

Ward, K., Longaker, A. J., Williams, J., Naylor, A., Rose, C. A., & Simpson, C. G. (2013). Incarceration within American and Nordic prisons: Comparison of national and international policies. *International Journal of Research and Practice on Student Engagement, 1*(1), 36–47.

Weber, M. (1919). *Politik als Beruf.* Munich, Germany: Duncker and Humblot.

Weisberg, R. (2012). Reality-challenged philosophies of punishment. *Marquette Law Review, 95*(4), 1203–1252.

West, H. C., & Sabol, W. J. (2008). *Prisoners in 2007.* Washington, DC: U.S. Department of Justice.

Wilper, A. P., Woodhandler, S., Boyd, J. W., Lasser, K. E., McCormick, D., Bor, D. H., & Himmelstein, D. U. (2009). The health and health care of U.S. prisoners: Results of a nationwide survey. *American Journal of Public Health, 99*(4), 666–672.

Wright, K. A. (2010). Strange bedfellows? Reaffirming rehabilitation and prison privatization. *Journal of Offender Rehabilitation, 49*(1), 74–90.

Wright, P., & Herivel, T. (2003). *Prison nation: The warehousing of America's poor.* New York, NY: Routledge.

Zatz, M. S. (2000). The convergence of race, ethnicity, gender, and class on court decision making: Looking toward the 21st century. *Criminal Justice, 3*(1), 503–552.

Zhang, L. (2008). Juvenile delinquency and justice in contemporary China: A critical review of the literature over 15 years. *Crime, Law and Social Change, 50*(3), 149–160.

Zimring, F., & Hawkins, G. (1993). *The scale of imprisonment.* Chicago, IL: University of Chicago Press.

11

International Law Approaches

Introduction

> If international law is, in some ways, at the vanishing point of law, the law of war is, perhaps even more conspicuously, at the vanishing point of international law.
> —*Hersch Lauterpacht,* Private Law Sources and Analogies of International Law *(1927)*

We now transition from criminal justice to law itself. Law is a system of rules and regulations that social institutions enforce to mediate relations at the individual, community, and international level, and can be an important means of addressing violence (Robertson, 2013). A collective legislature or a single legislator can create law through processes that jurisdictions have agreed upon, resulting in statutes, while private individuals can create legally binding contracts that hold up at court. Constitutions, written or tacit, may encode rights that form the foundation of laws. *International law*, which is the focus of this chapter, is a body of rules established by custom or treaty and recognized by nations as binding in their relations with one another (Swartz, 2013). It serves as a framework for the practice of stable and organized international relations, through treaties and conventions, and is primarily applicable to countries rather than individuals (Slomanson, 2011).

The international law approach is the second among the methods of intervention we are covering in this volume. It is becoming increasingly relevant as states have become more and more dependent on one another. This is attributable to the emergence and intensification of problems that reach far beyond national borders (Sztucki, 1974): matters of security, terrorism, human rights abuses, and armed conflict, as well as the mutual interdependence and vulnerability wrought by economic globalization, the environmental crisis, and the increasing movement of people across state boundaries (Samantha & John, 2010). These appear to have outrun the problem-solving capacity of any individual state to deal with adequately, necessitating interdependence and by extension regulations.

This chapter will briefly cover the history, successes, and challenges of international law. We will discuss what international law courts, such as the European Court of Human Rights and the International Criminal Court, have been able to accomplish. We will evaluate the need for agreements based on international cooperation, given the urgent issues of conflict and security, mass migrations, economic globalization, and the environmental crisis. We will review the limitations of international law in effectively preventing violence. While international legal structures and norms govern international life, whether they can effectively prevent violence at that level, rather than perpetuate the violence that occurs, remains to be seen. States still determine much of international law pertaining to the use of violence, as they also exercise

Violence: An Interdisciplinary Approach to Causes, Consequences, and Cures, First Edition. Bandy X. Lee.
© 2019 John Wiley & Sons, Inc. Published 2019 by John Wiley & Sons, Inc.

jurisdiction over prosecution of crimes within their territory or by their own citizens (Schiff, 2008). Whatever the future holds, we will consider how international law has developed into a complex field that has the potential to enable the global community to enact order in increasingly large domains.

Historical Background

A simple treaty or agreement between nations constitutes international law, and under this broad definition, international law has existed for thousands of years since city-states around Mesopotamia mutually agreed to keep boundaries (Shaw, 2008). Like all other laws, customs, etiquette, taboos, and moral principles play a role in defining socially emphasized and culturally valued practices about "proper relationships." Legal systems establish how wrongful behavior will be penalized, and represent a gradual evolution through the course of human civilization. During the sixteenth century, the proliferation of international practices, customs, rules, and treaties created a need for scholars to compile these instruments into organized treatises (Anand, 1982). Dutch jurist Hugo Grotius wrote *De jure belli ac pacis libri tres* (1625), the first codification of international law. Based on the legal status of war and on normative principles, *De Jure* holds it axiomatic that promises must be kept, and that harming another requires restitution (Grotius, 1625). In more recent years, post-World War institutions such as the United Nations (UN) and its judicial arm, the International Court of Justice (ICJ), have joined with institutions such as the International Criminal Court (ICC) and human rights treaty bodies (Samantha & John, 2010). The recognition of international law as a valid corpus of rules has been a gradual process (Jennings & Watts, 1992), developing through the consensus of states that recognize that they must respect and globally protect certain "values" amounting to valid legal norms (Lissitzyn, 1964).

The ICJ has defined the sources of modern international law as the following: international conventions; international customs; general principles of law agreed to by civilized nations; a supplementary source where applicable; and the teachings and decisions of the most qualified national publicists to determine legal rulings (Statute of the ICJ, 1945). Customary international law is law derived from universally held customs, or implied law as practiced out of legal obligation. Conventional international law can take almost any form, upon international agreement. Traditionally, international law considered only states, but the modern international legal system also includes individuals and international organizations (Shaw, 2010).

Over the past half-century, national governments have joined in signing a variety of international agreements that have direct relevance to violence prevention. These are important for setting standards for national legislation and norms of behavior. Some of the most important include: the *Convention on the Prevention and Punishment of the Crime of Genocide* (1948); the *Convention for the Suppression of the Traffic in Persons and of the Exploitation of the Prostitution of Others* (1949); the *Convention on the Elimination of All Forms of Racial Discrimination* (1965); the *International Covenant on Economic, Social and Cultural Rights* (1966a); the *International Covenant on Civil and Political Rights* (1966); the *Convention on the Elimination of All Forms of Discrimination against Women* (1979); the *Convention against Torture and Other Cruel, Inhuman or Degrading Treatment or Punishment* (1984); the *Convention on the Rights of the Child* (1989) and its two *Optional Protocols on the Involvement of Children in Armed Conflict* (2000) and *on the Sale of Children, Child Prostitution and Child Pornography* (2000). The *Rome Statute of the International Criminal Court* (1998) was also significant for international law.

In the 1990s, the UN led several commissions that created important documents such as the *Declaration on Elimination of Violence against Women* in 1993 (Qureshi, 2013). After publishing its *World Report* (Krug et al., 2002), the World Health Organization (WHO) convened major world players in the field through the Violence Prevention Alliance in order to respond to much of what it identified in the report (Ahmad, 2004). In a Global Campaign for Violence Prevention, the Alliance continues to meet every year, and every other year with WHO Member States to hold milestones meetings, with an informal influence on governmental policy and law (Lee, Leckman, & Mbwambo, 2014). There are many other campaigns at the international level, but as their importance grows, they are called to be more sensitive to local contexts (Zwi, 2004). Also notable is the *Journal of Peace Research*, which since 1964 has provided an academic process for encouraging peace in a multidisciplinary endeavor (Urdal, Ostby, & Gleditsch, 2014).

International Legal Structures

There are a number of substantive fields in international law, namely the economic, environmental, criminal, humanitarian, security, human rights, and diplomatic fields (Evans, 2014). The European Union (EU), the UN, and various other supranational organizations have established numerous legal bodies in the substantive fields of international law to provide sources of rules and regulations for member nations. These legal bodies attempt to improve legal standards in their respective fields and ensure that members are all held to an acceptable standard of law in their respective dealings with other states, international organizations, or individuals.

The *Universal Declaration of Human Rights* (UN, 1948), the *International Covenant on Economic, Social and Cultural Rights* (UN, 1966c), and the *International Covenant on Civil and Political Rights* (UN, 1966b) together make up the *International Bill of Human Rights*. These instruments emphasize the freedom and dignity of every human being. The *Universal Declaration* (UN, 1948) legally guarantees all humans their fundamental rights: to be free of tyranny; to be free from religious persecution; to enjoy freedom of speech; to be free from arbitrary arrest or exile; to be free from human trafficking; to be free from prosecution for acts in breach of a law before the law's existence; and to be free from arbitrary violation of one's privacy, among others. It is the first internationally accepted document acknowledging these rights and represents the first step toward broadening the scope of international law from nations to individuals within those nations. Its covenants stipulate obligations to create favorable living conditions for every person, including civil, political, economic, social, and cultural rights, and sanctions for not doing so. Recent peacekeeping operations, for instance, have effectively overcome obstacles and have played a role in the supervision of ceasefires and the maintenance of order, as well as in national conciliations. The UN and African Union peacekeeping operations protect civilians under the imminent threat of physical violence.

International economic law is a field of international law that covers both the conduct of sovereign states in international economic relations, and the conduct of private parties involved in cross-border business transactions. This includes, among other things, international trade law, law of international financial institutions, and private international law. The Association of Southeast Asian Nations (ASEAN) and the EU are prime examples of regional trade organizations that practice international economic law. Economic law includes the fields of regional economic integration, international law and development, international commercial arbitration, international intellectual property law, and international business regulation (Trachtman, 2008). International environmental law regulates the behavior of member states with regard to the environment (Rodgers, 1994).

International criminal law regulates the behavior of states, organizations, and individuals with respect to crimes. It is a body of public international law that prohibits conduct commonly viewed as serious atrocities. International crime includes genocide, crimes against humanity, war crimes, crimes of aggression, and any act considered by the court to violate internationally accepted norms from which no derogation is permitted (Bassiouni, 1998). *International humanitarian law* regulates armed conflict between states, groups, and individuals, and is one of the oldest fields of international law (International Committee of the Red Cross, 2004) that seeks to limit the harm of armed conflict and to protect persons who are not participating in hostilities. *International diplomatic law* covers the rights of diplomats in foreign nations (Von Glahn, 1992) such as through diplomatic immunity, which derives from state immunity, and is a field that goes back thousands of years. *International security law* focuses primarily on collective security measures involving both military and nonmilitary activities against both traditional and nontraditional security threats. It is arguably less clearly defined than the other substantive fields of international law: as international security is conceptually different from the type of security involving individuals or singular nations, it is necessary to view international security as collective security (Kelsen, 1957). In 1992, the UN Security Council expanded international security concerns to include economic, social, humanitarian, and ecological factors. In 2004, the UN High-Level Panel identified economic and social threats, transnational organized crime, interstate conflict, internal conflict, terrorism, and weapons of mass destruction as threats to global security (Nasu, 2011).

One institution that represents a major step in the attempt to combat human rights and criminal abuses such as war crimes and genocide within the global community is the ICC. Beginning in the 1920s, there were calls for a permanent international court for the prosecution of crime, and both Rwanda and Yugoslavia had set up temporary war crimes tribunals, as a permanent international body of criminal law was not yet available (Armstead & Holmes, 1998). One of the first steps toward the establishment of the ICC took place when the UN General Assembly adopted the *Convention on the Prevention and Punishment of the Crime of Genocide* (1948). Though the Cold War delayed an agreement by the international community on what constituted a crime of aggression, work on forming the ICC eventually picked up, and plans for the institution finalized in 1998 at the Rome Conference after only seven nations voted against it and 21 nations abstained. The *Rome Statute of the ICC* (1998) went into effect in 2002, after its ratification by the sixtieth state party. By 2006, 94 states have ratified the Rome statute; notably absent from this list are China, Russia, India, Pakistan, and the US.

The European Court of Human Rights (ECHR) came into existence after the Holocaust and was the first international legal institution that covered its substantive field. Its purpose was to ensure that a permanent international court existed, as nations deemed such a legal body urgently necessary after World War II (Artusy, 2014). The creation of the ECHR was groundbreaking in international law, permitting individuals, nongovernmental organizations, or groups of individuals to directly bring cases in court, as opposed to just states or intergovernmental organizations, as with the ICJ and the ICC. The ECHR's jurisdiction extends to all 47 member nations of the Council of Europe. The court has a pragmatic approach to ordering cases, respecting their importance and urgency, and the Chamber or President can exercise the power to give priority to cases that appear more pressing (Rules of Court, 2002). Given that the court has jurisdiction over all of the member nations of the Council of Europe, the member nations' status in the organization correlates with compliance.

The European Court of Justice (ECJ) was formed in 1953 on the assumption that all member states would maintain supreme courts, with the original court assigning one judge to each Supreme Court and one extra judge to ensure a decision without a tie (Artusy, 2014). The court covers all 27 member states of the EU and does not allow individuals to file petitions as the ECHR does. It is most similar, with respect to the legal scope of human rights protection, to the ECHR. The ECJ restricts itself from imposing laws that are found to conflict with member states' constitutions. Economic measures back ECJ judgments, and the legal protocols try to ensure that witnesses are inclined to cooperate, to take an oath to be truthful, and to give evidence.

The ICJ was founded to have global jurisdiction as the primary judicial body for the UN. While the ICJ has jurisdiction over member bodies, enforcement is contingent upon member states' consent to its authority. The ICJ allows only states to bring cases. The statutes of the ICJ give the Court the liberty to entrust any individual, body, bureau, commission, or other organization that it may select with the tasks of carrying out an inquiry or giving expert opinion. The ICJ allows itself flexibility in the way it handles cases, the imposition of deadlines, and the windows of time within which parties can make their arguments. The rulings of the court can be either advisory opinions, which are nonbinding but legally informed rulings, or binding resolutions after both parties have agreed to submit their case before the court (Rules of Court, 1978).

Challenges and Successes

We may consider it a positive step for humanity that legal institutions are being put in place to allow nations to apply legally many commonly held values concerning human rights, war crimes, international organized crime, and so on. However, in practice, it seems that the institutions created and expected to deliver these judgments often do not have adequate means to enforce them. For example, Omar Hassan Ahmad al-Bashir, Sudan's president, whom the ICC wanted for genocide, war crimes, and crimes against humanity, visited the nation of Chad in July 2010. As a member of the ICC, Chad was required to comply with the court's request to arrest al-Bashir, but refused, as this was during a rapprochement between the two neighboring nations that had previously strained relations between them (International Justice Resource Center, 2011). The African Union asked that the UN Security Council defer the prosecution of al-Bashir with the intention of avoiding dissension in Africa among African Union member states (Barnes, 2011).

This visit called into question whether it is possible to supersede all the existing values and priorities of member nations with appeals to morality or justice. One might assume that Chad sought to maintain its newly improved relations with its neighbor Sudan and that the African Union wished to avoid the potential instability of a power vacuum in its regional community. Chad's blatant lack of compliance with the requirement to abide by the Court's rulings called into question the power of the institution. The *Rome Statute* (1998) does not offer sufficient options regarding courses of action available to the ICC in the event of noncompliance by a party subject to its rulings, and as a result there is no clear punishment for violating it. Apart from executing judgments, it seems that the ICC does not achieve much in the way of convictions; it has achieved only two so far (Peet, 2015).

In the area of human rights law, there have been efforts to prevent violence by criminalizing international law—seeking to hold individuals, not states, responsible for crimes. One example is the ICC's prosecution of Joseph Kony, the leader of a child army in Uganda, in the case of *Prosecutor v. Kony, Otti, Odhiambo,* and *Ongwen* (2005). All four have been indicted with war crimes that include attacks against civilians, cruel treatment, enlisting of children, inducing of rape, murder, and pillaging; and crimes against humanity that include enslavement, inhumane acts, murder, rape, and sexual enslavement. Human rights lawyers hope that by holding Kony and other violators accountable, international law can deter future violence, build norms against violence, and restore trust and dignity to build a better, less violent society. Another instance includes the case of *Prosecutor v. Kunarac, Kovac, and Vukovic* (2001), where the defendants stood accused of detaining women against their will and raping them during the conflicts in Bosnia. The International Criminal Tribunal for the Former Yugoslavia updated the accepted definition of what constitutes slavery (Cdebaca, 2011). This understanding was changed from the original definition under the *Slavery Convention* (1926), which defined slavery in more narrow terms of ownership, buying, selling, exchange, and transport, to a more modern and all-encompassing term, including any scenario in which an individual's autonomy, freedom of movement, consent, or free will is restricted through means of threat or other coercion, physical or otherwise.

This expansion of the definition of slavery contrasts with what occurred in an earlier case that went before the United States Supreme Court, in which Ike Kozminski was accused of using coercion and deceit to take advantage of disabled men and have them work and live in sub-par conditions against their will. Since this coercion was not physical but psychological, the Supreme Court could not convict them of involuntary servitude without updated antislavery statutes that included non-physical coercion. This failure of justice helped to shape the UN *Protocol to Prevent, Suppress, and Punish Trafficking Persons, Especially Women and Children* (UN, 2000), also known as the *Palermo Protocol*.

There are several global attempts to prevent individual violence against women and children. Foremost among them is the *Declaration on Elimination of Violence against Women* (UN, 1993), which seeks to address the nexus between violence against women and their generally lower socioeconomic status, especially in low- and middle-income nations (Romany, 1993). It has led to several nations' legislatures adopting provisions to prohibit violence against women (Ortiz-Barreda & Vives-Cases, 2013). Another is the UN *Declaration of the Rights of the Child* (UN, 1959), which contains a similar anti-bullying program that has supported the passage of anti-bullying laws, inclusion into social networks, and educational reforms that help establish "reciprocal friendships" to protect students from isolation and victimization (Kolstrein & Jofre, 2013).

There are a growing number of studies on the topic and meta-analyses of anti-bullying interventions (Farrington & Ttofi, 2009; Ferguson, San Miguel, Kilburn, & Sanchez, 2007), as well as interventions conducted around the world (Olweus, 1991). However, intervention programs often face difficulties in a global context where there is cultural resistance, such as opposition to postwar reforms related to violence against women in Liberia (Abramowitz & Moran, 2012). International organizations, such as the Inter-American Development Bank, the World Bank, and the UN Educational, Scientific, and Cultural Organization (UNESCO) have begun collaborations on international violence intervention programs. These organizations and nations must work together to promote international treaties to establish international legal norms against violence, especially against women and children.

Abuses and the Difficulty of Enforcement

Similarly to the World Health Organization, the Pan American Health Organization has codified human rights throughout Latin America (Meier & Ayala, 2014). However, there has been concern over the abuse of international law by some nations; Israel, for example, was cited for "ad hoc legal entrepreneurialism" for its efforts to transform international law (Bisharat, 2013). These critiques mention the abduction of Nazi Adolf Eichmann, a German Nazi Lieutenant Colonel who played a major role in organizing the Holocaust. Another critique notes the increased precision in weapons and the "war on terror," which has shifted the damage costs from Israel's military to civilians on the other side. These create a "law of violence" which appears to conflict with human rights and with the legal framework that intends to alleviate violence, as American legal scholar Robert Cover (1986) presaged.

Some countries, such as Argentina, have adopted provisions in their Constitution directing the government to care for the physical and moral health of their citizenry. Such provisions have been read as a constitutional—not treaty-based—requirement to protect the human rights of citizens, creating legal accountability for compliance. In a Swedish study of intimate partner violence, researchers identified an important role of the political system as being to contribute to the change of societal norms and create social support structures. In state-run education systems, this change in societal norms should begin, according to focus groups in Europe, as early as preschool by teaching awareness of intimate partner violence (Jakobsson et al., 2013). Proposals for political legislative reforms, including global action for gun control, are happening through a country-by-country analysis, so as to help reduce gun crime, homicide, and likely suicide rates (Wolf, Gray, & Fazel, 2014). While gun legislation has not yet become global, the success of the Pan American Health Organization in leading 39 countries in the Americas to enact legislation addressing violence against women demonstrates that success through a global political structure may be possible (Ortiz-Barreda & Vives-Cases, 2013).

Global treaties regarding trade, finance, human rights, and conflict appear, according to qualitative studies, to succeed more often in shaping economic matters than in attempting to shape societal progress, likely due to the incentive of economic gain for countries, stakeholders, and other organizations (Hoffman & Rattingen, 2015). Therefore, coupling economic structure with violence reduction may be an effective route. A 169-country study of violence has demonstrated that greater income inequality positively correlates with robbery and homicide worldwide, although the correlation is small in high-income countries (Wolf et al., 2014). This supports previous and current sociological assertions that *anomie*, or diminishing social and ethical standards, and a lack of social cohesion lead to violence (Shaw & McKay, 1942; Wilkinson & Pickett, 2010). Nations that offer economic safety nets to reduce the effects of inequality or protect their citizens from falling prey to market forces have lower homicide rates (Savolanien, 2000). The World Bank (2000), in line with this argument, has recommended that governments institute labor market reforms, adjust fiscal policy, and increase support for small businesses in order to combat economic inequality.

Human rights treaty bodies have adopted new procedures, and additional protocols have been agreed upon to enhance protection and compliance. Recent additions are the protocols to the *International Covenant on Economic, Social and Cultural Rights* (1966a) and *Convention on the Rights of the Child* (1989), which provide a complaints procedure to use when these rights are violated. Despite this, a considerable number of states still fail to implement adequately their human rights obligations due to systemic and institutional shortcomings or to deliberate disregard. These states intentionally isolate themselves in a bid to violate human rights (Goedde, 2010)—a case in point is North Korea. The limits of the promotion and protection approach of the international human rights treaty and charter body system raise the question of whether force should be resorted to when there are serious violations. Although there are positive aspects to the existence of international courts, they are difficult to uphold as an ideal when states choose to follow or disregard the laws as a matter of convenience.

The growth of the international human rights regime has not been matched by an equally effective enforcement system. There are numerous instances where members of the international community disregard international legal bodies with few or no repercussions. In 1986, the US refused to acknowledge the authority of the ICJ and went home without defending a case (Schabas, 2004). The refusal of the US even to defend itself, and the lack of consequences for this blatant disregard, highlight the logic of foregoing altruistic levels of participation in international courts when such legal bodies do not have the necessary power to ensure that all nations comply with their rulings. What good is a court that does not have any enforcement power backing up its proclamations?

Another prevalent issue in the modern international system of law is the tendency for powerful subject states to try to use this law to the detriment of contentious nations. Vietnam and other nations that maintain that the Chinese incursion into the South China Sea is aggressive and illegal have brought the matter up in a Hague Tribunal, with the US calling for China to handle this matter within the framework of international law (Steinglass, 2014). The US's expectation that other nations abide by international law when it has disregarded legal authorities on a regular basis shows that international law is not objective and equitable legislation by which all nations can measure their and others' actions. Rather, international law can serve as subjective means to softly discredit and contain rival nations.

The ability of smaller nations to group together to launch an objection to the illegal acts of larger and more powerful nations will be a positive development in international law. Overall, it is already an advancement that such issues can be publicized and can enter the discussion at a global scale, but the power of international court rulings to have any real world effect continues to be insufficient. As long as the concept of sovereign nations exists, universal acceptance and stringent enforcement of a comprehensive international legal institution will be difficult, if not impossible. If the institution that issues a ruling implicitly or explicitly permits a choice with regard to compliance with that ruling, the ruling amounts to little more than an arbitrary formality and loses legitimacy, just as we have seen how selective enforcement of the law delegitimizes the criminal justice system within nations. While it is difficult for international law to codify norms and morality that are acceptable and applicable to all nations in all situations, the very attempt to do so marks the beginning of a system that may one day succeed if the bodies of the modern international legal system persist in trying to overcome these challenges.

With regard to interpersonal violence, countries where societal norms conflict with the desired legal framework that condemns violence will not likely adopt it (Hamilton, 1978). This difficulty is most apparent in traditionally male-dominated societies that struggle to develop legal codes against intimate partner violence (IPV) when those rules conflict with entrenched cultural norms (Malhotra & Schuler, 2005). Other social factors that may constrain municipalities and nations from resolving a violence problem include a culture of excessive alcohol consumption, as has been observed in the Kanak population in New Caledonia (Hamelin et al., 2009). It appears that nongovernmental organizations are attempting to combat this void. For instance, public institutions in Brazil, Thailand, Namibia, Bangladesh, and South Africa have provided crisis services to victims of IPV, with an aim of prevention (Chibber & Krishnan, 2011). Interestingly, those systems in developing countries have been more comprehensive and multilevel than systems in industrialized countries, possibly because of the efforts of nongovernmental organizations like the Pan American Health Organization to educate the public about IPV where the political system has not enacted sufficient legislation. While some nations, such as Switzerland, have proposed a World Court of Human Rights, opponents fear the "frighteningly broad powers" such a court could hold (Alston, 2014).

Changing Landscapes

International terrorism and international human rights raise especially difficult questions regarding international law. International law cannot on its own solve the world's problems. Its effectiveness depends on the international unlawful actions on the part of states, groups, and individuals. Terrorism invokes compelling emotional responses, which often lead to morally conflicting decisions. The fact that sovereign states are at liberty to enact counterterrorism measures that are consonant with their national interests does not preclude them from complying with their obligations under international law (Anwukah, 2016). Notwithstanding the emphasis on the need for concerted international action to confront the problem of terrorism, there is no coherent definition of terrorism as such in international humanitarian law, and abuses of the term can happen. In international criminal law, the international community has developed 13 conventions relating to the prevention and suppression of terrorism. Most of these treaties define specified acts as offenses and require states to criminalize them. The international criminal law provisions against terrorism have also been addressed in practice by international tribunals (Office of the UN High Commissioner for Human Rights, 2008).

International humanitarian law, based on the concepts of *jus ad bello*, is defined to be the law of wars. There are three types of violent conflicts that are recognized by international humanitarian law: international armed conflict, internationalized armed conflict, and non-international armed conflict. An *international armed conflict*, according to the *Geneva Conventions* of 1949, is a conflict between the legal armed forces of two different states, such as the North Korea–South Korea war of 1950. An *internationalized armed conflict* is a new phenomenon. It is a situation where a war occurs between two different factions fighting internally but with the support of two different outside states. A good example was the conflict in the Democratic Republic of Congo in 1998 when the forces from Rwanda, Angola, Zimbabwe, and Uganda intervened to support various groups in the country.

A *non-international armed conflict* means that one of the parties involved is nongovernmental in nature, and it has to meet two variables: the hostilities have to reach a certain minimum level of intensity, and there has to be a certain level of organization of the parties. Modern conflicts have drastically changed over the last few years with the introduction of new actors in conflict zones such as private military companies, multinational corporations, and transnational armed groups such as Al Qaeda and drug cartels. The picture has become more complex. For international humanitarian law to play an important part, it needs to adapt and continuously evolve to cater to the changing dynamics of conflicts today (Chelimo, 2011).

The global migration crisis has become an international political crisis. As migrants continue to journey across the Mediterranean, EU politicians are creating new, harmonized regulations governing migration. The UN persists in building two global agreements to assist migrants and refugees, the *Global Compact on Migration* (UN, 2017) and the *Global Compact on Refugees* (UN, 2017), which stem from the September 2016 UN Summit on Refugees and Migrants. The *Convention and Protocol Relating to the Status of Refugees* (1951) defines a refugee as a person who crosses an international border due to a well-founded fear of persecution, on the basis of race, religion, nationality, membership in a particular social group, or political opinion. This convention was born from the ashes of World War II, like many other foundational documents of international human rights law. The *Convention against Torture* (1984) prohibits sending anyone back to a place where they will be tortured or face other inhumane treatment. The term migrant is undefined in international law. The *International Convention on the Protection of the Rights of All Migrant Workers* (1990) relates only to workers who have contracts with employers abroad. Some regional agreements and *UN Guiding Principles* (UN, 2011) aim to help internally displaced people, but still, there is no binding international legal framework to protect them. Of course, these laws do not yet touch upon the causes of the global refugee crisis, which have to do with deteriorating conditions in low- and middle-income countries because of global economic inequities, human rights violations with impunity, and environmental devastations because of global warming.

The last of these causes gives rise to *environmental refugees,* who are people forced to leave their traditional habitat, temporarily or permanently, because of a marked environmental disruption that has jeopardized their existence and has seriously affected their quality of life. In legal terms, there is no such thing as a climate change refugee. There is, however, evidence that people are moving in response to the effects of climate change. Climate change often multiplies preexisting stressors, rather than being the sole cause of movement. It is important because climate change-driven displacements are projected to accelerate with time. The international protection regime is predicated on the idea of forced exile and is premised on the responsibility of other states to extend legal protection if a particular individual engages a state's non-refoulement obligations under international law. Migration, by contrast, does not enliven international legal duties beyond state obligations under human rights law generally. Thus, the nature of the movement and the motivation for it are significant when it comes to legal responses (Mcadam, 2012).

The growth of international environmental law as a separate area of public international law began with the Stockholm Conference on the Environment in 1972. The major sources of international environmental law are treaties and international agreements. An additional source is customary international law, which is often evidenced by national legislation, government statements, restatements of the law, and the interpretations of international tribunals such as the International Court of Justice and other arbitral bodies (Burnett, 2015). Although the drafting of much environmental legislation has been in response to catastrophes, preventing environmental harm is cheaper, easier, and less environmentally dangerous than reacting to environmental harm that has already taken place. Since the early 1970s, the "polluter pays" principle has been a dominant concept in environmental law. Many economists claim that producers largely cause environmental harm by externalizing the cost of their activities. Environmental protection requires consideration of the potential consequences of environmentally fateful decisions. Various jurisdictions and business organizations have begun to integrate environmental considerations into their decision-making through mandates on environmental impact assessments.

In 2017, an investor-state tribunal made history by ordering a mining company to pay 39 million US dollars to Ecuador for environmental cleanups. In 2016, Colombia posed three big questions to the Inter-American Court, roughly equivalent to the ECHR. If, Colombia asked, an individual living in Country A suffers a human rights violation due to ecological damage emanating from Country B, can she or he hold Country B responsible under the *American Convention* (1969)? There are pressing concerns, and not just in Colombia. One that is looming is Nicaragua's plan to build a Chinese-funded rival to the Panama Canal. Scientists fear it would literally muddy Caribbean waters, killing marine life and creating chemical pollution. The problem is that the main conventions oblige states to ensure the human rights of people only within their jurisdiction. Sooner or later, the courts will have to define what jurisdiction means in the context of transboundary environmental damage (Sands, 2014). Over the past two decades, it has become clear that, in order to understand the cross-border development of legal norms, we need to move beyond the limiting framework of international law. Although globalization has been an object of study for quite some time, most of this work has taken place in fields outside of law. The shift in focus from international law to law and globalization provides a new impetus for removing the artificial boundary between public and private international law (Schiff Berman, 2005).

International law today addresses the conduct of private corporations in a variety of areas. It regulates corporate conduct indirectly, by requiring states to enact and enforce regulations applicable to corporations and other non-state actors. In August 2003, the Sub-Commission of the Promotion of Human Rights of the UN Commission on Human Rights approved the *Norms* on the *Responsibilities of Transnational Corporations and Other Business Enterprises with Regard to Human Rights* (UN, 2003). The document purported to be a restatement of corporations' existing obligations under international human rights law. The most commonly proffered examples of international legal norms imposing obligations on corporations are in fact of the indirect variety. Reference is often made to the European concept *Drittwirkung,* or "third-party effect," under which certain provisions of the *European Convention of Human Rights* (1950) are understood to apply between private parties. The European authorities demonstrate that the state has an obligation in these circumstances to take steps to ensure that private parties behave in certain ways toward other private parties.

Also frequently cited is the decision of the Inter-American Court of Human Rights in the *Velásquez-Rodríguez* case (1988). The Inter-American Court recognized that the *American Convention on Human Rights* (1969) had a horizontal effect similar to that of the *European Convention* (1950). It affirmed the responsibility of the state for failing to prevent or punish private conduct that infringed human rights, but it did not hold that private individuals who inflict such injuries are guilty of violating the *Convention* (1969). However, establishing that certain norms have a horizontal effect, and adding to the list of such norms, could well represent an important advance in the protection of human rights. By imposing obligations on states, international law obviously disempowers states. It makes certain conducts states like to engage in unlawful. For example, if a treaty requires states to pass a minimum-wage legislation, it legally disables them from permitting the payment of lower wages (Vázquez, 2005).

International law has evolved into a particularly fascinating branch of law, the highest of them all, which might either break or make the world. It depends on negotiation, good offices, mediations, conciliation, and arbitration, and as a last resort on judicial settlements. After the fall of the League of Nations, the UN has been the most widely accepted body executing international law. The *Charter of the UN* (1945) has bound its member states through its various organs that work toward the single goal of establishing international law. A global economy has rapidly shrunk the world. Environmental issues are threatening the universe, but at the same time the world is becoming more aware that a united world is necessary to tackle despotic rule, hunger, poverty, ignorance, and natural catastrophes.

Case Studies

A and Others v. the UK (2004)

In 2004, the Grand Chamber of the European Court of Human Rights delivered its judgment in A and Others v. the United Kingdom. The case concerned the indefinite detention of foreign inmates in a prison, Belmarsh. The prisoners were held without trial under section 23 of the Anti-Terrorism, Crime and Security Act of 2001. These and subsequent detentions were challenged at the Court as incompatible with the European Convention on Human Rights. Nine people were threatened with deportation without trial on the basis that there was some evidence that they posed a threat to national security. They challenged the deportation decision and were later held indefinitely, without trial or deportation.

The inmates claimed that they were victims of inhuman or degrading treatment within the meaning of Article 3 of the European Convention on Human Rights and that they were denied an effective remedy for their complaints, in breach of Article 13 of the Convention. They complained that it was discriminatory and in breach of Article 14 to detain them when the UK suspected involvement with Al-Qaeda. They also complained that the procedure before the domestic courts did not comply with the requirements of paragraph 4 of Article 5. Regarding the complaint under Article 3, the Court stated that the applicants were not without any prospect or hope of release because they were able to bring proceedings to challenge the legality of their detention and found no violation of Article 3, alone or in conjunction with Article 13 (*A and Others v. the UK*, 2009).

However, the applicants successfully argued that their detention infringed the right to liberty found in Article 5 of the Convention. Although the state can deviate from Article 5 in time of war or other emergency, it may not go beyond what is strictly required. The Court found a breach of Article 5, paragraph 5, providing for the right to compensation for unlawful detention. The "rule of law" operates to protect citizens from arbitrary government decisions and is a part of balancing the constitution. This is a balanced judgment that took into account many disparate interests and affirmed that, whatever the political reasons, they cannot be used to justify discrimination based on nationality.

Bosnia and Herzegovina v. Serbia and Montenegro (2007)

Bosnia asked the Court, a judicial body of the United Nations, for formal recognition of its people's brutal fate and for financial compensation. The central argument was that Serbia and Montenegro violated the 1948 United Nations Convention on the Prevention and Punishment of the Crime of Genocide in the 1992–1995 war after the breakup of Yugoslavia.

The Court decided that after Montenegro's declaration of independence in 2006, Serbia, as Serbia and Montenegro's successor, was the only respondent party in the case. The Court recognized that the Srebrenica massacre was a genocide and that acts were committed with a specific intent to destroy, in part, the Muslims of Bosnia and Herzegovina. The Court found, although not unanimously, that Serbia was neither directly responsible for the Srebrenica genocide nor complicit in it, but it ruled that Serbia had committed a breach of the Genocide Convention by failing to prevent the genocide from occurring and not cooperating with the International Criminal Tribunal for the former Yugoslavia in punishing the offenders of the genocide. In reaching this decision, the court referred to the standard set by *Nicaragua v. United States* (1984), in which the US was found not to be legally responsible for the actions of the Contra guerrillas despite their common goal and publicized support.

The Bosnia ruling set important precedents. Genocide, without a paper trail, is difficult to prove in court. The issue is not how many people died during a certain event, but whether the killers had a specific intent to destroy a political, religious, or ethnic group. As in every criminal trial, the burden of proof is on the prosecution. This case highlighted that the International Court of Justice, which was set up to adjudicate disputes among states, may not be the proper forum for divided nations that need to be brought together on a more personal level.

Andriciuc and Others v. Banca Românească SA (2017)

Ruxandra Andriciuc and others received their income in Romanian lei (RON) and in 2007 and 2008 they took out loans denominated in Swiss francs (CHF) from a Romanian bank, Banca Românească. The exchange rate changed considerably to the detriment of the borrowers. The plaintiffs brought actions before the Romanian courts seeking a declaration that the terms according to which they must repay the loans in Swiss francs were unfair because the CHF fluctuates significantly against the RON and the bank failed to explain the exchange risk. At the time they executed the contracts, the bank pointed out only the benefits to the borrowers without calling attention to the potential risks and the likelihood of their occurring. Afterward, the Romanian Court of Appeal asked the European Court of Justice about the extent of banks' obligations to inform clients of exchange rate risks related to loans denominated in foreign currencies.

On September 20, 2017, the Court of Justice of the European Union entered a judgment, finding that lenders must be transparent with borrowers about the economic consequences of foreign-currency loans. The Court declared that the drafting of contractual terms must be in "plain intelligible language," and the contract must be set up in a way that makes transparent the mechanisms the particular terms relate to, so that the consumer can be in a position to evaluate the economic consequences that derive from the mechanisms. Any financial institution must thus provide borrowers with adequate information to enable them to make well-informed decisions. The Court judged that the bank had not fulfilled those obligations and that the national court must determine whether the bank failed to meet its obligations in good faith. This case established an important step in consumer protection.

F v. Bevándorlási és Állampolgársági Hivatal (2018)

Hungary has been in the spotlight due to "border walls" keeping refugees from entering Hungarian territory. The Court of Justice of the European Union and the European Court of Human Rights have both stated that Hungarian authorities have been enacting policies hostile to refugees. Hungary intended to resort to dubious means to evaluate the applications of individuals claiming asylum on grounds related to their sexual orientation. The Hungarian Administrative and Labor Court asked the Court of Justice of the European Union for a preliminary ruling in this case, which features a Nigerian national who had submitted an application for asylum in Hungary based on his sexual orientation. He had to deal with projective personality tests and other means of proving sexuality.

The Hungarian Court asked whether the application of Article 4 of Council Directive 2004/83/EC, concerning the assessment of applications for international protection, might be considered in light of Article 1 of the Charter of Fundamental Rights of the European Union, which states: "Human dignity is inviolable. It must be respected and protected." The question was whether this article precludes a forensic psychologist's expert opinions being based on projective personality tests in asylum adjudication when they relate to lesbian, gay, bisexual, transgender, and intersex (LGBTI) claimants.

The Court had handled Sexual Orientation and Gender Identity (SOGI) asylum claims in past cases, such as *X, Y, and Z v. Minister voor Immigratie* (2013) and *A, B, and C v. Staatssecretaris van Veiligheid en Justitie* (2014). This 2018 judgment is important because it establishes core principles of credibility and evidence assessment. The Court found that although the applicant's mere declarations are not sufficient to establish his sexual orientation, authorities must adhere to certain limits when evaluating SOGI asylum applications. The Court gave a "black list" of what authorities cannot do and made clear that there is no room for evidence that, by its nature, undermines human dignity and does not have probative value. This case has put back on the Court's agenda the evidentiary standards to be applied in SOGI asylum cases. Several practices have been criticized through the years, including stereotyped questioning and phallometry, whereby reactions of gay male asylum claimants to watching pornography were supposed to indicate their sexual orientation.

Quinteros v. Uruguay (1983)

María del Carmen Almeida de Quinteros had been arrested at her home in Uruguay in June 1976. She was held for 4 days incommunicado, until military personnel took her to a place in the City of Montevideo near the Embassy of Venezuela. Quinteros managed to jump over a wall and land inside the Embassy grounds. After striking the secretary of the embassy and other staff members, military personnel dragged her off the premises. Her detention had never been officially admitted. Her mother submitted a complaint but had not obtained any official information about her daughter's whereabouts. Additionally, Venezuela had suspended its diplomatic relations with Uruguay.

The Human Rights Committee, established under Article 28 of the International Covenant on Civil and Political Rights, found violations of Articles 7, 9, and 10.1 of the Covenant. It stated that the mother was also a victim of the violations of the Covenant her daughter suffered, because of the anguish and stress she endured due to the disappearance of her daughter and the continuing uncertainty concerning her whereabouts. The Human Rights Committee reiterated that the Government of Uruguay must conduct a full investigation into this matter to establish what has happened to Quinteros, bring to justice any persons found to be responsible for her disappearance and ill-treatment, pay compensation for the wrongs suffered, and ensure that similar violations do not occur in the future. Recommended remedies were similar to those in the case of *Bleier v. Uruguay* (1982).

Conclusion

International law has an increasingly important role to play in curbing violence at scales that exceed the reach of individual states. In this chapter, we discussed how international law is a way for social institutions to enforce rules at individual, community, national, and international levels to reduce violence based on custom or treaty. Issues of human rights, war crimes, international security, and the regulation of armed conflict enter the arbitration of international law courts such as the European Court of Human Rights and the International Criminal Court. However, international law, much as we have seen with the criminal justice system, has its limitations in effectively preventing violence, and in some cases may perpetuate violence through the sovereignty of nations and a lack of effective enforcement authority.

A system of international law and courts can solve many problems of violence in theory but in practice, to a large extent, states have often criminally harmed individuals and other states with impunity. The world community thus faces considerable challenges in implementing an international legal framework to prevent violence. While there have been successful applications of international law, often member states' unwillingness to comply renders rulings moot and the international legal institutions have low prosecution rates and cases that go on for many years without resolution. The attempt to arbitrate internationally fields such as human rights, war crimes, and armed conflict marks the start of a global effort to resolve disputes within a commonly accepted and fair legal forum with universally agreed-upon precedents and international customs and conventions. Nevertheless, global security, mass migrations, and economic and environmental crisis make international cooperation imperative and urgent. International legal institutions represent critical development of consensus through collaborative problem-solving and the upholding of commonly held customs and conventions, and should be supported at the same time as strengthening enforcement authority.

Reforms and procedural changes, in addition to more participation from signatories, are necessary for certain international bodies of law to reach their potential to rule effectively. Although international treaties such as conventions against torture or protecting women's and children's rights have provided guidelines that nations can implement, there is still a significant gap between the guidelines and enforceable laws. There are problems establishing programs that account for social norms unique to cultures or that respond to particular cultural problems, such as alcoholism in New Caledonia. While there is movement in international law toward peace—exemplified by the UN, the WHO, and the *Journal of Peace Research*—there is a corresponding movement in the direction of greater weapons development, such as in Israel,

North Korea, and the US; a lucrative global arms trade; and exploitation of military and economic power to gain more power. There are also theoretical constraints: there is little evidence that supports the efficacy of deterrence, especially with often irrational, symbolically-driven criminals; the fragmented and narrow focus of the moral-legal approach often misses the structural context and conditions that give rise to the crime; laws may suppress organic social movements; and finally, criminal law only acts *post mortem* after tragedies.

Legal foundations might therefore be considered in more proactive ways in collaboration, for example, with public health, as we will see in Chapter 12. *Therapeutic jurisprudence* is one example of where we consider not just the laws but their impact on the health and behavior of people. We know, for example, that reward and recognition are far more powerful in shaping behavior than threats and the fear of retribution, and legal sanctions and penalties may not be a sufficient means of preventing human rights abuses or of curbing violence. What is necessary, rather, is to elevate a society's level of health in ways that attract all players to constructive cooperation. This involves fostering a culture of caring, which laws can reflect as well as help build through protection. Given the ecological nature of violence, the passing of every law will have bearing on the rate of violent deaths, regarding which one can ask the question: does it reduce inequities or not? Considerations of greater social wellbeing and the benefits of collaboration over competition may allow for a focus beyond individual rights, to working toward a social and economic system that reflects justice and fairness and would help to reduce conditions that produce much violence.

Questions

1 How does law function to enforce rules at individual, community, national, and international levels?

2 What are some of the sources of international law?

3 What are some examples of the institutions of international law?

4 What are some of the challenges and the limitations of these institutions?

5 How might the global community strengthen international law?

References

A and Others v. the UK. (2004). UKHL 56.

A and Others v. the UK. (2009). Application No. 3455/05.

A, B, and C v. Staatssecretaris van Veiligheid en Justitie. (2014). Cases C-148/13 to C-150/13.

Abramowitz, S., & Moran, M. (2012). International human rights, gender-based violence, and local discourses of abuse in postconflict Liberia. *African Studies Review, 55*(2), 119–146.

Ahmad, K. (2004). Violence prevention receives international attention. *Lancet, 363*(9404), 220.

Alston, P. (2014). Against a world court for human rights. *Ethics and International Affairs, 28*(2), 197–212.

American Convention on Human Rights. (1969). Retrieved from https://www.cidh.oas.org/basicos/english/basic3.american%20convention.htm

Anand, R. P. (1982). *Origin and development of the law of the sea: History of international law revisited*. The Hague, Netherlands: Nijhoff.

Andriciuc and Others v. Banca Românească SA. (2017). Case C-186/16.

Anwukah, O. J. (2016). The effectiveness of international law: Torture and counterterrorism. *Annual Survey of International and Comparative Law, 21*(1), 1–28.

Armstead, J., & Holmes, J. (1998). The international criminal court: History, development and status. *Santa Clara Law Review, 38*(3), 745–835.

Artusy, D. V. (2014). The evolution of human rights law in Europe: Comparing the European court of human rights and the ECJ, ICJ, and ICC. *Inquiry Student Pulse, 6*(11), 1–4.

Barnes, G. P. (2011). The International Criminal Court's ineffective enforcement mechanisms: The indictment of president Omar Al Bashir. *Fordham International Law Journal, 34*(6), 1584–1619.

Bassiouni, M. C. (1998). *International criminal law*. Ardsley, NY: Transnational.

Bisharat, G. (2013). Violence's law. *Journal of Palestine Studies, 42*(3), 68–84.

Bleier v. Uruguay. (1982). Communication No. 30/1978.

Bosnia and Herzegovina v. Serbia and Montenegro. (2007). Judgment, ICJ Reports 2007, p. 43.

Burnett, A. (2015). *International environmental law*. Washington, DC: American Society of International Law.

Cdebaca, L. (2011). Successes and failures in international human trafficking law. *Michigan Journal of International Law, 33*(1), 37–51.

Chelimo, G. C. (2011). Defining armed conflict in international humanitarian law. *Inquiries Journal, 3*(4), 1.

Chibber, K. S., & Krishnan, S. (2011). Confronting intimate partner violence. *Mount Sinai Journal of Medicine, 78*(3), 449–457.

Convention against Torture and Other Cruel, Inhuman or Degrading Treatment or Punishment. (1984). Retrieved from https://www.ohchr.org/EN/ProfessionalInterest/Pages/CAT.aspx

Convention and Protocol Relating to the Status of Refugees. (1951). Retrieved from http://www.unhcr.org/en-us/3b66c2aa10

Convention for the Suppression of the Traffic in Persons and of the Exploitation of the Prostitution of Others. (1949). Retrieved from https://www.ohchr.org/EN/ProfessionalInterest/Pages/TrafficInPersons.aspx

Convention on the Elimination of All Forms of Discrimination against Women. (1979). Retrieved from http://www.un.org/womenwatch/daw/cedaw

Convention on the Elimination of All Forms of Racial Discrimination. (1965). Retrieved from https://www.ohchr.org/EN/ProfessionalInterest/Pages/CERD.aspx

Convention on the Prevention and Punishment of the Crime of Genocide. (1948). Retrieved from https://www.ohchr.org/EN/ProfessionalInterest/Pages/CrimeOfGenocide.aspx

Convention on the Rights of the Child. (1989). Retrieved from https://www.ohchr.org/en/professionalinterest/pages/crc.aspx

Council Directive. (2004). Retrieved from https://eur-lex.europa.eu/legal-content/EN/TXT/PDF/?uri=CELEX:32004L0083&from=ES

Cover, R. M. (1986). Violence and the word. *Yale Law Journal, 95*(8), 1601–1629.

Deady, C. W. (2014). *Incarceration and recidivism: Lessons from abroad*. Newport, RI: Pell Center for International Relations and Public Policy.

European Convention of Human Rights. (1950). Retrieved from https://www.echr.coe.int/Documents/Convention_ENG.pdf

Evans, M. D. (2014). *International law*. Oxford, UK: Oxford University Press.

Farrington, D. P., & Ttofi, M. M. (2009). School-based programs to reduce bullying and victimization. *Campbell Systematic Reviews, 6*.

F v. Bevándorlási és Állampolgársági Hivatal. (2018). Case C-473/16.

Ferguson, C. J., San Miguel, C., Kilburn, J. C., & Sanchez, P. (2007). The effectiveness of school-based anti-bullying programs a meta-analytic review. *Criminal Justice Review, 32*(4), 401–414.

Geneva Conventions. (1949). Retrieved from https://www.icrc.org/eng/assets/files/publications/icrc-002-0173.pdf

Goedde, P. (2010). Legal mobilization for human rights protection in North Korea: Furthering discourse or discord? *Human Rights Quarterly, 32*(3), 530–574.

Grotius, H. (1625). *De Jure belli ac pacis libri tres, in quibus jus naturae et gentium, item juris publici praecipua explicantur*. Paris, France: Buon.

Hamelin, C., Salomon, C., Sitta, R., Gueguen, A., Cyr, D., & Lert, F. (2009). Childhood sexual abuse and adult binge drinking among Kanak women in New Caledonia. *Social Science and Medicine, 68*(7), 1247–1253.

Hamilton, L. V. (1978). Who is responsible? Toward a social psychology of responsibility attribution. *Journal of Social Psychology, 41*(4), 316–328.

Hoffman, S., & Rattingen, J. (2015). Assessing the expected impact of global health treaties: Evidence from 90 quantitative evaluations. *American Journal of Public Health, 105*(1), 26–40.

International Committee of the Red Cross (2004). *International humanitarian law: Answers to your questions*. New York, NY: Author.

International Convention on the Protection of the Rights of All Migrant Workers and Members of Their Families. (1990). Retrieved from https://www.ohchr.org/EN/ProfessionalInterest/Pages/CMW.aspx

International Covenant on Civil and Political Rights. (1966). Retrieved from https://www.ohchr.org/en/professionalinterest/pages/ccpr.aspx

International Covenant on Economic, Social and Cultural Rights. (1966). Retrieved from https://www.ohchr.org/EN/ProfessionalInterest/Pages/CESCR.aspx

International Justice Resource Center. (2011). *Overview of the human rights framework*. San Francisco, CA: Author.

Jakobsson, A., von Borgstede, C., Krantz, G., Spak, F., & Hensing, G. (2013). Possibilities and hindrances for prevention of intimate partner violence: Perceptions among professionals and decision makers in a Swedish medium-sized town. *International Journal of Behavioral Medicine, 20*(3), 337–343.

Jennings, S. R., & Watts, S. A. (1992). *Oppenheim's international law*. London, UK: Longmans.

Kelsen, H. (1957). *Collective security under international law*. Washington, DC: U.S. G.P.O.

Kolstrein, A. M., & Jofre, M. I. T. (2013). Bullying: An analysis from the perspective of human rights, target groups, and interventions. *International Journal of Children's Rights, 21*(1), 46–58.

Krug, E. G., Mercy, J. A., Dalhberg, L. L., & Zwi, A. B. (2002). The world report on violence and health. *Lancet, 260*(933), 1083–1088.

Lauterpacht, H. (1927). *Private law sources and analogies of international law, with special reference to international arbitration*. London, UK: Longmans, Green, and Company.

Lee, B. X., Leckman, J. F., & Mbwambo, J. K. (2014). Violence and health: Current perspectives from the WHO violence prevention Alliance. *Aggression and Violent Behavior, 6*(19), 609–615.

Lissitzyn, O. J. (1964). Bilateral agreements on air transport. *Journal of Air Law and Commerce, 30*, 248–263.

Malhotra, A., & Schuler, S. R. (2005). Women's empowerment as a variable in international development. In D. Narayan-Parker (Ed.), *Measuring empowerment: Cross-disciplinary perspectives*. Washington, DC: World Bank.

Mcadam, J. (2012). *Climate change, forced migration and international law*. Oxford, UK: Oxford University Press.

Meier, B., & Ayala, A. (2014). The Pan American Health Organization and the mainstreaming of human rights in regional health governance. *Journal of Law, Medicine, and Ethics, 42*(3), 356–374.

Nasu, H. (2011). The expanded conception of security and international law: Challenges to the UN collective security system. *Amsterdam Law Forum, 3*(3), 15–33.

Nicaragua v. United States. (1984). Judgment of November 26, 1984, ICJ 39.

Office of the United Nations High Commissioner for Human Rights (2008). *Human rights, terrorism and counter-terrorism.* Geneva, Switzerland: Author. Retrieved from https://www.ohchr.org/Documents/Publications/Factsheet32EN.pdf

Olweus, D. (1991). Bully/victim problems among schoolchildren: Basic facts and effects of a school based intervention program. *Development and Treatment of Childhood Aggression, 17,* 411–448.

Optional Protocol to the Convention on the Rights of the Child on the Involvement of Children in Armed Conflict. (2000). Retrieved from https://www.ohchr.org/EN/ProfessionalInterest/Pages/OPACCRC.aspx

Optional Protocol to the Convention on the Rights of the Child on the Sale of Children, Child Prostitution and Child Pornography. (2000). Retrieved from https://www.ohchr.org/EN/ProfessionalInterest/Pages/OPSCCRC.aspx

Ortiz-Barreda, G., & Vives-Cases, C. (2013). Legislation on violence against women: Overview of key components. *Revista Panamericana de Salud Publica, 33*(1), 61–72.

Peet, E. (2015, June 15). Why is the International Criminal Court so bad at prosecuting war criminals? *Wilson Quarterly.*

Prosecutor v. Kony, Otti, Odhiambo, and Ongwen. (2005). International Criminal Court, ICC-02/04-01/05.

Prosecutor v. Kunarac, Kovac, and Vukovic. (2001). United Nations International Criminal Tribunal for the former Yugoslavia, IT-96-23 and 23/1.

Quinteros v. Uruguay. (1983). Communication No. 107/1981.

Qureshi, S. (2013). The recognition of violence against women as a violation of human rights in the United Nations system. *South Asian Studies, 28*(1), 187–198.

Robertson, G. (2013). *Crimes against humanity: The struggle for global justice.* New York, NY: New Press.

Rodgers, W. H. (1994). *Hornbook on environmental law.* Eagan, MN: West Group.

Romany, C. (1993). Women as aliens. *Harvard Human Rights Journal, 87*(6), 87–125.

Rome Statute of the International Criminal Court. (1998). Retrieved from https://www.icc-cpi.int/nr/rdonlyres/ea9aeff7-5752-4f84-be94-0a655eb30e16/0/rome_statute_english.pdf

Rules of Court of the European Court of Human Rights. (2002). Retrieved from http://www.echr.coe.int/documents/rules_court_eng.pdf.

Rules of Court of the International Court of Justice. (1978). Retrieved from http://www.icj-cij.org/documents/index.php?p1=4andp2=3and.

Samantha, B., & John, T. (2010). *Philosophy of international law.* Oxford, UK: Oxford University Press.

Sands, P. (2014). *Greening international law.* Abingdon, UK: Routledge.

Savolanien, J. (2000). Inequality, welfare state, and homicide: Further support for the institutional anomie theory. *Criminology, 38*(4), 1021–1042.

Schiff, B. (2008). *Building the international criminal court.* Cambridge, UK: Cambridge University Press.

Schiff Berman, P. (2005). *From international law to law and globalization.* Hartford, CT: University of Connecticut School of Law.

Shaw, C. R., & McKay, H. D. (1942). *Juvenile delinquency and urban areas.* New York, NY: Routledge.

Shaw, M. N. (2008). *International law*. Cambridge, UK: Cambridge University Press.

Shaw, M. N. (2010). *International law. Encyclopædia Britannica*. Chicago, IL: Encyclopædia Britannica.

Slavery Convention. (1926). Retrieved from https://www.ohchr.org/EN/ProfessionalInterest/Pages/SlaveryConvention.aspx

Slomanson, W. (2011). *Fundamental perspectives on international law*. Boston, MA: Wadsworth.

Statute of the International Court of Justice. (1945). Article 38, 1. Retrieved from http://legal.un.org/avl/pdf/ha/sicj/icj_statute_e.pdf

Steinglass, M. (2014, May 23). America and international law: Why the sheriff should follow the law. *The Economist*.

Swartz, J. J. (2013). *Oxford English dictionary* (2nd ed.). Oxford, UK: Per Linguam.

Sztucki, J. (1974). *Jus Cogens and the Vienna convention on the law of treaties: A critical appraisal*. Berlin, Germany: Springer-Verlag.

Trachtman, J. (2008). *Economic structure of international law*. Cambridge, MA: Harvard University Press.

United Nations. (1945). *Charter of the United Nations*. New York, NY: Author. Retrieved from http://www.un.org/en/charter-united-nations

United Nations. (1948). *Universal declaration of human rights*. New York, NY: Author. Retrieved from http://www.ohchr.org/EN/UDHR/Documents/UDHR_Translations/eng.pdf

United Nations. (1959). *Declaration of the rights of the child*. New York, NY: Author. Retrieved from https://www.unicef.org/malaysia/1959-Declaration-of-the-Rights-of-the-Child.pdf

United Nations. (1966a). *International covenant on economic, social and cultural rights*. New York, NY: Author. Retrieved from https://www.ohchr.org/EN/ProfessionalInterest/Pages/CESCR.aspx

United Nations. (1966b). *International covenant on civil and political rights*. New York, NY: Author. Retrieved from http://www.ohchr.org/Documents/ProfessionalInterest/ccpr.pdf

United Nations. (1966c). *International covenant on economic, social and cultural rights*. New York, NY: Author. Retrieved from http://www.ohchr.org/Documents/ProfessionalInterest/cescr.pdf

United Nations. (1993). *Declaration on the elimination of violence against women*. New York, NY: Author. Retrieved from http://www.un.org/documents/ga/res/48/a48r104.htm

United Nations. (2000). *Protocol to prevent, suppress and punish trafficking in persons especially women and children, supplementing the United Nations convention against transnational organized crime*. New York, NY: Author. Retrieved from https://www.ohchr.org/EN/ProfessionalInterest/Pages/ProtocolTraffickingInPersons.aspx

United Nations. (2003). *Norms on the responsibilities of transnational corporations and other business enterprises with regard to human rights*. New York, NY: Author. Retrieved from https://www.environmentandhumanrights.org/resources/Norms%20on%20the%20Responsibilities%20of%20Transnational%20Corporations%20and%20Other%20Business%20Enterprises%20with%20Regard%20to%20Human%20Rights.pdf

United Nations. (2011). *Guiding principles on business and human rights*. New York, NY: Author. Retrieved from https://www.ohchr.org/Documents/Publications/GuidingPrinciplesBusinessHR_EN.pdf

United Nations. (2017a). *Global compact for migration*. New York, NY: Author. Retrieved from https://www.ohchr.org/EN/Issues/Migration/Pages/GlobalCompactforMigration.aspx

United Nations. (2017b). *Global compact on refugees*. New York, NY: Author. Retrieved from https://refugeesmigrants.un.org/refugees-compact

Urdal, H., Ostby, G., & Gleditsch, N. P. (2014). *Journal of Peace Research Peace Review, 26*(4), 500–504.

Vázquez, C. M. (2005). *Direct vs. indirect obligations of corporations under international law.* Washington, DC: Georgetown University Law Center.

Velásquez-Rodríguez v. Honduras. (1988). Judgment of July 29, 1988, Inter-Am. Ct. H. R. (Ser. C) No. 4.

Von Glahn, G. (1992). *Law among nations: An introduction to public international law.* New York, NY: Macmillan.

Wilkinson, R. G., & Pickett, K. (2010). *Spirit level: Why greater equality makes societies stronger.* New York, NY: Bloomsbury.

Wolf, A., Gray, R., & Fazel, S. (2014). Violence as a public health problem: An ecological study of 169 countries. *Social Science and Medicine, 104,* 220–227.

World Bank. (2000). Making transition work for everyone: Poverty and inequality in Europe and Central Asia. Retrieved from http://documents.worldbank.org/curated/en/571801468037741599/pdf/multi-page.pdf

X, Y, and Z v. Minister voor Immigratie. (2013). Cases C-199/12 to C-201/12.

Zwi, A. B. (2004). How should the health community respond to violent political conflict? *PLoS Medicine, 1*(1), e14.

Cures (Continued)

Part VI   Prevention Framework

12

Public Health Approaches

Introduction

> Arguably the greatest technological triumph of the century has been the public-health system… fully half of us are alive today because of the improvements.
> —*Richard Rhodes,* Visions of Technology *(2012)*

We now transition from "law and order" approaches to those of "recovery and restoration," or of health. Public health is sometimes called the art of preventing disease and of promoting health (Berrigde, 2016). It focuses on the safety and wellbeing of communities and populations as a whole, where violence is a major burden. The shift from seeing human violence as an inevitable criminal justice and security issue, to which we can only respond, to seeing it as a preventable health problem that we can solve through scientific research is a major advance of just the past few decades. An *upstream–downstream* model (McKinlay, 1979) explains public health using the imagery of a swiftly flowing river, where upstream are preventive measures and health promotion interventions and downstream are disease and illness. Understanding that disease is a process, public health aims to intervene early at the upstream level, through disease prevention and health promotion, to allow for the greatest possible reduction of disease and suffering for whole populations at the downstream level. In violence prevention, this means the reduction of incidents and propensities for violence through changes in the causes and conditions that give rise to violence in the first place. The field involves much more than just proper intervention, to include advocacy and policymaking, and it relies on health assessment, health economics, and other important activities related to the overall promotion and protection of the population's general health. In this manner, the public health approach is a science-driven, population-based, interdisciplinary, and multisectoral response system that emphasizes prevention and focuses on providing the maximum benefit for the largest number of people.

The principles of public health provide a useful framework for investigating and understanding the extent and causes of violence. The population that public health addresses can be as small as a handful of people or as large as the total global population. Public health incorporates *epidemiology* (the study of the distribution and determinants of health and disease states), *biostatistics* (the analysis and interpretation of data relating to human health and disease), and *health services* (the maintenance and improvement of health through the prevention and treatment of injury and disease) and relies on scientifically tested and proven principles. Its approach to violence prevention involves improving the health and safety of all individuals by addressing underlying risk factors in a way that lessens the likelihood that individuals or groups will become victims or perpetrators of violence.

Violence: An Interdisciplinary Approach to Causes, Consequences, and Cures, First Edition. Bandy X. Lee.
© 2019 John Wiley & Sons, Inc. Published 2019 by John Wiley & Sons, Inc.

Just as public health efforts have prevented and reduced infectious diseases, pregnancy-related complications, workplace injuries, and illnesses resulting from contaminated food and water supplies, they can also reduce the incidence of violence by improving the larger social, cultural, political, economic, and environmental conditions. Modern public health practice is multidisciplinary, with the team consisting not only of public health workers and professionals, including physicians specializing in public health and preventive medicine, but also specialists as diverse as: epidemiologists, biostatisticians, nurses, midwives, nutritionists, microbiologists, neuroscientists, psychologists, sociologists, economists, lawyers, bioethicists, environmental health officers, education experts, and others (Joint Task Group on Public Health Human Resources, Advisory Committee on Health Delivery and Human Resources, & Advisory Committee on Population Health and Health Security, 2005).

In this chapter, we will show how the rapid developments over the past few decades have been instrumental in shifting toward a view of human violence as a preventable health problem. We will discuss how public health promotes interdisciplinary research and multisectoral collaboration. We will show how the ecological model, in particular, fosters an understanding of the commonality and interconnectedness of different types of violence, extending even further our initial bio-psycho-socio-environmental framework. We will discuss public health's typology of violence in terms of self-directed, interpersonal, and collective violence and its practice of identifying and responding to wide-ranging risk factors. Interdisciplinary and multisectoral efforts have shown that violence is preventable. Demonstrating through public health that it is possible to prevent violence, based on evidence and implementation, is perhaps one of the greatest achievements in our effort to curb human violence.

History

Public health has roots as deep as Antiquity, when the theory of *miasma*, or "bad air," gave leaders a role in regulating behavior as well as the environment to contain the spread of communicable diseases. By Roman times, proper diversion of human waste became a focus for urban areas, and the Ancient Chinese devised methods to slow the spread of smallpox through inoculation. Cramped and unsanitary conditions following the Industrial Revolution led to the establishment of public health institutions in the nineteenth century and the Poor Law Commission in the UK declaring that the large-scale governmental expenditures necessary for prevention "would ultimately amount to less than the cost of the disease now constantly engendered" (Rosen & Imperato, 2015). Subsequent actions led to the building of sewers, regular garbage collection, clean water supplies, and the drainage of standing water. English physician John Snow (1855) established the science of epidemiology, which tracks and analyzes disease patterns, their causes and effects, in defined populations. As germ theory gradually replaced that of miasma, methods for isolating bacteria and developing vaccines became a prevalent form of disease control, through the pioneering work of French chemist Louis Pasteur and German scientist Robert Koch. As the twentieth century saw a decrease in the prevalence of infectious diseases, public health began to focus more on issues such as infant mortality, cancer, and heart disease, and education on the behaviors and lifestyles that contribute to these conditions.

As violence, including homicide and suicide, emerged as a leading cause of death (CDC, 2009; Dahlberg & Mercy, 2009; Peden et al., 2000), it started to attract the attention of physicians and other health officials. Additionally, a variety of factors caused suicide and homicide rates to rise steadily through most of the second half of the twentieth century (Blumstein & Wallman, 2006; Wilson & Petersilia, 2010), necessitating a response from governments and the community (CDC, 1994; UNODC, 2011). While the US has been home to some of the most regressive responses to violence, such as its criminal justice system, it has also been home to some of the most progressive. It began with a 1979 report by then Surgeon General C. Everett Koop, who declared violence a public health problem (US Department of Health, 1979). Governmental and non-governmental institutions began to consider violence prevention as the responsibility of public health organizations and agencies. The US Centers for Disease Control and Prevention launched one of the world's first violence epidemiology departments in 1983 (Dahlberg & Mercy, 2009). Beginning with reports on youth violence and the necessity to involve healthcare workers to decrease it, violence was officially recognized as a public health problem, as epidemiological research methods were applied to homicide and suicide for the first time. In the 1990s, a new era began with setting and implementing preventive strategies to reduce youth violence and making impact assessments to highlight successes.

Global recognition of violence as a public health problem grew as similar efforts arose in countries around the world. Then a watershed moment happened in 1996, when the World Health Assembly (WHA, 1996) declared violence a public health priority. The World Health Organization (WHO) then took steps to create the Department of Violence and Injury Prevention and to assemble all available evidence up to that time in the *World Report on Violence and Health (WRVH)* (Krug et al., 2002). This document served as the foundation for subsequent scholarship and became a call to action by all nations and international organizations. Many scholars (Bloom, 2001; Slutkin, 2012) have since advocated a view of violence as an infectious disease that can spread among individuals, generations, and even populations in a global context. Researchers, community organizations, and policymakers began to use this scientific scholarship to inform the development of interventions and policies (WHO, 2010). Nowadays, it is well-established that violence is a complex problem that arises from biological, psychological, socioeconomic, cultural, and environmental conditions.

Framing violence as a worldwide health concern emphasized the need to move away from criminology, law, and politics toward public health, preventive medicine, and mental health. Beginning in the Global North but finding increasing traction in the Global South, violence has been increasingly taken seriously as a fundamental obstacle to human health and development (Bowman et al., 2008; Matzopolous et al., 2008). Systematic study showed the efficacy and cost-effectiveness of prevention, in contrast to retribution after the fact, highlighting community programs, mentorship, parenting classes, and better access to healthcare over policing, prisons, and military intervention. By placing the different types of violence—that is, self-directed, interpersonal, and collective violence—under the same rubric, the WHO welcomed efforts to understand them in totality, with an ecological perspective (Krug et al., 2002). This fostered an understanding of their commonalities and interconnections, as well as common causes and modes of intervention.

As the allied fields of health dramatically expanded their evidence base on the causes, manifestations, and prevention of violence through scientific study, social scientists, clinicians, and field implementers responded to a need to inform and sensitize awareness of the psychological and cultural dynamics behind the epidemiology and population trends. Because of the complex, multifaceted nature of violence, the public health approach emphasized a multisectoral response. Finally, it was a revolutionary step when the United Nations (2015) took on violence prevention as one of the central concerns in sustainable development. Cooperative efforts from diverse sectors such as health, social welfare, criminal justice, and education are now encouraged in order to solve a wide range of problems that give rise to violence, target vulnerable groups, or leave any marginalized groups behind. The underpinnings of a public health-oriented approach to violence prevention encapsulate around three basic principles: (a) the ecological framework; (b) a typology of violence; and (c) public health method, which we will discuss in the next few sections.

The Ecological Framework

Among the three basic principles of the public health approach to violence—(a) the ecological framework; (b) a typology of violence; and (c) the public health method—the first two have played a key role in structuring and broadening inquiry and are conceptual schemes. The third is more practical, and has helped to shape action in response to what has been learned about violence. The first conceptual scheme is *the ecological framework*, and it emphasizes the multifaceted nature of violence (see Figure 12.1). The layers that the WHO uses are as follows: individual, relationship, community, and societal. Derived from sociological models (Bronfenbrenner, 1979), this framework maintains that violence is a complex outcome of intersecting risk factors across the human lifespan, and no single factor can explain why some people or groups are at higher risk for violence than others. This model contrasts one that is called *reductionistic*, which is an approach to violence, disease, or any other phenomenon that claims that its ultimate source is one basic cause.

For example, let us take the example of youth violence. In order for a youth to engage in violence, what factors might be contributing to the violent behavior? At the individual level, there may be biological, neurological, and psychological factors: substance use, low intelligence, and history of victimization are possibilities. At the relationship level, conflict with a parent or a significant other may exist. At the family level, there may be low monitoring, poor family functioning, or harsh disciplinary practices. At the community level, high concentrations of impoverished residents, disruption and disorganization of neighborhoods, or ineffective schools can contribute. At the level of society, high levels of economic inequality and shaming, or cultural norms of gender and racial inequality can stimulate violence at the individual level. Thus, in order to understand an individual, the entire ecological system of the person's developmental context needs to be considered. Violence is the outcome of interactions between many different factors at many different levels, and a cross-disciplinary and developmental perspective is necessary. The ecological model highlights the influence of factors across levels, so that different dynamics can be happening simultaneously to produce a single result.

The ecological framework also applies to interventions; early research in high-income countries (Scott, 2008), for example, showed that actions at all levels for youth violence prevention are effective. Prenatal and infancy programs, early childhood education, parent training, after-school recreation, mentoring with contingent reinforcement, youth employment with education, organizational change in schools, community mobilization, school behavior management strategies, community and school policies, and media campaigns in five countries between 1989 and 2011 to prevent child physical abuse were all effective in reducing violence (Poole, Seal, & Taylor, 2014). Programs to prevent child violence, involving parents by helping them better communicate with their children, are proven to be particularly effective, as are early-childhood education programs in preventing violence-related consequences in the short

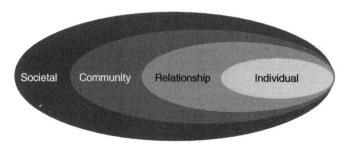

Figure 12.1 The Ecological Model explores the relationship between individual and contextual factors and considers violence as the product of multiple levels of influence.

and long term. Moreover, therapies such as cognitive behavioral therapy and policies that limit alcohol consumption to indirectly prevent related violence are highly effective as well (Sumner et al., 2015).

In light of this research, the ecological framework asserts that the only way to understand violence fully is to consider the parts in relation to the whole, and how the different tiers of risk or protective factors interact with one another within the whole. Different approaches therefore need always to be part of the conversation in order to attain a fuller understanding of the magnitude and nature of violence (Lee, Leckman, & Khoshnood, 2015). An obvious advantage of the ecological framework is that it offers a visual depiction of different levels of risk and protective factors all together (individual, relationship, community, and society). The disadvantage of the model is perhaps that it can depict only a limited number of dimensions, such that time and other underlying, dynamic processes are not simultaneously visible. It is therefore important to keep in mind that the model is fluid and suggestive of additional layers, rather than definitive.

A Typology of Violence

The ecological framework has also allowed for the study of different types of violence in relation to one another, and this brings us to our second concept in the public health approach to violence: a *typology of violence*. This is just one typology among many possible distinctions, since the emphasis is on unity and variety. Thus, the study of violence is no longer fragmented by field of study as before: for example, criminology for homicide; psychiatry for suicide; political science and history for warfare; and anthropology for culturally specific forms of violence. Rather, a broader health approach tries to understand violence in totality, where there is a continuum among the different types of violence in terms of shared root causes and common core characteristics as the various types of violence interact and interweave. It considers four modes in which violence might occur: physical, sexual, psychological, and through deprivation.

This typology further divides violence into three subtypes according to the victim—perpetrator relationship. *Self-directed violence* refers to violence in which the perpetrator and the victim are the same individual, and it is subdivided into self-abuse and suicide. *Interpersonal violence* refers to violence between individuals, and is subdivided into family, intimate partner, and community violence; the first two categories include child maltreatment, intimate partner violence, and elder abuse, while the third is divided into acquaintance and stranger violence and includes youth violence, assault by strangers, violence related to property crimes, and violence in workplaces and other institutions. *Collective violence* refers to violence committed by larger groups of people and can be subdivided into social, political, and economic violence. A major contribution of the *WRVH* has been to present this typology of violence under one rubric, allowing for unification—as well as systematic categorization—of the types of violence that had hitherto been considered separate and unrelated.

Prevailing cultural norms, poverty, social isolation, and factors such as substance abuse and access to firearms are risk factors for multiple types of violence. As a result, it is not unusual for some individuals at risk to experience more than one type of violence. Associations have been found between suicidal behavior and child maltreatment (Dube et al., 2001), intimate partner violence (Campbell, 2002), sexual assault (Joiner et al., 2007), and abuse of the elderly (Dong, 2005). In many countries that have suffered violent conflict, the rates of interpersonal violence remain high even after the cessation of hostilities. Cross-national and international studies reveal that combining suicide and homicide data can increase the robustness of results and reveal trends that may not have been apparent before (Lee et al., 2014; Lee, Wexler, & Gilligan, 2014).

The Public Health Method

The individual-to-collective typology of violence necessarily invokes a public health approach to methodology. *The public health method* is the last of the three basic principles of the public health approach to violence that we have described, after the ecological framework and a typology of violence. It is also the most practical, resting on the premise that improving the health of populations is as important as protecting that of individuals (Haegerich & Massetti, 2013). It is traditionally characterized in terms of three levels of prevention: *primary prevention*, or interventions that aim to prevent violence before it occurs; *secondary prevention*, or interventions that focus on the more immediate responses to violence, such as prehospital care and emergency services; and *tertiary prevention*, or interventions that focus on long-term care in the wake of violence, such as rehabilitation, reintegration, and attempts to reduce the long-term disability associated with violence (Gilligan, 2001). Public health emphasizes primary prevention, at the widest scale possible, aiming to prevent negative health outcomes before their occurrence rather than simply remedying those outcomes (DeGue et al., 2012). For example, primary prevention may result in improving health through altering the impact of social, environmental, and economic determinants of health (Boyce et al., 2010).

The practice of public health generally follows four steps: (a) describing and monitoring the problem, tracking trends; (b) identifying factors that increase risk and those that promote positive behavior; (c) developing and evaluating prevention policies to reduce risk factors and increase positive behavior; and (d) broadly disseminating and implementing these policies and strategies (Mercy et al., 1993). It emphasizes the need to monitor the effects of interventions on risk factors and on target outcomes through the surveillance of cases and health indicators, as well as to evaluate their impact and cost-effectiveness over extended periods of time. It also addresses the great disparity in healthcare access and building initiatives between high- and low-to-middle-income countries. It is currently working to address, for example, the troubling 90/10 gap, whereby 90% of published research comes from regions of the world where only 10% of global violence is occurring (Lee et al., 2016).

The public health approach has shown that the prevention of violence is possible, not as an article of faith, but based on evidence: examples of success abound around the world, from small-scale individual and community efforts to policy and legislative interventions at local, national, and international levels (World Health Organization [WHO], United Nations Office on Drugs and Crime [UNODC], & United Nations Development Programme [UNDP], 2014). Most countries acting at the sociocultural level, for example, have been able to prevent violence against women with the promotion of gender equality; youth violence usually responds to nurturing relationships and life skills development; and programs involving health professional support help reduce elder abuse. At the societal level, targeted strategies addressing the harmful and excessive use of alcohol intake and firearms possession are common (WHO, 2010).

Violence Prevention

Because of public health involvement, we have vastly grown in our awareness that violence is preventable, and that prevention is far more effective than intervention at a later stage. A major study found that educational programs for inmates led to long-term savings of up to six or seven times the investment cost, for example, mainly by lowering reincarceration and increasing employment after release (Davis et al., 2013). A series of briefings have summarized evidence for effective programs for advocates, program designers, and implementers into seven categories: (a) increasing safe, stable, and nurturing relationships between children and their parents and caregivers; (b) developing life skills in children and adolescents; (c) reducing the availability and harmful use of alcohol; (d) reducing access to guns, knives, and pesticides; (e) promoting gender equality; (f) changing cultural norms that support violence; and (g) victim identification, care, and support.

First, *developing safe, stable, and nurturing relationships* between children and their parents and caregivers in their early years that can prevent child maltreatment and reduce childhood aggression. They also help prevent lifelong consequences of child maltreatment in mental and physical health, social and occupational functioning, and individual and social development and security. Studies in high-income countries have shown that the Nurse Family Partnership home-visiting program and the Positive Parenting Program (PPP) reduce child maltreatment by providing health advice, child development education, and positive child management strategies (Prinz, Sanders, Shapiro, Whitaker, & Lutzker, 2009). Parent and child programs join parenting education with child education, social support, and other services.

Second, *developing life skills in children and adolescents* can prevent youth violence. Evidence shows that social, emotional, and behavioral skills acquired in social development programs can help children and adolescents deal effectively with the challenges of life. Programs that target children early in life can prevent involvement in violence, improve social skills, boost educational achievement, and improve job prospects. The effects are greatest in children from disadvantaged backgrounds (Heckman, 2006), but their applicability to low-income and middle-income countries is yet unclear. In the US, investments in high-quality programs early in an individual's life may last into adulthood.

Third, *reducing the availability and harmful use of alcohol* is thought to prevent violence, although randomized controlled trials are lacking. Most of the evidence comes chiefly from developed countries and some parts of Latin America. Regulation of alcohol availability can occur by restricting sale hours or days and by reducing retail outlets. Economic modeling suggests that raising alcohol prices can also lower consumption and associated violence. Interventions that use cognitive behavioral therapy have shown to reduce child maltreatment, intimate partner violence, and suicide (Bisson & Andrew, 2007). Some evidence is beginning to support interventions around drinking establishments that target crowding, comfort level, physical design, staff training, and access to late-night transport.

Fourth, *reducing access to guns, knives, and pesticides* appears to prevent homicides among young men of 15–29 years, suicides, and injuries, although more rigorous studies are needed. Jurisdictions with restrictive firearm legislation and lower firearm ownership have lower gun violence, while restrictive firearm policies—including bans, licensing restrictions, minimum buyer ages, and background checks—have shown effectiveness in Australia, Austria, Brazil, and New Zealand (Ozanne-Smith et al., 2004). Studies in Colombia and El Salvador show promise for enforced bans on carrying firearms in public. Safer pesticide storage, bans, and less-toxic replacements might help prevent many of the estimated 370,000 suicides by pesticide ingestion every year.

Fifth, *promoting gender equality* may help prevent violence against women. While further research is needed, social and educational programs could help promote gender equality by challenging stereotypes and cultural norms that give men power and control over women. Safe Dates in the US and the Youth Relationship Project in Canada address dating violence with positive results (Wolfe et al., 2003). Community interventions are also showing good outcomes, such as the Intervention with Microfinance for AIDS and Gender Equity (IMAGE) initiative in South Africa, which combines microfinance with gender equity training, and Stepping Stones in Africa and Asia, which is a life skills program in relationship skills, assertiveness training, and communication about the human immunodeficiency virus (HIV) (Kim et al., 2007).

Sixth, *changing cultural and social norms that support violence* can help reduce violence. Interventions that challenge rules or expectations of behavior within a cultural or social group are thought to reduce violence, but there is not yet much evidence for their effectiveness. Further rigorous evaluations of such interventions are required. Some evidence exists for the effectiveness of interventions challenging social and cultural norms related to gender in addressing dating violence and sexual abuse among teenagers and young adults. Other programs appear promising, including media campaigns that target youth education on violence through entertainment ("edutainment") to help reduce intimate partner violence (Fabiano et al., 2003).

Last, *victim identification, care, and support* programs can help break cycles of violence from one generation to the next. Improvements to emergency response systems and the ability of the healthcare sector to treat and rehabilitate victims; screening tools to identify victims of violence and referring them to appropriate services; ensuring that health, judicial, policing, and social services avoid repeat victimization; psychosocial interventions such as trauma-focused cognitive behavioral therapy; and social support and advocacy services that protect families at risk and reduce stress on caregivers have all shown to be effective (Sullivan, Bybee, & Allen, 2002). Policies that address social determinants of violence are also important, as much as violence has links with gender and social inequalities that place large segments of the population at risk. At the national level, legislative and legal reforms, communication campaigns that raise public awareness of the problem, training and monitoring of police and public officials, and educational or economic incentives for disadvantaged groups can all contribute. Social protection policies and programs are under considerable strain in many parts of the world as a result of globalization, debt and structural adjustments, the transition from planned to market economies, and armed conflicts. Many countries have seen real wages fall, basic infrastructures deteriorate, and the quality and quantity of healthcare, education, and social services decline. Given the established links between these conditions and violence, it is imperative that comprehensive violence prevention strategies not only address specific risk factors but also integrate policies directed at these macro-level societal factors (Butchart et al., 2004).

Multisectoral Collaboration

The complexity and diversity of human violence means that intervention requires the collaboration of multiple sectors, and public health provides a primary example. To go beyond disease prevention to enhance health promotion, for example, may involve collaboration with specialists in fields as diverse as geography, community planning, and media. Strategies must consider the cross-cutting issues of political, cultural, educational, and economic concerns. A multisectoral approach to decision-making creates room for systematic synthesis of research to affect the design of public health policies. Scientists and practitioners have the opportunity to get together and to link research and practice in ways that *overcome differences* in specialized language and be beneficial especially to a global effort to prevent violence (Degutis, 2012). Collaboration can also help relieve tensions in the growing gap in perspective between those who are working "from the top" and those who are personally affected by problems and policies "on the ground."

Multisectoral collaborations can be as effective in violence prevention as they are in tobacco control, acquired immunodeficiency syndrome (AIDS) prevention, and cardiovascular disease reduction. The government, the private sector, and civil society are the *key stakeholders* involved in executing various public health policies. In order to attain maximum effectiveness, all these parties have to engage one another actively and to allow for a proportionate distribution of roles. A lack of planning will imply duplication of roles and at the same time blindness to important aspects of service provision. Due to the large amount of ground that falls under the public health umbrella, the stakeholders must factor in a large network of sectors so as to enhance coordination.

Working with various sectors can allow for a *greater pool of expertise*, knowledge, and resources to come together. When the various players have a common objective, they will engage in endeavors that boost the efforts of the other parties (Pawinski & Lalloo, 2006) and have a better chance of attaining a comprehensive plan that will help achieve their goals as well as improve lives (Cooper, 2016). A common pool of resources will create greater flexibility and room in the operations that ensure services for a greater portion of the population. Moreover, the personnel in the various sectors who bring different expertise can contribute their knowledge to the development of a comprehensive implementation plan. Interactions create opportunities for innovation, and a team has a better chance of designing creative, more effective policies that meet the needs of the time. A deliberate plan on division of labor also reduces efforts while having the potential to increase interaction in comparison to isolated implementations of programs.

In relation to the educational objectives of public health, the collaborative process will create room for *tailoring messages* to target groups. Different geographic locations and cultural variations pose different types of needs and challenges. In recent decades, high-income countries have increased investment in violence prevention policies and evidence-informed programs. However, there has not yet been a response to the challenge of scaling up violence prevention investments in low- and middle-income countries. A sharing of financial resources and technical support for programming might flow from high- to low- and middle-income countries, while low- and middle-income countries can provide data and a better understanding of the global violence that disproportionately affects them.

Coordination among the various players enhances the specificity of the educational program. Paying attention to the issues involved and creating a process to work through them can help eliminate barriers and combat regional and societal inequities (Hamann et al., 2011). Above all, a consolidated team is more likely to create better approaches that have a significant influence on the target population (European Commission, 2017). Coordinated processes are more likely to take into account diversity issues in the workforce, allowing room for everyone to come to the table and leaving no person or sector behind. Furthermore, when the stakeholders adopt a common language, the target population will be more receptive, which increases the possibility of societal transformation.

Another advantage of multisectoral coordination is *improved infrastructure*. Coordination between public health and criminal justice agencies, for example, could improve, as the two arms of government that have the highest stakes in violence prevention. Efficient communication networks help fill gaps in services and reduce redundancies. The team can form service delivery organizations at state, local, tribal, and territorial levels of government (Guell et al., 2017). A clear communication protocol will ensure that program managers can easily respond to the needs of local populations. Geographical distributions of service centers further allow for analysis of the effectiveness of the various policies.

The level of *community involvement* will also go a long way in determining the effectiveness of joint undertakings. Multisectoral coordination must carry out a comprehensive study of target communities before embarking on any empowerment program. Many societies present distinct cultural practices that may contradict the methods of program implementers. Studying their belief systems will ensure that the collaborative team arrives at a plan that respects the community's choices while still addressing the target problems in an informed, evidence-based way. Public consultation and citizen juries form a credible means of information gathering. Working with members of the community in disbursing resources and providing education in a way that is sensitive to community needs has a higher chance of success (Yach et al., 2003). At global levels, recognizing the interconnectedness and interactions of global health is important, so that relationships can develop across regions to facilitate collaborative projects and research agendas.

Finally, stakeholders can organize *scientific research teams* to evaluate the problems on the ground before they embark on finding solutions (Bowen, 2004). Local research is first and foremost valuable for local violence prevention, but it is also an important component of the larger research effort that tries to understand violence on a global scale. Some global priorities might include: the common risk and protective factors that apply across different cultures and societies; promising prevention programs that have widespread implications; and the relationship between violence and the influence of globalization on economic, sociocultural, and environmental factors. Conducting retrospective studies to identify the measures that have a positive impact can help in the design of better methods that save time and resources in the future (Armstrong et al., 2006). Evaluating the intervention programs and modifying them according to research should be incorporated into every intervention design (Stover & Bassett, 2003). Of course, without multisectoral collaboration, there cannot be the kind of wide-scale, objective analysis and assessment of gaps that we currently have, not to mention the larger perspective and comprehensive approach inherent in a global study of violence. Applying the principles of public health allows for investigating and understanding the causes and consequences of violence at large scale, as well as for directly applying that knowledge to prevention programs, policy interventions, and advocacy. Multisectoral collaboration thus fosters a healthy culture that can grow through challenges and experiences of cooperation (Bowen, Martens, & Need to Know Team, 2005), and to build a healthy ethos that enhances alliances and environments conducive to concerted efforts.

The broader public health perspective reveals, furthermore, that violence prevention efforts can no longer remain within national boundaries but must vigorously take on the promotion of *global health*. The WHO has played a key role in this endeavor, by fostering the groupings of states, international agencies, and international networks of governmental and nongovernmental organizations. Additionally, it has convened major world players in the field through its Violence Prevention Alliance (VPA) in order to implement what it identified in the *WRVH* (Lee, Leckman, & Mbwambo, 2014). In a Global Campaign for Violence Prevention, the Alliance continues to meet every year, and every other year with WHO Member States to hold milestones meetings, with an education-based influence on policy and law.

The *WRVH* definition of violence emphasizes process over event, and power over simple physical force, widening the scope to include important forms of violence such as structural violence, of which the effects are less visible but no less harmful, as we see in instances of material deprivation or psychological damage (Galtung, 1969). The underlying social dynamics play a significant role, even in individual violence, which finally highlights the close connection between violence and basic human rights. Societies with high levels of inequality typically witness higher rates of violence, and increases in new forms of international violence are expected from the context of widening of wealth gaps between individuals and between countries.

Challenges and Possibilities

The public health approach to violence, as noted, has many advantages. However, its strengths can also become its deficits. Most notably, its reliance on epidemiology and other *quantitative methods* allows for the pooling of information from large populations, but it can also overlook nuances and important variations. Its models usually look for commonalities across different settings and populations, not providing for ethnic or cultural variations, which allows for widespread dissemination of programs but sometimes also insensitivity to local needs, inefficiency, and even harm. Finally, it is unable to measure characteristics or values that are of importance to individuals, and this can, in the name of care, unwittingly result in poor communication or a disregard for aspects that matter to the individuals actually receiving care. Collaborating with anthropologists and ethnographers can help mitigate through research based on *qualitative methods* that aid in understanding better the different cultures, social values, and experience (O'Campo & Dunn, 2012).

We mentioned in the section "The Ecological Framework" that the ecological model can depict only limited dimensions, leaving out gradations as well as invisible, dynamic processes. A result of this is that the model, while bringing to light important relationships between different levels, can also give a simplistic rendition regarding the quantity, proportion, and elasticity of those levels (Easterling, Ellner, & Dixon, 2000). A solution to this would be to emphasize less the actual categories as the concept of gradations itself. Just as we juxtapose the bio-psycho-socio-environmental model with the ecological model to offer a variation in perspective, there are multiple ways of devising divisions for the ease of study and awareness of variety. At the same time, we employ these schemes with the recognition that there is more than one way to partition a continuum that also functions as a whole.

The same holds true for the current typology of violence. While it is useful to subdivide violence, the subdivisions can become rigid and also result in silos (Lee et al., 2016). Social scientists have buffered this effect by adding other important layers and intersections for the consideration of violence, emphasizing the political, structural, symbolic, and everyday aspects of violence (Bourgois, 2001). These added dimensions help scholars to conceive of human violence in its complexity as well as to add nuances to the study of violence but need to be more central. The science-based yet practical focus of public health sometimes omits an intimate understanding of violence as a human phenomenon with great individual or cultural variation (Zwi, 2004). Peace promotion can also derive from a developmental perspective across the lifespan (Leckman, Panter-Brick, & Salah, 2014). A new kind of violence in the last few decades that involves global flows of images, capital, and identity formation within the same local world lies at the heart of contemporary ethnic or religious conflicts (Das, 2000) and cannot be considered without symbolic and subjective dimensions.

Even if great progress has occurred so far in addressing violence as a public health problem, research on violence and on implementation of prevention programs should continue, at both the macro level and the level of specific forms, with all their complexity. The *Global Status Report on Violence Prevention 2014* (WHO, UNODC, & UNDP, 2014) shows that actions on alcohol abuse are not sufficient in many countries; firearms policies are not homogeneous worldwide; violence against women and homicide are still poorly reported; and services specific to elderly violence prevention are absent in most countries, as are mental health services. The *Global Status Report* (WHO et al., 2014) informs us that violence of all types is not monitored for the general population in more than half of all countries; existing national action plans concern, most of the time, specific forms of interpersonal violence without relying on data; only some countries are acting on risk factors through social and educational measures; and even if laws against violence exist, they often lack application. At the international level, many UN agencies are involved, and the *2030 Agenda for Sustainable Development* (UN, 2015) is a critical step, but there is no coordinating agency. Despite the emphasis on standardizing data collection methods, available evidence can be of low quality (Khan et al., 2015).

Furthermore where substantial data are available, translating them into action at the provincial or national level is a challenge. A major obstacle is simply a lack of knowledge: for many decision-makers, the idea that violence is preventable is new or questionable. They may be very eager to make changes for prevention but have little access to the scientific evidence, or even when they do, they have difficulty understanding it, because it has not been made accessible. To others, since the majority of violence lies hidden, such as in the case of abuse of children, women, and the elderly, violence only seems a matter to deal with when it arrives at the doorstep, through some crisis or widely publicized event. For still others, since the problem of violence can be daunting, the solution may a priori seem difficult; this would be true if responses remained on a case-by-case basis, after the violence has occurred, but we now know that primary prevention is far more effective and far less costly, sometimes without any cost other than sound, informed policy.

This brings us to perhaps the greatest barrier, which is determination. Violence can be an emotionally charged issue, and some countries may be reluctant to take on initiatives that challenge long-established beliefs or practices. It may require considerable political courage to shift away from criminal justice toward community policing and public health programs. Understandably, in both high- and low-income countries, most efforts focus on tertiary prevention—dealing with the visible and immediate consequences of violence such as providing support to victims and punishing offenders. While important and in need of strengthening, these are the least efficient responses, allowing for much damage and suffering to happen before intervention. Even in high-income countries, where more evidence is available, public health officials struggle with massively constrained budgets (Rabarison et al., 2015), and while putting research into action curtails homicides and suicides (Frieden et al., 2005) and literally saves lives (Sistrom & Hale, 2006), funds for public health organizations continue to dwindle. This perpetuates the cycle wherein insufficient funding and resources to conduct appropriate research inhibits the improvement in communities' health in ways that could become costly (Massoudi et al., 2017). Violence prevention especially lags behind other areas of health in terms of the priority and resources it receives. Violence may also serve other functions, such as to scare populations into supporting certain policies that are in the interest of those in office. Because of these challenges, the close collaboration of public health officials, healthcare practitioners, academic institutions, and civil society organizations with policymakers is essential. There is much work to do to help develop sensible programs and policies, and to educate the public to build confidence in workable interventions.

Finally, rapid social change in response to strong global pressures can overwhelm existing social structures and controls over behavior on which public health programs depend. We have seen that the removal of market constraints and the increase in incentives for profits can result in much freer access to alcohol, drugs, and firearms, undermining efforts to reduce related violent incidents. All these effects can be explained through the public health model and addressed through: (a) universal interventions (approaches aimed at groups or the general population without regard to individual risk); (b) selected interventions (approaches aimed at those considered at heightened risk for violence); and (c) indicated interventions (approaches aimed at those who have already demonstrated violent behavior and need treatment or containment) (Tolan & Guerra, 1994).

Case Studies

A Prenatal Care Program

The Australian healthcare system appears remarkably successful in delivering good health outcomes at reasonable costs, and Australians enjoy one of the longest life expectancies. Its Medicare system invests heavily in prenatal care, offering a wide variety of options and encouraging choice with regard to type of care and place of giving birth. Midwives, obstetricians, and other doctors offer their services through this scheme in the hospital, the community clinic, the birth center, or any of the publicly funded homebirth programs. The government focuses a great deal of attention on how the woman must decide—if her pregnancy is going well—where to give birth and what type of care she wishes to receive. It created "publicly funded home births" in order to allow women to give birth in the comfort of their own homes. The public system runs these programs, and there are certain criteria to meet for eligibility: for example, the pregnant woman must live within a certain distance of a hospital in case something happens, and her pregnancy must be healthy and determined to be "low risk."

Regardless of where and how a woman decides to give birth, the government offers antenatal classes that include breastfeeding education, exercise regimes, and dietary information for expecting women. If a woman decides to give birth in her home, then she qualifies to receive postnatal care, which is when midwives and obstetricians go to her house to check up on her. These free home visits vary depending on the time of recovery needed. Sometimes a breastfeeding consultation is available to see there is a proper latch from the baby. Even though this program is not available in all Australian territory, in some areas it is underway and fully operating. In areas where this insurance is not in effect, the family can opt for a "sharing scheme"; midwives and doctors at their local maternity hospital will provide antenatal care, but the actual birth can take place where the family has decided, unless the mother must be transferred to a hospital (Craswell, Kearney, & Reed, 2016). Such planned focus on prenatal care at the governmental level is very effective and is a good investment at myriad levels, especially in violence prevention.

Family Violence Prevention

Previously known as the Family Violence Prevention Fund, Futures without Violence is a nonprofit organization that has been helping women, children, and men who have suffered from domestic and sexual violence by creating programs and policies, and campaigning worldwide alongside individuals and charity organizations that strive to end violence in each nation. Futures without Violence was behind the passage of the Violence Against Women Act in 1994, which was the US's first federal response to violence against communities and families, specifically as it affects women. Futures without Violence offers educational and training programs to doctors, coaches, judges, teachers, and nurses in order to be aware of signs of violence and of abuse in children. These types of programs have been around for many years, educating professionals for over 30 years, but recently they have started to gain more popularity as violence in schools has increased. Many studies have shown that when children see and experience violence in their homes, they are more likely to be aggressive toward other people in a different setting, for example, at school. Futures without Violence works with politicians, policymakers, and volunteers who are trying to build a self-sustained community that could lead the way and educate others about the importance of respect, healthy relationships, and self-esteem.

Some programs Futures without Violence has launched include the following:

- "Coaching Boys into Men" encourages boys to talk about their lives and the importance of respect. They do so while promoting and participating in different types of sports. This program has been exported from the US to South Africa, Canada, Australia, New Zealand, and India.
- "RESPECT!" is a campaign that has been designed to advocate for respect in relationships.
- "That's not Cool" is a national public service advertising campaign that makes heavy use of Futures without Violence mobile apps. It is aimed at informing teenage students about what violence is, how it is represented, and how it can happen in relationships.

Futures without Violence advocates resilience especially for children and for women who have suffered violence in the past. It also provides help in terms of healthcare, social services, and educational and judicial services (Chamberlain & Levenson, 2013).

School-Based Violence Prevention

The Universal School-Based Violence Prevention Program, based in the US, aims to reduce violence within all North American schools. It provides support and encourages the skills needed to have emotional self-awareness, working alongside therapists to promote self-esteem within the target population. It also teaches students how to solve social problems that may arise in their schools or neighborhoods, while practicing conflict resolution skills. Even though this program is "universal," its promotion has mainly been in schools across North America, despite the aim to make it an international school-based violence prevention program that will help to reduce violence and victimization among students and teachers. As a matter of fact, Universal School-Based Violence Prevention programs aim to make visible what it means to be violent, how youth react to it, and what the staff could do to help in stopping this type of behavior by inspiring young people to build emotional connections to one another in communicating their problems and their needs.

The implementation of this program usually occurs at the pre-kindergarten level up to high school, and the usual target schools are in high-risk areas with surroundings of high crime rates and low standards of living in comparison to other areas. A unique characteristic of this program is that it is taught in the familiarity of students' own classrooms, instead of as an extra session outside of their comfort zone. Research shows that violence prevention programs are most effective if they start at a young age. Violence decreases not only in the school environment but in other areas, such as the students' homes, at their jobs, and in their relationships (Hahn et al., 2007).

Bullying Prevention

Dan Olweus, a Norwegian psychologist at the University of Bergen, is a pioneer of bullying research. He has spent several decades researching the issue of bullying and is known for the most researched and widely adopted bullying prevention program. In the early 1970s, Olweus initiated the world's first systematic bullying research, viewing school safety as a fundamental human right. In 1981, he proposed enacting a law against bullying in schools so that students could be spared the repeated humiliation implied in bullying. By the mid-1990s, these arguments led to legislation against bullying by the Swedish and Norwegian parliaments. In 1983, three adolescent boys in Norway died by suicide, and the act was most likely a consequence of severe bullying by peers. The Norwegian Ministry of Education initiated a national campaign against bullying in schools and, as a result, the first version of the Olweus Bullying Prevention Program was developed (Smith, Pepler, & Rigby, 2004).

The Olweus Bullying Prevention Program is designed for students of the third to tenth grades. It is a program that requires some duration, since while it can be effective with younger students in as little as 8 months, with older students it may require several years. It is a school-wide program that is implemented at the school level, the classroom level, through individual students, and in the community. Under the assumption that a variety of risk and protective factors determine and reinforce bullying behavior, it intervenes at the level of the child, the peer group, the classroom, and the school. Teachers and school staff deliver the program through a range of activities after a schoolwide review of the amount and severity of bullying, using a questionnaire. A prevention program coordination committee implements schoolwide strategies to address the specific bullying problems the questionnaire identifies. Classroom-level activities include a series of rules aimed at discouraging bullying behaviors. Individual activities include specific rules and actions for addressing individual incidents of bullying through interventions with the victims, bullies, and their parents. The Olweus Bullying Prevention Program has been shown not only to reduce bullying, victimization, and antisocial behavior such as vandalism, fighting, theft, and truancy, but also to improve the social climate of classrooms (Olweus & Limber, 2010).

Firearm Restriction Policies

Jurisdictions with more restrictive firearm policies and lower firearm ownership are likely to experience lower levels of firearm violence. Australia, Austria, Brazil, and New Zealand offer examples of national reforms of firearm laws, while Colombia and El Salvador demonstrate their effects at the municipal level.

Australia: After a 1996 firearm massacre in Tasmania in which 35 people died, Australian governments united to remove semi-automatic and pump-action shotguns and rifles from civilian possession, as a key component of gun law reforms. More than a decade free of fatal mass shootings followed, alongside accelerated declines in firearm deaths, particularly suicides. Total homicide rates followed the same pattern (Chapman et al., 2006).

Austria: In 1997, Austria introduced new laws requiring purchasers of firearms to be at least 21, have a valid reason to purchase a firearm, and undergo background checks and psychological testing. In addition, the legislation requires a 3-day waiting period between licensing and purchasing, together with safer firearm storage. After the introduction of these laws, firearm suicides, which had been increasing, began to fall without an increase in suicides by other means. The new laws have also been associated with a falling demand for firearm licenses and a drop in gun homicides (Kapusta et al., 2007).

Brazil: Following some of the highest homicide rates in the world, Brazil reformed its firearm legislation in 2003. The new laws raised the minimum purchase age to 25, prohibited firearms outside the home or the workplace, made it illegal to own unregistered firearms, introduced buyer background checks, and controlled firearm imports. A voluntary disarmament scheme also returned over 450,000 firearms, and a 9% decrease in firearm homicides and suicides followed within 2 years of these laws. Additionally, accidental firearm deaths dropped by 15%, and firearm-related deaths of "undetermined intent" by 26% (Marinho de Souza et al., 2007).

New Zealand: After a mass shooting in 1990, the government instituted a rigorous licensing system requiring photos of firearm owners and regular renewals, tests to ensure that applicants understand the laws governing firearms, and police assessment of all applicants. It also calls for safe and locked storage of guns in areas separate from ammunition. The system has significantly reduced firearms suicides, particularly among people 25 years and under, although it is uncertain whether other forms of suicide increased during this time (Beautrais, Fergusson, & Horwood, 2006).

Colombia: Local legislation in Colombia banned the carrying of firearms in the cities of Cali and Bogotá on holidays, weekends following paydays, and election days. The bans were enforced with police checkpoints, searches during traffic stops, and routine police work. The incidence of homicides dropped in both cities on days when the ban was in place, compared to similar days when people were allowed to carry guns (Villaveces et al., 2000).

El Salvador: Municipalities in an Arms-Free Municipalities project, which began in August 2005, made it illegal to carry firearms in parks, schools, plazas, recreation centers, and other locations. The project also aimed to increase police capacity to enforce firearms bans, run a media campaign on the danger of guns and the nature of the new regulations, and implement a voluntary firearms surrender and collection scheme. The project initially reported a 47% reduction in homicides in participating municipalities and other successes, but reductions in homicides did not persist beyond the first year (Cano, 2006).

Conclusion

Public health tells us that, although violence has been with us since the dawn of history, it is not an inevitable part of the human condition, nor an intractable problem that we must learn to accept. On the contrary, there are very specific interventions that we can apply to reduce both its occurrence and its consequences. We might say that the type of violence is culture-dependent, but the level of violence is health-dependent. In this chapter, we reviewed how a better understanding of violence leads to a better capacity to prevent. We studied the ecological model that the WHO has put forth, with the layers of individual, relationship, community, and society, and the typology of violence, with the categories of self-directed, interpersonal, and collective violence. We discussed the interdisciplinary and multisectoral efforts that have shown violence to be preventable, although there are sometimes barriers to the implementation of measures. Yet, solutions in the form of partnerships and multilateral collaborations grow ever more promising, and prevention based on research and evidence all the more certain and efficient.

Although important information gaps still exist, we have learned useful lessons about the predictability and preventability of violence: approaching violence as a public health problem, rather than merely one of isolated individuals, can help identify factors that contribute to the prevalence of violence within certain populations, even where direct causality may be difficult to establish. There are associations between violence and individual or family factors—such as impulsivity, depression, poor parenting resources, strict gender norms, and domestic conflict—and between violence and macro-level factors—such as rapid social change, loss of social cohesion, sharp economic downturns, deteriorating public services, and rises in inequality. Local factors—such as high availability of weapons, certain patterns of drug dealing, and social acceptability of violence in particular neighborhoods—also play a role in producing violence. Identifying and measuring these factors can give timely warnings to decision-makers when action is necessary, and the tools for taking action are growing as research advances. Acting only after highly visible incidents of violence occur and then investing resources in short-term programs is highly inefficient in comparison to primary prevention efforts at the "upstream" level that allow for small investments to have large and long-lasting benefits.

Different types of violence are interlinked in many important ways and suggest a strong potential for partnerships: local government and community leaders, police and prison officials, social service providers, medical professionals, and researchers, as different as their fields are, can come together around common goals. Such partnerships allow for multifaceted, effective interventions; efficiency by avoiding duplication of efforts; enhancement of resources through the pooling of funds and personnel; and coordination of research and complementary expertise sharing that increases understanding. While much is possible through grassroots organizing, the success of public health efforts, including violence prevention, depends ultimately on political commitment at the national and international levels to ensure sustained support, funding, proper legislation, and legitimacy in the public consciousness. It recognizes that the health of a society is integrally linked with the successful prevention of violence against the self or another, or against one's own group or another, and the maintenance of security and peace. The goal of producing a healthier society for all allows for the joining of activities highly relevant to reducing violence, including those dealing with economic matters, access to healthcare, human rights, international law, and sustainable development. While public health practitioners and researchers contribute greatly by providing the public and policymakers with solid information on the prevalence, consequences, and effective management of violence, national governments, the UN, and bilateral development agencies have an important role to play in the development of sustained, multisectoral action plans.

Questions

1   What is the focus of public health, and how does this relate to violence prevention?

2   How has the health sector shifted in its view of human violence?

3   What are the main principles of public health?

4   What are the strengths of health promotion and multisectoral collaboration?

5   What are some of the challenges of public health?

References

Armstrong, R., Doyle, J., Lamb, C., & Waters, E. (2006). Multi-sectoral health promotion and public health: The role of evidence. *Journal of Public Health*, 28(2), 168–172.

Beautrais, A. L., Fergusson, D. M., & Horwood, L. J. (2006). Firearms legislation and reductions in firearm-related suicide deaths in New Zealand. *Australian and New Zealand Journal of Psychiatry*, 40(3), 253–259.

Berrigde, V. (2016). *Public health: A very short introduction*. Oxford, UK: Oxford University Press.

Bisson, J., & Andrew, M. (2007). *Psychological treatment of post-traumatic stress disorder*. New York, NY: Wiley.

Bloom, S. L. (2001). *Violence: A public health menace and a public health approach*. London, UK: Karnac Books.

Blumstein, A., & Wallman, J. (2006). *The crime drop in America*. New York, NY: Cambridge University Press.

Bourgois, P. (2001). The power of violence in war and peace: Post-Cold War lessons from El Salvador. *Ethnography*, 2(1), 5–24.

Bowen, S. (2004). *The Need to Know project evaluation, 2002–2004*. Winnipeg, MB: Manitoba Centre for Health Policy.

Bowen, S., Martens, P., & Need to Know Team (2005). Demystifying knowledge translation: Learning from the community. *Journal of Health Services Research & Policy*, 10(4), 203–211.

Bowman, B., Matzopoulos, R., Butchart, A., & Mercy, J. A. (2008). The impact of violence on development in low-to middle-income countries. *International Journal of Injury Control and Safety Promotion*, 15(4), 209–219.

Boyce, T., Peckham, S., Hann, A., & Trenholm, S. (2010). *A pro-active approach. Health promotion and ill-health prevention.* London, UK: King's Fund.

Bronfenbrenner, U. (1979). Contexts of child rearing: Problems and prospects. *American Psychologist, 34*(10), 844–850.

Butchart, A., Phinney, A., Check, P., & Villaveces, A. (2004). *Preventing violence: A guide to implementing the recommendations of the world report on violence and health.* Geneva, Switzerland: World Health Organization. Retrieved from http://apps.who.int/iris/bitstream/handle/10665/43014/9241592079.pdf?sequence=1

Campbell, J. C. (2002). Health consequences of intimate partner violence. *Lancet, 359*(9314), 1331–1336.

Cano, I. (2006). *Living without arms? Evaluation of the arms-free municipalities project: An experience in risk-taking in a risky context.* San Salvador, El Salvador: United Nations Development Project.

Centers for Disease Control and Prevention (1994). Homicides among 15-19-year-old males-United States, 1963–1991. *Morbidity and Mortality Weekly Report, 43*(40), 725–727.

Centers for Disease Control and Prevention (2009). *Leading causes of death, 1900–1998.* Washington, DC: Author.

Chamberlain, L., & Levenson, R. (2013). *Addressing intimate partner violence, reproductive and sexual coercion: A guide for obstetric, gynecologic and reproductive health care settings.* San Francisco, CA: Futures without Violence.

Chapman, S., Alpers, P., Agho, K., & Jones, M. (2006). Australia's 1996 gun law reforms: Faster falls in firearm deaths, firearm suicides, and a decade without mass shootings. *Injury Prevention, 12*(6), 365–372.

Cooper, A. (2016). *Governing global health: Challenge, response, innovation.* Abingdon, UK: Routledge.

Craswell, A., Kearney, L., & Reed, R. (2016). "Expecting and connecting" group pregnancy care: Evaluation of a collaborative clinic. *Women and Birth, 29*(5), 416–422.

Dahlberg, L., & Mercy, J. (2009). History of violence as a public health issue. *The Virtual Mentor: VM, 11*(2), 167–172.

Das, V. (2000). *Violence and subjectivity.* Berkeley, CA: University of California Press.

Davis, L. M., Bozick, R., Steele, J. L., Saunders, J., & Miles, J. N. (2013). *Evaluating the effectiveness of correctional education: A meta-analysis of programs that provide education to incarcerated adults.* Santa Monica, CA: RAND Corporation.

DeGue, S., Simon, T. R., Basile, K. C., Yee, S. L., Lang, K., & Spivak, H. (2012). Moving forward by looking back: Reflecting on a decade of CDC's work in sexual violence prevention, 2000–2010. *Journal of Women's Health, 21*(12), 1211–1218.

Degutis, L. C. (2012). The future of injury and violence prevention: Where are we going? *Journal of Safety Research, 43*(4), 231–232.

Dong, X. (2005). Medical implications of elder abuse and neglect. *Clinics in Geriatric Medicine, 21*(2), 293–313.

Dube, S. R., Anda, R. F., Felitti, V. J., Chapman, D. P., Williamson, D. F., & Giles, W. H. (2001). Childhood abuse, household dysfunction, and the risk of attempted suicide throughout the life span: Findings from The Adverse Childhood Experiences Study. *JAMA, 286*(24), 3089–3096.

Easterling, M. R., Ellner, S. P., & Dixon, P. M. (2000). Size-specific sensitivity: Applying a new structured population model. *Ecology, 81*(3), 694–708.

European Commission. (2017). *Thematic session 2: Multisectoral approaches to tackling health inequalities—Concept paper.* Brussels, Belgium: Author. Retrieved from https://ec.europa.eu/health/sites/health/files/social_determinants/docs/ev_20171107_co02_en.pdf

Fabiano, P. M., Perkins, H. W., Berkowitz, A., Linkenbach, J., & Stark, C. (2003). Engaging men as social justice allies in ending violence against women: Evidence for a social norms approach. *Journal of American College Health, 52*(3), 105–112.

Frieden, T., Das-Douglas, M., Kellerman, S. E., & Henning, K. J. (2005). Applying public health principles to the HIV epidemic. *The New England Journal of Medicine, 353*(22), 2397–2402.

Galtung, J. (1969). Violence, peace, and peace research. *Journal of Peace Research, 6*(3), 167–191.

Gilligan, J. (2001). *Preventing violence*. London, UK: Thames and Hudson.

Guell, C., Mackett, R., & Ogilvie, D. (2017). Negotiating multisectoral evidence: A qualitative study of knowledge exchange at the intersection of transport and public health. *BMC Public Health, 17*(1), 17.

Haegerich, T. M., & Massetti, G. M. (2013). Commentary on subgroup analysis in intervention research: Opportunities for the public health approach to violence prevention. *Prevention Science, 14*(2), 193–198.

Hahn, R., Fuqua-Whitley, D., Wethington, H., Lowy, J., Crosby, A., Fullilove, M., ... Snyder, S. (2007). Effectiveness of universal school-based programs to prevent violent and aggressive behavior: A systematic review. *American Journal of Preventive Medicine, 33*(2), S114–S129.

Hamann, R., Giamporcaro, S., Johnston, D., & Yachkaschi, S. (2011). The role of business and cross-sector collaboration in addressing the "wicked problem" of food insecurity. *Development Southern Africa, 28*(4), 579–594.

Heckman, J. J. (2006). Skill formation and the economics of investing in disadvantaged children. *Science, 312*(5782), 1900–1902.

Joiner, T. E., Sachs-Ericsson, N. J., Wingate, L. R., Brown, J. S., Anestis, M. D., & Selby, E. A. (2007). Childhood physical and sexual abuse and lifetime number of suicide attempts: A persistent and theoretically important relationship. *Behaviour Research and Therapy, 45*(3), 539–547.

Joint Task Group on Public Health Human Resources, Advisory Committee on Health Delivery and Human Resources, & Advisory Committee on Population Health and Health Security. (2005). *Building the public health workforce for the 21st century*. Ottawa, Canada: Public Health Agency of Canada.

Kapusta, N. D., Etzersdorfer, E., Krall, C., & Sonneck, G. (2007). Firearm legislation reform in the European Union: Impact on firearm availability, firearm suicide and homicide rates in Austria. *British Journal of Psychiatry, 191*(3), 253–257.

Khan, O., Ferriter, M., Huband, N., Powney, M. J., Dennis, J. A., & Duggan, C. (2015). Pharmacological interventions for those who have sexually offended or are at risk of offending. *Cochrane Database of Systematic Reviews, 2*, CD007989.

Kim, J. C., Watts, C. H., Hargreaves, J. R., Ndhlovu, L. X., Phetla, G., Morison, L. A., ... Pronyk, P. (2007). Understanding the impact of a microfinance-based intervention on women's empowerment and the reduction of intimate partner violence in South Africa. *American Journal of Public Health, 97*(10), 1794–1802.

Krug, E. G., Dahlberg, L. L., Mercy, J. A., Zwi, A. B., & Lozano, R. (2002). *World report on violence and health*. Geneva, Switzerland: World Health Organization. Retrieved from http://apps.who.int/iris/bitstream/10665/42495/1/9241545615_eng.pdf

Leckman, J. F., Panter-Brick, C., & Salah, R. (2014). *Pathways to peace: The transformative power of children and families*. Cambridge, MA: MIT Press.

Lee, B. X., Donnelly, P. D., Cohen, L., & Garg, S. (2016). Violence, health, and the 2030 agenda: Merging evidence and implementation. *Journal of Public Health Policy, 37*(S1), 1–12.

Lee, B. X., Gilligan, J., Kaaya, S. F., & Schuder, K. K. (2016). Violence and health: Implications of the 2030 agenda for South-North collaboration. *International Journal of Public Health, 61*(8), 861–862.

Lee, B. X., Leckman, J. F., & Khoshnood, K. (2015). Violence, health, and South-North collaborations: Furthering an interdisciplinary agenda. *Social Science and Medicine, 146*(1), 236–242.

Lee, B. X., Leckman, J. F., & Mbwambo, J. K. K. (2014). Violence and health: Current perspectives of the WHO violence prevention alliance. *Aggression and Violent Behavior, 19*(6), 609–615.

Lee, B. X., Marotta, P. L., Blay-Tofey, M., Wang, W., & de Bourmont, S. (2014). Economic correlates of violent death rates in forty countries, 1962–2008: A cross-typological analysis. *Aggression and Violent Behavior, 19*(6), 729–737.

Lee, B. X., Wexler, B. E., & Gilligan, J. (2014). Political correlates of violent death rates in the U.S., 1900–2010: Longitudinal and cross-sectional analyses. *Aggression and Violent Behavior, 19*(6), 721–728.

Marinho de Souza, M. F., Macinko, J., Alencar, A. P., Malta, D. C., & de Morais Neto, O. L. (2007). Reductions in firearm-related mortality and hospitalizations in Brazil after gun control. *Health Affairs, 26*(2), 575–584.

Massoudi, M. S., Marcelin, R. A., Young, B.-R., Bish, C. L., Henry, D., Hurley, S., ... Giles, W. H. (2017). Prevention research centers: Perspective for the future. *American Journal of Preventive Medicine, 52*(3), S218–S223.

Matzopoulos, R., Bowman, B., Butchart, A., & Mercy, J. A. (2008). The impact of violence on health in low-to middle-income countries. *International Journal of Injury Control and Safety Promotion, 15*(4), 177–187.

McKinlay, J. B. (1979). Epidemiological and political determinants of social policies regarding the public health. *Social Science and Medicine, 13*(5), 541–558.

Mercy, J. A., Rosenberg, M. L., Powell, K. E., Broome, C. V., & Roper, W. L. (1993). Public health policy for preventing violence. *Health Affairs, 12*(4), 7–29.

O'Campo, P., & Dunn, J. R. (2012). *Rethinking social epidemiology: Towards a science of change.* Dordrecht, Netherlands: Springer.

Olweus, D., & Limber, S. P. (2010). Bullying in school: Evaluation and dissemination of the Olweus bullying prevention program. *American Journal of Orthopsychiatry, 80*(1), 124–134.

Ozanne-Smith, J., Ashby, K., Newstead, S., Stathakis, V. Z., & Clapperton, A. (2004). Firearm related deaths: The impact of regulatory reform. *Injury Prevention, 10*(5), 280–286.

Pawinski, R. A., & Lalloo, U. G. (2006). Multisectoral responses to HIV/AIDS: Applying research to policy and practice. *American Journal of Public Health, 96*(7), 1189–1191.

Peden, M., McGee, K., & Krug, E. (2000). *Injury: A leading cause of the global burden of disease, 2000.* Geneva, Switzerland: World Health Organization. Retrieved from https://www.who.int/violence_injury_prevention/publications/other_injury/injury/en/

Poole, M. K., Seal, D. W., & Taylor, C. A. (2014). A systematic review of universal campaigns targeting child physical abuse prevention. *Health Education Research, 29*(3), 388–432.

Prinz, R. J., Sanders, M. R., Shapiro, C. J., Whitaker, D. J., & Lutzker, J. R. (2009). Population-based prevention of child maltreatment: The U.S. Triple P system population trial. *Prevention Science, 10*(1), 1–12.

Rabarison, K. M., Bish, C. L., Massoudi, M. S., & Giles, W. H. (2015). Economic evaluation enhances public health decision making. *Frontiers in Public Health, 3*(164), 1.

Rhodes, R. (2012). *Visions of technology: A century of vital debate about machines, systems and the human world.* New York, NY: Simon and Schuster.

Rosen, G., & Imperato, P. J. (2015). *A history of public health.* Baltimore, MD: Johns Hopkins University Press.

Scott, K. A. (2008). *Violence prevention in low-and middle-income countries: Finding a place on the global agenda, workshop summary.* Washington, DC: National Academies Press.

Sistrom, M., & Hale, P. (2006). Outbreak investigations: Community participation and role of community and public health nurses. *Public Health Nursing, 23*(3), 256–263.

Slutkin, G. (2012). Violence is a contagious disease. In D. M. Patel, M. A. Simon, & R. M. Taylor (Eds.), *Contagion of violence: Workshop summary* (pp. 94–111). Washington, DC: National Academies Press.

Smith, P. K., Pepler, D., & Rigby, K. (2004). *Bullying in schools: How successful can interventions be?*. Cambridge, UK: Cambridge University Press.

Snow, J. (1855). *On the mode of communication of cholera*. London, UK: John Churchill.

Stover, G. N., & Bassett, M. T. (2003). Practice is the purpose of public health. *American Journal of Public Health, 93*(11), 1799–1801.

Sullivan, C. M., Bybee, D. I., & Allen, N. E. (2002). Findings from a community-based program for battered women and their children. *Journal of Interpersonal Violence, 17*(9), 915–936.

Sumner, S. A., Mercy, J. A., Dahlberg, L. L., Hillis, S. D., Klevens, J., & Houry, D. (2015). Violence in the United States: Status, challenges, and opportunities. *JAMA, 314*(5), 478–488.

Tolan, P., & Guerra, N. (1994). *What works in reducing adolescent violence*. Boulder, CO: Center for the Study and Prevention of Violence.

US Department of Health, Education, and Welfare. (1979). *Healthy people: The Surgeon General's report on health promotion and disease prevention*. Washington, DC: Author.

United Nations. (2015). *Transforming our world: The 2030 agenda for sustainable development*. New York, NY: Author. Retrieved from https://sustainabledevelopment.un.org/content/documents/21252030%20Agenda%20for%20Sustainable%20Development%20web.pdf

United Nations Office of Drugs and Crime. (2011). *2011 Global study on homicide: Trends, contexts, data*. Vienna, Austria: Author. Retrieved from https://www.unodc.org/documents/congress/background-information/Crime_Statistics/Global_Study_on_Homicide_2011.pdf

Villaveces, A., Cummings, P., Espitia, V. E., Koepsell, T. D., McKnight, B., & Kellermann, A. L. (2000). Effect of a ban on carrying firearms on homicide rates in 2 Colombian cities. *JAMA, 283*(9), 1205–1209.

Wilson, J. Q., & Petersilia, J., 2010. *Crime and public policy*. New York, NY: Oxford University Press.

Wolfe, D. A., Wekerle, C., Scott, K., Straatman, A. L., Grasley, C., & Reitzel-Jaffe, D. (2003). Dating violence prevention with at-risk youth: A controlled outcome evaluation. *Journal of Consulting and Clinical Psychology, 71*(2), 279–291.

World Health Assembly. (1996). *Prevention of violence: A public health priority*. Geneva, Switzerland: World Health Organization. Retrieved from http://www.who.int/violence_injury_prevention/resources/publications/en/WHA4925_eng.pdf

World Health Organization. (2010). *Violence prevention: The evidence*. Geneva, Switzerland: Author. Retrieved from http://apps.who.int/iris/bitstream/10665/77936/1/9789241500845_eng.pdf?ua=1

World Health Organization, United Nations Office on Drugs and Crime, and United Nations Development Programme. (2014). *Global status report on violence prevention 2014*. Geneva, Switzerland: World Health Organization. Retrieved from http://www.who.int/violence_injury_prevention/violence/status_report/2014/en

Yach, D., Hawkes, C., Epping-Jordan, J. E., & Galbraith, S. (2003). The World Health Organization's framework convention on tobacco control: Implications for global epidemics of food-related deaths and disease. *Journal of Public Health Policy, 24*(3–4), 274–290.

Zwi, A. B. (2004). How should the health community respond to violent political conflict? *PLoS Medicine, 1*(1), e14.

13

Global Medicine Approaches

Introduction

> Medicine is a social science, and politics is nothing else but medicine on a large scale.
> —*Rudolf Virchow,* Die Medizinische Reform *(1848)*

The health approach to violence has helped to revolutionize our ability to predict, prevent, and intervene in the problem (Gilligan, 2001). As this approach takes on more systemic, international, and population proportions, providing the maximum benefit to the greatest number of people has become more efficient. However, human beings are not just all can be lost if we forget the end point of these endeavors: the person. It helps to return to the original intent of medicine. Contrasting and complementing the *utilitarianism* of public health should be the *autonomy, beneficence* (doing good), *non-maleficence* (not doing harm), and *justice* principles that underlie medical ethics. Giving care is central to this intent (Kleinman, 2015), and unlike legal motivations that are based on the fear of punishment, caring motivations are based on acts of love and are thus far more powerful. This means caring for those who are vulnerable, meeting their needs sensitively with all our ability, while respecting their human dignity. Caring responds to pain and suffering, and tries to alleviate the unendurable so that fellow human beings can lead lives of purpose and meaning and attain their potentials in communities and environments that foster them. Global medicine is the branch of medicine concerned with the influence of environmental, climatic, and topographic conditions on health and the prevalence of disease in different parts of the world (Segen, 2006).

This chapter focuses not on the skills that are necessary at global levels, such as in determining global health policy, but on the human-level practices that are ultimate focus and intent of medicine. Medicine is generally accepted as the art and science of maintaining health through diagnosing, understanding, preventing, and treating disease. The original word in Latin, *medicina*, emphasizes the art of healing, harking back to the original meaning of the term as *ars medicina*, or "the medical art." In an era of biotechnology, informatics, and cognitive science on the one hand and globalization and large-scale statistical measurements on the other, global medicine can play a role in bringing us back to this "art," especially in the area of violence prevention. Consider, for example, the disastrous industrialization of medicine in the US, which has happened without the input of those actually delivering the health care, let alone those receiving it; leaving out the social and human dimensions, in favor of large-scale business, industry, and profit, the US system has become the most inefficient among countries measured (Murray & Frenk, 2010). Being clear about the goal of health care (the person) can seem at first a diversion, but brings practicality even more effectively than focusing on practical aspects alone.

Violence: An Interdisciplinary Approach to Causes, Consequences, and Cures, First Edition. Bandy X. Lee.
© 2019 John Wiley & Sons, Inc. Published 2019 by John Wiley & Sons, Inc.

Global health is based on the public health model, emphasizing epidemiology and quantitative studies, and sometimes implementing large-scale policies that bear little consideration of what happens on the ground. However, there are aspects that relate to the person and the subjective, human experience that the global public health model will not be able to encompass; it is simply not within their paradigm. The perspectives of the medical practitioner, who engages intimately and has privy to information on the patient that no one else does, may provide a remedy. Medicine is grounded in the interaction with the person and the personal, and to emphasize these aspects, we will label this practice *global medicine*, meaning the hands-on practice of medicine as performed by any medical professional (certainly not just physicians), but put in global context. In more traditional cultures, physicians are leaders within their communities playing a social role, more so than a technical service provider, because of these close encounters.

Because violence is a human problem that is complex and multidimensional, we will review the topic in light of this original intent of *humanism* in medicine. Medicine faces the challenge of maintaining its mission of caring for the human in the face of burgeoning biomedical knowledge and the division of tasks among specialists and allied professionals. Indeed, the inexorable drive toward technological solutions has caused many to be concerned that the definition of well-being may be subsumed in a total "quantification of self" through a norm that attempts to submit the whole of life to numerical data (Fondation Télécom, 2015). However, technology does not address, as individual experience and collective subjectivity do, notions of sacredness, honor, and other values that may be important to the person, even if it is not well understood how the two domains interact (Tournay & Leibing, 2010).

Medicine, therefore, needs to be a training ground for caring as an operative agenda that is no longer able to ignore the roles of compassion, respect, empathy, and love. The emotional, ethical, and spiritual dimensions that these sensibilities bring are a part of the whole self that defies reduction into lesser parts. There is a difference between bringing a stethoscope to an unresponsive patient and building a personal connection through inquiry, conversation, and presence. The latter must be taught and supported among trainees, and maintained among seasoned practitioners, just as much as the rest of medical knowledge. Global practice, then, faces the challenge of maintaining local sensitivity and the human-centered purpose of medical care in the face of almost exclusive reliance on quantitatively "measurable" phenomena, which can easily turn into technicization, bureaucratization, and monetization (Hill-Taylor et al., 2013).

While a global perspective has allowed us to avoid the narrow focus of caring only for those within our own boundaries, this caring can get caught up in an abstract, globalized universe unless we continually look to the local for grounding in human understanding. In this chapter, we will explore ways of retaining the original medical principles of caregiving and a human-centered approach through juxtaposing local and global dimensions. We will discuss how a model for caring needs to be kept close to all practices, especially in wider-system applications. This entails sensitivity to cultural and psychological needs, certainly, but also to each person's universal humanity. We will discuss how the experience and knowledge that derive from close contact is essential for good governance, and that collaboration between healthcare givers and policymakers is critical. The global medicine approach, therefore, intends to encompass more globally the whole self, while spreading practices of the more local, intimate encounter that is the hallmark of medicine.

Historical Background

Medicine is a field that goes back many thousands of years, during most of which it has been an art with highly religious, symbolic, and human dimensions. The early medical practices of Egypt, Babylon, China, and India seldom separated themselves from mystical and philosophical traditions, even as they explored the examination, diagnosis, prognosis, and treatment of numerous physical ailments. The Greeks went further, introducing advanced medical ethics and the Hippocratic Oath, still taken by doctors today, after the influential Hippocrates of Kos in the fifth century BCE (Riddick, 2003). After Hippocrates, the next significant physician was Galen, who studied and traveled widely in Ancient Rome, composed the *Ars Medica* (*Arts of Medicine*), and remained authoritative well into the Middle Ages (Siegel, 1973). Islamic civilization rose to primacy in medicine by taking Ancient Indian, Greek, Roman, and Byzantine practices and developing them before spreading them throughout the Arab Empire.

Throughout the Middle Ages, Christian, Jewish, and Muslim thinkers alike strove toward a system of medical ethics that served both the physical and the spiritual needs of their patients. The European Renaissance beginning in the fourteenth century emphasized both humanism, mainly through *studia humanitatis* or the knowledge of Ancient Greek and Roman texts (Siraisi, 2007), and experimental investigation through the study of human anatomy by the Dutch anatomist Andreas Vesalius (Presti, 2010). Physicians rose to the forefront of scientific practice during the eighteenth-century Age of Enlightenment. The American Medical Association (AMA) adopted its initial code, based largely on English physician Thomas Percival's work, in 1847. Then, in the aftermath of horrors perpetrated during World War II, the *Nuremberg Code* (1947) and the *Declaration of Helsinki* (1964) were the first to insist that all people, regardless of race, ethnicity, or gender, were to be treated as equally human by all medical professionals around the world.

Rapid advances in science through the nineteenth century changed the practice of medicine, as well as the approaches of physicians, who relied more on systematic analyses of patients' symptoms and new chemical and laboratory techniques, although the decline of most lethal diseases was more attributable to improved hygiene and nutrition. By the twentieth century, the diminishing importance of the art of medicine became a great concern, and efforts to balance ever-advancing scientific knowledge and innovation with personal experience and wisdom continues to this day. A focus on humanism in medicine has risen in response to this trend, in order to safeguard the art and caring aspects of medicine. These principles are as old as medicine itself, and healthcare provision more generally. Christian principles of charity—to feed the hungry, give water to the thirsty, shelter the homeless, relieve the sick, and comfort prisoners—were what led religiously devoted people of different social classes to contribute to caring for people affected by the diseases and natural disasters that devastated medieval Europe. For Catholic women, life as a nun brought prestige, and wealthy families provided dowries that funded convents and free care for the poor, well into the early modern era (Fissell, 2008).

While an Egyptian woman of 2700 BCE, Merit Ptah, is recognized in an inscription as "chief physician," women mostly practiced medicine without formal training or recognition. As ancillary healers and midwives, they took on a more caring than technical role until the late twentieth century. Nineteenth-century English social reformer and founder of modern nursing Florence Nightingale wrote about caring attitudes (Nightingale, 1859). The first American woman physician Elizabeth Blackwell believed that humane female values would be the foundation of women's success in medicine (Morantz, 1982). Northern Europe adopted more secular humanistic and utilitarian philosophical approaches compared to Protestant Germany or Catholic countries, turning to municipal bodies for social and medical care (Safley, 2003). As combinations of city-run healthcare systems and church programs increasingly became the norm, the nobility's donations to administrative authorities dwindled in the absence of the strong spirituality that church charities offered (McGrew, 1985).

In the US, the twentieth century saw a growing movement of humanism in medicine, especially beginning in the 1960s, when public opinion started to view physicians as "impersonal technicians" and doctors became dissatisfied with their positions (Kutac, Osipov, & Childress, 2015). *Bioethics*, a field that studies the ethical issues arising from advances in biology and medicine, considers the promotion of life and health in the context of rapid changes (Petrini & Gainotti, 2008). The need to move away from pure science and technicity to give greater weight to the physician–patient relationship and the population as a whole became obvious, giving birth to *medical humanism* on the one hand and spawning the rebirth of religious principles on the other. Humanism in the context of global medicine begets other challenges. What does it translate to when caring for the world's population? What issues arise in considering migrants and refugees? How does it relate to human rights and social justice? *Postcolonial feminism*, which sees medicine in the context of its interrelations with race, gender, and other sociocultural factors, has asserted that health care must include in its epistemology concepts of identity, universality versus differences, and dialog to emphasize the unfinalizability of stereotypes (Racine, 2009).

When we talk about humanism in global medicine, do we mean in all circumstances for all situations? In some cases, global application of interventions that have seen success in one or a few localities has not worked. Economic strengthening through entrepreneurial and microenterprise development, for example, has mitigated poverty-based health disparities in some low-income countries, but similar programs for inner-city African-American male youth in the US have failed (Jennings, 2014). Even as globalization threatens humanism with its emphasis on individualism and consumerism, American economist Kenneth Arrow's (1963) health economics has envisioned a medical-care industry that values agency, knowledge, trust, and professionalism, so that actions on the best available evidence with health equity in mind should reorient medicine back to caring for whole persons.

Human-Centered Health Care

Paying attention to the patient *as a person* improves not only the experience of healthcare, but the overall patient health outcome (Al-Abri & Al-Balushi, 2014). In the West, medical ethics may have begun with the Hippocratic Oath, dating from the fifth century BCE (Riddick, 2003). Human-centered medicine has its roots in the notion of comprehensive health and of personalized approaches distinct in Eastern and Western civilizations. At the height of these civilizations, it also involved the cultivation of a practitioner's humanism through the humanities and the arts (Lee, 2013). The founder of *person-centered therapy* is, however, American psychologist Carl Rogers, whose influential ideas started shifting the focus of therapy from technique to relationship since the 1940's. He coined the term *client* in psychotherapy in line with his belief that the patient is equal to the therapist and that this recognition was paramount (Rogers, 1951).

Rogers believed that people are innately resourceful and capable, and thus are able to comprehend whatever it is that is making them unhappy. A therapist, according to this approach, is focusing on the person as opposed to the problem. For this reason, a therapist should be an instrument for change through being present with that person. Person-centered care takes into consideration people's desires, values, family solutions, and social circumstances, as well as lifestyles. Unlike in the past where a *patient* was expected to follow the set routines and practices that health and social services give them, person-centered care sees a person as an individual and enters into a dialog (McLeod, 2008). There are many reasons why person-centered care is important also at larger scale. Ensuring that people are at the center of care leads to improvement in the care's response to people's needs. Further, it helps people to become more active in looking after themselves, choosing for themselves healthy lifestyles with desired physical activity and proper nutrition, which then reduces some of the pressure on services.

The care relationship can then be more of a partnership than a top-down arrangement, which makes clients more content and improves the confidence and satisfaction of healthcare professionals (Health Innovation Network, 2017).

There has been growing theoretical support to justify the application of person-centered care in social domains to enhance a sense of social inclusion. Research has suggested that mental and emotional distress is linked to social and environmental causes. "Person-centered sociotherapy" is believed to help mitigate them. With the realization that the causes of emotional and mental distress are not intrinsic, endogenous, or solely intrapersonal but rather heavily social and environmental. Some scholars (Sanders, 2006) have argued that psychological distress always has social causes and that there is no such thing as mental illness apart from social conditions.

However, there can be exceptions. In mental illness, people may exhibit, on occasion, psychiatric symptoms or cognitive impairments that disrupt their decision-making capacity. This can make them legally incompetent to consent to or to refuse treatment. Applying a person-centered approach, the emphasis then turns to supporting "the person" within one's psychiatric condition. Revolving around a dialog that supports enhancing a person's living skills and environmental supports, this method aims to achieve goals that clients preferably set for themselves (Anthony et al., 2002). However, because of the nature of mental disease, this approach can sometimes raise ethical issues, especially where the goals that the clients set involve harm to self or to others. Psychiatry has integrated its knowledge into the rest of medicine to allow for the treatment of illness in context, through increased involvement of the individual as well as their next of kin (Hoyle & Leigh, 1982). In the most extenuating circumstances, the clinician may need to intervene to free the person from disease, in the case of certain mental disorders, since the goal is to allow the person to be as free and autonomous as possible to make his or her own decisions. This position has been explored extensively in the argument of right to treatment (Treffert, 1973), which exposes the complexity of respecting "the person."

The complexity of the human condition means that one cannot simply abide by ethical rules, but must often appeal to principles. A *rule* is an imperative that follows the structure of *modus ponendo ponens* (if P happens, then Q must follow), which deals with direct actions without the need of judgment. This is how criminal law proceeds: there is a penal typification of criminal conduct, based on past court rulings or on a penal code, and when there is a "guilty act" committed by the person, then the person is subject to criminal liability by virtue of having committed that act. A *principle*, on the other hand, is a more particular assertion, not necessarily imperative, that seeks to set a general standard on what is wrong and right, good and bad, and sometimes guides action as a "moral compass." In this case, the standard needs to very particular to the person or situation, relying heavily on judgment. Adhering to principles gives rise to statements such as: "Act in such a way that you treat humanity, whether in your own person or in the person of any other, never merely as a means to an end, but always at the same time as an end." Ancient Chinese Taoist philosopher Chuang-tzŭ put it this way: "One who knows the [Way] will surely penetrate the principle of things, and one who penetrates the principle of things will surely understand their application in various situations" (Chuang-tzŭ, 1889).

Following the same principle–the person–may therefore mean that the caregiver relinquishes the role of a paternalistic authority but trains to become a more effective coach or partner. This entails learning how to ask: "What matters to you?" as well as "What is the matter?" If healthcare providers can view the care experience through the recipients' eyes and share in decision-making processes, they will become more responsive to recipients' needs and, thereby, become better care providers (Barry & Edgman-Levitan, 2012). This approach translates, for larger societies, to respecting the culture's aspirations, traditions, language, and unique circumstances. Focus on a person's humanity and dignity, not as an afterthought or a peripheral concern, alters the meaning of the situation and gets to the core of the purpose of medicine.

A CARE Model

The lessons and guidelines of person-centered care are also applicable to violence. Because of the challenges and emotions usually involved in violence, we must examine more closely: what does it mean to *care*, or to give care? This concept is the foundation for the health professional's intimate and real knowledge of the person—including someone who has become violent. While society currently consigns little role for the treatment of violence perpetrators and courts restrict mental health professionals to doing individual violence risk assessments, an intimate encounter with individuals who become violent quickly reveals that their behavior is largely situational and social. They think and behave in ways that their background has shaped, they are most often victims of violence, and they damage others because they themselves are damaged. At the same time, such rudimentary understanding reveals the essential nature, importance, and transformative power of human engagement in caring: caring is the antithesis of violence and its best antidote. We return to the World Health Organization's definition of violence, or the intentional use of physical force or power, threatened or actual, against oneself, another person, or against a group or community, which either results in or has a high likelihood of resulting in injury, death, psychological harm, maldevelopment, or deprivation (Krug, Dahlberg, Mercy, Zwi, & Lozano, 2002).

We may then define caring as follows: the purposeful use of emotional capacity, expressed or enacted, to show kindness toward oneself, another person, or a group or community, which either results in or has a high likelihood of resulting in encouragement, healing, enhanced life, proper development, or abundance (Lee, 2014). The purposeful enhancement of life or thriving of life in human beings by human beings is a form of love, which can foster the achievement of the potential of an individual, society, or humanity as a whole. Yet, because it is not often amenable to empirical research or translatable into evidence-based policy, it is difficult to implement, let alone conceptualize—however, the most inconspicuous are sometimes the most powerful in overall effect. An intimate understanding of the underlying dynamics becomes useful: just as one must practice and train to go into battle with a violent offender, one must train in caring, possibly with greater effort. Given this difficulty, we will suggest doing what medical professionals do to remember and practice procedures: use an acronym.

Here we employ the acronym CARE to denote *Compassion, Altruism, Respect,* and *Encouragement. Compassion,* deriving from the Latin *compassionem,* or "sympathy" from *com* ("with, together") and *passion* ("suffering, enduring"), goes straight to the heart of the health approach. Medicine is about first doing no harm (*"primum non nocere"*), and then delivering direct, intimate care to alleviate harm. Sitting with the patient, sharing in the suffering, and helping to heal are some of the oldest ideals of the field. Compassion is a part of many religious traditions, including the suffering Christ in Christianity and the wounded healer in indigenous practices. A medical approach to the healing of violence would require suffering with those who are hurt, as well as those who have hurt. To view violence with anything less than compassion would be to ignore its tragic dimensions—that perpetrators and victims of violence are often the same persons, and doing further violence to those who manifest it only perpetuates the suffering of the world. The "togetherness" that compassion necessitates goes beyond humanism to encourage *humanitude*—standing up, exchanging glances, touching, smiling and laughing, having meals, and socializing, which are characteristics that make humans recognize others as one species with themselves (Phaneuf, 2007).

Empathy for other human beings in their suffering by putting oneself in their place has been a powerful driving force in the quest to understand violence for the sake of alleviating it while not condoning it, for it has hurt the perpetrator, too. This empathy for all people involved is the basis of violence prevention scholarship, which focuses on the problem that needs to be solved rather than on the individual who is responsible. *Altruism*, the *ism* ("doctrine, theory, practice") of the *altrui* ("other" in Old French, after the Latin *alteri*), is the opposite of egoism and denotes devotion to the welfare of others. Altruism is a form of love, or, among the Greek terms for love, *agape*. The best-guided caregiving efforts will ultimately be ineffective without the life-enhancing intent of love, while a lot of errors can be mitigated when they have still arisen out of love (Winnicott, 1964). Exercise of *agape* can then become a powerful healing and modeling force for those who have been deprived of love.

Patient perception of physician caring contributes to patient satisfaction, trust, and compliance with care (Hojat et al., 2010) and can determine even surgical success (Nagpal et al., 2010). Similarly, if one senses that the intent behind the deprivation and structural violence one experiences is egoism at large, or greed, then the harm will be greater. On the other hand, the moral foundation or "the goodness of the physician" can positively impact the patient's health (Finfgeld-Connett, 2008; Nuland, 2012). Hippocrates famously said that wherever the art of medicine is loved, there is also a love of humanity (Casey, 2007). Medicine is humanitarian in its goals (World Medical Association, 1948), and the ultimate promotion of health occurs out of a love for all humankind. It is therefore reasonable to assume that we must act on the highest and best we can offer—love—to the greatest extent possible—for humanity—when treating a problem as critical to survival as violence.

Respect, deriving from the Latin *respectus* from *re-* ("back") and *specere* ("to look at"), or "to look back at" with regard, relationship, and consideration, also connotes appreciation, admiration, and homage to another's humanity. Respect is important to global medicine, as it entails observing and listening to the care recipient's point of view and attending to the person's religion, culture, identity, and sources of meaning. With the modern world's mass human migrations and changing demographics, as well as its global refugee crisis, the local becomes global. Cultural awareness is no longer a luxury but a quintessential part of communicating respect, not to mention allowing for proper diagnosis and treatment at the same time as reducing racial and ethnic health disparities (Betancourt et al., 2003). Cultural considerations are also important for understanding the person and the person's attitudes and actions and for building rapport: reaching out to someone of different socioeconomic status, ethnic group, religious affiliation, gender, or age and making a personal connection can be an intensely powerful experience. And in the case of an individual who has become violent, it entails the ability to see dignity in the person. Cultural sensitivity can bring not only dignity but social inclusion and hope, especially to conditions of desperation. Religious involvement can also bring better health outcomes, including greater longevity, coping skills, quality of life, and protection from suicide (Mueller, Plevak, & Rummans, 2001).

Religious sensitivity can bring meaning and unity to the caring encounter: Christianity emphasizes loving and helping one's neighbor; Judaism teaches caring as part of a duty to repair the world and to support goodness; Islam instructs that caring for those in need is a deep obligation; Buddhism and Hinduism stress not harming but having compassion for all; indigenous religions feature caregiving as largely central to myths and rituals; and secular spirituality fosters a focus on advancing the well-being of all. In this manner, all the religions—and nonreligious humanism—have more in common than not. Most care recipients cite their spiritual life as being as important as their physical health, and spiritual needs are heightened in times of suffering. Awareness that a wide range of modalities of human life exist, and knowledge of cultural and religious nuances, can enlarge flexibility and choice for both the caregiver and the recipient.

Encouragement is the reinforcement of one's "heart, innermost feelings, inner strength" from Old French *corage*, whereby *cor* in Latin means "heart." At the same time that we are products of our social and cultural environments, human beings are complex agents in charge of our own identities and destinies. There is a core that defies the usual laws of physics and psychology, to rise to a level of symbolism, imagination, and creation. As the heart has reasons that surpass reason (Pascal, 1670), humans are not just abstract intellect but also emotion and spirit.

If respect is the removal of stereotyping, categorizing, and other limit-placing so that the care recipient has permission to be oneself, encouragement is active involvement in strengthening and fueling a person's core drive for life. This is not merely an intellectual exercise but an immersive experience, often facilitated through the engagement of visual art, music, dance, theater, and creative writing. Since the creative impulse that derives from a life-enhancing and death-defying drive is fundamental to human existence, as we noted in Chapter 4, "The Symbolism (or Spiritual Causes) of Violence," it is the culmination of human capacity as well as the most powerful mechanism for healing. Creative art-making is shown to be a therapeutic tool for finding symbolic ways of rising above trauma (Chazan & Cohen, 2010) and for promoting resilience as it teaches new ways of thinking and influences physical wellbeing, a fighting spirit, and even peace in the face of inevitability (Corley, 2010). Fostering creativity can also "inoculate" against further violence even in the most violent offenders (Gilligan & Lee, 2005), and the resilience and generativity that ensue can lead to a productive life.

Encouragement thus leads to *empowerment*, which means to infuse or to enable infusion with ability, mastery, and vigor, from the Old French verb *povoir* ("to be able"). This is where the notion of *power* needs reform: to turn away from its guise—violence—to true ability. The creative arts represent attempts to grasp the core of ability, where spirit or "life energy" is concerned. They are not only therapeutic but educational tools that enhance a caregiver's ability to observe, to empathize, and to endure the difficult work of caring (Perry, Maffulli, Willson, & Morrissey, 2011). Medical humanities as interdisciplinary education through courses in the humanities, residents' retreats, and practice of communication skills is a growing curriculum for medical trainees (Dellasega, Milone-Nuzzo, Curci, Ballard, & Kirch, 2007). The arts can also contribute to social justice: while education empowers populations by attuning them to oppression, esthetic practices do so by centering the heart in ways that make oppression unacceptable (Scarry, 1999). The arts can also represent the product of caregiving and recovery. The ability to have, to generate, and to share cathartic experiences, as opposed to mechanical and inauthentic exchanges, can be an expression of resilience and creative potential, and groping toward one of the highest expressions of humanity.

Caring is not just about sitting with but living among people, listening to their narratives, engaging them where they are in the world. This essence of caring should not change as implementation moves to societal scale; just as structural violence can damage its recipients in a manner much like direct violence, so can *structural caring* foster the flourishing of its recipients in a manner like direct caring. A growing observation, as we increase our understanding of violence, is that even the most "hopeless" cases can improve in some way; in other words, there is no human being who cannot be reached at some level if there is enough dedication and patience. No one is expendable. At the societal level, no group should be abandoned, and politics of caring should replace politics of power (punishment) if we wish to improve public health significantly. Even "dead souls" can be resurrected, and society has an obligation to care for them, not just to be good Samaritans to "poor murderers" but because doing so benefits society and the entire human race. Ultimately, we are trying to learn about violence, and we learn most from violent people. The interactionist model we apply to the disciplines also applies to human beings: *interaction* and inclusion help bring about a cure for violence.

The US has seen the detrimental consequences of a "health reform" that has happened without the involvement of those who actually deliver care, becoming no longer a healthcare system but a market system in health care. Management of the system has followed models of economics, business administration, and profit motives, leaving out the social, human, and human health dimensions and exacerbating the loss of human-centered care that accompanied technology and professionalization. Health systems need to be clear about their end goal as patients, not profits, and large-scale health approaches about their end goal as society, not the corporation that runs the system. Being clear about principles and purpose is more practical than fixation on practical aspects alone.

A Creative Model

Turning to the arts can be a means of bringing humanism as well as innovation to a healing environment, and we see this method gaining momentum in various care settings. There have been significant strides in the research on ways in which paintings and other works of art can help patients heal. A direct link exists between the content of the images and the brain's reaction to pain, stress, and anxiety, which has led many hospitals and clinics to consider choosing to display artworks as part of a caretaking priority (Landro, 2014). Use of the arts in health care is seen as a diverse and multidisciplinary way of transforming the healthcare experience. Connecting people with the power of art at defining moments in their lives can serve therapeutic and educational, as well as expressive purposes.

The arts promote recovery and restoration in many ways. Music, for instance, increases patients' comfort post-operatively. It reduces anxiety levels in children who are getting casts for orthopedic surgeries (Choi, Lee, & Lim, 2008). Music helps increase the heart rate as well as improve the behavioral score in pre-term infants in the neonatal intensive care unit, resulting in deeper sleep (Arnon et al., 2006). It also decreases the incidence of respiratory pauses in premature infants. Music can reduce anxiety, depression, and other mood disturbances in patients who are undergoing stem cell transplants (Cassileth, Vicker, & Magil, 2003). It is also effective in increasing salivary immunoglobulin, an antibody that provides defense against various infections.

Group music therapy has been shown to help women who have experienced intimate partner violence to experience significantly less depression and anxiety (Teague, Hahna, & McKinney, 2006). Music can also work as an anger management tool in prison populations (Hakvoort, 2002). Music therapy programs have also been designed to improve social interaction and relatedness, to increase self-expression and self-esteem, to decrease hostile and disruptive behavior, and to develop empathy and appropriate channels for energy release in juvenile offenders (Rio & Tenney, 2002).

Visual arts have several intrinsic and instrumental benefits in health care. Exposure to drawings and paintings has emerged as an effective way to help children with cancer deal with pain and other disturbing symptoms of illness and treatment (Rollins, 2005). In addition, engaging with art is also a way for people to be in control at a time where a lot of things are beyond their control, reducing their stress levels. Therapeutic use of artworks helps children who have had exposure to domestic violence to recount their stories in a less direct way and to reinforce positive expectations of the future (Kozlowska & Hanney, 2001). Visual arts also influence fatigue levels for patients on chemotherapy and reduce acute stress symptoms for pediatric trauma patients (Bar-Sela et al., 2007).

Moreover, there is evidence that art enhances certain skills of staff and caregivers. Drawing abilities and stereovision, including imagery and thinking three dimensionally, are an important aspect of neurosurgery and in the surgical profession in general (Pásztor, 1993). Russian short story writer Anton Chekhov made the humorous analogy of medicine as his lawful wife and literature his mistress, whereby when he gets tired of one, he spends the night with the other, illustrating the emotional benefits of having a creative outlet. Physician-writers such as Chekhov introduced the concept of narrative medicine. Narratives, whether literal or from pop culture, can enable patients and treaters to cope with illness and spawn resilience in the face of adversity (Charon, 2001).

The incorporation of art programs in correctional facilities has also shown a positive influence on prisoners. Creative expression within prisons through craft workshops, decorated envelopes, murals, and elaborate tattoos has always been popular (Bosworth, 2005). Inmates with low levels of education, especially literacy, can actively express themselves through non-verbal means, while also having a chance to improve their cognitive skills (Crighton & Towl, 2008). Art creates a portal through which inmates can develop their imagination, despite the adverse circumstances (Rose, 2011). By supporting a creative approach, art programs encourage inmates to educate themselves and conceive of unique means of resolving problems (Knott, 2011). Inmates who exhibit skill or express authentic emotion earn respect from fellow prisoners, while engaging in activities that have educational, communal, and therapeutic attributes. Participating in the arts may create a desire to do more for others, and with greater self-esteem, participants become more tolerant and more inclined to take peaceful approaches to conflict resolution (Gussak, 2013). Some institutions that have gone further to employ art therapy, and as a result have experienced a positive behavioral shift in a large percentage of participants (Gussak, 2017). A trained art therapist can actively engage inmates in ways that can help identify and overcome personal difficulties.

While the punitive approach to incarceration is largely counterproductive (Harvey & Smedley, 2012), art programs are a part of the restorative and therapeutic approach to behavior enhancement. The presence of art activities such as painting, music, and film facilitates institutional management, while allowing for greater freedom and diversity (Ellis & Gregory, 2011). Art programs can also emphasize a project-based approach, where the practice of art will lead to gratification from a publication, a performance, or a finished piece of art that everyone can celebrate. They can provide an avenue for inmate-artists to interact with the outside world through organized exhibitions, for example, and artistic endeavors by prisoners has long attracted public attention. Furthermore, developing creative skills, such as learning to paint or to play a musical instrument, can contribute to other areas of life (Daveson & Edwards, 2001). Activities such as these can have an immense effect in boosting confidence and in shaping social skills (Halperin et al., 2012), not to mention in enhancing feelings of connectedness, meaning, and hope.

The arts have also been employed for the development of leadership skills. Far from being impractical or irrelevant in the running of daily affairs, proper arts education can be the foundation for a humanistic orientation. It can build the capacity for ethical and empathic centering, social consciousness, compassion, and ultimately humane governance. High points of human civilization have recognized this power of the arts and considered cultivation in the arts essential, if not central, to the development of an educated individual in a civilized society. Ancient China and Renaissance Europe, for example, have respectively selected the best artists to be the highest government officials or actively involved them in the implementation of government. Ancient China selected its highest government officials based almost entirely on their accomplishment in calligraphy, poetry, and painting, promoting humanistic and compassionate rule. In Europe, the Renaissance era comes closest and remains an influential, productive period of creative cultural transformation. While our fast-paced, methods-oriented contemporary world seems distant from these legendary times, we can still harness the power of the arts for humankind (Lee, 2013).

Local and Global

We have noted the advantages of the health sector's involvement in violence prevention. But is there an advantage to the involvement of medical providers? Here, we should make a distinction between the local and the global. *The local* refers to aspects that a direct care provider would notice, such as individual characteristics, personal needs, a particular locale, a culture, a language, and a country. It refers to bearing witness and participating, and goes to the heart of what it means to be a human being, with unique personal experiences, backgrounds, thoughts and feelings, and identity. *The global* refers to aspects that are of concern in public health, as we have reviewed in the previous chapter, and include worldwide trends, epidemiologic analyses, the range of different settings, and the meeting of different worlds. It allows us to perceive a more abstract level, such as the whole of humanity, the continuum of circumstances, the variety of encounters, and what we hold in common. In an increasingly globalizing world, a global vision has certainly brought advantages, but the local vision risks either being subsumed in a larger picture of instrumentalities and numerical results or being lost in stereotype and caricature. Placing special emphasis on the local allows for greater attention to low- and middle-income country settings, where most of global violence occurs.

If not the emergency medicine physician sewing up wounds or the trauma surgeon repairing organs, the psychiatrist has been hard at work treating individuals who have experienced violence, and preventing their harm against self or other. Medicine's continued involvement in public health is essential for the hands-on, local perspective it brings: (a) physicians first identified interpersonal violence as a health problem because of their daily contact and care for victims and perpetrators of violence (Prothrow-Stith, 2004); (b) the medical professions have information, resources, and infrastructures for working with individuals at an intimate level that can lead to needed research, response, and prevention approaches; (c) much violence, such as child maltreatment, intimate partner violence, and elder abuse, occurs in private settings, and medical providers are often the first to detect it; (d) caregiver–recipient relationships, through their fully embodied, human presence, are as important to medical healing as to the understanding and prevention of violence; and (e) medical professionals have the expertise to extrapolate the magnitude, severity, urgency, and long-term consequences of behavioral violence, systematic deprivation, war, climate change, and nuclear devastation. Furthermore, in our day, most health problems the physician sees are because of human violence, rather than of natural causes. Even so-called "accidents" are not random, as there is often reckless behavior or societal neglect underlying them.

The person-centered approach of everyday healthcare practitioners can: (a) add qualitative, "human stories" to large-scale data and global policies; (b) apply pertinent modifications to interventions and prevention programs across individuals or cultures through their familiarity with local conditions and needs; and (c) ascertain through close contact the values that are important to specific persons or communities, such as spiritual beliefs or narratives of recovery. Healthcare systems should be helping the person and not the other way around. Doctors, nurses, and other healthcare personnel, therefore, by collaborating with public health officials, policymakers, and legislative bodies, can bring a unique voice of advocacy for those who are vulnerable. Policymakers do not have direct knowledge of the personal experience, but medical professionals see firsthand that the poor are the sickest; that psychosocial stress is perhaps the greatest risk factor for virtually all human ailments; and that health problems, including human violence, are often socioeconomic in nature. They witness that rigidly profit-driven models are especially destructive, as a large generator of structural violence and injustice that contribute to adverse health and premature death, leading to generations of illness and social disruption (Lynch et al., 2000). They observe that, as the world seems to be advancing as a whole, the poor are increasingly left behind, the wars are growing harsher where they are, and the violence of structures is ever more severe. Local populations once capable of fending for themselves are rendered vulnerable, and our approach should be a collaborative one of the Global North looking to mend the harms it has caused, and the Global South developing capacities to become self-reliant once again.

Understanding how the social determinants of health play out in everyday life can yield unique insights into the distress of one's global neighbors. The experience of local conditions and capacities can translate into global knowledge, as violence is ubiquitous and human suffering universal. Local experience highlights the importance of circumstances in which violence occurs—under specific gender norms, religious traditions, community risk and protective factors, particular manifestations and social acceptability of violence—which vary greatly from one context to another and are critical to consider when exporting interventions or when sharing resources. For example, successful initiatives in one region may face struggles with taboos elsewhere that prevent recognition of certain types of violence, such as that against women and children. At the same time, the local does well to be global; otherwise, it becomes a world apart, incapable of meeting challenges with innovation but constantly resisting change by becoming more extreme.

The comparative study of a diversity of country and resource settings allows consideration of the broader socioeconomic and political context at play in the local communities. A global perspective allows for the sharing of resources and capacity-building where necessary—but has the danger of perpetuating violence and inequality if little regard is given to specific local needs (Lee & Young, 2012). Local experience, furthermore, brings awareness that poverty and inequality are among the drivers of violent conflict, which in turn exacerbate poverty—leading to a vicious circle. The poorest people are generally the least served, even though their needs are the greatest, whether in a high- or a low-to-middle-income country, and increasingly in higher-income countries, issues of health inequity are becoming remarkably similar. All around the world, we share these fundamental issues of our time, and ultimately, in a globalizing world, local violence can easily transform into a global problem. We would thus do well to assume our collective responsibility for caring before global conditions force it.

Case Studies

Médecins Sans Frontières (Doctors Without Borders)

Amid the Parisian upheavals of May 1968, the French public saw frightening images on their black and white television screens. For the first time, there were broadcast scenes of children dying from hunger in remote corners of the world. In southern Nigeria, the province of Biafra had seceded. The territory was surrounded by the Nigerian army, and famine decimated the Biafran people. The French Red Cross issued an appeal for volunteers. Meanwhile, a group of young doctors decided to go and help victims of wars and major disasters. This new brand of humanitarianism would reinvent the concept of emergency aid. They were to become Médecins sans Frontières (MSF), known internationally as Doctors without Borders. The organization officially came into existence in 1971. It was founded on the belief that all people have the right to medical care regardless of gender, race, religion, or political affiliation and that the needs of people outweigh respect for national boundaries (Center for International Stabilization and Recovery, 1999).

MSF is an international, independent, medical humanitarian organization that delivers emergency aid to people affected by armed conflict, epidemics, natural disasters, and exclusion from health care. Medical ethics and the principles of neutrality and impartiality guide their actions (Vallaeys, 2004). The group was recipient of the 1999 Nobel Peace Prize. Today, MSF has offices worldwide and more than 2,000 volunteers. Its efforts have included intervention following the 2011 Turkish earthquake and continued assistance after the 2010 Haitian earthquake, providing healthcare to people living in tribal villages in central India caught up in the conflict between Maoist rebels and government forces, provision of health care in several countries following the aftermath of the Arab Spring, and fighting malaria in Africa (Jarudi, 2000).

Cure Violence

Cure Violence envisions a world without violence. Its mission is to reduce violence globally using disease control and behavior change methods. Central is a clear understanding that violence is a health issue, and community partners and strategic partnerships are its keys to success. Cure Violence has implemented its approach to reducing killings and shootings since 2000 in more than 25 cities, seven US states, and eight countries. Infectious disease physician Gary Slutkin at the University of Illinois at Chicago developed the Cure Violence model and still manages it there with his colleagues. The Cure Violence strategy uses outreach workers to work with friends and families of victims to identify, mediate, and prevent further violence and retaliation (Slutkin, Ransford, Decker, & Volker, 2015). The program relies on three key elements to stop the transmission of violent behavior: interrupting transmission directly, identifying and changing the thinking of potential transmitters (those at highest risk of perpetrating violence), and changing group norms regarding violence. The interruption of violence occurs by preventing retaliatory shootings, mediating ongoing conflicts, and continuing to follow up to keep the conflicts "cool." Outreach workers are key in this model. They need to have trusting relationships with the most high-risk individuals in the community, and it helps if they have had some prior involvement with the justice system (Butts, Roman, Bostwick, & Porter, 2015).

The University of California Davis Violence Prevention Research Program conducted the Reducing Urban Violence Study to estimate the relative impact of two leading approaches to violence prevention: targeted policing and the Cure Violence strategy. It found that investment in Cure Violence could actually achieve the same reduction in victimization as did a much larger investment in targeted policing (Blumstein & Wallman, 2006). In 2008, Cure Violence began its first international adaptation and replication of the methodology in Basrah, Iraq. Since then, international programs have been added in South Africa (Hanover Park), the UK (London), Kenya (Nairobi and Rift Valley), Honduras (San Pedro Sula), and Colombia (Barranquilla). Demand for the Cure Violence approach has been growing internationally, with interest in places such as Uganda, Jamaica, Colombia, El Salvador, Jordan, Israel, Palestine, Mexico, Brazil, Guatemala, Ecuador, and Canada. Violence occurs on every continent and in every city in the world, but the highest levels of violence are concentrated in a handful of countries in Latin America, the Caribbean, the Middle East, North Africa, Africa, and Southeast Asia. In its strategic plan is a proposal to establish a Global Violence Reduction Network, with a focus on two regions: Latin America and Caribbean as the first region; and the Middle East and Africa as the second. Their first priority in Latin America and the Caribbean is to prove the model in Honduras and Colombia, and their top priority for the Middle East and North Africa region is to continue to deepen the work with Syrian nationals. Outside these two priority areas, Cure Violence continues its existing programs in the United Kingdom, Canada, and South Africa (Cure Violence, 2013).

Mercy Corps

The organization was founded in 1979, as Save the Refugees Fund, a task force organized in response to the plight of Cambodian refugees fleeing the famine, war, and genocide of the "killing fields." Its mission has been to help people grappling with the toughest situations and to help communities turn crises around. Dan O'Neill and Ellsworth Culver formed Mercy Corps in 1982, shifting from simply providing relief assistance to focusing on long-term solutions to hunger and poverty. Its first development project began in Honduras. Since then, Mercy Corps has grown and evolved, gaining national and international recognition for quick-response, high-impact, cost-effective programs around the globe. Over the years, it has worked in more than 107 nations, delivering relief and development assistance such as food, shelter, healthcare, agriculture, water and sanitation, education, and small business loans.

Today, Mercy Corps helps more than 19 million people each year recover from disasters, build stronger communities, and find their own solutions to poverty. It has responded, for example, to the Indian Ocean tsunami, the wars in Afghanistan and Iraq, the food crisis in Niger, the displacement in Congo, and the earthquakes in China and Haiti. It has uniquely focused on using relief and development programs to strengthen civil society: rather than simply handing out food, building a school, or immunizing children, it has focused on working side-by-side with the poor, bringing diverse groups together to create societies that are more peaceful, more democratic, and economically strong (Mercy Corps, 2017).

One Acre Fund

Farmers have the potential to play a key role in reducing hunger and poverty. One Acre Fund helps farmers boost their farming productivity and provides them with startup financing, seeds, and fertilizer, agricultural training, and market facilitation to help maximize profit. Smallholder farmers comprise the majority of the world's poor. One Acre Fund's model increases revenue on the farm and gives the farmers the resources to continue improving their livelihoods by providing access to seed and fertilizer, finance, training, and post-harvest support (Clinton Global Initiative, 2017). The nonprofit organization currently serves farmers based in Kenya, Tanzania, Rwanda, and Burundi and Malawi. In 2015, it committed to scale its agricultural development model to reach one million smallholder farmers in Sub-Saharan Africa by 2020. One Acre Fund is on its way to representing Africa's largest network for smallholder farmers. By 2020, they will serve at least one million farm families, with more than five million people living in those families, and the farmers will produce enough food to feed another five million of their neighbors (The Life You Can Save, 2017).

One Acre Fund is different from other charities and agricultural programs. Traditional agricultural programs often provide help in just one area; for example, providing a small startup loan. One Acre Fund's multifaceted approach helps local farmers maximize agricultural profit and sustainability. The organization has conducted hundreds of trials on new crops and seed varieties, cost-effective farming techniques, and life-improving products. It is also offering some impactful non-agricultural products, such as solar lights and energy-efficient cooking stoves. As One Acre Fund also distributes tree seeds or seedlings, in 2016, farmers planted more than four million trees. Trees are a good source of income for farmers who can sell them for firewood or building materials, and in addition, trees prevent soil erosion, reverse the effects of deforestation, and reduce atmospheric carbon (Adelman, 2009).

The Library Project

Founder of the Library Project Tom Stader has been improving rural children's literacy in Asia since 2006. The Arizona native started his nonprofit project with just 500 US dollars in donations. The organization now donates books and libraries to underfinanced schools and orphanages in China and Vietnam. The Library Project relies on the principle that education is the key to change and breaking the cycle of poverty in the developing world. It involves the local community through book drives and awareness raising campaigns, while partnering with local charities and companies. An entire library costing just 1,500 US dollars can be a life-changer (Hatton, 2010).

In the attempt to reach schools of "greatest need," one of the project's big plans was to donate books to Liu Lin Primary School, a school on top of a mountain. The school was a mud and brick building with 60 students and eight teachers. It was not easy to reach. They had to take a train, two vans, and a boat, and then hike up a winding mountain trail. While at a loss as to how they would deliver an entire library, one of Stader's employees stood at the head of the classroom asking the children what kinds of books they would like to read, what their favorite subject was, and what it was like living in their village. From then on, this has been the organizational model. A month later they returned with 600 local language books, and as their boat pulled up to the base of the mountain, a group of 30 students was waiting for them. The older students had baskets on their backs that they filled with books, and the younger students each took a handful of books and walked up the mountain. In April 2015, the Library Project team donated their one-millionth book, and as of January 2017, they impacted their one-millionth child. They are donating on average one library every day. Their plans are to reach out to additional countries in the coming years (Stader, 2017).

Conclusion

There was a time when the medical community considered itself as playing an integral function in the program of social and human improvement. This chapter considers the application of medicine in that tradition. "Global medicine" stands for the intimate practice of medicine being applied to global levels, such as in determining global health policy, and emphasizes that intimate knowledge of the human experience is not only important but critical for the practicality of large-scale applications. Unlike public health, medicine is always rooted in the intimate, human level, and the dialectic interplay between society and person, between scholarship and practice, is both useful and enlightening.

Care of the human person, in the process of healing, is an art that is increasingly lost (Lown, 1996). While medicine is both a science and an art, globalization, overuse of technology, and market orientation threaten to cancel out the humanistic focus that has been its mainstay. Just as violence as a subject has helped to break down disciplinary boundaries, efforts to prevent violence and the human suffering it engenders can help shape the healthcare agenda. A global medicine approach is increasingly necessary to keep the care of individuals, communities, and societies local, while considering the complexity and wholeness of the individual person. In this chapter, we addressed the need to retain the original principles of caregiving and a human-centered approach, as has been the tradition of medicine. We emphasized the need for a model of caring that keeps close to all practices, including in wider-system applications. We proposed a CARE model of compassion, altruism, respect, and encouragement for the foundation of a person-centered, humanistic approach. Also, it is important to remember that the global needs grounding in the local, whereby sensitivity to local needs translates into cultural and psychological awareness in the context of each person's universal humanity. We underscored the need to preserve the knowledge that comes from close contact between providers and patients, especially in an ever-globalizing world.

Within a global economic system that perpetuates poverty and inequality, and a technicization that overwhelms what is human or natural, the person can all too easily become subordinate to healthcare systems, special interests, and bureaucratic and technical agendas. Those who are vulnerable and in need of care are especially without advocates, and the issue is exacerbated in cases involving violence. Public health has done a great deal to shift away from criminal justice and security approaches toward prevention and health promotion. Global medicine complements the public health approach by bringing in the local: taking into account human suffering, principles of caregiving, cultural and religious sensitivity, and fostering of resilience and creativity comes from intimate knowledge of the human being, and collaborations are necessary between healthcare givers and policymakers to bridge the gaps for effective governance. While public health aims to improve the health of whole populations through specific policy interventions, global medicine returns to medicine's original intent of understanding and giving care to the person through one's whole self.

The CARE principles are implicit in the long tradition of medicine, and they now require a conscious and explicit focus, recognizing that human beings are complex mixtures of body, mind, and spirit, with deeply embedded sets of values. A growing movement in medical humanism emphasizes the view of the human being as a whole, complex entity and appreciates human dignity, emotions, intelligence, and religious and moral commitments (Margolin, 2004). Medical providers are in a privileged and responsible position to help join individuals and communities with local and global policymakers. As in the rest of medicine, their task is to preserve the rightful place of the human being at the center of discourse. A human-centered approach does not condone violence but recognizes its reality and the need to free persons, including perpetrators, from it. As the application of a health approach to violence extends across the globe, there is an ever stronger need to preserve the knowledge that comes from this close contact, and to build collaborations between providers and policymakers (Degutis, 2012). Interestingly, we find that focusing on the most intimate parts of ourselves brings us to the most universal and comprehensive aspects of our humanity.

Questions

1   How can global medicine complement the public health approach to violence prevention?

2   What are the local and human aspects of medicine's tradition?

3   How do humanism and the art of medicine emphasize person-centered care?

4   What are the components of the CARE model?

5   How can local and global issues benefit from continued medical provider involvement?

References

Adelman, C. (2009). Global philanthropy and remittances: Reinventing foreign aid. *Brown Journal of World Affairs, 15*(2), 23–33.

Al-Abri, R., & Al-Balushi, A. (2014). Patient satisfaction survey as a tool toward quality improvement. *Oman Medical Journal, 29*(1), 3–7.

Anthony, A., Cohen, M., Farkas, M., & Gagne, C. (2002). *Psychiatric rehabilitation*. Boston, MA: Boston University Center for Psychiatric Rehabilitation.

Arnon, S., Shapsa, A., Forman, L., Regev, R., Bauer, S., & Litmanovitz, I. (2006). Live music is beneficial to preterm infants in the neonatal intensive care unit environment. *Birth, 33*(2), 131–136.

Arrow, K. J. (1963). Uncertainty and the welfare economics of medical care. *American Economic Review, 53*(5), 941–973.

Bar-Sela, G., Atid, L., Dans, S., Gabay, N., & Epelbaum, P. (2007). Art therapy improved depression and influenced fatigue levels in cancer patients on chemotherapy. *Psycho-Oncology, 16*(11), 980–984.

Barry, M. J., & Edgman-Levitan, S. (2012). Shared decision making—the pinnacle of patient-centered care. *New England Journal of Medicine, 366*(9), 780–781.

Betancourt, J. R., Green, A. R., Carrillo, J. E., & Ananeh-Firempong, O. II (2003). Defining cultural competence: A practical framework for addressing racial/ethnic disparities in health and health care. *Public Health Reports, 118*(4), 293–302.

Blumstein, A., & Wallman, J. (2006). *The crime drop in America*. Cambridge, MA: Cambridge University Press.

Bosworth, M. (2005). *Encyclopedia of prisons and correctional facilities*. Thousand Oaks, CA: Sage.

Butts, J. A., Roman, C. G., Bostwick, L., & Porter, J. R. (2015). Cure violence: A public health model to reduce gun violence. *Annual Review of Public Health, 36*, 39–53.

Casey, K. M. (2007). The global impact of surgical volunteerism. *Surgical Clinics of North America, 87*(4), 949–960.

Cassileth, B., Vickers, A., & Magill, L. (2003). Music therapy for mood disturbance during hospitalization for autologous stem cell transplantation: A randomized controlled trial. *Cancer, 98*(12), 2723–2729.

Center for International Stabilization and Recovery. (1999). Doctors without Borders. *The Journal of Conventional Weapons Destruction, 3*(3), 21.

Charon, R. (2001). Narrative medicine: A model for empathy, reflection, profession, and trust. *JAMA, 286*(15), 1897–1902.

Chazan, S., & Cohen, E. (2010). Adaptive and defensive strategies in post-traumatic play of young children exposed to violent attacks. *Journal of Child Psychotherapy, 36*(2), 133–151.

Choi, A., Lee, M., & Lim, H. (2008). Effects of group music intervention on depression, anxiety, and relationships in psychiatric patients: A pilot study. *Journal of Alternative and Complementary Medicine, 26*(5), 567–570.

Chuang-tzŭ (1889). *Chuang-tzŭ: Mystic, moralist, and social reformer*. Translated by H. A. Giles. London, UK: Quaritch.

Clinton Global Initiative. (2017). *One Acre Fund: Putting 1 million farmers first by 2020*. New York, NY: Clinton Foundation. Retrieved from https://www.clintonfoundation.org/clinton-global-initiative/commitments/one-acre-fund-putting-1-million-farmers-first-2020

Corley, C. (2010). Creative expression and resilience among holocaust survivors. *Journal of Human Behavior in the Social Environment, 20*(4), 542–552.

Crighton, D. A., & Towl, G. J. (2008). *Psychology in prisons*. Leicester, UK: British Psychological Society-Blackwell.

Cure Violence. (2013). *Strategic plan 2014–16*. Chicago, IL: Author.

Daveson, B. A., & Edwards, J. (2001). A descriptive study exploring the role of music therapy in prisons. *The Arts in Psychotherapy, 28*(2), 137–141.

Declaration of Helsinki. (1964). Retrieved from https://www.wma.net/wp-content/uploads/2018/07/DoH-Jun1964.pdf

Degutis, L. C. (2012). The future of injury and violence prevention: Where are we going? *Journal of Safety Research, 43*(4), 231–232.

Dellasega, C., Milone-Nuzzo, P., Curci, K. M., Ballard, J. O., & Kirch, D. G. (2007). The humanities interface of nursing and medicine. *Journal of Professional Nursing, 23*(3), 174–179.

Donohoe, M. T. (2012). *Public health and social justice.* San Francisco, CA: Jossey-Bass.

Ellis, J., & Gregory, T. (2011). *Demonstrating the value of arts in criminal justice.* New York, NY: Clinks.

Finfgeld-Connett, D. (2008). Meta-synthesis of caring in nursing. *Journal of Clinical Nursing, 17*(2), 196–204.

Fissell, M. E. (2008). Introduction: Women, health, and healing in early modern Europe. *Bulletin of the History of Medicine, 82*(1), 1–17.

Fondation Télécom. (2015). *L'Homme augmenté: Notre humanité en quête de sens.* Paris, France: Author.

Gilligan, J. (2001). *Preventing violence.* London, UK: Thames and Hudson.

Gilligan, J., & Lee, B. (2005). The Resolve to Stop the Violence Project: Reducing violence in the community through a jail-based initiative. *Journal of Public Health, 27*(2), 143–148.

Gunderman, R., and LeLand, B. (2016, May 23). Touch creates a healing bond in healthcare. *The Conversation.* Retrieved from http://theconversation.com/touch-creates-a-healing-bond-in-health-care-59637

Gussak, D. E. (2013). Art therapy in the prison subculture: Maintaining boundaries while breaking barriers. In P. Howie, S. Prasad, & J. Kristel (Eds.), *Using art therapy with diverse populations: Crossing cultures and abilities* (pp. 328–337). London, UK: Kingsley.

Gussak, D. E. (2017). The continuing emergence of art therapy in prisons. In B. S. Elger, C. Ritter, & H. Stöver (Eds.), *Emerging issues in prison health* (pp. 67–84). Dordrecht, Netherlands: Springer.

Hakvoort, L. (2002). A music therapy anger management program for forensic offenders. *Music Therapy Perspectives, 20*(2), 123–132.

Halperin, R., Kessler, S., & Braunschweiger, D. (2012). Rehabilitation through the arts: Impact on participants' engagement in educational programs. *Journal of Correctional Education, 63*(1), 6–23.

Harvey, J., & Smedley, K. (2012). *Psychological therapy in prisons and other settings.* Abingdon, UK: Routledge.

Hatton, C. (2010, December 18). Young Americans help China through non-profits. *CBS News.* Retrieved from https://www.cbsnews.com/news/young-americans-help-china-through-non-profits

Health Innovation Network. (2017). *What is person-centred care and why is it important?.* London, UK: Author.

Hill-Taylor, B., Sketris, I., Hayden, J., Byrne, S., O'Sullivan, D., & Christie, R. (2013). Application of the STOPP/START criteria: A systematic review of the prevalence of potentially inappropriate prescribing in older adults, and evidence of clinical, humanistic and economic impact. *Journal of Clinical Pharmacy and Therapeutics, 38*(5), 360–372.

Hojat, M., Louis, D. Z., Maxwell, K., Markham, F., Wender, R., & Gonnella, J. S. (2010). Patient perceptions of physician empathy, satisfaction with physician, interpersonal trust, and compliance. *International Journal of Medical Education, 1*, 83–87.

Hoyle, B., & Leigh, M. (1982). Comment: The role of psychiatry in medicine. *American Journal of Psychiatry, 139*(12), 1581–1587.

Jarudi, L. (2000). Doctors without borders. *Harvard International Review, 22*(1), 36–39.

Jennings, L. (2014). Do men need empowering too? A systematic review of entrepreneurial education and microenterprise development on health disparities among inner-city black male youth. *Journal of Urban Health, 91*(5), 836–850.

Kleinman, A. (2015). Care: In search of a health agenda. *Lancet, 386*(9990), 240–241.

Knott, G. A. (2011). Cost and punishment: Reassessing incarceration costs and the value of college-in-prison programs. *Northern Illinois University Law Review, 32*(1), 267–293.

Kozlowska, K., & Hanney, L. (2001). An art therapy group for children traumatized by parental violence and separation. *Clinical Child Psychology and Psychiatry, 6*(1), 49–78.

Krug, E. G., Dahlberg, L. L., Mercy, J. A., Zwi, A. B., & Lozano, R. (2002). *World report on violence and health.* Geneva, Switzerland: World Health Organization. Retrieved from http://apps.who.int/iris/bitstream/10665/42495/1/9241545615_eng.pdf

Kutac, J., Osipov, R., & Childress, A. (2015). Innovation through tradition: Rediscovering the "humanist" in the medical humanities. *The Journal of Medical Humanities, 37*(4), 371–387.

Landro, L. (2014, August 18). More hospitals use the healing powers of public art. *Wall Street Journal.* Retrieved from https://www.wsj.com/amp/articles/more-hospitals-use-the-healing-powers-of-public-art-1408404629

Lee, B. X. (2013). From human destructiveness to creativity. In C. McLean (Ed.), *Creative arts in humane medicine.* Toronto, Canada: University of Toronto Press.

Lee, B. X., & Young, J. L. (2012). Building a global health ethic without doing further violence. *American Journal of Bioethics, 12*(12), 59–60.

Lown, B. (1996). *Lost art of healing.* Boston, MA: Houghton Mifflin.

Lynch, J. W., Smith, G. D., Kaplan, G. A., & House, J. S. (2000). Income inequality and mortality: Importance to health of individual income, psychosocial environment, or material conditions. *British Medical Journal, 320*(7243), 1200–1204.

Margolin, J. C. (2004). Apologie pour l'humanisme: De la globalization à la sectorisation d'un concept socio-historique. *Peninsula: Revista de Estudos Ibéricos, 1*, 15–36.

McGrew, R. E. (1985). *Encyclopedia of medical history.* New York, NY: McGraw-Hill.

McLeod, S. A. (2008). Person centered therapy. Simply Psychology. Retrieved from https://www.simplypsychology.org/client-centred-therapy.html

Mercy Corps. (2017). *Our history.* Edinburgh, UK: Author. Retrieved from www.mercycorps.org.uk/u/about-us/our-history

Morantz, R. M. (1982). Feminism, professionalism, and germs: The thought of Mary Putnam Jacobi and Elizabeth Blackwell. *American Quarterly, 34*(5), 459–478.

Mueller, P. S., Plevak, D. J., & Rummans, T. A. (2001). Religious involvement, spirituality, and medicine: Implications for clinical practice. *Mayo Clinic Proceedings, 76*(12), 1225–1235.

Murray, C. J., & Frenk, J. (2010). Ranking 37th—Measuring the performance of the US health care system. *New England Journal of Medicine, 362*(2), 98–99.

Nagpal, K., Vats, A., Ahmed, K., Smith, A. B., Sevdalis, N., Jonannsson, H., … Moorthy, K. (2010). A systematic quantitative assessment of risks associated with poor communication in surgical care. *Archives of Surgery, 145*(6), 582–588.

Nightingale, F. (1859). *Notes on nursing.* London, UK: Duckworth.

Nuland, S. B. (2012). Yale University's Interdisciplinary Center for Bioethics lecture.

Nuremberg Code. (1947). Retrieved from https://history.nih.gov/research/downloads/nuremberg.pdf

Pascal, B. (1670). *Pensées de M. Pascal sur la religion, et sur quelques autres sujets.* Paris, France: Guillaume Desprez.

Pásztor, E. (1993). Parallels between three-dimensional thinking in neurosurgery and the development of perspective in art. *Acta Neurochirurgica, 124*(2–4), 176–178.

Perry, M., Maffulli, N., Willson, S., & Morrissey, D. (2011). The effectiveness of arts-based interventions in medical education: A literature review. *Medical Education, 45*(2), 141–148.

Petrini, C., & Gainotti, S. (2008). A personalist approach to public-health ethics. *Bulletin of the World Health Organization, 86*(8), 624–629.

Phaneuf, M. (2007). Le concept d'humanitude: Une application aux soins infirmiers généraux. Infiressources, 1–21.

Presti, R. L. (2010). Anatomy as epistemology: The body of man and the body of medicine in Vesalius and his ancient sources (Celsus, Galen). *Renaissance and Reformation, 33*(3), 27–60.

Prothrow-Stith, D. (2004). Strengthening the collaboration between public health and criminal justice to prevent violence. *The Journal of Law, Medicine and Ethics, 32*(1), 82–88.

Racine, L. (2009). Examining the conflation of multiculturalism, sexism, and religious fundamentalism through Taylor and Bakhtin: Expanding post-colonial feminist epistemology. *Nursing Philosophy, 10*(1), 14–25.

Riddick, F. (2003). The code of medical ethics of the American medical association. *Ochsner Journal, 5*(2), 6–10.

Rio, R. E., & Tenney, K. S. (2002). Music therapy for juvenile offenders in residential treatment. *Music Therapy Perspectives, 20*(2), 89–97.

Rogers, C. (1951). *Client-centered therapy: Its current practice, implications and theory.* London, UK: Constable.

Rollins, J. (2005). Tell me about it: Drawing as a communication tool for children with cancer. *Journal of Pediatric Oncology Nursing, 22*(4), 203–221.

Rose, M. (2011). *A new leaf: The benefits of arts education in prisons.* Bloomington, IN: Indiana University.

Safley, T. M. (2003). *Reformation of charity: The secular and the religious in early modern poor relief.* Boston, MA: Brill.

Sanders, P. (2006). Why person-centred therapists must reject the medicalization of distress. *Self and Society, 34*(3), 32–39.

Scarry, E. (1999). *On beauty and being just.* Princeton, NJ: Princeton University Press.

Segen, J. C. (2006). *Concise dictionary of modern medicine.* New York, NY: McGraw-Hill.

Siegel, R. E. (1973). *Galen's system of physiology and medicine.* Basel, Switzerland: Karger.

Siraisi, N. G. (2007). *History, medicine, and the traditions of renaissance learning.* Ann Arbor, MI: University of Michigan Press.

Slutkin, G., Ransford, C. L., Decker, B., & Volker, K. (2015). *Cure violence—An evidence based method to reduce shootings and killings.* New York, NY: World Bank.

Stader, T. (2017). *Our story.* Phoenix, AZ: The Library Project. Retrieved from https://www.library-project.org/about/story

Teague, A. K., Hahna, N. D., & McKinney, C. H. (2006). Group music therapy with women who have experienced intimate partner violence. *Music Therapy Perspectives, 24*(2), 80–86.

The Life You Can Save. (2017). *We can do it … You can help: The life you can save's 2017 strategic plan.* Princeton, NJ: Author.

Tournay, V., & Leibing, A. (2010). *Les technologies de l'espoir: La Fabrique d'une histoire à accomplir.* Québec, Canada: Presses Universitaire de Laval.

Treffert, D. A. (1973). Dying with their rights on. *American Journal of Psychiatry, 130*(1), 9.

Vallaeys, A. (2004). *Médecins Sans Frontières: La biographie.* Paris, France: Fayard.

Verghese, A. (2009). A touch of sense. *Health Affairs, 28*(4), 1177–1182.

Virchow, R. (1848). *Die Medizinische Reform, 2.*

Winnicott, D. W. (1964). *The child, the family, and the outside world.* New York, NY: Penguin.

14

Nonviolence Approaches

Introduction

> Nonviolence is a weapon of the strong.
>
> —*Mohandas Gandhi,* Words of Gandhi *(1982)*

This chapter is the last on interventions in this volume. Extending the transition from "law and order" to the health model, nonviolence is the logical continuation and perhaps the most effective principle yet. To review, criminal justice establishes that we can centralize and organize the use of violence, while the law shows that we can regulate society, nationally and internationally. Public health demonstrates that we can prevent violence before it happens, while medicine underscores that we can care for others at the human level, locally and globally. Nonviolence may seem an odd and "toothless" choice of method to counter a problem as serious as violence, but we will see that it is one of the most powerful antidotes. It represents a growing revelation that we can employ our essential humanity to cure our violent tendencies, even society-wide. In Chapter 13, "Global Medicine Approaches," we argued that effective global approaches require close contact with the person and the local. Regard for the full, inextinguishable dignity of the person does not end there. It begins with the caregiver–receiver relationship but ends when the circle completes and the hierarchy disappears, in the expression of reverence for all life (Schweitzer, Winston, & Winston, 1965). Suffering may bring a person to a moment of need, but greater power and insight can emerge from the process of becoming, which is the purpose of being (Maslow, 1962).

Empowerment thus happens when the person recovers, rises, and recreates a situation where the affliction or oppression not only may not recur, but where that overcoming power has the potential to uplift the world (Mollica, 2006). To get to the core of preventing violence means to arrive not just at peace*keeping* but at peace*building* that grows out of the creativity, generativity, and life-giving energy that are the hallmark of health. How, then, does personal empowerment translate into popular empowerment? Personal transformation provides insight into the seemingly daunting change humanity needs to reverse its relentless trend of violence (Nhất Hạnh, 1993). Oppressed peoples around the world, themselves wounded healers, can take on the task of healing the world through the method of nonviolence. Just as a shift has been happening in our way of dealing with violence from the "law and order" approach (meeting violence with violence) to the "health and humanism" approach (meeting violence with healing), a collective shift in consciousness from violence to nonviolence might be possible.

Nonviolence derives from the Sanskrit word *ahimsa*, or "lack of desire to harm or kill," and refers to: (a) the principle or practice of abstaining from the use of violence (Simpson & Weiner,

Violence: An Interdisciplinary Approach to Causes, Consequences, and Cures, First Edition. Bandy X. Lee.
© 2019 John Wiley & Sons, Inc. Published 2019 by John Wiley & Sons, Inc.

1989); or (b) the use of peaceful means, not force, to bring about political or social change (Simpson & Weiner, 1993). The negative or absence of something, however, does not imply the same in the English-speaking culture as in many Eastern traditions, where spaces of absence carry great significance, sometimes more than material presence, and hence the absence of an act can be more momentous than the act itself (Connolly, 2015). Mohandas Gandhi, leader of the Indian independence movement and pioneer of nonviolence in the twentieth century, preferred the expression *satyagraha*, which is Sanskrit for "holding firmly to" (*agraha*) "truth" (*satya*). Apart from terminology, the relative weakness of the concept of nonviolence is also attributable to preconceptions.

For example, history abounds with examples of nonviolence as a way of ending violence, which often are far more successful in achieving social and political ends than violence, but we do not "see" these successes (Howes, 2013) because of our prevailing paradigm of violence. In other words, our general framework of how the world works revolves around violence, and therefore we are more likely to persist and to insist on violent methods, no matter how little success they demonstrate and even in the face of great failure (Pape, 1996). However, just as the prevention of violence has turned out to be not only possible but effective and cost-effective (Gilligan, 2001), nonviolence has proven to be not only utopian but also powerful and enduring (Gregg, 1934). A discerning discussion of approaches to preventing violence, as well as how to think about violence in order to prevent it effectively, must include nonviolence, the history, application, and basic tenets of which we will review in this chapter.

Historical Basis

Examples of successful nonviolence are harder to find than those of successful violence in history books, not because they are rare, but because our prevailing paradigm of violence "recognizes" violent episodes more readily than the less dramatic but more durable instances of nonviolence (Bartkowski, 2013). However, scholars of nonviolence are beginning to document and explain better the power of nonviolence, especially in the past 150 years (Cortright, 2008). The seeds of nonviolent practices trace back to prehistory and humanity's first civilizations, which include individual actions as well as the influences of the major world religions (Adolf, 2009). All the major Indian religious traditions (Hinduism, Buddhism, and Jainism), as well as as the major Abrahamic religions (Judaism, Christianity, and Islam) emphasize nonviolence as a way of life. While Hinduism pioneered and perfected the principles of *ahimsa*, Mahavira (599 BCE to 527 BCE) of Jainism first coined the term. The *Chandogya Upanishad* of the *Upanishads*, or part of Hinduism's principal scriptures dating back to the eight or seventh century B.C.E., instructs in nonviolence toward all creatures (*sarvabhuta*) (Tähtinen, 1964). Buddhism's founder, Siddhartha Gautama (ca. 563/480 BCE to ca. 483/400 BCE), put forth the Noble Eightfold Path: right understanding, right intention, right speech, right action, right livelihood, right effort, right mindfulness, and right concentration (Gelsey, 2014), which commits one to the pursuit of enlightenment, based on unity, universality, and loving-kindness toward all beings (metta) (Keown, 2005). Taoism explains that those who are in harmony with the Tao engage in completely natural, effortless action (*wu-wei*) that does not harm (Creel, 1970).

Tikkun olam, which in Hebrew means "repairing the world," is a key aspect of Judaism that considers nonviolent kindness to be a foundation for fixing what is wrong with the world (Gottlieb, 2011). Christianity arose out of predictions of an eternal, peaceful reign embodied in the *Messiah* Jesus (ca. 4 BCE to ca. CE 30/33), who would meet violent hate with nonviolent love (Anders, 2016). Islam also begins with nonviolence: the word itself means "peace," which begins with its founder Muhammad (ca. 570–632) revealing the reward of submission to *Allah*, or "the Lord" (Esposito, 1994); the Arabic terms for nonviolence as a life decision are *islam*, as a method *jihad* ("struggle for justice"), and as a principle underlying both *tawhid* ("affirmation of the unity of God") (Harris, 2010). Also significant are modern pagan traditions (Madden, 2005) and the philosophy of American author Henry David Thoreau (1817–1862), who had a major impact on Russian author Leo Tolstoy, Gandhi, and American Civil Rights activists.

Successful nonviolent campaigns have been recorded since the plebeians withdrew from Rome in the fifth century BCE. Another example is William of Orange's 1688 Glorious Revolution against King James II of England, which saw James' larger army dissolve within a week, and a political victory occurred without military conflict. In the 1850s and 1860s, statesman Ferenc Deák led the Hungarians into a massive nonviolence resistance against despotic Austrian rule in a way that made the opponents' repression rebound and undermine their own power. Nonviolent action has served to secure the workers' right to organize, women's rights, universal suffrage, abolition of slavery, national independence, democracy, civil rights, racial integration, and greater equality for all. By far the most influential nonviolent struggle is the Indian independence movement (Nagler, 2001). Gandhi drew from his Hindu background "the greatest force in the world," or "the one constructive process of Nature in the midst of incessant destruction going on about us" (Gandhi, 1993b, p. 240). Its power dawned on him in 1906 at a meeting on migrant Indian community rights in Durban, South Africa. The community had gathered in a theater and was about to vote on whether to refuse to register themselves, as the government was requiring in order to gain control over them. A member of the crowd stood up and suggested that they not only vote on the issue but also take an oath not to register. This greatly impressed Gandhi, who saw the enormous difference in binding force between a simple vote and a personal oath—which called on a much deeper personal commitment, unto death.

This is the kind of commitment that lies behind nonviolent acts (Downton & Wehr, 1998), and what gave Gandhi the inspiration to return to India in 1915 and to lead a movement that eventually brought down the British Raj. His actions subsequently led to the downfall of imperialism, which at the time claimed most of the world. Most famous among his campaigns is the 26-day Salt March in 1930 in resistance to the British-imposed salt tax. When he and 4,000 followers arrived at the sea, Gandhi took a brief swim and scooped up salt and saltwater in his hands, and 83 volunteers dug and carried off salt deposits in bags (Sharp, 2005). This broke the Salt Act, eventually leading to Great Britain's grant of Indian independence in 1947.

More Recent Examples

In the United States, the Civil Rights Movement of the 1950s and 1960s, also known as the Black Freedom Struggle, is one of the most successful, protracted periods calling upon nonviolent action in the country (Morris, 1986). At a time when, according to the law in Alabama, African-Americans had to pay their fare and then sit in the back of the bus, Rosa Parks's refusal to yield her seat to a white man sparked the Montgomery Bus Boycott in 1955, whereby people refused to take the bus until the law changed. At the front was Baptist minister Martin Luther King, Jr., who drew directly from Gandhi's philosophy and Christian inspiration, and in the back was educator Septima Clark, who supported the movement through literacy and citizenship workshops, who together emerged as the primary leaders. Nonviolent protests and civil disobedience gave rise to the Civil Rights Act of 1957 (desegregation of public schools), the Civil Rights Act of 1960 (penalties for voter obstruction), the Civil Rights Act of 1964 (outlawing of discrimination based on race, color, religion, sex, or national origin), the Voting Rights Act of 1965 (prohibition of racial discrimination in voting), and the Civil Rights Act of 1968 (equal housing opportunities regardless of race, creed, or national origin).

Other struggles for justice soon followed, including the Women's Liberation Movement, the American Indian Movement, anti-nuclear protests, anti-Vietnam War protests, and rallies for gay rights, environmental protection, and continued workers' rights. Campaigns of the latter category included the California grape workers' strike and boycott in 1965; these workers suffered from abject poverty, displacement, homelessness, economic exploitation, and a lack of union representation (Merriman, 2009). The Agricultural Workers Organizing Committee (AWOC) joined with a young Chicano leader, Cesar Chavez, and his Mexican-based National Farm Workers Association (NFWA) to lead a nonviolent movement, and the Delano growers finally agreed to a pay increase in 1970. These movements inspired many regions of the world to similarly pursue desegregation and greater justice. These examples show that nonviolence is good not only for dissolving oppressive regimes but also for reforming democratic ones; both outcomes have happened numerous times throughout American history.

Meanwhile, the same kind of dramatic result was happening with the Solidarity Movement in Poland 1977 and in Czechoslovakia from the 1960s to the 1980s—movements that eventually led the collapse of the Soviet Empire (Bernhard, 1993). The Polish Solidarity Movement began with a nongovernmental trade union in the early 1980s and soon became a broad, nonviolent, anti-Communist social movement that contributed greatly to the fall of Communism around half the world. Lech Wałęsa, a former shipyard worker and electrician, together with other workers' representatives, formed Solidarity, the first independent labor union in a Soviet-bloc country. Over time, 9–10 million workers, intellectuals, and students joined, and soon 80% of the total Polish work force voluntarily belonged to a single organization, for the first time in history (Cirtautas, 1997). In reaction, Poland's Communist government instituted martial law, but the movement went underground and generated the disintegrative force that eventually drove the Soviet Union and its Empire into oblivion. After several years of political repression the government was forced to negotiate, leading to semi-free elections in 1989. A Solidarity-coalition government was formed, and Wałęsa was elected president. A dismantling of the Communist governmental system and Poland's transformation into a modern democratic state led to a spread of anti-Communist ideas and movements throughout the Eastern Bloc, weakening Communist strongholds and culminating in the Revolutions of 1989 (Kenney, 2002). These were not small events in history but involved the great empires of their day. Nonviolence did not remain in the margins of history but became a source of movements that shook the world.

An enormous wave of nonviolent, democratic movements at the end of the twentieth century followed, in the Philippines, Greece, Spain, Portugal, Chile, Argentina, and about two dozen more countries around the world (Markoff, 2015). Concurrently, the cruder, territorial types of imperialism that girdled the globe in the early twentieth century and onward universally disappeared. Although there were violent movements as well, nonviolence was at the center of this progress, such as in the collapse of the apartheid regime in South Africa and the highly influential Truth and Reconciliation Commission that followed. Other recent successes include the nonviolent campaigns of Leymah Gbowee and the women of Liberia, who were able to peacefully end a 14-year civil war and bring to power the country's first female president (Fuest, 2009). Others are the 2003 Rose Revolution of Georgia, the 2004 Orange Revolution of Ukraine, and the 2011 Jasmine Revolution of Tunisia. Nonviolent movements played a critical role in 50 of 67 transitions from authoritarianism between 1966 and 1999 (Ackerman & DuVall, 2000), and now a staggering two-thirds of humanity benefits (Ives, 2001).

Looking at all known campaigns for self-determination between 1900 and 2006, nonviolent actions were twice as likely to succeed as violent ones (Chenoweth & Stephan, 2011). Nonviolent movements also increased the chances that peace and democratic rule would succeed the overthrow of the authoritarian regime, and this applied even to highly authoritarian and repressive countries where nonviolent resistance is usually expected to fail. Movements that opt for violence, on the other hand, often unleash terrible destruction and bloodshed, often without realizing their end goals (Stephan & Chenoweth, 2008). Nonviolent resistance has been shown to succeed, not because it melts the hearts of dictators and secret police, but because it is better than armed struggle at attracting mass participation and diverse tactics, imposing unsustainable costs on a regime.

We cannot ignore the major role of women in nonviolent movements. Legend and history tell of their facing violence with the power of spirit: Saccedina of Morocco subdued a Muslim army of 6,000 men through wisdom, Saint Geneviève saved Paris from the Huns through prayer, and Saint Clare protected Assisi from the Saracens through sacraments, to give just a few examples. Contemporary accounts are not lacking: a study of 40 peace processes over the last three decades showed that when women were allowed to influence a peace process, an agreement was almost always reached, and the peace was more likely to endure (O'Reilly, Súilleabháin, & Paffenholz, 2015). Women's empowerment in general is overwhelmingly associated with peace in a society (Caprioli, 2000; Gizelis, 2011; Hudson et al., 2012; Regan & Paskeviciute, 2003), and greater female participation in parliament reduces the risks of war (Caprioli & Boyer, 2001) and human rights abuses (Melander, 2005). Women are more effective at defying terrorism, being among the first targets of fundamentalism (Bennoune, 2014), and preventing violent extremism in the first place through cooperation, dialog, and trust (Disney & Reticker, 2015). Women serving in police forces are more successful than militaries at combating terrorism (O'Neill & Vary, 2010), while other women more readily report gender-based violence to them (Peters, 2014). Meanwhile, women are more likely than their male counterparts to deescalate tensions and to refrain from using excessive force (Lonsway et al., 2002).

Parties in conflict may see women as less threatening because they are typically acting outside of formal power structures and are not commonly assumed to be mobilizing fighting forces (Anderlini, 2007). Women frequently elicit broader societal participation, mobilizing across ethnic, religious, political, and cultural divides, building coalitions and political legitimacy (Chang et al., 2015). Women are less likely to take up arms, but they die in higher numbers from war's indirect effects (Kuehnast, de Jonge Oudraat, & Hernes, 2011)—the breakdown in social order, human rights abuses, the spread of infectious diseases, and economic devastation—and thus raise different priorities during peace negotiations (Page, Whitman, & Anderson, 2009). Having suffered subordination through much of history, it would not be surprising if women—and other disadvantaged groups—had special access to what Czech statesman Václav Havel (1985) called, "the power of the powerless."

Criticisms

Nonviolence is not the prevailing paradigm, and thus is *ipso facto* difficult to visualize. The starting point being violence, there is no shortage of moral and practical dilemmas skeptics are able to raise as impediments to taking nonviolence seriously; hence, we start here with criticisms before an explanation of the basic concepts. Three criticisms are the most prominent: (a) that nonviolence is passive; (b) that it is ineffective; and (c) that it denies one the right to self-defense.

The first criticism is that nonviolence is passive. Conventional wisdom dictates that violence is the supreme force, the decider of fates. If you shun it, it may feel good, but your family will be killed, your country will be overrun, you will worship a foreign god—and you will lose everything and be wiped out. Therefore, nonviolence may even be *immoral*, because it involves abdication of principle.

The second criticism is that nonviolence is ineffective. Often emphasized are the failures to effect political change in Tibet, Burma, China, and Palestine. Critics say that nonviolence is ineffective in bringing about real change, since it does not exercise "real power," or the power of the state and the military. Others go so far as to say that violent movements defend life, while nonviolent ones sacrifice it through beatings, arrests, tortures, or the self-defeating reluctance to finish off an opponent. Feminist critiques have been similar: in a patriarchal structure, women were expected to accept suffering and practice patience in the face of male violence, and such an approach has merely left them in a second-class position. English novelist George Orwell (1949) expressed the most common criticism when he stated it would be very difficult to see how nonviolent methods could be useful in countries without freedom of the press or the right of assembly.

The third criticism is that nonviolence denies the right to self-defense. Russian revolutionary Leon Trotsky, psychiatrist Frantz Fanon of Martinique, Indian nationalist Subhas Chandra Bose, and American activist Malcolm X were among fervent critics who viewed nonviolence and pacifism as attempts to impose bourgeois morals on the proletariat to deny the fundamental right to defend oneself. Black Panther member George Jackson (1994) described King's nonviolent tactics as "a false ideal [presupposing] the existence of compassion and a sense of justice on the part of one's adversary." Anarchist Peter Gelderloos (2007) argues that nonviolence expects "oppressed people, many of whom are people of color, to suffer patiently under an inconceivably greater violence." In other words, nonviolence is a deliberate attempt to render resurgent groups harmless.

All these are understandable criticisms. However, we will argue here that they presuppose a unidimensional concept of power, as that manifesting in violence. We propose a different notion of power, one that American political theorist Hannah Arendt (1970) called the opposite of violence, and therefore would be expected to emerge as violence disappears.

Basic Tenets

Gandhi likened the rigorous preparation for and ongoing practice of nonviolent discipline to the training of a soldier (Gandhi, 1993a). Contrary to surface appearance, starting within the individual may require more courage than waging war, for one is generating the preconditions for peace through *justicemaking* and rebellion in defiance of the status quo (Adams et al., 1990). Indian journalist Krishnalal Shridharani wrote in *War without Violence* (1939) that nonviolent action resembles military action, except it uses psychological, social, political, and economic pressures rather than violence. It is also nonconformist: by emulating as little as possible the army that one fights, one is refusing to reproduce the violence while usurping "the greatest weapon in the hands of the oppressor," which is the mind of the oppressed (Biko and Stubbs, 1978). It is the opposite of passive submission, impotence, or acceptance and should not be confused with it because of surface appearances. Defenders of the status quo, rather, have pacifist tendencies in that they prefer conciliation over disruption of existing notions—since "war" as a concrete concept actually gives a sense of familiarity and comfort. American writer D. A. Clarke clarifies that nonviolent tactics will be of little or no use to groups that are traditionally considered incapable of violence, since nonviolence will be in keeping with expectations for them.

Nonviolence, far from doing nothing, represents a radical break from "business as usual" and requires courage as well as inventiveness and active imagination. Mobilizing the power of the mind allows for violence to lose its power of deception. Gandhi (1993a) cautioned that those who embrace a life of nonviolence must commit all aspects of their lives to this approach. To be nonviolent in some domains but not in others would be a policy, not a life force. Nonviolence is one step above violence-as the renunciation of one's capacity for violence, while violence is one step above cowardice, which is the capacity for neither. He offered several simple axioms for nonviolence:

a) Nonviolence implies complete self-purification as is humanly possible.
b) The strength of nonviolence is in exact proportion to the ability, not the will, of the nonviolent person to inflict violence.
c) Nonviolence is without exception superior to violence; that is, the power at the disposal of a nonviolent person is always greater than one would have if one were violent.
d) There is no such thing as defeat in nonviolence; the end of violence is the surest defeat.
e) The ultimate end of nonviolence is the surest victory, if such a term may be used of nonviolence (in reality, there is no sense of defeat or of victory).

Nonviolent action starts with individual transformation, and has the power of simultaneously being rooted in the universal as well as being highly responsive to the immediate plight of groups. King (1963) notes that everyone must decide whether to walk in the light of "creative altruism" or in the darkness of "destructive selfishness"—and since only light can drive out darkness, the act of loving is what is revolutionary, not the countering of hate with hate. American political scientist Gene Sharp (2005) views nonviolent action as a technique that rejects passivity and submission to violence but questions how to wield power effectively through wise strategy and tactics. The effectiveness of nonviolent struggles has even been demonstrated against the Nazi regime (Stoltzfus, 2001): it is not only a more moral but also a more effective way of achieving political aims, without alienating opponents and bystanders.

Nonviolence does not seem as powerful as violence by impression, even in the word itself that only describes what it is not. However, complete absence of violence is not inaction, as history itself has witnessed, and the negative term can be misleading, as it originates from a culture that accepts that some concepts are indescribable: *ahimsa* in Sanskrit follows a tradition that sometimes names obliquely, according to the next highest order (as nonviolence is to violence) (Salgado et al., 1996). Other traditions believe that eternal concepts are categorically unnamable (Laozi, 1853), which does not imply nonexistence but rather a form of *hyper*existence beyond the categories of naming (Johansen, 2007). As American psychologist Abraham Maslow noted, we may fear to know the fearsome and unsavory aspects of ourselves, but we fear even more to know the godlike in ourselves (Galardi, 2009).

The minimal characterization may evoke the need for evolution: we are still transitioning from the renouncing of destructive tendencies to the embracing of constructive ones. We know from the chapter, "The Symbolism of Violence," that the symbolism attached to violence is strong enough to give rise to it even when there is no tangible benefit; this principle in human beings can also render physical violence powerless in the face of greater meaning (Tolstoy, 1948). Where violence is life energy gone awry, nonviolence can be a form of positive, healthy energy that affirms life as opposed to invites death. Since violence is a reaction against powerlessness, those who are drawn to true power are less likely to need a guise but focus directly on content. Meekness and gentleness are not weaknesses but strength under control—and having strength as content, outward displays are unnecessary.

Applications

Once a group has decided to move forward with nonviolent action, myriad strategies are available. Sharp (2005) identified nearly two hundred; examples include nonviolent protest, noncooperation, nonviolent intervention, constructive programming, and voluntary association

(Schell, 2003). *Nonviolent protest* is a symbolic action a group of people performs to show their support or disapproval of a policy, group, or government. The goal is to bring public awareness to an issue, to persuade, to influence a particular group of people, or to facilitate future action. Methods include speeches, processions, public communications, petitions, art, and other public assemblies.

Noncooperation, or civil resistance, is the purposeful withholding of support through one's activity, time, finances, and verbal allegiance to authorities. One may practice civil disobedience, stop paying taxes, engage in sit-ins, boycott, break laws that are unjust, strike, and resign from posts in administrations that one opposes. By an act of conscience, one is stating that while one cannot actively fight against all the injustices of the world, at the very least one can withdraw one's share of resources from an unjust system. As it turns out, this is a powerful political act: as Gandhi noted, if the government does not receive the active support of its officials, its soldiers, its police, and its citizens, it cannot endure (Pantham, 1983). Of course, civil disobedience is not easy: one practicing it risks losing one's job, being rejected by the larger community, being jailed, tortured, or even killed. However, if enough people choose the simple act of ceasing to participate in an unjust system, the government is left just making noise, and that will be the end of the regime. States and institutions draw power from the support that people give them, and with its withdrawal, they collapse.

Nonviolent intervention or disruption is a more direct method of nonviolent action (Sharp, 1967). Its strategies actively disrupt the normal operation of policies or systems by deliberate physical, psychological, social, economic, or political interference. This is often more immediate and effective than noncooperation, but also more difficult for the resisters to sustain and harder on the opponents. It encompasses fasting or hunger strikes, occupations, blockades, exposure to the elements, sit-ins, pray-ins, nonviolent raids, truck cavalcades, alternative markets, and other parallel systems. Tactics have to take into account political and cultural circumstances with a strategic larger plan, and the knowledge that they can provoke speedier and more severe repression than either protest or noncooperation. A powerful method of nonviolent intervention is to provoke public or international scrutiny of the oppressors by meeting violent repression with nonviolence: if the police or military attempt to repress nonviolent resisters with violence, power shifts from the oppressors to the resisters. Resisters' fearlessness and willingness to suffer have a profound effect on those acting on behalf of the oppressor, and the police or military will have to accept that they no longer have authority over their opponents (Sharp, 1973). Sharp (2005) notes that participants in a nonviolent struggle often suffer harsh penalties for their defiance, but victories in nonviolent struggle generally have fewer casualties than violent struggles with similar objectives, and sometimes none.

Constructive programming is what Gandhi called "silent plotting" (Schell, 2004). He advised, instead of directing fire at the destructive regime, just going out and doing the things that one believes need doing: if the environment is dirty, clean it up; if people do not have enough income, give them some money; if people are not participating in politics, then organize the village. In other words, rather than waiting to seize power and then pass some legislation, one starts in one's own community and does the things that one can. With action on behalf of one's beliefs, and above all when acting together with others, one generates power. Those in the Solidarity Movement in Poland acted in this way, engaging in what they called "social work"; they began to organize universities, environmental groups, and social justice groups—there was an explosion of civil society. They called themselves "the self-limiting revolution," meaning that they were not going to seek state power but let the government remain in its formal apparatus. However, they discovered, much to their own amazement, that if they were running society, then power eventually fell into their hands. In 1989, that is exactly what happened: while they were doing their social work and helping out workers who were in trouble, they were generating political power—and soon had to be prime minister, minister of justice, and then the government. The existing government realized at a certain point that it was unable to govern Poland without the support of Solidarity. It had nominal power but not real power and had to turn to Solidarity for help, until it simply disintegrated, with the whole Soviet Union falling suite.

Voluntary association or, on a larger scale, nonviolent revolution, is the phenomenon of spontaneous organization that seems to arise out of nowhere and suddenly spring into existence in revolutionary situations (Diamond, 1994). It happened with the American Revolution: even before 1776, so-called "committees of correspondence," or parallel forms of government, simultaneously came into existence in all the towns, the cities, and the states. It is this period which founder John Adams referred to as the Revolution, not the subsequent war, which merely defended what came before (Diemand, 2015). The real revolution occurred when the colonists took over their own lives and formed their own political structures. It happened even more rapidly with the Solidarity Movement: the association began with one shipyard, then all shipyards, and 3 days later all of Poland was on strike and in touch with one another, organizing and developing into a 10-year movement. The Soviet Union ended at that moment, and the rest was a playing out of the inevitable.

Very much the same thing happened at the beginning of the Arab Spring, in Tunisia and Egypt especially, when suddenly people emerged as if from nowhere in Tahrir Square and organized: they had medical centers, food delivery, wound care, communication with one another, and social media (Bellin, 2012). Hannah Arendt (1963) describes similar "counsel systems" in the early days of the Russian, German, American, and French Revolutions, when workers and other ordinary people just got together in their factories or wherever they were, sat down to deliberate, to decide what actions to take as their own "counsels," and to act on those decisions. They are closely related to constructive programming, but there is an additional aspect of embryonic institution-building, as any of their actions could later become institutions. Many American democratic institutions arose from scratch in this manner. French diplomat Alexis De Tocqueville (1835) described this in the concept of civil society: he observed that, as soon as there was a need for something, Americans would organize—to form a temperance league, to fix the roads, or to accomplish some other goal. Voluntary association is unique to nonviolent action, and when it evolves into parallel government, revolution ensues.

Case Studies

A Beacon of Hope Amid Racial Discrimination

Nelson Mandela was a South African anti-apartheid revolutionary and political leader who served as the first black president of South Africa from 1994 to 1999 and changed the face of his nation by dismantling institutionalized racism and fostering racial reconciliation. There were many life-changing moments that steered his journey—but where did it all start? Mandela was born as Rolihlahla (his birth name) into a royal family of the Thembu tribe in the village of Mvezo. His role in the tribal leadership can be credited to Jongintaba Dalindyebo, a high-ranking Thembu regent who adopted Mandela after his father's demise in 1927. Hearing the elders' stories of his ancestors gave him a rich sense of African self-government and heritage, and he dreamed of making his own contribution to the freedom struggle of his people.

Mandela was the first in his family to receive a formal education. He attended primary school in Qunu where his teacher gave him the name Nelson, in accordance with the custom of giving all schoolchildren "Christian" names. Change started trickling into Mandela's life when he entered the elite University of Fort Hare, the only Western-style institute for higher education open to South African blacks in 1939. He did not complete his degree, as he was expelled for joining in a student protest. Then, Mandela ran away from an arranged marriage and found himself in Johannesburg, where the whites were prosperous and the blacks were discriminated against and poor. He ended up taking a variety of jobs, such as guard and clerk, and experienced racial discrimination for the first time. He completed his Bachelor of Arts degree through the University of South Africa and went back to Fort Hare for his graduation in 1943. Meanwhile, he began studying for a law degree at the University of the Witwatersrand but completed it only in 1989, in the last months of his imprisonment, from the University of South Africa.

In Johannesburg, his eyes were opened to the state of segregation in South Africa, and he decided it was time to break from the chains of white supremacy. After the white-only government established apartheid, a system of racial segregation that privileged whites, he became active in the anti-apartheid movement. He joined the African National Congress (ANC) in 1943. Within the ANC, he helped found the African National Congress Youth League. In 1944 he married Evelyn Mase, a nurse. They had two sons, Madiba Thembekile and Makgatho, and two daughters both called Makaziwe, the first of whom died in infancy. Mandela went on to found the Mandela and Tambo law firm to provide legal counsel to unrepresented blacks. Mandela rose through the ranks of the ANC, which adopted a more radical policy in 1949. In 1952, a campaign of civil disobedience against six unjust laws led to his and 19 others' being sentenced to 9 months of hard labor, suspended for 2 years.

The petitioning became a mass grassroots movement. Mandela's tireless nonviolent campaigns went on for 20 long years against the South African government's racial politics. Then came the big blow. In 1956, Mandela and 150 others were charged with treason for their political advocacy. This was Mandela's greatest turning point, after which he achieved great things, including becoming a model of courage through 28 years in prison, leading South Africa to a multiracial democracy, and pursuing peaceful reconciliation as the country's first black president in 1994 (Nelson Mandela Foundation, 2017). He was intent on healing the destructive human divisions that the abhorrent practice of apartheid had spawned.

At a speech in 2007 addressing a conference of top leaders and other Nobel laureates, Mandela called on the world to solve conflicts by reinventing Gandhi's nonviolent approach. The 88-year-old described Gandhi as "the sacred warrior" who combined ethics and morality with a steely resolve that refused to compromise with the oppressor. "In a world driven by violence and strife, Gandhi's message of peace and non-violence holds the key to human survival in the twenty-first century," he said (Bhalla, 2007). We recall words from his autobiography, *Long Walk to Freedom*: "No one is born hating another person because of the color of his skin, or his background, or his religion. People must learn to hate, and if they can learn to hate, they can be taught to love, for love comes more naturally to the human heart than its opposite" (Mandela, 1994). Having emerged from almost three decades of incarceration without a hint of bitterness, and leading his country into a peaceful transition without retribution, Mandela proved himself a nonviolent warrior who continues to inspire generations.

Fighting the Good Fight

A teacher and a civil rights activist, Septima Clark's citizenship schools enfranchised African-Americans in ways that history had not known before. Coming from a young woman, it was hard for many to accept and to understand, and the magnitude of her contribution is still difficult to conceive today. A star was born among the eight children of Peter Poinsette, her father, who was forced to serve as a messenger to Confederate troops as a young slave during the Civil War. Clark grew up on lessons of love and patience. Well educated, she went on to become a teacher. Not long after she acquired her teaching license, segregation and racial discrimination hit her hard. Black teachers were not allowed to teach any students in South Carolina's capital, and this was a moment of change. Her love of teaching rather took her to John's Island until 1919, when she decided to return to her hometown and she went from door to door, collecting signatures of black parents who wanted black teachers to educate their children in Charleston schools. Two-thirds of the city's black population signed the petition, and a year later, Charleston's ban on black teachers was overturned. She not only taught young students, but she held informal literacy classes for adults. Alongside this, she pushed an education and equal rights agenda in numerous organizations such as the Young Women's Christian Association (YWCA), Federation of Women's Clubs, Council of Negro Women, and, most importantly, the National Association for the Advancement of Colored People (NAACP).

Clark could have settled into life as an elementary school teacher, but she kept pushing. Along with other NAACP members, she began to fight for higher salaries for black teachers. It took her more than 20 years to help win equal pay for her colleagues, but in 1945, teacher pay was equalized. In 1956, when South Carolina made it illegal for public servants to participate in civil rights movements, Clark lost her teaching job and pension because she would not give up the cause. She next led literacy and civil rights workshops for black students at a Tennessee school. Clark and her cousin Bernice Robinson created the first citizenship school to educate blacks in literacy, state government, and election procedures. The state of Tennessee revoked the school's charter, forcibly closing down its buildings and arresting teachers on bogus charges. Clark was accused of illegal alcohol possession and arrested, though later released from jail. She continued her work in Georgia, and the "citizenship school" model she started became a juggernaut (Blakemore, 2016).

Traveling throughout the South, Clark trained teachers for citizenship schools and assisted in Southern Christian Leadership Conference (SCLC) marches and protests, working with Martin Luther King Jr. and the pastor Andrew Jackson Young Jr. It helped fill the educational gaps of segregated school systems for black students, producing smart new voters and changing the course of the Civil Rights Movement. Among her mentees was Rosa Parks, who sparked a decisive movement. With Clark, NAACP racked up many victories and changed the course of the nation's history. King acknowledged Clark when he received the Nobel Peace Prize in 1964 by insisting that she accompany him to Sweden (Black Past, 2017).

In 1979, President Jimmy Carter honored her with a Living Legacy Award. South Carolina, which once threw her out of her job, crowned her with its highest civilian honor in 1982, the Order of the Palmetto. "The greatest evil in our country today is not racism, but ignorance," Clark wrote in her autobiography (Clark & Brown, 1990). Clark understood the underlying work that was necessary before a movement could be possible, which is the essence of nonviolence. By offering black citizens literacy, the confidence to think and then to claim the rights of citizenship, she cultivated the spirit of one of the greatest nonviolent movements of her nation's history. Thus starting as a daughter of a slave, she became a teacher and "the queen mother" of the American Civil Rights Movement.

The Father of a Nation

Who would have thought that a rebellious teenager from India who desired to be a British gentleman would then return to become a revered leader of an independence movement in his home country? Mohandas Gandhi, activist leader of the Indian independence movement against British rule who came to inspire nonviolent civil disobedience movements throughout the world, was born in the princely state of Porbandar in 1869. His father worked for the government as the chief minister of Porbandar, and his mother was a deeply pious woman who spent a lot of her time at temple and went on frequent fasts. She instilled in Gandhi a strong

Hindu ethic, with an emphasis on vegetarianism, religious tolerance, a simple lifestyle, and nonviolence. At the age of 13 Gandhi married Kasturba, a local girl of 14. He was a rebellious teenager—drinking, eating meat, and womanizing—but when he left his father on his deathbed to have sex with his wife and missed the moment of his death, it marked him. He subsequently moved to London to study law, dressed in Western clothes, and tried his best to become a gentleman.

The real turning point in Gandhi's life, however, came when he went to South Africa in 1893. The lawyer from London, who was traveling on a contract to lend services to help Sheikh Abdulla, a Gujarati servant, faced racial discrimination from the moment he landed. When Gandhi landed in Durban, he took a train to reach his destination, traveling first class. The train halted at Pietermaritzburg where an Englishman entered the compartment. Custom dictated that Gandhi vacate the compartment for the "white man" and move to third class. He did not know this and fought for his rights. He argued that he had paid for the ticket, and it was his legal right to travel first class. Gandhi was dragged and pushed out of the train along with his luggage. At an odd hour, in a country he did not know, he was cold and puzzled. The station master even took his luggage, and Gandhi spent a sleepless night fighting the cold and thinking. That incident changed his life. He realized that the injustice was not about education or personal grudges; it was a deep-rooted social disease.

In 1913, Gandhi organized a strike against a tax on people of Indian descent. For the first time, he led working-class Indians in a 2,221-person march from Natal into the Transvaal. Gandhi was arrested and sentenced to 9 months in prison, but the strike spread and the British were forced to drop the tax and to release him. He returned to India in 1915 with determination and a vision. He joined the Indian National Congress and transformed it from an elite group to a party of mass appeal (Hardiman, 2017). He wanted a free India based on religious tolerance and acceptance of all. Indians of all classes and religions came to embrace his calls for nonviolent protests. His unorthodox advocacy included the call to wear *khadi*, or homespun cloth, instead of British-made textiles, and he himself spent much time spinning *khadi*. When rioting broke out as a result of the Jallianwala Bagh Massacre, where British forces open fired and killed hundreds of innocent civilians, Gandhi criticized the protesters instead, urging them to use love and to help also "liberate" the British of themselves (Cultural India, 2017). He called for a deeper strength than violence, stating: "The weak can never forgive. Forgiveness is the attribute of the strong" (Gandhi, 1958). By redefining victory by violence as tantamount to defeat, he allowed for Indians and countless others after him to envision a more enduring triumph that was accessible even to the common people. In this manner, the humble man who dressed and lived like the poorest of impoverished India became a *mahātmā*, or a great soul, the father of a nation, and an inspiration for the world.

Lessons From a War Zone

Florence Nightingale was an English social reformer and the founder of modern nursing who, through her far-sighted ideas influenced the very nature of modern healthcare. She fought for much that has become standard today: open-air hospitals, nursing as an honored profession, and data-driven research (Sweet, 2014). She was born in 1820 into an affluent, well-connected British family. Raised in a fairytale setting, she defied social expectations by becoming a nurse and transforming the profession into a respectable one for women. She became famous for her presence in the devastating Crimea War, as a compassionate figure who attended to sick and wounded soldiers. She arrived at the war in November 1854. With no beds or blankets for the wounded, and rats and fleas everywhere, she realized that soldiers were dying of preventable diseases from bad health care, not from battle wounds. Cholera, typhus, and many diseases flourished as a result of unsanitary and inhumane living conditions, but above all, there were no substantial medical records to refer to. There were no records of the deaths, or the causes of death, of hundreds of soldiers. This was a moment of change for Nightingale.

She started collecting data. She employed others to join her and to record the numbers of those who were killed, injured, or died of other causes on the field. When she journeyed back from Crimea to London, it was with statistics supporting proposed medical reforms. She began getting in touch with government officials and people with scientific training. Her statistical records saw the light of the day when she decided to come up with a comprehensive diagram depicting the reasons for soldiers' deaths. She revealed shocking facts that people had guessed but no one could quantify. She vividly communicated that more men had died from disease than from their wounds. She then instigated a Royal Commission into the health of the army, which led to a large number of improvements and saved the lives of many. Nightingale is credited with inventing the pie chart and was the first woman to be elected to the Royal Statistical Society. She was also the first woman to be awarded the Freedom of the City of London, which she received in 1909. She campaigned tirelessly to improve health standards, publishing over 200 books, reports, and pamphlets on hospital planning and organization that are still widely read today, including her most famous work, *Notes on Nursing: What It Is and What It Is Not* (Nightingale, 1859). She also wrote some 13,000 letters as a part of her campaigns (Florence Nightingale Museum, 2017).

Nightingale's influence on today's healthcare ranges from her ward designs (known as Nightingale Wards), which were developed in response to a realization that hospital buildings themselves could affect the health and recovery of patients, to pioneering infection control measures and the championing of nutrition as a key factor for recovery. In her own words: "The very first requirement in a hospital [was] that it should do the sick no harm" (Nightingale, 1859). In 1860, she established the first professional training school for nurses, Nightingale Training School at Saint Thomas's Hospital. Its reputation soon spread, and Nightingale nurses were requested to start new schools all over the world, including Australia, America, and Africa. She also believed in the need for specialist midwifery nurses and established a School of Midwifery nursing at King's College Hospital, which became a model for the country. She inspired the founding of the International Red Cross, which still awards the Nightingale Medal for nurses who demonstrate exceptional care to the sick and wounded in war or peace. Her works thus influenced many reforms and became the paragon of prevention, saving many lives but also critical to the advancement of public health and of women's education—both of which are now powerful contributors to peace.

The Monk With a Cause

Dalai Lamas, the spiritual and temporal leaders of the Tibetan people, are manifestations of the patron saint of Tibet and believed to be the reincarnation of Avalokitesvara, an important Buddhist deity and the personification of compassion. The present Dalai Lama, Tenzin Gyatso, calls himself "a simple Buddhist monk". He was born to farmers as Lhamo Dhondup in 1935 in Taktser, China. He was the fifth of 16 children. The 13th Dalai Lama identified him as the next spiritual master at the age of two, citing many spiritual signs. He was renamed Tenzin Gyatso when he became the 14th Dalai Lama. Things changed for Tenzin in 1950, when he was called upon to assume full political responsibility as head of the state and government, and the People's Republic of China invaded Tibet. In 1954, he went to Beijing to hold peace talks with Mao Tsetung and other Chinese leaders. In 1956, while visiting India to attend the 2500th birth anniversary of the Buddha, he had a series of meetings with the Indian prime minister about the deteriorating situation in Tibet.

Despite his efforts to bring about a peaceful solution to the Sino-Tibetan problem, Beijing's ruthless policy in eastern Tibet ignited a popular uprising, and in 1959, the capital of Tibet, Lhasa, exploded with a massive demonstration for Tibet's independence. Fearing assassination, the Dalai Lama and thousands of followers fled to Dharamsala in northern India, where they established an alternative government. Today more than 120,000 Tibetan refugees are in India, Nepal, Bhutan, and the West. In the early years of exile, the Dalai Lama appealed to the United Nations, which resulted in the General Assembly's adoption of three resolutions, in 1959, 1961, and 1965, calling on China to respect the human rights of Tibetans and their right to self-determination. Since then, the Dalai Lama has worked tirelessly to establish peace around the world and for the cause of a free Tibet. The monk who fled from his own hometown is now celebrated around the world for his humanitarian efforts. The Dalai Lama was awarded the Nobel Peace Prize in 1989 for his lectures and workshops devoted to peace.

The citation of the Norwegian Nobel Committee stated:

> The Dalai Lama in his struggle for the liberation of Tibet has consistently opposed the use of violence. He has instead advocated peaceful solutions based upon tolerance and mutual respect in order to preserve the historical and cultural heritage of his people. The Dalai Lama has developed his philosophy of peace from a great reverence for all things living and upon the concept of universal responsibility embracing all mankind as well as nature. *(Office of Tibet, 2011)*

He has managed to apply to his time and place the Buddhist quest for decisive knowledge of the human condition, or the recognition that life is an endless cycle of suffering, disease, death, and rebirth, bred of ignorance and an ingrained misconception of reality, and that liberation or enlightenment comes when, through the training of the mind, the mind itself is transcended. This brings us to fulfillment and peace: "Love and compassion [which] are necessities, not luxuries. Without them, humanity cannot survive" (Lama & Cutler, 1998). The Dalai Lama's role as a preeminent monk is today almost universally acknowledged among the different schools of Buddhism. In a battle between capitalist materialism and Buddhist spiritualism, between the power of the gun and the power of wisdom and compassion, the Dalai Lama reaches out to the world with messages of wisdom, compassion, and, increasingly, environmental sustainability (Biography, 2011).

Conclusion

Recent history refutes the argument that violence is inevitable, and nonviolence may be the most powerful antidote to violence yet known. This is not the absolute, infinite concept of peace and goodwill of fantasies but a rational, practical peace that is attained through an effective solving of problems. It is rather the current system that is unsustainable. If we were to consider the most prominent aspects of how our current civilization maintains order and operates the economy, and of its overall structure, it would not be an exaggeration to say that it is violence: we organize everything through violence, or the threat of violence. We therefore live in a violent world, and even the ability to "see" nonviolence requires active imagination, a letting go of the familiar, and an ability to believe. We can then recognize that a vast portion of the world's population now enjoys the benefits of nonviolent action, which has proven to be effective in many domains. It is the first demonstration that a change of consciousness can not only dramatically reduce human violence but improve conditions of life. To understand better, it is necessary to study nonviolence in rigorous ways; this requires more than the reductionism into existing concepts or conformity with the methods of "hard" science, but openness and responsiveness to the actual phenomenon. We learn, for example, that while human beings are unique in their capacity for violence, they are also unique in their capacity for greater good. A study of violence can help to improve recognition of this power in history, to characterize it, and to apply it systematically to future situations. Nonviolence is part of the natural progression of our pursuit of how to think about violence as we move away from merely meeting violence with more violence to considering underlying causes and prevention. If humanity is to overcome violence, we need first to identify it as a problem and not a given; we must recognize the alternative possibilities of nonviolence. Not merely different principles, nonviolence is about shifting to a different battleground and different goals. Just as violence requires imagination in order to occur, so does nascent peace. States prefer violence, since states have a monopoly on it: no matter how much violence protesters use, the regime will use more. The power of the people is, instead, in popular mobilization and in nonviolence, and that is the greater power.

In this chapter, we showed that, contrary to current assumptions, far from being passive or ineffective, nonviolent methods have been demonstrated to bring down empires, to topple regimes, and to effectuate long-lasting peace—at a greater frequency than violent means. It is the greatest force at the disposal of humankind, more powerful than any weapon of destruction. Starting with the personal level, and drawing on the various spiritual traditions, nonviolence may delve into the depths that are necessary for countering our complex tendency for violence. Nonviolence gives us the lesson that peace is possible, not just by stemming destructive forces, but through fostering constructive ones.

While this truth of nonviolence has existed since the dawn of humankind, our most pressing concern and challenge for humanity is how to adopt it widely enough to transform a pervasive world culture of violence into a culture of peace. We are in a state where either humankind will take control of its own destiny and will concern itself with community interests, through values of solidarity and compassion for others; or, alternatively, there will be no destiny for anyone to control. A strategy as well as a way of life, nonviolence is beginning to offer convincing ways of countering the violence of our contemporary world. Successful campaigns of the last two centuries provide the foundation and the justification for further experimentation in the twenty-first century, so that nonviolent action in the future not only contributes to the reduction of violence but to the expansion of democratic practices, political freedom, and social justice. Characteristics of this state might include connection to self, to others, and to the natural world; deep spiritual roots; the art of really listening to each other; and a rising global, spiritual consciousness (Perpetual Peace Initiative, 2016). Perhaps then we will have achieved what seventeenth-century Dutch philosopher Baruch de Spinoza (1670) understood when he said that peace is not an absence of war but a virtue, and a disposition for benevolence and justice. Will humanity decry its course of violence and seize upon this opportunity? A viable, powerful, and productive alternative seems to lie in nonviolence, and it is up to us to choose it.

Questions

1 How is nonviolence powerful and successful in ending violence?

2 According to the major spiritual traditions, where does nonviolence begin?

3 What are some of the characteristics of nonviolence?

4   What are some examples of the application of nonviolence?

5   How does nonviolence make use of constructive forces?

References

Ackerman, P., & DuVall, J. (2000). *A force more powerful: A century of non-violent conflict.* New York, NY: St. Martin's Press.

Adams, D., Barnett, S. A., Bechtereva, N. P., Carter, B. F., Delgado, J. M. R., Diaz, J. L., Eliasz, A., Genoves, S., Ginsburg, B. E., Groebel, J., & Ghosh, S. K. (1990). Seville Statement on Violence. *American Psychologist, 45*(10), 1167.

Adolf, A. (2009). *PEACE: A world history.* Malden, MA: Polity Press.

Anderlini, S. N. (2007). *Women building peace: What they do, why it matters.* Boulder, CO: Lynne Rienner.

Anders, T. M. (2016, January 23). [Letter to S. Rochen]. Nonviolent activism, Denver, CO.

Arendt, H. (1963). *On revolution.* New York, NY: Viking Press.

Arendt, H. (1970). *On violence.* New York, NY: Harcourt, Brace, Jovanovich.

Bartkowski, M. J. (2013). *Recovering nonviolent history: Civil resistance in liberation struggles.* Boulder, CO: Rienner.

Bellin, E. (2012). Reconsidering the robustness of authoritarianism in the Middle East: Lessons from the Arab Spring. *Comparative Politics, 44*(2), 127–149.

Bennoune, K. (2014). *Your fatwa does not apply here: Untold stories from the fight against Muslim fundamentalism.* New York, NY: Norton and Company.

Bernhard, M. (1993). Civil society and democratic transition in East Central Europe. *Political Science Quarterly, 108*(2), 307–326.

Biko, S. B., & Stubbs, A. (1978). *I write what I like.* San Francisco, CA: Harper and Row.

Bhalla, N. (2007, January 29). Mandela calls for Gandhi's non-violence approach. *Guardian.* Retrieved from https://www.reuters.com/article/us-india-gandhi-mandela/mandela-calls-for-gandhis-non-violence-approach-idUSDEL34219720070129

Biography. (2011, March 12). Dalai Lama biography: Activist, religious figure (1935-). *Biography.* Retrieved from https://www.biography.com/people/dalai-lama-9264833

Black Past. (2017). Clark, Septima Poinsette (1898–1987). Seattle, Washington: Black Past. Retrieved from http://www.blackpast.org/aah/clark-septima-poinsette-1898-1987

Blakemore, E. (2016, February 16). The woman who schooled the Civil Rights Movement. *Time.* Retrieved from http://time.com/4213751/septima-clark-civil-rights-movement

Caprioli, M. (2000). Gendered conflict. *Journal of Peace Research, 37*(1), 53–68.

Caprioli, M., & Boyer, M. (2001). Gender, violence, and international crisis. *Journal of Conflict Resolution, 45*(4), 503–518.

Chang, P., Alam, M., Warren, R., Bhatia, R., & Turkington, R. (2015). *Women leading peace: A close examination of women's political participation in peace processes in Northern Ireland, Guatemala, Kenya, and the Philippines.* Washington, DC: Georgetown Institute for Women, Peace and Security.

Chenoweth, E., & Stephan, M. J. (2011). *Why civil resistance works: The strategic logic of nonviolent conflict.* New York, NY: Columbia University Press.

Cirtautas, A. M. (1997). *Polish solidarity movement: Revolution, democracy and natural rights.* London, UK: Routledge.

Clark, S. P., & Brown, C. S. (1990). *Ready from within: Septima clark and the civil rights movement.* Trenton, NJ: Africa World.

Clarke, D. A. (1993). A woman with a sword: Some thoughts on women, feminism, and violence. In E. Buchwald, P. R. Fletcher, & M. Roth (Eds.) *Transforming a rape culture* (pp. 393–404). Minneapolis, MN: Milkweed Editions.

Connolly, T. (2015). *Doing philosophy comparatively*. London, UK: Bloomsbury.

Cortright, D. (2008). *Peace: A history of movements and ideas*. Cambridge University Press.

Creel, H. G. (1970). *What is Taoism?* Chicago, IL: University of Chicago Press.

Cultural India. (2017). Mahatma Gandhi. Retrieved from https://www.culturalindia.net/indian-history/modern-history/mahatma-gandhi.html

De Spinoza, B. (1670). *Tractatus theologico-politicus: Continens dissertationes aliquot, quibus ostenditur libertatem philosophandi non tantum salva pietate, and reipublicae pace posse concedi, sed eandem nisi cum pace reipublicae, ipsaque pietate tolli non posse.* Apud Henricum Kunraht: Hamburgi [i.e. Amsterdam]. Netherlands: Künraht [i.e. Jan Rieuwertsz].

De Tocqueville, A. (1835). *De la démocratie en Amérique*. Paris, France: Librairie de Charles Gosselin.

Diamond, L. J. (1994). Toward democratic consolidation. *Journal of Democracy, 5*(3), 4–17.

Diemand, K. A. (2015). *'Life, liberty ... and the law: John Adams' political thought during the American revolution.* Durham, NH: University of New Hampshire.

Disney, A., and Reticker, G. (2015, September 8). When it comes to "networks of death," women don't need saving—they are our saviors. *New York Times*. Retrieved from http://nytlive.nytimes.com/womenintheworld/2015/09/08/when-it-comes-to-networks-of-death-women-dont-need-saving-they-are-our-saviors.

Downton, J., & Wehr, P. (1998). Persistent pacifism: How activist commitment is developed and sustained. *Journal of Peace Research, 35*(5), 531–550.

Esposito, J. L. (1994). Islam in the world and in America. In J. Neusner (Ed.), *World religions in America: An introduction* (pp. 243–257). Louisville, KY: Westminster/Knox Press.

Florence Nightingale Museum. (2017). *Florence nightingale biography*. London, UK: Author. Retrieved from http://www.florence-nightingale.co.uk/resources/biography/?v=7516fd43adaa

Fuest, V. (2009). Liberia's women acting for peace: Collective action in a war-affected country. In S. Ellis, & I. van Kessel (Eds.), *Movers and shakers* (pp. 114–137). Leiden, Netherlands: Brill.

Galardi, T. (2009). *The lifequake phenomenon: How to thrive (not just survive) in times of personal and global upheaval*. Tucson, AZ: Wheatmark.

Gandhi, M. (1958). *All men are brothers; life and thoughts of Mahatma Gandhi*. Paris, France: UNESCO.

Gandhi, M. (1993a). Axioms of non-violence. In R. Iyer (Ed.), *The essential writings of Mahatma Gandhi* (p. 240). New Delhi, India: Oxford University Press.

Gandhi, M. (1993b). The greatest force in the world. In R. Iyer (Ed.), *The essential writings of Mahatma Gandhi* (p. 240). New Delhi, India: Oxford University Press.

Gandhi, M., & Attenborough, R. (1982). *The words of Gandhi*. New York, NY: Newmarket Press.

Gelderloos, P. (2007). *How nonviolence protects the state*. Cambridge, MA: South End Press.

Gelsey, R. C. (2014). *Mending our broken world: A path to perpetual peace*. Denver, CO: PlanDocs Press.

Gilligan, J. (2001). *Preventing violence*. London, UK: Thames and Hudson.

Gizelis, T. I. (2011). A country of their own: Women and peacebuilding. *Conflict Management and Peace Science, 28*(5), 522–542.

Gottlieb, L. (2011). Tikkun Olam: The art of nonviolent civil resistance. *Tikkun, 26*(11), 42–43.

Gregg, R. B. (1934). *Power of non-violence*. London, UK: J. B. Lippincott.

Hardiman, D. (2017). Gandhi: Reckless teenager to father of India. BBC. Retrieved from www.bbc.co.uk/timelines/zpdqmp3

Harris, R. T. (2010). On Islamic nonviolence. *Fellowship, 76*(1–3), 26.

Havel, V. (1985). *Power of the powerless: Citizens against the state in Central-Eastern Europe.* London, UK: Hutchinson.

Howes, D. (2013). The failure of pacifism and the success of nonviolence. *Perspectives on Politics, 11*(2), 427–446.

Hudson, V., Ballif-Spanvill, B., Caprioli, M., & Emmett, C. F. (2012). *Sex and world peace.* New York, NY: Columbia University Press.

Ives, S. (2001). *No fear: Breaking the cycle of violence, creating circles of peace.* Palo Alto: CA: Peace Center.

Jackson, G. (1994). *Soledad brother: The prison letters of George Jackson.* Chicago, IL: Chicago Review Press.

Johansen, J. (2007). Nonviolence: More than the absence of violence. In C. Webel, & J. Galtung (Eds.), *Handbook of peace and conflict studies* (pp. 143–159). London, UK: Routledge.

Kenney, P. (2002). *A Carnival of revolution: Central Europe 1989.* Princeton, NJ: Princeton University Press.

Keown, D. (2005). *Buddhist ethics: A very short introduction.* Oxford, UK: Oxford University Press.

King, M. L. (1963, August). A letter from a Birmingham Jail. *The Atlantic.*

Kuehnast, K., de Jonge Oudraat, C., & Hernes, H. (2011). *Women and war: Power and protection in the 21st century.* Washington, DC: United States Institute of Peace.

Lama, D. XIV, & Cutler, H. C. (1998). *The art of happiness.* New York, NY: Riverhead Books.

Laozi. (1853). *Tao te dhing chu.* Nanhai, China: Wu Shih.

Lonsway, K., Wood, M. I., Fickling, M. E., DeLeon, A. L., Moore, M., Harrington, P., ... Spillar, K. A. (2002). *Men, women, and police excessive force: A tale of two genders.* Los Angeles, CA: National Center for Women and Policing.

Madden, K. (2005). *Exploring the pagan path: Wisdom from the elders.* Franklin Lakes, NJ: New Page Books.

Mandela, N. (1994). *Long walk to freedom.* Boston, MA: Little, Brown.

Markoff, J. (2015). *Waves of democracy: Social movements and political change.* London, UK: Routledge.

Maslow, A. H. (1962). *Toward a psychology of being.* Princeton, NJ: Van Nostrand.

Melander, E. (2005). Political gender equality and state human rights abuse. *Journal of Peace Research, 42*(2), 149–166.

Merriman, H. (2009). Theory and dynamics of nonviolent action. In M. Stephan (Ed.), *Civilian jihad: Nonviolent struggle, democratization, and governance in the Middle East* (pp. 17–29). New York, NY: Springer.

Mollica, R. F. (2006). *Healing invisible wounds: Paths to hope and recovery in a violent world.* Orlando, FL: Harcourt.

Morris, A. D. (1986). *The origins of the civil rights movement.* New York, NY: Simon and Schuster.

Nagler, M. N. (2001). *Is there no other way? The search for a nonviolent future.* Berkeley, CA: Berkeley Hills Books.

Nelson Mandela Foundation. (2017). *Biography of Nelson Mandela.* Houghton, South Africa: Author. Retrieved from https://www.nelsonmandela.org/content/page/biography

Nhất Hạnh, T. (1993). *Love in action: Writings on nonviolent social change.* Berkeley, CA: Parallax Press.

Nightingale, F. (1859). *Notes on nursing: What it is, and what it is not.* London, UK: Harrison.

Office of Tibet. (2011). *Biography of His Holiness the 14th Dalai Lama, Tenzin Gyatso.* Washington, DC: Author. Retrieved from http://tibetoffice.org/h-h-the-dalai-lama/biography-14th-dalai-lama

O'Neill, J., & Vary, J. (2010). Allies and assets: Strengthening DDR and SSR through women's inclusion. In M. A. Civic, & M. Miklaucic (Eds.), *Monopoly of force: The Nexus of DDR and SSR* (pp. 77–108). Washington, DC: National Defense University.

O'Reilly, M., Súilleabháin, A. Ó., & Paffenholz, T. (2015). *Reimagining peacemaking: Women's roles in peace processes*. New York, NY: International Peace Institute.

Orwell, G. (1949). Reflections on Gandhi. *Partisan Review, 16*(1), 85–92.

Page, M., Whitman, T., & Anderson, C. (2009). *Strategies for policymakers: Bringing women into negotiations*. Washington, DC: Institute for Inclusive Security.

Pantham, T. (1983). Thinking with Mahatma Gandhi: Beyond liberal democracy. *Political Theory, 11*(2), 165–188.

Pape, R. A. (1996). *Bombing to win: Air power and coercion in War*. Ithaca, NY: Cornell University Press.

Perpetual Peace Initiative. (2016). *Moving forward in the second axial age: News from the Perpetual Peace Initiative World*. Denver, CO: Perpetual Peace Initiative.

Peters, A. (2014). *Countering terrorism and violent extremism in Pakistan: Why policewomen must have a role*. Washington, DC: Institute for Inclusive Security.

Regan, P. M., & Paskeviciute, A. (2003). Women's access to politics and peaceful states. *Journal of Peace Research, 40*(3), 287–302.

Salgado, N., Vidal, D., Tarabout, G., & Meyer, E. (1996). Violences et non-violences en Inde. *The Journal of Asian Studies, 55*(1), 206–207.

Schell, J. (2003). *The unconquerable world: Power, nonviolence, and the will of the people*. London, UK: Penguin.

Schell, J. (2004). *The unconquerable world: Power, nonviolence, and the will of the people*. New York, NY: Macmillan.

Schweitzer, A., Winston, R., & Winston, C. (1965). *The teaching of reverence for life*. London, UK: Owen.

Sharp, G. (1967). The technique of nonviolent action. In A. Roberts (Ed.), *Civilian resistance as a national defence: Non-violent action against aggression* (pp. 107–127). London, UK: Penguin Books.

Sharp, G. (1973). *Politics of nonviolent action*. Boston, MA: Porter Sargent.

Sharp, G. (2005). *Waging nonviolent struggle: 20th century practice and 21st century*. Manchester, NH: Extending Horizons Books.

Shridharani, K. (1939). *War without violence: A study of Gandhi's method and its accomplishments*. New York, NY: Harcourt, Brace.

Simpson, J. A., & Weiner, E. S. C. (1989). *Oxford English dictionary* (2nd ed.). Oxford, UK: Clarendon Press.

Simpson, J. A., & Weiner, E. S. C. (1993). *Oxford English dictionary additions series*. Oxford, UK: Clarendon Press.

Stephan, M. J., & Chenoweth, E. (2008). Why civil resistance works: The strategic logic of nonviolent conflict. *International Security, 33*(1), 7–44.

Stoltzfus, N. (2001). *Resistance of the heart: Intermarriage and the Rosenstrasse protest in Nazi Germany*. Rutgers, NJ: Rutgers University Press.

Sweet, V. (2014, March 3). Far more than a lady with a lamp. *New York Times*. Retrieved from https://www.nytimes.com/2014/03/04/health/florence-nightingales-wisdom.html

Tähtinen, U. (1964). *Non-violence as an ethical principle: With special reference to the views of Mahatma Gandhi*. Turku, Finland: Turun Yliopisto.

Tolstoy, L. (1948). *The law of love and the law of violence*. New York, NY: Rudolph Field.

Conclusion

Part VII   Overview and Analysis

15

Synthesis and Integration

Introduction

> These rules … drawing upon several sciences and arts [are] capable of expressing and establishing interrelationships between the content and conclusions of nearly all scholarly disciplines.
>
> —*Hermann Hesse*, Das Glasperlenspiel *(1943)*

This final chapter attempts to synthesize and integrate the knowledge we have gained about violence from major fields of study. Emphasizing the object of study over the boundaries of disciplines, this text seeks an interdisciplinary as well as transdisciplinary understanding. A subject is more than an area of study; it is also a worldview—a view that can contribute to a better understanding of the whole. For example, biology gives us an awareness of the diversity and malleability of human beings. Psychology shows us that we are more than we appear to be on the surface. Semiotics reveals the importance of meaning and symbolism. The social sciences demonstrate the dominant role of social and cultural forces in individual behavior. Political science and economics highlight two influential institutions that shape social dynamics. A study of structural violence shows that invisible violence can be the deadliest, while environmental and nuclear violence establish that humans are the greatest threat to our own survival. A review of the consequences of violence shows the costs of violence to be enormous. The interventions we have examined at are our responses so far: criminal justice's centralizing use of violence; law's establishment of norms; public health's prevention efforts through empirical study; medicine's healing through the enhancement of individual humanity; and nonviolence's ability to neutralize violence through true power. Any combination of these disciplines can bring awareness that there are as many modes of intervention as there are causes of violence. While new information is always useful, there is also a need to step back and assess what our aggregated knowledge tells us about how to think about violence.

What lessons can we draw from an integration of the fields? The first chapter introduced violence as a topic of complexity; this chapter emphasizes the need for synthesis and simplicity. Knowledge is more than information, requiring more than content: a framework that addresses the deeply ingrained outlook that compromises human life and potential. A meta-perspective naturally emerges out of the integration and discernment of patterns, and the student will find that we have now arrived at a level quite beyond what one might have expected at the onset. Nevertheless, this level of understanding is critical to cultivate. First, it allows for scholarly integrity and consistency. Second, it is efficient for avoiding duplication of efforts or a tilting of perspective. Third, it is accurate: understanding the interrelationship between the different

Violence: An Interdisciplinary Approach to Causes, Consequences, and Cures, First Edition. Bandy X. Lee.
© 2019 John Wiley & Sons, Inc. Published 2019 by John Wiley & Sons, Inc.

forms of violence will help elucidate much more than the study of an isolated area can achieve. Most importantly, in the case of violence prevention, a correct understanding will save lives.

Two important themes emerge from earlier chapters: the continuum of life and the power of insight. The continuum of life illustrates that life and death, or health and disease, fall on a spectrum; what we understand about violence will determine whether we steer ourselves closer to one end or to the other; the bio-psycho-socio-environmental paradigm or interconnected ecology will mean that no action is insulated, and that all actions have a rippling effect. Violence, along this scheme of life and death, is an obstacle to life, and its suitability as a solution, no matter how attractive in theory, eventually breaks down. Mounting evidence of the practicality of nonviolent methods makes this irrefutable (Chenoweth and Stephan, 2011; Paige, 2009). Consciousness of violence as a problem is the first step: recognizing the abyss for what it is allows for a vision beyond it (Lifton, 1987). Looking into our death-dealing tendencies allows access to our ability to pivot toward life-promotion. This is called *insight*: knowing fully where we are and deciding where not to stay. Confrontation of the truth can cause distress; the whole truth, however, reveals a greater human capacity for transformation.

The Endgame of Violence

To look fully into the abyss is to recognize our current condition of violence. Violence penetrates all areas of society, as the military–industrial complex, the prison–industrial complex, excessive police force, civil strife, and structures that concentrate wealth and resources indicate. The prevailing paradigm of violence, or the age-old view of violence as an acceptable solution, generates a cycle that continues to add violence to our already violent ecology. Evidence shows that meeting violence with violence only leads to more of it. Far from a world that is growing more peaceful after a repetition of a "war to end all wars" (Wells, 1914), or enjoying the most peaceable era of all time (Pinker, 2011), violence finds continual evolution in the new millennium. New forms of civil wars, terrorism, genocide, structural violence, and ultimately flirtation with environmental and nuclear catastrophe threaten our survival. A vivid example of violence begetting more violence is the 2001 US invasion of Afghanistan. Rather than mitigating extremist groups, a military-based approach led to mutual counterattacks that escalated and prolonged the conflict (Richards, 2015). Since the US and the UK invaded Iraq in 2003, the world has seen an upsurge of terrorist attacks, and the Middle East has descended into great instability. Invasion and bombing as a means of bringing "democracy" have instead created fertile breeding grounds for the rise of militia groups, raising the specter of terrorism and fear that is often the seed of autocratic rule. Destabilizing governmental structures, furthermore, has caused massive hardship and dispersion among inhabitants of the invaded countries, spreading resentment and recruitment potential for extremist groups.

These are predictable results, since the risk of war-torn societies experiencing further violent conflict is very high, due to what is called a "conflict trap" (Collier et al., 2003). Militant groups such as Al Qaeda, for example, have radicalized into the Islamic State of Iraq and the Levant (ISIL) and have mounted escalating retaliatory moves against the US and the UK (Chan & Card, 2012). Attacks such as the bombing in London that killed 52 people and the beheading of Western journalists in Iraq have been undertaken by groups identifying themselves as *jihadist* (engaged in a "holy war") (Mirza, 2007). Perpetrators of the 2013 Boston marathon bombing claimed to act to revenge the American wars in Afghanistan and Iraq (Gessen, 2015). Governmental studies spectacularly show that an average of 28.3 terrorist attacks per year before the US invasion of Iraq steadily rose to almost 12,000 attacks per year, with more than 28,000 deaths and 35,000 injuries annually, reflecting a more than 400-fold global increase

(National Consortium for the Study of Terrorism and Responses to Terrorism, 2015). "The war on terror" hence precipitated a "fueling of terror."

The cycle of violence also transpires in the lifetime of an individual. Studies in the last few decades show that adverse childhood experiences affect violence perpetration later in life (Dube et al., 2001; Yexley, Borowsky, & Ireland, 2002). Abusive environments interrupt normal development and spawn violent propensities (Lynch & Cicchetti, 1998). There is much evidence of a relationship between a history of having been abused and suicide attempts (Silverman, Reinherz, & Giaconia, 1996) and between abuse and violent arrests (Lansford et al., 2007). Other forms of maltreatment, such as racial discrimination, also predict violent behavior (Estrada-Martinez et al., 2012). Wars, furthermore, no longer involve just soldiers and the battlefield but increasingly civilians in cities, towns, villages, and even private spaces.

Attitudes and values not only cause direct harm but determine the social and cultural use of violence to solve conflicts at all levels. When children observe adults behaving violently, particularly within a culture that portrays violence as acceptable or even praiseworthy, they will see violence as something that brings desired outcomes and emulate it (Bandura, 1973). Adolescents, in their longing for an identity and a place in the world, become vulnerable targets for youth gangs or for militant groups and governments that recruit them as "pupils of war." The violence and destruction are seen as ways to discharge the hopelessness, the despair, and the shame of lacking education and employment in the form of glorified terror (Joshi & O'Donnell, 2003).

A major way in which society deals with individual violence is through the criminal justice system and the police—and this may seem to decrease the incentive for violence by reducing its "rewards". However, we see in the biggest carceral nation of the world, the US, "backfire" effects that promote violence and crime in ways that overwhelm any small gains these systems produce. Juvenile arrests not only increase future arrests and later involvement in crime (Liberman, Kirk, & Kideuk, 2014) but amplify deviant attitudes that accept violence as a viable approach (Wiley & Esbensen, 2013). Cities that employ aggressive policing tactics amass complaints of police abuse, excessive force, and discourtesy (Conklin, 2003) without appreciable gains in violent crime drop compared to cities with more positive, community-oriented activities (Currie, 1999). Since a small minority of offenders commits a vast proportion of violent crime, increasing incarceration effectively creates "schools of crime" that are criminogenic for less violent individuals through exposure and exploitation by serious offenders in the absence of equally powerful rehabilitation programs. The disastrous disruptions to the lives of offenders and their communities reverberate culturally and intergenerationally (Petersilia, 2010). Furthermore, as the funds for imprisonment are taken from education, healthcare, welfare, and crime prevention programs (Chambliss, 1999), the detrimental effects multiply. It is not surprising, therefore, that states with the fastest-growing prison population achieve no better crime reduction than those with slower growth or reductions (Lynch, 2007).

As of 2009, the US incarceration rate was five times that of the UK, more than six times that of Canada, eight times that of Belgium, and almost nine times that of Germany (Walmsley, 2016), but at the same time the least effective in the world in terms of recidivism, with 7 out of 10 rearrests and 50% reincarceration within 3 years (Durose, Cooper, & Snyder, 2014). Escalating incarceration, additionally, has not changed the sevenfold risk of dying by violent crime in the US compared to other high-income countries (United Nations Office on Drugs and Crime, 2013). In a culture where two-thirds of gun owners have self-protection in mind (Masters, 2016), Americans are 10 times more likely to die by guns than people in other developed countries, while gun murder rates are 25 times higher overall, and 49 times higher for 15–24-year-olds (Grinshteyn & Hemenway, 2016). A cyclical argument—whereby one views the violence as justifying more violence to defend or "to protect"—adds to the cycle of violence, with a resulting cascade that continues to increase the chances of victimization with each victimization.

The concept of deterring war with weapons is similarly self-defeating. There is no doubt that the twentieth century killed more people than any other century, with animosities mounting to major world wars. While some may believe that war is inevitable, we now recognize that if we thought creatively enough in advance—diplomatically, politically, socially, and culturally— violence as a "solution" would not be necessary. Apart from the principles or moral objections of pacifism, violence is not as effective as we would believe it to be—in fact, with careful scrutiny, we find that it is almost never effective. Violence is ultimately a destructive and self- destructive act. With each stage of the twentieth-century wars, more parties entered in the belief that further force would overwhelm the enemy and end the cycles of violence. It was in this context that the first fission, or atomic, bomb appeared (Smyth, 1945). While the project may have begun with "benevolent" intent—to obtain the weapons before Germany under the fascist dictator Adolf Hitler and use them against fascist-leaning Japan—it did not end war. After the bombing of Hiroshima and Nagasaki and the end of World War II, Soviet dictator Joseph Stalin, upon seeing the destructive possibilities of the bomb, created a crash program for the Soviet Union's own weaponry. A nuclear arms race began, and the US developed the first fusion, or hydrogen, bomb in 1951, with the Soviet Union soon following in 1954. The first test revealed an explosive power 500 times greater than that of the fission bomb that leveled Hiroshima (Morland, 2004).

The assurance of mutual destruction and a devastating nuclear holocaust may have briefly deterred the use of thermonuclear weapons during the Cold War, but the culture of proliferation did not end with the cessation of hostilities between the two superpowers. As the number of warheads in these two nations was going down, the number of nations jumping on board to possess such weapons went up. The mere existence of the weaponry has created a psychological attraction affecting previously non-nuclear nations, such as North Korea, Japan, Israel, Iran, India, and Pakistan (Schell, 2007). The danger of global nuclear catastrophe has thus escalated since the Cold War, both because proliferation has not stopped and because the technology has become more accessible. Now, the target is not just bipolar but involves the entire world.

The former superpowers, rather than dispatching their nuclear arsenals, held onto them, refurbished them, and built new generations of them. Even if deterrence theory were to hold, it is hardly arguable that the world is safer, since the effectiveness of deterrence relies on a willingness to use the weapons under certain conditions. Especially after September 11, 2001, the idea of stopping proliferation by force, and by nuclear force if necessary, became official policy in the US (Leffler, 2005), which France and the UK also adopted. However, the side effects of using nuclear arsenals to stop nuclear proliferation require reconsideration. Since threat engenders a greater justification for defense, as the world grows more replete with nuclear technology, with approximately 27,000 nuclear weapons in existence, the horrifying prospect of a terrorist group acquiring one or several nuclear weapons only becomes likelier (Schell, 2007). Deterrence has little meaning to a terrorist who intends to inflict the greatest harm possible in the process of self-destruction, and the concept that an aspirin-size mass can, in a nuclear explosion, destroy a whole city if not a whole planet, becomes especially compelling.

Escalating structural violence is similarly unsustainable. Economic development may have increased the wealth of many individuals and many nations, but it has also increased structural violence, or the potential for harm through structures that socioeconomically favor some persons or groups over others (Galtung, 1969; Gilligan, 1996). While much of structural violence occurs without direct awareness on the part of players, a growing proportion is a deliberate institution of structures that concentrate advantage (Pogge, 2008). Hunger, malnutrition, and poverty kill far more people per year than all the high-profile shootings, stabbings, and bombings combined, which are but a fraction of violent deaths (Høivik, 1977). The structures that funnel wealth from the poorest to the most prosperous are the same structures that accelerate environmental degradation, the devastation of vulnerable regions, the spread of diseases, conflicts, and ever-growing refugee crises (Reuveny, 2007).

Structural violence, through human-induced climate catastrophe, is now a threat that rivals thermonuclear war in its capacity to imperil all of life on earth (Kunstler, 2007). Economic hegemony topples governmental structures, civil societies, national capacities, and even the ability of ordinary citizens to obtain correct information about their plight. Structures have the function of organizing and stabilizing at some levels, and therefore psychological resistance develops against criticizing or toppling them, no matter the damage and the promotion of inequity. Furthermore, while injustice and exploitation might have benefited some—no matter the zero-sum outcome or net loss—all becomes moot with the possibility that the entire human species will perish (Hansen, 2010). Structural violence is therefore not only the most lethal form of violence but also the most indirectly dangerous, as it insidiously facilitates the likelihood of ultimate violence; this kind of violence that affects all humankind might be labeled *collective suicidality*. Thermonuclear war and environmental degradation together represent our precipitous drive toward collective suicide, and a growing attraction to these, alongside diminishing insight and conscious identification of these problems, are alarming signs that elevate risk.

The Threat of Nuclear War

What is the current likelihood of dying from a thermonuclear world war? This may seem an odd question, but an American professor emeritus of engineering at Stanford University has sought precisely to answer this question. Applying risk analysis to a potential failure of nuclear deterrence, Martin Hellman claims that the risk of a child born today suffering an early death due to nuclear war is at least 10% (Blackman, 2009). Just as manufacturers assess the risk of injury to drivers, and engineers assess potential risks of a new nuclear power plant, he has assessed the risk of nuclear war based on our current arms strategy. While almost everyone agrees that thermonuclear weapons cannot be used to advantage because using them would be annihilation, the policy of nuclear deterrence requires that those weapons be ready for use under "hair-trigger alert" (McNamara, 2005). Deterrence, therefore, is a gamble that we will never do what we are always ready to do.

To review some history, it is commonly believed that the risk of thermonuclear war was greatest during the Cold War. The Cold War was a state of geopolitical tension after World War II between the Soviet Union and its satellite states to the East and the US, its North Atlantic Treaty Organization (NATO) allies, and others to the West. It is thought to have begun around 1947, when the US pledged to aid nations that Soviet expansionism threatened, and ended either in 1989, when Communism fell in Eastern Europe, or in 1991, when the Soviet Union collapsed. It was "cold" because the two superpowers did not engage directly in armed combat, but they were heavily prepared for a possible all-out thermonuclear war. The countries avoided such a war on the basis that such an attack would imply total destruction of the attacker, while the struggle for dominance happened via proxy wars around the globe.

The Cuban Missile Crisis was a 13-day confrontation between the US and the Soviet Union in October 1962 and is considered to be when the Cold War was closest to becoming a full-scale thermonuclear war. Americans had deployed ballistic missiles in Italy and Turkey, and the Soviet Union deployed them in Cuba in response. An Air Force plane brought back images of ballistic missile facilities, and US President John Kennedy made it clear that he would use military force if necessary to neutralize this perceived threat. After tense negotiations, Kennedy reached an agreement with Soviet leader Nikita Khrushchev, who offered to remove the Cuban missiles in exchange for the US promising not to invade Cuba, while Kennedy agreed to remove US missiles from Turkey. *Probability theory* is the branch of mathematics that measures the probability of something by expressing it through a set of axioms or premises, and is a natural fit for evaluating the nuclear gamble. Consider a game in which A repeatedly tosses a coin and B calls heads or tails each time. The game continues until B guesses incorrectly, at which point B is shot. The chance of surviving 30 tosses is roughly one in one billion. What does pistol roulette have to do with nuclear war? During the Cuban Missile Crisis, Kennedy estimated that the odds of nuclear war were "somewhere between one out of three and even." Thus, the Cuban Missile Crisis would be equivalent to nuclear roulette, a version of pistol roulette in which the entire world is at stake, with a two- or three-chambered revolver. Every "small war" pulls the trigger in nuclear roulette (Hellman, 1986).

When nuclear tensions between the US and the former Soviet Union ran high, the risk of nuclear inadvertence was much greater than had been recognized. In other words, it is not the threat of a nuclear war but any inadvertent incident that can lead to a catastrophic scenario. The Union of Concerned Scientists (2015) lists many dozens of such incidents involving nuclear warheads in the US alone, and estimates many more that have not been made public. Even though the Soviet Union no longer exists, and the Cold War is over, nuclear inadvertence remains an issue of contemporary relevance. The end of the Cold War did not bring the nuclear standoff to a final, irreversible end, but the two countries continued to develop and modernize weapons, while other nations around the world joined in (Busch, 2015). Nuclear threats have now been increasing from Russia, China, and North Korea, with ongoing conflicts in the Middle East.

A poll of 50 experts concluded that there is a 6.8% chance of catastrophic nuclear war in the next 20 years, killing more people than World War II. This means that our children have a greater chance of dying from the consequences of nuclear war than from a car crash. The longer nuclear weapons exist, the higher is the likelihood of a nuclear explosion, be it accidental, mistaken, or authorized. India and Pakistan have a 40% chance of war and a 9% chance of nuclear exchange (Project for the Study of the 21st Century, 2017). Cities in the Middle East may be even more vulnerable. The US invasion demolished Baghdad, while Aleppo, Damascus, and other cities of Syria have fared even worse. Despite the nuclear deal between Iran and the world's major powers, experts still saw a 27% risk of some kind of conflict between Tehran and its enemies. More than a quarter of a century after the fall of the Berlin Wall, Russia and the US, with roughly 1950 and 1650 active strategic nuclear weapons respectively, together possess more than 90 percent of the world's nuclear arsenals. The survey estimated a 21% chance of NATO and Russia fighting at least a limited conventional war in the next 20 years, and a 4% chance it might go nuclear. The risk of the US fighting China is 12%, with a 2% chance of going nuclear. Japan does not currently have a nuclear weapon program, but experts say it could probably build one in a hurry if it believed it needed it (Apps, 2015).

We now see how critically these numbers have risen against public apathy and reduced threat perception after the Cold War. Changing the situation would also depend on our consciousness more than on any technological ability or actual circumstances. The current military strategy of "mutually assured destruction," aptly abbreviated "MAD," is a doctrine that ensures the full-scale use of nuclear weapons against any nuclear attack and is incompatible with humanity's continued survival. The immediate consequences of a single thermonuclear weapon explosion are well known: fireball radiation, prompt neutrons, gamma rays, blasts, and fires. The Hiroshima bomb that killed between 100,000 and 200,000 people was a fission device of about

12-kt yield (the explosive equivalent of 12,000 tons of trinitrotoluene [TNT]). A modern thermonuclear warhead uses a device like the Hiroshima bomb as the trigger (Sagan, 1983). The only possible conclusion is that the way to survive this pistol roulette is to put the gun down (Hellman, 1986).

The Threat of Climate Catastrophe

We are now dangerously close to being too late to avoid climate catastrophe. Irreversible damage has already begun. The only question now is whether we will be able to embrace the few imperfect options we have left. The year 2016 was the hottest on record (US National Aeronautics and Space Administration [NASA], 2017), and according to the US National Oceanic and Atmospheric Administration (2017), seven of the 10 warmest years fell in the 2010s and nine of the 10 since 2000. Rajendra Pachauri, former chairman of the Intergovernmental Panel on Climate Change (IPCC) who accepted the 2007 Nobel Peace Prize alongside former American vice president Albert Gore, stated that, unless we begin to make fundamental reforms by 2012, we can expect to watch the climate system spin out of control. NASA scientist James Hansen, who was the first to blow the whistle on global warming in the late 1980s, said that we must stop burning coal by 2030 (Crist, Rinker, & McKibben, 2009).

Humans have contributed to global warming by burning fossil fuels like coal and oil, altering the earth's energy balance between incoming solar radiation and outgoing infrared radiation (European Environment Agency, 2015). One way to reduce the carbon dioxide we release into the atmosphere is to switch energy sources from fossil fuels to renewable resources such as wind and solar power. The greatest uphill battle, however, is not in a lack of knowledge or conflicting scholarship but in political will and misinformation campaigns (Giddens, 2009).

The UK Climate Impacts Programme (UKCIP) scenarios, which the Hadley Centre for Climate Change and the Tyndall Centre for Climate Change Research have developed, are the most up to date, detailed, and reliable depictions of the future. The scenarios indicate that changes to our climate will start to become evident by the 2050s, with significant changes occurring by the 2080s (McEvoy, 2007). A collaborative global response to climate change launched the Paris Agreement (United Nations, 2015), with a goal of reducing emissions. It aims to keep the global temperature rise to just 1.5°C, which would significantly reduce the risks and impacts associated with climate change. Multiple studies show that a massive 97% of researchers believe global warming is happening and agree that trends observed over the last century are due to human activity. Unfortunately, ideologically driven political campaigns have minimized the dangers, and climate change is considered only the third most serious issue facing the world, behind international terrorism and poverty, hunger, and the lack of drinking water (Plummer & McGoogan, 2017). Citizens around the world are suing their own governments and some of the world's biggest oil and energy companies over failing to protect them from the risks and consequences of climate change (Brändlin, 2016).

In addition to the impacts of global warming, the increasing level of carbon dioxide in the atmosphere is contributing to another potentially devastating process. Seawater acidity is changing with a rapidity that is almost unprecedented. Marine life has survived large climate and acidification variations in the past, but the projected rates of global warming and ocean acidification over the next century are much greater than ever before. Since the Industrial Revolution, ocean pH has gone down by 0.1 units, which translates into a 30% surge in acidity. Scientists predict that pH will go down another 0.14–0.35 units by the end of this century (Sponberg, 2007).

The oceans are the largest carbon sinks on earth, absorbing nearly one-third of anthropogenic carbon dioxide emissions. As the atmospheric concentration increases, the ocean absorbs more carbon dioxide, which lowers the pH of seawater, making it more acidic. The altered chemistry of the ocean will affect the ability of some marine organisms to form shells and skeletons, threatening already vulnerable coral reefs, shellfish, and the plankton that form the base of the ocean's food web. The first noticeable impacts will probably be widespread loss of coral reefs. These reefs act as buffers against tropical storms that are expected to increase in frequency and severity as a result of global warming. And because reducing the atmospheric concentration of carbon dioxide is the only way to mitigate ocean acidification on a global scale, some strategies to combat global warming (for instance, those that focus on non-carbon dioxide greenhouse gasses) could have negligible effects on the acidification of the ocean (US Environmental Protection Agency, 2009).

The Threat of Escalating Inequality

We discussed in Chapter 7, "Structural Violence," the lethality of structural violence and its stimulation of other forms of violence make it one of the most important forms of violence. In a similar manner, it undergirds nuclear and climate devastations in inextricably intertwined ways. While less an immediate emergency than nuclear or climate threats, income and wealth inequality is an urgent form of structural violence we need to address for its rapidity of acceleration and stimulation of both nuclear and environmental violence.

The income inequality crisis is worsening. Just eight men own the same wealth as the poorest half of the world as economics drive society to an extreme, unsustainable, and unjust point (Oxfam International, 2017). As growth benefits the richest, the rest of the world—especially the poorest—suffers. Since 2015, the richest 1% has owned more wealth than the rest of the planet (Crédit Suisse, 2016). The incomes of the poorest 10% of people increased by less than 3 US dollars a year between 1988 and 2011, while the incomes of the richest 1% increased 182 times as much (Hardoon, Ayele, & Fuentes-Nieva, 2016). A Financial Times Stock Exchange 100 Index (FTSE-100) chief executive officer earns as much in a year as 10,000 people working in garment factories in Bangladesh (Oxfam International, 2017). In the US, the growth in the incomes of the bottom 50% has been zero over the last 30 years, whereas incomes of the top 1% have grown 300% (Cohen, 2016). The rising inequality threatens to pull our societies apart through increases in crime and insecurity (Seery & Caistor Arendar, 2014). While hundreds of millions of people have been lifted out of poverty in recent decades, one in nine people still go to bed hungry (World Food Programme, 2017). Had growth been pro-poor between 1990 and 2010, 700 million more people, most of them women, would not be living in poverty today (Hardoon & Slater, 2015). In fact, research finds that three-quarters of extreme poverty could be eliminated today using existing resources, through an increase in taxation and a reduction in military and other regressive spending (Hoy & Sumner, 2016).

Large corporations and the superrich are driving the inequality crisis, squeezing workers and producers in pursuit of delivering high returns to those at the top while dodging taxes that would benefit everyone (Harrington, 2016). As a consequence, far from trickling down, they are sucking up income and wealth at an alarming rate. In extreme cases, forced labor or slavery can be used to keep corporate costs down; the International Labour Organization estimates that 21 million people are forced laborers, generating 150 billion US dollars in profits each year. Africa alone loses 14 billion US dollars in tax revenues due to superrich tax havens—which would be enough to pay for the healthcare that could save the lives of four million children and to employ enough teachers to get every African child into school. Thirty-one corporations from several sectors—finance, extractives, garment manufacturers, pharmaceuticals, and others—use their power and influence to ensure that regulations and national and international policies are shaped in ways that ensure their profitability. While some billionaires owe their fortunes predominantly to hard work and talent, Oxfam's analysis has found that one-third of the world's billionaire wealth is derived from inherited wealth, while 43% can be linked to cronyism (Oxfam International, 2017).

To pay as little tax as possible, they make active use of a secretive global network of tax havens (Zuchman, 2015). Countries compete to attract the superrich, compromising their sovereignty. In the US, the top rate of income tax was 70% as recently as 1980; it is now 40% (Data 360, 2017). In low-and middle-income countries, taxation on the rich is lower still. Many of the superrich also use their power, influence, and connections to "buy" politics and to ensure that the rules are written for them: they use their fortunes to help buy the political outcomes they desire, seeking to influence elections and public policy. The Koch brothers, two of the richest men in the world, have had an enormous influence over politics in the US, supporting influential conservative think tanks and the Tea Party movement (Mayer, 2017) and contributing heavily to discrediting the case for action on climate change. This active political influencing by the superrich and their representatives directly escalates inequality by constructing "reinforcing feedback loops" in which the winners of the game gain yet more resources to win even bigger next time (Meadows, 2008).

In this setting, it is no wonder that violence in general increases, but especially threatening are environmental and nuclear violence. First, structural violence will erode the trust and cooperation that are necessary to tame the planet's climate or to reduce nuclear weapons. Additionally, income and wealth gaps accelerate the environmental crises. In 2002, the European Commission drew attention to the increasingly uneven level of consumption, and the fact that many natural resources are already being exploited at or beyond their limits (Commission of the European Communities, 2002). If the scale of an economy is too large and its speed too rapid, then natural cycles cannot produce the resources or absorb or assimilate industrial residues such as, for instance, heavy metals, phosphorous, carbon dioxide, and radioactive waste (Martinez-Alier, 2002). Failures to reach consensus have often been due to, among other factors, conflicting policies of rich and poor countries, which disagree on the implementation of mitigation measures (Vasconcelos, Santos, Pacheco, & Levin, 2014). They bring awareness to the reality that global environmental governance and world policies for poverty reduction go hand-in-hand. With globalization and population pressures putting ever more demand on the earth's resources, the emphasis of change needs to be on the use of sustainable habitats. By forming alliances, the Global South could strengthen its representation in the media, in scientific studies, and in political discourse (Davey, 2009).

That economic inequality contributes to spawning violent conflicts within and between nations has been explained in Chapter 7, "Structural Violence." One form of structural violence can give rise to others: the division of a society into "superior" and "inferior" groups shames the inferior group, so that it will desperately seek sources of self-meaning, such as in race, ethnicity, and gender—often qualities that no one can usurp. This explains why racism, nativism, and sexism—and the subsequent hate crimes, domestic abuse, and other forms of violence—are more prevalent in societies that are experiencing income and wealth inequality. When there is greater income and wealth inequality between nations, social and cultural gaps grow, fragmenting the global community and increasing a perceived need for military defense, including nuclear weapons for nations that could afford them. Hence, we see again that the different forms of violence are highly interconnected and that we will not get rid of one form of violence without getting rid of the others—that we must work on all forms simultaneously.

The Fruits of Integration

Humanity has the knowledge and the means to destroy itself, and its major task now is learning how to live (Masters & Way, 1946). As noted in Chapter 4, "The Symbolism (or Spiritual Causes) of Violence," humans are inveterate symbolizers, and once we recognize that our own consciousness underlies most of the crises of conflict and war, we have already taken the most crucial step. When we are at a place where we can face the perils (as we do when reading a text such as this!) and name them "violence," we are ready for a critical intervention reality. In other words, we can only overcome what we see. Understanding violence for what it is results in denouncing it so that it cannot continue to take root everywhere (Anderson & Menon, 2009). It is indeed a strange paradox that, when one is ready for peace, one begins by recognizing the horrors of war. As murderers who are capable of committing more murders as long as they feel no remorse, we cannot expect to overcome our own violence unless we overcome our desire to deny reality.

How do we understand reality? Until now, we have tried to do so by having each discipline carve out smaller and smaller portions in order to carry out rigorous and "original" scholarship, and this has, to a certain degree, served us well. However, we are now at a dangerous point where we are losing the forest for the trees. Efficiency started to become barriers that divided disciplines, and ease turned into traps; the knowledge gained became more a product of these trappings than the actual subject of study. Taking divisions for facilitating investigation for "joints in nature" themselves, world views arose from methodology and practice alone (Lee, 1995). Useful findings within one's own domain generated blindness to other areas of inquiry and a closing of the mind (Casadevall and Fang, 2014). Silos have made it feasible to avoid obvious questions by declaring them not ours to answer (Haney & Zimbardo, 1998; Milgram, 1969). This is the kind of myopia that has set a relentless course of an atomic and then a nuclear age in motion, as well as the kind of capitalism that could pursue "the bottom line" no matter the environmental or human devastation. Mindless technicity came to be mistaken for scholarship, and literally the surrounding world could collapse, but the process would continue, as partial operations have taken over as the whole. We now know that this fragmentation of knowledge diminishes critical consciousness that could become an agent of history. We can recognize the value of minding the whole when we consider the cancer cell, which has mastered its own reproduction, ends by destroying the very organism on which it is dependent for survival. An antidote to this is to apprehend fragments as interacting constituents of a whole that we need to consider in context, while recognizing that the whole is always a work in progress. This is not to resist the rigorous methods of each discipline but to set them to a higher standard, even if it first means facing how little we actually know.

The better we understand reality, the more capable we are of moving from describing to *prescribing*: the capacity to imagine what does not exist, and to change our future. If humankind has chosen a course that, in total sum, defies its own logic and own life, is it not proof that our method is flawed? How can the fields of scholarship, in their near-frenetic activity to add to an ever-expanding knowledge base, help us to approach the answers, rather than drawing us away? How can we direct our disciplines so that knowing more does not lead to understanding less? Fragmentation is the very disposition on which violence thrives. As long as humankind is divided against itself, perceiving that there is always an "enemy" to defeat, it will continue to beget violence until it achieves self-destruction (Rai, Valdesolo, & Graham, 2017). When awareness changes, the significance of violence changes, and there is a chance that true strength will replace its guise. War and militarism do not lead to security, and their power will diminish as the tacit agreement from which violence derives its force dissipates. To understand is not to condone, but rather to expose the falsehoods in favor of peacebuilding methods that are actually more effective, powerful, and enduring. Knowledge should be operable before the most urgent and basic questions confronting humankind, and scholarly disciplines exist for purposes beyond serving their own frameworks (Reader, Fornari, Simon, & Townsend, 2015). The best efforts of the human species, in the drive to improve life and to protect its own (Aboelela et al., 2007), should not end up useless for its own preservation.

Integration of scholarship into a whole, like integration of an individual, a family, a community, or a society into a cohesive whole, is the first step toward health and true strength. And where there is true strength, violence becomes unnecessary. This is a form of *insight*, which does not supplant fragments of knowledge but "sees" them together in perspective (Wallerstein & Bernstein, 1988). Rather than avoid reflection in fear of speculative bias, the inclusion of insight brings about humility and an opening of the mind that allows for a dialectic between datum and design, between piece and picture (Campbell, 1957), so that the whole might be seen. We are at a critical time in history, when our ability to see will determine our own fate. Leader of the Indian independence movement Mohandas Gandhi saw truth as something that is multifaceted, necessitating the pieces of others' truths in order to grasp the greater truth, which led him to believe in the inherent worth of dialogue with opponents. We may apply this to scholarship: a healthy and rigorous approach at this time entails integration, which occurs when disciplines start talking to one another. The study of violence especially highlights this need, for we now have a great deal of information in piecemeal, but still absent is a coherent and cogent, overarching theory that could help us to use our knowledge to recreate and transform reality. We hope that this text will have provided the student a launching pad for that and not an endpoint. If, rather than providing specific answers, it has led the student to thinking about violence coherently and systematically, in the direction of learning to identify the right questions, then it will have been successful. Questions are quests for understanding, and while information fills the mind, transformation molds the mind. Information remains external, but transformation is internal and can lead to wisdom. To this end, this volume has proposed a structure for violence studies as a discipline in its own right, capable of integrating knowledge and converting it into comprehensive insight. As Greek philosopher Aristotle (1909) noted, those who are educated in a subject are good judges of that subject, but those who have an all-round education are good judges in general. The healthy state of wholeness, moreover, will naturally give rise to the creativity and ingenuity necessary for overcoming hitherto insurmountable challenges. Perhaps, then, just as the world eradicated smallpox through a comprehensive and concerted effort, we can do the same with violence.

The Power of Unity

The awareness of violence means that we are at the verge of change. Insight carries with it a newfound ability to: (a) perceive where we are; (b) apprehend what we have; and (c) comprehend what we can do. Gaining insight is an intensely internal process (Gandhi, 1993), but from the depths of reflection arises a power that can transform society and humankind. Development of insight occurs alongside a progression in consciousness that is crucial for effective violence prevention. In Chapter 4, "The Symbolism (or Spiritual Causes) of Violence," we reviewed Kohlberg's stages of moral development. Here, we create a similar progression in the conceptualization of violence:

1a) Obedience and submission (*I of course obey those who are violent*)
1b) Self-focus and victimhood (*why are they being violent to me?*)

2a) Interpersonal modeling and conformity (*how can I avenge what was done to me? how can I use this same violence to my benefit?*)

2b) Cooperation and assistance (*this violence is keeping us together, and so it must be necessary*)

3a) Opposition and resistance (*this violence is doing harm, and so I will fight against it*)

3b) Universal principles in human existence (*the violence is wrong, but there needs to be forgiveness and healing to overcome it*).

From this, we can also conceive of a scheme for societal progression:

1a) Oneness with the offender (*I identify with those who oppress me*)

1b) Separation from the offender (*I am suffering from this oppression*)

2a) Modeling and conformity (*how can I mimic the oppressor and no longer be oppressed?*)

2b) Collusion and social oppression (*these oppressive structures are what keep society together, and so they must be legitimate*)

3a) Solidarity and revolution (*repairing injustices increases the welfare of all, and this also benefits me, and so I will fight for it*)

3b) Universal principles in human existence (*injustices are a sad fact, but universal essence is greater, and its abundance absorbs the destructiveness in the perpetrator and the bitterness in the victim*) (Lee, personal notes, 2014).

British economist and educator Kenneth Boulding (1995) makes a similar observation couched as "three faces of power": threat, exchange, and integrative power. Those who subscribe to a paradigm of the world as threatening and fragmented will perceive each party as either right or wrong, and so if they can prove the other wrong, they will be right and "win" while the other "loses." Under the paradigm of wholeness, however, conflict arises as a natural result of diversity and is an opportunity for mutual learning, reconciliation, and eventual unity. An expanding notion of the self, or broadening ego boundaries, makes this possible (Singer, 2011). From this view, those who oppress others also oppress themselves as they lose access to the greatest source of power; the greater, integrative power is always on the side of the governed (Hume, 1742). This is the reason reconciliation and unity often occur from the bottom up, and evolved perceptions unleash a capacity that we do not yet fully know: human history has only seen glimpses of an immensely generative force that is the very fuel of life and the basis of nonviolence.

The truth is not reducible, but it is simple. As an ancient Chinese philosopher has said: "in the pursuit of knowledge, everyday something is added; in the pursuit of wisdom, everyday something is dropped" (Laozi, 1853). We return to an earlier dictum: "A flower cannot bloom without sunshine, and a human cannot live without love" (Müller, 1857, p. 15). As great as the drive toward violence seems to be, the impulse for love is greater; indeed, we have learned earlier that violence arises out of a need for love. This drive, when directed properly, facilitates reconciliation, wholeness, and human blossoming beyond our current comprehension. Death can be dramatic, but life is more vibrant and more powerful. Paradigms and methods determine what we see (Kuhn, 1967), and we must look beneath the surface separation and the fragmentation to see the broader principles that unite the diverse disciplines, including our common humanity. It is therefore important to know the reasons we cannot progress beyond disintegration and destruction, in the same manner that we cannot move beyond Newtonian mechanics and the laws of thermodynamics without a model for alternative imagination (Lee & Wexler, 1999).

We have highlighted two manifestations of human potential: creativity and compassion. We have the capacity for immense creativity, flexibility, and generativity that can bring us far beyond simple violence prevention and peacekeeping to peace*making* and peace*building*. We have seen how we largely lose the battle of trying to reduce violence with more violence, such as through retribution, coercion, and cruelty. We might achieve greater progress through means that do not employ violence, but even greater progress could be achieved with the active employment of creativity and compassion. Creative consideration that goes beyond our current paradigm of separation, for example, might spark our capacity to exist at a more life-affirming level. We only have a glimpse of what is possible in the realms of creativity and compassion, but we may extrapolate their explosive potential from the progression from violence to nonviolence (see Figure 15.1).

According to Gandhi (1993), nonviolence is closer to violence than to inaction. Studies of human genetics show that the gene associated with violence shows lower-than-normal levels of activity in the absence of a coupling environment (Caspi et al., 2002). Psychological dynamics make possible an explanation of violence as life energy gone awry, as we have seen in Chapter 3 "The Psychology of Violence." The superficial similarity between violence and energy, between destructiveness and power, ends at the surface: creativity and compassion are derivatives of a life impulse, while violence and antipathy of a death drive; inactivity and indifference underlie both. Nonviolence, or the opposite of violence, is thus highly creative and deeply compassionate, being the farthest removed from passivity. We conclude, therefore, that love, the principal source of nonviolent power, underlies creativity, defined as generativity that brings forth value (Runco & Jaeger, 2012), and compassion, which originates in a condition of abundance. Love and justice therefore form the foundation for lasting peace and not mere absence of violence. These can achieve what violence can only pretend to do: provide and accomplish. A new theory of violence is thus a new theory of humankind, which is at our disposal to choose.

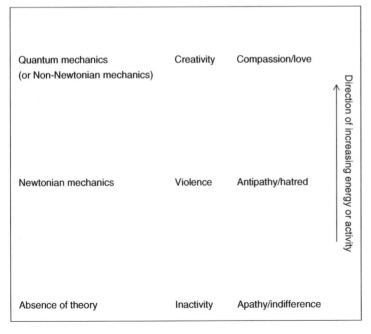

Figure 15.1 Progression from violence to creativity.

Conclusion

Interest in the study of violence has been sweeping through multiple fields, generating an explosion of information. More urgently needed than greater quantities of information is addressing the question of how to think about violence. This is not a question for a single field or the subfield of a scholarly subject but one for a composite of all fields, and the critical consciousness, or wisdom, that they yield together. We learned from biology that human beings are adaptable, from psychology that they are complex, and from sociology and anthropology that they are products of socialization. Meanwhile, we have moved away from framing violence as purely a concern of criminology, law, and politics to it being one of public health, mental health, and preventive medicine, and to our general investment in promoting human thriving for peace. If criminal justice can do violence to all involved, humane approaches to violence can enhance the collective whole. Better access to healthcare, disarmament, and international cooperation, are not only more effective in preventing violence but are generative of improved conditions for life. Therefore, we progress from merely trying to organize and control violence through further violence, to preventing it from arising in the first place, and finally to caring for each person and empowering one another in ways that diminish any need for violence.

These efforts could not be more timely. Humanity is at a crossroads, whereby its capacity for destruction has never been greater, but so has its potential for re-creation and renewal. What we need is readiness and willingness to address a problem that is human-caused and human-solvable. Rather than choose retaliation, we can choose affiliation, reconciliation, and a stance of solving problems rather than perpetuating them. This requires courage, to have a full look at where we are through the *Gestalt* or global whole of all knowledge in order to change our *Weltanschauung*, or world view. As a new perspective emerges, so does a new vision for human existence, and initial instability can give way to greater equilibrium. Meanwhile, the violence paradigm has reached its limits, having achieved the ability to destroy our world many times over, and movements to "denuclearize" and to salvage our natural environment are growing, not out of ideological preference, but out of a critical last attempt at survival. We also come face-to-face with the uncomfortable truth that violence is a human issue, and we are all responsible, not just a limited number of select offenders. A change of humanity will be necessary, for anything less would be dealing merely with symptoms.

As unsettling as these moments are, they can also be chances for creative breakthrough (Nissani, 1997). We can think more innovatively about the way we organize our world, and the paradigms that we bring. Will we continue to resort to violence of our own to respond to others' violence, or will we look at our collective violence, as a society, and rightly declare it a problem? The very act of creation often involves bringing together previously conflicting ideas in unusual ways (Koestler, 1964). Highly creative artists and thinkers who span several disciplines, or Archimedes's celebrated "eureka" moment in a single discipline, have all involved creatively bringing together previously unthought-of combinations (Simonton, 1988). The drive behind purposeful creativity is, furthermore, an impulse for life, or the betterment of life. Since disciplinary boundaries are not demarcated in nature, the challenges that come from intellectual crossovers can stimulate fresh vision for the subject matter (Klein, 2010). This does not replace routine preparation but rather arises out of it, as preservation and innovation go hand-in-hand in sound scholarship. The resulting, unexpected "insight" or net understanding approaches wisdom in the context of the whole. American physicist Thomas Kuhn, for example, found a remarkable resemblance between breakthroughs in awareness, as in psychology, and paradigmatic shifts, as in the history of science (Kuhn, 1962).

Thus, after decades of effort, the field of violence studies is reaching a critical time. In light of accumulating information on the topic, it is important to take a step back, to synthesize and integrate the vast knowledge we already have available, and to create a conceptual framework that can direct us toward proper action—for a study of violence is necessarily practical. Academia has been an important global player in this era of emphasis on science-based practices, for evidence can serve as a potent initiative where implementation of primary prevention is politically and emotionally difficult (Gilligan, 2001). It can also mediate where professional networks operate in isolation and where the benefits of a long-range view can motivate cooperation and a common, overarching perspective. Interdisciplinary sharing and integration of knowledge among academics thus has the potential to serve as a starting point for the much-needed collaboration between scholars, practitioners, and policymakers in the domains of social services, government, justice, and healthcare. It is hence timely for violence studies to emerge as a field of its own, in order to cross boundaries actively and concertedly, to transcend traditional disciplinary divisions, and to help unify different sectors of intervention. Moving beyond our spheres and regional biases will allow us to avoid duplicating efforts or proceeding with incomplete information, and to address our common major concerns at hand. It is with this purpose and hope that this text has been conceived, with the conviction that the genesis of a new consciousness obliges no less than this level of synthesis. We are approaching a decisive moment in human history, and the more pressing the problem, the more urgent the task of employing the best of our intellect and our most thoughtful reflections to undertake this immense challenge.

Questions

1   How can synthesis and integration of diverse disciplines help to end violence?

2   What is the endgame of violence?

3   How can synthesis be a solution to violence?

4   How is unity relevant to compassion, creativity, love, and peacebuilding?

5   How can the integration of knowledge from multiple disciplines help to shape our collective consciousness?

References

Aboelela, S. W., Larson, E., Bakken, S., Carrasquillo, O., Formicola, A., Glied, S. A., ... Gebbie, K. M. (2007). Defining interdisciplinary research: Conclusions from a critical review of the literature. *Health Services Research*, 42(1 pt.1), 329–346.

Anderson, P., & Menon, J. (2009). *Violence performed: Local roots and global routes of conflict.* Basingstoke, UK: Palgrave Macmillan.

Apps, P. (2015, November 13). Which cities are at greatest risk of nuclear war? *City Metric.* Retrieved from https://www.citymetric.com/horizons/which-cities-are-greatest-risk-nuclear-war-1586

Aristotle (1909). *Aristotle's Nicomachean ethics* (D. Ross, Trans.). London, U.K.: Paul, Trench, Trübner, and Company.

Bandura, A. (1973). *Aggression: A social learning analysis.* Englewood Cliffs, NJ: Prentice-Hall.

Blackman, C. (2009, July 20). Chance of nuclear war is greater than you think: Stanford engineer makes risk analysis. *Phys.* Retrieved from https://phys.org/news/2009-07-chance-nuclear-war-greater-stanford.html

Boulding, K. E. (1995). *Three faces of power*. Newbury Park, CA: Sage.

Brändlin, A.-S. (2016, November16). Citizens across the world are suing their governments over climate change. *Deutsche Welle*. Retrieved from http://www.dw.com/en/citizens-across-the-world-are-suing-their-governments-over-climate-change/a-36413833

Busch, N. E. (2015). *No end in sight: The continuing menace of nuclear proliferation*. Lexington, KY: University Press of Kentucky.

Campbell, N. R. (1957). *Foundations of science: The philosophy of theory and experiment*. New York, NY: Dover.

Casadevall, A., & Fang, F. C. (2014). Specialized science. *Infection and Immunity, 82*(4), 1355–1360.

Caspi, A., McClay, J., Moffitt, T. E., Mill, J., Martin, J., Craig, I. W., ... Poulton, R. (2002). Role of genotype in the cycle of violence in maltreated children. *Science, 297*(5582), 851–854.

Chambliss, W. J. (1999). *Power, politics, and crime*. Boulder, CO: Westview Press.

Chan, D. K., & Card, C. (2012). *Beyond just war: A virtue ethics approach*. Basingstoke, UK: Palgrave Macmillan.

Chenoweth, E., & Stephan, M. J. (2011). *Why civil resistance works: The strategic logic of nonviolent conflict*. New York, NY: Columbia University Press.

Cohen, P. (2016, December 6). A bigger economic pie, but a smaller slice for half of the U.S. *New York Times*. Retrieved from https://www.nytimes.com/2016/12/06/business/economy/a-bigger-economic-pie-but-a-smaller-slice-for-half-of-the-us.html?smid=tw-nytimesbusiness&smtyp=cur

Collier, P., Elliott, V. L., Hegre, H., Hoeffler, A., Reynal-Querol, M., & Sambanis, N. (2003). *Breaking the conflict trap: Civil war and development policy*. Washington, DC: World Bank.

Commission of the European Communities. (2002). *Communication from the commission to the European Parliament, the council, the economic and social committee and the committee of the regions: Towards a Global Partnership for Sustainable Development*. Brussels, Belgium: Author. Retrieved from http://ec.europa.eu/regional_policy/archive/innovation/pdf/library/globalpartner_sustaindev_en.pdf

Conklin, J. (2003). *Why crime rates fell*. Boston, MA: Allyn and Bacon.

Crédit Suisse. (2016). *Global wealth databook 2016*. Zurich, Switzerland: Author. Retrieved from http://publications.credit-suisse.com/tasks/render/file/index.cfm?fileid=AD6F2B43-B17B-345E-E20A1A254A3E24A5

Crist, E., Rinker, H. B., & McKibben, B. (2009). *Gaia in turmoil: Climate change, biodepletion, and earth ethics in an age of crisis*. Cambridge, MA: MIT Press.

Currie, E. (1999). Reflections on crime and criminology at the millennium. *Western Criminology Review, 2*(1), 1–13.

Data 360 (2017). *Top U.S. federal tax rates on regular income and capital gains*. San Francisco, CA: Webster Systems. Retrieved from http://www.data360.org/dsg.aspx?Data_Set_Group_Id=475

Davey, I. (2009). Environmentalism of the poor and sustainable development: An appraisal. *Journal of Administration and Governance, 4*(1), 1–10.

Dube, S. R., Anda, R. F., Felitti, V. J., Chapman, D. P., Williamson, D. F., & Giles, W. H. (2001). Childhood abuse, household dysfunction, and the risk of attempted suicide throughout the life span: Findings from the adverse childhood experiences study. *JAMA, 286*(24), 3089–3096.

Durose, M. R., Cooper, A. D., & Snyder, H. N. (2014). *Recidivism of prisoners released in 30 States in 2005: Patterns from 2005 to 2010*. Washington, DC: U.S. Department of Justice.

Estrada-Martinez, L., Caldwell, C., Bauermeister, J., & Zimmerman, M. (2012). Stressors in multiple life-domains and the risk for externalizing and internalizing behaviors among African Americans during emerging adulthood. *Journal of Youth and Adolescence, 41*(12), 1600–1612.

European Environment Agency. (2015). *Atmospheric greenhouse gas concentrations*. Copenhagen, Denmark: Author. Retrieved from https://www.eea.europa.eu/data-and-maps/indicators/atmospheric-greenhouse-gas-concentrations-4/assessment

Galtung, J. (1969). Violence, peace, and peace research. *Journal of Peace Research, 6*(3), 167–191.

Gandhi, M. (1993). Axioms of non-violence. In R. Iyer (Ed.), *The essential writings of Mahatma Gandhi* (pp. 240). New Delhi, India: Oxford University Press.

Gessen, M. (2015). *Tsarnaev brothers: The road to a modern tragedy*. Brunswick, Australia: Scribe Publications.

Giddens, A. (2009). *Politics of climate change*. Cambridge, UK: Polity Press.

Gilligan, J. (1996). *Violence: Our deadly epidemic and its causes*. New York, NY: Putnam.

Gilligan, J. (2001). *Preventing violence*. London, UK: Thames and Hudson.

Grinshteyn, E., & Hemenway, D. (2016). Violent death rates: The U.S. compared with other high-income OECD countries, 2010. *American Journal of Medicine, 129*(3), 266–273.

Haney, C., & Zimbardo, P. (1998). The past and future of US prison policy: Twenty-five years after the Stanford Prison Experiment. *American Psychologist, 53*(7), 709.

Hansen, J. (2010). *Storms of my grandchildren: The truth about the coming climate catastrophe and our last chance to save humanity*. London, UK: Bloomsbury.

Hardoon, D., Ayele, S., & Fuentes-Nieva, R. (2016). *An economy for the 1%: How privilege and power in the economy drive extreme inequality and how this can be stopped*. Oxford, UK: Oxfam International. Retrieved from http://policy-practice.oxfam.org.uk/publications/an-economy-for-the-1-how-privilege-and-power-in-the-economy-drive-extreme-inequ-592643

Hardoon, D., & Slater, J. (2015). *Inequality and the end of extreme poverty*. Oxford, UK: Oxfam International. Retrieved from https://policy-practice.oxfam.org.uk/publications/inequality-and-the-end-of-extreme-poverty-577506

Harrington, B. (2016). *Capital without borders: Wealth managers and the one percent*. Cambridge, MA: Harvard University Press.

Hellman, M. E. (1986). *Nuclear war: Inevitable or preventable?*. Vancouver, Canada: University of British Columbia.

Hesse, H. (1943). *Das Glasperlenspiel*. Zurich, Switzerland: Fretz and Wasmuth.

Høivik, T. (1977). The demography of structural violence. *Journal of Peace Research, 14*(1), 59–73.

Hoy, C., & Sumner, A. (2016). *Gasoline, guns, and giveaways: Is there new capacity for redistribution to end three quarters of global poverty?*. Washington, DC: Center for Global Development. Retrieved from https://www.cgdev.org/sites/default/files/gasoline-guns-and-giveaways-end-three-quarters-global-poverty-0.pdf

Hume, D. (1742). *Essays and treatises on several subjects. 1, part I. Essays, moral, political, and literary*. London, UK: A. Millar, in the Strand and A. Kincaid and A. Donaldson, at Edinburgh.

Joshi, P. T., & O'Donnell, D. A. (2003). Consequences of child exposure to war and terrorism. *Clinical Child and Family Psychology Review, 6*(4), 275–292.

Klein, J. T. (2010). A taxonomy of interdisciplinarity. In R. Frodeman, J. T. Klein, & C. Mitcham (Eds.), *Oxford handbook of interdisciplinarity* (pp. 15–30). Oxford, UK: Oxford University Press.

Koestler, A. (1964). *The act of creation*. London, UK: Hutchinson.

Kuhn, T. S. (1962). *The structure of scientific revolutions*. Chicago, IL: University of Chicago Press.

Kuhn, T. S. (1967). *Structure of scientific revolutions*. Chicago, IL: University of Chicago Press.

Kunstler, J. H. (2007). *The long emergency: Surviving the end of oil, climate change, and other converging catastrophes of the twenty-first century*. New York, NY: Grove Press.

Lansford, J. E., Miller-Johnson, S., Berlin, L. J., Dodge, K. A., Bates, J. E., & Pettit, G. S. (2007). Early physical abuse and late violent delinquency: A prospective longitudinal study. *Child Maltreatment, 12*(3), 233–245.

Laozi (1853). *Tao te ching chu*. Nanhai, China: Wu Shih.

Lee, B. X. (1995). *Toward a new psychiatry: Quantum physical implications for psychiatric theory and practice*. New Haven, CT: Yale School of Medicine.

Lee, B. X., & Wexler, B. E. (1999). Physics and the quandaries of contemporary psychiatry: Review and research. *Psychiatry, 62*(3), 222–234.

Leffler, M. P. (2005). 9/11 and American foreign policy. *Diplomatic History, 29*(3), 395–413.

Liberman, A. M., Kirk, D. S., & Kideuk, K. (2014). Labeling effects of first juvenile arrests: Secondary deviance and secondary sanctioning. *Criminology, 52*(3), 345–370.

Lifton, R. J. (1987). *The future of immortality and other essays for a nuclear age.* New York, NY: Basic Books.

Lynch, M. (2007). *Big prisons, big dreams.* Piscataway, NJ: Rutgers University Press.

Lynch, M., & Cicchetti, D. (1998). An ecological-transactional analysis of children and contexts: The longitudinal interplay among child maltreatment, community violence, and children's symptomatology. *Development and Psychopathology, 10*(2), 235–257.

Martinez-Alier, J. (2002). *The environmentalism of the poor. United nations research institute for social development and University of Witwatersrand.* Johannesburg, South Africa: University of Witwatersrand. Retrieved from http://www.unrisd.org/80256B3C005BCCF9/(httpAuxPages)/5EB03FFBDD19EA90C1257664004831BD/$file/MartinezAlier.pdf

Masters, D., & Way, K. (1946). *One world or none.* New York, NY: McGraw-Hill.

Masters, K. (2016, September 19). Fear of other people is now the primary motivation for American gun ownership, a landmark survey finds. *The Trace.* Retrieved from https://www.thetrace.org/2016/09/harvard-gun-ownership-study-self-defense

Mayer, J. (2017). *Dark money: The hidden history of the billionaires behind the rise of the radical right.* New York, NY: Anchor Books.

McEvoy, D. (2007). Climate change and cities. *Built Environment, 33*(1), 4–9.

McNamara, R. S. (2005). Apocalypse soon. *Foreign Policy, 148*, 29–35.

Meadows, D. H. (2008). *Thinking in systems: A primer.* Hartford, VT: Chelsea Green Publishing.

Milgram, S. (1969). Interdisciplinary thinking and the small world problem. In M. Sherif, & C. W. Sherif (Eds.), *Interdisciplinary relations in the social sciences* (pp. 103–120). Chicago, IL: Aldine.

Mirza, R. M. S. (2007). *The rise and fall of the American empire: A re-interpretation of history, economics and philosophy: 1492–2006.* Victoria, Canada: Trafford.

Morland, H. (2004). Born Secret. *Cardozo Law Review, 26*(4), 1401–1408.

Müller, F. M. (1857). *Deutsche Liebe: Aus den Papieren eines Fremdlings.* Leipzig, Germany.

National Consortium for the Study of Terrorism and Responses to Terrorism (2015). *Annex of statistical information: Country reports on terrorism 2014.* College Park, MD: Department of Homeland Security Science and Technology Center of Excellence.

Nissani, M. (1997). Ten cheers for interdisciplinarity: The case for interdisciplinary knowledge and research. *Social Science Journal, 34*(2), 201–216.

Oxfam International. (2017). *An economy for the 99%.* Oxford, UK: Author.

Paige, G. D. (2009). *Nonkilling global political science.* Honolulu, HI: Center for Global Nonkilling.

Petersilia, J. (2010). Community corrections. In J. Q. Wilson, & J. Petersilia (Eds.), *Crime and public policy.* Oxford, UK: Oxford University Press.

Pinker, S. (2011). *The better angels of our nature: Why violence has declined.* New York, NY: Viking.

Plummer, L., & McGoogan, C. (2017, September 4). 11 terrifying climate change facts. *Wired.* Retrieved from www.wired.co.uk/article/climate-change-facts

Pogge, T. (2008). Growth and inequality: Understanding recent trends and political choices. *Dissent, 55*(1), 66–75.

Project for the Study of the 21st Century. (2017). *PS21 survey: Experts see increased risk of nuclear war.* London, UK: Author. Retrieved from https://projects21.org/2015/11/12/ps21-survey-experts-see-increased-risk-of-nuclear-war

Rai, T. S., Valdesolo, P., & Graham, J. (2017). Dehumanization increases instrumental violence, but not moral violence. *Proceedings of the National Academy of Sciences of the United States of America, 114*(32), 8511–8516.

Reader, S., Fornari, A., Simon, S., & Townsend, J. (2015). Promoting Faculty Scholarship—An evaluation of a program for busy clinician-educators. *Canadian Medical Education Journal*, 6(1), e43–e60.

Reuveny, R. (2007). Climate change-induced migration and violent conflict. *Political Geography*, 26(6), 656–673.

Richards, A. (2015). *Conceptualizing terrorism*. New York, NY: Oxford University Press.

Runco, M. A., & Jaeger, G. J. (2012). The standard definition of creativity. *Creativity Research Journal*, 24(1), 92–96.

Sagan, C. (1983). Nuclear war and climatic catastrophe: Some policy implications. *Foreign Affairs*, 62(2), 257–292.

Schell, J. (2007). *The seventh decade: The new shape of nuclear danger*. New York, NY: Macmillan.

Seery, E., & Caistor Arendar, A. (2014). *Even it up: Time to end extreme inequality*. Oxford, UK: Oxfam International. Retrieved from https://www.oxfam.org/sites/www.oxfam.org/files/file_attachments/cr-even-it-up-extreme-inequality-291014-en.pdf

Silverman, A. B., Reinherz, H. Z., & Giaconia, R. M. (1996). The long-term sequelae of child and adolescent abuse: A longitudinal community study. *Child Abuse and Neglect*, 20(8), 709–723.

Simonton, D. K. (1988). *Scientific genius*. Cambridge, UK: Cambridge University Press.

Singer, P. (2011). *The expanding circle: Ethics, evolution, and moral progress*. Princeton, NJ: Princeton University Press.

Smyth, H. D. (1945). Atomic energy for military purposes. *Reviews of Modern Physics*, 17(4), 351–471.

Sponberg, A. F. (2007). Ocean acidification: The biggest threat to our oceans? *American Institute of Biological Sciences Bulletin*, 57(10), 822–822.

Union of Concerned Scientists. (2015). *Close calls with nuclear weapons*. Boston, MA: Author.

United Nations. (2015). *Paris agreement*. New York, NY: Author. Retrieved from https://unfccc.int/sites/default/files/english_paris_agreement.pdf

United Nations Office on Drugs and Crime. (2013). *Global study on homicide 2013: Trends, contexts, data*. Vienna, Austria: Author. Retrieved from https://www.unodc.org/documents/gsh/pdfs/2014_GLOBAL_HOMICIDE_BOOK_web.pdf

U.S. Environmental Protection Agency. (2009). *Economics of climate change*. Washington, DC: Author. Retrieved from https://www.epa.gov/environmental-economics/economics-climate-change

U.S. National Aeronautics and Space Administration. (2017). *NASA, NOAA data show 2016 warmest year on record globally*. Washington, DC: Author. Retrieved from https://www.nasa.gov/press-release/nasa-noaa-data-show-2016-warmest-year-on-record-globally

U.S. National Oceanic and Atmospheric Administration. (2017). *Global climate report—Annual 2017*. Washington, DC: Author Retrieved from https://www.ncdc.noaa.gov/sotc/global/201713

Vasconcelos, V. V., Santos, F. C., Pacheco, J. M., & Levin, S. A. (2014). Climate policies under wealth inequality. *Proceedings of the National Academy of Sciences*, 111(6), 2212–2216.

Wallerstein, N., & Bernstein, E. (1988). Empowerment education: Freire's ideas adapted to health education. *Health Education Quarterly*, 15(4), 379–394.

Walmsley, R. (2016). *World prison population list*. London, UK: Institute for Criminal Policy Research.

Wells, H. G. (1914). *The war that will end war*. London, UK: Frank and Cecil Palmer.

Wiley, S. A., & Esbensen, F.-A. (2013). The effect of police contact: Does official intervention result in deviance amplification? *Crime and Delinquency*, 62(3), 283–307.

World Food Programme. (2017). *Zero hunger*. Rome, Italy: Author. Retrieved from http://www1.wfp.org/zero-hunger

Yexley, M., Borowsky, I., & Ireland, M. (2002). Correlation between different experiences of intrafamilial physical violence and violent adolescent behavior. *Journal of Interpersonal Violence*, 17(7), 707–720.

Zuchman, G. (2015). *The hidden wealth of nations*. Chicago, IL: University of Chicago Press.

Index

Violence: An Interdisciplinary Approach to Causes, Consequences, and Cures, First Edition. Bandy X. Lee.
© 2019 John Wiley & Sons, Inc. Published 2019 by John Wiley & Sons, Inc.

Printed in Poland
by Amazon Fulfillment
Poland Sp. z o.o., Wrocław
15 October 2020

9f463b1f-0311-4905-a6b1-1acbaa0722fbR01